Marketing and Globalization

This concise text focuses squarely on the issues facing marketers in an increasingly global world. It identifies several trends, linking them together, and positioning them as marketing practices that companies implement as a way of responding to the major consequences of globalization. The book also includes case studies to illustrate new practices and allow students to discuss issues of market selection, entry modes, segmentation, targeting, and positioning, as well as product, price, distribution, promotion, and corporate communication policies in a globalized world.

Durand's unique approach moves beyond marketing management and strategy issues and provides students with the broader context to understand the marketing practices they'll use in the real world.

This book will prove to be an essential resource for any student of marketing and international business working to stay ahead in an increasingly competitive and global industry.

Aurélia Durand is an associate professor of international business at HEC Montréal, Canada. She earned a BBA in Entrepreneurship and holds an MBA as well as a PhD in Management. She has worked in the consulting industry in her native country of France and has held academic positions in Argentina and Chile.

Marketing and Globalization

Aurélia Durand

NEW YORK AND LONDON

First published 2019
by Routledge
711 Third Avenue, New York, NY 10017

and by Routledge
2 Park Square, Milton Park, Abingdon, Oxon, OX14 4RN

*Routledge is an imprint of the Taylor & Francis Group, an
informa business*

© 2019 Taylor & Francis

The right of Aurélia Durand to be identified as author of this
work has been asserted by her in accordance with sections 77 and
78 of the Copyright, Designs and Patents Act 1988.

All rights reserved. No part of this book may be reprinted
or reproduced or utilised in any form or by any electronic,
mechanical, or other means, now known or hereafter invented,
including photocopying and recording, or in any information
storage or retrieval system, without permission in writing from
the publishers.

Trademark notice: Product or corporate names may be
trademarks or registered trademarks, and are used only for
identification and explanation without intent to infringe.

Library of Congress Cataloging-in-Publication Data
Names: Durand, Aurélia, author.
Title: Marketing and globalization/Aurélia Durand.
Description: New York : Routledge, 2018. | Includes
  bibliographical references and index.
Identifiers: LCCN 2018000432 | ISBN 9781138202337
  (hardback) | ISBN 9781138202344 (pbk.) | ISBN
  9781315474175 (ebook)
Subjects: LCSH: Marketing. | Marketing—Technological
  innovations. | Internet marketing. | Globalization—Economic
  aspects.
Classification: LCC HF5415 .D867 2018 | DDC 658.8/4—dc23
LC record available at https://lccn.loc.gov/2018000432

ISBN: 978-1-138-20233-7 (hbk)
ISBN: 978-1-138-20234-4 (pbk)
ISBN: 978-1-315-47417-5 (ebk)

Typeset in Sabon
by Apex CoVantage, LLC

Visit the eResources: www.routledge.com/9781138202344

Contents

Figures	vii
Tables	xiii
Preface	xv
Contributor Bios	xvii
Acknowledgments	xxii

1 Globalization	1
2 Internationalization	34
3 Standardization and Adaptation	70
4 Geographic and Psychic Distances	98
5 Cultural Distance	138
6 Administrative Distance	181
7 Economic and Technological Distances	236
8 Bottom of the Pyramid Marketing	286
9 Reverse Innovation	333
10 Mobile Marketing	376
11 Origin-Based Marketing	431

vi *Contents*

12 Cause-Related Marketing   497

Overall Book Conclusion   548

Acronyms   549
Index   552

Figures

1.1	Illustrating Chapter 1	2
1.2	Books supporting the idea that "distance is dead"	3
1.3	Positioning Chapter 1 in the overall book structure	5
1.4	Illustrating the growth of exports of goods and services in absolute numbers (1960–2015)	7
1.5	Illustrating the growth of exports of goods and services in proportion of global GDP (1960–2015)	8
1.6	Portrait of Theodore Levitt	11
1.7	The "Convergence Club" in 1850	15
1.8	The "Convergence Club" in 1900	16
1.9	The "Convergence Club" interwar period	17
1.10	The "Convergence Club" early 2000s	18
1.11	Illustrating separatism and the use of media to defend local identities as counter evidence to cultural convergence	19
1.12	Depicting globalization, its mechanisms and main outcomes for marketers	20
1.13	Portrait of Pankaj Ghemawat	21
1.14	Book supporting the idea that "distance is not dead"	22
1.15	Illustrating the concept of semi-internationalization	23
1.16	Illustrating degrees of globalization of corporate functions and marketing activities in the automotive industry	24
1.17	Weighting the pros and cons of globalization	30
2.1	Illustrating Chapter 2	35
2.2	Positioning Chapter 2 in the overall book structure	36
2.3	Presenting the Uppsala or "U-model" of internationalization	38
2.4	Overview of various international entry modes	40
2.5	Comparing entry modes in terms of rate of return and foreign involvement	40
2.6	Presenting a typical decision tree for entry modes	42
2.7	Illustrating licensing for cereals	44
2.8	Illustrating licensing for fragrances	44
2.9	Examples of franchises	45
2.10	Portrait of John Dunning	48
2.11	Portrait of Oliver Williamson	52
2.12	Detailing transaction costs in international trade	53

viii *Figures*

2.13	Structuring an international marketing plan	57
3.1	Illustrating Chapter 3	71
3.2	Positioning Chapter 3 in the overall book structure	73
3.3	Portrait of Philip Kotler	75
3.4	Illustrating the complexity of international marketing compared to domestic marketing	77
3.5	Illustrating drivers of AdaptStand decisions	85
3.6	Illustrating adaptation of IKEA's brand name in Russian, Thai, Arabic, and Mandarin	90
4.1	Illustrating Chapter 4	99
4.2	Positioning Chapter 4 in the overall book structure	101
4.3	Representing psychic distance	103
4.4	Memorizing important country-based theories with symbols	109
4.5	Memorizing important firm-based theories with symbols	112
4.6	Illustrating the reduction of communication and transportation costs (1920–2015)	114
4.7	Representing tariffs reduction (1947–1993)	115
4.8	Illustrating transaction costs involved in imports–exports with the Buy-Ship-Pay model	116
4.9	Illustrating varying costs and risks according to selected Incoterms®	118
4.10	Categorizing dimensions of proximity	123
4.11	Calculating trade flows between countries with the gravity model of international trade	125
4.12	Representing world trade flows in a gravity perspective	127
4.13	Proposing a nomological network for geographic and psychic distances	131
5.1	Illustrating Chapter 5	139
5.2	Positioning Chapter 5 in the overall book structure	141
5.3	Portrait of Geert Hofstede	142
5.4	Comparing countries in terms of intergenerational earnings elasticity	146
5.5	Illustrating the diversity of languages in the world	149
5.6	Illustrating the diversity of meaning in gestures	151
5.7	Categorizing cultures according to the task/relationship model	155
5.8	Symbols of the four most practiced religions in the world: Christianity, Islam, Hinduism, and Buddhism (in this order)	156
5.9	Representing the proportion of major religious groups in . the global population	156
5.10	Mapping the diversity of religions in the world	157
5.11	Illustrating religious restrictions on products	158
5.12	Situating cultural clusters	160
5.13	Presenting the reasoned action model	165
5.14	Illustrating the process through which values help translate beliefs into attitudes and behaviors	165

Figures ix

5.15	Proposing a nomological network for cultural distance	175
6.1	Illustrating Chapter 6	182
6.2	Positioning Chapter 6 in the overall book structure	183
6.3	Illustrating nationalization with the case of Spanish Electropaz in Bolivia (2012)	188
6.4	Mapping country risk across the world	189
6.5	Mapping corruption across the world	192
6.6	Mapping legal systems in the world	198
6.7	Illustrating varying degrees of integration in regional trade agreements	201
6.8	Mapping the geographic diversity of regional integration with selected agreements	202
6.9	Presenting the logos of important international organizations	206
6.10	Presenting selected threats in the business world as perceived by global CEOs	211
6.11	Illustrating international commercial disputes	212
6.12	Mapping disputes between WTO members	213
6.13	Example of plain packaging for cigarettes	220
6.14	Proposing a nomological network for administrative distance	227
7.1	Illustrating Chapter 7	237
7.2	Positioning Chapter 7 in the overall book structure	239
7.3	Illustrating the interdependence between demand and production factors with the "National Diamond of Competitive Advantage" model	242
7.4	Classifying countries by income levels (2016)	244
7.5	Mapping the diversity of development levels	245
7.6	Representing the income distribution within one country: the example of Canada	246
7.7	Representing the global income distribution in 2010	247
7.8	Mapping Human Development Index scores (2014)	248
7.9	Comparing the GNI per capita at PPP (in current international dollar): the examples of Armenia, Ethiopia, the Russian Federation, Spain, and Sweden	250
7.10	Illustrating the global digital divide by looking at the proportion of households with Internet access in various regions	254
7.11	Illustrating the importance of intellectual property protection with trademarks and patents for an Oral-B toothbrush	256
7.12	Presenting selected excerpts of US4802255, D434563, and D347736 patents, held by Gillette (in charge of commercializing Oral-B toothbrushes and a company belonging to P&G)	257
7.13	Illustrating the anticipated shift in global economic power from developed to emerging economies	265

x Figures

7.14	Illustrating "intra-grouping heterogeneity" with the value of exports (in Billion USD) from the BRIC countries toward selected trade partners	268
7.15	Proposing a nomological network for economic and technological distances	279
8.1	Illustrating Chapter 8	288
8.2	Positioning Chapter 8 in the overall book structure	290
8.3	Illustrating the concept of segmentation	291
8.4	An example of geographic segmentation with ice cream spending in the US	292
8.5	Illustrating the concept of positioning	294
8.6	Proposing a positioning map in the automotive industry	295
8.7	Proposing a positioning map in the cosmetics industry	295
8.8	Illustrating the drastic growth of middle-income populations in Asia, South America, and Eastern Europe	297
8.9	Contrasting the shares of several developed and emerging economies in global middle-class consumption (2000–2050)	298
8.10	Contrasting spending patterns among various income levels	300
8.11	Comparing the proportion of various income segments in the global population	301
8.12	Portrait of Coimbatore Krishnao Prahalad (1941–2010)	302
8.13	Representing the world income pyramid	304
8.14	Illustrating the distribution of income in the world	305
8.15	A Cemex BOP initiative: Patrimonio Hoy	307
8.16	Presenting Grameen Danone Foods, a joint-venture between Danone and Grameen Bank	308
8.17	Portrait of Muhammad Yunus with Aurélia Durand (book author) at the first Social Business Forum held at HEC Montréal on May 24, 2017	309
8.18	Presenting a Nokia BOP initiative: Nokia Life Tools	311
8.19	Presenting a Philips's BOP initiative: the LifeLight range of products	313
8.20	Illustrating the three pillars of Schneider Electric's "Access to Energy program" (formerly called the BipBop program)	314
8.21	Presenting Grameenphone, a joint-venture between Telenor and Grameen Telecom	316
8.22	Presenting Unilever's logotype	318
8.23	Presenting a range of products: Unilever's "Pureit" water purifiers	319
8.24	Presenting Vodafone's logotype	320
8.25	Illustrating the M-Pesa mobile phone-based money transfer	321
8.26	Illustrating the heterogeneity of the BOP segment	323
8.27	Proposing a nomological network for BOP marketing	327
9.1	Illustrating Chapter 9	334
9.2	Positioning Chapter 9 in the overall book structure	336
9.3	Illustrating a variety of "processes" in food services	338
9.4	Representing regular and augmented "proof" for transportation services	339
9.5	Illustrating intrinsic and extrinsic food product attributes	343

9.6	Examples of firms offering international services	344
9.7	Illustrating Roger's theory of innovation diffusion	346
9.8	Illustrating the Product Life Cycle (PLC)	347
9.9	Illustrating the International Product Life Cycle (IPLC)	349
9.10	Representing the rise of foreign competition in the export cycle	350
9.11	Illustrating the concept of reverse innovation	352
9.12	Comparing high-technology exports of China, Japan, and the US (1991–2015)	353
9.13	Comparing patent applications by residents in China, Japan, and the US (2006–2014)	354
9.14	Illustrating the use of an ECG machine in developing vs. developed economic contexts	358
9.15	Presenting the LifeStraw line of products and different uses in developing and developed contexts	365
9.16	Highlighting linkages between globalization and reverse innovation	367
9.17	Proposing a nomological network for reverse innovation	371
10.1	Illustrating Chapter 10	377
10.2	Positioning Chapter 10 in the overall book structure	379
10.3	Listing important decisions involved in international distribution policies	381
10.4	Presenting various intermediaries and lengths of distribution channels	382
10.5	Illustrating the growth of global Internet retailing (1999–2012)	385
10.6	Contrasting Internet statistics in different regions	386
10.7	Illustrating global diversity in terms of popular social media networks and instant messengers	388
10.8	Distinguishing between digital, online, mobile, social, and viral marketing	393
10.9	Presenting a simplified Technology Acceptance Model (TAM)	395
10.10	Presenting Costco's mobile application	400
10.11	Presenting a visual of Dan-On	401
10.12	Illustrating one functionality of the FIAT 500e mobile app: location of charging stations	402
10.13	Presenting Frank And Oak's logotype	403
10.14	Illustrating the use of mobile technology by Frank And Oak	405
10.15	Presenting IKEA's store app	408
10.16	Proposing a nomological network for mobile marketing	421
11.1	Illustrating Chapter 11	432
11.2	Positioning Chapter 11 in the overall book structure	434
11.3	Illustrating the use of cues (product category: cars)	435
11.4	Presenting the four pillars of brand equity	437
11.5	Illustrating the effect of origin: China vs. Swiss-made (product categories: watches and textiles)	439
11.6	Distinguishing the three facets of country image	440
11.7	Illustrating markings (product category: cameras)	441

xii *Figures*

11.8	Contrasting different levels of place branding	446
11.9	Illustrating the diversity of stakeholders in managing a country brand	448
11.10	Situating place branding as one of the antecedents of the country-of-origin effect (COE)	449
11.11	Presenting Canada Goose's logotype	452
11.12	Presenting IKEA logotype	454
11.13	Presenting Victorinox logotype	456
11.14	Presenting the logotype used for the Volkswagen car brand from 2007 to 2015	456
11.15	Presenting Australia's country brand	465
11.16	Presenting Slovenia's country brand	471
11.17	Measuring country brand equity	474
11.18	Illustrating the evolution of country brands rankings	477
11.19	Proposing a nomological network for origin-based marketing	488
12.1	Illustrating Chapter 12	498
12.2	Positioning Chapter 12 in the overall book structure	500
12.3	Illustrating the three pillars of sustainable development	502
12.4	Illustrating the virtuous circle of sustainable consumption and production	502
12.5	Presenting a "responsible" product with emphasis on the "organic" process cue on packaging (juice)	503
12.6	Presenting the pyramid of corporate social responsibility	505
12.7	Contrasting organic and fair trade business (per capita consumption and retails sales) in the top ten consuming countries	508
12.8	Presenting a conceptual framework explaining why organic food consumption differs across countries	509
12.9	Presenting the pink ribbon and logotype of the National Breast Cancer Foundation (US)	512
12.10	Presenting Fjällräven's logo in the shape of its namesake, the Arctic fox	516
12.11	Presenting Subaru's "Share the Love" cause-related marketing campaign	518
12.12	Featuring the bilingual logos (English/French) of Aldo's campaign against AIDS	519
12.13	Illustrating P&G's "Dawn Saves Wildlife" initiative	522
12.14	Presenting P&G Purifier of Water packets	524
12.15	Proposing a nomological network for cause-related marketing	538

Tables

1.1	Measuring globalization through countries' openness to the world	25
1.2	Ranking countries according to their degree of globalization	27
2.1	Using the OLI framework to choose among entry modes	54
3.1	Comparing domestic and international marketing	78
3.2	Headquarters orientation toward subsidiaries	83
3.3	Illustrating AdaptStand decisions for Apple and the iPhone	88
3.4	Illustrating AdaptStand decisions for McDonald's	91
4.1	Measuring psychic distance with an objective approach (focal country: Australia)	104
4.2	Ranking selected countries in terms of psychic distance (focal country: Australia)	105
4.3	Measuring psychic distance based on a subjective approach	106
4.4	Illustrating varying costs according to selected transportation means	119
4.5	Illustrating varying costs and cross-border price escalation according to selected entry modes	120
4.6	Illustrating the paradox of proximity	128
5.1	Defining important study fields in nonverbal communication	150
5.2	Classifying universal values	163
5.3	Illustrating mixed evidence for the convergence of cultural values	168
6.1	Assessing the institutional landscape	194
6.2	Comparing the number of judges, lawyers, and suits filed across selected countries	196
6.3	Illustrating the NAICS hierarchical structure with a focus on the Agriculture, Forestry, Fishing and Hunting sectors	208
7.1	Measuring differences in development levels with selected indicators from the World Bank's "Economy and Growth" category	249

xiv *Tables*

7.2	Measuring differences in resources with selected indicators from the World Bank's "Agriculture and Rural Development," "Energy and Mining," and "Financial Sector" categories	251
7.3	Measuring differences in technological development with selected indicators from the World Bank's "Infrastructure" category	253
7.4	Assessing technological distance between selected countries (China, Japan, South Korea, and Vietnam)	253
7.5	Measuring differences in intellectual property development with selected indicators from the World Bank's "Science and Technology" category	258
7.6	Comparing several market groupings on selected indicators: the G7, BRIC, MIST, and CIVETS	263
7.7	Illustrating "intra-regional heterogeneity" with selected countries in the Americas	267
8.1	Profiling Cemex (Mexico)	306
8.2	Profiling Danone (France)	308
8.3	Profiling Nokia (Finland)	310
8.4	Profiling Royal Philips (Netherlands)	312
8.5	Profiling Schneider Electric (France)	314
8.6	Profiling Telenor (Norway)	316
8.7	Profiling Unilever (US)	318
8.8	Profiling Vodafone (UK)	320
9.1	Overview of the extended marketing-mix (7Ps)	341
9.2	Differentiating among types of reverse innovation and corporate examples	356
9.3	Profiling General Electric (US)	357
9.4	Profiling Harman (US)	360
9.5	Profiling Tata Group (India)	361
9.6	Profiling Vestergaard (Switzerland) in 2015	364
10.1	Ranking global retailers	383
10.2	Comparing social media penetration rates in selected countries	388
10.3	Listing traditional and digital media	389
10.4	Profiling Costco (US)	399
10.5	Profiling FIAT Chrysler Automobile (Italy)	402
10.6	Profiling Foote Cone & Belding (US)	409
10.7	Profiling Uber (US)	411
11.1	Profiling Canada Goose (Canada)	450
11.2	Profiling IKEA (Sweden)	455
11.3	Profiling Victorinox (Switzerland)	457
11.4	Profiling the Volkswagen Group (Germany)	459
11.5	Illustrating the variability in brand origin recognition	480
12.1	Profiling The Coca-Cola Company (US)	515
12.2	Profiling Procter & Gamble (US)	521
12.3	Comparing sponsorship spending in different regions of the world	534

Preface

This book is born from a pedagogical challenge. A challenge shaped by three types of hurdles related to: content, format, and audience.

In terms of content, the need for this book emerged after I was hired in the International Business department at HEC Montréal (Canada) in 2011. I was then asked to redesign an existing course in the MSc program and integrate "interesting marketing practices with a global scope." I quickly identified five of them that I found fascinating (i.e., BOP Marketing, Reverse Innovation, Mobile Marketing, Origin-Based Marketing and Cause-Related Marketing), but, at first, I did not know how to present them in a cohesive manner. Each one of these approaches had already been described and analyzed in many books and scientific articles. Each approach seemed to be a different strategy, adopted by firms for different reasons. And nowhere could I find an explanation as to why companies deployed several of them, often simultaneously. Yet, my own research interests soon led me to realize that adopting the lens of *distance* was the missing common thread. Indeed, my central proposal in this book is that the above-mentioned practices can be considered as solutions to overcome one or several dimensions of distance—i.e., geographic distance as well as political, administrative, legal, cultural, economic, and technological differences—between companies' home and foreign markets. In addition, they are all corporate reactions to one major consequence of globalization: the need to become ever more competitive, both abroad and at home.

In addition to rising up to the challenge of *content*, I also had to face the challenge of *format*, since our MSc program prepares two types of students, those who later pursue doctoral studies and those who enter into the job market as analysts with proficient research skills. In this context, reading two to five academic articles each week as preparatory work was quite standard and needed to be preserved, as well as having discussions around the issues outlined in these articles. Nevertheless, practical examples also needed to be incorporated to increase relevance for students soon to be "out there, in the real world." I also wanted to provide a consistent structure to enhance memorization and practical tips on available (and free) Internet resources, to encourage students to dig further into topics on their own time. My interest in "flipping the classroom" (i.e., giving access to all lecture material to students prior to class, so that our time together would be dedicated to contrasting opinions and debating issues) required a versatile format: a text that could be given to read prior to, or after, class.

xvi   *Preface*

Finally, another challenge—that we all face in the profession—came from the profile of students who had backgrounds in international business, marketing, management, and, sometimes, in entirely different fields of study (e.g., engineering and psychology). In order to favor a deep understanding of the five selected practices, I needed to provide the students with a common vocabulary and knowledge about globalization, internationalization of companies, standardization and adaptation of marketing policies, and, of course, an in-depth analysis of *distance* in its multiple dimensions. Furthermore, students were also diverse in their geographic origins. As a non-native English speaker myself, I know well the despair that can arise from trying—and failing—to absorb ideas from texts while being dazzled by highly sophisticated wording. Consequently, it was important to keep simplicity in mind when writing.

Marketing and Globalization is my best attempt to address all of these pedagogical challenges. It follows a maieutic logic by being written in the form of a dialogue: each paragraph starts with a question that readers can ponder for a minute and answer for themselves before reading my proposed answers and eventually joining others in class to contrast and enrich their thinking with different points of view and experiences. Some of the questions raised are purposefully left unanswered, but, most often, proposed answers are "hidden" in later parts of the text to encourage attention and information retention. Each chapter comes with a set of recommended readings (and specific questions), all of them scientific articles that were selected for being either old or recent, seminal or controversial. Overall, the software used to manage the bibliography reveals that the information presented in this book relies on no fewer than 722 peer-reviewed articles, 150 books, 130 newspaper articles, 354 webpages, 112 reports from organizations, 30 case studies, six working papers, and seven dissertations, for a total of 1,511 references. Practical examples are provided throughout the book (with numerous references made to websites and YouTube videos that can be accessed in or outside of the classroom) and forty-six companies provide illustrations for the presented concepts and discussed issues. The cases of several of these companies (e.g., Danone, Disney, IKEA, Starbucks, and Volkswagen) have been purposefully utilized in multiple chapters in order to help readers create linkages between topics.

Contributor Bios

Thomas André is in charge of the Access to Energy program strategy at Schneider Electric. He started his career as an electronic hardware engineer and project manager in a French SME. After studying sustainability, Thomas joined Schneider Electric in 2010 to work on its inclusive business program. He first covered coordination and then business development activities, in parallel with writing his doctoral dissertation, focusing on the interactions between Base of the Pyramid, sustainability, and corporate strategies. Thomas holds an Engineering degree from ESME Sudria, an MSc in Sustainability from HEC Paris, and a PhD in Economics from Ecole Polytechnique.

Catherine Archambault is a PhD Student at University of Lille (France). She holds a BAA in Marketing and a MSc in Management from HEC Montréal (Canada). Her research interests focus on business models, business model innovation and experimentation. Her work aims to understand how incumbent firms achieve to create and capture value in novel ways. Catherine's teaching experience includes Master and Bachelor level courses on the topics of strategy and business models.

Ari Van Assche is associate professor and chair of the International Business department at HEC Montréal (Canada), as well as research fellow at the research centers CIRANO and IRPP. He holds a BA and an MA in Chinese Studies from the Katholieke Universiteit Leuven and a PhD in Economics from the University of Hawaii at Manoa. His research focuses on the organization of global value chains and their implications for trade and industrial cluster policy. On this topic, he has published widely in academic journals and has consulted for various Canadian and international governmental organizations, including Global Affairs Canada, Transport Canada, the Asian Development Bank and the World Bank.

Patrick Cohendet is full professor at HEC Montréal in the International Business Department. His research interests include Theory of the Firm, Economics of Innovation, Economics of Knowledge, Economics of Creativity, and Knowledge Management. He is the author of twenty books and more than 120 articles in refereed journals, such as *Research Policy, Organization Science, Industrial and Corporate Change, Journal of Economic Geography, Long Range Planning*, etc. He has been the supervisor xviii *Contributor Bios*

of more than seventy PhD students. He has conducted a series of studies on the economics of innovation for different international organisations, such as the European Commission, the Council of Europe, the European Space Agency and the Canadian Space Agency. He is currently co-director of the research group Mosaic at HEC Montréal on the management of innovation and creativity, and co-editor of the academic journal *International Management*.

Aude Le Cottier earned her MSc in Management from ESSEC Business School (France) in 2004. After several years in auditing, banking, and strategy consulting in Singapore, Paris, Morocco, and Dubai, she moved to Madrid to start her doctorate in Strategy. She is currently an Assistant Professor in International Management at HEC Montréal. Her research lies at the intersection between International Corporate Governance and International Management. She studies in particular how firm ownership, in several of its dimensions, impacts firms' strategy and performance.

Danilo Dantas is associate professor of marketing at HEC Montréal. His expertise revolves around electronic commerce, database marketing, and music marketing. He received a BAA in Administration from UFRGS in Brazil, a DESS, DEA, and doctorate from the Université de Grenoble II in France. His research has been published in peer-reviewed journals such as the *Canadian Journal of Administrative Sciences*, *Gestion*, *International Journal of Arts Management*, *Management Decisions and Marketing Intelligence & Planning*.

Jonathan Deschenes is associate professor of marketing at HEC Montréal. He received his PhD from Concordia University. He is co-founder and member of the executive committee of HEC's IDEOS strategic hub. His research has been presented in international conferences such as the *Association for Consumer Research Conference*, the *European Marketing Academy Conference* and the *International Conference Promoting Business Ethnics*. He has been published in academic journals such as the *Journal of Consumer Psychology*, *Journal of Business Research*, *Psychology and Marketing, and Journal of Consumer Culture*. His current research, which he carries out with various co-authors, focuses on solicitation of money and reciprocity in the charity sector, volunteering and legitimacy, as well as responsible consumption and circular economy. His fieldwork mostly focuses on Canada and China.

Pouya Ebrahimi holds an MSc (economics) from Université de Montréal and is a doctoral candidate in International Business at HEC Montréal. His research focuses on the impact of international taxation on the operations of multinational firms, in particular on their transfer pricing and global production decisions. His work has been presented in the annual meetings of the American Economic Association, Canadian Economics Association, and Strategic Management Society.

Contributor Bios xix

Verena Gruber is assistant professor of Marketing at HEC Montréal. Previously she has been assistant professor at WU Vienna (Austria), where she received her PhD in Marketing. Her research has been published in academic journals such as the *Journal of Public Policy and Marketing*, *Journal of Business Ethics*, *Journal of Advertising Research*, *Psychology & Marketing*, and *International Marketing Review*. Her research interests revolve around topics of consumer behavior and sustainability, with a particular focus on message framing and the impact of sustainability on well-being.

Ashraful Hassan has been working with Grameen Group since 1984. He currently serves as Managing Director of Grameen Telecom and is engaged in promoting and providing easy access to GSM cellular services in rural Bangladesh. He also serves as Managing Director of Grameen Distribution Ltd. and Grameen Shamogree, of which Grameen Distribution Ltd. is a large Social Business Company. He gained extensive and diversified knowledge in various industrial sectors especially in the field of textiles focusing on resource efficient and energy saving production with exposure in the industrial management, export market and labor management arenas. Ashraful also serves as a member of the Board of Directors of several enterprises that play commendable roles in the fields of renewable energy, health care, food & nutrition, information and communication technology, employment generation and so forth. He holds a Bachelor of Science in Engineering from Khulna University of Engineering and Technology, Bangladesh.

Renaud Legoux is associate professor of marketing at HEC Montréal. He holds the Professorship on big data for the arts and culture. He is the codirector of the Data Philanthropy Hub, an initiative of IVADO. He received his PhD in Management with a concentration in Marketing from McGill University (Canada). Before his academic career, he worked as a manager in the cultural field. His current research interests include consumer behavior, arts marketing, and customer satisfaction.

Pengfei Li is an assistant professor in the Department of International Business at HEC Montréal. He taught at the University of Toronto and East China Normal University in Shanghai. His research focuses on industrial clusters, knowledge and industrial evolution, and regional economic development. His work has been published in the *Journal of Economic Geography and Regional Studies*.

Marcelo Vinhal Nepomuceno is an associate professor in marketing at HEC Montréal. He has a Master's degree in Psychology from the University of Brasilia (Brazil) and a PhD (valedictorian) in Business Administration from Concordia University (Canada). He has also been an Assistant Professor of Marketing at ESCP Europe (Paris Campus). He has published papers in the *Journal of Consumer Psychology*, *Journal of Business Ethics*, *Journal of Business Research*, *Journal of Advertising Research*, *International Journal of Advertising*, *Journal of Consumer Affairs*, and *Journal*

xx   *Contributor Bios*

of Retailing and Consumer Services, Personality and Individual Differences, among other journals. Marcelo's research interests revolved around social psychology, consumer behavior, and evolutionary psychology. He is particularly interested in anti-consumption, materialism, social media, and the influence of hormones on behavior.

David Pastoriza is associate professor of international business at HEC Montréal. He received his PhD from IESE Business School (Spain). His research has been published in academic journals such as the *Journal of Economics & Management Strategy, the International Business Review, and Journal of Business Ethics.* His current research focuses on the Liability of Foreignness on the PGA Tour.

Marlei Pozzebon is full professor at HEC Montréal and associate professor at FGV/EAESP (Brazil). Some keywords of her research are social change, citizen creativity, social technologies, global-local dialogue, and post-development. Her research interests are linked to the relationship between technology and society and to the possibilities of better understanding and promoting social change using practice-based theoretical lenses and qualitative research methods. Marlei has been published in journals such as *Organization Studies, Journal of Management Studies,* and *Business and Society and Public Administration,* among others, and in leading Brazilian journals such as *Revista de Administração de Empresas.*

Polona Prešeren holds a BA in international relations and MSc in political science from the University of Ljubljana, Slovenia. As the Undersecretary at the Government Communication Office of the Republic of Slovenia and the "I feel Slovenia" Brand Manager, she is responsible for coordinating brand management processes. Polonoa started her career in journalism, writing for several Slovenian magazines and newspapers. She was aslo an editor of *Sinfo* magazine and www.slovenia.si.

Mina Rohani is an assistant professor of marketing at the Edwards School of Business (University of Saskatchewan, Canada). She completed her postdoctoral fellowship and PhD in Marketing at the HEC Montréal. Her research interests are in services marketing, online public complaining, consumer revenge and forgiveness. Her research has been presented at prestigious marketing conferences, such as the Service Frontiers (2015 and 2012), American Marketing Association Conference (2015 and 2013), Association for Consumer Research (2013), Advertising and Consumer Psychology Conference (2013), and La Londe Conference (2012). Before her doctoral studies, she worked in the telecommunications industry as a marketing product manager. She holds a bachelor in Computer Hardware Engineering, an MSc in Systems Engineering, and an EMBA.

Ekaterina Turkina holds a PhD in Public and International Affairs from the University of Pittsburgh (US). She is associate professor at HEC Montréal and a holder of Professorship in International Business Networks. Ekaterina is also an associate editor of the *Journal of Small Business and Entrepreneurship,* as well as a member of the International Advisory Board of

International Journal of Productivity Management and Assessment Technologies. Her main research areas are socio-cultural and politico-economic contexts in international business, innovation and inter-firm networks, international entrepreneurship, and industrial clustering. Among other journals, she has published in *World Economy Journal, Journal of Business Venturing, Journal of Common Market Studies, Journal of Business Research, Journal of European Integration*, and *Cross Cultural Management: an International Journal*.

Thierry Warrin is associate professor of international business at HEC Montréal and a faculty affiliate at the MOC Network (Harvard Business School). He is also a Fellow (former Vice-President Strategy and International Economics) at CIRANO (Canada) and a Researcher at CERIUM (University of Montreal). He completed his PhD in monetary economics and finance at the Essec Business School in Paris. He subsequently held positions in academic institutions like Middlebury College USA, Polytechnique Montreal, Sun Yat Sen University Guangzhou, Essec Business School Paris, HEC Paris, La Sorbonne, and UIBE Beijing. His research revolves around international economics and finance topics, with a particular focus on the European economic integration, while using Data Science as his main methodological approach.

Acknowledgments

During the four years it took to put this book together, from inception to completion, I benefited from the expertise and the help of a number of people and entities that I would like to warmly thank.

In regard to content, fourteen of my colleagues at HEC Montreal in the departments of International Business and Marketing either directly contributed by writing a paragraph or two, based on their respective fields of expertise, or suggested someone with recent publications on the topics at hand. The idea of inviting this great number of internal contributors stems from my belief that, at HEC Montreal, we have a collective expertise (about issues that firms face in a global world) with strong connections. Often, these connections are not self-evident because, as researchers, we each publish in our specialized domains. However, a textbook with a strong academic flavor could best reveal these connections and show how intertwined all of our research interests really are. Thus, my gratitude goes to: Patrick Cohendet, Danilo Dantas, Jonathan Deschenes, Yany Gregoire, Verena Gruber, Aude Le Cottier, Renaud Legoux, Pengfei Li, Marcelo Nepomuceno, David Pastoriza, Marlei Pozzebon, Ekaterina Turkina, Ari Van Assche, and Thierry Warin for having contributed with their time and knowledge. It also goes to the three former students in the MSc and PhD programs who now pursue academic careers elsewhere, as well as the three practitioners who kindly accepted to participate: Thomas Andre, Catherine Archambault, Pouya Ebrahimi, Ashraful Hassan, Mina Rohani, and Polona Prešeren.

For twelve consecutive university trimesters, I have worked with fifteen motivated assistants, all hand-picked among our best Msc and PhD students. My thanks go to: Catherine Archambault, Didier Chanut, Pouya Ebrahimi, Bazhena Ivanova, Andriana Hnatykiw, Tara Mcgrath, Shoma Patnaik, Nebojsa Radovic, Houda Sbaa, and Julio Natal Sequeira, who helped me with research and writing tasks. Julio Natal Sequeira is to be particularly commended for his hard work in helping create a total of 242 original figures and tables to illustrate this book. He also contributed directly by posing as a model in photographs to illustrate concepts of nonverbal communication (Figure 5.6) and commercial disputes, along with Tara Mcgrath and Marc-Antoine Hébert (Figure 6.11). In turn, the administrative work of Emmanuel Bou, Marianne Deschenes, Pouya Ebrahimi, Marc-Antoine Hébert, Vincent Limoges, and Jean-Nicolas Yacoub has been key in compiling all of my teaching notes, as well as contacting and tracking the answers from 145

Acknowledgments xxiii

organizations in order to finally obtain seventy permissions to reproduce proprietary material (company logos, product pictures, and authors' portrays). Between January 2012 and April 2017, I have taught the course 6–014–13 Marketing and Globalization in English and French nine times and would like to thank all of the students who have taken this course for their sharp questions and useful comments.

On the practical side of things, the financial support of both the Department of International Business and the Direction de la Recherche at HEC Montreal (in the form of grants and paid assistantships) has been elemental in moving the book forward. The understanding and encouragement of my Department Head, Ari Van Assche, has been invaluable. The trust and continuous support of publishing experts at Taylor and Francis/Routledge, in particular Sharon Golan, Erin Arata, and Alston Slatton were also instrumental. Finally, I cannot emphasize enough the skills and infinite patience of the English editing and proofreading of Gabrielle Ciquier, Tara Mcgrath, and Sarah Pierpoint.

From a personal point of view, I would like to dedicate this book to readers who want to learn. Not in my capacity as a professor, but as a student myself. Someone accused me one day in a rather spiteful manner of being "an eternal student." I want to thank that person: it was in fact the nicest compliment I could receive. I have work experience and degrees in fields others than international business and marketing. When I graduated, I knew little about globalization. Since then, I have read, I have talked to others, and I have learned. This book encapsulates a lot of this gathered knowledge. It represents many hours of hard work, and I am grateful to family members and friends who offered comforting words during this time. I hope that my daughter, Vita, born in the last year of writing this book, will grow to appreciate the efforts—and rewards—of learning. My wish is to inspire other eternal students.

1 Globalization

Table of Contents

1 Globalization

Introduction: What Does Globalization Mean for Marketers? 2
- 1.1 *Definitions*...4
  - 1.1.1 *An Increase in Scale*..4
  - 1.1.2 *Historical Perspective* 9
  - 1.1.3 *In the Business World (Levitt)* 10
- 1.2 *Drivers* 11
  - 1.2.1 *Politics and Integration* 12
  - 1.2.2 *Technology and Convergence* 14
- 1.3 *Issues at Stake and Examples* 20
  - 1.3.1 *Scope and Measurement* 21
  - 1.3.2 *Corporate Examples: New Balance and Nike; Tata Motors; Nokia and Ericsson; Amazon, Apple, Google, and Facebook* 26
  - 1.3.3 *Ambivalence of Outcomes*.................................30

Conclusion: For marketers, globalization means an increase in the scale of activities, supported by convergence and integration. It forces them to understand changing degrees of distance between markets and find new ways to differentiate from rising competition.
References

Recommended Reading

- Levitt, Theodore (1983). The Globalization of Markets. *Harvard Business Review*, 61(3), 92–102

2 *Globalization*

Figure 1.1 Illustrating Chapter 1
Source: Own elaboration

Introduction: What Does Globalization Mean for Marketers?

One of the ideas often associated with globalization is that distance represents less and less of an impediment to international business in general, and to international marketing in particular. In this view, the world is considered borderless and firms can market their products and services anywhere. Illustrated in Figure 1.2, examples of publications bearing this idea include Cairncross's (2001) book entitled *The Death of Distance 2.0: How Communication Revolution Will Change Our Lives*, and *The World Is Flat: A Brief History of the Twenty-First Century* by Friedman (2005).

However, the question **"Is distance dead?"** still receives much attention. The notion of distance refers to more than just physical distance between two geographical locations. We are, in fact, talking about various kinds of differences between countries (cultural, administrative, economic, and technological) that are routinely studied for impeding, slowing down, or making international business more difficult, costly, and hazardous. Authors such as Ghemawat (2001) do not hesitate to claim that *"distance still matters."*

Thus, asking the question **"What does globalization mean for marketers?"** leads us not only to wonder about firms' internationalization and marketers' skills and tools in this context (Chapters 2–3), but also to question whether distance in all its forms is actually increasing or decreasing worldwide (Chapters 4–7). We also use this question to set the stage for the study of marketing practices that have been developed in reaction to the globalization phenomenon (Chapters 8–13).

Figure 1.2 Books supporting the idea that "distance is dead"

Source: The jacket design of *The Death of Distance* by Cairncross (2001) is reprinted by permission of Harvard Business Publishing; The jacket design of *The World Is Flat* by Friedman (2005) is reprinted by permission of Farrar, Straus and Giroux. Jacket design by Dean Nicastro copyright © 2005. Jacket art: Digital image of the earth © 1996 CORBIS; Image courtesy of NASA/CORBIS.

4   *Globalization*

The objectives of this chapter are to first define globalization and reflect on its origins. Second, we look at the drivers of globalization (politics and technology) and the important mechanisms through which globalization operates (integration and convergence). Finally, we discuss related issues (such as the scope and measurement of globalization, as well as conflicting opinions about its outcomes) and consider its impact on marketing decisions. Figure 1.3 indicates the position of this chapter in the overall book structure.

1.1 Definitions

This section addresses the following questions:

- What is globalization?
- When did globalization start?
- Who popularized the term in the business world?

1.1.1 An Increase in Scale

What is globalization? A great number of definitions of *globalization* exist and a variety of perspectives can be found in the literature. It is not easy to find a consensual definition, due to the complexity of the phenomenon. However, most authors agree on the fact that it is a process, not a "state." Put simply, the following statements capture common ways of defining globalization: i) "This thing is everywhere now" (pointing to an increase in scale—or extent—of availability), ii) "Everything is becoming interrelated" (pointing to the mechanism of integration), and iii) instead of "everything is becoming similar" (pointing to the mechanism of convergence). In fact, integration and convergence are the reasons why "something" is found in an increasing number of places around the world. Distinguishing the causes from the actual phenomenon is important. Thus, we define globalization as the increasing scale of an object's availability beyond the borders of its territory of origin. An object can be many "things." Flows across national borders include exchanges (imports and exports) of goods and services, capital, information, ideas and technology, not to mention jobs (Griffin & Pustay, 2006). For this reason, the notion of *borders* is central to defining globalization, an inherently territorial phenomenon. Yet, a territory is not only geographic/tangible and its borders are not only at the national level. We address this point later on.

What are some formal definitions of globalization? Globalization has been described as "the increased mobility of goods, services, labor, technology and capital throughout the world" and add that, from the viewpoint of the firm, as "the process of doing something that is worldwide in scope" (Cateora, Gilly, & Graham, 2011, p. 11). Croucher (2004, p. 10) presents globalization as "the process of transformation of local or regional phenomena into global phenomena driven by a combination of economic, technological, socio-cultural and political forces."

What is the common idea in these definitions? The notion of an increase in scale. The question concerning where can an object be found becomes central

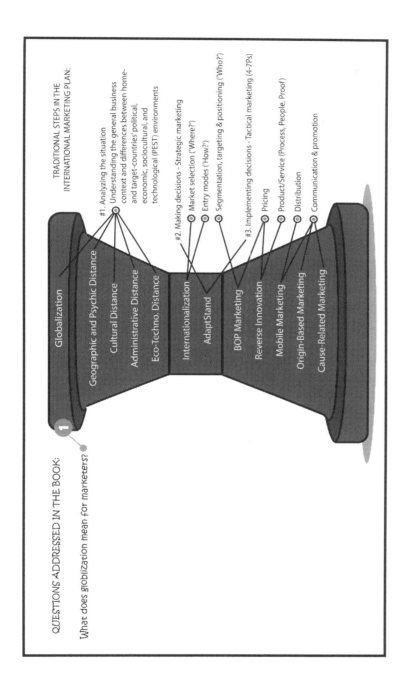

Figure 1.3 Positioning Chapter 1 in the overall book structure

Source: Own elaboration

6 Globalization

to defining globalization. If the answer is "worldwide," then the object in question is "global." Yet, since all things that are being "globalized" are not necessarily found everywhere, a finer definition is needed. Globalization is more about the "displacement" of an object, across borders, from a specific origin to a wider destination. One example of this increase in scale is the phenomenal growth of international trade of goods and services, as illustrated next.

What data supports this idea of an increase in scale? The growth of exports of goods and services in absolute numbers (see Figure 1.4) shows a rather spectacular increase. For instance, exports value was tripled in twenty years (from ~2.5 trillion USD to ~7.95 trillion USD between 1980 and 2000) and then tripled again in the next fourteen years (reaching a peak of 24 trillion USD in 2014) (World Bank, 2016d). Yet, the phenomenon of increase in scale is best illustrated by the growth of exports as a ratio of the world's GDP. Indeed, Figure 1.5 indicates a sharp increase in the proportion of value represented by exports compared to the overall value created in the world (measured by all countries' cumulated GDP). It has more than doubled in the 1960–2015 timeframe, increasing from ~12 percent to ~29 percent in 2015 (World Bank, 2016a).

What could be other examples of "things" that have been displaced to a larger scale? For instance, do you, like Levitt (1983), think that pizza and jazz are good examples of the globalization of markets? It is safe to say that you can eat pizza (originally from Italy) and listen to live jazz (originally from the US) in any major city around the globe. But can you do so in smaller towns? Or in rural areas of East-Asian countries? Probably not. Another example would include celebrations; fifteen years ago, Halloween was still a very North American celebration. However, nowadays, European children and teenagers increasingly dress up and trick-or-treat on October 31 every year. Does it mean that this celebration has been globalized? Yes. Does it mean that it is now celebrated everywhere? No. We also often hear about various events that used to be contained within national or regional borders and that have now spread at a much larger scale. Examples of these types of events include financial crises and epidemics, etc.

What is an important observation that can be made based on these examples? The point is that the scale to which "something" is available (or present) far away from its place of origin varies. Its presence can be either extensive or moderate. What matters in defining globalization is the expanding scale of that presence. Another compelling example is to count the number of countries in which "something" must be present to be considered "global." Again, the purist community on globalization would say that that "something" must be present "worldwide." But hold that thought for a minute. **First, we must ask ourselves the following question: how many countries are there in the world?** Depending on the way we recognize sovereign countries, there is a total of between 180 and 220 countries in the world. The United Nations was made up of 193 Member States, as of 2018 (UN, 2018).

So, from which number of countries can "something" be considered global? Is it really 190 and not below? What if Starbucks only sells in about seventy

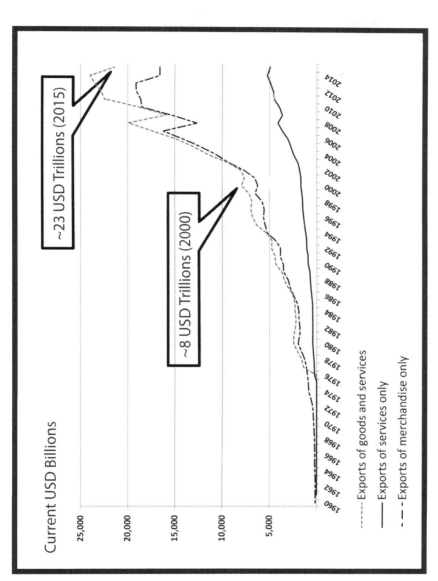

Figure 1.4 Illustrating the growth of exports of goods and services in absolute numbers (1960–2015)

Source: World Bank (2016b, 2016c, 2016d)

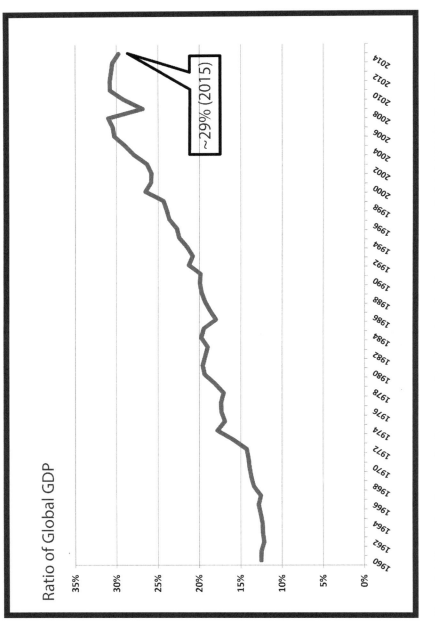

Figure 1.5 Illustrating the growth of exports of goods and services in proportion of global GDP (1960–2015)

Source: World Bank (2016a)

countries (Starbucks, 2017)—should it not be considered a global company? There is no easy answer. The industry of fast-moving consumer goods (FMCG) flaunts multinational corporations (MNCs) (e.g., Nestlé, Unilever, and Coca-Cola) that sell their products in more than 150 countries. In contrast, the retailing industry is proud of its multinational giants, like Carrefour or Walmart, even though they operate in only about forty countries. As such, there is no consensual rule about how extensive the scale must be to be characterized as globalization. The increased scale of "where" products (or any other object) are made available is what matters in defining globalization. Before turning to integration and convergence as drivers of globalization, we need to look further into its historical development.

1.1.2 Historical Perspective

When did globalization start? Thinking about the beginnings of globalization, we instinctively jump back to the mid-1990s, with the advent of the Internet and all the new information and communication technologies (ICT) that flourished at the time. With not only the global circulation of products, but also circulation of ideas and information, we could also identify the 1950s, post-World War II, as a period when cross-border flows started to significantly increase in volume and speed.

Could we go further back in time? Starting in the 1750s, the waves of industrial revolutions coexisted with the formation of the economies of modern "nations" and with global circuits of capital. Then, what about the affairs of Old Europe colonial states (e.g., Spain and Portugal) in the Americas? What about the colonization of the Indies? Did it not result in products, capital, and ideas being used far away from their birthplace? Following this logic, we could say that globalization started sometime in the fifteenth to eighteenth centuries. But then, what about Marco Polo's travels? Did the Silk Road (1295) not reignite the interest for commerce between Europe and the Far East? Indeed, there is no reason to stop here and not go back in time as far as the Mongol Empire (c. thirteenth to fourteenth century), the Islamic Golden Age (c. seventh to twelfth century), or even the Roman Empire (c. first to fourth century)!

Is there any limit in dating the phenomenon of globalization? Why not then include the early migrations of humanity? We could indeed. It is hard to date precisely the time when globalization started. What is important to remember is that throughout history, we have observed waves of globalization in very different locations on the planet. From an occidental perspective, we often hear about the following phases: i) early forms of globalization (from the beginnings of humanity to about the Renaissance, fourteenth century), ii) an expanding globalization (fifteenth to eighteenth century), and iii) modern globalization (nineteenth century to present) (Griffin & Pustay, 2006). Other chronologies are also put forward in trying to describe a phenomenon that is intrinsically intertwined with the development of humanity.

Therefore, it is also useful to turn toward the fields of history, sociology, and philosophy. In particular, one needs to contrast the "stages" of society and their foundations in the premodern (valuing the past and traditions), modern and hypermodern (valuing the future, individualism, and progress), and postmodern (valuing the present and hedonism) eras to better comprehend the

10 *Globalization*

phenomenon of globalization. A good starting point for someone with no previous background in the matter would be Wikipedia entries about "modernity" and "postmodernity" (Wikipedia, 2017a, b).

What is an important lesson that we can learn from this excursion outside the realm of business administration? It is important to be cognizant of the timeframe by which we decide to look at the phenomenon of globalization. Indeed, we are talking about an evolution that occurred in phases and that spanned several centuries. We often get the feeling that disruptions of the "established order" have been more and more frequent in the past decades, hence the fact that periods of stability (i.e., periods of time sharing homogeneous features) are shorter and shorter, and that history has been accelerating. However, a time period of ten years or even thirty years is probably too short to provide a clear understanding of what is going on, let alone the timeframe of a few months or years that most articles in business magazines or the general media employ when covering the topic of globalization. Globalization evolves over time according to beliefs about how society functions. These beliefs take a long time to settle and change.

1.1.3 In the Business World (Levitt)

Back to the field of business administration, who popularized the term "globalization"? Theodore Levitt is often mentioned as the person who coined and helped diffuse the term *globalization,* thanks to a seminal article entitled: "The Globalization of Markets," published in the Harvard Business Review (HBR) in May–June 1983. An inquiry in Google Scholar (March 2018) shows that this article had been cited more than 6,800 times.

Who was Theodore Levitt? Levitt (1925–2006) was an American economist and professor at Harvard Business School (Boston, Massachusetts). He was also editor of the *Harvard Business Review* (HBR) from 1985 to 1989 (Harvard University Gazette, 2006). HBR was created in 1922 and is considered one of the most influential reviews in business administration. It is ranked nineth in a list of the top-fifty journals (Financial Times, 2016). Contrary to most scientific journals making the list of the *Financial Times,* HBR mainly targets CEOs as an audience, before scholars. Usually, articles in HBR are written by established scholars, often in collaboration with practitioners in large companies, and their content is expunged of technical vocabulary and methods to focus solely on managerial implications of studies and observations conducted by their authors.

What are the benefits of globalization? This question deserves to be debated. We can start by acknowledging what Levitt had to say about the topic in his 1983 article (see "Food for Thought").

Food for Thought 1.1

- In reference to Levitt (1983), what are the benefits of globalization? What is the difference between a global and a multinational company? What is the central concept used for this distinction?

Globalization 11

Figure 1.6 Portrait of Theodore Levitt

Source: Screen capture from a YouTube video available with search words: "Global Markets by Theodore Levitt," posted by PRSmith1000, retrievable at www.YouTube.com/watch?v=h52W3D-tuf0

One avenue to start answering the "Food for Thought" lies in a direct quote from Levitt (1983, p. 92): "The globalization of markets is at hand. With that, the multinational commercial world nears its end, and so does the multinational corporation [. . .] The multinational corporation operates in a number of countries, and adjusts its products and processes in each, at high relative cost [. . .] The global corporation operates with resolute constancy . . . it sells the same things in the same way everywhere." Thus, the concept of standardization, enabled by technological progress, is put at the core of the globalization phenomenon. Levitt's prediction about a vastly standardized marketing has been the object of much criticism. Even global companies like Coca-Cola and McDonald's, with highly standardized products and processes, do not "sell the same thing the same way everywhere," but adapt to local conditions to a certain extent (see Chapter 3 for more details on the AdaptStand debate).

1.2 Drivers

This section addresses the following questions:

- What are the main drivers of globalization? In particular, what is integration and what is convergence?
- How do the various perspectives of globalization (scale, integration, and convergence) relate to one another?

Globalization is such a complex phenomenon that it is hard to disentangle its drivers (i.e., the reasons why it is occurring) from its outcomes. Here, we

12 Globalization

focus on the most recent phase of globalization as we know it, when globalization adopted a faster pace at the turn of the twenty-first century. We start by comparing the situation before and after this change.

1.2.1 Politics and Integration

What did the world look like in the 1980s from a Western perspective? In the 1980s, we had a strong opposition between two models of society based on radically different economic systems: liberalism and the market economy (marked by deregulations and privatizations of many activities, including manufacturing, transports, communication, financial system, banking, etc.)—probably best personified by Ronald Reagan and Margaret Thatcher, and communism and the state economy (marked by centralization, planning, etc.) in what was known as the USSR. The latter also characterized China at the time, but the country was looking inward and not participating much as an actor in the international scene. Other countries in Asia, Africa, and Latin America did not hold much political power or economic weight.

What are the world dynamics like since the 1990s? The USSR collapsed and most countries have transitioned or are still transitioning toward a market economy. It appears that capitalism has become the mainstream economic system. However, it starts to be seriously questioned with the incipient notion of a "social economy." In addition, the merits of democracy and secularism, as opposed to autocracies and religious states, are at the forefront of international debate and the source of many conflicts (e.g., the Arab Spring in 2011). Another divide has appeared: developed economies vs. emerging economies. Acronyms to design new groups of countries sharing similar characteristics in their development stage have appeared as these countries have started to weigh-in, in the world's economic situation—like the BRICs (Brazil, Russia, India, and China), the CIVETS (Colombia, Indonesia, Vietnam, Egypt, Turkey, and South Africa) and the MIST (Mexico, Indonesia, South Korea, and Turkey). The longstanding 80/20 split of the world's GDP between developed and emerging economies is rapidly evolving toward a 50/50 ratio (sometime between 2015 and 2020), and most likely toward a shift in power soon afterward (The Economist, 2011).

What is at the root of these two different pictures of the world dynamics (1980s and 2010s)? The answer would be changes in politics. States have stopped fighting on one front, to fight on another. They have agreed to reduce the thickness of their borders and to increase cross-border flows. They have ceded part of their authority to transnational institutions that have taken on a more active role (e.g., the World Trade Organization, WTO, created in 1995). In parallel, another type of major change related to technology has occurred: the advent of the Internet (roughly dated in 1995, when it reached significant diffusion). Advances in communication and transportation have procured the means to increase cross-border flows. It is perhaps wiser not to get caught up in the chicken-or-egg debate about which had precedent over the other (technology or politics), but simply note that the end of the Cold War (and the fall of the Berlin Wall in 1989 as a symbolic event) as well as the advent of the Internet mark the transition toward an episode of fast-paced

Globalization   13

globalization. Looking further back in the history of globalization, it is safe to say that changes in politics and in technology explain various phases in globalization and are, as such, key drivers of the phenomenon.

What is integration? Researchers have been interested in integration for many decades. For instance, Mitrany (1933) defines international *integration* as the collective governance and the interdependence between nations. In turn, regional integration is seen as a process in which nations enter an agreement in order to improve regional cooperation through institutions and norms (Rosamond, 2000). Both of these sources (selected among many other available definitions) explain that integration is notably due to a change in the structure and locus of authority. On the one hand, we find that the power of states is eroding. The notion of "state" is built on a principle of territorialism; it is increasingly seen as obsolete as a form of social organization. On the other hand, we observe that "knowledge" (embodied by academics and experts) is weighing more and more in the decision-making process. This type of authority (i.e., "the more knowledgeable one decides") contrasts with the more ancient type of authority that was based on strength (i.e., "the more belligerent one decides"). Traditionally, strength has been linked to military power, which is also a territorial concept. Nowadays, states have lost control of military power (e.g., independent armed groups—including terrorists groups—are found in many countries).

In terms of examples, we need to distinguish among examples that expose integration (i.e., the interrelation between objects or "things") and examples that are symptomatic of this integration. In the former category, we can find examples in regional blocks (e.g., the North American Free Trade Agreement, NAFTA) and supranational institutions (e.g., the World Trade Organization and the United Nations, which count 164–193 state members and, respectively, aim to enhance international commerce and peace). To become members, nations abdicate part of their sovereign power to comply with policies emitted by these supranational institutions. In the latter category, financial crises spread because financial systems of a great number of countries are pegged to one another. In this way, one could say that integration is a cause for the increase in scale.

What is the key concept to remember here? The notion of boundaries is fading. Interdependence and unity (e.g., among countries) results from this process of integration. Yet, we have only discussed boundaries from the perspective of national borders. **Are there any other types of fading boundaries, more abstract ones, that illustrate the mechanism of integration?** An example of a more abstract type of boundary is the one that previously separated different spheres of human activity, like the "public" and "private" spheres. Before the existence of social networks like Facebook and Renren, what we had for breakfast, for instance, was usually known by a very restricted number of people. It was private. Today, a few dozen or even hundreds of "friends" can be privy to this delicious oatmeal bowl. In the same vein, if someone drank too much at a party, only the circle of people who had attended the party knew about that person's drunkenness. Today, pictures or videos of this drunken person can be diffused to millions of strangers and may even be found by future employers. Many aspects of individuals' private

14 Globalization

lives can now be made public. To some extent, this example illustrates the disappearance of boundaries in social life.

1.2.2 Technology and Convergence

What is convergence? *Convergence* refers to the mechanism by which different economies, cultures, or technologies evolve into becoming more similar or uniform. For instance, the global economic convergence has been defined as a process by which different economies of the world become more alike (in terms of access to common technology, similar capital–labor ratios, real wage levels, productivity levels, and standards of living) (Dowrick & DeLong, 2003). Figures 1.7–1.10 represent the chronological evolution of countries becoming members or falling out of membership of the so-called "Convergence Club." **Can we conclude with certainty that we observe economic convergence at a global level?** Probably not. Over time, there are signs of convergence and signs of divergence.

Second, we can take a look at cultural convergence. **What are examples of cultures becoming more similar?** The emergence of global consumers, in other words, people sharing sets of important symbols related to the consumption culture (e.g., consumption of coffee and fast-food, use of credit cards, studying in coffee shops) is a good example. However, this is a complex question, because people also strengthen their cultural identity (e.g., immigrants, sport supporters, defenders of national independence) and do not hesitate to use social media to do so. For instance, we can find numerous initiatives on Twitter or Facebook, such as "Canadians living in Qatar," that help communities share and reinforce their sense of belonging to a specific culture. Many on-going movements for separatism and gaining national independence (e.g., Quebec from Canada, Scotland from the UK, Casamance from Senegal and Catalonia from Spain) contradict the thesis that the world is smoothly converging toward a homogeneous culture. Figure 1.11 illustrates demonstrations held in Barcelona in 2015 with more than one million people protesting for the right to a vote for independence.

Can we conclude with certainty that we observe cultural convergence at a global level over a long period of time? Probably not. There are also signs of convergence and signs of divergence. Specialists even talk about cultural "crossvergence" (see Chapter 5 for more details), blurring even more our chances for a straightforward answer.

As a conclusion, what are the keywords that are worth remembering when defining globalization? Defining globalization suggests to adopt a scale perspective (the key concept is *increase in scale*, with objects being displaced further away from their point of origin, crossing borders, and becoming available at a larger scale), an integration perspective (the keywords being *unity* and *interdependence*, with the disappearance of borders), and a convergence perspective (the keywords are then *uniformity* and *homogeneity*, with systems like economies and cultures becoming more alike). At an anecdotal level, the advertising "Write the Future" (Nike, 2010) released in the context of the soccer World Cup adequately illustrates the mechanisms of increase in scale, integration, and convergence.

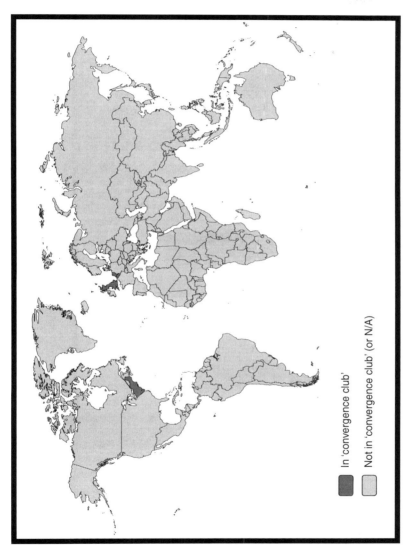

Figure 1.7 The "Convergence Club" in 1850
Source: Adapted from Dowrick and DeLong (2003, p. 197)
For the color version, see the eResource at www.routledge.com/9781138202344

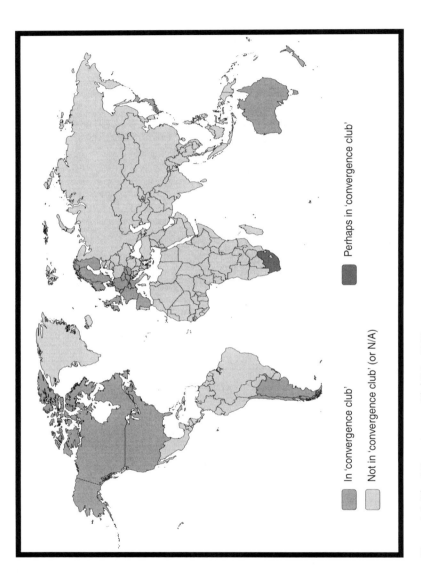

Figure 1.8 The "Convergence Club" in 1900
Source: Adapted from Dowrick and DeLong (2003, p. 199)
For the color version, see the eResource at www.routledge.com/9781138202344

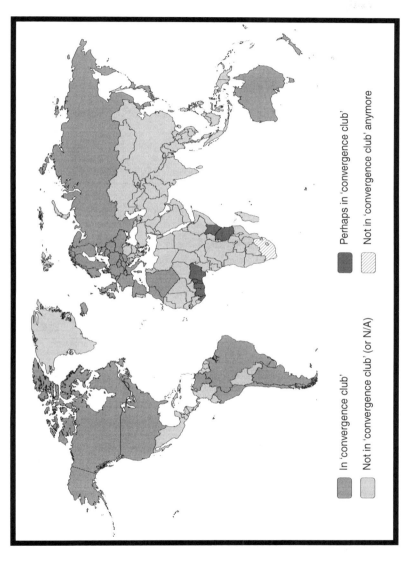

Figure 1.9 The "Convergence Club" interwar period
Source: Adapted from Dowrick and DeLong (2003, p. 200)
For the color version, see the eResource at www.routledge.com/9781138202344

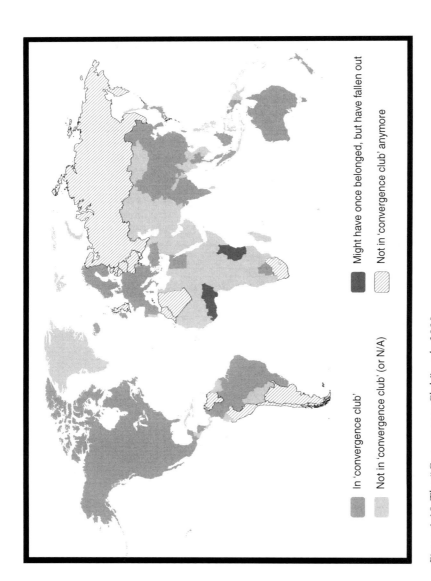

Figure 1.10 The "Convergence Club" early 2000s
Source: Adapted from Dowrick and DeLong (2003, p. 202)
For the color version, see the eResource at www.routledge.com/9781138202344

Figure 1.11 Illustrating separatism and the use of media to defend local identities as counter evidence to cultural convergence

Source: Screen capture from a YouTube video available with search words: "España-Cataluña #1: Una explicación imparcial del deseo de independencia," posted by El Contexto Magazine, retrievable at www.YouTube.com/watch?v=Xeeg_fKCv6k

Can we link these perspectives of globalization (scale, integration, and convergence) to one another? Figure 1.12 proposes a simplification of the complex linkages between these concepts. First, we can look at the scale increase as a result of integration (it is because borders are opening that objects can cross them). In turn, convergence can be seen as a possible outcome of the scale increase of cross-border flows (objects being increasingly available everywhere, local specificities are diluted). Integration and convergence mutually reinforce each other (the more interdependent the nations and the fewer the exchange barriers between them, the more likely convergence will happen; in turn, the more standards and preferences converge across borders, and the more likely governments are to facilitate integration). For companies, the combination of these mechanisms has two main consequences. First, distance between markets changes in a dual manner. Distance increases because of the change of scale, in the sense that companies can go further and further away from their home base and are thus confronted with wider differences in target markets than ever before. At the same time, distance also decreases because of integration and convergence. Hence, the necessity for marketers to accurately evaluate which distances are increasing and which are decreasing. Finally, competition is on the rise. Integration means that companies can go and compete more efficiently in foreign markets against local companies, but that they also have to defend their own traditional territories against foreign competitors. Convergence entails the need to further differentiate and become better than competitors at addressing similar needs. It can be argued that the level of consolidation observed in certain industries (e.g., automotive and telecommunication sectors) in which a few major global players emerged would

20 *Globalization*

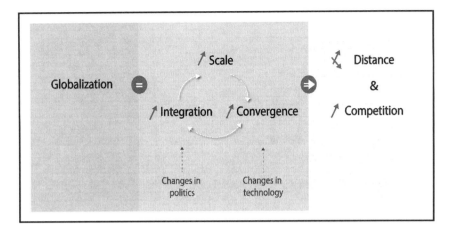

Figure 1.12 Depicting globalization, its mechanisms and main outcomes for marketers
Source: Own elaboration

instead suggest a decrease in competition. This is correct in terms of the number of competitors, but the level of competitive intensity that these remaining actors are experiencing is unprecedented. Overall, a significant increase in the level of competitive rivalry among firms is probably one of the most challenging issues related to globalization. Its central mechanisms (increase in scale, integration, and convergence) all result in the need for companies to differentiate themselves from foreign competitors (both at home and abroad).

Next, we reflect on the impact of convergence and integration on marketing managers' tasks (see "Food for Thought").

Food for Thought 1.2

- To what extent do the mechanisms of convergence and integration help the marketer in his/her tasks overseas?

1.3 Issues at Stake and Examples

This section addresses the following questions:

- To what extent is the world globalized?
- How can we measure globalization?
- Is globalization a good or a bad thing?
- How do integration and convergence affect companies?

Figure 1.13 Portrait of Pankaj Ghemawat
Source: Courtesy of Pankaj Ghemawat

1.3.1 Scope and Measurement

To what extent is the world globalized? In the Western world, we tend to think that globalization is extensive (i.e., that the phenomenon has reached the most remote parts of the globe). However, reality checks remind us that this is far from being the case. Pankaj Ghemawat, a professor who was on the faculty at Harvard Business School (from 1983 to 2008) and has been working at the Stern School of Business (New York City) and IESE Business School (Barcelona), rejects a general tendency to assume (or predict) a nearly complete internationalization and rather talks about "semi-internationalization."

For instance, he proposed in his book *Redefining Global Strategy: Crossing Borders in a World Where Differences Still Matter* (2007) to look at the degree of internationalization of various activities (such as foreign direct investment (FDI), patenting, etc.). The ratios presented in Figure 1.15 are obtained by measuring the proportion of activities conducted outside the home country compared to the activities conducted within the home country (in 2004). In this way, we can read the figure in the following manner: fewer than 5 percent of all telephone calls made are international phone calls.

What is this graph telling us? According to this study, the level of internationalization of various activities is far from reaching 100 percent on the internationalization scale. This observation echoes the illustration presented in Figure 1.5 about the value of exports as a ratio of global GDP. In spite of a sharp increase in the past decades, this ratio also stays below the 35 percent threshold. This reminds us that, although international trade is growing fast, the vast majority of business is still done domestically.

Ghemawat (2007) supports the idea that differences between countries are larger than generally recognized and that, as a result, corporate strategies

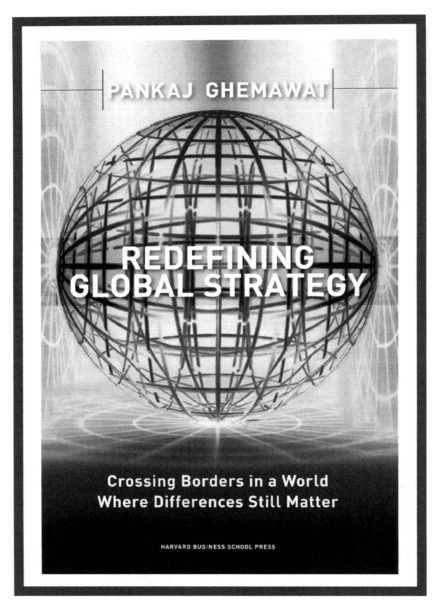

Figure 1.14 Book supporting the idea that "distance is not dead"
Source: The jacket design of *The Death of Distance* by Ghemawat (2007) is reprinted by permission of Harvard Business Publishing

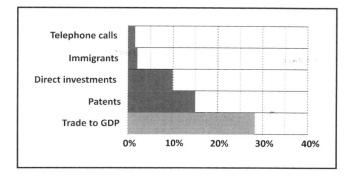

Figure 1.15 Illustrating the concept of semi-internationalization
Source: Adapted from Ghemawat (2007, *Fig. 1.1*)

based on a complete global integration tend to put too much emphasis on standardization and scalar expansion. We will develop further on this topic in Chapter 3.

Other authors use different angles to study the scale of globalization. For instance, París (2008) looks at the degree of globalization of various functional activities in the automotive industry. Figure 1.16 shows that Research & Development and Sourcing are two of the most globalized corporate functions. Other functions can be considered regionalized (e.g., Finance and Production), while still others are still localized (Sales and After-Sales Service). Finally, we can zoom in and focus on one specific function, in this case the marketing function, and observe that various activities or policies are characterized by different scales. If decisions related to Product management can be considered being taken at a regional and global level, Price management remains a very local activity.

While we explore the idea that globalization is a process through which the scale of "something" (e.g., a corporate function) expands from a local, to a regional, to a global reach, we must ask ourselves how we can measure the progress of this reach.

How can we measure globalization? Have you heard of any indexes of globalization? We find an increasing number of attempts to aggregate indicators and propose an evaluation of the degree of globalization in the world. These attempts rely on a country-level of analysis and take globalization to mean "openness to the world" (as opposed to being closed up and protectionist). In a way, the integration perspective is adopted here, since the measures capture the permeability of national borders. Among several other initiatives, the Swiss Federal Institute of Technology has developed the KOF Index of Globalization since 2002, the University of Warwick in UK proposes the CSGR Globalization Index (with data going as far back as 1982) and Ernst & Young has collaborated with the Economist Intelligence Unit (EIU) to publish a Globalization Index (1995–2012).

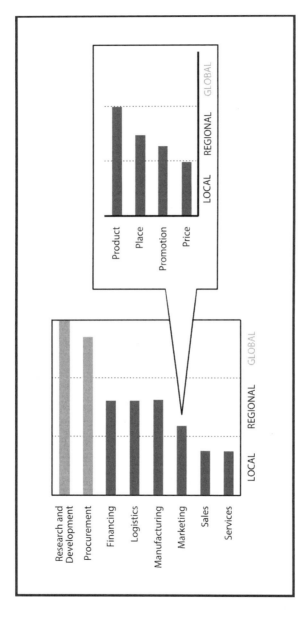

Figure 1.16 Illustrating degrees of globalization of corporate functions and marketing activities in the automotive industry

Source: Adapted from Paris (2008, p. 33)

Globalization   25

For instance, the latter index calculated the extent to which the sixty largest countries (in terms of GDP) were connected to the rest of the world according to five categories: openness to trade, movements of capital, exchange of technologies and ideas, movements of labor, and cultural integration. It was based on an online survey of business executives across the world (e.g., 520 in 2009; 1,050 in 2010) as well as in-depth interviews with business executives and high-profile experts (e.g., 30 in 2009; 20 in 2010). Table 1.1 illustrates how this index was computed, including the indicators used to measure each of the five categories, the sources of information (primary with scoring from the EIU analysts or secondary with statistics from various

Table 1.1 Measuring globalization through countries' openness to the world

Category and Selected Indicators	Source
Movement of goods and services (Weighting: 22%)	
☐ Total trade (exports and imports) as % of GDP	National Accounts
☐ Trade openness (5=very high)	Scored on 1–5 scale by Economist Intel. Unit analysts
☐ Tariff and non-tariff barriers (5=low)	Scored on 1–5 scale by EIU analysts
Movement of capital and finance (Weighting: 21%)	
☐ FDI Flows (in and out, % of GDP)	National Accounts
☐ Government policy toward FDI (5=very encouraging)	National Accounts
☐ Expropriation risk (5=non-existent)	Scored on 1–5 scale by EIU analysts
Exchange of technology and ideas (Weighting: 21%)	
☐ R&D trade (in and out, as % of GDP)	Balance of payments and EIU estimates
☐ Broadband subscriptions (per 100 people)	International Telecommunications Union
☐ Internet subscriptions (per 100 people)	International Telecommunications Union
Movement of labor (Weighting: 19%)	
☐ Net migration (% of total population)	Balance of payments and EIU estimates
☐ Current transfers (in and out, as % of GDP)	International Telecommunications Union
☐ Hiring of foreign nationals (5=easy)	International Telecommunications Union
Cultural integration (Weighting: 17%)	
☐ Tourism (in and out, per 1,000 people)	World Tourism Organization
☐ International communication	International Telecommunications Union
☐ Openness of national culture to foreign influence	Scored by EIU analysts

Source: Adapted from Ernst and Young (2012)

26 Globalization

organizations like the United Nations or the International Communication Union, for instance), as well as the weight (relatively equivalent) of each dimension in the overall measure.

So, which are the countries that are particularly open to the world? Table 1.2 presents the 2017 KOF Globalization Index and its ranking of countries. **Is it surprising not to see the US appear as one of the most globalized country? Why is that?** To understand this, we need to remember that what is measured here are the flows in and out of national borders. We observe that none of the large countries (e.g., China, Russia, and the US) make it to the top of the ranking because their important domestic markets somewhat "dilute" the relative importance of their exchanges with other countries. This is the first limitation of the way we have managed to measure globalization so far, providing only a partial picture of the extent to which countries are integrated into the world. Another limitation lies in the choice of variables to build these indices. In particular, some dimensions (like culture) are so difficult to capture that indices rely on less-than-ideal variables. The index developed by the EUI for Ernst & Young relies on an evaluation of "openness of national culture to foreign influence" by analysts that is most likely a highly subjective evaluation. In turn, the KOF index relies on the number of existing McDonald's and IKEA stores per capita to capture "cultural proximity" (or, rather, openness in terms of culture). This choice illustrates how difficult it is to find quantifiable indicators to compute a measure of globalization that reflects its multidimensionality.

What is a valuable lesson when interpreting data from globalization measurement? Before jumping to conclusions about the facts (e.g., "The world is globalized," and, "This country is more open or connected to the world than this one"), we must make sure we correctly understand the information that is presented to us. We need to always check "when" the information was collected/analyzed, "who" (which type of organization) is providing the information, and "why" (their motivations) as well as "how" this information was compiled or computed to make an informed interpretation of data. This is especially important when we study a phenomenon that is as complex and ambivalent as globalization.

1.3.2 Corporate Examples: New Balance and Nike; Tata Motors; Nokia and Ericsson; Amazon, Apple, Google, and Facebook

In this section, we look at examples that help us answer the following question: "How do the mechanisms of integration and convergence, two fundamental pillars of globalization, impact companies' marketing activities?" We focus on the economic and technological dimensions of integration and convergence, the cultural dimension being further studied in Chapter 5.

How does economic integration affect companies? Starting with economic integration, the main benefits of regional trade agreements (e.g., European Union (EU), NAFTA, Mercosur, and Trans-Pacific Partnership (TPP)—see Chapter 6) for companies in terms of marketing include: increase in sales (access to a larger pool of consumers), improvement in price competitiveness (costs reduction with the lowering or elimination of trade barriers),

Table 1.2 Ranking countries according to their degree of globalization

	country	Globalization		country	Economic Globalization		country	Social Globalization		country	Political Globalization
1	Netherlands	92.84	1	Singapore	97.77	1	Singapore	91.61	1	France	97.29
2	Ireland	92.15	2	Ireland	94.65	2	Switzerland	91.13	2	Italy	97.25
3	Belgium	91.75	3	Luxembourg	94.06	3	Ireland	90.99	3	Belgium	95.79
4	Austria	90.05	4	Netherlands	93.06	4	Netherlands	90.71	4	Sweden	95.56
5	Switzerland	88.79	5	Malta	91.74	5	Austria	90.62	5	Netherlands	95.41
6	Denmark	88.37	6	Belgium	90.08	6	Belgium	90.34	6	Spain	95.23
7	Sweden	87.96	7	Hungary	88.75	7	Puerto Rico	89.98	7	Austria	95.15
3	United Kingdom	87.26	8	United Arab Emirates	88.06	8	Canada	89.22	s.	United Kingdom	94.67
9	France	87.19	9	Mauritius	88.01	9	Denmark	87.54	9	Brazil	94.3
10	Hungary	86.55	10	Estonia	87.54	10	Cyprus	87.17	10	Switzerland	93.4
11	Canada	86.51	11	Bahrain	87.37	11	France	87.11	n.	Denmark	92.84
12	Finland	86.3	12	Slovak Republic	87	12	Norway	86.31	12	Norway	92.74
13	Portugal	85.04	13	Czech Republic	86.9	13	United Kingdom	85.33	13	Argentina	92.61
14	Cyprus	85	14	Cyprus	86.64	14	Germany	85.49	14	Egypt. Arab Rep.	92.46
15	Czech Republic	84.S3	15	Denmark	85.76	15	Croatia	85.29	15	Canada	92.45
16	Germany	84.57	16	Austria	85.5	16	Sweden	84.66	16	Finland	92.34
17	Spain	84.56	17	Sweden	85.48	17	Australia	84.13	17	Turkey	91.88
I8	Slovak Republic	84.36	IS.	Finland	84.2	18	Finland	83.31	IS.	Germany	91.71
19	Luxembourg	84.21	19	Georgia	83.01	19	Portugal	83.39	19	US	91.43
20	Singapore	83.64	20	United Kingdom	82.99	20	Spain	83.38	20	Russian Federation	91.34

Source: Courtesy of the Swiss Federal Institute of Technology (2017)

28 *Globalization*

and facilitation of international product policies (homogenization of standards, technical regulations, and approval processes for cross-border flows of goods, data, and services among partnering countries). On the other hand, economic integration means that local manufacturers are less protected from foreign competition due to the lowering of tariff and non-tariff barriers and, thus, could end up with uncompetitive pricing and sales decrease.

New Balance and Nike[1]—The footwear industry provides an example of two leading companies in the US with opposing views on the TPP (i.e., the Trans-Pacific Partnership proposed in 2016 between twelve countries bordering the Pacific, including the US and Vietnam). To understand the ambivalence of outcomes for companies, we focus on trade between the US and Vietnam. Between 1997 and 2012, Vietnam's export of footwear to the US increased more than 23 percent to reach nearly 2.5 billion USD. In 2013, manufacturers exporting from countries with no specific agreement with the US, such as Vietnam (i.e., under "the most favored nation" treatment), were subjected to an ad valorem tariff of 20 percent per pair of athletic shoes (HS. 6404.11.90) with a FOB value of more than 12 USD. For New Balance, the protective import tariff that the TPP threatens to remove would be a significant blow, as it is already estimated that producing in the US is already 25–35 percent more expensive than is producing in Vietnam. Indeed, the company has branded itself in the US as having a strong "local" component (see the slogan: "American-made. That's our story" on New Balance's website). Even though it relies on foreign contractors in Vietnam for other markets worldwide, it operates five factories in the US to serve the local market. The company also contracts US suppliers (representing an estimated 7,000 people) and generates indirect employment in many cities where it operates. The situation is very different for Nike; in 2013 it employed fewer than one hundred workers for footwear production on US soil, but had more than 230,000 workers in twenty-nine factories located in Vietnam. Thus, Nike would benefit from exporting to the US from Vietnam with preferential tariffs. For the marketing of these two US companies (and especially for pricing), economic integration represents either good or bad news, depending on the structure and location of their global value chains.

Tata Motors[2]—Moving on to the automotive industry and onto another regional agreement, the EU, the case of Tata Motors speaks—by default—to the benefits of economic integration. The company, a subsidiary of Tata Group (India), acquired Jaguar Land Rover in 2008. With the UK's exit from the EU (the Brexit), the company could incur a revenue decrease of nearly 1.37 billion USD. Indeed, Jaguar Land Rover could be subjected to a 4 percent levy to import vehicle parts for production in the UK, and to a 10 percent levy to export cars to countries belonging to the EU. The British government could eventually decide to offset the impact of these tariffs with incentives to automakers, but in the meantime, the company would have to decide between transferring the cost increase onto consumers (through higher prices) or to absorb a loss in profits, resulting from a lower average revenue per vehicle sold in the EU.

How do technological integration and convergence affect companies?[3] The evolution of mobile technology reflects a general trend—albeit met with resistance—toward the homogenization of technical standards across the world. In the 1980s, the first-generation (1G) networks were characterized

Globalization 29

by fragmented standards, limited competition, and high tariffs. In the early 1990s, the second generation (2G) was the object of much convergence as EU countries adopted a common standard, the Global System Mobile (GSM). First deployed in Finland (1991), then adopted in Germany, Denmark, Portugal, Sweden, Italy, and France, the GSM network was already available in forty-eight countries by 1993. In 1995, it had a presence in eighty-six countries, spanning Africa, Asia, and Eurasia. In 2016, the GSM network had become the global standard for mobile communications, even if differences among countries were still noticeable. For instance, Canada, the US, Mexico, and several Central and South American countries function with 850/1900Mhz frequency bands instead of 900/1800Mhz, as everywhere else.

Nokia and Ericsson[4]—The convergence toward a common technology platform represented tremendous gains in terms of economies of scale and efficiencies for equipment vendors, network operators, system integrators, and software developers. For instance, Nokia (Finland) and Ericsson (Sweden) took advantage of their expertise in building GSM networks in the EU to sell their GSM infrastructure projects into emerging markets, such as those of Eastern Europe.

Amazon, Apple, Google, and Facebook[5]—It is somewhat difficult to distinguish the effect of technological integration (interdependence) from technological convergence (homogenization) when it comes to the Internet economy. Indeed, the frontiers between industrial domains that were previously clearly defined (e.g., phones and computers were two different businesses) are increasingly blurred. In addition, there is convergence toward the use of mobile devices (tablets and phones). Both mechanisms have allowed companies to diversify into connected businesses. In this way, original equipment manufacturers (OEM) like Apple and Nokia, software companies like Microsoft, search engines and online advertisers like Google, online retailers like Amazon, and social networks like Facebook, all implement strategies to become "Internet and mobile ecosystems." For instance, Google (founded in the US in 1998) acquired video storage and distribution with YouTube (2006), launched the Android mobile-phone operating system (2007), and acquired Motorola Mobility, a manufacturer of handsets (2011). In turn, Amazon proposed cloud-computing services to firms—including storage, analytics, and deployment services, for instance—with its Amazon Web Services platform (2006); started distributing digital content on its Kindle Platform (2007); gave consumers access to movies, TV shows, songs, books, magazines, apps, and games with its Fire Tablets (2011); made an incursion into the phone and television businesses with its Fire Phone and Fire TV (2014); and launched the hands-free voice device Echo (2014), which allows the ability to ask for information, music, news, sports scores, and weather from across the room and get answers instantly. Apple (a US hardware manufacturer founded in 1976) also became a music provider with the iTunes software and complementary iPod music player (2001), in addition to commercializing its notorious iPhone (2007) and iPad (2010), both supported by the iOS, a proprietary mobile operating system (2007). Finally, Facebook (created in 2005) has announced various initiatives that extend its core business of connecting people, including: Facebook AI Research (FAIR)—started in 2015, this project aims to facilitate information search using image and speech recognition, natural language processing, and physical and logical infrastructure required to run artificial

30 Globalization

intelligence systems—and Marketplace, introduced in 2016 to help people discover, buy, and sell items in their community.

In addition to illustrating technological integration and convergence, the case of these four giants highlights a paradoxical effect on competition. On the one hand, these companies have entered a cutthroat race for innovations that benefit consumers. On the other hand, their size and speed could also be used to choke competition, something that antitrust regulations should closely monitor.

1.3.3 Ambivalence of Outcomes

Because globalization is a phenomenon that has quite a current and fast-changing impact on our lives and jobs, it is important to form an opinion about it (see "Food for Thought"). To answer this challenging question, we recommend structuring pros and cons of globalization according to different levels of analysis or stakeholders (e.g., society at large, national governments, industries, companies, and, finally, individuals as workers and consumers). Once you have compiled your list of pros and cons, can you identify **a stakeholder, in particular, for whom the advantages of globalization seem more obvious than for others (i.e., more pros than cons)**?

Food for Thought 1.3

- What do you think: Is globalization a good or bad thing? For whom?

Figure 1.17 Weighting the pros and cons of globalization
Source: Own elaboration

In the remainder of this book, we will focus our attention on the level of companies while studying the new marketing practices they put in place. However, this focus will not prevent us from noting the many linkages that exist between firms, their new marketing practices and the other important stakeholders (society, governments, and individuals). Firms and their activities cannot be considered in isolation from the rest of human activities.

Conclusion: For Marketers, Globalization Means an Increase in the Scale of Activities, Supported By Convergence and Integration. It Forces Them to Understand Changing Degrees of Distance Between Markets and Find New Ways to Differentiate From Rising Competition

Going back to one of the initial questions: "**Is distance dead?**" we highlighted that it is impossible to claim that indeed the effect of distance (i.e., not only physical distance, but also the many economic, cultural, and technological differences between countries) has disappeared in cross-border business. The world is not fully globalized: the extent of the "scale increase" as well as the integration and the convergence processes are still the object of much debate. The path to integration and convergence is far from steady and straight-forward. Evidence shows a pendulum-like movement in terms of how these mechanisms unfold historically. In the postmodern era of globalization, some barriers (differences) have been lowered (allowing for flows to "go further"), whereas others remain or have even increased (simply because distant places and customers are now technically reachable).

So, what does globalization mean for marketers? Globalization forces market-ers to understand changing degrees of distance between markets (Chapters 4–7) and to find new ways to differentiate from competition (Chapters 8–12). The five marketing trends studied in this book (i.e., bottom of the pyramid mar-keting, reverse innovation, mobile marketing, origin-based marketing, and cause-related marketing) are ways for companies to overcome issues related to distance in marketing abroad and fight against increasing competition. We explore this answer throughout the remainder of the book. In the next chapter, we look into the topic of internationalization.

Notes

1 The example of Nike and New Balance is based on: RICG (2014).
2 The example of Tata Motors relies on: Forbes (2016).
3 In Section 1.3.3., the paragraph entitled "How do technological integration and convergence affect companies?" is based on: INS 127 (2013); ITU (2007); Worldtimezone.com (2016).
4 The paragraph about Nokia and Ericsson is based on: INS 127 (2013).
5 The example about Amazon, Apple, Facebook, and Google is based on: Ama-zon (2016); Facebook (2016); HBS 9–513–060 (2013); INS 127 (2013).

32 Globalization

References

Amazon (2016). Our Innovations. Retrieved September 2016, from www.amazon. com/p/feature/tv76jef8gz289rm?ref_=aa_navb_4&pf_rd_r=N1F12ZHWE73 AFDVBD5RM&pf_rd_p=2ca95a3a-be2c-470a-a4b6-e969bc07540d

Cairncross, Frances (2001). *The Death of Distance: How the Communications Revolution Is Changing our Lives*. Boston: Harvard Business School Press (p. 320).

Cateora, Philip, Gilly, Mary & Graham, John (2011). *International Marketing* (2nd ed.). New York: McGraw-Hill/Irwin (p. 742).

Croucher, Sheila (2004). *Globalization and Belonging: The Politics of Identity in a Changing World* (Vol. 229). Lanham, MD: Rowman & Littlefield (p. 240).

Dowrick, Steve & DeLong, Bradford (2003). Globalization and Convergence. In *Globalization in Historical Perspective*, Michael Bordo, Alan Taylor, and Jeffrey Williamson (Editors). Chicago: University of Chicago Press (pp. 191–226).

The Economist (2011, August 4th). Economic Focus—Why the Tail Wags the Dog. Retrieved from www.economist.com/blogs/dailychart/2011/08/emerging-vs-developed-economies

Ernst & Young (2012). Looking Beyond the Obvious—Globalization and New Opportunities for Growth. Retrieved March 2017, from www.ey.com/gl/en/issues/driving-growth/globalization—-looking-beyond-the-obvious—-2012-index

Facebook (2016). News Room. Retrieved March 2017, from http://newsroom. fb.com/?s=introducing+AI&post_type=any

Financial Times (2016, September 12th). 50 Journals Used in FT Research Rank, *By Laurent Ormans*. Retrieved from www.ft.com/content/3405a512-5cbb-11e1-8f1f-00144feabdc0

Forbes (2016, June 27th). Why 'Brexit' Might Be Bad News For Tata Motors? *By Trefis Team*. Retrieved from www.forbes.com/sites/greatspeculations/2016/06/27/why-brexit-might-be-bad-news-for-tata-motors/#3010ad49338b

Friedman, Thomas (2005). *The World is Flat—A Brief History of the Twenty-First Century*. New York: Farrar, Straus & Giroux (p. 488).

Ghemawat, Pankaj (2001). Distance Still Matters: The Hard Reality of Global Expansion. *Harvard Business Review*, 79(8), 137–147.

Ghemawat, Pankaj (2007). *Redefining Global Strategy: Crossing Borders in a World Where Differences Still Matter*. Boston: Harvard Business School Press (p. 272).

Griffin, Ricky & Pustay, Michael (2006). *International Business*. Upper Saddle River, NJ: Prentice Hall (p. 672).

Harvard University Gazette (2006). Professor Theodore Levitt Legendary Marketing Scholar and Former Harvard Business Review Editor. Retrieved March 2017, from http://news.harvard.edu/gazette/story/2006/07/professor-theodore-levitt-legendary-marketing-scholar-and-former-harvard-business-review-editor-dead-at-81/

HBS 9–513–060 (2013). *Amazon, Apple, Facebook, and Google*. Case written by: John Deighton and Leora Kornfeld. Boston: Harvard Business School (p. 18).

INS 127 (2013). *Nokia and the New Mobile Ecosystem: Competing in the Age of Internet Mobile Convergence*. Case written by: Wei-Ru Chen, Javier Gimeno, Aon Dirk Verbeek, Maciej Workiewicz, and Juan Jose de la Torre. Fontainebleau: INSEAD (p. 24).

ITU (2007). *3G Mobile Licensing Policy: GSM Case Study*. Case written by: Audrey Selian. Geneva: International Telecommunication Union (p. 50). www. itu.int/osg/spu/ni/3G/casestudies/GSM-FINAL.doc

Globalization 33

Levitt, Theodore (1983). The Globalization of Markets. *Harvard Business Review*, 61(3), 92–102.

Mitrany, David (1933). *The Progress of International Government*. New Haven: Yale University Press (p. 176).

Nike (2010). Write The Future—World Cup Commercial. Nike Soccer. Retrieved March 2017, from www.YouTube.com/watch?v=igUF8Aa2OL0

París, José Antonio (2008). *Marketing Internacional—Desde la Optica Latinoamericana*. Buenos Aires, Argentina: Errepar (p. 576).

RICG (2014). Nike Versus New Balance: Trade Policy in a World of Global Value Chains. Case Written by: Simon Brodeur and Ari Van Assche. Institution: HEC Montréal—International Journal of Case Studies in Management 9-00-2014-001 (p. 16).

Rosamond, Ben (2000). *Theories of European Integration*. Basingstoke: Palgrave Macmillan (p. 240).

Starbucks (2017). Starbucks Coffee International. Retrieved March 2017, from www.starbucks.com/business/international-stores

Swiss Federal Institute of Technology (2017). KOF Globalization Index. Retrieved April 2017, from http://globalization.kof.ethz.ch/

UN (2018). Overview of the United Nations. Retrieved May 2018, from www.un.org/en/sections/about-un/overview/

Wikipedia (2017a). Postmodernity. Retrieved March 2017, from https://en.wikipedia.org/wiki/Postmodernity

Wikipedia (2017b). Modernity. Retrieved March 2017, from https://en.wikipedia.org/wiki/Modernity

World Bank (2016a). Exports of Goods and Services (Percentage of GDP). Retrieved March 2017, from http://data.worldbank.org/indicator/NE.EXP.GNFS.ZS?view=chart

World Bank (2016b). Merchandise Exports (Current US$). Retrieved March 2017, from http://data.worldbank.org/indicator/TX.VAL.MRCH.CD.WT?view=chart

World Bank (2016c). Service Exports (BoP, Current US$). Retrieved March 2017, from http://data.worldbank.org/indicator/BX.GSR.NFSV.CD?display=graph

World Bank (2016d). Exports of Goods and Services (BoP, Current US$). Retrieved March 2017, from http://data.worldbank.org/indicator/BX.GSR.GNFS.CD?display=graph

Worldtimezone.com (2016). GSM World Coverage Map. Retrieved March 2017, from www.worldtimezone.com/gsm.html

2 Internationalization

Table of Contents

2 Internationalization

Introduction: Why, Where, and How Do Companies Go Abroad?...35
    2.1   *Definitions*...37
        2.1.1   Internationalization Process: From Classical Theory to Born Globals 37
        2.1.2   Entry Modes (Exports, Licenses, Franchises, Foreign Direct Investments) 39
    2.2   *Drivers* 47
        2.2.1   Motivations for Internationalizing.....................48
        2.2.2   On the Location of Production (Dunning) and Transaction Costs (Williamson)...................50
        2.2.3   On Psychic Distance and the Liability of Outsidership (Johanson and Vahlne)..............53
    2.3   *Issues at Stake and Examples* 55
        2.3.1   Building an International Marketing Plan..........55
        2.3.2   Corporate examples: Abercrombie & Fitch, Amazon, Coca-Cola, Disney, IKEA, McDonald's, Netflix, Starbucks, Tesla, Uber, Vice Media, and Volkswagen............................59

Conclusion: In their foreign expansion, companies follow four main motives, go where they can learn faster, and have a variety of entry modes at their disposal.
References

Recommended Readings

- Cavusgil, Tamer & Knight, Gary (2015). The Born Global Firm: An Entrepreneurial and Capabilities Perspective on Early and

> Rapid Internationalization. *Journal of International Business Studies*, 46(1): 3–16.
> - Dunning, John (2009). Location and the Multinational Enterprise: A Neglected Factor? *Journal of International Business Studies*, 40(1): 5–19.
> - Johanson, Jan & Vahlne, Jan-Erik (1977). The Internationalization Process of the Firm-A Model of Knowledge Development and Increasing Foreign Market Commitments. *Journal of International Business Studies*, 8(1): 23–32.
> - Johanson, Jan & Vahlne, Jan-Erik (2009). The Uppsala Internationalization Process Model Revisited: From Liability of Foreignness to Liability of Outsidership. *Journal of International Business Studies*, 40(9): 1411–1431.

Introduction: Why, Where and How Do Companies Go Abroad?

Asking the question: **"Why, where and how do companies go abroad?"** is central to understanding marketing in the context of globalization. It is important to have an overview of the implications of decisions made in regard to market selection and entry modes in the internationalization process before elaborating further on distance analysis (see Figure 2.2). Indeed, these decisions (i.e., "where?" and "how?" to expand abroad) justify the need and purpose for analyzing in detail the many differences/distances that exist among countries (Chapters 4–7).

Figure 2.1 Illustrating Chapter 2

Source: Own elaboration

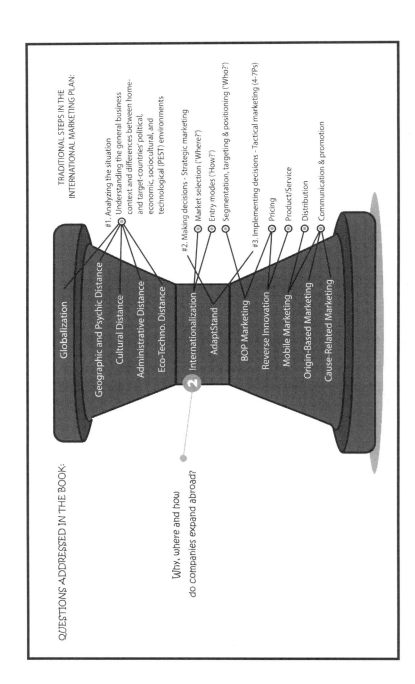

Figure 2.2 Positioning Chapter 2 in the overall book structure

Source: Own elaboration

The objectives of this chapter are first to define important concepts by discussing the typical process followed in firms' internationalization, as well as the main entry modes at their disposal. Then, we cover important theories that help explain some of the core drivers of the process and sequence of internationalization (i.e., which countries do firms choose for their expansion, and in which order), as well as choice among entry modes. Next, we look into some important issues related to the internationalization of firms: we review the structure and tools used to build an international marketing plan, and, finally, we provide corporate examples to illustrate internationalization in various industries and according to different paces (traditional vs. born globals).

2.1 Definitions

In this section, we examine the following questions:

- What are the main models and variables used to explain internationalization?
- What is a *born global company* and how does it contrast with companies following a traditional path to internationalization?
- What are the various entry modes that firms use to expand abroad? What are their dis/advantages and how to choose among them?

2.1.1 Internationalization Process: From Classical Theory to Born Globals

For a company, internationalization represents the process through which its value offerings are made available in foreign markets.

What variables are important in explaining the internationalization process of companies? In a critical analysis of models explaining the internationalization process, Andersen (1993, p. 213) outlines the existence of the Uppsala model (called by contraction "U-model") and of many models that he calls "I-models" by contraposition, standing for "innovation-related models" of internationalization. I-models describe the internationalization process as if it were an innovation that firms gradually adopt. Over all, these models emphasize the notions of risk, control, commitment, and knowledge as central variables to explain the internationalization process.

In particular, how is the Uppsala model explaining internationalization? This model is named after a city and university, bearing the same name, in Sweden to identify several scholars who have investigated the topic early on. Researchers in the Department of Business Studies at Uppsala University in the mid-1970s made empirical observations that contradicted the established international business literature of the time (Johanson & Vahlne, 2009). Until then, firms were expected to choose the optimal mode to enter a market by analyzing their costs and risks based on both market characteristics and on their own resources. If a firm with large resources were interested in a high-opportunity and low-risk market, there was no reason to theorize why it should not, or could not, readily and massively enter this market. Instead, the

38 *Internationalization*

Uppsala model posits that firms often develop their international operations in small steps rather than by making large foreign production investments at a single point in time. First, firms start with no commitment in markets abroad, then continue with a low-commitment mode of entry (e.g., indirect exports); they then use an export agent or distributor, after which they open a commercial office and eventually establish a wholly-owned subsidiary abroad (Johanson & Wiedersheim-Paul, 1975). This approach assumes that firms follow a path toward gaining more control and accept taking on more risks.

As illustrated in Figure 2.3, the model relies on two main variables to steer the direction of geographic expansion: the level of market knowledge, and the level of desired commitment in a particular host country (Johanson & Vahlne, 1977). The underlying assumptions of the 1977 model are uncertainty and bounded rationality (Johanson & Vahlne, 2009). These assumptions are captured by the concepts of psychic distance (here, the factors preventing a good understanding of a foreign environment) and liability of foreignness (i.e., costs and risks that foreign firms incur because they have to overcome the challenges of managing across distance and time zones, limited local knowledge and possible discrimination). At a given time (T), early in the process, the internationalizing company selects a market—typically characterized by low degrees of psychic distance—based on its current knowledge. It commits resources to this market depending on its attractiveness (i.e., size and growth potential) and, according to obtained results—submitted to the liability of foreigness/outsidership—makes the decision at T+1 to select another market—typically characterized by larger degrees of psychic distance—and then repeats the process.

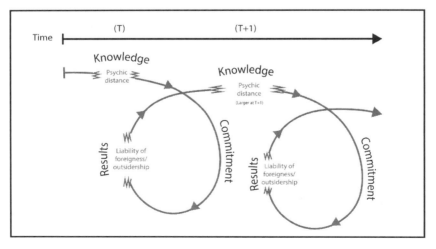

Figure 2.3 Presenting the Uppsala or "U-model" of internationalization
Source: Adapted from Johanson and Vahlne (1977, p. 26)

Internationalization 39

Before further exploring the phenomenon of "born global" companies, we can reflect on the way this phenomenon relates to the Uppsala model of internationalization (see "Food for Thought").

Food for Thought 2.1

- In reference to Johanson and Vahlne (2009) and Cavusgil and Knight (2015), to what extent is the *born global* phenomenon in rupture with classical internationalization theory (Uppsala model)?

What is a born global company?[1] The internationalization of the firm had been traditionally seen as a gradual process—once firms have consolidated in their domestic market, they start to build activities abroad, first by exporting and later by investing abroad. *Born global* firms challenge this conventional view (Knight & Cavusgil, 2004; Oviatt, Philips McDougall, & Loper, 1995). Born global firms are international from inception; they do not wait to consolidate or dominate their domestic market before expanding abroad. From or near founding, they obtain a substantial portion of total revenue from sales in international markets. In their review of the literature, Freeman, Hutchings, and Chetty (2012) note a divergence between studies defining the born global firm based on the process of internationalization (starting two, three, six, and up to eight years after inception), the scope of internationalization (foreign sales reaching 25 percent of total sales within a few years of inception, 75 percent within two years of inception, or else reaching 50 percent outside of the home continent) or the modes of entry (some studies focusing on exports while others consider that much overseas FDI defines born globals).

The irruption of born global firms cannot be explained by one single factor. Some of the most frequently researched drivers are the homogenization of buyer preferences (making the positioning of products in foreign markets easier) (Moen, 2001), technological advances (i.e., better telecommunications that make worldwide communication easier) (Knight & Cavusgil, 2004), or the entrepreneurial personality of the founder (Andersson & Ingemar, 2003).

2.1.2 Entry Modes (Exports, Licenses, Franchises, Foreign Direct Investments)

What are the main entry modes available for foreign expansion? Different options are available to firms willing to commercialize their value offerings in foreign markets. These options are called "entry modes" in the case of a first commercialization abroad, or "expansion modes" if the company has already sold in a specific country but penetrates it further by using other available options. As illustrated in Figure 2.4, these entry or expansion modes

40 *Internationalization*

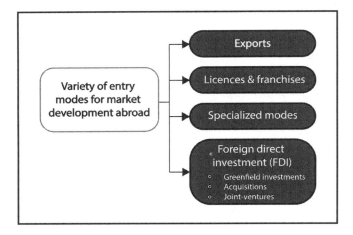

Figure 2.4 Overview of various international entry modes
Source: Adapted from Griffin and Pustay (2015, p. 342)

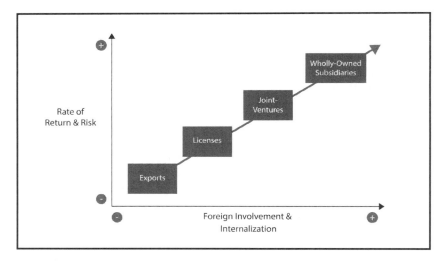

Figure 2.5 Comparing entry modes in terms of rate of return and foreign involvement
Source: Adapted from Dunning (1981, p. 399)

include: exports and contractual agreements (such as licenses, franchises and specialized modes), as well as foreign direct investments (including wholly or partially owned ventures such as "greenfield" projects, which evoke an untouched piece of land, mergers and acquisitions, and partnerships and alliances like joint-ventures).

Figure 2.5 compares these entry modes in terms of the amount of risk to which they expose firms and the potential return on investment they represent.

Internationalization 41

It illustrates the fact that some entry modes are higher risk (but also higher return) than others. Above all, it illustrates the role of time in the internationalizing process, as captured in the I- and U-models. In a traditional perspective, firms gradually move on from low-risk and low-commitment modes (such as exports) to high-risk and high-commitment modes (such as direct investments).

What is the typical reasoning or decision-making process used when choosing among entry modes? Figure 2.6 outlines a typical decision tree. Starting with the decision to commercialize abroad, firms must decide whether they will keep producing from home (and thus, export to foreign markets) or produce from foreign locations. If they decide to produce from abroad, firms must decide whether to externalize or internalize the production. Externalizing production means the firm would grant some other company the responsibility to undertake it. Contractual agreements, such as licenses and franchises or other more specialized contracts (which will be further explained), are thus established with other companies located abroad. Internalizing production, on the other hand, means that the firm remains in control and in charge of production (it stays "within" the boundaries of the organization), even if it is performed abroad. To do this, firms can establish assets abroad through "foreign direct investments" (FDI). Obviously, these investments require much more capital than the previous entry modes. Here they have two main options. One option is to increase existing production capacity by acquiring or merging with another company. The other option is to build new production capacity—either from scratch (the so-called "greenfield" projects, building on new land) or by remodelling existing production facilities (the so-called "brownfield" projects, evoking a piece of land that had already been ploughed to some extent). In both cases (building or acquiring production capacity), the level of control can be partial (in the case of a joint-venture or the acquisition of a minority stake in the equity of a foreign company) or full (in the case of wholly owned subsidiaries).

Overall, what are the main factors involved in choosing an entry mode in foreign markets? We have seen with the I- and U-models that levels of risk, control, commitment, and knowledge were central in choosing among entry modes. Because some of these modes are more costly than others, the financial resources of companies naturally determine this choice as well. Last but not least, the vision and objectives of decision-makers, in other words, what they expect and want from international expansion, will also influence their choice (notably because it will change their level of risk acceptance) (Cateora, Graham, & Bruning, 2006, Chap. 9). Examples of objectives can be "surviving a temporary domestic crisis" or "becoming the world leader in a specific industry." Obviously, these goals entail very different levels of required risk, control, commitment, and knowledge of foreign markets.

Exports: What are the different forms of exports? Exporting is about making value offerings (i.e., products or services) available in foreign markets by crossing national borders. There are three common ways of exporting: directly, indirectly, or through intracorporate transfers in the case of multinational corporations (MNCs). In *direct export*, the seller handles the process until the buyer, located abroad, purchases the goods/services. In *indirect*

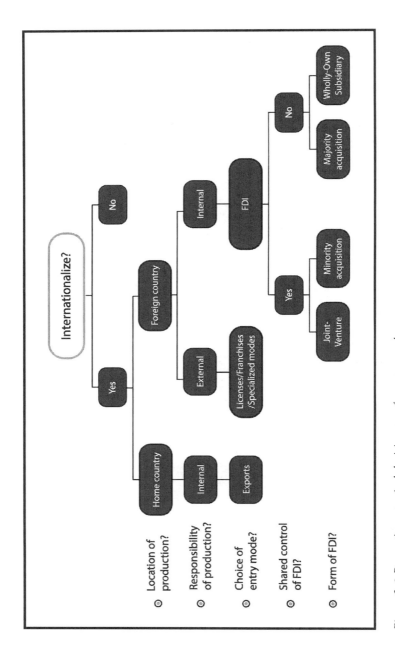

Figure 2.6 Presenting a typical decision tree for entry modes

Source: Adapted from Czinkota, Ronkainen, and Moffett (2005, *Fig.* 5.6)

exports, the seller uses an intermediary, such as an agent or a distributor, who will take charge of the process of selling abroad. The term is also used for products (e.g., components and parts) that are first sold to a domestic buyer who then sells to a foreign buyer (for instance, Intel sells microchips to Dell, another US company, which then exports worldwide). Finally, MNCs have subsidiaries located in various countries. These subsidiaries may sell/buy inputs or services to/from other subsidiaries or to/from the headquarters through what is called *intracorporate transfers*. For instance, Jaguar Land Rover (UK) may export jaguars to Tata Motors (India), but the goods remain within the same holding company. Incidentally, the inputs (i.e., components or semi-finished products), finished products, or services that are exchanged within MNCs are often exchanged at prices that are above or below market value. Indeed, MNCs fix prices for themselves differently than they would do for outsider firms. It is the issue of "transfer pricing" with which international lawyers and accountants are familiar. This practice is a way to manage taxes across the globe: the general idea is to lower profits as much as possible in countries where taxes are high by paying high prices for purchased goods/services and, in turn, to pay lower prices for purchased goods/services (resulting in higher declared profits) in countries with lower taxation rates. When executed properly, this practice represents a tremendous source of savings for MNCs, or a fiscal and legal liability in the contrary case (many MNCs have been severely fined for not respecting fiscal laws of home or host countries).

What are the pros and cons of exports as an entry mode? Exporting is one of the minimally risky modes of entry. If something goes wrong in a specific foreign market (e.g., a war impeding distribution or galloping inflation eroding profit margins), a company just needs to pull the plug and stop sending their products to that country. Of course, this may result in losses (e.g., losing revenues and customers to competitors), but nothing compared to what it would be if the company had been producing directly from this market (e.g., costs associated to shutting down a plant and firing employees). It is also fairly easy to set up, compared to other entry modes, like FDI. However, it does not yield the same return. Indeed, one of the limitations of exports as an entry mode is the potentially reduced profit margin at the end of the sale process, since transportation costs and many governmental taxes are incurred (not only to cross borders but also every time the goods change hands, for instance).

License: What is a license and how does it work? Licensing is the practice of conceding a licence, specifically a right that is often limited to a set of conditions and bound in time to other companies so that they can use what is called *intellectual property* (e.g., a technology, a brand, a patent). *Licensing* occurs when a firm, called the *licenser (or licensor)*, permits another firm, called the *licensee*, to use its *intellectual property* in exchange for royalties (Griffin & Pustay, 2015, Chap. 12). The term *licensing* might sound obscure or unfamiliar, but you have seen countless examples of this practice. In the food products industry, Oreo—a brand owned by Nabisco, a US manufacturer of cookies, chocolates, and sweets—relies heavily on licenses from entertainment companies (e.g., Marvel Entertainment, DreamWorks, and Paramount Pictures) to insert characters like the Hulk, Shrek, and Transformers onto their packaging. Another example is illustrated in Figure 2.7

44 *Internationalization*

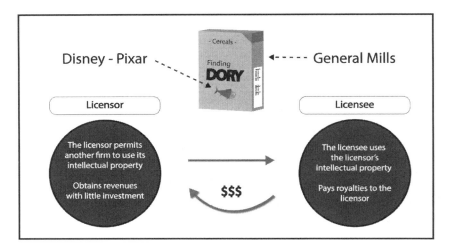

Figure 2.7 Illustrating licensing for cereals
Source: Own elaboration

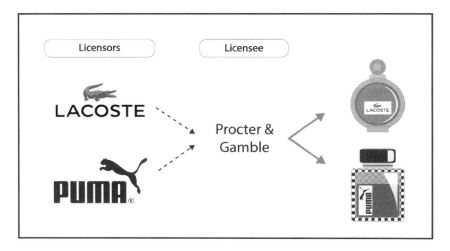

Figure 2.8 Illustrating licensing for fragrances
Source: Own elaboration with images received as courtesy of Puma and Lacoste (©LACOSTE S.A. 2017)

with the Dory character (from *Finding Nemo*), the intellectual property of Disney-Pixar, being used on a cereal box produced by General Mills (US).

The cosmetics industry also provides examples with perfumes from fashion/apparel companies. Do companies like French Lacoste and German Puma have the facilities and knowledge to produce fragrances? Probably not. However, Procter & Gamble and Coty (US) or L'Oréal (France) do, and thus have licensed the trademarks of the companies to commercialize perfumes in their name. P&G

Internationalization   45

was a licensee for Puma (2003–2015, then replaced by L'Oréal) and for Lacoste (2001–2016, then replaced by Coty) (Basenotes, 2015; License Mag, 2014).

What are the pros and cons of licensing as an entry mode? Licensing is among the easiest ways for companies to commercialize their products abroad. For a minimal investment of resources (money, time, and energy), royalties are realized and the hassle of commercialization is "externalized" (i.e., handled by a third party). Compared to other entry modes with higher degrees of involvement and control, however, revenues remain limited. In addition, finding the right business partner may not be easy, and there are risks involved in sharing one's intellectual property. Beyond possible mistakes—resulting in poor product quality, for instance, which could be harmful to the firm's brand and reputation—the entrusted partner could also use the acquired knowledge for his own benefit (e.g., developing a competing technology) and diluting the firm's competitive advantage in the future.

Franchises: What is a franchise and how does it work? Franchising is a type of licensing extended to a whole business model. It is the practice of conceding the rights—although limited to a set of conditions and bound in time—to other companies to run a business under your brand name. Griffin and Pustay (2015, p. 358) explain that a *franchise* allows either an independent entrepreneur or an organization, called the *franchisee*, to *exploit a company under the brand name of another*, called the *franchisor*, in exchange for royalties. Again, examples abound (see Figure 2.9). The food industry is particularly suited for this practice (e.g., Subway, McDonald's, Pizza Hut,

Figure 2.9 Examples of franchises

Source: Courtesy of The Body Shop and Subway. Subway® is a registered trademark of Subway IP Inc.

46 Internationalization

and Starbucks Coffee from the US, Tim Hortons and La Belle Province from Canada, or Havanna from Argentina). Yet, players in other industries have also taken up this expansion strategy, both in domestic and foreign markets. Examples include car repair and maintenance (e.g., Midas from the US is present in more than fifteen countries), personal care, hotels, and many more.

The beauty retailer The Body Shop, originally from the UK, has more than 2,600 locations across sixty-five countries, and is growing across the world, with a franchise network of more than 1,500 stores (The Body Shop, 2014). This means that its stores you may have seen on commercial streets, in shopping malls, or in airports are either the property of the company or a franchise owned by an independent entrepreneur, just like you. If you were interested in opening a franchise of The Body Shop, the company website informs that you could do so starting with only 55,000 Euros (including minimal start-up costs of €50,000 and a franchise fee of €5,000). You would then have to pay royalties to the company, but, in exchange, it would provide you with "tailored promotional plans to drive traffic in-store and retail and operational training to run your store" (The Body Shop, 2014), among other things. In most countries, you will find franchise associations, such as the Canadian Franchise Association. These associations inform on opportunities and financial requirements, and thus help franchisors and franchisees find each other.

What are the pros and cons of franchising as an entry mode? Since franchising can be considered an extended form of licensing, it brings about similar risks and benefits. Yet, the level of risks and benefits may be elevated. Since we talk here about a whole business model, the franchisee may face increased complexity in performing well, and the commitment from the franchisor to provide support is often more significant than from the licensor. In terms of benefits, many companies use franchising in addition to wholly owned operations. Consider the following explanation: "Franchising enables an individual to own a restaurant business and maintain control over staffing, purchasing, marketing, and pricing decisions, while also benefiting from the strength of McDonald's global brand, operating system, and financial resources. One of the strengths of this model is that the expertise gained from operating Company-owned restaurants allows McDonald's to improve the operations and success of all restaurants while innovations from franchisees can be tested and, when viable, efficiently implemented across relevant restaurants" (McDonald's Corporation, 2015, p. 1).

Specialized entry modes: what are some of the main ones? Here, we briefly broach three other types of entry modes that are often industry-specific: subcontracting, management contract, and turnkey projects. *Subcontracting* abroad implies that the firm will supply technical specifications to a subcontractor or to a local manufacturer. It allows the firm to specialize itself in the design of the product while entrepreneurs accept the responsibility of the manufacturing installations. The example of Nike is often given to illustrate this practice. In turn, a *management contract* is an agreement whereby a company provides management assistance, technical expertise, or specialized services to a second company for an agreed amount of time in exchange for monetary compensation (fixed amount or a percentage of sales). Many hotel chains function this way (e.g., Marriot and Hilton). They do not own all of

Internationalization 47

the buildings in which they are established, but sign management contracts with the building owners to operate the buildings as hotels. Finally, a *turnkey project* is a contract whereby a company designs, builds, and fully equips a facility and then presents the project to the buyer when it is ready to operate. This is a practice particularly suited for complex projects, such as the construction of a nuclear power plant, an airport, an oil refinery, etc. See Keegan and Green (2008, Chap. 9) for more details on specialized entry modes.

What is Foreign Direct Investment (FDI) and its main forms? FDI stands for Foreign Direct Investment. It represents the partial or complete operations of a company outside of its country of origin (Griffin & Pustay, 2015). When a company wants to make investments abroad, it can do so using two mechanisms: portfolio investments or direct investments. Both types of investment can take the form of purchasing shares in the equity of a foreign company. Yet, the difference resides in the degree of control obtained and the durability of the investment. When a company makes a *portfolio investment*, it looks for returns and a passive role in the administration of the company. On the contrary, when a company makes a *direct investment* abroad, it looks for control and an active role in the management of decision, with real power in influencing executive decisions. In addition, it will not be able to disinvest as easily as in the case of a portfolio investment. The International Monetary Fund and the United Nations Conference on Trade and Development (UNCTAD) puts the threshold to be considered a direct investment (as opposed to a portfolio investment) at 10 percent of the capital of a local company. However, national regulations can fix higher thresholds, such as in the UK (20 percent) and Germany (25 percent). FDI can take the following forms: starting new operations (greenfield and brownfield projects), merging with or acquiring an existing business (i.e., full or partial acquisition of the assets of a foreign company, through the acquisition of minority or majority equity in the company), and strategic alliances and joint ventures.

What are the pros and cons of FDI? By comparison to other entry modes, the three forms of FDI represent higher degrees of risk and commitment (notably in terms of financial and human resources), while also yielding more benefits (revenues and knowledge gained in foreign markets, in particular). Among the three forms, there is a gradation in terms of commitment and risk. Obviously, the shared form of direct investment through strategic partnerships and alliances (e.g., joint-venture where a new legal entity is created) with a local partner is less demanding than when a company goes alone. Acquiring a company may be more risky and expensive, but not as much as building one from scratch as in the case of greenfield projects.

2.2 Drivers

This section addresses the following questions:

- Who is considered the father of international business management?
- Why do companies expand abroad; what are their main motives?
- What are the factors driving decisions of how and where firms internationalize?

48 *Internationalization*

2.2.1 Motivations for Internationalizing

Who is considered the father of international business management? John Dunning (1927–2009) was a British economist and Reading University professor with a worldwide reputation for his work on international business management. He developed the eclectic paradigm, also known as the OLI framework, which is one of the most-used theories to explain MNC choices for international expansion by foreign direct investments.

What are the main motives for companies to expand abroad, what are they looking for? Dunning developed a typology of motives for firms to expand abroad that is discussed in the recommended reading; can you identify it (see "Food for Thought")?

Figure 2.10 Portrait of John Dunning
Source: John Dunning and Edward Elgar Publishing Ltd.

Food for Thought 2.2

- In reference to Dunning (2009), why are firms expanding abroad? What are they looking for?

Internationalization 49

The keyword when considering the motives for internationalization is *access*. Most of the time, companies go abroad because they are looking to access new markets (i.e., clients who will purchase their goods or services). To do so, they can use any entry modes, exports included. Companies can also look for resources, gains in efficiency or strategic assets, and in this case will likely operate abroad (i.e., have facilities) and expand by using foreign direct investments (Dunning, 1981, 1998). In sum, a company expands abroad because it is market-seeking, resource-seeking, efficiency-seeking, and/or strategic asset-seeking. The last three types of motivations are better pursued with investments made directly abroad (i.e., FDI) as entry modes.

Focusing solely on "market-seeking" as a motivation, what are the different reasons that justify the need for companies to expand internationally? We can think of reactive motivations, such as being limited by the size of their own domestic market or perhaps being "attacked" by foreign competitors at home. The latter can also underlay a proactive effort to monitor competitors and possibly retaliate against aggressive moves (e.g., imagine that a foreign competitor lowers prices in your home market, which forces you to do the same and lose revenues; if you are present in other markets where you can do the same against that competitor, they may not engage in this practice for fear of entering a downward spiral where they would lose revenues as well). A more proactive motivation is simply the desire to expand through "market development" (see Ansoff's Matrix) and to exploit new geographic markets. In the case of companies expanding through FDI, other market-seeking motivations include getting to better know consumers' preferences, adapt more rapidly to changes, and provide support services (e.g., after-sale service, repair and maintenance) as well as bypass trade regulations that would restrict imports in specific markets.

Now, focusing on "resource-seeking" as a motivation, what are the various types of resources that a country can offer to companies? Companies can look for resources elsewhere because they are more available or more affordable than in their home country. These resources fall into the physical, human, or financial categories. Among *physical resources*, we can think of raw materials (e.g., minerals or agricultural products) or any kind of inputs (e.g., semi-finished products or components) needed in industrial activities not only to produce but also to run, or cool, manufacturing or assembly processes (e.g., energy or water). For *human resources*, companies can be attracted to specific countries—or locations within countries such as regions or cities—because of the presence or low costs of unskilled, semi-skilled, or skilled labor. Finally, access to financial resources is another incentive, especially for companies coming from countries where financial markets are not fully developed or efficient—financing through stock markets or venture capital, for instance. All of the resources that are available in specific countries constitute part of their "location advantage" (i.e., the reasons why foreign companies would have an advantage to locate their operations there, either in full or in part).

What is "efficiency-seeking" as a motivation, and what is the rationale behind looking to increase efficiency though internationalization? Expanding abroad allows the ability to build up business volume. Through volume,

50   *Internationalization*

economies of scale are achieved. This is a major interest for MNCs. The "New Theory of Trade" (Krugman, 1980) has focused on economies of scale (and scope) to explain the very existence of MNCs. Another major interest to having production and/or sales in many different points of the globe is risk diversification. Indeed, economic cycles (e.g., growth or recession periods) as well as financial crises (e.g., the Mexican peso crisis in 1994 and the Asian financial crisis in 1997) are generally seen at the levels of regions (e.g., Europe, Asia, etc.) rather than the whole planet, even though we have started to see global episodes with the financial crisis of 2008. Even in this case, all countries were not equally affected. In Argentina, for instance, the crisis remained largely unfelt at the time. The fact that economies are affected differently over time allows companies with multinational presence to rely on revenues from places that are doing better, and to eventually offset or limit the damages occurring in other parts of the world. The Mexican cement company Cemex, for instance, is known for having better survived the 1994 peso crisis because it was already internationalized at the time.

Focusing on the latest category of motivations (strategic asset-seeking), what are the various strategic assets that companies look for in other countries? Assets that are important to companies and that can be found overseas include new product lines, new technologies, ideas, or any kind of intellectual property. For instance, brand names or patents can help companies strengthen their innovatory or production competitiveness. Knowledge, in general, is an important asset that companies look to obtain. This is why they are called "strategic" assets. A good example of a company looking for such assets among all the above-mentioned motivations is L'Oréal, which expands internationally through acquisitions of other companies. The desire to acquire well-established and recognized brand names has always been important for L'Oréal. It notably allows them to save costs and efforts in targeting all consumer segments in the beauty industry (by adding luxury brands to their portfolio, such as Shiseido or mid-range brands such as Maybelline). They also learn from business models that are very different from their original core business (e.g., with Kiehl's model of word-of-mouth promotion or with the Body Shop's model of franchising). Other benefits falling into this category of strategic assets include economies of common governance (e.g., several companies belonging to the same group save costs by employing only one Research and Development center).

2.2.2 *On the Location of Production (Dunning) and Transaction Costs (Williamson)*

Why do MNCs engage in international production? One theoretical approach to the existence of MNCs is situated at the crossroad between country- and firm-based theories of internationalization. Since it draws from both levels of analysis, it has been called the "Eclectic theory" (or paradigm).

What is the Eclectic theory about, who proposed it, and when? The Eclectic paradigm revolves around a powerful framework, the OLI framework, which is particularly useful in understanding why companies internationalize,

Internationalization 51

where they locate their production, and how they enter foreign markets (selection of entry modes) (Dunning, 1977, 1981). The OLI framework focuses on three types of advantages that companies can benefit from when producing abroad: the Ownership advantage (Why?), Location advantage (Where?), and Internalization advantage (How?). Next, we review them one at a time.

First, what is the Ownership (O-type) advantage about? An ownership advantage exists when a firm has a valuable asset that creates a national competitive advantage which can then be used to enter foreign markets (Griffin & Pustay, 2015, Chap. 6). In this way, it can explain "why" a company is successful in foreign markets. Examples of such an advantage include: superior technology, a well-known brand name, economies of scale, etc. Here is a more-detailed presentation structure of ownership advantages according to their type: organizational (e.g., operating structures, brands, relationships with external actors), financial (e.g., preferential access to capital), technological (e.g., technology, patents, processes), physical (e.g., preferential access to land, raw materials and natural resources), and human ownership advantages (e.g., experience, training, individual ideas, etc.).

Second, what is the Location (L-type) advantage about? A location advantage exists when the undertaking of production activities is more profitable for the company abroad than in the domestic market (Griffin & Pustay, 2015, Chap. 6). In this way, this advantage raises the question of "where" (i.e., market selection) the company should locate its operations. Sources of location advantage include: the allocation of production factors and conditions, access to resources, proximity/access to supply and consumer markets, state regulations, and levels of country risk. Where the company finds the most advantageous conditions for its operation determines the existence of a location advantage abroad. Naturally, this advantage influences the choice of an entry mode: where there is no location advantage, the company is better off with a low-commitment entry mode (e.g., exports or licenses), while, on the contrary, a high-commitment entry mode (i.e., FDI) yields important benefits in the presence of a strong location advantage.

Before we broach the I-type advantage (i.e., the internalization advantage), it is useful to first make a slight detour to understand the basics of yet another theory known as the *transaction costs theory*.

What is the transaction costs theory about, who proposed it, and when? The American economist and Berkeley professor Oliver Williamson (1932–) developed the transaction cost theory (also known as the transaction costs analysis) in the mid-1970s. His work (for which he received a Nobel Memorial Prize in 2009) has been used in many ways. Here, we limit ourselves to understanding the core concept of transaction costs. This concept provides an explanation for the existence of formal relationships between companies through contracts (between customers and suppliers, for instance). Indeed, firms develop long-term relationships and sign contracts with other firms to lower transaction costs.

What are transaction costs then? When a transaction occurs, there are direct costs for the buyer (i.e., the price paid for the purchased goods or services) but also indirect costs, such as the time and energy spent in searching for the right supplier, negotiating with this potential supplier, formalizing and signing an

52 Internationalization

Figure 2.11 Portrait of Oliver Williamson

Source: With permission of Oliver Williamson, screen capture from a YouTube video available with search words: "UC Berkeley Professor Oliver Williamson wins the 2009 Nobel Prize in Economics," posted by: UC Berkeley Events, retrievable at: www.YouTube.com/watch?v=SSYYe-x9r68

agreement, enforcing the agreement if it is not respected, and so on (Williamson, 1975, 1979). These costs are referred to as *transaction costs*. Sellers incur transaction costs as well, since they spend time searching for clients, communicating and negotiating with them, monitoring relationships, etc. At a later point, we will discuss the transaction costs in international exchange in further detail (Chapter 4). At this stage, it suffices to remember that transaction costs are the costs incurred in finding and organizing the exchange process with a business partner. Figure 2.12 provides a visual structure for various types of transaction costs.

Back to the OLI framework, what is the I-type advantage about? The I-type refers to the advantages of internalizing—instead of externalizing—certain value-adding activities (e.g., procurement, production, or distribution). An internalization advantage exists when transaction costs or specific risks (e.g., poor product quality, malpractice) are (too) high. Fighting against opportunism from third parties is also one of the reasons why firms internalize activities (Williamson, 1975). In this case, it is advantageous to internalize certain activities (i.e., keeping them "internal" or inside the organizational boundaries while retaining an important control over them). Therefore, the internalization advantage lies in integrating several activities along the value-chain,

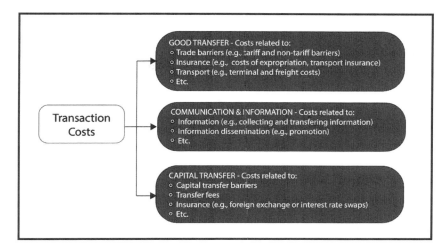

Figure 2.12 Detailing transaction costs in international trade
Source: Adapted from Amelung (1990, p. 6)

such as distribution or manufacturing and exports, in order for companies to reduce transaction costs. This type of advantage raises the question of "how" companies enter foreign markets (i.e., entry mode selection) with low-commitment entry modes (e.g., exports or licenses), because there is no real internalization advantage (transaction costs or risks are acceptable), or with high-commitment entry modes (e.g., acquisitions or greenfield projects), because of a strong internalization advantage.

Which entry mode is best suited for a company? The OLI framework is useful at the time of choosing among entry modes. As illustrated in Table 2.1, a company first must answer positively to the question of possessing or being able to develop an O-type advantage in order to be successful abroad. The firm may then consider if it has an advantage in controlling internally its operations (internalization advantage) and in operating directly in foreign markets (location advantage). A company deriving no advantage from operating in foreign countries but gaining from internalizing activities would logically produce at home and export. However, a company with no location advantage and no specific gain from internalizing activities (or with mechanisms in place to mitigate the risk of externalizing production) should not hesitate to grant licenses to foreign producers. Finally, a company that sees a strong advantage in locating production abroad and in keeping internal control of its activities would opt for foreign direct investments.

2.2.3 On psychic distance and the liability of outsidership (Johanson and Vahlne)

What is psychic distance? The concept of psychic distance has been introduced by Jan Johanson and Jan-Erik Vahlne in their 1977 seminal article entitled "The Internationalization Process of the Firm: A Model of Knowledge

54 *Internationalization*

Table 2.1 Using the OLI framework to choose among entry modes

TYPE OF ADVANTAGE				
O—Ownership advantage	Question:	**Does the company own specific assets that will favor success in international markets?** E.g., economies of scale, expertise and resources.		
	Answer:	**YES**	**YES**	**YES**
L—Location advantage	Question:	**Is there an advantage for the company to locate production in this country?** E.g., price and quality of resources such as labor, energy and materials; favorable regulations and infrastructure; proximity to other markets.		
	Answer:	**NO**	**NO**	**YES**
I—Internalization advantage	Question:	**Is there an advantage for the company to internalize production?** E.g., to reduce transaction costs; to control supplies and quality of products.		
	Answer:	**YES**	**NO**	**YES**
		↓	↓	↓
CHOICE OF ENTRY MODE		**EXPORTS**	**LICENSES**	**FDI**

Source: Adapted from Dunning (1981, p. 111)

Development and Increasing Foreign Market Commitments" (cited nearly 12,000 times as of March 2018, according to an inquiry in Google Scholar!). It is a central notion that we have broached superficially in Section 2.1.1 when presenting the Uppsala model. We cover this notion in more detail in Chapter 4. Still, we know enough at this stage to question its role in the internationalization process (see "Food for Thought"). It is particularly interesting to contrast the 1977 article with Johanson and Valhne's 2009 article, entitled "The Uppsala internationalization process model revisited: From liability of foreignness to liability of outsidership" (already cited over 3,000 times as of March 2018 according to Google Scholar). In the thirty years separating the publication of these two articles, did the role of psychic distance change in the way firms internationalize (see "Food for Thought")?

Food for Thought 2.3

- In reference to Johanson and Vahlne (1977, 2009), what is psychic distance? What role does it play in the internationalization of firms?

Internationalization 55

What is liability of outsidership?[2] It is well known that firms face difficulties when internationalizing into new markets. Business scholars have used various concepts to capture this, each with their own nuance.

Hymer (1976) is the first scholar to argue that foreign firms face "costs of doing business abroad" (CDBA) which local firms do not experience. They face additional costs related to geographic distance (transport, coordination), national borders (tariffs, exchange rate risks), unfamiliarity with the local environment (lack of connections), and differential treatment by host country actors (discrimination). It is precisely due to these CDBA that foreign firms need firm-specific advantages to overcome the home-court advantages of local firms and become competitive.

Eden and Miller (2004) decompose CDBA into two categories: *activity-based costs* and *liability of foreignness* (LOF). Activity-based costs are the economic costs related to doing business at a geographic distance. These include transportation costs, trade barriers, and costs associated with foreign exchange transactions. LOF, in contrast, are the disadvantages of being a "stranger in a strange land." Foreign firms face unfamiliarity hazards due to their lack of knowledge of the home country's institutions. In addition, they face discriminatory hazards, as they are treated differently by the host government, consumers, or the general public.

Johanson and Vahlne (2009) pointed out that many of the disadvantages captured by LOF are not because a firm is foreign, but rather because it faces a "liability of outsidership" (LOO). Since it does not have relationships with one or several actors in the host market, it does not know who the business actors are, or how they are related to each other. A key research question is thus, whether and when the main problem in foreign market entry is being foreign or being an outsider.

In conclusion, what are the factors driving decisions of how and where firms internationalize? These factors have been listed when considering the choice of entry modes but they are also valid for market selection. Overall, we need to remember that companies make decisions of how and where to go abroad based on:

- Managers' vision and attitude toward risk
- The available resources (e.g., financial and human resources)
- How much control is desired
- How much knowledge of target markets is possessed

2.3 Issues at Stake and Examples

This section proposes avenues to answer the following questions:

- How to structure a plan for international marketing expansion?
- What are examples of companies that have internationalized according to a "traditional" or a "born global" path?

2.3.1 Building an International Marketing Plan

How can firms plan an expansion into foreign markets? One of the main tools to do so is the international marketing plan. It is a document that structures

56   Internationalization

and presents the results of different tasks that international marketers must undertake to plan for an expansion abroad (as a first entry or as a means to further penetrate existing markets).

What are the tasks that international marketers must undertake to build an international marketing plan? Three important tasks should be considered:

- **Analyzing the situation** in which the company is embedded. A good start is to study its current business environment as well as the foreign environment in which the company plans to commercialize its products/services. Multiple analytical tools are available to complete this first task.
- **Defining a solution,** in other words, making decisions. This requires the exact issue or problem that needs to be taken care of to first be identified (e.g., Is it a first move abroad? Is it a selection between several potential markets? Is it deciding on the best segment market to target abroad?), and to then identify and compare the various options or alternative solutions that will address this precise problem and reach the objectives. In summary, decisions often revolve around market selection (where to go?), entry modes (how to expand abroad?) and targeting (who should we target?).
- **Implementing the chosen solution.** This boils down to considering the various impacts of the solution on the marketing function, as well as the other functions of the company (e.g., production, logistics, finance, human resources). Important decisions must be made regarding the desired degree of adaptation versus standardization of the marketing-mix and the degree of centralization (at headquarters) versus delegation (to foreign subsidiaries) for decision-making. In particular, the marketing-mix consists of policies regarding the 4Ps (an acronym which stands for "product," "price," "place"–or distribution, and "promotion") or the 7Ps (an acronym that also includes policies concerning "processes," "personnel," and "physical evidence," whether the value offering is a service instead of a product). In addition, it is important to propose a timeline defining how the solution will be rolled out in time and a budget that will detail the expected costs and revenues generated by the solution, as well as how the solution will be financed. Finally, the last step requires outlining a contingency plan. Upon the completion of all these tasks, the international marketer puts together a complete document.

Figure 2.13 illustrates the main activities involved in structuring an international marketing plan. It highlights different analytical tools that can be used for a situation analysis. For instance, the 5Cs (Company, Context, Collaborators, Clients, and Competitors) and EPRG (Ethnocentric, Polycentric, Regiocentric and Geocentric orientations) frameworks provide information about the context and vision of the company for which the plan is made. Concepts and models developed by Michael Porter and others in the field of strategic management (e.g., value chain, five forces of the competitive environment, diamond of national advantage, key success factors, and competitive advantage) offer a more specific description of its position within its industry. In turn, the Ansoff Matrix and the SWOT (Strengths, Weaknesses,

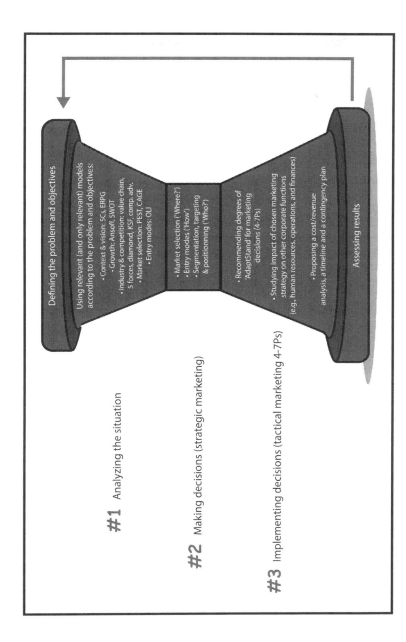

Figure 2.13 Structuring an international marketing plan

Source: Own elaboration

58 *Internationalization*

Opportunities and Threats) analysis help with growth avenues. To make a market selection decision, the best tools are a PEST or a CAGE analysis (i.e., analyzing the Politico-legal, Economic, Sociocultural and Technological environment of the target country or the Cultural, Administrative, Geographic and Economic distance between the home and the target country). Finally, the OLI framework (standing for Ownership, Location and Internalization advantages) helps to document entry mode decisions. In this book, we review a few of these tools (OLI in the present chapter, EPRG in Chapter 3, CAGE in Chapter 4). The figure also illustrates the proposed path between the three building blocks: 1) analyzing the situation, 2) defining a solution (i.e., making decisions), and 3) implementing the chosen solution. In the figure, note the retroactive arrow going from the implementation back to the defining objectives and analyzing the situation. It illustrates the importance of monitoring the results of the implementation and benchmarking these results against the plan's objectives. After implementing a solution, it is often useful to go back to analyzing the situation and see if the issues detected were initially well addressed.

Is this the only way to structure an international marketing plan? This is not a normative model for an international marketing plan. It is only one of the possible ways of structuring such a plan. In many cases, the problem is obvious and does not require analyzing the situation at home first. In other cases, it is only after a careful analysis of the situation at hand that the actual problem and relevant alternative solutions can be identified. Furthermore, decisions at the strategic level may have already been taken and the marketing plan only comprises the implementation section. Also, it could well be that needs for specific analysis about foreign markets only arise when considering decisions for implementing the chosen marketing strategy. Thus, what is important to remember is the existence of those three main activities: 1) analyzing, 2) defining a strategy (i.e., making decisions at the strategic level), and 3) implementing (i.e., making decision at the tactic level). Here, the structure for an international marketing plan is presented in a static manner to ease its comprehension. In real life, the order in which each activity is undertaken needs to be selected carefully. Several iterations and a dialogue in a dynamic approach between each activity should be sought after.

Aren't plans overrated? Experience shows that things rarely go according to plan. Does this mean that plans in general, and international marketing plans in particular, are worthless? One of the drawbacks of an international marketing plan is that it is time consuming and sometimes hazardous to put together (because of a lack of information on foreign markets, for instance). Unforeseeable conditions (e.g., financial crisis, wars, earthquakes), market volatility, speed of change in an industry, and many other events or conditions can render the plan obsolete before it is even completed.

Why then is it useful to build an international marketing plan? The international marketing plan presents at least three advantages. First, it helps deal with uncertainty. Indeed, decision-making is a process that is inhibited by uncertainty. Making decisions requires controlling for uncertainty to a certain extent. This extent is determined by individuals' level of tolerance for risk-taking, in other words, their aversion to risk, which is a key aspect of personality. Considering that significant amounts of money are usually at stake when planning for marketing strategies and tactics abroad, and that success or failure impact decision-makers' professional career, trying to reduce uncertainty as much as possible is a rational thing to do. Putting together a document, the international marketing plan, fulfills this need. Second, it helps to convince others. A document is a basis for discussing with colleagues to get their input and to ultimately agree upon specifics. Once it is considered final, it is instrumental to communicate with others inside and outside the company (e.g., with subordinates to get their commitment, superiors to get their approval and investors to get financing). Finally, it helps to deal with change. A written document such as the international marketing plan acts as a snapshot of the conditions surrounding the moment in which it was elaborated. It is like taking a picture of reality. In business and administration sciences, reality is much more subjective than in "hard" sciences. Like for any other social science (e.g., history, law, psychology), it is not easy to agree upon one "truth" about how "things" or conditions were at a specific moment in time. In addition, conditions change fast and memories can be evasive. Because a written document has authors and a timestamp, it later allows managers to acknowledge how much has changed compared to "the" truth or reality as experienced at the time and by the people involved. It is an essential tool to determine whether the picture taken at the time was accurate or not. It allows us to benchmark the results against the intentions. With no written trace of specific situations and intentions, it is much harder to reassess objectives and eventually correct a course of action.

2.3.2 Corporate Examples: Abercrombie & Fitch, Amazon, Coca-Cola, Disney, IKEA, McDonald's, Netflix, Starbucks, Tesla, Uber, Vice Media, and Volkswagen

In this section, we look at examples that illustrate why, where and how companies internationalize their activities. They are presented in alphabetical order but some of these companies have clearly internationalized according to the traditional model while others are considered born global companies. Can you tell (see "Food for Thought")?

Food for Thought 2.4

- Among the examples listed below (and others that you may have heard of), which companies have put in practice the "classical theory of internationalization" and which can be called "born global" firms?

Abercrombie & Fitch[3]—Established in 1892, the US clothing company A&F Co. started its international expansion over a century later by entering

60   Internationalization

Canada in 2006, with stores in Edmonton and Toronto. One year later, the company entered the UK (London). By 2011, the firm had added twenty stores in the UK and opened fifty-four stores across Europe (e.g., Denmark, Germany, Italy, and Spain), Asia (e.g., Japan, China, Hong Kong, and Singapore), and Central America (e.g., Puerto Rico). By the end of 2012, the company had increased its international points of selling from 54 to 139.

Amazon[4]—Amazon started as a small online bookstore in the US (1995). Its international expansion came only a few short years after being founded, when it moved simultaneously into the UK and Germany (1998). Soon after, Amazon launched in Japan and France, which became a European market hub where local, as well as customers from other countries, could make purchases (2000). The last two markets, of the company's initial global expansion, to be entered were Canada (2002) and China (2004). A second wave of growth began with an increased presence in Europe, for example, in Italy (2010) and Spain (2011). Seventeen years after inception, Amazon entered emerging markets such as India and Brazil (2012), with international sales then representing 43 percent of revenue. In terms of entry modes, Amazon either established subsidiaries directly (e.g., in France, Japan, Canada, and Brazil), or used acquisitions first such as in the UK with Bookpages.co.uk, Germany with ABC Bucherdienst/Telebuch.de and China with Joyo.com, to later establish country-specific websites (subsidiaries) in these markets. By the end of 2015, Amazon was generating 107 billion USD in sales and had subsidiaries establish in thirteen countries including those mentioned above, Australia, Mexico and the Netherlands.

Coca-Cola[5]—The Coca-Cola company was founded in 1886 in Atlanta (US) and sold its products domestically until 1904. By 1905, the firm made its debut in five countries: Canada, Panama, Cuba, Puerto Rico, and France. Over the next twenty years, the number of countries where the company operated increased to fifty-three (1940). It was during the next twenty years, in the post-World War II period, that the international expansion of the company grew significantly to reach a global presence in one hundred and twenty countries (1960). Since then, international expansion has never stopped, and Coca-Cola advertises selling its beverages in more than two hundred countries, virtually everywhere on the planet. In terms of entry modes, Coca-Cola has used licenses, wholly owned operations and acquisitions. For instance, the company had been in India from 1970 to 1977. After deciding to leave due to changes in government policies, it reentered the country through the acquisition of the main local player Parle (1993).

Disney[6]—The Walt Disney Company has a number of business units, including parks and resorts, studio entertainment, media networks, and consumer products. Focusing on amusement parks, Disneyland was first built in the US (1955). Thirty years later, it started to internationalize its operations with a ten- to fifteen-year period in between each new entry. The company entered Asia with a park in Tokyo (1983), Europe with a park in Paris (1992), and then continued its Asian expansion with a park in Hong Kong (2005) and in Shanghai (2016).

Disney Parks and Resorts are a good example of the use of multiple entry modes, including licenses, joint-ventures, management contracts, and greenfield investments. In Japan, the company granted a license to a local firm, which in return paid 5 percent royalties from gross revenues from food and merchandise, and a fee of 10 percent of admissions and sponsorship agreements. In France, Disney established a new company, Euro Disney SCA, with a distinctive legal structuring, and made it public by launching an IPO to raise capital while maintaining a 39 percent stake in the company. In China, it made a joint-venture with the Hong Kong government (43 percent stake), which proved to be a valued partner, granting a low-interest loan to build the park and undertaking important infrastructure improvements (in particular, transportation). For the Shanghai location, Disney formed another joint-venture with a state-owned holding company as well with a management company (responsible for creating, developing and operating the resort on behalf of the owner companies), retaining a 43 percent stake in the former and a 70 percent stake in the latter.

IKEA[7]—Founded in 1943 by seventeen-year-old Ingvar Kamprad, IKEA opened its inaugural store in 1958 and its first flagship store in Stockholm, Sweden's capital, in 1965. The company made its first contact outside of its home base for procurement in Denmark and Poland (1961). Its international expansion started twenty years after inception, with stores opened in Norway (1963) and in Denmark (1969). The first store outside Scandinavia was opened in Switzerland (1973) and afterward in Germany (1974). It entered the US in 1985. Although the company's traditional strongholds have been Europe and North America, it has been moving into newer markets, such as China (1998). In 2016, the company had three hundred and forty stores in twenty-eight countries, twenty-two Pick-up and Order Points in eleven countries, forty-one Shopping Centres in fifteen countries, and thirty-eight Distribution sites in eighteen countries. As foreign entry modes, IKEA has used a combination of wholly owned and franchised stores (e.g., in Saudi Arabia since 1983).

McDonald's[8]—McDonald's started its operations in the US shortly after World War II (1948). Twelve years later, the fast food company had more than one thousand national franchises. The internationalization process started nineteen years after inception, with the opening of a restaurant in Canada and in Costa Rica (both in 1967). Only a few years later, the firm was present in Japan, Holland, and Australia (early 1970s). McDonald's then entered the South American market with Brazil (1979), and pursued its global expansion by entering the Arab world with Morocco (1992). From there, the internationalization sped up and by the end of the 1990s, the firm sold hamburgers in one hundred countries, with Belarus being the hundreth country with a McDonald's (Time, 2009). In 2016, McDonald's had more than thirty-six thousand restaurants in one hundred and nineteen countries.

In terms of entry modes, the company relies heavily on franchising. Indeed, only 16.8 percent of McDonald's restaurants were company owned in 2016. The rest were operated by franchisees (about eighteen thousand restaurants abroad and twelve thousand in the US). Several types of arrangements are used: conventional franchises, developmental licenses, and minority acquisitions. Under the conventional arrangement (average franchise length is twenty years), McDonald's either owns the land and the building or has a

62 Internationalization

long-term location lease; in turn, the franchisee co-invests by paying for the equipment, signs, seating, and décor. McDonald's receives a grant for the opening of the new restaurant and royalty fees based on a percentage of sales. Under the developmental license arrangement, the licensee is responsible for paying the entire business, including real estate, royalty fees based on sales, and the license grant. This structure is used in more than seventy countries, with a total of 5,500 restaurants. For instance, the largest licensee operates 2,100 restaurants in nineteen countries in Latin America and the Caribbean. Under the minority acquisitions scheme, McDonald's makes an equity investment in what they call *affiliates*. In that case, the affiliate pays only a percentage of sales. The largest of the affiliates can be found in Japan, with three thousand restaurants.

Netflix[9]—This US company started in 1997 as a DVD-by-mail service, but shifted its business model to Internet streaming and video on demand (VOD) in 2007. Due to a saturated domestic market, it began an aggressive internationalization strategy three years later, with entry into Canada, Europe, and Latin America (2010). They soon added sixty new markets (2010–2015), and in 2016, announced their intention to expand into another one hundred and thirty countries, which means reaching global market coverage with one hundred ninety countries served, less than ten years after initiating their geographic expansion. In terms of entry modes, Netflix invests heavily in partnerships and joint-ventures with local content creators in order to provide specific offerings for local audiences. For instance, Netflix partnered with Japanese talent agency Yoshimoto Kogyo to obtain exclusive streaming rights for programs developed by the agency in exchange for development funding. In 2015, Netflix employed 3,500 people for total revenues upwards of 6.78 billion USD, and an estimated 74 million subscribers worldwide.

Starbucks[10]—The coffee company and coffeehouse chain opened its first store in 1971 in Seattle (US). Sixteen years later, Starbucks crossed the Canadian border (a two-hour drive from Seattle) and entered its first foreign market in Vancouver (1987). The company waited another nine years before opening its first stores outside of North America, in Japan and in Singapore (1996). Then, its internationalization process started to speed up in 1998–99 with entries in Europe (e.g., UK), Asia and Australasia (e.g., China, Malaysia, New Zealand, Taiwan, Thailand, and South Korea), and the Middle East (e.g., Kuwait and Lebanon). In 1998, the company had about 1,880 stores. The search for new customers (market-seeking motivation) then became very active in the following fifteen years (2000–2015), as the company opened over 22,500 selling points in fifty-four countries. In 2016, the company focus has turned toward the PAC region (China and Asia-Pacific) as it has opened close to 2,300 stores in one hundred Chinese cities and is targeting the opening of 3,400 stores by 2019. Although only seventy-five stores were opened between 2012 and 2015, India also appears as a substantial target for future growth.

Entry modes include wholly owned and licensed stores in a roughly 50/50 proportion. For instance, Starbucks had 10,394 co-operated stores and 10,125 licensed stores worldwide in 2014. The company develops proprietary ventures (for instance, it has its own coffee farm in China), but also uses

Internationalization 63

partnerships to develop foreign markets (for instance, it has entered the Indian market in partnership with Tata Global Beverages, a subsidiary of the Tata Group). Wholly owned subsidiaries include Teavana, which operates some three hundred Heaven of Tea retail stores (tea-related products, such as gourmet loose-leaf teas and teapots). Finally, Starbucks also licenses its brand for such products as ice cream (made by Dreyer's Grand Ice Cream, a subsidiary of Nestlé), coffee flavored liqueur (Beam), and bottled Frappuccino (PepsiCo).

Tesla[11]—Tesla was founded in 2003 as an automotive company dedicated to producing fully electric cars. The company began by conducting all sales either via the phone, online, or in person, but by the end of 2012, Tesla had opened twenty-four company-owned stores across North America, another thirteen stores in Europe and three in Asia. They continued to grow the number of showrooms, with a presence in Australia, Japan, China, Mexico, the UK, Scandinavia, and most Western European countries. Unlike other automobile companies, Tesla does not license franchise dealers in order to sell their vehicles, but rather manages all sales and services in-house.

Uber[12]—Uber was founded in San Francisco (US) in 2009 and officially launched in 2010, after founders Travis Kalanick and Garrett Camp had an impossible time getting a taxi while overseas in Paris. The company's exponential growth was fueled by funding from angel investors, venture capital groups, and major investment banks. After raising 12 million USD from Benchmark Capital in the early stages, Uber raised a further 32 million USD from other investors, including Menlo Ventures, Bezos Expeditions, and Goldman Sachs just eighteen months after its launch. A 258 million USD investment by Google and others followed in 2013. Uber's valuation then jumped from $330 million in 2011 to $3.4 billion in 2013, revealing investors' confidence in the company's ability to maintain its exponential growth rate. Although the company did not disclose official figures, Uber was said to have reported sales of $125 million in 2013, with an 18 percent monthly growth rate and four hundred employees worldwide. With Uber having secured another $4 billion in investments in 2015, estimates bring the transportation start-up to a valuation of $41 billion USD.

Uber first had three drivers cruising the streets of San Francisco on its test run in June 2010. Late in 2011, it was introduced in Paris—thought to have a similar traffic situation as San Francisco (e.g., low taxi accessibility, a considerable smartphone penetration, and the well-recognized use of the PayPal system), followed by the UK in 2012. It quickly spread across geographic regions in 2013–2014, including Australia, Canada, Chile, Colombia, China, India, Mexico, Russia, Singapore, South Korea, South Africa, and Taiwan. By February 2016, Uber was operating in sixty-eight countries and more than four hundred cities. As of July 2017, the company operated in 634 cities (279 in North America, 128 in Central and South America, 105 in Asia—including 39 cities in South-East Asia, 37 in South Asia, 20 in Australia and New Zealand, and 9 in East Asia, 94 in Europe, 15 in Africa, and 13 in the Middle East). In its domestic market, the company operates under Uber USA, LLC, and its subsidiaries and affiliates are collectively known as "Uber." Internationally, Uber B.V. is a private limited liability company established in the Netherlands.

64   *Internationalization*

The fast pace of internationalization was supported by a standardized mobile technology model that could be easily replicated everywhere.

Vice Media[13]—Vice Media began as a small locally distributed newsprint and culture magazine in Canada (1995). It started its international expansion only six years after inception, noting that advertising interest was limited in one single market. Vice quickly started serving a niche market in the US (1996), and moved its head office to New York City (1998). Four years later, it moved into the UK, Australia, and Japan (2002). The rest of Europe followed from 2004–2007, although certain Eastern European markets (e.g., Bulgaria and Romania) were too small to support the expansion. It pursued its internationalization with emerging markets such as Brazil, Mexico, South Africa, and Russia (2008–2013). The company's initial strategy of using partnerships to set up a magazine and then expand into other business lines was abandoned in the late 2000s, opting instead for acquisitions and wholly owned subsidiaries. In 2016, it had offices in twenty-eight countries.

Volkswagen[14]—Founded in Germany in 1934, Volkswagen was proudly Teutonic until the end of World War II with the division of Germany, when the company passed into British administration in 1954. By 1950, it was exporting to eighteen countries, chiefly Sweden, Belgium, the Netherlands, Switzerland and, in a departure from its mainly European markets, Brazil. The company entered a period of further internationalization between the 1950s and 1960s, creating a sales and customer service network in Canada (1952) and its first foreign production plant in Brazil (1953). By 1954, it had established eighty-two sales agencies outside Germany, with the majority of sales coming from Belgium, Sweden, the Netherlands, and Switzerland. In 1955, the company entered the US cautiously as a market research and observation agency. Next entries included: Australia (1957), France (1960), Mexico (1964), erstwhile Yugoslavia (1972), Nigeria (1973), Spain (1981), Japan (1982), China (1985), Poland (1998), Russia (2006), and India (2007). As of 2016, the Volkswagen Group sold its vehicles in 153 countries, with 120 production plants (located in twenty European countries and eleven countries in the Americas, Asia and Africa).

In addition to exports, Volkswagen has often used acquisition as a market entry mode. For instance, it entered South Africa (1956) through the acquisition of South African Motor Assemblers and Distributors Ltd., Argentina (1980) through its acquisition of Chrysler, and the Czech Republic (1991) via a 30 percent stake in Skoda (eventually raised to 100 percent).

Conclusion: In Their Foreign Expansion, Companies Follow Four Main Motives, Go Where They Can Learn Faster, and Have a Variety of Entry Modes at Their Disposal

The short answer to the question guiding this chapter: **"Why, where, and how do firms internationalize?"** is that companies usually expand abroad for four main motives (market-seeking, resource-seeking, strategic-asset seeking, and efficiency-seeking); they go where they can learn faster (whether it is because of low degrees of psychic distance or because they

Internationalization 65

have access to knowledge through networks of local partners); and they have a variety of avenues at their disposal for how to proceed (exports, licenses, franchises, specialized modes, and foreign direct investments, including alliances and joint-ventures, acquisitions, and greenfield projects). The choice among entry modes is driven by important notions, such as the location of production and the internalization of transaction costs (Cf. OLI framework).

Over all, decisions related to market selection (where) and choice of entry modes (how) are central to the internationalization of firms. The hourglass presented in the introduction shows that this chapter was directed to the level of strategic marketing (i.e., the central part of the hourglass where these "where" and "how" questions are addressed). The reason for this jump over the detailed analysis of distance is to help understand the very reason for a situation analysis. Because of the central role of market knowledge in the internationalization process, marketers need to conduct a thorough analysis of differences between home and foreign environments (Chapters 4–7). This is key in selecting target markets and entry modes, as well as in deciding on the degree of "AdaptStand" of marketing activities. The extent to which marketing should be adapted to foreign markets and/or standardized across markets is the topic of the next chapter.

Notes

1 In Section 2.1.1, the paragraph entitled: "What is a born global company?" has been written in collaboration with David Pastoriza, Associate Professor in International Business (HEC Montréal, Canada), whose research interests include internationalization and the multinational corporation.
2 In Section 2.2.3, the paragraph entitled "What is liability of outsidership?" has been written in collaboration with Ari Van Assche, Associate Professor in International Business (HEC Montréal, Canada), whose research interests include international trade and global value chains.
3 The Abercrombie & Fitch example relies on: Forbes (2015); Ivey W12342 (2012).
4 The example of Amazon is based on: Amazon (2015); Ivey W14784 (2015).
5 The Coca-Cola example is based on: IMB 387 (2012); The Coca-Cola Company (2016).
6 The example of Disney relies on: HKU 885 (2010); Shanghai Disney Resort (2016).
7 IKEA example is based on: HBS 9–116–015 (2016); HBS 9–504–094 (2004); IKEA (2016a, 2016b); Inter IKEA Systems (2016).
8 The example of MacDonald's is based on: Entrepreneur.com (2016); McDonald's Corporation (2015, 2016).
9 Netflix example is based on: Ivey W16236 (2016).
10 Starbucks example relies on: HBS 9–314–068 (2014); Hoovers (2016); Starbucks Corp. (2015); Trefis (2016).
11 Tesla example is based on: MH 0017 (2015); Tesla (2016).
12 The example of Uber relies on: Business Insider (2013); Forbes (2014); Fortune (2013); Inc.com (2016); Ramaswami and Lyons (2013); The Michael Report (2015); Uber (2015, 2016, 2017).
13 Vice Media example is based on: Ivey W14037 (2014); Vice Media (2016).
14 The example of Volkswagen based on: IMD 141 (2002); Volkswagen AG (2008, 2016).

References

Amazon (2015). Annual Report. www.annualreports.com/Company/amazoncom-inc

Amelung, Torsten (1990). *Explaining Regionalization of Trade in Asia Pacific: A Transaction Cost Approach*. Kiel Working Papers, No. 423. Kiel Institute for the World Economy. Retrieved from http://econpapers.repec.org/paper/zbwifwkwp/423.htm

Andersen, Otto (1993). On the Internationalization Process of Firms: A Critical Analysis. *Journal of International Business Studies*, 24(2), 209–231.

Andersson, Svante & Ingemar, Wiktor (2003). Innovative Internationalization in New Firms: Born Globals—the Swedish Case. *Journal of International Entrepreneurship*, 1(3), 249–275.

Basenotes (2015). All of Procter & Gamble's Fragrance Acquisitions and Divestures 1990–2015. Retrieved April 2017, from www.basenotes.net/features/3165-all-of-procter-and-gambles-fragrance-acquisitions-and-divestures-1990-2015

The Body Shop (2014). Franchising. Retrieved January 2015, from www.thebodyshop.com/content/services/franchising.aspx

Business Insider (2013, August 22nd). On-Demand Driver Startup Uber Receives Investment At A $3.5 Billion Valuation From TPG, *By Allison Shontell*. Retrieved from www.businessinsider.com/uber-raises-at-a-35-billion-2013-8

Cateora, Philip, Graham, John & Bruning, Edward (2006). *International Marketing*. Whitby, Canada: McGraw-Hill Ryerson Higher Education (p. 536).

Cavusgil, Tamer & Knight, Gary (2015). The Born Global Firm: An Entrepreneurial and Capabilities Perspective on Early and Rapid Internationalization. *Journal of International Business Studies*, 46(1), 3–16.

The Coca-Cola Company (2016). From 1886 to the Present Day, This Is the Story of Coca-Cola. Retrieved September 2016, from www.coca-cola.co.uk/stories/from-1886-to-the-present-day—this-is-the-story-of-coca-cola#

Czinkota, Michael, Ronkainen, Ilkka & Moffett, Michael (2005). *International Business* (7th ed.). Ithaca: Thomson/South-Western (p. 782).

Dunning, John (1977). Trade, Location of Economic Activity and the MNE: A Search for an Eclectic Approach. In *The International Allocation of Economic Activity: Proceedings of a Nobel Symposium Held at Stockholm*, Bertil Ohlin, Per-Ove Hesselborn, and Per Mangus Wijkman (Editors). London: The Macmillan Press Ltd. (pp. 395–418).

Dunning, John (1981). *International Production and the Multinational Enterprise*. London: Georges Allen & Unwin Ltd. (p. 440).

Dunning, John (1998). Globalization and the New Geography of Foreign Direct Investment. *Oxford Development Studies*, 26(1), 47–69.

Dunning, John (2009). Location and the Multinational Enterprise: A Neglected Factor? *Journal of International Business Studies*, 40(1), 5–19.

Eden, Lorraine & Miller, Stewart (2004). Distance Matters: Liability of Foreignness, Institutional Distance and Ownership Strategy. In *Theories of the Multinational Enterprise: Diversity, Complexity and Relevance*, Michael Hitt and Joseph Cheng (Editors). Bingley: Emerald Group Publishing Limited (Vol. 16, pp. 187–221).

Entrepreneur.com (2016). McDonald's Units (Locations). Retrieved April 2017, from www.entrepreneur.com/franchises/mcdonalds/282570

Forbes (2014). Uber's Global Expansion in Five Seconds. Retrieved September 2016, from www.forbes.com/sites/ellenhuet/2014/12/11/ubers-global-expansion/#643 fcbc87a7a

Forbes (2015). Why Abercrombie & Fitch's International Expansion Makes Sense Despite Europe Concerns. Retrieved September 2016, from www.forbes. com/sites/greatspeculations/2015/08/13/why-abercrombie-fitchs-international-expansion-makes-sense-despite-europe-concerns/#7aec09462d2d

Fortune (2013, July 23rd). Video and transcript: Uber CEO Travis Kalanick, *By Jessi Hempel*. Retrieved from http://fortune.com/2013/07/23/video-and-transcript-uber-ceo-travis-kalanick/

Freeman, Susan, Hutchings, Kate & Chetty, Sylvie (2012). Born-Globals and Culturally Proximate Markets. *Management International Review*, *52*(3), 425–460.

Griffin, Ricky & Pustay, Michael (2015). *International Business* (8th ed.). New Jersey: Pearson (p. 624).

HBS 9–116–015 (2016). *IKEA in Saudi Arabia (A)*. Case written by: Karthik Ramanna, Jerome Lenhardt, and Marc Homsy. Boston: Harvard Business School (p. 23).

HBS 9–314–068 (2014). *Starbucks Coffee Company: Transformation and Renewal*. Case written by: Nancy Koehn, Kelly McNamara, Nora Khan, and Elizabeth Legris. Boston: Harvard Business School (p. 71).

HBS 9–504–094 (2004). *IKEA Invades America*. Case written by: Youngme Moon.Boston: Harvard Business School (p. 13).

HKU 885 (2010). *Disney: Losing Magic in the Middle Kingdom*. Case written by: Ali Farhoomand. Hong Kong: Asia Case Research Centre (p. 31).

Hoovers (2016). Starbucks Corporation. Subsidiary of Dun & Bradstreet. Retrieved April 2017, from http://cobrands.hoovers.com/company/STARBUCKS_CORPORATION/rhkchi-1-1njhxf.html

Hymer, Stephen (1976). *The International Operations of National Firms: A Study of Direct Foreign Investment*. Cambridge: MIT Press (p. 253).

IKEA (2016a). IKEA History—How It All Began. Retrieved September 2016, from www.ikea.com/ms/en_GB/about_ikea/the_ikea_way/history/

IKEA (2016b). IKEA Group Yearly Summary. 51. www.ikea.com/ms/en_CA/pdf/yearly_summary/IKEA_Group_Yearly_Summary_2016.pdf

IMB 387 (2012). *Coke and Pepsi: From Global to Indian Advertising*. Case written by: Seema Gupta. Bangalore: Indian Institute of Management (p. 18).

IMD 141 (2002). *Globalizing Volkswagen: Creating Excellence on All Fronts*. Case written by: Jan Kubes and George Radler. Lausanne: International Institute for Management Development (p. 35).

Inc.com (2016). 4 Design Challenges Uber Had to Overcome to Take Its App Global. Retrieved September 2016, from www.inc.com/kevin-j-ryan/how-uber-designed-one-app-that-makes-sense-in-70-different-countries.html

Inter IKEA Systems (2016). Milestones in Our History. Retrieved September 2016, from http://inter.ikea.com/en/about-us/milestones/

Ivey W12342 (2012). *Abercombie and Fitch*. Case written by: Cameron Mahi, David Anderson, Gracie Boelsems, and John Garrison. London, Ontario: Ivey Publishing 9B12A033 (p. 15).

Ivey W14037 (2014). *Vice Media: Competitive Advantage and Global Expansion*. Case written by: Alvi Farzad. London, Ontario: Ivey Publishing 9B14M039 (p. 13).

68 Internationalization

Ivey W14784 (2015). *Amazon Goes Global*. Case written by: Li Yong and Li Jing. London, Ontario: Ivey Publishing 9B14M122 (p. 15).

Ivey W16236 (2016). *Netflix: International Expansion*. Case written by: Won-Yong Oh and Duane Myer. London, Ontario: Ivey Publishing 9B16M070 (p. 11).

Johanson, Jan & Vahlne, Jan-Erik (1977). The Internationalization Process of the Firm-A Model of Knowledge Development and Increasing Foreign Market Commitments. *Journal of International Business Studies*, 8(1), 23–32.

Johanson, Jan & Vahlne, Jan-Erik (2009). The Uppsala Internationalization Process Model Revisited: From Liability of Foreignness to Liability of Outsidership. *Journal of International Business Studies*, 40(9), 1411–1431.

Johanson, Jan & Wiedersheim-Paul, Finn (1975). The Internationalization of the Firm: Four Swedish Cases. *Journal of Management Studies*, 12(3), 305–322.

Keegan, Warren & Green, Mark (2008). *Global Marketing* (5th ed.). New Jersey: Pearson Prentice Hall (p. 643).

Knight, Gary & Cavusgil, Tamer (2004). Innovation, Organizational Capabilities, and the Born-Global Firm. *Journal of International Business Studies*, 35(2), 124–141.

Krugman, Paul (1980). Scale Economies, Product Differentiation, and the Pattern of Trade. *American Economic Review*, 70(5), 950–959.

License Mag (2014). Puma, L'Oréal Sign Beauty Deal. Retrieved January 2015, from www.licensemag.com/license-global/puma-loreal-sign-beauty-deal

McDonald's Corporation (2015). Annual Report. Retrieved from http://corporate. mcdonalds.com/content/dam/AboutMcDonalds/Investors%202/2015%20 Annual%20Report.pdf

McDonald's Corporation (2016). Company Profile. Retrieved September 2016, from http://corporate.mcdonalds.com/content/mcd/investors/company-overview/company-overview-segment-information.html

MH 0017 (2015). *Tesla Motors (in 2013): Will Sparks Fly in the Automobile Industry?* Case written by: Frank Rothaermel and Erin Zimmer. New York: McGraw-Hill Education (p. 26).

The Michael Report (2015). Finally Revealed: This Is Ethically Questionable Strategy Uber Uses To Win Its Wars. Retrieved December 2015, from http:// themichaelreport.com/2015/02/25/the-uber-playbook/

Moen, Oystein (2001). The Born Globals: A New Generation of Small European Exporters. *International Marketing Review*, 19(2), 156–175.

Oviatt, Benjamin, Philips McDougall, Patricia & Loper, Marvin (1995). Global Start-Ups: Entrepreneurs on a Worldwide Stage. *The Academy of Management Executive*, 9(2), 30–44.

Ramaswami, Vivek & Lyons, Connor (2013). Disrupting the Dispatch: How Uber Can Succeed in the Race for Mobile Taxi Supremacy. Retrieved July 2017, from http://iveybusinessreview.ca/cms/1773/disrupting-the-dispatch/

Shanghai Disney Resort (2016). About Our Company. Retrieved April 2017, from https://shcorporate.shanghaidisneyresort.com/en/category/company-over view-en

Starbucks Corp (2015). Annual Report. Retrieved from http://investor.starbucks. com/phoenix.zhtml?c=99518&p=irol-reportsannual

Tesla (2016). Find Us—Stores. Retrieved April 2017, from www.tesla.com/findus#/ bounds/45.575182,-73.23168299999998,45.481297,-73.32265899999999?sea rch=store

Internationalization 69

Time (2009). McDonald's Abroad. Retrieved September 2016, from http://content.time.com/time/world/article/0,8599,1932839,00.html

Trefis (2016). Starbucks Focuses on Expansion in Asian Markets. Retrieved April 2017, from www.trefis.com/stock/sbux/model/trefis?easyAccessToken=PROVIDER_ee302f87ca2ab31d744b2d33f816fe974868bd1f&from=widget:slideshow

Uber (2015). UBER B.V. Terms and Conditions. August 2017, from www.uber.com/legal

Uber (2016). Locations. Retrieved September 2016, from https://newsroom.uber.com/locations/

Uber (2017). Find a City. Retrieved July 2017, from www.uber.com/en-CA/cities/

Vice Media (2016). About Us. Retrieved April 2017, from www.vice.com/en_ca/pages/about

Volkswagen AG (2008). Historical Notes: Becoming a Global Player. Volkswagen Aktiengesellschaft, Corporate History Department. from www.volkswagenag.com/presence/medien/documents/HN7e_www2.pdf

Volkswagen AG (2016). Volkswagen Production Plants. Retrieved May 2016, from www.volkswagenag.com/content/vwcorp/content/en/the_group/production_plants.html

Williamson, Oliver (1975). *Markets and Hierarchies*. New York: Free Press (p. 286).

Williamson, Oliver (1979). Transaction-Cost Economics: The Governance of Contractual Relations. *The Journal of Law and Economics*, 22(2), 233–261.

3 Standardization and Adaptation

Table of Contents

3 Standardization and Adaptation

Introduction: To What Extent Should Companies Standardize or Adapt Marketing Activities in Foreign Markets? 71
3.1 *Definitions* 74
    3.1.1 Differences Between Domestic, International and Global Marketing (Kotler) 74
    3.1.2 Pros and Cons of Standardization and Adaptation 79
3.2 *Drivers* 80
    3.2.1 Country-Level Factors 80
    3.2.2 Industry- and Product-Level Factors 81
    3.2.3 Firm-Level Factors 82
3.3 *Issues at Stake and Examples* 86
    3.3.1 Organizational Design and Centralization/ Delegation Decisions 86
    3.3.2 Corporate Examples: Apple, Abercrombie & Fitch, Coca-Cola, Disney, Ikea, McDonald's, Netflix, Starbucks, and Volkswagen 87

Conclusion: The extent to which companies should standardize or adapt their marketing activities depends on a variety of country-, industry-, product-, and firm-level factors. It needs to be carefully analyzed on a case-by-case basis, using an AdaptStand approach.
References

Recommended Readings

- Buzell, Robert (1968). "Can You Standardize Multinational Marketing?" *Harvard Business Review*, 46(6), 102–113.
- Quelch, John & Hoff, Edward (1986). Customizing Global Marketing. *Harvard Business Review*, 64(3), 59–68.

- Levitt, Theodore (1983). The Globalization of Markets. *Harvard Business Review*, 61(3), 92–102. [Also recommended in Chapter 1]
- Perlmutter, Howard (1969). The Tortuous Evolution of the Multinational Corporation. *Columbia Journal of World Business*, 4(1), 9–18.
- Tan, Qun & Sousa, Carlos (2013). International Marketing Standardization. *Management International Review*, 53(5), 711–739.
- Vrontis, Demetris; Thrassou, Alkis & Lamprianou, Iasonas (2009). International Marketing Adaptation versus Standardisation of Multinational Companies. *International Marketing Review*, 26(4/5), 477–500.

Introduction: To What Extent Should Companies Standardize or Adapt Marketing Activities in Foreign Markets?

Determining the right degree of adaptation to local conditions or standardization of marketing activities is a key competence that marketers need in order to be successful in international markets. Reformulated, the question addressed in this chapter could be: **"How far is too far?"** How far should companies push for standardization? From a cost perspective,

Figure 3.1 Illustrating Chapter 3
Source: Own elaboration

72 Standardization and Adaptation

the more standardized the marketing of a company's offering, the further away the company can expand (i.e., the more countries it can enter). In Chapter 1, we saw that Levitt (1983, p. 92) captures well this idea with global corporations selling "the same things in the same way everywhere." Thus, the need for adaptation often sets limits on firms' expansion. However, costs are far from being the only determining factor of success and many companies have failed abroad exactly because of a lack of adaptation. Examples of unexpected losses include big names such as eBay in China and Walmart in Japan. eBay was confronted with heavyweight competition from TaoBao, its Chinese archrival. One of the reasons why TaoBao was more successful was due to the importance of trust, which had been developed and nurtured through customer relationship management. In China, customers wanted to be in touch with sellers through text messaging so as to communicate with them easily and to be able to see their online status (International Business Guide, 2013). Efforts from Walmart to expand in Japan through a partial acquisition of the Seiyu Company (37 percent in 2002) resulted in losses of $117 million USD in 2004 (more than triple its earlier projections). One likely explanation is that Japanese consumers associated low prices with low quality and were not convinced they could get good value for their money (Bloomberg Businessweek, 2005).

Thus, asking the question: **"To what extent should companies standardize or adapt marketing in foreign markets?"** leads us to look into the central topic of AdaptStand decisions. Here, we borrow this term from Vrontis and colleagues (e.g., Vrontis, 2003; Vrontis, Thrassou, and Lamprianou, 2009) to encompass the many options that companies have in terms of combining adaptation and standardization (at both the strategic level of marketing with decisions regarding market selection, entry modes, targeting and positioning, and the tactical level with decisions regarding implementation of the marketing-mix with the 4/7Ps). In the perspective of an international marketing plan, and in the continuation of Chapter 2, we jump ahead of distance analysis between markets (Chapters 4–7) in order to truly understand the *raison d'être* for such analysis. Figure 3.2 situates this chapter in the overall book structure.

The objectives of this chapter are to first distinguish among domestic, international, and global marketing. Defining these terms provides us with a common vocabulary for the remainder of the book. Next, we reflect on the benefits and risks of standardization and adaptation, based on seminal articles on the topic. Looking into the drivers that influence decisions in this matter, we then differentiate between country-, industry-, product-, and firm-related factors. In the last subsection, we consider one important issue related to the extent to which marketing managers can push for standardization, namely the fact that their decisions are not taken in isolation from the overall structure and strategy of companies. We also examine several corporate examples that help us realize what companies do in real life when confronted with the AdaptStand issue.

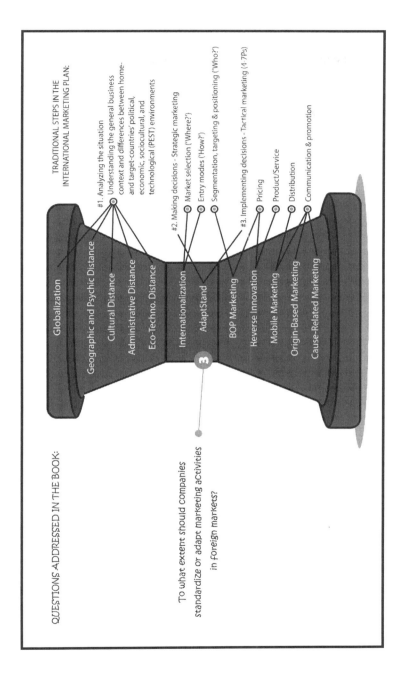

Figure 3.2 Positioning Chapter 3 in the overall book structure

Source: Own elaboration

74 *Standardization and Adaptation*

3.1 Definitions

This section raises the following questions:

- What is marketing and how does domestic marketing differ from international marketing and global marketing?
- Who is Philip Kotler?
- What are the advantages and disadvantages of standardization and adaptation of marketing activities across countries?

3.1.1 Differences Between Domestic, International, and Global Marketing (Kotler)

For starters, what is domestic marketing? Marketing is the object of countless definitions. We can consider a few from both professional associations and academics, which help circumscribe one fundamental notion around the "marketing concept." For instance, The Chartered Institute of Marketing (CIM) in the UK states that: "Marketing is the management process which identifies, anticipates and fulfills consumer requirements in a profitable way" (Chartered Institute of Marketing, 2014). The American Marketing Association (AMA)—which is one of the most recognized and active entities in promoting research and business practice in marketing—defines it as, "The activity, set of institutions, and processes for creating, communicating, delivering, and exchanging offerings that have value for customers, clients, partners, and society at large" (American Marketing Association, 2013). Two formulations by Kotler at an interval of ten years are also enlightening: "Marketing is the human activity which is directed toward satisfying human needs and wants through an exchange process," (Kotler, 1980) and, "Marketing is a social and managerial process by which individuals and groups obtain what they want and need thanks to the creation, the offer and the exchange of products of value with others" (Kotler, 1989).

Who is Philip Kotler? Philip Kotler (1931—) is an American professor of International Marketing at the Kellogg School of Management at Northwestern University in Chicago. He is one of the most prominent figures in the field of marketing and has been writing about a large variety of topics (e.g., international marketing, planning and organization, and marketing strategy) over the past forty years. One of his books, *Marketing Management*, has been re-issued fifteen times so far and ranks among the classics of marketing.

What do these definitions have in common to circumscribe the "marketing concept"? The first common element is the idea that marketing is an activity aimed at fulfilling the requirements, needs, and wants of people (whether individuals, groups, or society at large). This point is the object of considerable debate in the field of marketing since it relates to the issue of answering versus creating needs. For instance, Levitt (1983, p. 98) criticizes companies that adapted too much to consumers' desires and called it the "perverse practice of the marketing concept." The argument made is that consumers do not always know what they want. And you? What do you think about this debate (see "Food for Thought")?

Figure 3.3 Portrait of Philip Kotler

Source: With permission of Philip Kotler, S. C. Johnson Distinguished Professor of International Marketing, screen capture from a YouTube video available with search words: "Philip Kotler: Future of business is doing good (and the four Ps are safe)," posted by Marketing Magazine, retrievable at www.YouTube.com/watch?v=9Pn6om4NGRQ with permission of Philip Kotler

---

Food for Thought 3.1

- What do you think about the debate of answering versus creating consumer needs? Which other common elements do you see in the definitions of marketing provided above?

From here, how can we define international marketing? In their textbook about international marketing, Cateora, Gilly, and Graham (2015, p. 10) slightly adapt the definition provided by the AMA and describe it as "the performance of business activities designed to plan, price, promote, and direct the flow of a company's goods and services to consumers or users in more than one nation for a profit." According to this definition, the only difference between marketing and international marketing is the addition of a geographical precision, in other words, "in more than one country." This precision emphasizes the role of national borders as determinants to being

76 Standardization and Adaptation

"international." Thus, cross-border activities in distribution and commercialization characterize international marketing. It also underlines the absence of required thresholds or rules about the number of countries a company needs to be present in to be considered involved in international marketing. A company conducting marketing activities in its domestic market and in at least one foreign country is deemed active in international marketing.

So, is international marketing just the same thing as domestic marketing but applied to more than one country? Although this definition is fairly simple at first sight, Cateora et al. (2015) underline that it conceals a deep complexity. They illustrate this complexity by first identifying variables with a direct impact on marketing activities that companies can control (e.g., firm characteristics such as size and resources, R&D activities, and decisions made about the product, price, distribution, and promotion). Then, they include variables present in the domestic and foreign markets on which companies have little (eventually gained through lobbying governments) to no control. At home, the competitors, economic climate, and political and legal forces impact marketing activities. In a foreign market, the same variables influence marketing, along with additional variables. In particular, differences in the geographic and technological environment (e.g., temperatures, sea access, and infrastructure), cultural environment (e.g., language and norms), and business environment (e.g., structure of distribution and competitive rivalry) significantly influence marketing activities. All of these variables are likely to differ in each foreign market. Thus, the juxtaposition of all of these foreign environments results in greater complexity for the firm, as illustrated in Figure 3.4.

In summary, how is international marketing different from domestic marketing? The existence of differences and the degree of these differences between the domestic (or home) market and foreign markets (i.e., the extended notion of "distance") is central to understanding the essence of international marketing. In this book, we propose that: **international marketing pursues the same purpose as domestic marketing, while being characterized by higher degrees of complexity due to differences (distance) between countries at both macro and micro levels of analysis.**

As a direct result of this complexity, international marketers must address two dilemmas. One is deciding on the right degree of local adaptation (or localization) versus standardization of marketing activities, and the other one is finding the right degree of delegation versus centralization for making decisions. We can think about these dilemmas in terms of the *tensions* existing between the two extremes of a continuum. The notion of tension better reflects the various and sometimes multiple positions that firms take along these continuums. Put in simple terms, the first one is the "what-do-we-do" continuum (e.g., do we adapt all of our marketing policies or do we standardize them across countries? Otherwise, do we only standardize a few policies, like product and distribution management and adapt others like pricing and promotion activities?). The second one is the "how-do-we-coordinate" continuum (e.g., do we charge subsidiaries in foreign markets with the responsibility to make decisions about marketing

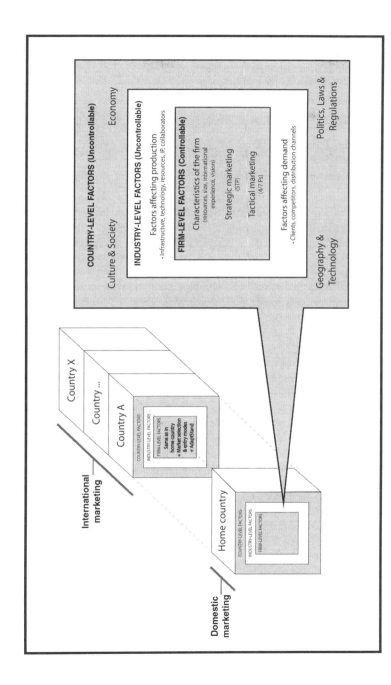

Figure 3.4 Illustrating the complexity of international marketing compared to domestic marketing

Source: Adapted from Cateora et al. (2015)

78 Standardization and Adaptation

activities or do we centralize all decisions at the headquarters?). When activities are standardized, the headquarters of companies are in charge of making decisions. When activities are adapted, both the headquarters and local subsidiaries can make decisions about what should be adapted. Depending on degrees of delegation, decisions can be left to marketers in foreign subsidiaries who are more knowledgeable about the local business environment, for instance. This illustrates that these two dilemmas work hand in hand.

Table 3.1 summarizes the questions under scrutiny in domestic marketing, on the left-hand side. They relate to the business environment analysis, the segmentation, targeting, and positioning (STP) process, as well as the marketing policies (4Ps for the marketing of products and 7Ps for the marketing of services). On the right-hand side of the table, we see that marketing "in more than one country" requires conducting the exact same activities, in addition to raising another set of questions. These questions relate to entry mode selection (i.e., how to go abroad?) and market selection (i.e., where to go?), and the two tensions about how to coordinate marketing activities (i.e., centralization versus delegation) and what to offer in terms of products and services (i.e., standardization versus adaptation).

What about global marketing? In fact, we do not need anything else to characterize global marketing. Global marketing includes the same activities as international marketing, but is characterized by a large-scale/wide

Table 3.1 Comparing domestic and international marketing

	'Single Country' Marketing	→	'More Than One Country' Marketing
Analyzing the situation			
	Understanding the business environment	→	Idem + *Understanding differences across countries*
Making decisions—Strategic marketing			
	Segmenting, targeting and positioning (STP) the offer (Who?)	→	Idem + *Market selection (Where?)* + *Entry modes (How?)*
Implementing decisions—Tactical marketing			
	Defining the marketing-mix (4 or 7Ps): product, price, place (distribution), promotion, people, physical evidence, processes	→	Idem + *Standardizing or adapting the mix?* + *Centralizing or delegating decisions?*

Source: Own elaboration

Standardization and Adaptation 79

scope in market selection, high degrees of standardization of marketing policies, and high degrees of centralization in the coordination of marketing activities.

Keegan and Green (2016, p. 232) further distinguish three forms of global marketing: standardized, concentrated, and differentiated global marketing. *Standardized* global marketing is "analogous to mass marketing in a single country. It involves creating the same marketing-mix for a broad mass of potential buyers." One example could be Coca-Cola's beverages. *Concentrated* global marketing "involves devising a marketing-mix to reach a niche. A niche is simply a single segment of the global market" and is best illustrated by Chanel's cosmetics or Louis Vuitton's hand bags. Finally, *differentiated* global marketing or multisegment targeting "entails targeting two or more distinct market segments with multiple marketing-mix offerings." One example is Danone's yogurt, sold with different marketing-mixes in developed economies (e.g., Dannon and Activia brands) and in developing economies (e.g., Shokti Doi and Dolima brands).

In the remainder of this book, we posit that global marketing raises the same questions as international marketing but provides answers favoring standardization and centralization over adaptation and delegation. Moreover, global marketing tends to be performed by "global companies," which brings forth the topic of organizational structure, discussed later in more details.

Overall, the topic of standardization versus adaptation is central to (international and global) marketing, more so than the centralization versus delegation topic which is being widely researched in (international and global) management instead. We now examine the reasons why firms would rather standardize or adapt (i.e., localize) their marketing activities abroad.

3.1.2 Pros and Cons of Standardization and Adaptation

Why would companies pursue global marketing (i.e., highly standardized marketing activities)? Now that we have started situating global marketing in regards to international marketing by higher degrees of standardization in marketing policies, it is interesting to wonder why companies would pursue global marketing. From various articles recommended as complementary to this chapter, we gather that standardizing marketing activities brings several advantages to firms. But so does adaptation. What are the pros and cons of each approach (see "Food for Thought")?

Food for Thought 3.2

- In reference to Buzell (1968), Levitt (1983), Quelch and Hoff (1986) and Tan and Sousa (2013), what are the advantages and disadvantages of standardizing marketing activities? Conversely, what are the advantages and disadvantages of local adaptation?

80 *Standardization and Adaptation*

3.2 *Drivers*

This section aims to provide avenues to answer the following questions:

- What are the factors which influence decision-making in regards to adaptation and standardization?
- In particular, what is the ERPG scheme and how does it relate to marketing?

Deciding on the degree of standardization and adaptation of marketing activities (from strategic to tactic) is one of the most important decisions that marketing managers must make. In the vast literature addressing the issue, a plethora of driving factors have been put forward. Facing such complexity, a solution is to structure our analysis by using a macro, meso, and micro perspective (e.g., looking into these factors using different levels of analysis, such as the country-, industry-, product-, and firm-level of analysis). Can you use this structure to answer the question in "Food for Thought"?

Food for Thought 3.3

- According to Tan and Sousa (2013), Vrontis et al. (2009), Perlmutter (1969), and Buzell (1968), what are the factors that influence decision-making regarding the degree of standardization and local adaptation?

3.2.1 *Country-Level Factors*

What are the country factors which drive AdaptStand decisions? In their literature review of international adaptation versus global standardization, Vrontis et al. (2009) put forward macro factors, such as economic, legal, cultural, physical, and demographic differences between countries, that will force companies to adapt. On the contrary, if distances between countries are thought to be low, managers will be inclined to standardize marketing activities. In this vein, Tan and Sousa (2013, p. 714) note that "similar environments indicate a homogenized demand in home and host markets, thus increasing the feasibility of a standardized marketing strategy."

It is important to observe that differences across countries may affect only specific marketing activities, not the whole marketing-mix. Cultural differences, for instance, were shown to influence promotion—thus forcing adaptation—but had little influence over product, price, place, or process (Chung, 2007). Differences in physical conditions and technological environments can strongly affect distribution (Buzell, 1968).

Standardization and Adaptation 81

For instance, tropical climates and poor logistics infrastructures can represent a real challenge for distributing products requiring a cold chain. Economic differences between rich and poor countries can obviously force companies to adapt their prices or else change their positioning (e.g., appliances perceived as inexpensive staples in developed economies are perceived as luxuries in developing economies) (Buzell, 1968). In turn, legal and political differences (e.g., product regulations, openness to foreign investments) can impede the distribution and promotion of restricted products (e.g., alcohol in Muslim countries, pharmaceutical products in France), and specific entry modes (e.g., the only way to invest directly in China was through joint-ventures until the country joined the WTO in 2001). Often, different regulations across countries dictate modifications in product design (e.g., safety standards on electrical products such as irons in Europe being more stringent than in the US) (Buzell, 1968).

3.2.2 Industry- and Product-Level Factors

What are the factors at the industry-level of analysis which drive AdaptStand decisions? The structure and intensity of competition influence AdaptStand decisions. In less-competitive markets, marketing managers may have more room for standardization, while particularly vigorous competition usually forces them to locally adapt in order to be more reactive and relevant to customers (Buzell, 1968; Tan & Sousa, 2013).

The availability, costs, and competencies of marketing intermediaries (e.g., distributors and advertising agencies) will also determine if local adaptation is needed (e.g., Douglas & Wind, 1987). For instance, Buzell (1968, p. 112) points out that "differences in the number, size, dispersion of distributive outlets call for differences in promotional methods, and differences in prevailing wholesale and/or retail margins may require vastly different price and discount structures."

Finally, the extent to which an industry is considered to be technology intensive, also called the "industry technological orientation," has been studied for its impact on standardization (e.g., Cavusgil, Zou, & Naidu, 1993). The idea is that standardized marketing is more likely to happen in technology-intensive industries, such as medical equipment or computers. Recent examples with electronic platforms (e.g., Airbnb, Netflix, and Uber) suggest that marketing decisions are indeed easier to replicate in a similar fashion across markets (at least some of these decisions, such as the product, processes, distribution, and promotion decisions).

What are the factors at the product-level of analysis that drive Adapt-Stand decisions? Cavusgil et al. (1993) argue that characteristics of the product, such as its "uniqueness" (i.e., the extent to which the product satisfies unique needs, as opposed to universal needs) and its "type" (i.e., a product sold in a B2C or B2B business model) influence these decisions. Universal products and industrial products (B2B model) should be easier to commercialize with a standardized marketing-mix, as opposed

82 *Standardization and Adaptation*

to "unique" products and consumer goods (B2C model). However, the empirical evidence does not always support these propositions (Tan & Sousa, 2013).

Buzell (1968) and others also argue that the "product life cycle" could be a determinant. Indeed, companies selling products reaching different cycle stages in international markets could be forced to adapt. For instance, promotion should be geared toward raising awareness and educating customers in markets where products are still in the introduction stage, while it can be deployed to differentiate these products from competition in markets where they have already reached the maturity stage.

3.2.3 Firm-Level Factors

What are the factors at the firm-level of analysis which drive AdaptStand decisions? First, we briefly review some of the most important factors identified in the literature, such as firms' organizational design and international experience. Next, we focus on another important factor, firms' strategic orientation, using the EPRG framework.

Firms' organizational design matters, as it impacts the relationship between headquarters and subsidiaries. For this reason, the degree of centralization of companies and the ownership structure of subsidiaries have been found to influence the extent to which marketing activities could be standardized. For instance, Quelch and Hoff (1986, pp. 9–10) observe that, "by coordinating programs with the field, headquarters can balance the company's local and global perspectives. Even a decentralized multinational may decide, however, that to protect or exploit some corporate asset, the center of gravity for certain elements of the marketing program should be at headquarters. In such cases, management has two options: it can send clear directives to its local managers or permit them to develop their own programs within specified parameters and subject to headquarters approval. With a properly managed approval process, a multinational can exert effective control without unduly dampening the country manager's decision-making responsibility and creativity." Doing so, they highlight some of the benefits of standardizing (e.g., maintaining control) and some of the risks (e.g., demotivating local managers who would rather favor adaptation), as discussed previously. If Vrontis et al. (2009) do include "easier planning and control" in their list of benefits for standardization, they do not put much emphasis on the mechanism behind this positive effect: centralization. Defined as "the extent to which headquarters control subsidiaries' management in terms of strategic decision-making" (Tan & Sousa, 2013, p. 715), centralization is conducive to standardization.

International experience at the levels of firms and their decision-makers is also a recognized driver of AdaptStand decisions. Defined as "the amount of experience management has accumulated as an international business player" (Cavusgil et al., 1993, p. 486), it is expected that a company with more experience (which translates, for instance, in larger international market coverage) is more willing and capable to adapt its marketing activities.

Standardization and Adaptation 83

Tan and Sousa (2013) did find that foreign market coverage along with the increased international experience inhibited standardization of promotion.

Several authors (e.g., Buzell, 1968; Vrontis et al., 2009) do not put much emphasis on the importance of AdaptStand drivers at the level of the firm. Yet, it is reasonable to think that marketing departments do not have full authority over international decisions and that many of these decisions are constrained by the structure and strategy of the firm. For this reason, we now highlight the importance of the strategic orientation of the firm using the EPRG framework.

What are the EPRG strategic orientations and how can they impact marketing decisions? The EPRG framework proposes a typology of strategic orientations that firms adopt when expanding abroad. This framework was developed by Howard Perlmutter, a professor at the Wharton School of the University of Pennsylvania in Philadelphia (US) and colleagues (e.g., Heenan & Perlmutter, 1979; Perlmutter, 1969; Wind, Douglas, & Perlmutter, 1973). The seminal article "The Tortuous Evolution of the Multinational Corporation" by Perlmutter (1969) presents different relationships that headquarters can develop with their foreign subsidiaries, as illustrated in Table 3.2.

Table 3.2 Headquarters orientation toward subsidiaries

Organization Design	Ethnocentric	Polycentric	Geocentric
Communication and information flow	High volume from headquarters to subsidiaries	Little to and from headquarters; little between subsidiaries	Both ways and between subsidiaries
Evaluation and control	Standards from home country	Determined in host countries	Find standards which are global and local
Identification	Nationality of owner	Nationality of host country	Truly international but identifying with national interests
Locus of decision-making	Headquarters	Subsidiaries	Aim for a collaborative approach between headquarters and subsidiaries
Recruiting and developing staff	Recruit and develop people of home country for key positions everywhere in the world	Develop people of local nationality for key positions in their own country	Develop best people everywhere in the world for key positions everywhere in the world

Source: Adapted from Perlmutter (1969, p. 12)

84 *Standardization and Adaptation*

Although the framework was originally targeting management decisions (e.g., evaluation and control, recruitment and staffing), it can be extended to marketing decisions abroad. According to Cateora et al. (2015, Chapter 1), a company with an ethnocentric strategic orientation considers foreign marketing activities as a simple extension of domestic marketing activities. Managers in the firm believe that home country marketing practices will succeed elsewhere without having to adapt and view international operations as secondary to domestic operations. Often, being present abroad is motivated by selling excess domestic production. In turn, a firm with a polycentric strategic orientation undertakes "multidomestic" marketing. This means that managers believe that country markets are vastly different, and that an almost-independent marketing program for each country is required in order to succeed. Then, subsidiaries tend to operate independently of one another when establishing marketing objectives and plans. Products are adapted to each market, with little coordination with other country markets. Advertising campaigns, pricing, and distribution decisions are all localized. Lastly, firms with a regiocentric or geocentric strategic orientation implement global marketing.

Why did the framework evolved from EPG to EPRG? Perlmutter's original work (1969) only presented the "geocentric" orientation, not the "regiocentric" orientation. It is subsequent work that helped recognize that firms tend to standardize their activities at a regional level more so than at the level of the entire planet (Wind et al., 1973). Yet, the idea is fundamentally the same between the "regiocentric" and "geocentric" orientations. They both translate into what is considered today as global marketing: a company tends toward standardizing its marketing activities at the scale of an entire region or throughout the world (whenever it is profitable) and adapts them only when and where local conditions dictate.

Figure 3.5 captures the variety of factors influencing AdaptStand decisions. It highlights the fact that companies choosing adaptation often do so because of country-level and industry-level factors, whereas companies choosing standardization mainly consider firm-level factors. To summarize, we can also use a slightly different structure, such as the one proposed by Theodosiou and Katsikeas (2001), who regroup these factors as follows: macroenvironmental factors (economic, legal, cultural, physical and demographic elements), microenvironmental factors (customer characteristics, competition, and intermediaries), firm-specific factors (centralization, strategic orientation, international experience, and subsidiary's ownership structure), and product and/or industry factors (nature of product, uniqueness, cultural specificity, stage in the life cycle, conditions and patterns of product use, product familiarity, and industry technology orientation).

In conclusion, decisions about the degree of standardization/adaptation are complex and influenced by a multitude of factors that must be considered carefully on a case-by-case basis. International marketers must decide which elements of the marketing-mix they should standardize or adapt, under what conditions, and to what degree (Theodosiou & Katsikeas, 2001). Thus, "deciding on the 'balance' between standardization and adaptation is difficult to achieve and a challenging conundrum of an ongoing nature" (Vrontis et al., 2009, p. 491).

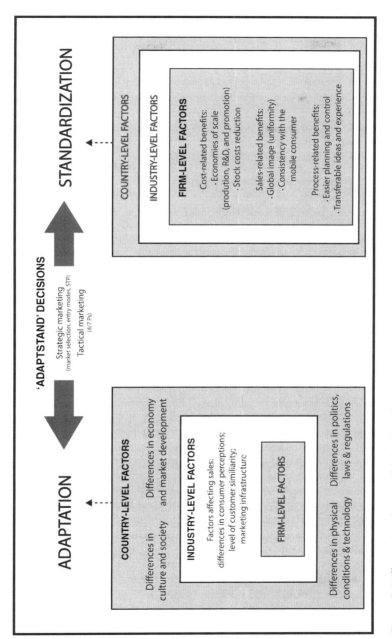

Figure 3.5 Illustrating drivers of AdaptStand decisions

Source: Adapted from Vrontis et al. (2009)

86 Standardization and Adaptation

3.3 Issues at Stake and Examples

This section addresses the following questions:

- Should firms centralize decision-making, or should they delegate decisions to subsidiaries located in foreign markets?
- Among companies known for being widely internationalized, what is the extent to which they have adapted or standardized their marketing activities?

3.3.1 Organizational Design and Centralization/Delegation Decisions

In general, should firms centralize decision-making or should they delegate decisions to subsidiaries located in foreign markets?[1] Answers are to be found in the field of management (strategy and organizational behavior), as they largely depend on organizational structure (e.g., relationship headquarters and foreign subsidiaries).

Each multinational subsidiary operates in a different national environment. In countries where forces calling for national responsiveness are high, subsidiaries must adapt their offerings and strategy to local customers, governments, and local competitors' moves. Food and beverages, or tobacco, would be examples of industries that demand adapted national responses. These are called "multinational environments" (Bartlett & Ghoshal, 1991). In multinational environments, the headquarters decentralize decision-making and resources to subsidiaries (e.g., manufacturing, marketing strategies), because the latter are the best positioned to react to local market specificities, and national environments are too different among themselves for the headquarters to interfere (Ghoshal & Nohria, 1993).

On the other extreme of the spectrum, the forces for national responsiveness can be low in some countries. Subsidiaries do not have to adapt their offer to local market specificities and they can focus on reaching global integration; that is, trying to gain a competitive advantage by offering the same high-quality product worldwide and benefiting from economies of scale. Aeronautics and heavy engineering are examples of industries that do not demand adapted national responses. These are called "global environments" (Bartlett & Ghoshal, 1991). In global environments, the headquarters concentrate decision-making and resources. Subsidiaries are mere implementers (i.e., they distribute and sell) and they are tightly coordinated from the headquarters (Ghoshal & Nohria, 1993).

So, are decisions in the marketing department bound by decisions made at the level of the firm's overall strategy? Yes, marketing managers often have to play by the rules set by high executives in charge of corporate strategy. Here, a dialogue can be established and the extent to which the marketing department is able to influence the overall strategy is likely to depend on the degree of "market orientation" of the firm. Overall, this influencing factor situates us exactly at the intersection between the fields of marketing and management. Entry modes and organizational structures are indeed core topics in

Standardization and Adaptation 87

international management, strategy, and organizational behavior. Several frameworks developed in the field of management are widely used to better understand the topic of marketing in foreign markets. In this regard, Michael Porter and Christopher Bartlett—two other famous professors at Harvard Business School—come to mind: the former because of his generic strategies to gain a competitive advantage (i.e., cost leadership and differentiation) (Porter, 1985), and the latter because of his work (with various colleagues) on organizational forms (i.e., international, multinational, transnational and global companies) (Bartlett & Ghoshal, 2002) that raise discussions about the required levels of centralization and delegation of marketing activities, as discussed previously. What we need to remember here is that marketing managers are not free to make decisions solely based on distances between countries, industry, or product factors. The strategic orientation of firms and their "market orientation" also conditions the degree of AdaptStand of their marketing activities abroad.

3.3.2 Corporate Examples: Apple, Abercrombie & Fitch, Coca-Cola, Disney, Ikea, McDonald's, Netflix, Starbucks, and Volkswagen

In this section, we look at examples that help us answer the following question: "To what extent do companies standardize and/or adapt their marketing activities in foreign markets?" These examples are presented in alphabetical order but some of these companies have clearly standardized their marketing more than others. Can you tell why (see "Food for Thought")?

Food for Thought 3.4

- Among the examples listed below (and others that you may have heard of), to what extent would you say that marketing activities are standardized? How would you explain these companies' choices?

Apple—The well-known US technology company is often cited for its standardized products, positioning, and communication style across markets. Yet, it also adapts various aspects of its marketing activities, as illustrated in Table 3.3.

Abercrombie & Fitch[2] —When the American apparel brand opened its first retail store in Japan (Tokyo) in 2010, it used a mix of adaptation and standardization. Pricing, for instance, was adapted and almost double compared to prices in the US, which was not well received by Japanese consumers. Standardized elements were also a source of concern. Although foreign apparel firms usually hire local staff in order to meet Japanese expectations, the company wanted to make the in-store experience as American as possible, resulting in few people on the sales floor that could be considered as

88 *Standardization and Adaptation*

Table 3.3 Illustrating AdaptStand decisions for Apple and the iPhone

Marketing-mix	Standardization (worldwide)	Adaptation (region-wide or nationwide)
Customer service	• Standard protocol to attend to customers: highly customized	• Interactions with customers adapted to cultural preferences
Price		• In 2017, the iPhone 7 was sold for 649 USD in the US; 5,388 CYN (~780 USD) in China; 255,990 HUF (~870 USD) in Hungary, and 3,499 BRL (~1,110 USD) in Brazil
Positioning	• "Hype" culture, fashion, creativity, personality and design	
Product	• Design (functionality and look)	• Power supply • Specificities of Telecom companies • E.g., iPhone 6 Supports 16–20 long-term evolution bandwidths (LTE bands), enabling fast downloads in other regions
Store	• High visibility and traffic	• Facilities fit with culture and architectural environment
Website	• Design, look and feel	• Translation (and edition when necessary) of text by local editors

Source: Adapted from Apple (2017), Brand Quarterly (2014), and The Telegraph (2016)

Japanese. The staff addressed buyers in English, which is considered particularly rude there. They also behaved in ways that could be expected on Fifth Avenue in New York (e.g., being flashy while dancing and singing all over the store) but not in retail shops in Japan. As a singular sign of brand differentiation for new openings at Abercrombie & Fitch stores, male staff went shirtless, which is considered another misalignment with fashion habits and culture in Japan.

Coca-Cola[3]—The Coca-Cola brand name (a registered trademark in the US since 1944) is standardized to a great extent: it appears in white lettering on a red background in all countries. However, the lettering is adapted to various alphabets and is often given the desired connotation in the target language. In this way, it reads as "delicious" and "happiness" in Mandarin. In terms of advertising, the company has launched a series of global campaigns, highly standardized, such as "Always Coca-Cola" and "Coca-Cola enjoy." The company also launched adapted campaigns, with local stars acting in settings that consumers can recognize and identify with. For instance, the "Thanda matlab Coca-Cola" (2003) was launched with local film actor and producer Aamir Khan, for the Indian market (videos representative of

Standardization and Adaptation 89

the adaptation efforts are available on YouTube with search words: "Coke ad—Thanda matlab Coca Cola.flv").

Disney[4]—From the start, the Tokyo park (1983) presented a high degree of standardization, resembling a typical park in the US. Only signage and food were adapted. Its immediate success has been attributed to the strong interest for American culture in the Japanese population. In Paris (1992), however, the company was criticized by opponents in regards to cultural imperialism and their unhealthy American style of consumerism. Efforts in localization were then higher. They included serving wine in restaurants and widening choices for food (e.g., English, German, and Italian customers had complained that only French sausages were available). In addition, prices were lowered for some menu items, as well as for admission and lodging. Learning from past mistakes, the company undertook even more significant efforts in localization for the Hong Kong (HK) Disneyland (2005). First, it consulted with a local *feng shui* master for the construction, and manifested interest in local beliefs by putting forward the number eight, which is considered auspicious in Chinese culture (e.g., one of the ballrooms in a hotel was designed to be exactly 888 square meters) or by removing green hats, which would symbolize infidelity of one's spouse. Moreover, foods were not only adapted to Chinese tastes but also to Japanese and Indian ones, all the while serving classic American items. The staff was trilingual, to attend to HK visitors in Cantonese, mainland China visitors in Mandarin, and foreign tourists in English. After still facing severe criticism in its first years of operations—for reasons ranging from being overcrowded to environmental damage to poor workers' conditions—HK Disneyland kept reinforcing the adaptation of its product offering. For instance, it celebrated the Chinese New Year in 2008 with many special features (e.g., costumes for Mickey and Minnie characters were redesigned in red; gods of wealth, health, and longevity greeted visitors with traditional chocolate gold coins).

IKEA[5]—IKEA has been generally perceived to take a very standardized approach throughout its international markets. The company's product offer of around ten thousand items tends to be standardized, as is their promotion via the annual catalogue. Its stores tend to be concentrated on the outskirts of cities, often requiring access by cars. The selling and service environment is also more or less similar, and features layouts particular to the company, such as room settings to exhibit the furniture, food courts with Swedish cuisine, and a child care center. IKEA also emphasizes a 'Do-It-Yourself' (DIY) culture among its customers, requiring them to take an active role in the company's low-price positioning.

However, even with these standardized elements, there are adaptations. For instance, IKEA's logo is an example of highly standardized brand name. The company has chosen to present the original color scheme and appearance and if the meaning stays literal, the lettering is often adapted, as illustrated in Figure 3.6.

The largely standardized product offering was tweaked to adapt to local conditions. In China, IKEA introduced items such as woks and chopsticks. Specialized items were also added for local festivals, such as the Chinese New Year and Ramadan in Saudi Arabia. Similarly, store layouts reflect

Figure 3.6 Illustrating adaptation of Ikea's brand name in Russian, Thai, Arabic, and Mandarin

Source: Used with the permission of Inter IKEA Systems B.V.

local cultural and religious considerations. Chinese stores are comparatively more centrally located, reflecting the fact that Chinese consumers have lower access to cars. The room-settings in Chinese stores are often smaller and feature furnishings for balconies. Meanwhile in Saudi Arabia, stores include segregated dining areas and prayer rooms run by chiefly male employees. The recipe for its famous Swedish meatballs was adapted to conform to Islamic halal regulations. Even core values such as the low-price, DIY model had to be relaxed for markets such as China, where IKEA was perceived as an aspirational model and where, culturally, customers expected assistance in the delivery and assembly of furniture. While IKEA's catalogue was published in twenty-nine different languages, it was further adapted in certain markets. In China, it was supplemented by more-frequently published brochures.

Certain concessions were also made to cater to local tastes in European and North American markets, although cultural and economic distances with Sweden were lower. For example, in the UK there is greater reliance on the Internet as a market communication tool, and advertising caters to British humor. Similarly, in the US, the sizes of kitchenware had to be increased in keeping with American serving sizes. When IKEA entered the US (1985), customers had also complained about the hardness of sofas, the lack of fit of beds and kitchen cabinets with American sheets and appliances, and the fact that product dimensions were displayed in centimeters and not in inches. In Russia, smaller living spaces with multiple generations of the same family led the company to introduce a wider range of sofa beds.

Incidentally, not all of these adaptations to local tastes were appreciated at the global scale. For instance, IKEA drew flak in 2012 for digitally erasing women out of its catalogues in Saudi Arabia, in keeping with the country's strict gender segregation. Consumers in Europe, for instance, were shocked by this practice when the company regularly cites women's rights and gender equality as core values. This illustrates yet another facet of the challenges faced by companies in the AdaptStand debate, when adaptation to local preferences can draw criticism and tarnish a company's reputation in other markets.

McDonald's[6]—McDonald's is probably one of the most cited example of a highly standardized marketing. Examples include the distribution practice of privileging restaurants in high traffic areas and offering emblematic products such as the Big Mac. Another highly standardized "P" in the marketing-mix

Standardization and Adaptation   91

is the "Process" through which service is delivered in restaurants (a highly codified process, replicated in similar ways everywhere). For a rough idea, the total training in restaurant for a franchisee (including the management courses) takes approximately nine months to two years to complete.

However, it is easy to find other examples that illustrate how McDonald's adapts to local conditions. In terms of product, a potato burger is offered for the mainly vegetarian Indian market. Also, the company has nicknames that differ widely from country to country. The prices of a Big Mac vary from a low 1.75 USD in India to a high 6.76 USD in Switzerland. Of course, differences in labor costs can explain why burger prices are cheaper in poor versus richer countries. Nevertheless, they are also adapted to the purchasing power of target customers. Table 3.4 captures the AdaptStand balance achieved by the company.

Interestingly, *The Economist* has published a "Big Mac Index" to monitor global exchange rates since 1986! This index offers an easy comparison between the price of a Big Mac and the GDP per capita in many countries. This is a tool that can be remembered when measuring economic distance between countries (see Chapter 7). Humorously referred to as "Burgernomics," the index is not a "precise gauge of currency misalignment, merely a tool to make exchange rate theory more digestible." Here, the Big Mac represents a "basket of goods and services." According to the Parity Purchasing-Power theory, currencies would evolve over the long run toward exchange

Table 3.4 Illustrating AdaptStand decisions for McDonald's

Marketing-mix	Standardization (worldwide)	Adaptation (nationwide)
Product	• Big Mac	• McAloo Tikka potato burger (India); Rye McFeast (Finland)
Promotion	• Brand name	• Slang nicknames: Macca's (Australia), Mäkkäri (Finland), MacDoof (Germany), MakDo (Philippines)
	• Advertisement campaign: "I'm lovin' it"	• Video campaigns on YouTube: "Not without Canadian farmers" (Canada)
Place	• Restaurants in high-traffic public areas	• McDelivery: available in China, India, Japan, and other countries, but not, for instance, in France or Spain
		• *National rail system: Switzerland*
Price	• Entry-level menu items everywhere	• Big Mac price varies (in USD and at PPP, 2016): 2.05 (Russia), 4.78 (Brazil), 6.59 (Switzerland)

Source: Adapted from Keegan and Green (2016, p. 16) and including examples of adapted promotion from: www.YouTube.com/watch?v=Wy9I4Lc53U4, adapted prices from: www.economist.com/content/big-mac-index, and adapted distribution from: https://en.wikipedia.org/wiki/McDelivery

92 Standardization and Adaptation

rates that equalize the price of a Big Mac if they were not over- or under-evaluated. Beyond the usefulness of this tool for benchmarking currencies against their "real" value, the simple fact that *The Economist* has chosen a product like MacDonald's Big Mac for this tool is a sign that it is considered fairly comparable, hence standardized, across countries.

Netflix[7]—Netflix's strategy for entering international markets included offering select titles, after which they adapt the content and services available based on the markets' reaction in the testing period. Netflix has adapted its content services in twenty different languages, which is a step toward bridging cultural gaps, but still short of satisfying audiences' strong preference for local-language and local-content service offerings across the 190 countries. Thus, the company also invests heavily in creating region-specific programming, to the tune of $5 billion USD internationally. Netflix's profitability within a market depends on the price and availability of Internet, for which less than one-third of households in developing countries have access. Underdeveloped infrastructure for Internet and wireless services represent a barrier in certain markets, such as India. Finally, Netflix must abide by strict regulations imposed by the US government, as well as restrictions by governments in each country into which it expands. This forces the company to adapt (or exclude) offerings to new markets. In Indonesia, Vietnam, and Malaysia, for example, censorship agencies deemed much of Netflix's content unfit for local audiences.

Starbucks[8]—Under the leadership of Howard Schultz, the company was focused on differentiating itself as a specialized experience and "affordable luxury," not as an everyday commodity. With more than 22,500 stores in sixty-seven countries (2015), Starbucks has standardized many aspects of its value proposition. In terms of positioning, the brand stood not just for quality coffee, but also for a welcoming community experience, knowledgeable baristas, and an eco-conscious outlook. It focused on transferring the same brand power to other markets. Its location strategy consisted of opening several point of sales in one particular city area. Promotion was based on word-of-mouth over mass media campaigns, whether in the US or in Japan. Nevertheless, local realities have also led the company to adapt, sometimes with less success than others. For instance, the company entered Israel in 2001 and left in 2003. Upon entry, Starbucks had changed its location strategy and decided to open stores in five distant areas. They also targeted the business community while entering supermarkets at the same time, which resulted in confusion in regards to the company's positioning. Some product offerings were lacking adaptation, such as seasonal pumpkin-spice lattes (where the fall season goes unnoticed and is not a cause of traditional celebration such as in North America). Learning that consumer consumption preferences might not always evolve fast enough to suit a particular corporate offer, the company has acquired Teavana (US) and started to deploy the brand in India, a predominantly tea drinking country (2016).

Volkswagen[9]—The company has balanced standardization and adaptation carefully in its international marketing strategy. For instance, it has emphasized its core values as an "innovative, valuable and responsible" company in India, while at the same time adapting its product design and promotions

Standardization and Adaptation 93

to local conditions. Volkswagen took into consideration cultural differences, providing additional space on the cars' dashboards for idols of Hindu gods, or incorporating more chrome into the cars as per Indian tastes. Similarly, the product design reflected adaptation to geographical conditions, such as the elimination of heavy car roofs (originally meant to withstand snowfall) and more-powerful cooling to better suit the hot climate in most of India. While it has continually used its traditional strategy of snappy, clear-cut, and detail-oriented ads, it has tailored them to pop culture in each market—such as its Star Wars campaign for the Passat in the US, or using Bollywood stars to promote its product offering in India. Positioning was also adapted. Far from being the "people's car" as it was in Europe, it was positioned as an aspirational brand, chiefly targeted at wealthy, urban Indians.

Conclusion: The Extent to Which Companies Should Standardize or Adapt Their Marketing Activities Depends on a Variety of Country-, Industry-, Product-, and Firm-Level Factors. It Must Be Carefully Analyzed on a Case-By-Case Basis, Using an AdaptStand Approach

Thus, what is the answer to the question raised in this chapter: "To what extent should companies standardize or adapt their marketing in foreign markets?" or put differently: "How far is too far?" An answer to this question necessarily starts with: "It depends," and should include careful considerations about the company, the product, the industry, and the differences between the home and host countries' business environments.

The extent to which firms push for standardization can determine the scale and scope of their expansion abroad. "Too far" is the place where unsatisfying results make the expansion abroad unsustainable, forcing companies to retract. It is a difficult place to locate *ex ante*. Marketing managers know *a posteriori* that they have gone too far in standardizing marketing activities when market shares or sales objectives are unmatched (for instance, due to a lack of appeal to foreign customers in terms of products, pricing, or promotion or due to ineffective distribution). On the other hand, too much adaptation translates into costs that can also endanger a company's long-term presence abroad in the face of local competition.

The "contingency perspective" recommends a mixture of standardization and adaptation (the AdaptStand approach) and makes it clear that some aspects of strategic marketing can be standardized (e.g., market selection with a fixed set of criteria that target countries need to match to be considered for entry), while others are to be adapted (e.g., entry modes). The same applies to tactical marketing, with some elements in the mix standardized (e.g., products and distribution) while others are adapted to local specificities (e.g., promotion and price). Striking the right balance and working with an AdaptStand approach is really a key competence that international marketers must develop to be successful in international markets.

Is the AdaptStand approach different from "glocalization"? Vrontis et al. (2009) elaborate on the AdaptStand approach, initially proposed in Vrontis (2003). In their view, the AdaptStand approach applies to the tactical level of

94 Standardization and Adaptation

marketing only, while *glocalization* concerns both the strategic and tactical levels of marketing. They explain that companies adopting the AdaptStand approach will standardize tactics (i.e., the marketing-mix) where possible and adapt them only where necessary. In turn, companies putting glocalization in practice will be thinking globally and adapt their marketing-mix locally.

In this book, this nuance is simplified. The AdaptStand approach refers to the difficult exercise that marketing managers undertake in finding the right combination of local adaptation and global standardization for both strategic marketing activities (market selection, entry modes, targeting and positioning) and tactical marketing activities (the 4/7Ps). Beyond the lemma "think global, act local," the term *glocalization* encapsulates the combination of global (i.e., standardized) and local (i.e., adapted) activities. In Section 3.3.2., we illustrated that most companies tend to do exactly that: adapt certain activities while standardizing others. This suggests that the "contingency perspective" is indeed more widely applied than either one of the extremes on the standardization/ adaptation continuum.

Now that we have discussed "what globalization means for marketers" (Chapter 1) and introduced two of the main topics needed to understand marketing in a globalizing context ("why, where, and how firms internationalize" in Chapter 2, and "the extent to which firms should standardize or adapt marketing" in Chapter 3), it is time to start studying in more detail what makes it so difficult to market in foreign countries ("distance analysis" in Chapters 4–7). In the next chapter, we begin with the most tangible and intangible types of distances: geographic distance and psychic distance.

Notes

1 In Section 3.3.1, the paragraph entitled "In general, should firms centralize decision-making or should they delegate decisions to subsidiaries located in foreign markets?" has been written in collaboration with David Pastoriza, Associate Professor in International Business (HEC Montréal, Canada), whose research interests include internationalization and the multinational corporation.
2 The example of Abercrombie & Fitch is based on: The Business of Fashion (2010).
3 The example of Coca-Cola is based on: IMB 387 (2012); Keegan and Green (2008).
4 Disney example relies on: HKU 885 (2010).
5 IKEA example is based on: Burt, Johansson, and Thelander (2011); HBS 9–116–015 (2016); HBS 9–504–094 (2004); Johansson and Thelander (2009).
6 The example of McDonald's relies on: Keegan and Green (2016); McDonald's (2017); The Economist (2017).
7 The example of Netflix is based on: Ivey W16236 (2016).
8 Starbucks examples relies on: Haaretz (2015); HBS 9–801–361 (2005); Justfood.com (2002); Starbucks (2017); Trefis (2016).
9 Volkswagen case is based on: IMB 443 (2013).

References

American Marketing Association (2013). Definition of Marketing. Retrieved October 2014, from www.ama.org/AboutAMA/Pages/Definition-of-Marketing.aspx

Apple (2017). Price Comparison of iPhone 7 (Apple Websites in Brazil, China, Hungary, and the US). Retrieved April 2017, from www.apple.com/br/shop/buy-iphone/iphone-7 www.apple.com/cn/shop/buy-iphone/iphone-7 www.apple.com/hu/shop/buy-iphone/iphone-7 www.apple.com/shop/buy-iphone/iphone-7

Bartlett, Christopher & Ghoshal, Sumantra (1991). Global Strategic Management: Impact on the New Frontiers of Strategy Research. *Strategic Management Journal*, *12*(S1), 5–16.

Bartlett, Christopher & Ghoshal, Sumantra (2002). *Managing Across Borders: The Transnational Solution* (2nd ed.). Boston: Harvard Business School Press (p. 391).

Bloomberg Businessweek (2005, February 28th). Japan Isn't Buying The Walmart Idea, *By Ian Rowley*. Retrieved from www.businessweek.com/stories/2005-02-27/japan-isnt-buying-the-Walmart-idea

Brand Quarterly (2014). Globalization: Apple's One-Size-Fits-All Approach. Retrieved June 2016, from www.brandquarterly.com/globalization-apples-one-size-fits-approach

Burt, Steve, Johansson, Ulf & Thelander, Åsa (2011). Standardized Marketing Strategies in Retailing? IKEA's Marketing Strategies in Sweden, the UK and China. *Journal of Retailing and Consumer Services*, *18*(3), 183–193.

The Business of Fashion (2010). In Tokyo, Abercrombie Misses Its Mark. Retrieved September 2016, from www.businessoffashion.com/articles/intelligence/in-tokyo-abercrombie-misses-its-mark

Buzell, Robert (1968). Can You Standardize Multinational Marketing? *Harvard Business Review*, *46*(6), 102–113.

Cateora, Philip, Gilly, Mary & Graham, John (2015). *International Marketing* (17th ed.). New York (US): McGraw-Hill/Irwin (p. 704).

Cavusgil, Tamer, Zou, Shaoming & Naidu, G. M. (1993). Product and Promotion Adaptation in Export Ventures: An Empirical Investigation. *Journal of International Business Studies*, *24*(3), 479–506.

Chartered Institute of Marketing (2014). Glossary. Retrieved October 2014, from www.cim.co.uk/Resources/JargonBuster.aspx

Chung, Henry (2007). International Marketing Standardisation Strategies Analysis. *Asia Pacific Journal of Marketing and Logistics*, *19*(2), 145–167.

Douglas, Susan & Wind, Yoram (1987). The Myth of Globalization. *Columbia Journal of World Business*, *22*(Winter), 19–29.

The Economist (2017). The Big Mac Index. Retrieved May 2018, from www.economist.com/content/big-mac-index

Ghoshal, Sumantra & Nohria, Nitin (1993). Horses for Courses: Organizational Forms for Multinational Corporations. *Sloan Management Review*, *34*(2), 23–35.

Haaretz (2015, October 11th). Why You Won't Find Starbucks in Israel, *By Ben Sales*. Retrieved from www.haaretz.com/israel-news/business/1.679724

HBS 9–116–015 (2016). *IKEA in Saudi Arabia (A)*. Case written by: Karthik Ramanna, Jerome Lenhardt, and Marc Homsy. Boston: Harvard Business School (p. 23).

HBS 9–504–094 (2004). *IKEA Invades America*. Case written by: Youngme Moon. Boston: Harvard Business School (p. 13).

HBS 9–801–361 (2005). *Howard Schultz and the Starbuck Coffee Company*. Case written by: Nancy Koehn. Boston: Harvard Business School (p. 40).

Heenan, David & Perlmutter, Howard (1979). *Multinational Organization Development*. Reading (US): Addison-Wesley (p. 194).

96 Standardization and Adaptation

HKU 885 (2010). *Disney: Losing Magic in the Middle Kingdom*. Case written by: Ali Farhoomand. Hong Kong: Asia Case Research Centre (p. 31).

IMB 387 (2012). *Coke and Pepsi: From Global to Indian Advertising*. Case written by: Seema Gupta. Bangalore: Indian Institute of Management (p. 18).

IMB 443 (2013). *Volkswagen in India*. Case written by: Seema Gupta. Bangalore: Indian Institute of Management (p. 33).

International Business Guide (2013). 10 Successful American Businesses That Have Failed Overseas. Retrieved October 2014, from www.internationalbusinessguide.org/10-successful-american-businesses-that-have-failed-overseas/

Ivey W16236 (2016). *Netflix: International Expansion*. Case written by: Won-Yong Oh and Duane Myer. London, Ontario: Ivey Publishing 9B16M070 (p. 11).

Johansson, Ulf & Thelander, Åsa (2009). A Standardised Approach to the World? IKEA in China. *International Journal of Quality and Service Sciences*, 1(2), 199–219.

Just-food.com (2002). Starbucks in Israel: What Went Wrong? Retrieved September 2016, from www.just-food.com/analysis/what-went-wrong_id93573.aspx

Keegan, Warren & Green, Mark (2008). *Global Marketing* (5th ed.). New Jersey: Pearson Prentice Hall (p. 643).

Keegan, Warren & Green, Mark (2016). *Global Marketing* (9th ed.). New Jersey: Pearson (p. 624).

Kotler, Philip (1980). The Marketing of Social Clauses: The First Ten Years. *Journal of Marketing*, 44(4), 24–33.

Kotler, Philip (1989). From Mass Marketing to Mass Customization. *Strategy and Leadership*, 17(5), 10–47.

Levitt, Theodore (1983). The Globalization of Markets. *Harvard Business Review*, 61(3), 92–102.

McDonald's (2017). Purchasing Your Franchise. Retrieved April 2017, from www.mcdonalds.ca/ca/en/our_story/corporate_info/franchising/purchasing_your_franchise.html

Perlmutter, Howard (1969). The Tortuous Evolution of the Multinational Corporation. *Columbia Journal of World Business*, 4(1), 9–18.

Porter, Michael (1985). *Competitive Advantage: Creating and Sustaining Superior Performance*. New York: The Free Press (p. 557).

Quelch, John & Hoff, Edward (1986). Customizing Global Marketing. *Harvard Business Review*, 64(3), 59–68.

Starbucks (2017). Starbucks Company Profile. Retrieved April 2017, from www.starbucks.com/about-us/company-information/starbucks-company-profile

Tan, Qun & Sousa, Carlos (2013). International Marketing Standardization. *Management International Review*, 53(5), 711–739.

The Telegraph (2016, September 10th). How Much Does the iPhone 7 Cost Around the World? *By Cristina Criddle*. Retrieved from www.telegraph.co.uk/technology/2016/09/10/how-much-does-the-iphone-7-cost-around-the-world/

Theodosiou, Marios & Katsikeas, Constantine (2001). Factors Influencing the Degree of International Pricing Strategy Standardization of Multinational Corporations. *Journal of International Marketing*, 9(3), 1–18.

Trefis (2016). Starbucks Focuses on Expansion in Asian Markets. Retrieved April 2017, from www.trefis.com/stock/sbux/model/trefis?easyAccessToken=PROVIDER_ee302f87ca2ab31d744b2d33f816fe974868bd1f&from=widget: slideshow

Vrontis, Demetris (2003). Integrating Adaptation and Standardisation in International Marketing: The AdaptStand Modelling Process. *Journal of Marketing Management*, *19*(3–4), 283–305.

Vrontis, Demetris, Thrassou, Alkis & Lamprianou, Iasonas (2009). International Marketing Adaptation versus Standardisation of Multinational Companies. *International Marketing Review*, *26*(4/5), 477–500.

Wind, Yoram, Douglas, Susan & Perlmutter, Howard (1973). Guidelines for Developing International Marketing Strategies. *Journal of Marketing*, *37*(2), 14.

4 Geographic and Psychic Distances

Table of Contents

4 Geographic Distance and Psychic Distance

Introduction: Why Do They Matter? Are They Decreasing?.............99
4.1 *Definitions and Measurement*...*100*
    4.1.1 Geographic or Physical Distance *100*
    4.1.2 Psychic Distance *102*
4.2 *Drivers of Psychic Distance*...*106*
    4.2.1 Country-Level Factors (Ghemawat).................*107*
    4.2.2 Firm- and Individual-Level Factors.................*107*
4.3 *Central Role of Costs and Knowledge*..........................*108*
    4.3.1 International Trade Patterns: A Detour
          by Economics.. *108*
    4.3.2 Costs: A Distance Perspective *113*
    4.3.3 Knowledge: A Proximity Perspective *121*
4.4 *Issues at Stake* *124*
    4.4.1 On the Persistence of Distance Effects.............*124*
    4.4.2 Paradoxes of Distance and Proximity.............*126*
    4.4.3 Impact on Marketing decisions *128*

Conclusion: Geographic and psychic distances matter because they generate costs and inhibit knowledge. They should be decreasing, yet. . .
References

Recommended Readings

- Boschma, Ron (2005). Proximity and Innovation: A Critical Assessment. *Regional Studies*, 39(1), 61–74.

- Dunning, John (2009). Location and the Multinational Enterprise: A Neglected Factor? *Journal of International Business Studies*, 40(1), 5–19. [**Also recommended** in Chapter 2]
- Ghemawat, Pankaj (2001). Distance Still Matters: The Hard Reality of Global Expansion. *Harvard Business Review*, 79(8), 137–147.
- Johanson, Jan & Vahlne, Jan-Erik (1977). The Internationalization Process of the Firm-A Model of Knowledge Development and Increasing Foreign Market Commitments. *Journal of International Business Studies*, 8(1), 23–32. [**Also recommended in** Chapter 2]
- Johanson, Jan & Vahlne, Jan-Erik (2009). The Uppsala Internationalization Process Model Revisited: From Liability of Foreignness to Liability of Outsidership. *Journal of International Business Studies*, 40(9), 1411–1431. [**Also recommended in** Chapter 2]
- O'Grady, Shawna & Lane, Henry (1996). The Psychic Distance Paradox. *Journal of International Business Studies*, 27(2), 309–333.
- Porter, Michael (1998). Clusters and the New Economics of Competition. *Harvard Business Review*, 76(6), 77–90.

Introduction: Why Do They Matter? Are They Decreasing?

Asking the question: "**Why do geographic and psychic distances matter in marketing activities?**" is about further detailing the question regarding the

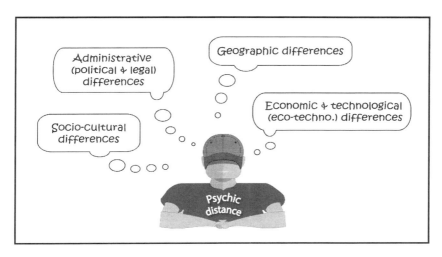

Figure 4.1 Illustrating Chapter 4

Source: Own elaboration

100 *Geographic and Psychic Distances*

"death" of distance broached in Chapter 1. We have started to see that it "still matters," and Ghemawat (2001) makes a strong case for it.

To push further the debate about "when" distance matters, we examine its impact on marketing activities (Chapters 4–7). Thus, this chapter and the three following ones each focuses on specific dimensions of distance (i.e., psychic, geographic, cultural, administrative, economic and technological distances). They all ask the same questions: "Why do these specific dimensions matter?" and "Are they increasing or decreasing?" The objective with this approach is to have a balanced view of the changes occurring for marketers, as a consequence of globalization, when contrasting home and foreign markets (at the country level of analysis). In terms of distance, this is about highlighting the ambivalence of these changes (some distances are increasing while, at the same time, others decrease).

Figure 4.2 situates the present chapter in the overall book structure. It also shows that distance analysis constitutes an element in the first building block or step in crafting an international marketing plan ("Analyzing the situation").

The objectives of this chapter are to define, measure, and evaluate the outcomes of geographic and psychic distances for international marketing. To answer the introductory question and ultimately reflect on whether geographic and psychic distances between firms and their markets decrease in a globalizing world, we start by examining definitions and measurements of both types of distance. After covering important drivers of psychic distance, we turn toward geographic distance. In order to understand the evolution of thoughts about the role of geographic location, we connect the dots with economics and some of the prominent theories of international trade. Next, we inquire into the fields of industrial economy and economic geography (alternatively taking a distance perspective and a proximity perspective) to study the central role of costs and knowledge in explaining why location matters (and thereby psychic and geographic distances). Finally, we broach such important issues as the puzzling persistence of the distance effect, and the existence of a paradox of both distance and proximity. We conclude with an overview of the impact of both types of distance on marketing decisions.

4.1 Definitions and Measurement

In this section, we address the following questions:

- What is geographic distance, and how can we measure it?
- What is psychic distance? How can we measure it and how does it differ from the CAGE distance?

4.1.1 Geographic or Physical Distance

What is geographic distance, and how can we measure it? A basic definition of geographic distance between home and target country refers to their degree of physical separation. In the same vein, Boschma (2005, p. 63) defines

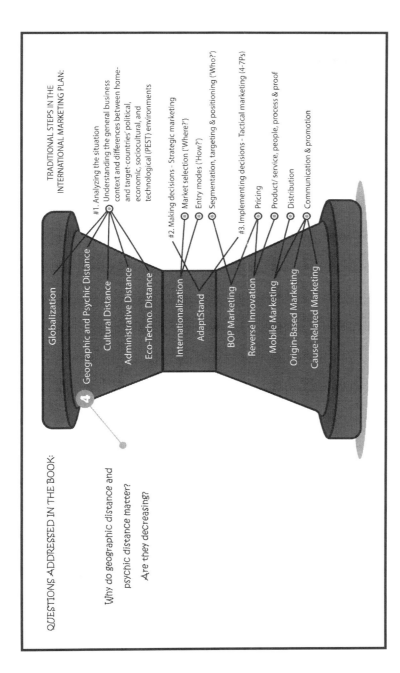

Figure 4.2 Positioning Chapter 4 in the overall book structure

Source: Own elaboration

102 *Geographic and Psychic Distances*

geographic proximity as "spatial distance between actors." Thus, one of the first ways to measure geographic distance is to evaluate the physical remoteness in terms of how many kilometers separate Country A from Country B.

However, Ghemawat (2001) argues that other factors, such as climate, topography (e.g., access to water, presence of mountains), and different factors related to the technological environment (e.g., transportation and telecommunication infrastructure), are all important in evaluating differences in terms of geographic distance. It can, therefore, stem from physical remoteness, a lack of a common border, a lack of sea or river access, the sheer size of a country (e.g., compared to Belgium, major cities in Russia are likely to be further away from major cities in neighboring countries), weak transportation or communication links, as well as from differences in climates and seasonality (e.g., the fact that Southern and Northern hemispheres have opposite seasons can require important adjustments for companies with a presence in both Europe and South Africa).

4.1.2 Psychic Distance

What is psychic distance? Before answering this question in more details, we can start reflecting on seminal articles on the topic (see "Food for Thought").

Food for Thought 4.1

- In reference to Johanson and Vahlne (1977, 2009) and Ghemawat (2001), what is psychic distance and how does it differ from the CAGE distance?

According to Johanson and Vahlne's (1977) seminal article, which was followed up by much subsequent work from researchers at the Uppsala University, for example Nordstrom and Valhne (1994), psychic distance emerges from factors that interfere with the way firms (i.e., managers) learn about and understand foreign environments. Their initial proposition was: "Psychic distance is defined as the sum of factors preventing the flow of information from and to the market. Examples are differences in language, education, business practices, culture, and industrial development" (Johanson & Vahlne, 1977, p. 24). This definition needed refinement, as it captured what creates psychic distance but not necessarily what psychic distance is.

Some researchers have since defined psychic distance as the extent to which managers were familiar with differences between their home country and foreign countries, or to the extent that they find these differences problematic (e.g., Bello, Chelariu, & Zhang, 2003; Leonidou, Barnes, & Talias, 2006). Others have focused on managers' perceptions of dissimilarity/differences between their home country and foreign countries (e.g., Durand, Turkina, & Robson, 2016; Griffith & Dimitrova, 2014). The latter approach

Geographic and Psychic Distances 103

brings more clarity to the concept and led Katsikeas, Skarmeas, and Bello (2009, p. 154) to conceptualize psychic distance as the "degree of dissimilarity in the parties' operating environments."

Simply put, we define psychic distance as the dissimilarity between countries' PEST environments. The debate about whether this dissimilarity is actual or perceived is broached next. The notion of degree is important here. High psychic distance means a high degree of dissimilarity (and conversely). To illustrate the concept, Figure 4.3 uses a scale and situates the foreign country's environment in relation to the home country's environment, with varying degrees of divergence on the scale.

How to measure psychic distance? Because of various conceptualizations, the literature is conflicted about measuring psychic distance. Aligned with seeing psychic distance as dissimilarity between countries' environments, an "objective" approach and a "subjective" approach coexist. They both rely on capturing distance through different dimensions of countries' PEST/CAGE environments, but use different data collection techniques.

First, the objective approach looks into secondary data. Articles by Dow and Karunaratna (2006) and Brewer (2007a) illustrate the efforts made in

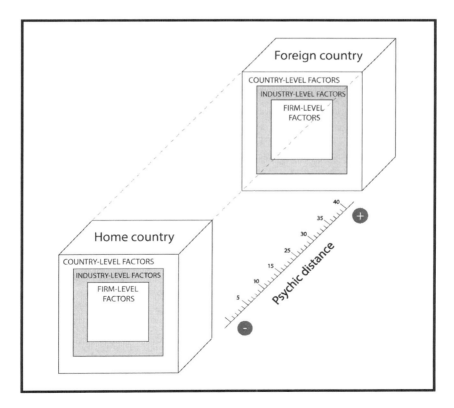

Figure 4.3 Representing psychic distance
Source: Own elaboration

104   *Geographic and Psychic Distances*

building indices that capture psychic distance as objectively as possible. Table 4.1 presents how Brewer (2007a) measured Australia's commercial, political, historic, economic, social, and information ties with twenty-five other countries, using inventive ways of quantifying data that is not as easily counted as, for instance, the number of trade agreements between countries. For instance, taking colonial relationships as an indicator of political ties (or administrative distance), the researcher rated countries with no past colonial relationship with Australia as 0, countries belonging to the same (British) empire as .5, and the country with a direct colonial relationship with Australia as 1. This is one common method that researchers use to build indices with indicators that are difficult to quantify. As a result, the UK ranks first in terms of closeness (i.e., low psychic distance) to Australia, followed by New Zealand and the US (see Table 4.2). The disconnection between geographic and psychic distances is obvious here, since countries like Papua New Guinea

Table 4.1 Measuring psychic distance with an objective approach (focal country: Australia)

Indicators	Measurement
Administrative Dimension	
• Trade agreements	The number of formal bilateral or regional free-trade treaties in operation between Australia and each country in 2002–2003 (normalized).
• Value of aid programs	The dollar value of official Australian aid programs to each country in 2004–2005 (normalized).
• Trade representations offices	The number of Austrade offices in each country in 2003 plus the number of trade offices from each country in Australia (normalized).
• Colonial relationship	Direct colonial relationship = 1, membership of the same empire = .5, and no colonial relationship = 0. Values are added for each country and normalized.
• Shared wars	World War I: ally = 2, neutral = 1, and enemy = 0; World War II: ally = 2, neutral = 1, and enemy = 0. Values for each war are added for each country and normalized.
• Level of corruption	Transparency International corruption index (normalized)
Economic Dimension	
• Two-way trade	The proportion of total Australian exports going to each country in 2002–2003 (expressed as a decimal fraction) plus the proportion of total Australian imports sourced from each country (expressed as a decimal), normalized.
• Stock of foreign investment	The total Australian outward FDI stock invested in each country in 2001–2002 (expressed as a decimal fraction of the total outward FDI stock) plus the proportion of total inward FDI stock into Australia in 2001–2002 from each country (expressed as a decimal), normalized.

Indicators	Measurement
• Level of development	The United Nations human development index (normalized).
Geographic Dimension	
• Geographic proximity	The direct distance between the closest two major port cities in Home and Away in kilometers (normalized).
Socio-Cultural Dimension	
• Cultural similarities	The cultural distance index that Fletcher and Bohn (1998) developed (normalized).
• Sport preferences	A country that regularly plays against Australia in cricket, rugby union, rugby league, and tennis is allocated 1 for each sport. These values are added and normalized.
• Language similarities	English is widely spoken = 0, English is widely spoken in business = .25, other languages that use the Roman alphabet are spoken = .5, and other languages that use other alphabets are spoken = 1.
• Information availability	Value equals the number of catalog entries for each country in the University of Queensland library (normalized).
• Immigration	The number of Australians living in each country, plus the number of Australians visiting each country in 2001, plus the number of residents of Australia originating from each country, plus the number of visitors to Australia from each country in 2001 (normalized).

Source: Adapted from Brewer (2007a)

Table 4.2 Ranking selected countries in terms of psychic distance (focal country: Australia)

Rank	Countries	PD Index
1	United Kingdom	10.65904
2	New Zealand	10.00606
3	US	9.90284
4	Singapore	7.23377
5	Hong Kong	7.13230
6	Japan	7.09080
7	Canada	6.81389
8	Papua New Guinea	6.59794
9	Fiji	5.73842
10	Malaysia	5.64549
. . .		
20	Taiwan	4.26083
21	United Arab Emirates	4.25294
22	Kuwait	3.95784
23	Kenya	3.79584
24	Thailand	3.76592
25	South Korea	3.75037

Source: Adapted from Brewer (2007a)

106   *Geographic and Psychic Distances*

and Fiji, which are much closer geographically to Australia, only rank in eighth and ninth positions.

Second, the subjective approach uses primary data in order to collect managers' perceptions (e.g., Evans, Mavondo, & Bridson, 2008; Sousa & Lages, 2011; Sousa & Bradley, 2006). In this approach, psychic distance has also been referred to as "psychological" distance. Regardless of actual differences between countries, managers have their own perceptions of existing differences between their home country and their target markets. The following quote by Evans and Mavondo (2002, p. 516) illustrates this approach: "It is not the simple presence of external environmental factors, which determines the degree of psychic distance. Rather, it is the mind's processing, in terms of perception, of cultural and business differences that forms the basis of psychic distance."

Table 4.3 presents the items included in a questionnaire sent by Sousa and Lages (2011) to managers in charge of international business operations and activities in a little more than three hundred Portuguese companies. For each item, respondents had to rate the extent to which they perceived their home country to be different from the foreign country (their largest market abroad). Originally, these items fell in two dimensions (country- and people-related) to capture psychic distance. These items were reordered here according to the PEST/CAGE dimensions. In this view, any factor that interferes with managers' knowledge about foreign countries increases psychic distance.

4.2 Drivers of Psychic Distance

In this section, we look into the following question:

* What are the factors at the country-, firm- and individual-level of analysis driving psychic distance?

Table 4.3 Measuring psychic distance based on a subjective approach

	Measure: 5-point scale from 1 (very similar) to 5 (very different)
Administrative Dimension	
• Legal regulations	1–5 scale
• Technical requirements	1–5 scale
Economic Dimension	
• Communications infrastructure	1–5 scale
• Marketing infrastructure	1–5 scale
• Market competitiveness	1–5 scale
• Level of economic and industrial development	1–5 scale
• Per-capita income	1–5 scale
• Purchasing power of customers	1–5 scale
Socio-Cultural Dimension	
• Consumer preferences	1–5 scale
• Level of literacy and education	1–5 scale
• Lifestyles	1–5 scale

Source: Adapted from Sousa and Lages (2011)

Geographic and Psychic Distances 107

4.2.1 Country-Level Factors (Ghemawat)

At the country-level of analysis, which are the factors that determine levels of psychic distance? Previously, we discussed the CAGE distance framework proposed by Ghemawat (2001). Within this framework, distances are to be understood as differences between countries in terms of their cultural, administrative, geographic, and economic (CAGE) environments. It is interesting to wonder if the CAGE distance drives psychic distance. The answer depends on the stand we take in terms of an objective or subjective approach to the latter (see Section 4.1.2).

In an objective approach, the CAGE framework can simply be seen as a way to structure the various dimensions forming psychic distance. As a reminder, the CAGE offers an acronym to help structure a comparative analysis between domestic and foreign environments in terms of distances. Each one of the CAGE dimensions relate closely to those present in the PEST framework, also used to analyze foreign environments. Indeed, the politico-legal and administrative dimension, and the technological and geographic dimension can easily be regrouped together for dealing with connected issues. In this objective perspective, CAGE distance and psychic distance are one and the same.

However, in a subjective approach, the CAGE framework organizes the factors (at a country-level of analysis) that ultimately create psychic distance (at an individual-level of analysis). It is because managers perceive important differences in terms of culture, regulations, or economic development between their home country and a foreign country that they will develop high levels of psychic distance in regard to that country. On the contrary, it is because managers believe that the foreign country is rather similar to their home country that they will display low levels of psychic distance. In this case, the CAGE distances can be considered as drivers (i.e., determinants) of psychic distance.

One interesting point to note is the fact that, more and more, the home country of firms and the home country of their managers are not the same. This leads us to consider factors at the firm- and individual-level of analysis.

4.2.2 Firm- and Individual-Level Factors

Besides factors at the country-level of analysis, which other factors are known to drive psychic distance? Since psychic distance is a perception-based concept, factors related to individuals must be acknowledged.

First, managers' personal characteristics and familiarity with foreign countries have received some support in the literature as drivers of psychic distance. For instance, Dichtl, Koeglmayr, and Mueller (1990) study firms' "international orientation" as an antecedent to export success and look into the linkages between psychic distance and both objective characteristics of managers (e.g., age, level of education, command of foreign languages, vacations and longer stays abroad) and subjective characteristics (e.g., attitude toward risk, rigidity, and willingness to change). In this vein, cross-cultural training, trips abroad, and language courses are commonly cited methods

108 *Geographic and Psychic Distances*

that can be used to reduce psychic distance (e.g., Leonidou et al., 2006; Leonidou, Palihawadana, Chari, & Leonidou, 2011).

Next, the international experience of firms has also been studied for its impact on psychic distance, yet with mixed empirical evidence. While most employees' experience culminates at forty-five to fifty years, at best, some companies enjoy an international experience that is spanning a century or more. Investigating the antecedents and outcomes of psychic distance, Evans et al. (2008) assume that the amount of experience acquired by an organization when operating in foreign markets would affect that organization's perception of the similarities and differences between markets. They measure international experience in terms of the number of years operating in foreign markets and the number of foreign markets in which the organization had operations. Limited international experience would lead companies to overestimate the similarities between their home market and a foreign market. In contrast, internationally experienced organizations would develop a better sense of the unique subtleties in each foreign market. Surprisingly, the result of their study fails to confirm a link between firms' international experience and psychic distance, as perceived by managers.

This suggests that more research is needed to fully understand the drivers of psychic distance at the individual- and firm-level of analysis. In particular, psychological factors, such as managers' motivation to succeed in foreign markets and beliefs about foreign countries (e.g., country image), represent interesting avenues for future research in determining the antecedents to psychic distance (Durand et al., 2016). All in all, the concept of knowledge still appears to be central (i.e., how much managers or firms "know" about foreign markets as a determinant of psychic distance).

4.3 *Central Role of Costs and Knowledge*

In this section, we address the following questions:

- Why interest ourselves with international trade theories in marketing?
- Why would geographical location be important for marketing in an international context?

4.3.1 *International Trade Patterns: A Detour by Economics*

What are the issues that economics and international trade theories explain and help resolve? Traditionally, we divide these theories in two levels of analysis: those that were first formed at the country level of analysis, and those that were developed afterward, at the firm level of analysis. At the country level, the theories answer important questions like: "Which goods and services should be imported and/or exported?" and, "In which quantity and with which countries to trade?" At the firm level, they respond to questions such as: "Why do multinationals exist?" and, "Which firms will succeed on the global scene?" Although governments are more directly interested in these questions compared to individual marketers, having a basic understanding of international trade theories gives a broader view on mechanisms

Geographic and Psychic Distances 109

at play in marketing in an international context. A Wikipedia entry about "internationalization" (Wikipedia, 2017) provides a good departure point.

Figure 4.4 provides simple symbols to help you remember three of the main country-based theories: mercantilism, absolute, and comparative advantages. A brief account of each one follows.

Figure 4.4 Memorizing important country-based theories with symbols
Source: Own elaboration

110   *Geographic and Psychic Distances*

What is the rationale behind mercantilism? In Figure 4.4, the treasure box symbolizes *mercantilism*. This perspective on ways to organize economic activities was prominent in Western Europe in the sixteenth to eighteenth centuries. It stipulated that the wealth of a nation depends on the accumulation of hard currencies, such as gold and silver. In order to accumulate wealth, a country had to export as much as possible, and import as little as possible (in order to avoid paying for foreign goods and deplete reserves of currencies). This dominant approach started to decline with the rise of a different economic rationale to ensure the creation and appropriation of wealth by countries, "the Absolute Advantage Theory," which is symbolized here by a winner standing on a podium.

What is the absolute advantage theory? Scottish economist and moral philosopher Adam Smith is famous for his views largely presented in the seminal book entitled *An Inquiry into the Nature and Causes of the Wealth of Nations* (shortened title *The Wealth of Nations*) (Smith, 1776). In a nutshell, *the absolute advantage theory* says that countries should identify what they are best at producing, and focus on manufacturing as much as possible of this product to dominate the market and export these goods. However, several issues with this theory were subsequently discussed. One dead-end was: **Can a country with no absolute advantage whatsoever still engage in trade with others?** Many such countries in the world are poorly endowed (e.g., being small, without sea access, with few resources) and yet they still engage in international trading. David Ricardo, an Englishman born only a few years before Smith wrote the *Wealth of Nations*, later proposed a nuance to the absolute advantage theory known as the "Comparative Advantage" theory.

What is the comparative advantage theory about? Even without an absolute advantage, a country can have a *comparative advantage* (Ricardo, 1817). The illustration consists of two survivors on a deserted island. Here, the river separating them symbolizes the border between two countries. The younger man is likely to be fast and agile, compared to the older man. According to the theory, he should specialize in activities requiring these skills, such as hunting and fishing. In turn, the older man should instead specialize in activities for which he possesses the relevant skills. He can still contribute to their survival by cooking, making crafts from waste, and so on. It is a simple image to understand that even though a country does not have an absolute advantage at producing a given good, it can still participate in international trade by focusing on what it can do best comparatively to others (and trade against products for which it is not so good at producing, comparatively to others).

Which country has a comparative advantage? The idea of "dotation" or "endowment" in production factors is important here to explain why a country has a comparative advantage. It was further developed by Bertil Ohlin (1933) and his doctoral dissertation supervisor, Eli Heckscher. A country should export the goods for which it has a strong endowment in production factors (such as natural resources, skilled or unskilled labor, etc.) and import those for which factors are scarce.

Why did new theories—known as "firm-based theories"—appear? Just after World War II, new theories started to appear (Griffin & Pustay, 2015). First of all, several researchers such as Leontief (1954) failed to empirically

Geographic and Psychic Distances   111

validate the Heckscher-Ohlin theory, casting a shadow on its relevance. Then, country-based theories did not explain the existence and growth of intra-industry exchange (i.e., the imports and exports of goods pertaining to the same industry, like the automotive industry for instance) and the growing importance of a new form of organization: the multinational corporation (with production facilities in different locations across the world). Figure 4.5 provides simple symbols to help you remember three of the main firm-based theories: demand similarity, international product life cycle, and global strategic rivalry. A brief account of each one follows.

What is the "demand similarity theory" about? To represent the phenomenon of intra-industry trade, the illustration features the example of two well-known carmakers, from Germany and Japan, respectively. With country-based theories, there was little explanation as to why Germany would simultaneously export BMW cars and import Toyota cars, for instance. Cars are products for which both countries are considered having favorable factor endowments and a comparative advantage. A Swedish economist, Staffan Linder (1961) put forth the hypothesis that this phenomenon occurred because the demand structure of both countries (e.g., tastes and purchasing power of consumers) was similar. Prominent companies in industries for which factor endowment is favorable can then internationalize targeting foreign consumers similar to their domestic consumers.

Why do intra-industry trade flows change over time (i.e., Why do countries start importing goods they were previously exporting)? Vernon (1966, 1979), another US economist and Harvard professor, developed the "International Product Life Cycle" (IPLC) theory to explain the evolution of import/export patterns from a different angle. Instead of looking at explanatory factors at the country-level of analysis, he proposed to look at factors at the industry- or product-level of analysis. Innovative countries (such as the US) first start by exporting products that they have developed and then import them (instead of producing them) when products reach the maturity phase and become more standardized (see Chapter 9 for more details).

Why have some countries developed internationally competitive industries often driven by powerful "champion" firms? Two sets of important new ideas that help answer this question were developed in the 1980s by professors Paul Krugman and Michael Porter. The illustration for both is a chess board, which symbolizes the importance of strategy in order to be successful internationally.

What is the "New Trade Theory" about? With articles like "Scale Economies, Product Differentiation, and the Pattern of Trade" (Krugman, 1980) and "Strategic Trade Policy and the New International Economics"(Krugman, 1986), US economist—and Princeton and London Business School professor—Paul Krugman emphasized the importance of "scale economies" to explain new patterns in trade and the fast-growing development of foreign direct investment (i.e., multinational companies are interested in producing and commercializing abroad because it allows them to save costs through economies of scale). He won the Nobel Prize in Economics in 2008.

What is the "Global Strategic Rivalry" about? This approach is also often referred to as the *competitive advantage theory*, which is not to be confused

112 *Geographic and Psychic Distances*

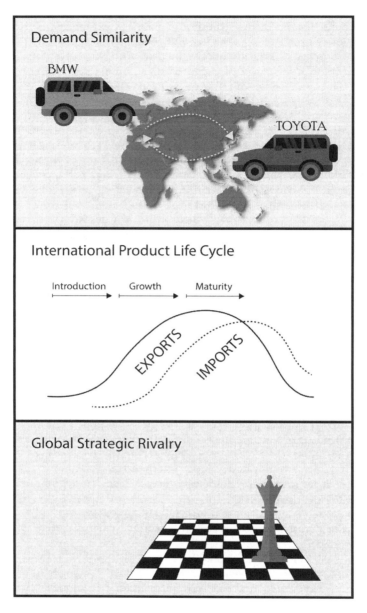

Figure 4.5 Memorizing important firm-based theories with symbols
Source: Own elaboration

with the comparative advantage theory seen previously. Simply put, MNCs struggle to develop some sustainable competitive advantages (like scale economies or valuable intellectual property), which they can then exploit to dominate the global marketplace. A competitive advantage is, thus, an asset that

Geographic and Psychic Distances   113

distinguishes a company from competitors and establishes its superiority. The US strategist, and Harvard professor, Michael Porter is famous for texts like "Competitive Advantage: Creating and Sustaining Superior Performance" (Porter, 1985) and "The Competitive Advantage of Nations" (Porter, 1990).

Now that we have covered the basic description of several important theories at both the country- and firm-level of analysis, we can better understand why Dunning's OLI paradigm (see Chapter 2) is called "eclectic": it drew from both levels of analysis. Indeed, the existence of MNCs (firms engaging in international production) is explained with one factor at the country-level of analysis (Location advantage) and two factors at the firm-level of analysis (Ownership and Internalization advantages).

Why interest ourselves in economics and international trade theories in marketing? Theories developed and used in international economics are useful to understand marketing in a globalized context as they look to resolve several issues that have an impact on business sectors and consequently on companies within these sectors. Indeed, companies do not act in isolation from other companies in their industry (e.g., pricing, outsourcing, delocalizing) nor in isolation from governments who make decisions that regulate their activities (see Chapter 6). For instance, welcoming or protecting against foreign direct investment, lowering custom duties and participating in regional trade agreements, or designing incentives to enhance specific industrial clusters have direct repercussions on firms' costs and access to knowledge. We now take the perspective of two branches of economics, economic geography and industrial economy, alternatively, to look more into the topics of costs and knowledge.

4.3.2 Costs: A Distance Perspective

For companies willing to expand abroad, which costs have significantly reduced over the past decades? With the information and communication technologies (ICT) revolution in the mid-1990s, the required time, energy, and financial resources to generate, send, and receive information (for market research, establishing potential contacts with business partners, maintaining efficient headquarters-subsidiaries relations, etc.) has become significantly lower. Not only is communication cheaper, but transportation is too. With the development of better infrastructures (roads, airports, etc.), numerous ground, air, and maritime routes, advanced technologies to handle and move charges, and more efficient logistic systems, getting goods from one point of the globe to another has become increasingly faster and cheaper. Figure 4.6 illustrates the continuous and drastic reduction of both air and maritime transport costs, as well as communication costs, during the 1930–2000 period.

Finally, crossing borders has also become easier and cheaper. The reduction of trade barriers (at the regional and global levels) has been and is still actively pursued, in particular with WTO activities. Figure 4.7 shows the efforts of successive rounds of negotiation among the members of the General Agreement on Tariffs and Trade (GATT) to reduce average tariffs that were about 40 percent right after World War II, to about 5 percent in the 1990s (HBS 9–703–015, 2002; WTO, 2015, p. 16). It is another straightforward

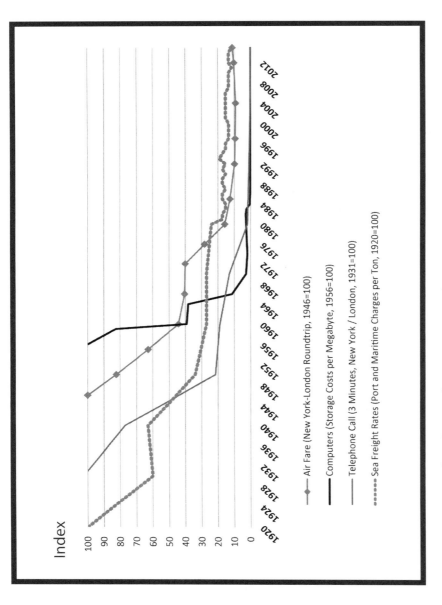

Figure 4.6 Illustrating the reduction of communication and transportation costs (1920–2015)

Source: Data provided by Jean-Paul Rodrigue, based on Rodrigue (2017) and Rodrigue, Comtois, and Slack (2017)

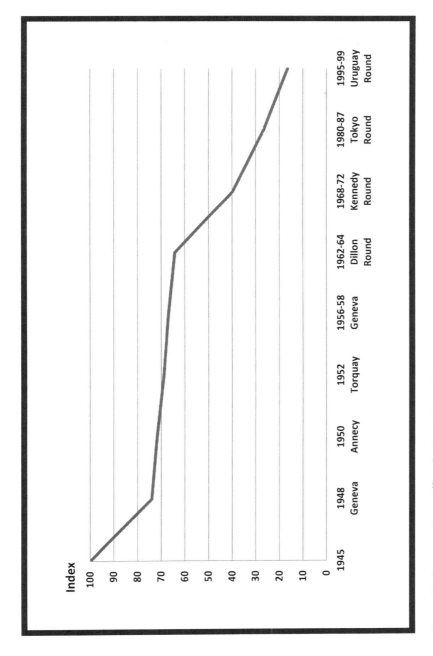

Figure 4.7 Representing tariffs reduction (1947–1993)
Source: WTO (2007, p. 207)

advocacy for a drastic reduction of the weight of geographic and administrative distances.

While transportation, communication, and administrative costs have undergone a phenomenal reduction (with direct consequences in the ability of firms to lower prices for final consumers on foreign markets), crossing borders is still costly, due to other transaction costs. The "Buy-Ship-Pay" (BSP) model proposed by the United Nations Centre for Trade Facilitation and Electronic Business (2014) offers an interesting illustration of the various transaction costs incurred in the context of international exchange.

How does the Buy-Ship-Pay model illustrate transaction costs in crossing borders? The BSP model describes several of the main tasks that companies commercializing abroad must undertake. All of the procedures detailed in Figure 4.8 must be performed and, evidently, paid for (either by remunerating employees or by paying specialized third parties). A narrow view would limit transaction costs to commercial procedures. A larger view would also include the costs generated by transport, regulatory, and financial procedures as part of transaction costs.

As an example, we can go through the procedure described in the model as an importer. The goal of the importer is to buy goods abroad, have them shipped, and pay for them. For that, several commercial procedures are needed (i.e., ordering goods with information on delivery times and conditions, establishing the contract with the price, quantity, and terms of commerce—the Incoterms® described below—and setting the payment

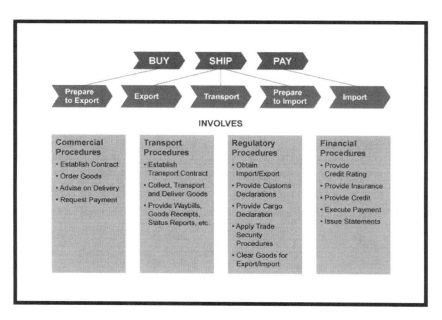

Figure 4.8 Illustrating transaction costs involved in imports–exports with the Buy-Ship-Pay model

Source: UNECE (2001) and UN/CEFACT (2014)

Geographic and Psychic Distances   117

requirements). Then, the export and transport phases involve procedures related to regulations and transportation (e.g., determining under which industrial classification code the goods are to be imported and submitted to which tariffs). Thinking of the amount of hours that people spend establishing transport contracts, collecting and transporting the goods, providing all the paper work (e.g., goods receipt, waybills, customs and cargo declarations), applying all the trade security procedures, and then clearing goods at the border gives an idea of the costs involved. Financial procedures also apply with obtaining insurance and eventually a rating and line of credit, executing the payments, and issuing related statements. All of these procedures involve money, time, and energy.

What are Incoterms® and why are they important? Incoterms®, short for "International Commercial Terms," provide internationally accepted definitions and rules of interpretation for most common commercial terms used in contracts for the sale of goods (ICC, 2010). They define when the responsibilities of the seller stop and when those of the buyer start, and as such, are all about defining the costs and risks (e.g., errors in handling causing delays or accidents, machinery breakdowns, fires, robbery) that both parties are willing to assume. These costs and risks arise while goods are packed and uploaded from their production facilities onto trucks or trains; transported via roads or rail tracks either directly to the border or to domestic harbors, ports, or airports; warehoused and inspected by customs officers; and then uploaded once again onto boats or planes; transported for hours, days, weeks or months; and then downloaded, inspected, transported again, and delivered to the buyer's facilities. An additional source of costs are the multiple types of insurance that need to be acquired to cover incurred risks. Evidently, the buyer generally tries to take responsibility at the latest moment possible, while on the contrary, the seller pushes for the buyer to take responsibility at the earliest moment possible in the whole process. Examples of common Incoterms are free-on-board (FOB) and cost-insurance-and-freight (CIF). Figure 4.9 illustrates various Incoterms and the different moments along the transportation process when the responsibility is transferred from the seller to the buyer. In sum, Incoterms define the moment when property ownership changes hands. The negotiated Incoterms may then have an impact on prices to reflect costs and risks incurred.

If you have never thought about Incoterms before, just imagine that you are a salesperson in a pharmaceutical company and that you have managed to sell 10 million USD worth of important medicinal drugs to a foreign importer. Obviously, you are eager to celebrate. However a few weeks later, your boss calls you, asks you about the Incoterm you had negotiated (which you did not negotiate, since you had agreed unknowingly to a DDP— "Delivered Duty Paid"—one of the less protective arrangements for sellers) and informs you that the boat transporting the merchandise encountered a tropical storm on its way and is now lost at sea. In addition to having lost the 10 million USD, there is an angry customer who threatens to sue if the company does not pay hundreds of thousands of dollars in fines for not having delivered the merchandise. This anecdote should give you a good idea of the importance of Incoterms in outlining international contracts properly. Other

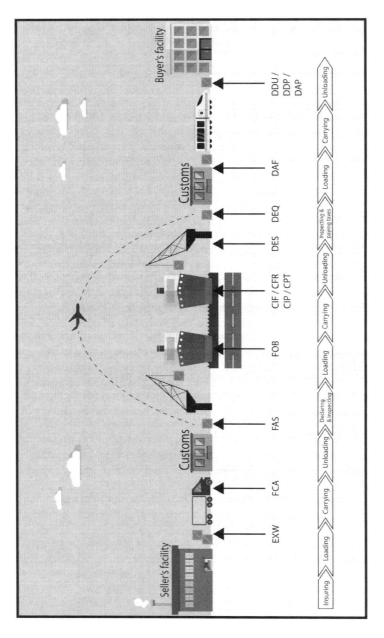

Figure 4.9 Illustrating varying costs and risks according to selected Incoterms®

Source: Adapted from ICC (2010)

Geographic and Psychic Distances   119

costs, related to transportation means and entry modes, should also be taken into account, as illustrated by the following examples.

Would you rather ship a container of computer parts from Singapore to North America by air cargo or by ocean? Table 4.4 shows a rather counter-intuitive answer to this trick question, since airfreight is the cheaper solution in this example provided by Cateora, Gilly, and Graham (2015). Although actual transport costs are indeed much higher by airplane, it also takes far less time for goods to reach their destination (three days instead of three weeks). This ends up making a big difference because of other time-sensitive costs incurred, like warehousing and financing costs for in-transit goods. Obviously, this is not to be generalized (the weight-to-value ratio of goods can also make a big difference, for instance). Yet, this example reminds us of the importance of working with a team of logistics experts who will make the right decisions, as transportation costs have a massive impact on pricing to end-consumers (thus affecting marketing people in the end).

To keep your prices competitive, would you rather produce at home (and export) or produce in the foreign country? In Chapter 2, we studied a typical decision tree for selecting entry modes. One of the main factors motivating companies to produce in foreign markets instead of at home is lower costs, which then allows for more competitive prices to end-users. Not only are production factors (e.g., material and labor costs) important to consider, but so are administrative costs related to changes in ownership. Every time goods change ownership (e.g., from the hands of the manufacturer to those of the wholesaler, to those of the retailer, to those of the final consumer), a turnover tax may apply. In addition, each actor involved in the process takes a profit margin for having facilitated distribution to end-consumers. Table 4.5 offers an example of *price escalation*, the phenomenon that results from this situation very common in exports. Consequently, prices that foreign customers pay are significantly higher than for domestic customers. The case of Telemetrix (fictitious name), a French-Canadian company willing to commercialize its technology to Brazil, illustrates how entry modes impact prices on foreign markets because of various taxes and degree of intermediation of the supply chain (RICG, 2016). The company could either be exporting to Brazil, subcontracting the manufacturing process to a local company (another partner

Table 4.4 Illustrating varying costs according to selected transportation means

COSTS	OCEAN	AIR
Transport costs	$31,890 (**in transit 21 days**)	$127,160 (**in transit 3 days**)
In-transit inventory financing costs	*$44,289*	*$6,328*
Total transportation costs	$76,179	$133,488
Warehousing inventory costs, Singapore and US	$126,540 (60 days at $2,109 per day)	
Warehouse rent	*$6,500*	
Real physical distribution costs	**$209,219**	**$133,488**

Source: Cateora et al. (2015, p. 392)

Table 4.5 Illustrating varying costs and cross-border price escalation according to selected entry modes

BRL		Exporting	Sub-contracting	Licensing
Cost of parts	$	235.23	245.35[2]	245.35[2]
Administration costs	+ $	04.23	39.28[1]	39.28
Transportation costs	+ $	01.76		
Manufacturer's profit	+ $	04.12		
Labour	+ $	120.25	114.00[2]	114.00[2]
Cost of materials supplied by manufacturer	+ $	230.00	230.00[2]	230.00[2]
Total manufacturing and assembly costs	= $	365.59	398.63[2]	398.63[2]
Local taxes[2]	+ $	80.40	160.70[2]	160.70[2]
Cost price (including taxes)	= $	675.99	789.33[2]	789.33[2]
Telemetrix's profit margin (30%)	+ $	202.80	236.80[2]	236.80[2]
Price by manufacturer	= $	**878.79**	**1,026.12[2]**	**1,026.12[2]**
Import taxes on NCM classified products 8517.62.59 (25%)[3]	+ $	219.70		
IPI tax (15%)	+ $	164.77	153.92[2]	
PIS tax (1.65%)	+ $	20.84	19.47[2]	
COFINS tax (8.60%)	+ $	110.43	103.16[2]	
ICMS tax (18%)	+ $	251.02	234.48[2]	
Price by importer/ distributor	= $	**1,645.56**	**1,537.15[2]**	**1,026.12[2]**
Distributor's margin[4]	+ $	246.83	230.57[2]	102.61[2]
IPI tax (15%)	+ $	283.86	265.16[2]	169.31[2]
PIS tax (1.65%)	+ $	35.91	33.54[2]	21.42[2]
COFINS tax (8.60%)	+ $	190.25	177.71[2]	113.47[2]
ICMS tax (18%)	+ $	432.43	403.95[2]	257.93[2]
Retail price	= $	**2,834.84**	**2,648.09[2]**	**1,690.87[2]**

Source: Adapted from RICG (2016)

1 The estimate provided by Brazilian potential partner gives a cost including administrative costs, transportation costs, and profit margin
2 Local taxes: In Quebec: QST + GST: 13.5%; Brazil: cascading taxes (ICMS 12%, PIS 1.65%, COFINS 7.6%, CSLL and IRRF 2.5%)
3 List of acronyms: COFINS (Contribução para o da Financiamento Seguridade Social): federal tax for the financial contribution to social security; CSLL (Contribução Social sobre o Lucro Líquido): profit tax; ICMS (Imposto sobre circulação of Mercadorias e Serviços): State tax on movement of goods and services; IPI (Impostos sobre produtos Industrializados) federal tax on industrialized products; IRRF (Imposto Renda): profit tax; NCM (Nomenclatura Comum do Mercosul): Mercosul common nomenclature; PIS (Programa social Integração): federal tax for fund for employees of private companies; QST: Quebec sales tax; GST: Goods and services tax
4 In the case of subcontracting, the partner has a 15% distribution margin; in the case of licensing, the partner has a 10% distribution margin

Geographic and Psychic Distances   121

would then distribute), or licensing (both manufacturing and distribution). The table shows that a product that could be sold at home for about 880 BRL in 2016 (i.e., ~270 USD) would end up costing twice as much (1,690 BRL, i.e., ~520 USD) with licensing, and more than three times as much (2,835 BRL, i.e., ~870 USD) through exports.

4.3.3 Knowledge: A Proximity Perspective

Adopting a proximity perspective, we can start by wondering why would it matter in relation to marketing and take a look at some important work in economic geography and industrial economy—all the while making links with international business research (see "Food for Thought").

Food for Thought 4.2

- In reference to Porter (1998) and Boschma (2005), as well as Dunning (2009), why would geographic proximity be important for marketing activities?

Noticing that Porter (1998) and Boschma (2005) talk about proximity instead of distance, what is the difference between the two concepts? Ibert (2010, p. 188) provides one of the few clarifications on distinguishing *distance* from *proximity*: "Distance and proximity express the same circumstances: two or more entities are interrelated in their contemporaneity. Whenever entities share a common position on the time axis, they are only discernible (and thus entities, rather than an entity) when regarded as co-constitutive (Massey, 2005). Proximity and distance differ mainly with respect to the intensity and sharpness which they ascribe to the respective distinction: 'proximity' thereby denotes a smaller, whereas 'distance' means a greater, degree of divergence along the same, gradually increasing, scale."

From this definition, we can take away that researchers who focus on concepts of distance and proximity are investigating the same phenomenon, only observed from a different angle. On the one hand, researchers (like Porter and Boschma) interested in the impact of proximity on companies look at differences from a narrower perspective (using a figurative magnifying glass). They focus on business at the industry- or firm-level of analysis. They may prefer questions like how "close" should companies be for them to be successful? They often work in the fields of economic geography, industrial economy, and strategic management. On the other hand, researchers investigating the impact of distance on companies look at differences from a wider perspective (using a figurative pair of binoculars). They prioritize questions such as how "far" can companies go to be successful? They tend to focus on trade and business at the country-level of analysis and often work in the fields of international economics and international business management.

122 *Geographic and Psychic Distances*

Incidentally, research in international marketing has adopted both approaches. All of these researchers are interested in factors that cut companies from their customers and other stakeholders and in how to overcome them. Schematically, the main explanation and solution proposed by tenants of the "distance approach" lies in "non-spatial" dimensions (e.g., reducing administrative barriers to trade, converging toward similar economic conditions, and institutional or technological standards). Quite amusingly, the main explanation/solution provided by tenants of the "proximity approach" resides in the spatial dimension, in particular in geographic "co-location."

Why is there such circularity between the distance approach and proximity approach? What is the core concept that has a fundamental influence on decision-making? Regarding the distance approach, we have discussed knowledge as a core mechanism in the internationalization process (Chapter 2). Regarding the proximity approach, knowledge diffusion has too been at the center of discussions for a long time. As far back as the late-nineteenth century, English economist Alfred Marshall proposed that the physical proximity of firms within a common industry affects how well knowledge travels among firms and facilitates innovation and growth. American economists Kenneth Arrow and Paul Romer further extended Marshall's theory, and their ideas became known as the MAR approach, an acronym comprising their surnames Marshall-Arrow-Romer. They had observed that employees from different firms in an industry exchanged ideas about new products and new ways to produce goods (Marshall, 1890). About a century later, Michael Porter researched clusters and industrial districts and focused on the fact that competition promotes innovation. Knowledge spillovers stimulate growth in specialized industries that are geographically concentrated (where firms are "co-localized," i.e., sharing the same location) (Porter, 1985, 1990, 1998). We all hear about Silicon Valley, Hollywood, and other clusters that put entire industries on the global map, and for which countries or regions are well-recognized. Firms are therefore motivated to locate close to other firms because of the very nature of knowledge.

What is it about knowledge that "being close" becomes so important? First, knowledge is tacit. Think about it. If you have mastered an art or a sport, or invented something, for instance, you may find it hard to explain to someone else how you do what you do. Why this specific gesture needs to be done with this specific timing, for instance. The corporate world goes to great lengths to make tacit knowledge explicit and transmit it (e.g., write manuals and procedures, organize training seminars). Second, knowledge is not transmitted instantly to the exposed population but is rather diffused over time (see Chapter 9 for more details on the diffusion of innovations). Some people learn or adopt new ideas and practices faster than do others. Because of these two characteristics of knowledge, firms benefit from geographic proximity with other firms (e.g., suppliers, customers, and even competitors). Indeed, knowledge "spillovers" are enhanced by frequent and personal interactions. This is simply illustrated by thinking about the occasions we may remember to tell something to someone because we see them. For instance, we may have been thinking about communicating an idea to someone but had not taken the time and energy to write it down in an email. Yet, we would likely remember to tell them if we saw them in the corridor or in a restaurant. Thus, spatial proximity is determinant in how frequent and personal the interactions between firms and people can be. To a certain extent, it is a solution to reduce non-spatial dimensions of distance. In Boschma (2004, p. 8), "Proximity means a lot more than just geography. It is a broad concept that incorporates similarity or adherence between actors or organizations. It includes spatial and non-spatial dimensions."

What are these "non-spatial" dimensions of proximity? Here, *non-spatial distance* refers to all the existing differences between the places of production (including design, manufacturing, assembly, branding activities, and so on), purchase, and consumption that create gaps, difficulties, costs, and risks for companies. One of the first sources of differences that generally comes to mind is culture. Another one lies in different institutions and legal contexts of countries (like differences in degrees of institutions' independence from the executive power and freedom from corruption, for instance). Soon, we think of the PEST framework to structure differences in the political, economic, sociocultural and technological environments of countries and Ghemawat's (2001) CAGE framework. Cultural, institutional, and administrative, as well as economic, differences constitute important "non-spatial" dimensions. Researchers have even established the role of more types of non-spatial dimensions, such as organizational, social, relational, or cognitive dimensions of distance (Boschma, 2005; Knoben & Oerlemans, 2006), as illustrated in Figure 4.10.

Finally, could that explain why international trade fairs are still so important nowadays?[1] In the early times of capitalism, before the establishment of global finance and logistics systems, a considerable part of international trade was transacted periodically in trade fairs as temporary markets (Milgrom, North, & Weingast, 1990; Epstein, 1994). Later, as commerce flourished, mobile vendors stopped travelling and temporary trade fairs turned into permanent marketplaces, and eventually cities (Weber, 1978). In our days, e-commerce platforms (e.g., Amazon) create online marketplaces for

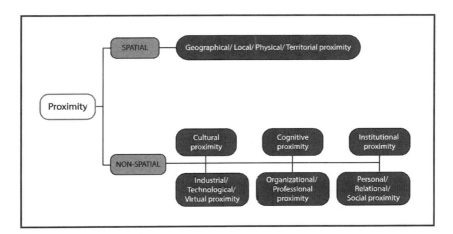

Figure 4.10 Categorizing dimensions of proximity

Source: Adapted from Knoben and Oerlemans (2006, p. 74)

124 *Geographic and Psychic Distances*

firms to showcase their products worldwide. It seems reasonable that trade fairs should be trivial for business.

However, the reality shows an opposite trend. The Global Association of the Exhibition Industry (2014) estimates that about thirty-one thousand trade fairs are organized every year, a number that has grown steadily, even since the 2008–09 global crisis. China, Germany, and the US host the lion's share of these events. Flagship exhibitions (e.g., the Consumer Electronics Show, Paris Fashion Week, and Art Basel) have become must-go destinations for leading firms, even though deal-making does not account for a major reason for some of them to be there. Borghini, Golfetto, and Rinallo (2006) call these fair-goers who do not look for orders on site "atypical" participants.

Recent literature explains the resurgence of trade fairs by emphasizing that temporary gatherings enable knowledge sharing, trust building, and consensus making between buyers and sellers (Bathelt, Golfetto, & Rinallo, 2014; Li, 2014; Rinallo, Bathelt, & Golfetto, 2017). Being close to peers intensifies competition and benchmarking pressure for producers to innovate, so as to differentiate themselves in the buyers' screening. In fact, firms at exhibitions interact in similar ways as they do in industrial clusters. Maskell, Bathelt, and Malmberg (2006) therefore describe trade fairs as *temporary clusters*. Even in the digital era, close physical proximity is still sought.

4.4 *Issues at Stake*

In this section, we address the following questions:

- Why is the effect of geographic distance persistent in spite of transportation and communication costs reduction?
- What are the paradoxes in the distance and proximity approaches, and why should we care?
- What is the impact of geographic distance and psychic distance on international marketing decisions?

4.4.1 *On the Persistence of Distance Effects*

Why is the effect of geographic distance persistent? The reduction of communication, transportation, and administrative costs has prompted several authors to declare geographic distance as being "dead" (Cairncross, 2001), or the world as being "flat" (Friedman, 2005) (see Chapter 1). However, much research has been conducted to investigate this major change, and the effect of geographic distance has been found to be surprisingly persistent, to the point where academics have used playful titles for their articles such as "Distance Is Alive and Well," or "The Puzzling Persistence of the Distance Effect." In addition to Ghemawat's (2001) "Distance Still Matters: The Hard Reality of Global Expansion," a few examples of these articles are listed here:

- Carrière and Schiff (2005), On the Geography of Trade: Distance is Alive and Well. *Revue Economique,* 56(6), 1249–74.
- Berthelon and Freund (2008), On the Conservation of Distance in International Trade. *Journal of International Economics,* 75(2), 310–310.

Geographic and Psychic Distances   125

- Disdier and Head (2008), The Puzzling Persistence of the Distance Effect on Bilateral Trade. *Review of Economics and Statistics*, 90(1), 37–48.
- Jacks (2009), "On the Death of Distance and Borders: Evidence from the Nineteenth Century." National Bureau of Economics Research Working Paper 15250.

These examples suggest that even though costs related to geographic distance have reduced, the effect of distance has still not disappeared. This persistence has been explained by the importance of other types of differences, illustrated by the CAGE framework. In particular, administrative distance has been shown to play an important role with a "border effect" (i.e., trade volume between cities and regions cut by a national border is less than between cities and regions located in the same country). The technological distance/proximity (e.g., presence of infrastructures) also affects the costs related to geographic distance. Other factors related to the economic dimension have been shown to play a role. In economic geography, there has been a lot of work around a "gravity theory" of international trade, developed to explain the intensity of trade flows between countries (i.e., why certain countries trade much more with some countries than others).

What is the "gravity theory" of international trade about? Economists like Walter Isard (1954) and Jan Tinbergen (1962) propose to consider international trade flows as a function of the economic mass of markets and distance. The *gravity theory* uses the metaphor of "mass" to portray markets (or countries) as planets. A basic understanding of astrophysics suggests that the larger the mass (in other words, the bigger and denser the planets are), the stronger the force (i.e., gravity) with which they attract celestial bodies. Thus, this theory stipulates that the intensity of trade flows between two countries varies according to their respective economic mass (measured with their GDP, for instance) and according to the distance between them. Figure 4.11 illustrates a basic gravity model.

Much attention in economics has been dedicated to empirically testing gravity models of international trade. One example lies in the work by

$$F_{ij} = G \frac{M_i M_j}{D_{ij}}$$

With:

F: Trade flow
ij: Country i and j
M: Economic mass, for example GDP
D: Distance
G: Constant

Figure 4.11 Calculating trade flows between countries with the gravity model of international trade

Source: Adapted from Tinbergen (1962)

126 *Geographic and Psychic Distances*

Krempel and Plümper (2002). They provided an interesting visual representation of global trade in 1994, with the mass of markets/countries represented by different size of bubbles (the bigger the bubble, the larger the economy), and the intensity of trade flows represented by the width of links between bubbles (the larger the link, the more intense the international commerce between the economies). Interestingly, at that time the bubble representing China was about the same size as the bubble for Hong Kong. Today, China's weight in global trade is represented by a far bigger bubble, as illustrated in Figure 4.12.

Why is the notion of gravity useful to understand the importance of the economic dimension (and the persistence of distance)? The core notion that underlies gravity models is that in addition to geographic distance, economic weight of countries matter in explaining international trade flows. This spotlight on economic power, or attractiveness of markets, suggests that geographic distance is tempered by economic motives. In other words, managers and policy makers make decisions to trade with foreign countries, despite costs related to geographic distance, when the volume of (current and potential) business makes it worthwhile. This is an important aspect to remember when making market selection decisions.

4.4.2 Paradoxes of Distance and Proximity

What is the paradox of psychic distance? The "paradox of psychic distance" is a term coined by O'Grady and Lane (1996) in an article that was cited 1,100 times (as of March 2018, according to Google Scholar). It prompts us to contrast it with the notion of "paradox of proximity" (see "Food for Thought").

Food for Thought 4.3

- In reference to O'Grady and Lane (1996), what is the paradox of psychic distance? Does it relate to the paradox of proximity highlighted by Boschma (2005)?

What is the paradox of proximity? Although proximity in its many dimensions is supposed to yield positive results, Boschma (2005) highlights some of the problems that occur in terms of innovation when there is either too little or too much of it between partnering firms. For instance, too little cognitive proximity with a business partner most likely results in misunderstandings. However, it is unlikely that any novel idea will emerge from exchanging with a partner characterized by too much cognitive proximity. Table 4.6 presents possible solutions to this paradox. Interestingly, many researchers involved in the phenomenon of proximity converge toward a similar conclusion: it is not an issue in and of itself in international business or marketing. What

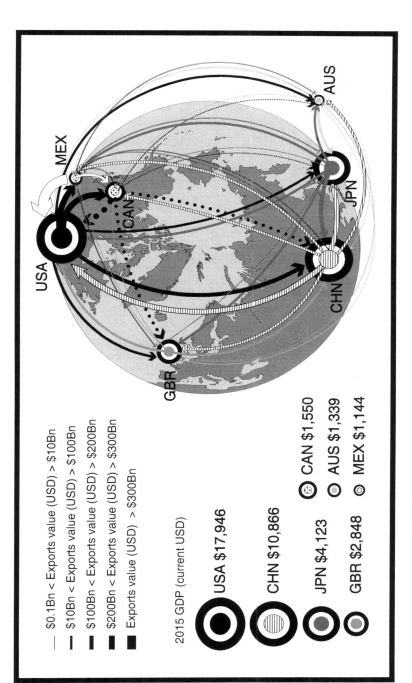

Figure 4.12 Representing world trade flows in a gravity perspective

Source: Own elaboration based on UN Comtrade (2016) and inspired by Krempel and Plümper (2002)

For the color version, see the eResource at www.routledge.com/9781138202344

128   *Geographic and Psychic Distances*

Table 4.6 Illustrating the paradox of proximity

Forms of proximity	Key dimension	Too little proximity	Too much proximity	Possible solutions
1. Cognitive	Knowledge gap	Misunderstanding	Lack of sources of novelty	Common knowledge base with diverse but complementary capabilities
2. Organizational	Control	Opportunism	Bureaucracy	Loosely coupled system
3. Social	Trust (based on social relations)	Opportunism	No economic rationale	Mixture of embedded and market relations
4. Institutional	Trust (based on common institutions)	Opportunism	Lock-in and inertia	Institutional checks and balances
5. Geographical	Distance	No spatial externalities	Lack of geographical openness	Mix of local 'buzz' and extra-local linkages

Source: Boschma (2005, p. 71)

matters is either finding ways to overcome distance/proximity issues, or finding the appropriate amount of distance/proximity for enhancing chances of success.

4.4.3 *Impact on Marketing Decisions*

What is the impact of geographic distance on international marketing decisions? Overall, geographic distance can impact all marketing decisions, at both the strategic and tactical level. Differences in climate, for instance, can affect market selection and product policies (e.g., for a company specializing in winter equipment). Differences in urban vs. rural concentration of the population can affect targeting (e.g., for a company providing fertilizers). Differences in seasons (Northern vs. Southern hemispheres) can affect the promotion of any product or service affected by weather (e.g., a clothing company needs to adjust the timing for promoting its fall/spring collections).

In the literature, geographic distance has received particular attention for the costs it generates in international transactions (in particular for transporting goods, crossing national borders, and exchanging information). These costs particularly impact pricing, entry modes, and distribution channels for goods. First, these costs must be reflected in pricing whenever possible (i.e., transferred to customers), although competition in the foreign market might

Geographic and Psychic Distances 129

not allow this adjustment mechanism. Prohibitive costs might also encourage companies to opt for producing closer to their markets and thereby privilege FDI instead of exports. Long distribution channels (i.e., with a large number of intermediaries) represent additional costs. This price escalation also influences firms in their choice of distribution channels (i.e., how they want to give access to their value offerings to customers in foreign markets). For instance, they can integrate certain activities along the supply chain, i.e., "integrate vertically" by acquiring distributors. In turn, changes in pricing and distribution may affect targeting, positioning, and demand, with obvious repercussions on corporate revenues.

The impact of geographic distance on product innovation is another aspect of marketing that has received a fair deal of attention (e.g., Ganesan, Malter, & Rindfleisch, 2005; Shearmur & Doloreux, 2009; Johnson & Lybecker, 2012). The general position in the literature about clusters and "localized agglomerations" is that geographic distance inhibits innovation. This position is debated, in particular in relation to services, as opposed to manufactured goods. For instance, Shearmur and Doloreux (2009) find that innovation in Knowledge-Intensive Business Services (KIBS) (e.g., management and engineering consultancy, computer systems and design) first decreased with distance from the core of metropolitan areas but then increased again, after 30–50 km (with different patterns according to subsectors).

To keep it simple, let us remember that geographic distance can impact marketing as a whole, but has a particularly important effect on product policies (in particular new product development by, arguably, inhibiting knowledge sharing and innovation) as well as on pricing and distribution (by raising costs).

What is the impact of psychic distance on international marketing decisions? Since it encompasses managers' perceptions of differences across markets, psychic distance also has the potential to affect all AdaptStand decisions at the strategic and tactical level of marketing.

In the literature, it has received plenty of attention for its impact on market selection, with researchers looking to assess the validity of the Uppsala model of internationalization (e.g., Alexander, Rhodes, & Myers, 2007; Brewer, 2007b; Cyrino, Barcellos, & Tanure, 2010; Dow, 2000; Stottinger & Schlegelmilch, 1998). Another area in which the concept was particularly investigated is B2B relationships (i.e., industrial buyers and sellers), in particular to assess firms' success in collaborating with foreign partners (e.g., importers and retailers) (e.g., Conway & Swift, 2000; Katsikeas et al., 2009; Johnston, Khalil, Jain, & Cheng, 2012; Durand et al., 2016), which in turn affects the product, price, distribution, and promotion policies. The influence of psychic distance on AdaptStand issues has received some attention and several authors have shown that high psychic distance led firms to further adapt to local conditions in foreign markets (e.g., Evans & Bridson, 2005; Sousa & Lages, 2011). Finally, researchers also investigated the impact of psychic distance on the overall performance of companies in their ventures abroad since it is an overarching concept (Evans & Mavondo, 2002; Evans et al., 2008; Sousa & Lengler, 2009).

130 *Geographic and Psychic Distances*

The nature of its effect (positive or negative) has been widely debated, first because of issues related to its operationalization and then because of conflicting empirical findings. The dominant position in the literature is that psychic distance is an individual level, subjective influence on marketers, and that it renders decision-making more difficult. In context of high psychic distance with foreign markets, marketing managers are expected to make more risk-adverse decisions (e.g., selecting less-distant markets or opting for a low-commitment entry mode). However, researchers have also examined at length O'Grady and Lane's (1996) "psychic distance paradox" and a surprising positive relationship between psychic distance and, for instance, export performance (e.g., Sousa & Lengler, 2009).

Beyond these ongoing debates in the academic literature, we can remember that psychic distance has a potential effect on all aspects of AdaptStand decisions, and has been particularly studied for its impact on market selection.

Conclusion: Geographic and Psychic Distances Matter Because They Generate Costs and Inhibit Knowledge. They Should be Decreasing, Yet. . .

What would a nomological network for geographic and psychic distances look like? A *nomological network* has been defined as the representation of the constructs of interest in a study, their observable manifestations, and the interrelationships among and between them (Cronbach & Meehl, 1955). Figure 4.13 encapsulates the concepts reviewed in this chapter by proposing a nomological network for both types of distance in relation to marketing. For parsimonious purposes, we look at both geographic and psychic distances at the same time, but each one could well be the object of a separate nomological network. They do relate to one another since geographic distance constitutes one dimension of psychic distance. This relationship is not captured in the conceptual model to keep it simple.

Moving on with the figure description, its center shows both types of distances as the phenomena under scrutiny. It specifies that geographic distance is a concept studied at the country-level of analysis, whereas psychic distance can be both conceptualized at the country-level of analysis (objective approach) or at the individual-level of analysis (subjective approach). The figure also reminds us that geographic distance is defined as the degree of dissimilarity between a firm's home and target country in terms of their geographic environments. In turn, psychic distance is defined as the degree of dissimilarity between a firm's home and target country in terms of their whole country environment, captured by the CAGE or PEST acronyms.

The left-hand side of the figure represents the drivers of both types of distance, specifying that they are to be conceptualized at the country-level of analysis except in a subjective approach of psychic distance when factors related to managerial knowledge (individual- and firm-level of analysis) will then also determine psychic distance.

The right-hand side of the figure captures the fact that outcomes of both distances can be found at all levels of marketing with an impact on

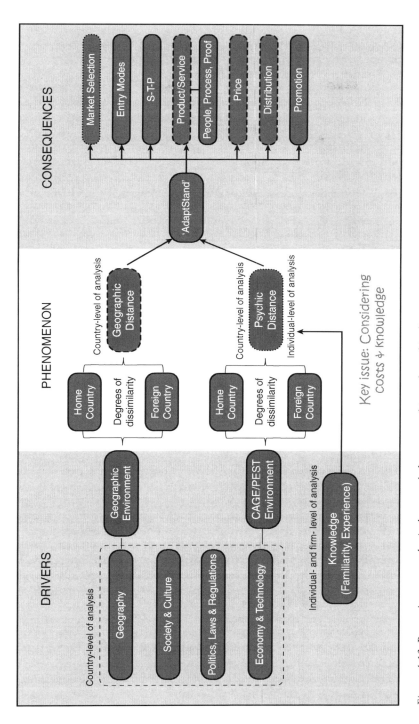

Figure 4.13 Proposing a nomological network for geographic and psychic distances

Source: Own elaboration

132   *Geographic and Psychic Distances*

AdaptStand decisions. It also represents the particular interest found in the literature for the impact of geographic distance on product policies (in particular innovation and new product development), price and distribution, on the one hand, and for the impact of psychic distance on market selection, on the other.

So, why do geographic and psychic distances matter for marketing decisions in a globalizing context? Throughout this chapter, we emphasized the multidimensionality of distance to understand the complexity of its impact on marketing activities in international settings. We can conclude that geographic distance matters because it **raises costs** and **inhibits knowledge** (more specifically, the acquisition and sharing of knowledge). Its effect must be considered along with the effect of other dimensions of distance (e.g., cultural, economic, technological, and administrative distances). In turn, psychic distance, an intangible aggregate of all types of distances that is formed in the minds of managers, matters because it **inhibits decision-making and learning** (i.e., knowledge acquisition) about foreign markets. Simply put, the key issue for marketers when looking at foreign markets from the angle of geographic and psychic distances is then: carefully "**considering incurred costs and required knowledge**" (see Figure 4.13).

Finally, is geographic distance decreasing? What about psychic distance, is it decreasing? The intangible aspects of geography are obviously not changing. Nevertheless, the reduction of transportation and communication costs makes a reasonable argument in favor of a "shrinking" geographic distance. This is to put in perspective with the still-persistent effect of geographic distance due to the fact that it is almost impossible to entirely disentangle it from the effect of the other distances involved (e.g., cultural and economic). So, the answer leaves room for debate.

As for a possible reduction of psychic distance, the answer is also quite challenging. In a way, we can argue that, with the reduction of transportation and communication costs, the diffusion of knowledge is increasingly facilitated. Managers can learn faster and in a more precise way than ever before about foreign markets. Yet, more knowledge does not necessarily mean less psychic distance. Knowledge can better "shape" psychic distance (and paradoxically reinforce it). Perceptions of differences between home and target countries become finer. The only mechanisms that could eventually reduce psychic distance for sure are integration and convergence (see Chapter 1). If countries actually converge (culturally, economically, and technologically), and if borders continue to disappear with integration, then actual and perceived differences between countries should diminish, as should psychic distance. This is a question that we will continue to discuss in the remainder of the book (in particular in Chapters 5, 6, and 7). For now, what we need to remember as marketers is to avoid dismissing the effect of geographic and psychic distances. One can argue that their effect on marketing might be decreasing, but they will still be very present for years to come.

In the next chapter, we tackle cultural distance and raise again the question of shrinking distances by examining the literature on cultural convergence.

Note

1 In Section 4.3.3, the paragraph entitled "Finally, could that explain why international trade fairs are still so important nowadays?" has been written in collaboration with Pengfei Li, Assistant Professor in International Business (HEC Montréal, Canada), whose research interests include economic geography, and local and international business networks.

References

Alexander, Nicholas, Rhodes, Mark & Myers, Hayley (2007). International Market Selection: Measuring Actions Instead of Intentions. *The Journal of Services Marketing*, 21(6), 424–434.

Bathelt, Harald, Golfetto, Francesca & Rinallo, Diego (2014). *Trade Shows in the Globalizing Knowledge Economy*. New York: Oxford University Press (p. 330).

Bello, Daniel, Chelariu, Cristian & Zhang, Li (2003). The Antecedents and Performance Consequences of Relationalism in Export Distribution Channels. *Journal of Business Research*, 56(1), 1–16.

Berthelon, Matias & Freund, Caroline (2008). On the Conservation of Distance in International Trade. *Journal of International Economics*, 75(2), 310–320.

Borghini, Stefania, Golfetto, Francesca & Rinallo, Diego (2006). Ongoing Search Among Industrial Buyers. *Journal of Business Research*, 59(10), 1151–1159.

Boschma, Ron (2004). Proximité et innovation. *Économie rurale*, 280, 8–24.

Boschma, Ron (2005). Proximity and Innovation: A Critical Assessment. *Regional Studies*, 39(1), 61–74.

Brewer, Paul (2007a). Operationalizing Psychic Distance: A Revised Approach. *Journal of International Marketing*, 15(1), 44–66.

Brewer, Paul (2007b). Psychic Distance and Australian Export Market Selection. *Australian Journal of Management*, 32(1), 73–94.

Cairncross, Frances (2001). *The Death of Distance: How the Communications Revolution Is Changing our Lives*. Boston: Harvard Business School Press (p. 320).

Carrière, Céline & Schiff, Maurice (2005). On the Geography of Trade: Distance Is Alive and Well. *Revue Économique*, 56(6), 1249–1274.

Cateora, Philip, Gilly, Mary & Graham, John (2015). *International Marketing* (17th ed.). New York (US): McGraw-Hill/Irwin (p. 704).

Conway, Tony & Swift, Jonathan (2000). International Relationship Marketing—The Importance of Psychic Distance. *European Journal of Marketing*, 34(11/12), 1391–1414.

Cronbach, Lee Joseph & Meehl, Paul (1955). Construct Validity in Psychological Tests. *Psychological Bulletin*, 52(4), 281–302.

Cyrino, Alvaro, Barcellos, Erika & Tanure, Betania (2010). International Trajectories of Brazilian Companies. *International Journal of Emerging Markets*, 5(3/4), 358–376.

Dichtl, Erwin, Koeglmayr, Hans-Georg & Mueller, Stefan (1990). International Orientation as a Precondition for Export Success. *Journal of International Business Studies*, 21(1), 23–40.

Disdier, Anne-Célia & Head, Keith (2008). The Puzzling Persistence of the Distance Effect on Bilateral Trade. *Review of Economics and Statistics*, 90(1), 37–48.

134 *Geographic and Psychic Distances*

Dow, Douglas (2000). A Note on Psychological Distance and Export Market Selection. *Journal of International Marketing*, 8(1), 51–64.

Dow, Douglas & Karunaratna, Amal (2006). Developing a Multidimensional Instrument to Measure Psychic Distance Stimuli. *Journal of International Business Studies*, 37(5), 578–602.

Dunning, John (2009). Location and the Multinational Enterprise: A Neglected Factor? *Journal of International Business Studies*, 40(1), 5–19.

Durand, Aurélia, Turkina, Ekaterina & Robson, Matthew (2016). Psychic Distance and Country Image in Exporter-Importer Relationships. *Journal of International Marketing*, 24(3), 31–57.

Epstein, Stephan (1994). Regional Fairs, Institutional Innovation, and Economic Growth in Late Medieval Europe. *Economic History Review*, 47(3), 459–482.

Evans, Jody & Bridson, Kerrie (2005). Explaining Retail Offer Adaptation Through Psychic Distance. *International Journal of Retail & Distribution Management*, 33(1), 69–78.

Evans, Jody & Mavondo, Felix (2002). Psychic Distance and Organizational Performance: An Empirical Examination of International Retailing Operations. *Journal of International Business Studies*, 33(3), 515–532.

Evans, Jody, Mavondo, Felix & Bridson, Kerrie (2008). Psychic Distance: Antecedents, Retail Strategy Implications, and Performance Outcomes. *Journal of International Marketing*, 16(2), 32–63.

Friedman, Thomas (2005). *The World Is Flat—A Brief History of the Twenty-First Century*. New York: Farrar, Straus & Giroux (p. 488).

Ganesan, Shankar, Malter, Alan J. & Rindfleisch, Aric (2005). Does Distance Still Matter? Geographic Proximity and New Product Development. *Journal of Marketing*, 69(4), 44–60.

Ghemawat, Pankaj (2001). Distance Still Matters: The Hard Reality of Global Expansion. *Harvard Business Review*, 79(8), 137–147.

Global Association of the Exhibition Industry (2014). Exhibition Industry Statistics. Retrieved April 2017, from www.ufi.org/wp-content/uploads/2016/01/2014_exhibiton_industry_statistics_b.pdf

Griffin, Ricky & Pustay, Michael (2015). *International Business* (8th ed.). New Jersey: Pearson (p. 624).

Griffith, David & Dimitrova, Boryana (2014). Business and Cultural Aspects of Psychic Distance and Complementarity of Capabilities in Export Relationships. *Journal of International Marketing*, 22(3), 50–67.

HBS 9–703–015 (2002). *The World Trade Organization*. Case written by: David Moss and Nicholas Bartlett. Boston: Harvard Business School (p. 28).

Ibert, Oliver (2010). Relational Distance: Sociocultural and Time-Spatial Tensions in Innovation Practices. *Environment & Planning*, 42(1), 187–204.

ICC (2010). Incoterms. International Chamber of Commerce. Retrieved November 2016, from www.iccwbo.org/products-and-services/trade-facilitation/incoterms-2010/the-incoterms-rules/

Isard, Walter (1954). Location Theory and Trade Theory: Short-Run Analysis. *Quarterly Journal of Economics*, 68(2), 305–320.

Jacks, David (2009). On the Death of Distance and Borders: Evidence From the Nineteenth Century. *Economics Letters*, 105(3), 230–233.

Johanson, Jan & Vahlne, Jan-Erik (1977). The Internationalization Process of the Firm-A Model of Knowledge Development and Increasing Foreign Market Commitments. *Journal of International Business Studies*, 8(1), 23–32.

Johanson, Jan & Vahlne, Jan-Erik (2009). The Uppsala Internationalization Process Model Revisited: From Liability of Foreignness to Liability of Outsidership. *Journal of International Business Studies*, 40(9), 1411–1431.

Johnson, Daniel & Lybecker, Kristina (2012). Does Distance Matter Less Now? The Changing Role of Geography in Biotechnology Innovation. *Review of Industrial Organization*, 40(1), 21–35.

Johnston, Wesley, Khalil, Shadab, Jain, Megha & Cheng, Julian Ming-Sung (2012). Determinants of Joint Action in International Channels of Distribution: The Moderating Role of Psychic Distance. *Journal of International Marketing*, 20(3), 34–49.

Katsikeas, Constantine, Skarmeas, Dionysis & Bello, Daniel (2009). Developing Successful Trust-Based International Exchange Relationships. *Journal of International Business Studies*, 40(1), 132–155.

Knoben, Joris & Oerlemans, Leon (2006). Proximity and Inter-Organizational Collaboration: A Literature Review. *International Journal of Management Reviews*, 8(2), 71–89.

Krempel, Lothar & Plümper, Thomas (2002). Exploring the Dynamics of International Trade by Combining the Comparative Advantages of Multivariate Statistics and Network Visualizations. *Journal of Social Structure*, 4(1), 1–22s.

Krugman, Paul (1980). Scale Economies, Product Differentiation, and the Pattern of Trade. *American Economic Review*, 70(5), 950–959.

Krugman, Paul (1986). *Strategic Trade Policy and the New International Economics*. Boston: MIT Press (p. 128).

Leonidou, Leonidas, Barnes, Bradley & Talias, Michael (2006). Exporter-Importer Relationship Quality: The Inhibiting Role of Uncertainty, Distance, and Conflict. *Industrial Marketing Management*, 35(5), 576–588.

Leonidou, Leonidas, Palihawadana, Dayananda, Chari, Simos & Leonidou, Constantinos (2011). Drivers and Outcomes of Importer Adaptation in International Buyer-Seller Relationships. *Journal of World Business*, 46(4), 527–543.

Leontief, Wassily (1954). Domestic Production and Foreign Trade: The American Capital Position Re-examined. *Economia Internazionale*, 2(1), 3–32.

Li, Peng-Fei (2014). Global Temporary Networks of Clusters: Structures and Dynamics of Trade Fairs in Asian Economies. *Journal of Economic Geography*, 14(5), 995–1021.

Linder, Staffan (1961). *An Essay on Trade and Transformation*. Stockholm, Sweden: Almqvist and Wiksell (p. 167).

Marshall, Alfred (1890). *Principles of Economics*. London: Macmillan & Co. (p. 754).

Maskell, Peter, Bathelt, Harald & Malmberg, Anders (2006). Building Global Knowledge Pipelines: The Role of Temporary Clusters. *European Planning Studies*, 14(8), 997–1013.

Massey, Doreen (2005). *For Space*. Thousand Oaks: Sage Publications (p. 232).

Milgrom, Paul, North, Douglass & Weingast, Barry (1990). The Role of Institutions in the Revival of Trade: The Law Merchant, Private Judges, and the Champagne Fairs. *Economics and Politics*, 2(1), 1–23.

Nordstrom, Kjell & Valhne, Jan-Erik (1994). Is the Globe Shrinking? Psychic Distance and the Establishment of Swedish Sales Subsidiaries During the Last 100 Years. In *International Trade: Regional and Global Issues*, Michael Landeck (Editor), London: Macmillan (pp. 41–56).

O'Grady, Shawna & Lane, Henry (1996). The Psychic Distance Paradox. *Journal of International Business Studies*, 27(2), 309–333.

136　*Geographic and Psychic Distances*

Ohlin, Bertil (1933). *Interregional and International Trade*. Boston: Harvard University Press (p. 617).

Porter, Michael (1985). *Competitive Advantage: Creating and Sustaining Superior Performance*. New York: The Free Press (p. 557).

Porter, Michael (1990). The Competitive Advantage of Nations. *Harvard Business Review*, 68(2), 73–93.

Porter, Michael (1998). Clusters and the New Economics of Competition. *Harvard Business Review*, 76(6), 77–90.

Ricardo, David (1817). *On the Principles of Political Economy and Taxation*. London: John Murray (p. 589).

RICG (2016). Telemetrix (B)—Telemetrix in Brazil: Indirect Export, Subcontract, or Licence? Case Written by: Aurélia Durand and Eleonore Kuentz. International Journal of Case Studies in Management—HEC Montréal 9-00-2015-003B (p. 10).

Rinallo, Diego, Bathelt, Harald & Golfetto, Francesca (2017). Economic Geography and Industrial Marketing Views on Trade Shows: Collective Marketing and Knowledge Circulation. *Industrial Marketing Management*, 61, 93–103.

Rodrigue, Jean-Paul (2017). Transport and Communications Costs Indexes, 1920–2015. Deptartment of Global Studies & Geography, Hofstra University. Retrieved April 2017, from https://people.hofstra.edu/geotrans/eng/ch1en/conc1en/priceevol.html

Rodrigue, Jean-Paul, Comtois, Claude & Slack, Brian (2017). Transport and Communications Costs Indexes, 1920–2015. In *The Geography of Transport Systems*, New York: Routledge (4th ed., p. 429).

Shearmur, Richard & Doloreux, David (2009). Place, Space and Distance: Toward a Geography of Knowledge-Intensive Business Services Innovation. *Industry and Innovation*, 16(1), 79–102.

Smith, Adam (1776). *An Inquiry into the Nature and Causes of the Wealth of Nations*. London: W. Strahan (p. 510).

Sousa, Carlos & Lages, Luis Filipe (2011). The PD Scale: A Measure of Psychic Distance and Its Impact on International Marketing Strategy. *International Marketing Review*, 28(2), 201–222.

Sousa, Carlos & Bradley, Frank (2006). Cultural Distance and Psychic Distance: Two Peas in a Pod? *Journal of International Marketing*, 14(1), 49–70.

Sousa, Carlos & Lengler, Jorge (2009). Psychic Distance, Marketing Strategy and Performance in Export Ventures of Brazilian Firms. *Journal of Marketing Management*, 25(5/6), 591–610.

Stottinger, Barbara & Schlegelmilch, Bodo (1998). Explaining Export Development Through Psychic Distance: Enlightening or Elusive? *International Marketing Review*, 15(5), 357–372.

Tinbergen, Jan (1962). *Shaping the World Economy: Suggestions for an International Economic Policy*. New York: Twentieth Century Fund. (p. 330).

UN Comtrade (2016). Exports of Selected Countries in 2015 (Current USD). *United Nations Commodity Trade Statistics Database*. Retrieved May 2017, from http://comtrade.un.org/data/

UN/CEFACT (2014). Buy-Ship-Pay Model. United Nations Centre for Trade Facilitation and Electronic Business. Retrieved September 2014, from http://tfig.unece.org/contents/buy-ship-pay-model.htm

UNECE (2001). Recommendation No. 18—Facilitation Measures Related to International Trade Procedures. United Nations—Economic Commision for

Europe Retrieved March 2017, from www.unece.org/fileadmin/DAM/cefact/recommendations/rec18/Rec18_pub_2002_ecetr271.pdf

Vernon, Raymond (1966). International Investment and International Trade in the Product Cycle. *The Quarterly Journal of Economics*, 80(2), 190–207.

Vernon, Raymond (1979). The Product Cycle Hypothesis in a New International Environment. *Oxford Bulleting of Economics and Statistics*, 41(4), 255–267.

Weber, Max (1978). *Economy and Society*. Berkeley: University of California Press (p. 1469).

Wikipedia (2017). Internationalization. Retrieved April 2017, from http://en.wikipedia.org/wiki/Internationalization

WTO (2007). World Trade Report 2007. © World Trade Organization. www.wto.org/English/res_e/booksp_e/anrep_e/world_trade_report07_e.pdf

WTO (2015). Understanding the WTO. © World Trade Organization—Information and External Relations Division. www.wto.org/english/thewto_e/whatis_e/tif_e/understanding_e.pdf

5 Cultural Distance

Table of Contents

5 **Cultural Distance**

Introduction: Why Does It Matter? Is It Decreasing? 139
5.1 Definitions...140
5.2 Drivers 143
    5.2.1 Social Organization 143
    5.2.2 Verbal and Non-Verbal Communication
        (Hall and Hall)...147
    5.2.3 Religion   154
    5.2.4 Beliefs, Values and Norms (Ronen and
        Shenkar; Hofstede; Schwartz) 159
5.3 Central Role of Behaviors 164
    5.3.1 Theory of Reasoned Action/Planned
        Behavior (Fishbein and Ajzen) 164
5.4 Issues at Stake 167
    5.4.1 Cultural Convergence 167
    5.4.2 Points of Contention in Assessing Cultural
        Distance...168
    5.4.3 Impact on Marketing Decisions with
        Corporate Examples: Disney, HSBC,
        Ikea, Kellogg's, Microsoft, McDonald's,
        Pinterest, and Starbucks...................................169

Conclusion: Cultural distance matters because it prevents companies from understanding and influencing different behaviors. Its evolution over time escapes our grasp.
References

Recommended Readings

- Dow, Douglas & Karunaratna, Amal (2006). Developing a Multidimensional Instrument to Measure Psychic Distance Stimuli. *Journal of International Business Studies*, 37(5), 578–602.

- Ralston, David (2008). The Crossvergence Perspective: Reflections and Projections. *Journal of International Business Studies*, 39(1), 27–40.
- Shenkar, Oded (2012). Cultural Distance Revisited: Toward a More Rigorous Conceptualization and Measurement of Cultural Differences. *Journal of International Business Studies*, 43(1), 1–11.
- Sousa, Carlos & Bradley, Frank (2006). Cultural Distance and Psychic Distance: Two Peas in a Pod? *Journal of International Marketing*, 14(1), 49–70.

Introduction: Why Does It Matter? Is It Decreasing?

There is little doubt that cultural distance matters, as we are constantly reminded of different behaviors among people from various origins. However, asking the follow-up question: "**Is cultural distance decreasing?**" is rather ambitious.

Before delving deeper into the topic of cultural convergence, we should ensure we know how to study the cultural environment in foreign markets and measure distance between countries in this regard. To do so, we first define culture and cultural distance, while differentiating it from psychic distance. Then, we consider important factors through which cultural differences manifest, including social organization, verbal and non-verbal communication, religion, and finally, beliefs, values, and norms. Next, we move on to further explore the central role of attitudes and behaviors in understanding why cultural distance matters for marketing activities in an

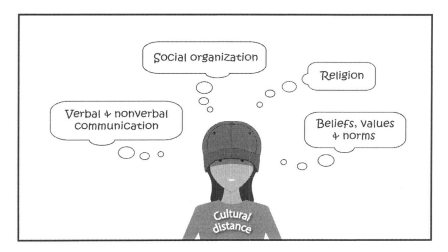

Figure 5.1 Illustrating Chapter 5
Source: Own elaboration

140   *Cultural Distance*

international context. Finally, we explore the theme of cultural convergence, several points of contention in the literature about the conceptualization and measurement of cultural distance, and the extent to which this specific dimension of distance impacts marketing decisions.

Overall, the objectives of this chapter are to define, measure, and evaluate the outcomes of cultural distance for international marketing. Figure 5.2 situates this chapter in the overall book structure.

5.1 Definitions

In this section, we examine the following questions:

- What is culture?
- What is cultural distance? How is it different from psychic distance?
- Which are the important components of the socio-cultural environment that create distance (i.e., that differ across countries)?

How can we define culture? Classical definitions of *culture* include Linton (1945, p. 32) who states, "it is the configuration of learned behaviour and results of behaviour whose component elements are shared and transmitted by the members of a particular society." Hall (1959, p. 43) declares, "For anthropologists culture has long stood for the way of life of a people, for the sum of their learned behavior patterns, attitudes, and material things." Finally, Goodenough (1971) presents culture as a set of beliefs or standards, shared by a group of people, that help the individual decide what is, what can be, how to feel, what to do, and how to go about doing it.

What do these definitions have in common? These definitions have in common the idea that culture is learned, transmitted, and shared among people, and that culture translates into behaviors. These definitions indicate how important culture is in guiding individuals through life. Another definition by one of the prominent researchers on culture, Geert Hofstede, encapsulates this importance by establishing an analogy with computer programming.

Who is Geert Hofstede? Geert Hofstede (Figure 5.3) (born in 1928) is a Dutch social psychologist, former IBM employee, and a professor at Maastricht University in the Netherlands (Wikipedia, 2017d).

Hofstede's work on cultural dimensions is renowned and has been used as a basis for countless studies. For instance, a search on Google Scholar performed in March 2018 indicates that his book *Culture's Consequences: International Differences in Work-Related Values* (Hofstede, 1980), has been cited more than fifty-two thousand times. A second edition of this book, *Culture's Consequences: Comparing Values, Behaviors, Institutions and Organizations Across Nations* (Hofstede, 2001), has also been cited more than 24,000 times. In a more recent book, *Cultures and Organizations*, Hofstede, and Minkov (2010, p. 6), Hofstede proposed that "culture is the collective programming of the mind that distinguishes the members of one category of people from those of another." The subtitle of the book is *Software of the Mind*, which is a powerful image to illustrate how culture configures individuals and defines what they can do and how they do it.

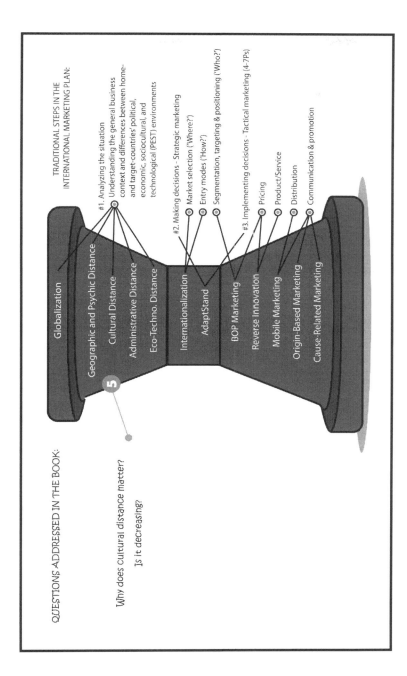

Figure 5.2 Positioning Chapter 5 in the overall book structure

Source: Own elaboration

Figure 5.3 Portrait of Geert Hofstede
Source: Courtesy of Geert Hofstede

What do we mean here by "category of people"? With the term *category*, Hofstede (2010) is referring to all sorts of human groupings, such as nations, ethnic groups, gender groups, organizations, families, etc. We all can think of "what we do or say in our [family/company/school]" for instance, which differs from what others do in their own [family/company/school]. Another way to put it is to try to complete the following sentence: "My [family/company/school] is different because we [believe/say/do] . . ." The ability to complete this sentence underlines differences that are rooted in one's culture. Culture develops in all human groups. However, in the remainder of this text, we will focus on culture at the level of countries or nations, which has received more empirical attention and is of particular interest for the purpose of marketing in a context of globalization.

What is cultural distance? Cultural distance has been defined as "the degree to which cultural values in one country differ from those in another country" (Sousa & Bradley, 2006, p. 52), or else "the extent to which cultures are similar or different" (Shenkar, 2012, p. 519), as well as "the extent to which the cultural norms and values of one nation differ from those of another nation" (Moon & Park, 2011, p. 20). From these definitions, a consensus appears as to defining cultural distance as the degree of dissimilarity between countries in regard to their social and cultural environments.

How different is cultural distance from psychic distance? In the literature, many studies seem to use both concepts of cultural and psychic distance interchangeably, prompting us to wonder how similar they really are (see "Food for Thought").

Cultural Distance 143

Food for Thought 5.1

- In reference to Sousa and Bradley (2006) and Dow and Karunaratna (2006), are cultural distance and psychic distance synonymous?

5.2 Drivers

Culture being so important and omnipresent, what should we look at to understand cultural distance among countries? Griffin and Pustay (2015) suggest classifying the main components of culture into four broad categories: social organization, verbal and nonverbal communication, religion, and, finally, values, beliefs, and attitudes. This proposition aligns with the elements that Ghemawat (2001, p. 5) attributes to creating cultural distance: "different languages, ethnicities, religion, and social norms." Next, we examine each one of the factors driving cultural distance: social organization, communication, religion, and, finally, beliefs, values, and norms (illustrated in Figure 5.1).

To this end, we examine questions such as:

- What should we know about social organization? Why does the role of individuals within groups matter in marketing? What is social mobility and how does it vary across countries?
- How important is communication as a driver of cultural distance? How diverse is the world in terms of languages? What is the purpose of the "high/low context" approach? What characterizes monochronic- and polychronic-time cultures? Finally, why does verbal and nonverbal communication matter for marketing in a globalizing context?
- What are the main religions in the world? Why does religion matter for marketing decisions in a globalizing context?
- What are the differences between values, beliefs, attitudes, and norms? What are the "work-related dimensions" that help differentiate national cultures? Beside Hofstede's work, what is another well-known theory used to measure cultural distance based on values?

5.2.1 Social Organization

What should we know about social organization? Important topics to consider in relation to social organization are the role of individuals within groups (such as families), social stratification, and social mobility (Griffin & Pustay, 2015).

How does the role of individuals within groups vary? First, the very definition of such groups varies. For instance, the questions "What is a family?" or "How many people are expected in a family reunion?" receive different answers in North America or Northern Europe (where families often

144 *Cultural Distance*

comprise only a handful of people, such as parents and siblings, sometimes grandparents), and in South American, African, or Arab countries (where families may include dozens of people, adding elders, uncles and aunts, cousins, and even family friends). Second, people from different cultures have different answers as regards the role (e.g., duties and rights) of individuals. For instance, the respect granted to elderly members of a family or to senior colleagues of a company is much stronger in Japan and in many other Asian countries than it is in Western cultures. Finally, the importance of groups and the sense of belonging differ widely from country to country. In France, for instance, it is not customary for teenagers to look forward to spending Sundays with their families. Activities with friends outside the family circle tend to be preferred. By contrast, in Argentina, spending the day gathered around an *asado* (barbecue) with the extended family is normal and desirable, even for teenagers, who get to invite their friends as well.

Why does the role of individuals within groups matter in marketing? Overall, international differences in the matter are pervasive in many aspects of marketing policies, especially at the strategic (in the STP decisions) and tactic levels (promotion activities). Indeed, studying these differences helps gain a better understanding of purchasing decisions (who makes them and for whom) and helps tailor promotional campaigns to the buyers' culture and values so they can better relate to the product (e.g., a positioning based on family values will be better achieved if promotional material, such as TV spots for instance, depicts the type of family that people relate to best). For a deeper look into the role of individuals within groups and how it affects marketing, see Usunier and Lee (2005).

What is social stratification and how does it vary? *Stratification* refers to stratas or layers of people having homogenous characteristics in a society. It is notably used in relation to standards of living and "status" (low, average, or high status). Belonging to a specific strata has a great impact on individuals' lives, since it may open, restrict, or even suppress a wide range of life opportunities (e.g., education, marriage, jobs). Understanding stratification is required to grasp what is "given to" and "expected from" their members. For more details, see Berreman (1972). Stratification is easily represented using the figure of a pyramid, which represents various layers according to numbers of people (from the most numerous at the base of the pyramid to the least numerous at the top).

What is an example of a society that is heavily stratified? India is always an example that comes to mind because of the caste system. Part of the complexity of understanding the Indian culture for foreigners comes from stratification and the existence of these *castes*. For a broad overview, see a Wikipedia (2017b) entry on the caste system in India. According to the Asia Society website (an organization dedicated to facilitate exchanges between the US and Asia, founded in 1956 by John D. Rockefeller III), the ranking of castes is based on purity and pollution, often associated with functions of the human body. Roles associated with the head – such as thinking, talking, teaching, and learning – are considered pure. Consequently, Brahmins at the top of the purity scale were scholars who traditionally taught and presided at religious functions. Activities associated with waste, feet, and skin are considered polluting. Untouchables, at the bottom of the scale, cleared away human waste, collected garbage, cut hair, skinned animals, and washed

Cultural Distance 145

clothes (Asia Society, 2014). Elsewhere in the world, castes are also to be found in various regions of Africa (Wikipedia, 2017a).

In Western cultures, what is an example of strata? The notion of *social class* comes to mind and income is often used as a proxy to distinguish "lower" from "middle" and "higher" classes in societies. A simple way to understand how caste and social class compare is to note that members of a caste can be recognized by the way they look (e.g., features, height, body shape). By contrast, it is unusual to detect social class from physical attributes. Rather, we tend to recognize people from a certain social class by the way they dress or behave in society. The notion of castes goes a little further than that of classes because it may include genetically based features. In sum, strata in different societies can be labeled under different names (e.g., caste, class, tribes). They all define possibilities (or lack thereof) given to individuals according to the group of people they are born into.

What is social mobility and how does it vary across countries? *Social mobility* is the ability of individuals to move up or down strata or classes in a given society. Factors influencing intergenerational mobility include a country's policies and institutions in terms of education, labor, product market, and redistribution of wealth (Causa & Johansson, 2010). Many international studies have compared countries and shown important differences in terms of how "mobile" societies can be. For instance, Corak (2016) compared the US to many other countries in terms of the degree of elasticity (i.e., variation) of earnings when comparing generations, as illustrated in Figure 5.4.

Intergenerational elasticity of earnings reflects the extent to which sons' earning level reflect those of their fathers. The estimated elasticity lies from zero to one, with a value of zero when parents' and their (adult) children's positions in income distribution are completely unrelated (i.e., complete mobility), and a value of one when parents' and adult children's positions in income distribution are identical (i.e., complete immobility) (Statistics Canada, 2016). In this way, the higher the intergenerational earnings elasticity, the less mobile the society (e.g., Peru has the highest score with 0.67, compared to Denmark with a score of 0.15). In Figure 5.4, Denmark has a low score because it is a rather "egalitarian" country compared to Canada, for instance, which in turn is more egalitarian than the US, which is more egalitarian than Peru; a country situated at the other extreme. Finally, the probability that young adults in Canada earn significantly more (or less) than their parents is much higher than in China, which is a country characterized by a high "intergenerational immobility", like Peru or Brazil.

Figure 5.4 also illustrates some counterintuitive data, such as the discrepancy between the idea that is often associated with the US as the "land of opportunity and self-made men," and a ranking that places other countries, such as Scandinavian countries as well as Singapore, New Zealand, and Australia ahead of the US by offering a better chance for individuals to move away from the earning levels of their parents. This figure also reveals similarities between Pakistan and Switzerland in regards to social mobility (this is a small reminder of the importance of looking at data before assuming anything when it comes to differences among countries).

Other visual representations of social mobility include the "Great Gatsby curve" (in reference to the American novel written in 1925 by Francis Scott

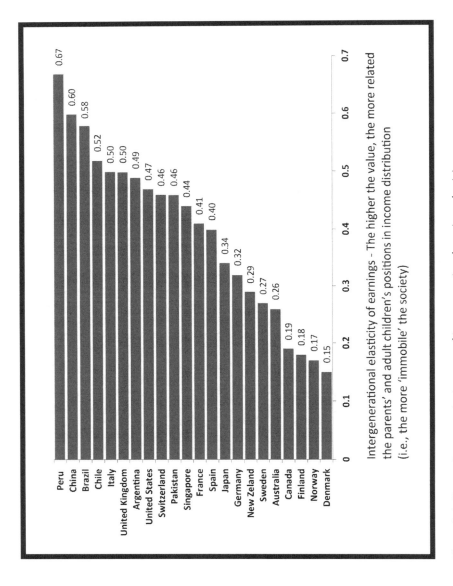

Figure 5.4 Comparing countries in terms of intergenerational earnings elasticity
Source: Adapted from Corak (2016, p. 11)

Fitzgerald), available for a quick look in Wikipedia (2014b). It ranks countries according to intergenerational earning elasticity and a well-known indicator of economic inequalities, the Gini index. The Gini index indicates how wide the gap in revenues is between the poorest and the richest people in one country. This other approach shows that rich people in Brazil are much richer compared to poor people in Brazil, in contrast with rich people in Denmark compared to poor people in Denmark.

To conclude, why do social stratification and mobility matter in marketing? Knowing about the existence of rigid or loosely structured social classes and about their degree of permeability—the possibility to enter or exit social classes (i.e., move up or down in society)—is primarily important for a general understanding of foreign cultures. When coming from a mobile society, it may be difficult to accept constraints/limitations imposed on individuals based on their birth and social background in more-rigid societies. In turn, people from less-mobile societies may tend to reject products or services that clash with established rules. This will notably impact positioning strategies and communication policies (as well as product development and pricing, indirectly), because value offerings need to correspond to targeted segments' aspirations and possible roles in society.

5.2.2 Verbal and Nonverbal Communication (Hall and Hall)

How important is communication as a driver of cultural distance? By contrast to social organization, the importance of verbal and nonverbal communication for cultural distance in general and for marketing purposes in particular is rather evident. Starting with verbal communication, language is one of the first, if not the first, cultural delineator. Language organizes the way members of a society think about the world (Griffin & Pustay, 2015). It filters observations and perceptions and affects the understanding of messages between individuals. In turn, nonverbal communication consists of messages that are transmitted by means other than language. It may account for as much as 80–90 percent of all information transmitted and is, thus, of major importance in facilitating exchanges (Griffin & Pustay, 2015). Next, we review aspects of both verbal and nonverbal communication that differ across countries.

How diverse is the world in terms of languages? In 2016, there were an estimated 7,100 languages spoken in the world (CIA World Factbook, 2016b). Approximately 2,300 languages were spoken in Asia, 2,140 in Africa, 1,310 in the Pacific, 1,060 in the Americas, and 290 in Europe. Yet, 80 percent of these languages were spoken by fewer than one hundred thousand people. Only one hundred and fifty to two hundred languages had more than a million speakers. In fact, the United Nations' six languages (Arabic, Mandarin, English, French, Russian, and Spanish) were the mother tongue or second language of about half of the world's population. Taking into account "first language" speakers only, the world population thus mainly spoke Mandarin Chinese (12.2 percent), Spanish (5.8 percent), English (4.6 percent), Arabic (3.6 percent), Hindi (3.6 percent), Portuguese (2.8 percent), Bengali (2.6 percent), Russian (2.3 percent), Japanese (1.7 percent), Punjabi (1.2 percent) and Javanese (1.2 percent) (CIA World Factbook, 2016b). Most countries have

148 Cultural Distance

only one official language, with exceptions such as Canada (two), Switzerland (four), South Africa (eleven), and India (only two at the federal level but twenty-two at the state level). Communities that are isolated from each other in mountainous regions often develop a much greater number of languages. Papua New Guinea, for example, boasts about 840 separate languages (CIA World Factbook, 2016b). Figure 5.5 illustrates the diversity of the world in terms of languages, with large geographic zones speaking common languages (e.g., Spanish-speaking Latin America) and other highly heterogeneous zones (e.g., sub-Saharan Africa).

Diversity of languages is one thing, but what about diversity of meanings? Indeed, verbal communication varies not only because of differences in spoken languages but also in the meaning of words said in any particular language. For instance, some words have a literal translation that is very straightforward from one language to another, but what they mean is actually lost in translation. A good example of a word with an easy translation but that is not used in the same way in different cultures is *tomorrow* (*mañana*) or *right away* (*ahorita*). In Mexico or other Latin American countries, these terms are not used as literally as they are in North America, for instance. Imagine you are working in a company and make a call to someone for assistance. In North America, if the person tells you, "This will be done tomorrow," you can reasonably expect that the said task will be completed the next day. By contrast, if you hear "Mañana, sin problema," while working in Latin America, it would be unreasonable to actually expect the task to be completed the following day. In such a situation, the term could also translate as *later* or *in the next few days*.

Another well-known example is the use of *yes* and *no*, which varies greatly across cultures. For instance, saying yes does not mean "I agree" in all countries. In Japan and other Asian countries, saying yes to punctuate a conversation may mean, "Yes, I understand what you are telling me," not necessarily, "Yes, I agree with what you are telling me." These subtleties in languages bring to mind an anecdote regarding the huge disappointment American businessmen may experience after a long meeting with Japanese businessmen. Although the latter may have spent the whole meeting saying yes to every business proposition, they nonetheless end up refusing to sign the contract. They understood what was being proposed but did not buy into the arguments, causing disarray in the American team, who thought they were geared toward success (Griffin & Pustay, 2015, p. 92).

The meaning of *no* in many Asian countries also carries much more weight than in Western cultures, where being told no is often not offensive but factual: "No, you cannot obtain this." In Japan, however, saying no to someone in a conversation is confronting. To save someone from the embarrassment or shame (i.e., from "losing face") that a confronting no can cause, Japanese people have developed many ways to avoid directly saying no. Ueda (1974) has documented sixteen different such ways (e.g., opposing silence or a counter question, criticizing the question itself, or refusing the question altogether). As you can imagine, the diversity in the meaning of words that otherwise translate easily is the cause of many misunderstandings and

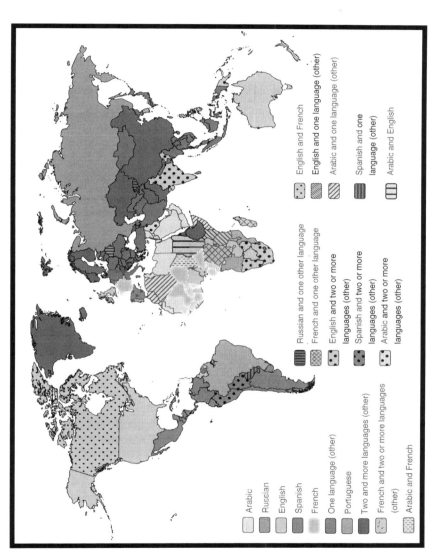

Figure 5.5 Illustrating the diversity of languages in the world

Source: Own elaboration based on CIA World Factbook (2016b)

For the color version, see the eResource at www.routledge.com/9781138202344

150 *Cultural Distance*

difficulties in cross-cultural interactions. Another source of great diversity (and misunderstanding) is nonverbal communication.

What are some examples of nonverbal communication? Many cues serve as nonverbal communication. We can group these cues together according to the senses to which they appeal. For instance, visual cues include gestures, facial expression, posture and stance, walking behavior, hair/clothing style, use of cosmetics, eye contact, and color/graphic symbolism (e.g., positive or negative associations with specific colors or shapes, such as the triangle and circle). Auditory cues by which we transmit and receive information include the way we speak (i.e., rate, pitch, inflection, volume) as well as the timing and use of pauses or silences. They are very informative to other people. Different *chronemics*, as it is called, can be the source of massive confusion and frustration among people from different cultures. Cues involving touch (*haptics*) and positioning in space (*proxemics*), as well as olfactive cues (e.g., strength or absence of smell), are also very important in the way we transmit and receive information and are marked by high diversity across cultures. Table 5.1 presents some of the important areas involved in studying nonverbal communication.

Going over a few examples of visual cues, gestures are often obvious signs of nonverbal communication. They can be single-handed or two-handed gestures or can be performed with other body parts (e.g., shoulders, elbows)—see a Wikipedia (2017c) entry for a list of gestures across cultures. Although there are many sources of information where one can learn the meaning of specific gestures in foreign cultures (especially books, magazines, websites, blogs, and forums targeting travelers), it is unfortunate that systematic cataloging is not available for all cultures. Causes for misunderstanding are numerous! Figure 5.6 is inspired from *A Dictionary of Argentine Gestures* by Indij (2007). From the upper-left corner, going clock-wise, the meaning conveyed by these gestures are: "It was crowded," "What are you telling me?," "I have no idea!," and "Hurry-up!" Someone unfamiliar with the Argentine culture could either be clueless as to what a certain gesture means or completely misinterpret the gesture. For instance, the gesture expressing "I have no idea!" is likely to be interpreted as an insult in Italy and several North African countries (e.g., Morocco and Tunisia). In the latter countries, the sign for "What are you telling me?" means "Wait a minute" or "Slow down." Finally, the gesture meaning "Hurry up" in Argentina is very close to what

Table 5.1 Defining important study fields in nonverbal communication

Study Fields	
• Chronemics	Timing of verbal exchanges
• Haptics	Use of touch (e.g., hand on the forearm or shoulder) while conversing
• Kinesics	Movement of parts of the body to communicate
• Oculesics	Use (or avoidance) of eye contact
• Proxemics	Use of space (e.g., interpersonal distance) in communication

Source: Adapted from Albaum, Duerr, and Josiassen (2016, Table 12.1)

Cultural Distance 151

Figure 5.6 Illustrating the diversity of meaning in gestures
Source: Own image inspired by Indij (2007)

French people would understand as "Boy, you are in trouble." All interpretations trigger very different reactions, obviously.

In terms of expressiveness, people from Latin countries can get frustrated when interacting with people from Scandinavian or Asian countries due to their inability to "read" them (because joy, frustration, or boredom will not be apparent through facial expressions). In turn, people who are used to less body language might interpret the numerous facial expressions and use of hand gestures in Latin people as rather hysterical and lacking a desirable restraint.

Posture and stance, meaning the way our body is positioned in space or in movement (e.g., walking behavior), say something about us as persons and about our present state of mind/mood. For instance, a straight back and

152 *Cultural Distance*

open shoulders can convey a sense of interest, self-confidence, or pretention, whereas an arched back and slumped shoulders can translate as a state of boredom, laziness, or tiredness. People from diverse cultures pay different attention to these details. For instance, the way our body is positioned when eating is subject to different interpretations across cultures because of various "dos" and "don'ts" in each culture (i.e., proper etiquette). The respect of such codes is big in France, for instance, and people will infer about your social upbringing according to your table manners. In France, if you are a right-handed person, the correct way to place your left hand, when unused, is with the wrist on the table next to your plate and fork. No elbows on the table and no left hand under the table, ever! This would be an important custom to be aware of if you were to have a business lunch with Frenchmen and would want to avoid being looked down on. It would also be a challenge if you were used to different habits (such as in North America, where the left hand tends to be placed under the table when unused) or simply from a culture where such rules are not taken so seriously.

The same observation applies for clothing and hairstyles or with the use of cosmetics. For instance, the extent to which clothing items and products associated with seduction are used (e.g., revealing neckline and makeup for women, hair products and perfumes for men) can be assets or liabilities, depending on cultural preferences and on whether business counterparts pay close attention to these elements.

In addition, eye contact is a well-known example of a behavior that carries different meanings across cultures. The study of *oculesics* (eye behavior) shows that the impression made by someone making and sustaining eye contact could not be more drastically distinct between South Korea and the US, for instance. In South Korea, sustaining eye contact can be interpreted as offensive and as a sign of disrespect or confrontation (and as such, is best avoided), while in the US, it is often deemed as trustworthy and honest. Eye contact is one of the aspects of body language/micro expressions that are subtle yet essential in adapting one's nonverbal communication when interacting with people from other cultures.

Finally, many studies have reported differences in the use of colors, numbers, and graphic symbolism. A few well-known examples include the different associations made with the colors white and red. For example, while white is used for weddings in Western countries, as it is a symbol of purity and beginnings, it is used for funerals in several Asian countries, as a symbol of death. In contrast, red is the color associated with funerals and death in some African countries, while it is often perceived as an energetic and passionate color in Western countries (think of the Coca-Cola or Red Bull logos).

What is the purpose of the "high/low context" approach? Hall and Hall (1990) propose an approach to understanding communication based on the relative emphasis on verbal and nonverbal cues to transmit meaning. This approach helps contrast cultures to the extent to which information is only conveyed through verbal and explicit messages, or *low context* (i.e., where the context is not necessarily needed to derive meaning, such as in Switzerland, Germany, Canada, and the US), and through nonverbal and implicit

Cultural Distance 153

messages, or *high context* (i.e., where the context matters tremendously to properly interpret information, such as in Japan, China, and Middle Eastern countries).

Going back to examples given previously about nonverbal communication, high-context cultures are those where proper etiquette exists for many aspects of life—from greetings to table manners, etc. For instance, appropriate clothing, hairstyle, and cosmetic use vary depending on whether the event is work related, pertaining to a special occasion (e.g., wedding), or for leisure (e.g., concert). Interpretation of a message also depends heavily on the context in which words are spoken, for instance: "who says what" (i.e., in which role: subordinate, colleague, friend, mentor), "where it is said" (i.e., in a private or public setting for instance, or in front of whom), and "how things are said" (i.e., the tone or facial expressions often play an important role in interpreting the spoken information and may change its meaning).

On the other hand, communication in countries with low-context cultures depends more on explicit, verbally expressed thoughts. In turn, people's appearances do not matter as much, because it is not as important a source of information (e.g., it is not used as a signal about who people are, how they should be treated). Thus, these cultures often allow a greater freedom than do high-context cultures (coupled with indifference, to some extent) in terms of clothing, hairstyle, cosmetics, tattoos, or piercing jewelry. For instance, in Germany it would not be particularly shocking to attend a summer class in which the university professor is dressed in Bermuda shorts and sandals. However, this would be unthinkable in Latin America or in Arab countries where suits and closed shoes are required, even though the weather is much hotter.

Another example of differences between low- and high-context cultures lies in business negotiations. As messages are more or less explicit and specific, the importance of context translates into different degrees of reliance on legal paperwork. In low-context cultures, there is a strong focus on nonpersonal documentation of credibility. By contrast, high-context cultures often put less emphasis on legal paperwork but focus on personal reputation instead. When the parties have solid reputations for being trustworthy, the "given word" can be considered a sufficient reassurance to conclude business deals.

High/low-context categorization is linked to another cultural difference affecting communication: time perception. Indeed, most low-context cultures operate on monochronic-time (also referred to as "M-time") and most high-context cultures operation on polychronic time (P-time).

What characterizes monochronic- and polychronic-time cultures? In *M-time cultures*, individuals tend to concentrate on one thing at a time. They divide time into small units and are concerned with promptness. These are cultures in which expressions such as "saving time," "wasting time," "biding time," "spending time," and "losing time" have some meaning, as if time were a currency. The desire to get straight to the point and get down to business is a manifestation of an M-time culture, as are other indications of directness. Time can be visually represented by a straight line, and sequences can be clearly cut out from this line with a specific beginning and ending (Hall, 1983).

154 *Cultural Distance*

In *P-time cultures*, holding to schedules is less important than completing human transactions. For instance, students in a classroom in Argentina could see no problem in being released after the time scheduled for the end of the class in order to finish a discussion when, on the contrary, students in a classroom in Canada will consider it more important to interrupt an interesting discussion in order to be on time for their next activity. P-time is characterized by the simultaneous occurrence of many things and people are put in the forefront.

Time perceptions translate into several differences that affect communication. For instance, people from P-time cultures are used to being interrupted in conversations and, in turn, do not hesitate to interrupt others. Something that is often considered extremely rude in M-time cultures and can offend people (e.g., Quebec people tend to resent Frenchmen for this cultural habit). Conversations between people from M-time cultures are more paced (a little like trains on rails with regular stops of various duration), while conversations in P-time cultures often take new directions abruptly and resemble fireworks.

Inspired from research in leadership and intercultural negotiation, the task/relationship model (see Figure 5.7) captures the interrelation of time and context. Once more, cultures are ranked along an axis presenting a computer at one extreme (to symbolize the emphasis put on "performing the task at hand" in Northern European or North American cultures, for instance) and faces at the other extreme (to symbolize the importance of developing and maintaining strong relationships, such as in Asian or Middle Eastern cultures). A typical manifestation lies in differences in the way people from different cultures handle a phone call to a business partner. In task-oriented cultures, it is perfectly fine to call someone and, after saying hello, jump right into the topic at hand. In relationship-oriented cultures, it would be rude to start off right away and not spend a few minutes (sometimes much more than a few!) inquiring about the health, the family, the weekend activities, or any other topic that shows that one cares and connects on some personal level.

Finally, why does verbal and nonverbal communication matter for marketing in a globalizing context? Communication is a key aspect in business in general. The many activities involved in running a marketing department depend on successful communication. First, communication impacts international relationships between buyers and sellers (B2B and B2C), and thus affects directly entry modes and sales/services. In addition, promotion is particularly sensitive to variations in verbal and nonverbal communication across cultures. Advertising, for instance, requires the use of appropriate cues to which targeted consumers will respond. In the eventuality of failed communication, financial and time investments are lost, and the brand image and corporate reputation can suffer serious damages. Overall, all facets of marketing activities are impacted by communication, with a particular importance on advertising and promotion policies.

5.2.3 *Religion*

Moving on to another important influencing factor, what are the main religions in the world? The main religions in terms of numbers of followers are Christianity,

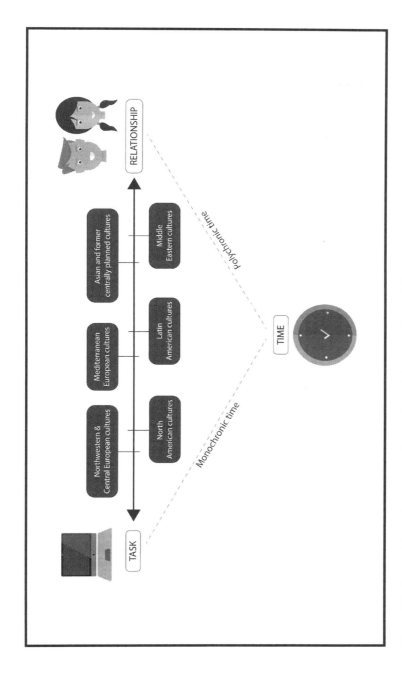

Figure 5.7 Categorizing cultures according to the task/relationship model

Source: Adapted from Schuster and Copeland (1999, p. 65)

156 *Cultural Distance*

Islam, Hinduism, and Buddhism—for more details, see the Pew Forum on Religion & Public Life (2012). Figures 5.8 and 5.9 present their respective symbols, as well as the proportion they represent in the global population.

In a similar fashion as with languages, Figure 5.10 illustrates the fragmentation of the world in terms of religions, with large geographic zones having

Figure 5.8 Symbols of the four most practiced religions in the world: Christianity, Islam, Hinduism, and Buddhism (in this order)

Source: Google Images

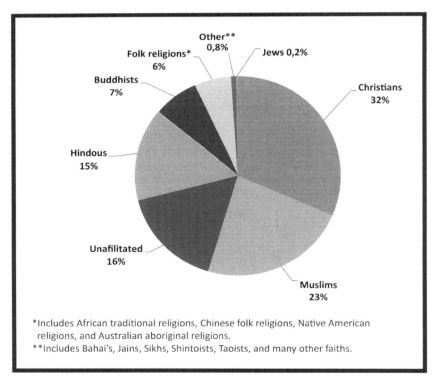

Figure 5.9 Representing the proportion of major religious groups in the global population

Source: Pew Forum on Religion & Public Life (2012)

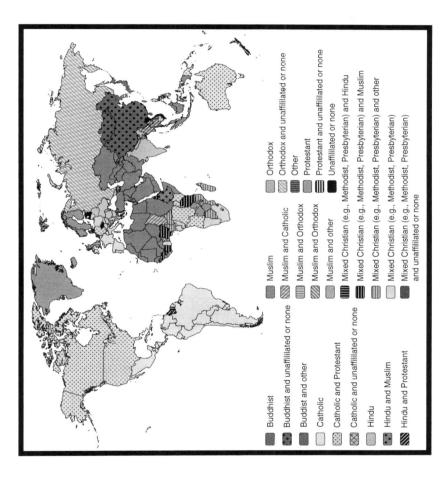

Figure 5.10 Mapping the diversity of religions in the world
Source: Own elaboration based on CIA World Factbook (2016a)
For the color version, see the eResource at www.routledge.com/9781138202344

Figure 5.11 Illustrating religious restrictions on products
Source: Own elaboration

common religions (e.g., Latin America or North Africa and Middle East), while other regions show higher degrees of diversity (e.g., Europe and South-East Asia).

Why does religion matter for marketing decisions in a globalizing context? Religion matters in marketing because it generates many variations between international markets regarding: 1) the type of products that consumers can or cannot purchase (the "what"), 2) the role of individuals in society ("who" buys what), and 3) the timing and contents of various celebrations, holidays, and rituals with an influence on specific product categories ("when" to buy what). An example that illustrates the "timing" of purchases (for consumption and gifts) of specific products is the Muslim celebration of *Aïd El-Fitr*, with dates that are offered generously. Figure 5.11 illustrates different types of beverages and food that people strictly following Hinduism (beef), Catholicism (meat on Fridays during Lent), Islam (alcohol), and Judaism (fish without fins and scales, such as shrimp) would not consume.

Overall, religion affects the roles of individuals in society (which can in turn affect the segmentation, targeting, and positioning process), product and distribution management, and much more (e.g., financing).

Cultural Distance 159

5.2.4 Beliefs, Values, and Norms (Ronen and Shenkar; Hofstede; Schwartz)

What are the differences between values, beliefs, attitudes, and norms? According to Cateora, Gilly, and Graham (2015, p. 120), a *belief* can be defined as "a mental acceptance of and conviction in the truth, actuality, or validity of something." Here, "something" can be anything really: an idea, a fact, an object, etc. According to the same source, a *value* is "an enduring belief that a specific mode of conduct or end-state of existence is personally or socially preferable to an opposite or converse mode of conduct or end-state of existence." Thus, the notion of persistence over time is key to understanding the difference between beliefs and values. Next, an *attitude* is defined as a "mental predisposition to view a particular person, object, or idea in either positive or negative terms." Anecdotally, a positive attitude is symbolized by the "thumbs up" pictogram, made so famous by Facebook. Finally, a *norm* is defined as "a standard of proper or acceptable behavior," according to the online Merriam-Webster dictionary.

On which basis can we group countries and talk about cultural clusters? Ronen and Shenkar (1985) propose to cluster countries based on similar means of communication and common values. As illustrated in Figure 5.12, this work is suggestive of cultural proximity between countries that are either geographically close (e.g., Arab cluster or the European clusters) or, on the contrary, quite distant (e.g., the Anglo cluster which regroups Australia, Canada, Ireland, New Zealand, South Africa, the UK, and the US). In this sense, it grounds Ghemawat's (2001) arguments for the persistence of cultural and administrative links between countries, notably due to colonization. This work also shows the existence of quite a few differences in a relatively small geographic area—Europe—with the coexistence of no less than four clusters (e.g., Anglo, Germanic, Latin, and Nordic).

What do we observe from Figure 5.12? One of the most obvious observations relies on the few countries that cannot be grouped with others. It is interesting to note that two of these "independent" countries, Brazil and India, are large countries, whereas the other two, Israel and Japan, are of more modest sizes. In relation to common values and communication styles, each one of these countries is extremely specific, yet for different reasons. Japan is characterized by high degrees of ethnocentrism and a highly cohesive social system, for instance, whereas religion and language are probably what most distinguish Israel. Brazil also stands alone in the South American continent for language reasons (as a Portuguese- rather than Spanish-speaking country) and because of its African influences due to different migratory patterns. Finally, India is characterized by an unusual variety of ethnic groups and languages. As we have seen previously, it also has a very specific social system based on castes.

If this study had been conducted today, which countries would most likely be included and why? Another interesting observation derives from the countries that were not surveyed in Ronen and Shenkar's (1985) original study. It is likely that Russia and China, as well as Eastern Europe, would now be part of the sample of surveyed countries. Whether for political motives,

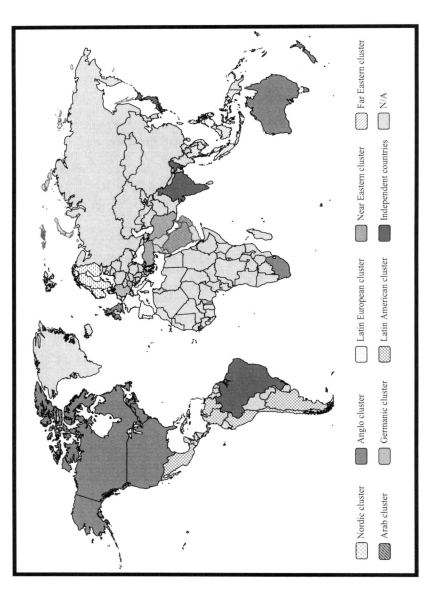

Figure 5.12 Situating cultural clusters

Source: Adapted from Ronen and Shenkar (1985)

For the color version, see the eResource at www.routledge.com/9781138202344

Cultural Distance 161

administrative barriers (i.e., difficulty of accessing information), or lack of interest, several countries were excluded (the vast majority of Africa not being the least). Since then, politics have largely evolved with the opening of these countries to the rest of the world (and to the market economy), administrative barriers have subsided, and economic interests have surged. It is important that, as marketers, we develop the reflex to ponder who conducted the studies we are exposed to and why. Here, the authors, Ronen and Shenkar, worked at New York University and Tel Aviv University, respectively. In a way, their sampling of countries also reflects their interests and possibilities in the mid-1980s. This observation helps us to remember that scientific inquiries are not disconnected from the economic and political landscape at the time they were undertaken.

What are the "work-related dimensions" that help differentiate national cultures? The most widely known and used studies about cultural differences in business are found in Geert Hofstede's work (1980, 2001). Over the past thirty years, Hofstede and colleagues have worked on capturing values or "dimensions" that help to differentiate national cultures. These dimensions include:

- Group orientation (collectivism vs. individualism)
- Power orientation (power respect vs. distribution)
- Uncertainty orientation (uncertainty avoidance vs. acceptance)
- Goal orientation (passive/feminine vs. agressive/masculine)
- Time orientation—added in 1991 (long-term vs. short-term)
- Gratification orientation—added in 2010 (indulgence vs. restraint)

Many resources are available to understand the details of each dimension, in particular Hofstede's personal website: https://geerthofstede.com/. Other resources include Hofstede Insights created in 2017 from a merger between the Hofstede Centre and the consultancy firm ITIM (Institute for Training in Intercultural Management) This website offers a useful tool for comparing national scores for each dimension (select Our models/Country comparison tool). Score differences are all relative and subject to interpretation. Instead of debating about a few points difference, it is more interesting to remember the nature of the proposed continuums or "orientations" when exposed to a new culture.

Why is the study presented in terms of "orientations"? The concept of *orientation* reflects the idea that values are present in all cultures, but to different degrees. Taking the example of the first dimension, *group orientation*, it is possible to conceptually represent this dimension by drawing a continuum between two extremes: on one hand, the group, and on the other hand, the individual. In all cultures, a tension exists between the interests of individuals and the interests of the group (e.g., a company). In some cultures, there will be a clear tendency toward putting more value on the interests of the group, while in other cultures it is socially accepted and even anticipated that the interests of individuals come first. All dimensions can be represented by a continuum in the same way, and opposite values tend to be found at the extremes of these continuums.

162 *Cultural Distance*

How useful is this study? Overall, Hofstede's work-related research has been criticized for a number of methodological issues and for inappropriate generalizations (cf. Kirkman, Lowe, & Gibson, 2006). Nevertheless, work is ongoing and the core dimensions are extremely useful to marketers because they give matter for reflecting on cultures as well as a strong basis to compare them. Indeed, we often want to learn about foreign consumers' culture, but it is such a vast topic that it is sometimes hard to know where to start and what to inquire about, beyond the usual food and musical traditions. How well regarded is it to value individual over collective interests, short-term over long-term projects, assertiveness over modesty, etc.? On the basis of the proposed Hofstede dimensions, these questions and many more allow us to gain a deeper understanding of other national cultures in a work context. In addition, recent work by Beugelsdijk, Maseland, and Hoorn (2015) examines how country scores on Hofstede's dimensions have developed over time. Results indicated that contemporary societies do score differently compared with the 1970s when data was initially collected by Hofstede (e.g., higher scores on individualism and indulgence and lower scores on power distance), but that countries' scores relative to the scores of other countries had not changed significantly. Thus, cultural differences between countries seem generally stable over time.

However, it is central to use Hofstede's dimensions in a meaningful manner. Some dimensions may be more or less relevant, depending on the type of decisions they aim to inform (e.g., choice of entry mode, AdaptStand decisions for promotion, sales, and services), or the type of business and industry, for instance. It is strongly recommended to carefully analyze the applicability of each dimension according to the matter at hand before using Hofstede's country scores.

Are there any follow-up studies to Hofstede's work-related dimensions? A recent extension of cultural dimensions in the workplace is proposed in the GLOBE (Global Leadership and Organizational Behavior Effectiveness) study (House, Hanges, Javidan, Dorfman, & Gupta, 2004). This research program was conceived in 1991 by Robert J. House of the Wharton School (University of Pennsylvania, US), and 170 co-investigators based in sixty-two different cultures helped to collect data from 17,300 middle managers in 951 organizations (Wikipedia, 2014a). Their approach builds upon Hofstede's (1980) research findings and looks into the following cultural dimensions: power distance, uncertainty avoidance, collectivism (institutional), collectivism (in-group), gender egalitarianism, future orientation, humane orientation, assertiveness, and performance orientation. One aspect that differs from the Hofstede approach is that the GLOBE study measures both cultural values and beliefs (i.e., how things "should be") and cultural practices (i.e., how things "actually are").

Finally, what is another well-known theory used to measure cultural distance based on values? One of the prominent theories is the *universal values theory* proposed by Shalom Schwartz (1992). Schwartz is a social psychologist, now retired from academic positions in psychology and sociology departments in the US and Israel (Wikipedia, 2017e). Table 5.2 classifies ten values that can be considered universal, but which importance will vary depending on culture. Here, they are presented in alphabetical order, but the original theory tested a circumplex structure because the items that operationalize each value occupied a distinct region—with no substantial empty

Cultural Distance   163

Table 5.2 Classifying universal values

Motivational Types of Values	Items
Power	
Social status and prestige, control or dominance over people and resources.	Authority, social power, wealth, preserving my public image.
Achievement	
Personal success through demonstrating competence according to social standards.	Ambitious, successful, capable, influential.
Hedonism	
Pleasure or sensuous gratification for oneself.	Pleasure, enjoying life, self-indulgent.
Stimulation	
Excitement, novelty, and challenge in life.	Daring, a varied life, an exciting life.
Self-direction	
Independent thought and action—choosing, creating, exploring.	Creativity, freedom, independent, choosing own goals, curious.
Universalism	
Understanding, appreciation, tolerance, and protection for the welfare of all people and for nature.	Equality, social justice, wisdom, broadminded, protecting the environment, unity with nature, a world of beauty.
Benevolence	
Preservation and enhancement of the welfare of people with whom one is in frequent personal contact.	Helpful, honest, forgiving, loyal, responsible.
Tradition	
Respect, commitment, and acceptance of the customs and ideas that traditional culture or religion provide.	Devout, respect for tradition, humble, moderate.
Conformity	
Restraint of actions, inclinations, and impulses likely to upset or harm others and violate social expectations or norms.	Self-discipline, politeness, honoring parents and elders, obedience.
Security	
Safety, harmony, and stability of society, of relationships, and of self.	Family security, national security, social order, clean, reciprocation of favors.

Source: Adapted from Schwartz and Boehnke (2004, p. 239)

spaces between regions—in the plotting space when conducting statistical analyses (Schwartz & Boehnke, 2004). There are four of these regions or "higher-order type" of values: openness to change (self-direction and stimulation values), conservation (conformity, tradition, and security values), self-enhancement (achievement and power values) and self-transcendence

164   *Cultural Distance*

(benevolence and universalism values). According to Schwartz and Boehnke (2004, p. 236), *openness to change* forms a bipolar dimension with *conservation* in a way that captures "the extent to which these values motivate people to follow their own emotional and intellectual interests in unpredictable and uncertain directions (openness) versus to preserve the status quo and the certainty it provides (conservation)." In turn, *self-enhancement* forms a bipolar dimension with *self-transcendence* in a way that captures "the extent to which they motivate people to enhance their own personal interests even at the expense of others (self-enhancement) versus to transcend selfish concerns and promote the welfare of others, close and distant, and of nature (self-transcendence). Hedonism values share some elements of both openness and self-enhancement. Consequently, hedonism is located between these two higher-order types."

5.3 *Central Role of Behaviors*

This section aims to develop our understanding of the central role of beliefs and values in influencing attitudes and ultimately in determining behaviors. In turn, understanding differences in behaviors is key to understanding the impact of cultural distance in marketing. Questions raised include:

- How do beliefs, values, attitudes, and norms relate to individuals' behaviors?
- Why is it important in marketing to consider differences in beliefs and values across countries?

5.3.1 *Theory of Reasoned Action/Planned Behavior (Fishbein and Ajzen)*

How do beliefs, values, attitudes, and norms relate to individuals' behaviors? A well-known theory, the *theory of reasoned action*—later developed into the *theory of planned behavior*—explains how behaviors develop from intentions that are determined by attitudes, which in turn derive from a combination of beliefs and norms (Ajzen & Fishbein, 1980; Fishbein & Ajzen, 1975, 2010). Beliefs are, thus, central in understanding differences in attitudes and behaviors across cultures. Figure 5.13 presents a simplification of the reasoned action model. It captures the idea that "people are said to perform a behavior because they intend to do so, they have the prerequisite skills and abilities, and there are no environmental constraints to prevent them from carrying out their intentions (i.e., they have favorable intentions and actual behavioral control)" (Fishbein & Ajzen, 2010, p. 21). An array of background factors at the level of individuals, society, and access to information influences the formation of *behavioral* (e.g., "Eating healthy foods will enable me to lower my cholesterol"), *normative* (e.g., "My partner expects me to eat more healthy foods"), and *control* beliefs (e.g., "I can afford to buy healthy food"). In turn, these beliefs influence the attitude toward the behavior (e.g., "I like eating healthy foods") and perceptions about the norm and behavioral control (e.g., "I should and I can eat healthy foods"). An

Cultural Distance 165

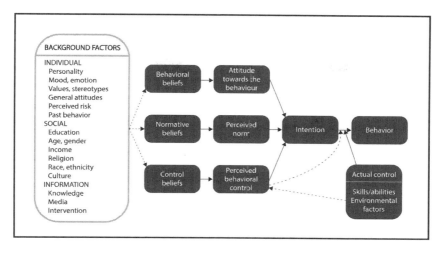

Figure 5.13 Presenting the reasoned action model
Source: Fishbein and Ajzen (2010, p. 22)

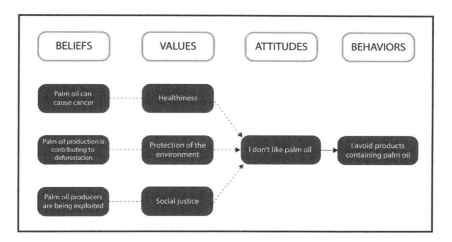

Figure 5.14 Illustrating the process through which values help translate beliefs into attitudes and behaviors
Source: Own elaboration

intention is formed (e.g., "I intend on eating healthy foods for lunch today"), which is transformed into a behavior (e.g., "I am eating healthy foods at the cafeteria right now"), depending on the degree of actual control (e.g., "My boss insisted that we skipped lunch instead").

Figure 5.14 provides a simple example of the process through which values also help translate beliefs into attitudes and behaviors. In this example,

166 *Cultural Distance*

three beliefs about palm oil turn into a negative attitude toward palm oil when filtered through the values of healthiness, protection of the environment, and social justice. In turn, a negative attitude translates into a behavior that consists of avoiding purchasing products containing palm oil (e.g., Nutella). Interestingly, beliefs can be of an opposite nature (e.g., palm oil is a source of vitamins, palm oil is increasingly harvested in a sustainable manner, and palm oil production is an important source of revenues for local farmers), and when filtered through the same values (or different ones, such as pleasure) lead to a positive attitude about palm oil. The corresponding behavior is seeking to consume products containing palm oil.

Usunier and Lee (2005) propose a synthetic model representing the impact of cultural dynamics within persons, on interactions between persons, and finally on people's attitude toward action. In this model, basic assumptions on the nature of reality relate to time and space perceptions—*space* being a notion related to social space and not geographical space, meaning for instance the notion of in-group and out-group (i.e., who belongs to a social circle), as well as to the conceptualization of the self and others. This model relies on the same principles that link beliefs to behaviors. Assumptions or beliefs "within persons" (about the self-concept, time, and space) affect interactions between persons, which in turn affect the attitude toward actions from persons and their behavior in the world.

Why is it important in marketing to consider differences in beliefs and values across countries? It is fundamental because they impact individuals' attitudes and behaviors, which include purchasing, re-purchasing, product evaluation, willingness-to-pay, recommendations to others through word-of-mouth, etc. In marketing, we aim to influence individual and organizational behavior. In other words, we invite end-consumers or industrial buyers (e.g., distributors or retailers) to try out a product/service and then buy it for the first time, purchase it over and over again, prefer it against competing offerings, recommend it to others, etc. In order to influence behaviors, marketers thus have no choice but to understand beliefs, values, and norms, and eventually to work at changing existing beliefs or promoting new values.

Examples of companies relying on belief and value differences across countries to advertise their understanding of cultural distance include the bank HSBC, which had an impactful advertising campaign and positioning as "The world's local bank" (2002–2011). Examples of videos are available on YouTube with the search keywords: "HSBC Culture Difference Personal Space."

Moreover, the reasoned action theory suggests that intention is the best single predictor of behavior (Fishbein & Ajzen, 2010). This detail is central since, up until recently, marketers could more easily measure consumers' intention (e.g., with surveys) rather than actual behavior. However, this is evolving fast with the development of "Big Data" capability building which increasingly allows companies to better monitor consumers' behaviors (e.g., purchases and recommendations) in real time.

Cultural Distance 167

5.4 Issues at Stake

This section aims to raise the following questions:

- Is cultural distance decreasing? Are we heading toward cultural convergence?
- Do we have a good grasp on cultural distance? What are the points of contention in academic studies about measuring cultural distance?
- What is the impact of cultural distance on marketing decisions in an international context?

5.4.1 Cultural Convergence

Is cultural distance increasing or decreasing worldwide? This question is an enduring one, as it was raised as early as in Webber (1969). To this day, it remains a particularly challenging one. To examine this question, we turn to Ralston and colleagues, who have worked on the concepts of convergence, divergence and crossvergence (see "Food for Thought").

Food for Thought 5.2

- In reference to Ralston (2008), can we conclude that cultural convergence is happening?

According to Ralston, Gustafson, Cheung, and Terpstra (1993, p. 251), *convergence* is captured by the idea that "managers in industrialized nations will embrace the attitudes and behaviors common to managers in other industrialized nations despite cultural differences," *divergence* by the fact that "individuals will retain diverse, culturally based values despite any economic and social similarities between their nations" and finally, *crossvergence* is the notion that "when two cultures meet, a blending may result in some new cross-bred form of values." According to their work, two main factors drive the way values evolve overtime: sociocultural influences and business ideology influences (which regroup economic, political, and technological influences).

In a subsequent study, Ralston (2008) reports on prior work on the evolution of values comparing the US, Russia, Japan, and China over a little more than a decade (1989–2001). As illustrated in Table 5.3, the US and Russia were chosen for being representative of Western cultures (individual-oriented culture) and China and Japan for being representative of Eastern cultures (group-oriented culture). In terms of business ideology, the US and Japan were considered representative of capitalism (individual-oriented business ideology), while Russia and China were deemed representative of socialism (group-oriented business ideology).

168 Cultural Distance

Table 5.3 Illustrating mixed evidence for the convergence of cultural values

Evolution Between 1989 and 2001	Values Dimensions
Convergence	• Integration
Crossvergence	• Confucian work dynamism • *Human-heartedness* • *Locus of control* • *Intolerance of ambiguity* • *Moral discipline*
Divergence	• Dogmatism • Machiavellianism

Source: Adapted from Ralston (2008)

The values under investigation were: integration (i.e., tolerance for others), human-heartedness (i.e., compassion toward others), Machiavellianism (i.e., willingness to use social power), locus of control (i.e., feeling of self-control), Confucian work dynamism (i.e., search for virtue and need to order relationships by status and respect the order established by status), moral discipline (i.e., moderation, prudence, and adaptability), intolerance of ambiguity (i.e., ability to function and make decisions in uncertain environments), and, finally, dogmatism (i.e., inflexibility and lack of openness to new ideas). In this study, Ralston (2008) highlights the coexistence of convergence, divergence, and crossvergence, depending on the values under examination. Table 5.3 illustrates the diversity of their findings and the impossibility to have a definite answer about convergence of values (i.e., the reduction of cultural distance in terms of values).

Other studies display similarly ambiguous results. For instance, De Mooij and Hofstede (2002) investigate degrees of convergence in various European countries in terms of consumption habits for eighteen different products and services. They find that only five product categories (i.e., television sets, telephone mainlines, automobiles, cleaning products, and soft drinks) seemed to evolve toward similar consumption patterns.

Not only is the phenomenon of cultural convergence a challenge to measure scientifically, but the available results nuance drastically the assumption that cultures in general are becoming more similar, and that cultural distance is generally decreasing worldwide. This does not imply that specific segments of the population across countries could not be converging in terms of their consumption habits (e.g., Generation Y and Z), yet more academic studies are needed to establish this as a fact.

5.4.2 Points of Contention in Assessing Cultural Distance

Do we have a good grasp on cultural distance? Cultural differences across countries have received intense scrutiny for several decades now. Still, experts such as Oded Shenkar question the methods used and results obtained.

Transposed to the context of marketing, do you think that the concept of "distance" is misleading when studying the impact of cultures? (see "Food for Thought").

Food for Thought 5.3

- In reference to Shenkar (2012), what are the points of contention in academic studies about assessing cultural distance? Do you agree that, in the context of marketing, the concept of "distance" might be misleading when studying the impact of cultures?

5.4.3 Impact on Marketing Decisions With Corporate Examples: Disney, HSBC, Ikea, Kellogg's, Microsoft, McDonald's, Pinterest, and Starbucks

To what extent does cultural distance impact marketers' decisions in an international context? Cultural distance affects all aspects of marketing in international settings. Because of the weight that cultural distance has in creating psychic distance, market selection is highly impacted. Because of the challenges in understanding foreign environments and future partners, entry modes are also highly impacted by cultural distance (e.g., negotiation with governments to establish a greenfield investment or with partners in the context of a joint-venture). Targeting and positioning may need to be adapted as cultures assign different roles and designate different behaviors to specific groups (e.g., according to age and gender). At the tactical level, pricing, distribution, and promotion – without forgetting the very definition and design of products, services, and brands – are all affected by differences in culture. A few of the hundreds of available corporate examples are presented below, adding to or complementing those proposed in Chapter 3 (internationalization background is provided only for the examples that have not been previously introduced). These examples also illustrate cultural adaptation for different marketing activities; can you tell which ones (i.e., market selection, entry modes, targeting/positioning, and the 4/7Ps) (see "Food for Thought")?

Food for Thought 5.4

- Among the examples listed below (and others that you may have heard of), which marketing activities are mostly impacted by cultural distance?

Disney[1]—The Walt Disney Company has put Chinese culture at the center of its Shanghai Disneyland (opened in 2016). First, the company sent teams around China researching ways to incorporate Chinese cultural elements. It

170   Cultural Distance

also hired Chinese architects and designers, with Disney Chief Executive Bob Iger reportedly saying that the resort would be "authentically Disney and distinctly Chinese." Other cultural adaptation included a large garden—instead of the traditional "Main Street U.S.A."—which featured Disney versions of the Chinese Zodiac animals. In this garden, a sizeable glass sculpture of a peony blossom—a symbol of good fortune and majesty—is presented at the center of a fountain. Due to China's former one-child policy (ended in 2015), extended families often travel together with few children (e.g., four adults for every child). To adapt to this situation, the company designed more viewing areas in open spaces and more seating space in restaurants (as Chinese adults seem to enjoy live entertainment perhaps more than rides, and linger longer over meals). Having learned its lesson from its first year of operations in Hong Kong, Disney offers in Shanghai a mobile phone app for visitors allowing them to receive updates on waiting times and warnings if the park is at capacity.

HSBC[2]—A major global bank, HSBC (UK) has attempted to adapt to the religious preferences of its Muslim consumers, not only abroad (e.g., Indonesia, Malaysia, and several of its Middle East markets) but also at home. In 2003, it started offering Sharia-compliant home financing products through HSBC Amanah.

The Sharia is a set of religious principles that form the basis of Islamic law. In this legal system, charging interest on lent money is not permitted, because it is deemed unfair. Instead, Islamic banks make money through profit or rent on three types of Home Purchase Plans: *Ijara* (i.e., "lease" in Arabic), *Musharaka* ("partnership"), and *Murabaha* ("profit"). An *Ijara* is a lease-to-own plan (i.e., the bank purchases the property the customer wants and leases it out to the customer; when the term is over, the bank transfers ownership to the customer). Under a *Musharaka* plan, the customer purchases the property jointly with the bank and gradually buys the bank out of it. In a *Murabaha* plan, the bank buys the property and sells it right away to the customer with a profit margin (the customer then pays fixed monthly repayments but with no interest to pay back). Islamic banking is growing globally at a fast rate (e.g., owned assets globally were estimated to be ~800 billion USD in 2010 and 1.1 trillion USD only two years later).

Despite important growth perspectives, HSBC Amanah pulled out from six of its markets in 2012 (Bahrain, Bangladesh, Indonesia, Mauritius, Singapore, the United Arab Emirates, and the UK), only maintaining Sharia-compliant offerings in Malaysia and Saudi Arabia. This decision followed a strategic review of operations around the world (which also led to abandoning about twenty mainstream retail banking markets with poor performance). Indeed, growth and profits are two different things. Costs and competition could explain this step back. First, many Islamic financial products come with higher charges because of complex structuring and legal overheads, thus reducing profits. Second, the increasing presence of Islamic banks in the UK (e.g., Ahli United Bank and United National Bank)—as well as in other countries, such as Noorassur in France which opened in 2015—added to the strong foothold of local players (e.g., Saudi Al Rajhi Bank, Kuwait Finance House, and Dubai Islamic Bank) might make it too difficult for international banks like HSBC to be profitable in Islamic retail banking.

Cultural Distance   171

IKEA[3]—Opening its first store in India at the end of 2017, IKEA hopes to appeal to younger generations that shop for furniture differently than older generations. This may explain their market selection choice of the southern city of Hyderabad as its first store location, since it is home to some four hundred thousand IT professionals—all young, wealthy, and well travelled. In the past, furniture in India was considered an investment, like gold and silver. It was typically offered during weddings, had to be heavy and ornate to convey value, and lasted for decades. Although young Indians seem more open to self-assembly than do their parents, IKEA might have to implement a similar strategy as in China where the company offers home delivery and furniture assembly, since the DIY concept was hard to accept there. To prepare for its foray into India, the company conducted primary data collection and visited more than five hundred homes in Hyderabad, with questions related to what people wanted: "We see their bedrooms, toilets, kitchens, and then we sit down and then we talk. And then we ask: 'What would you like to change?'"

Kellogg's[4]—The Kellogg Company or Kellogg's (US) manufactures food products (e.g., cereals, cookies, and crackers) in about eighteen countries and has a commercial presence in more than one hundred and eighty countries. When it entered India in 1994, it encountered significant cultural hurdles. Indeed, the company launched a brand of unsweetened crispy flakes—that would go soggy when consumed with hot milk and that would not allow added sugar to dissolve properly when consumed with cold milk, while the local habits were to consume milk hot and sweetened. The offering of a dish that was bland, sweet, and cold was also the opposite of Indian consumers' habit of consuming varied, substantial, spicy and hot foods for breakfast (e.g., buttery fried *parathas* and deep-fried *vadas*, with chutneys and pickles). Since then, Kelloggs' has adapted its product offering (e.g., with Frosties, already sweetened flakes), the range of product sizes (e.g., individual packs), its pricing as well as promotion (to reposition the cereals as a fun choice rather than just a nutritious one). This has been a winning strategy and the company now benefits from a substantial market share of the Indian market.

In other locations, Kellogg's broadcasts interesting commercials with varying degrees of cultural adaptation. One example of a TV spot where standardization is high (e.g., similar scripts, layout, and actors' clothing) and only a few localization elements are implemented (i.e., language translation and humor) is for the brand All Bran. Videos available on YouTube with search word "ALL BRAN ® FibraRica" (posted in 2009) for the version in Spanish, and "All-Bran Commercial" (posted in 2007) for the version in Australian English show the same role play. A young man is being interviewed by an older and rigorous-looking man equipped with a lie detector. The choice of actors for the young man reflects some localization effort: brown-haired for the Latin character and blond-haired for the Australian character but both in their twenties/early thirties, with an apparent "cool" attitude. Questioned about their eating habits and opinions of All Bran, the young men try to, but cannot, lie (due to the detector) about finding All Bran delicious. However, humor elements are adapted as both young men want to conclude the interview by pretending they need to go

172 *Cultural Distance*

and do something else: the lie detector reveals that the Latin character needs to pick up his mother and not his girlfriend, as initially pretended, while the Australian character needs to go and wax his chest and not his surfboard, as he first claimed. Another example, this time a highly adapted execution of a TV spot, is found in the "Detox challenge" (while the message stays the same: "eat All Bran for ten days and you will feel better"). Videos on YouTube show entirely different scripts, choice of actors, and settings for US, Australian, and French-speaking audiences. They are respectively available with search words "All-Bran Construction Worker" (posted in 2007), "Kellogg's All Bran ad by JWT Sydney" (posted in 2009), and "Kellogg's All-Bran Detox Challenge" (posted in 2007). Interestingly, the degree of abstraction used to mention digestive improvements varies in a rather obvious manner, with the US and Australian versions being far more explicit than the French-speaking version. This can be explained by the low/high-context approach, previously explained in this chapter. For instance, the actors in the Australian version, playing the role of a happily married couple, directly refer to some "sit downs" making them feel much better with the All Bran challenge. By contrast, the version in French depicts a woman walking in the city streets with random things clinging onto her (e.g., a pan, a Christmas tree, and many other junk items) and making her slow down. With the All Bran challenge, she is suddenly liberated from all this dragging weight: a rather elaborate, poetic, and visually sophisticated way to implicitly refer to bowel movements.

Microsoft[5]—Microsoft and other global technology companies (e.g., Adobe, Apple, Google, IBM, Mozilla, and Oracle) all take steps to ensure their products are not culturally misunderstood when developing software applications and websites for international audiences. For instance, Microsoft recalls that in early user interfaces, the rural mail box used to indicate mail was not well received outside of the US: "When the image was introduced in Europe, most people wanted to know what a breadbox sitting on a pole had to do with mail. A much better choice would have been – and still is – using an outline of a postal letter, since most people who understand the concept of mail would understand this image." Regarding the use of images and visuals across cultures, the Apache Open Office's globalization guide (from the Apache Software Foundation) also states that: "The problem with human figures is manifold: is it female or male, what is it wearing, what color is its skin and hair, what position is the body in, what is the figure doing? Obviously in some cultures, certain types of dress are inappropriate, whereas they are standard in other cultures. People of one sex may not be allowed to perform certain tasks in some cultures, but in others they are the primary performers of these tasks. In different parts of the world, people identify with different skin and hair color on the figures. The only acceptable human figure is a stick figure with no clothes, no hands with fingers, and no hair. With body parts, the difficulty lies not only in which body part is being represented, but what position it is in, where it is cut off, and how it is cut off. Hands—don't even try. There's not a hand position around which isn't offensive somewhere."

Cultural Distance   173

McDonald's[6]—This company is known to support its foreign expansion with research and investment in products adapted to local tastes. In countries so diverse as India, cultural differences are not only analyzed at the country level, but also at the regional level. Since Big Macs were never going to succeed in a country where 80 percent of the population do not eat beef, the company decided to conduct in-depth analyses in several states. For instance, in states where most people are vegetarian, like Gujarat, it offered vegetarian burgers and other Indian dishes (e.g., samosas). By contrast, it introduced meat burgers for non-beef eaters in New Delhi, like the Maharaja Mac, with lamb or chicken.

Pinterest[7]—A web and mobile application best described as "the world's catalog of ideas" or an "online bulletin board for images of fashion, food, and furniture," Pinterest (US) was launched in different phases from 2009–2011. It started its international expansion as early as 2012 and was expected to have to shift from a largely female, Midwestern-skewing audience to different user niches in each new market. Although the choice of Japan as its first foreign market made sense because of customers' high interest in social media, it initially raised questions about the cultural interest in DIY. Indeed, the platform was largely used in its home market to post home improvement and design inspirations, but home renting is more common in Japan and housing units tend to be much smaller, suggesting that people might not find the app as useful. Later on, Pinterest seemed to appeal to a different audience in France (i.e., urban early adopters with a balance in terms of gender), while in Brazil there was a risk of incompatibility, since people appeared to be more interested in what their friends were doing instead of looking at images that would only reflect what they liked. The company put great effort into better localizing the search for images. Indeed, too much American content could deter foreign users. For instance, when a British person looked for "food" and "chips" in the early stages of expansion, they were likely to find an image of a Lay's potato chip bag, while they were expecting to see steak fries. Pinterest had to surface pins from British websites first, so that people could find images that matched their cultural expectations. Another example of localization is the addition of the category "Featured Collections," which tailors content to each country (e.g., recipes from local celebrity chefs and the latest merchandise from local retailers) for users in Brazil, France, Germany, Japan, and the UK. In 2016, Pinterest seemed to have managed the localization challenge with more than half of its 100 million monthly active users located overseas.

Starbucks[8]—In China, the company implemented a unique multimillion-dollar program for its forty thousand employees: the extension of health coverage to their parents. Indeed, Starbucks had noticed an increasing number of requests for financial assistance from employees to help cover parents' health costs and employee surveys found that 70 percent of workers were concerned about the health of their elderly parents. This program is a response to traditional Chinese values where children often care for their parents and grandparents. In addition, it is a strategic move to retain employees and create goodwill toward the company at a time of increasing political tensions between the US and China.

174   *Cultural Distance*

Conclusion: Cultural Distance Matters Because It Prevents Companies from Understanding and Influencing Different Behaviors. Its Evolution Over Time Escapes Our Grasp

What would a nomological network for cultural distance look like? A *nomological network* has been defined as the representation of the constructs of interest in a study, their observable manifestations and the interrelationships among and between them (Cronbach & Meehl, 1955). Figure 5.15 captures important variables when it comes to cultural distance and marketing. In the center of the proposed nomological network, cultural distance is positioned as the phenomenon under scrutiny. On its left-hand side, we find the above-mentioned drivers of cultural distance at the country-level of analysis. On the right-hand side, the figure reflects the overall impact of cultural distance on all AdaptStand decisions, i.e., on the degree to which companies need to adapt to cultural preferences or can standardize their marketing activities across markets.

So, **why does cultural distance matter for marketing decisions in a globalizing context?** In this chapter, we have exposed that cultural distance represents the degree of dissimilarity in the sociocultural environment between the home- and foreign-country. Central to cultural distance is the variety of behaviors of people across the world. These behaviors are driven by factors such as beliefs, values, and norms stemming from different social organization, religion, and ways of communicating. In all, cultural distance matters because it prevents companies from understanding and influencing behaviors of foreign consumers and business partners. As marketers, our role is indeed to offer an attractive product/service (at the right price and with easy access through efficient distribution), but also to influence whenever possible the psychological processes associated with buying (in the pre-purchase, purchase, and post-purchase phases) through promotion. Whether to create awareness, encourage trial, inform about a benefit, create an image, remind, or reassure consumers, communicating with clients is key. Since culture is pervasive to all human actions, it has a tremendous influence on marketing activities at both the strategic and tactical levels. Simply put, the key issue for marketers when looking at foreign markets from the angle of cultural distance is then: **"understanding and influencing behaviors"** (see Figure 5.15).

Cultural distance has a strong impact on marketing activities, but is it decreasing at all? A short answer would be: "Yes, absolutely, and . . . no, too hard to say." Again, this question suggests a nuanced answer, since stories of corporate success abroad and reports by the media of increasing cultural convergence clash with scientific studies trying to prove the phenomenon. Indeed, rigorous investigation into measuring whether cultural distance diminishes at the global scale has been confronted with significant conceptual and methodological issues. In terms of values and behaviors, studies and examples covered in this chapter indicate the coexistence of convergence ("yes, cultural distance is shrinking"), divergence ("no, cultural distance is actually increasing"), and crossvergence ("neither increasing or decreasing,

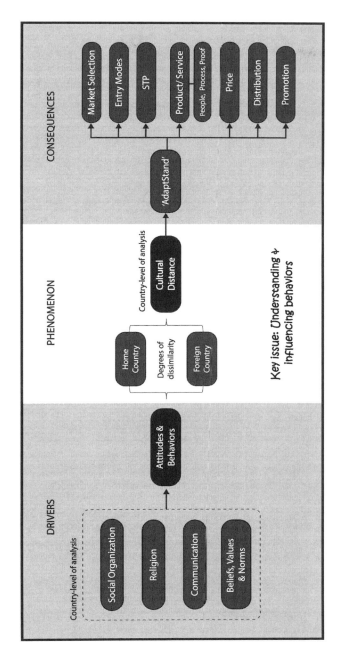

Figure 5.15 Proposing a nomological network for cultural distance
Source: Own elaboration

176 *Cultural Distance*

just evolving due to the combination of cultures into something new"). Perhaps the evolution over time of the phenomenon is just too complex for us to entirely grasp.

The take-away here is that marketers cannot assume anything. Obviously, behaviors evolve in, for instance, many emerging markets that are showing "occidentalization" or "westernization" patterns in people's consumption habits. By contrast, innovation also stems from the developing world and diffuses to the developed world, as we will later see in Chapter 9. With the adoption of these innovative products and services, cultures in the developed world are also likely to significantly evolve in the decades to come. Economic, technological, and political influences, combined with sociocultural influences, are driving changes in values (e.g., Ralston, 2008), and, consequently, in behaviors. Thus, marketers must humbly do their cultural homework and be ready to be surprised either way: in the enthusiastic adoption of offerings far from cultural traditions or in the fierce resistance against it. Being well informed and prepared to invest overtime is key to succeed in overcoming or adjusting to cultural distance.

Notes

1 Disney example is based on: Los Angeles Times (2016); UV 7197 (2016).
2 HSBC example is based on: Financial Times (2012); Huffington Post (2015); The Guardian (2008).
3 IKEA example is based on: BBC News (2016); Burt, Johansson, and Thelander (2011).
4 Kellogg's example is based on: Translate Media (2015); Usunier and Lee (2009, Chapter 13).
5 Microsoft example is based on: Apache Open Office (2017); Deseret News (2013); Microsoft (2017).
6 McDonald's example is based on: Financial Times (2010).
7 Pinterest example is based on: Advertising Age (2012); Fortune (2016); Recode (2015).
8 Starbucks example is based on: Bloomberg (2017).

References

Advertising Age (2012, June 15th). How Pinterest Must Adapt to Conquer Global Markets, *By Cotton Delo*. Retrieved from http://adage.com/article/global-news/pinterest-adapt-conquer-global-markets/235202/
Ajzen, Icek & Fishbein, Martin (1980). *Understanding Attitudes and Predicting Social Behavior*. Englewood Cliffs: Prentice-Hall (p. 278).
Albaum, Gerald, Duerr, Edwin & Josiassen, Alexander (2016). *International Marketing and Export Management* (8th ed.). Harlow: Pearson Education Limited (p. 744).
Apache Open Office (2017). Globalization in Software Design. Retrieved May 2017, from www.openoffice.org/specs/collaterals/guides/I18n_in_Software.html#mozTocId574537
Asia Society (2014). Social Stratification in India. By Donald Johnson and John Johnson. Retrieved October 2014, from http://asiasociety.org/countries/traditions/social-stratification-india

Cultural Distance 177

BBC News (2016, August 12th). IKEA Paves Way for First Indian Store. Retrieved from www.bbc.com/news/business-37057254

Berreman, Gerald (1972). Race, Caste, and Other Invidious Distinctions in Social Stratification. *Race*, *13*(4), 385–414.

Beugelsdijk, Sjoerd, Maseland, Robbert & Hoorn, André (2015). Are Scores on Hofstede's Dimensions of National Culture Stable Over Time? A Cohort Analysis. *Global Strategy Journal*, *5*(3), 223–240.

Bloomberg (2017, April 11th). Starbucks Extends China Health Coverage to Workers' Parents, *With Assistance by Rachel Chang and Hui Li*. Retrieved from www.bloomberg.com/news/articles/2017-04-11/starbucks-offers-health-insurance-for-parents-of-chinese-workers

Burt, Steve, Johansson, Ulf & Thelander, Åsa (2011). Standardized Marketing Strategies in Retailing? IKEA's Marketing Strategies in Sweden, the UK and China. *Journal of Retailing and Consumer Services*, *18*(3), 183–193.

Cateora, Philip, Gilly, Mary & Graham, John (2015). *International Marketing* (17th ed.). New York: McGraw-Hill/Irwin (p. 704).

Causa, Orsetta & Johansson, Åsa (2010). Intergenerational Social Mobility in OECD Countries. Organisation for Economic Co-operation and Development. www.oecd.org/eco/labour/49849281.pdf

CIA World Factbook (2016a). Field Listing: Religions. Retrieved October 2016, from www.cia.gov/library/publications/the-world-factbook/fields/2122.html

CIA World Factbook (2016b). Field Listing: Languages. Retrieved June 2016, from www.cia.gov/library/publications/the-world-factbook/fields/2098.html

Corak, Miles (2016). *Inequality From Generation to Generation: The US in Comparison*. Discussion Paper Series, No. 9929. Institute for the Study of Labor. Retrieved from http://ftp.iza.org/dp9929.pdf

Cronbach, Lee Joseph & Meehl, Paul (1955). Construct Validity in Psychological Tests. *Psychological Bulletin*, *52*(4), 281–302.

De Mooij, Marieke & Hofstede, Geert (2002). Convergence and Divergence in Consumer Behavior: Implications for International Retailing. *Journal of Retailing*, *78*(1), 61–69.

Deseret News (2013, June 7th). Top 10 Cultural Adaptation Tips from Technology Giants, *By Adam Wooten*. Retrieved from www.deseretnews.com/top/1554/0/Top-10-cultural-adaptation-tips-from-technology-giants.html

Dow, Douglas & Karunaratna, Amal (2006). Developing a Multidimensional Instrument to Measure Psychic Distance Stimuli. *Journal of International Business Studies*, *37*(5), 578–602.

Financial Times (2010, July 19th). Navigating Cultural Differences, *By Emma Jacobs*. Retrieved from www.ft.com/content/f3e2f464-937e-11df-bb9a-00144feab49a

Financial Times (2012, October 7th). HSBC's Islamic Closures Highlight Dilemma, *By Patrick Jenkins and Camilla Hall*. Retrieved from www.ft.com/content/bdb5f212-0f1c-11e2-9343-00144feabdc0

Fishbein, Martin & Ajzen, Icek (1975). *Belief, Attitude, Intention, and Behavior: An Introduction to Theory and Research*. Reading: Addison-Wesley (p. 578).

Fishbein, Martin & Ajzen, Icek (2010). *Predicting and Changing Behavior—The Reasoned Action Approach*. New York: Taylor and Francis (p. 538).

Fortune (2016, April 27th). Pinterest Crosses Key Milestone In Quest To Be a Truly Global Business, *By Kia Kokalitcheva* Retrieved from http://fortune.com/2016/04/28/pinterest-international-users/

178 Cultural Distance

Ghemawat, Pankaj (2001). Distance Still Matters: The Hard Reality of Global Expansion. *Harvard Business Review*, 79(8), 137–147.

Goodenough, Ward (1971). *Culture, Language and Society*. Reading: Modular Publications (p. 134).

Griffin, Ricky & Pustay, Michael (2015). *International Business* (8th ed.). New Jersey: Pearson (p. 624).

The Guardian (2008, June 29th). Sharia-Compliant Mortgages Are Here—And They're Not Just for Muslims, *By Huma Qureshi*. Retrieved from www.theguardian.com/money/2008/jun/29/mortgages.islam

Hall, Edward (1959). *The Silent Language*. New York: Doubleday and Company (p. 240).

Hall, Edward (1983). *The Dance of Life: The Other Dimension of Time*. New York: Anchor Press/Doubleday and Company (p. 250).

Hall, Edward & Hall, Mildred (1990). *Understanding Cultural Differences*. Yarmouth: Intercultural Press (p. 193).

Hofstede, Geert (1980). *Culture's Consequences: International Differences in Work-Related Values*. Beverly Hills: SAGE Publications (p. 328).

Hofstede, Geert (2001). *Culture's Consequences: Comparing Values, Behaviors, Institutions and Organizations Across Nations* (2nd ed.). Thousand Oaks: SAGE Publications (p. 596).

Hofstede, Geert, Hofstede, Gert Jan & Minkov, Michael (2010). *Cultures and Organizations: Software of the Mind* (3rd ed.). New York: McGraw-Hill (p. 576).

House, Robert, Hanges, Paul, Javidan, Mansour, Dorfman, Peter & Gupta, Vipin (2004). *Culture, Leadership, and Organizations: The GLOBE Study of 62 Societies*. Thousand Oakes: SAGE Publications (p. 848).

Huffington Post (2015, December 23rd). Islamic Banking In Canada Touted As Next Big Thing For Financial Services Sector, *By Alexandra Posadzki, The Canadian Press*. Retrieved from www.huffingtonpost.ca/2015/12/23/canada-well-positioned-to-become-islamic-banking-hub-according-to-report_n_8867238.html

Indij, Guido (2007). *Sin Palabras: Speechless: A Dictionary of Argentine Gestures/ Gestiario Argentino*. Buenos Aires (Argentina): La Marca Editora (p. 240).

Kirkman, Bradley, Lowe, Kevin & Gibson, Cristina (2006). A Quarter Century of Culture's Consequences: A Review of Empirical Research Incorporating Hofstede's Cultural Values Framework. *Journal of International Business Studies*, 37(3), 285–320.

Linton, Ralph (1945). *The Cultural Background of Personality*. New York: Appleton-Century-Crofts (p. 157).

Los Angeles Times (2016, June 9th). Shanghai Disney Opens Next Week, and It's Working Hard to Avoid Cultural Faux Pas, *By Hugo Martin and Julie Makinen*. Retrieved from www.latimes.com/business/la-fi-disney-shanghai-culture-adv-snap-story.html

Microsoft (2017). Globalization Step-by-Step Guide—Using Images and Icons. Retrieved May 2017, from https://msdn.microsoft.com/en-us/globalization/mt712571

Moon, Tae Won & Park, Sang Il (2011). The Effect of Cultural Distance on International Marketing Strategy: A Comparison of Cultural Distance and Managerial Perception Measures. *Journal of Global Marketing*, 24(1), 18–40.

Cultural Distance   179

Pew Forum on Religion & Public Life (2012). The Global Religious Landscape. Retrieved November 2011, from www.pewforum.org/2012/12/18/global-religious-landscape-exec/

Ralston, David (2008). The Crossvergence Perspective: Reflections and Projections. *Journal of International Business Studies*, 39(1), 27–40.

Ralston, David, Gustafson, David, Cheung, Fanny & Terpstra, Robert (1993). Differences in Managerial Values: A Study of U.S., Hong Kong and PRC Managers. *Journal of International Business Studies*, 24(2), 249–275.

Recode (2015, October 8th). Pinterest Is Localizing Search Because Half of Its Users Live Abroad, *By Carmel De Amicis*. Retrieved from www.recode.net/2015/10/8/11619374/pinterest-is-localizing-search-because-half-of-its-users-live-abroad

Ronen, Simcha & Shenkar, Oded (1985). Clustering Countries on Attitudinal Dimensions: A Review and Synthesis. *Academy of Management Review*, 10(3), 435–454.

Schuster, Camille & Copeland, Michael (1999). Global Business Exchanges: Similarities and Differences Around the World. *Journal of International Marketing*, 7(2), 63–80.

Schwartz, Shalom (1992). Universals in the Content and Structure of Values: Theoretical Advances and Empirical Tests in 20 Countries. *Advances in Experimental Social Psychology*, 25, 1–65.

Schwartz, Shalom & Boehnke, Klaus (2004). Evaluating the Structure of Human Values With Confirmatory Factor Analysis. *Journal of Research in Personality*, 38(3), 230–255.

Shenkar, Oded (2012). Cultural Distance Revisited: Toward a More Rigorous Conceptualization and Measurement of Cultural Differences. *Journal of International Business Studies*, 43(1), 1–11.

Sousa, Carlos & Bradley, Frank (2006). Cultural Distance and Psychic Distance: Two Peas in a Pod? *Journal of International Marketing*, 14(1), 49–70.

Statistics Canada (2016). Intergenerational Income Mobility: New Evidence from Canada. Economic Insights by Wen-Hao Chen, Yuri Ostrovsky, and Patrizio Piraino. Retrieved March 2017, from www.statcan.gc.ca/pub/11-626-x/11-626-x2016059-eng.htm

Translate Media (2015, March 16th). How Kellogg's Failed, and Then Won, in India. Retrieved from www.translatemedia.com/translation-blog/how-kelloggs-failed-and-then-won-in-india/

Ueda, Keiko (1974). Sixteen Ways to Avoid Saying "No" in Japan. In *Intercultural Encounters in Japan*, John Condon and Mitsuko Saito (Editors). Tokyo (Japan): Simul Press (pp. 185–192).

Usunier, Jean-Claude & Lee, Julie Anne (2005). *Marketing Across Cultures*. London: Prentice Hall (p. 573).

Usunier, Jean-Claude & Lee, Julie Anne (2009). *Marketing Across Cultures*. New Jersey: Pearson Education (p. 479).

UV 7197 (2016). *The Walt Disney Company: Mickey Mouse Visits Shanghai.* Case written by: Stephen Maiden, Gerry Yemen, and Elliott Weiss. Charlottesville: Darden School of Business (p. 11).

Webber, Ross (1969). Convergence or Divergence. *Columbia Journal of World Business*, 4(3), 75–83.

Wikipedia (2014a). Project GLOBE. Retrieved November 2014, from http://en.wikipedia.org/wiki/Global_Leadership#Project_GLOBE

180 *Cultural Distance*

Wikipedia (2014b). The "Great Gatsby Curve". Retrieved October 2014, from http://en.wikipedia.org/wiki/Social_mobility#Country_comparison

Wikipedia (2017a). Caste System in Africa. Retrieved May 2017, from http://en.wikipedia.org/wiki/Caste_system_in_Africa

Wikipedia (2017b). Caste System in India. Retrieved May 2017, from http://en.wikipedia.org/wiki/Caste_system_in_India

Wikipedia (2017c). List of Gestures. Retrieved May 2017, from http://en.wikipedia.org/wiki/List_of_gestures

Wikipedia (2017d). Geert Hofstede. Retrieved May 2017, from http://en.wikipedia.org/wiki/Geert_Hofstede

Wikipedia (2017e). Shalom Schwartz. Retrieved May 2017, from https://en.wikipedia.org/wiki/Shalom_H._Schwartz

6 Administrative Distance

Table of Contents

6 Administrative Distance

Introduction: Why does it matter? Is it decreasing? 182
- 6.1 *Definitions* 184
- 6.2 *Drivers* 186
  - 6.2.1 *Political Risk* 186
  - 6.2.2 *Institutional Landscape (Khanna and Palepu)* 191
  - 6.2.3 *Legal System* 195
  - 6.2.4 *Regional Integration* 200
- 6.3 *Central Role of Governments and Global Organizations* 205
  - 6.3.1 *Administrating International Trade* 205
  - 6.3.2 *Solving International Disputes* 211
- 6.4 *Issues at Stake* 214
  - 6.4.1 *Administrative Convergence* 214
  - 6.4.2 *Impact on Marketing Decisions* 216
  - 6.4.3 *Challenges and Opportunities in Overcoming Administrative Distance* 223

Conclusion: Administrative distance matters because it generates uncertainty and complexity. It could be decreasing, yet. . .

References

Recommended Readings

- Ghemawat, Pankaj (2001). Distance Still Matters: The Hard Reality of Global Expansion. *Harvard Business Review*, 79(8), 137–147. [Also recommended in Chapter 4]

- Khanna, Tarun & Palepu, Krishna (2005). Spotting Institutional Voids in Emerging Markets. *Harvard Business Review Background Note 106–014 (August 2005)*, 11.
- Turkina, Ekaterina & Postnikov, Evgeny (2014). From Business to Politics: Cross-Border Inter-Firm Networks and Policy Spillovers in the EU's Eastern Neighbourhood. *Journal of Common Market Studies*, 52(5), 1120–1141.

Introduction: Why Does It Matter? Is It Decreasing?

This chapter aims to define, measure, and estimate the outcomes of administrative distance in international marketing. In this context, it addresses the following overarching question: **Why does administrative distance matter?**

To answer this question and ultimately reflect on whether administrative distance between markets increases or decreases in a globalizing world, we first define important concepts and then consider administrative distance driving factors in the political, legal, and institutional arenas (e.g., levels of political risk, variety of legal systems, and regional integration). Next, we focus on the central role of governmental and nongovernmental institutions in creating or reducing distance across countries through the administration of international trade, the establishment of standards and classification, and the resolution of commercial disputes. Finally, we address some of the issues at stake, such as the debated convergence toward global rules, the numerous impacts on marketing, and the challenges in overcoming administrative distance.

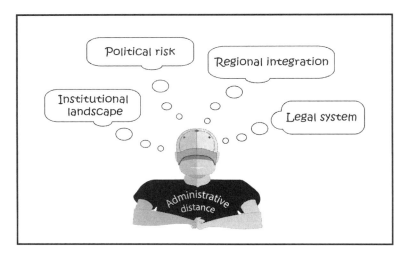

Figure 6.1 Illustrating Chapter 6
Source: Own elaboration

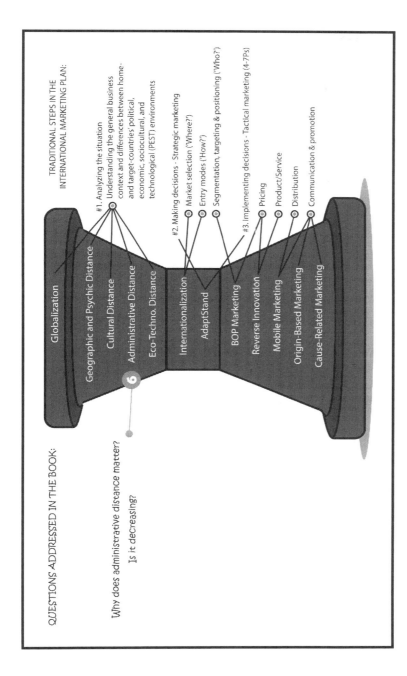

Figure 6.2 Positioning Chapter 6 in the overall book structure

Source: Own elaboration

184　*Administrative Distance*

6.1 Definitions

This section addresses the following questions:

- What are institutions?
- What is institutional distance? How does it differ from administrative distance?

How can we define institutions? Since we emphasize the role of governmental and nongovernmental institutions in creating or reducing administrative distance in this chapter, we start by considering a definition of *institutions* found in a seminal book by W. Richard Scott entitled *Institutions and Organizations*, which first edition in 1995 has been cited more than 16,600 times, according to an inquiry in Google Scholar (January 2017). "Institutions comprise regulative, normative and cultural-cognitive elements, that together with associated activities and resources, provide stability and meaning to social life" (Scott, 2014, p. 56).

In this well-known approach, institutions are thus conceptualized as comprising three "pillars." The *regulative pillar* is translated in society through indicators such as rules, laws, and sanctions. According to a simple definition from the online Merriam-Webster dictionary, a *regulation* is "a rule or order issued by an executive authority or regulatory agency of a government and having the force of law," while, in turn, a *law* is a "rule made by the government of a town, state, country, etc." The *normative pillar* is represented by values and norms that govern people's behavior and is visible through indicators such as accreditation and certification. Finally, the *cognitive-cultural pillar* consist of the way people in a given society create meaning through common frames of reference and shared conceptions about the nature of social reality. It is arguably the most difficult pillar to understand, but thinking of indicators such as symbols, common beliefs, and shared logics for action should help. This aspect refers directly to the work of one of the founders of the field of sociology, Max Weber (1864–1920). As noted by Scott (2014, p. 67): "Meanings arise in interaction and are maintained and transformed as they are employed to make sense of the ongoing stream of happenings. [. . .] Weber regarded action as social to the extent that the actor attaches meaning to the behavior. To understand or explain any action, the analyst must take into account not only the objective conditions but the actor's subjective interpretation of them. Extensive research by psychologists over the past three decades has shown that cognitive frames enter into the full range of information-processing activities, from determining what information will receive attention, how it will be encoded, how it will be retained, retrieved and organized into memory, to how it will be interpreted, thus affecting evaluations, judgments, predictions, and inferences."

As such, the notion of institution is more complex than usually thought in relation to business and marketing. We tend to think only of "global institutions," such as the United Nations or the WTO. It helps to remember that marriage, family, or education, for instance, are also considered institutions. It is then easy to realize how deeply embedded institutions and culture are.

Finally, Scott (2014, p. 60) proposes to look at the basis of legitimacy for action and the affective response of people, among other aspects, to understand the multi-dimensionality of institutions. In an institutional perspective, an action is legitimate when it is legally sanctioned (regulative pillar), morally governed (normative pillar), and comprehensible and recognizable (cultural-cognitive pillar). In turn, behaviors trigger affective reactions such as fear and guilt vs. innocence (regulative pillar), shame vs. honor (normative pillar), and certainty vs. confusion (cultural-cognitive pillar).

What is institutional distance? How does it differ from administrative distance? To reflect on this topic, see "Food for Thought."

Food for Thought 6.1

- In reference to Khanna and Palepu (2005) and Ghemawat (2001), what are institutional and administrative distances?

Considering the definition of institutions provided above, it comes as no surprise that institutional distance has been defined as the "difference between the institutional profiles of two countries" (Kostova, 1999, p. 316), the "differences between the host and home institutional environments" (Yang, Su, & Fam, 2012, p. 41), and "the extent of dissimilarity between the regulative, normative, and cognitive institutions of two countries" (Xu, Pan, & Beamish, 2004, p. 286). When it comes to administrative distance, Ghemawat (2001) equates it with "political distance" and relies on indicators such as the presence and strength of monetary, historical and political associations, preferential trade agreements, colonial linkages, political hostility, legal and financial institutions, and national protectionism to assess administrative distance between countries. In this perspective, the level of government involvement drives the increase or reduction of this type of distance. Industries particularly sensitive to administrative distance tend to be heavily regulated, because the government wants to protect national independence and competitiveness (e.g., electricity, telecommunications, aerospace), domestic workers (e.g., farming), consumers (e.g., alcohol and drugs), or natural resources (e.g., oil and mining).

Overall, administrative distance is a simplification of institutional distance and is a more "business-orientated" notion. Academically, there are differences, but in this chapter, we can group them together and remember that this type of distance refers to the role played by governmental and nongovernmental institutions in facilitating trade among countries. In this spirit, we define administrative distance as the degree of dissimilarity between the home- and foreign-country political, legal, and institutional environments. For this reason, we now look at four important drivers of administrative distance (illustrated in Figure 6.1): varying conditions across countries in terms of political climate, institutional landscape, legal system, and regional integration.

186 *Administrative Distance*

6.2 *Drivers*

In this section, we look at the drivers of administrative distance, i.e., the important components of the political, legal, and institutional environments that differ across countries. We address the following questions:

- What are political risk and country risk? What are the factors that increase the risk of doing business in a foreign country? Which are the information sources and indicators that can help us assess this risk?
- What is the institutional landscape in a country? What are institutional voids and how to spot them? How easy is it to assess the institutional landscape of a foreign country?
- Why is it important to know about the legal environment of each foreign market? What are the main legal systems in the world? What is the rule of law and which information sources can we use to assess differences across countries?
- What are the main regional integration forms between countries? Which are the important regional trade agreements around the planet? Will regional integration keep increasing and why is it a driver of administrative distance?

6.2.1 *Political Risk*

What are political risk and country risk? According to Wagner (2012), these terms are often used interchangeably, but they bear different meanings. Although the term *country risk* generally refers to the risks assumed by operating in another country, it has more of a financial flavor than does *political risk*, and points to the likelihood that a sovereign state may be unable or unwilling to fulfill its obligations toward one or more lenders (Krayenbuehl, 1985). In turn, political risk concerns "political and social developments that can have an impact upon the value or repatriation of foreign investment or on the repayment of cross-border lending. [. . .] This includes arbitrary or discriminatory actions taken by governments, political groups, or individuals that have an adverse impact on trade or investment transactions" Wagner (2012, p. 44). The obligations that governments have toward foreign companies mainly involve protection (of physical and intellectual property) and freedom (to hire, to lay-off, to purchase, to borrow, to repatriate dividends, etc.). Other terms such as *credit risk* and *operational risk* are also often used to evaluate different aspects of the nature of risk related to doing business in foreign countries for companies. Overall, the political climate that helps companies commercialize and invest in a country is mainly characterized by stability, one that is nurtured by a friendly government (Czinkota, Ronkainen, & Moffett, 2011, Chapter 6). Often, uncertainty about potential changes is indeed more damaging for business than are difficult conditions, as companies can learn to deal with or work their way around established hurdles but can do little when conditions change frequently and abruptly.

What are the factors that increase the risk of doing business in a foreign country? Focusing on political risk, factors mainly relate to instability that is either due to changes in governmental decisions (e.g., nationalization, currency devaluation, tax increase, change in labor laws), to events or trends that are partly independent of a government's control (e.g., inflation, economic turndown, campaigns against foreign goods), or to events that are entirely escaping governmental control (e.g., wars, civil wars, kidnappings and terrorist threats). While examples of drastic business events, such as nationalizations (when a government decides to appropriate private ownership of companies), abound in history in both developed and developing economies, most recent illustrations are coming from emerging and developing countries. For instance, the government of Argentina decided to renationalize the oil company YPF in 2012 by expropriating the Spanish company Repsol, which had held more than 51 percet stake in the company since 1999 (a compensation of 5 billion USD was finally granted after much legal and political turmoil). This decision has been seen as one of the main causes in the 41 percent drop of FDI in the country between 2013 and 2014 (La Nación, 2015). Five years later, a state visit to Spain by the subsequent president of Argentina was still bearing the stigmata of the event and was described as "an act of reconciliation" between the two countries in the press (La Nación, 2017). Another example is illustrated in Figure 6.3, when the government of Bolivia also decided to nationalize several Spanish assets in 2012. The photograph shows military power deployed around the newly nationalized company Electropaz, specialized in electricity distribution.

Which information sources can help us assess political risk in foreign countries? Many private information sources are available (for a fee), such as the *International Country Risk Guide* (ICRG) published by the Political Risk Services (PRS) Group, *Business Risk Reports* published by the Business Environment Risk Intelligence (BERI), Euromoney, and the Economist Intelligence Unit (EIU). For instance, the EIU evaluates a wide range of risks, including: political risk (credit risk posed by the political system), sovereign risk (risk of default on public, domestic and external debt), currency risk (risk of a devaluation), banking risk (risk of a systematic banking crisis), and economic structure risk (risk posed by structural economic indicators). One of the few sources providing information, free of charge, is COFACE, with several interesting publications, such as their "country panoramas" and "country risk assessment maps." Published every quarter, these maps help track the evolution of risk in one hundred and sixty countries, as illustrated in Figure 6.4. Revealing the world's fragmentation, the first quarter of 2017 shows parts of the world, such as North America, Western Europe, and Australasia, presenting low country risk levels, whereas most of Africa, Asia, Latin America, and the Middle East present moderate to high country risk levels. Diversity within regions can also be observed with, for instance, the contrast offered by Portugal, Spain, and Greece in Europe with relatively higher risk levels, or Chile in South America with a significantly lower risk level compared to the other countries in the region.

Are there any other indicators that can give us a sense of risk or challenges in the political, legal, and institutional environments in foreign countries? Other useful indicators are provided by a number of transnational organizations (e.g., the World Bank jointly with the International Finance Corporation

188 *Administrative Distance*

Figure 6.3 Illustrating nationalization with the case of Spanish Electropaz in Bolivia (2012)

Source: Screen capture from a YouTube video available with search words: "Morales expropriates Spanish energy subsidiaries", posted by: Associated Press Archive, retrievable at: www.YouTube.com/results?search_query=nationalization+Electropaz

and their *Doing Business Index*), think tanks (e.g. the Heritage Foundation and their *Economic Freedom Index*), and finally, watchdog organizations and nongovernmental organizations (NGOs; e.g., Freedom House with their annual reports on *Freedom in the World*, and Transparency International with their *Corruption Perceptions Index*). These indices, presented hereafter, do not focus solely on political risk, but still provide a sense of how difficult and risky doing business in countries around the world can be.

- The *Doing Business Index* is of particular interest to firms wanting to undertake FDI. Since 2004, it ranks one hundred and ninety countries comparing the ease of doing business (i.e., the easiness of starting a business, registering property, dealing with construction permits, getting credit and electricity, protecting minority investors, paying taxes, enforcing contracts, resolving insolvency, trading across borders, and

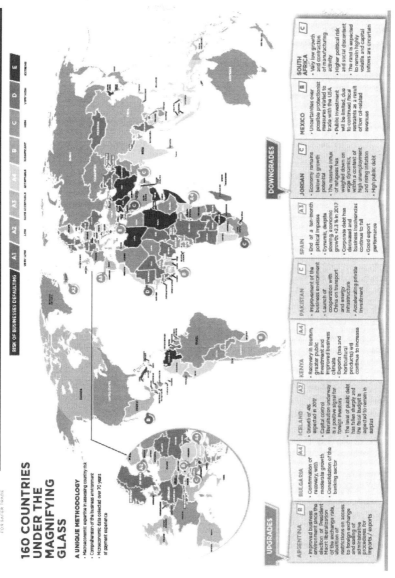

Figure 6.4 Mapping country risk across the world
Source: Coface (2017)
For the color version, see the eResource at www.routledge.com/9781138202344

190   *Administrative Distance*

labor market regulation). A high ease of doing business ranking reflects a regulatory environment that is more conducive to the starting and operation of a local firm. In 2017, the five countries at the top of this ranking were New Zealand, Singapore, Denmark, Hong Kong, and South Korea, while the five countries at the bottom were South Sudan, Venezuela, Libya, Eritrea, and Somalia (World Bank, 2017a).

- The *Economic Freedom Index* covers one hundred and eighty-six countries and reflects various degrees of economic and financial liberalization (free, mostly free, mostly unfree, and repressed economies). It has been measured for more than twenty years by the Heritage Foundation, a conservative organization in the US. The data is available for download on the organization's website, starting in 2006. The index is built on the following variables: rule of law (property rights, government integrity, judicial effectiveness), government size (government spending, tax burden, fiscal health), regulatory efficiency (business freedom, labor freedom, monetary freedom), and open markets (trade freedom, investment freedom, financial freedom). In 2017, the top five "free countries" were: Hong Kong, Singapore, New Zealand, Switzerland, and Australia, and the top five "repressed countries" were: Eritrea, Republic of Congo, Cuba, Venezuela, and North Korea (Heritage Foundation, 2017). This index focuses on companies as the main stakeholder.

- The annual reports entitled *Freedom in the World* are studies of political rights and civil liberties across one hundred and ninety-five countries and fourteen disputed territories (e.g., Crimea, Tibet, and Western Sahara). Unlike the prior example, this index places individuals (not companies) as the main stakeholder, and therefore provides only a general context to evaluate the state of political risk. Published since 1973 by Freedom House, a US-based NGO (established in 1941), it evaluates countries as "free," "partly free," or "not free." Scores are calculated based on ten political rights indicators (tapping into the electoral process, political pluralism and participation, and functioning of government) and fifteen civil liberties indicators (covering freedom of expression and belief, associational and organizational rights, rule of law, personal autonomy, and individual rights). In 2017, the five countries with the worst scores were: Syria, Tibet, Eritrea, North Korea, and Turkmenistan; in turn, the five countries with the best scores were: Sweden, Norway, Finland, the Netherlands, and Canada (Freedom House, 2017).

- Finally, the *Corruption Perceptions Index* is presented by Transparency International, a German NGO established in 1993. On its website, the organization defines corruption as "the abuse of entrusted power for private gain" and distinguishes *grand corruption* (acts committed at a high level of government that distort policies or the central functioning of the state, enabling leaders to benefit at the expense of the public good) from *petty corruption* (the everyday abuse of entrusted power by low- and mid-level public officials in their interactions with ordinary citizens, such as in hospitals, schools, or police departments), and *political corruption* (a manipulation of policies, institutions, and rules in the allocation of

Administrative Distance 191

resources and financing by political decision-makers who can then abuse their position to sustain their power and wealth). The 2016 index relied on answers to specific questions about corruption by experts working in thirteen different organizations with a wide international presence. These experts were involved in the EIU's *Country Risk Ratings*, Freedom House's *Nations in Transit* reports, the PRS's *International Country Risk Guide*, HIS Markit's *Global Insight Country Risk Ratings*, Bertelsmann Foundation's *Sustainable Governance Indicators* and *Transformation Index*, the Institute for Management Development's (IMD) *World Competitiveness Yearbook*, the World Bank's *Country Policy and Institutional Assessment*, the World Economic Forum's *Executive Opinion Survey*, the World Justice Project's *Rule of Law Index*, the Varieties of Democracy (V-Dem) Project at University of Gothenburg (Sweden), as well as the African Development Bank *Governance Ratings and the Political and Economic Risk Consultancy Asian Intelligence*. In 2016, the *Corruption Perceptions Index* included one hundred and seventy-six countries and territories, among which the least corrupted appeared to be Denmark, New Zealand, Finland, Sweden, and Switzerland, while the most corrupted were Yemen, Syria, North Korea, South Sudan, and Somalia (Transparency International, 2017). The corresponding map of corruption perceptions worldwide is presented in Figure 6.5.

6.2.2 Institutional Landscape (Khanna and Palepu)

What is the institutional landscape of a country? The term is equivalent to a country's *institutional infrastructure*, broadly defined as "the set of arrangements that shape the 'rules of the game' and the incentives for the economic agents" (Cherchye & Moesen, 2003, p. 3). Economic agents (i.e., people or organizations) have an influence on the economy of a country by producing, buying, or selling something (e.g., information, goods, and services). A favorable institutional infrastructure rewards their efforts and encourages them to engage in productive activities (e.g., accumulating skills, investing in physical capital, developing product- and process-innovations), while an unfavorable institutional infrastructure deters these efforts (e.g., in the presence of theft, corruption, or political instability, and in the absence of a clear definition of property rights, the maintenance of law and order, and an equitable civil service) (Cherchye & Moesen, 2003). Overall, the institutional landscape or infrastructure represents the way institutions and actors are organized in a country in order to sustain its economy.

What are institutional voids and how to spot them? Khanna and Palepu (2005) refer to weak institutions and the absence of important actors as *institutional voids*. In addition to a country's political and social system and openness to the world (in particular, in terms of FDI), they focus on actors present in three markets: capital, product, and labor. In their view, we can spot institutional voids in foreign countries by inquiring about the presence and degree of sophistication of six types of actors in these three markets: regulators, adjudicators, information analyzers and advisors, aggregators and

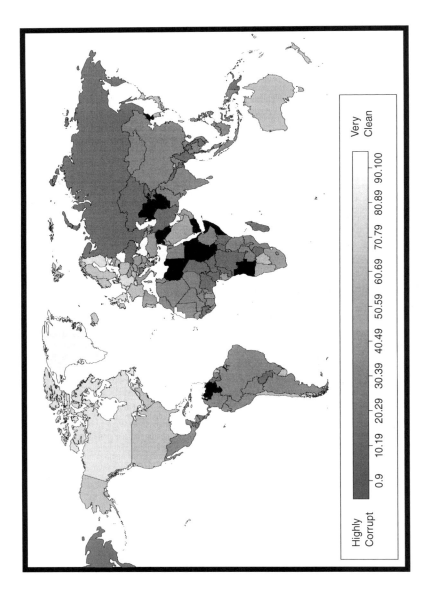

Figure 6.5 Mapping corruption across the world

Source: Corruption perceptions index © 2017 by Transparency International. Licensed under CC-BY-ND 4.0
For the color version, see the eResource at www.routledge.com/9781138202344

Administrative Distance 193

distributors, transaction facilitators, and credibility enhancers. Each type is briefly described here (for more details, see Khanna & Palepu, 2005, Table A):

- *Regulators* create and enforce regulations. Examples in the product market can be found in agencies across countries that regulate food safety, for instance. The Canadian Food Inspection Agency (CFIA) within Health Canada, the Food and Drug Administration (FDA) in the US, or the European Food Safety Authority (EFSA) are a few among these regulators.
- *Adjudicators* constitute all the courts and arbitrators whose role is to solve disputes, in particular commercial disputes. Their number and efficiency is essential for speedy rulings and for maintaining trust in a fair system.
- *Information analyzers and advisors* provide information about producers and consumers and guide decisions. Examples in the capital markets include the financial press (e.g., *Cinco Días* in Spain, *Financial Post* in Canada, the *Hong Kong Economic Times*, and *Valor Econômico* in Brazil, to name a few) and credit rating agencies (e.g., Standard & Poor's, Moody's, and Fitch Group). In product markets, the press and consumer magazines are primary information analyzers, as well as industry analysts and market research companies (e.g., Euromonitor International, and Forrester) among others. In labor and talent markets, an example of these types of actors would be publications ranking universities and programs such as the Times Higher Education's world university rankings and the Economist's MBA ranking.
- Credibility enhancers certify claims made in markets by suppliers and customers. Examples of such important actors are found in financial markets with auditing companies (e.g., Deloitte, PwC, Ernst & Young, and KPMG), in product markets with certification organizations (e.g., ISO), and in talent markets with organizations accrediting business schools (e.g., EQUIS and AACSB) or tests asserting students' levels in management studies or languages (e.g., GMAT and TOEFL).
- *Aggregators and distributors* provide value-added services and match buyers and sellers through expertise and economies of scale. In financial markets, examples of such institutional actors are banks (e.g., Bank of China, HSBC, JPMorgan Chase & Co., and BNP Paribas) and insurance companies (e.g., AXA, Zurich Insurance Group, and China Life Insurance). In product markets, trading companies (e.g., Vitol, Glencore, and Cargill) and mass retailers (e.g., Walmart, Carrefour, and Amazon) are good examples. We can also consider universities and labor unions, for instance, as actors matching demand and supply in talent markets.
- Finally, *transaction facilitators* are platforms where customers and suppliers can exchange information, goods and services and receive support for conducting transactions. There is a wide diversity of actors in this category, including brokerage houses (e.g., LPL Financial) in financial markets, or platforms like eBay and PayPal in product markets, as well as job announcement websites (e.g., Linkedin, Indeed, and SimplyHired).

How easy is it to assess the institutional landscape of a foreign country?
From the sheer number and diversity of the above-mentioned actors, we

194 *Administrative Distance*

understand that evaluating the state and degree of sophistication of institutions in any given country is a challenging and lengthy exercise. Khanna and Palepu (2005) list no fewer than one hundred and ten questions to assess a country's capital, product, and labor markets, as well as its openness to the world and political and social system (see Table 6.1). Answering these questions often requires asking local experts (e.g., policy makers, accountants, and lawyers) and mastering the local idiom (or have access to people who do) to review the press, find, and analyze information.

Table 6.1 Assessing the institutional landscape

Indicators	Examples of questions to ask in order to measure administrative distance
Political and social system	
• Governmental interference	Does the government go beyond regulating business to interfering in it or running companies?
• Judiciary independence	Is the judiciary independent? Do the courts adjudicate disputes and enforce contracts in a timely and impartial manner? How effective are the quasi-judicial regulatory institutions that set and enforce rules for business activities?
• Media independence	How vibrant and independent is the media? Are newspapers and magazines neutral or do they represent sectarian interests?
• NGOs dynamism	Are nongovernmental organizations, civil rights groups, and environmental groups active in the country?
Openness	
• Governmental restrictions	What restrictions does the government place on foreign investment? Are those restrictions in place to facilitate the growth of domestic companies, to protect state monopolies or because people are suspicious of multinationals? Are there restrictions on portfolio investments by overseas companies or on dividend repatriation by multinationals?
• Easiness to do business	How long does it take to start a new venture in the country? How cumbersome are the government's procedures for permitting the launch of a wholly foreign-owned business?
• Trade agreements	Has the country signed free-trade agreements with other nations? If so, do those agreements favor investments by companies from some parts of the world over others?
Product markets	
• Market research	Can companies easily obtain reliable data on customer tastes and purchase behaviors? Are there cultural barriers to market research? Do world-class market research firms operate in the country?
• Infrastructure quality	How strong are the logistics and transportation infrastructures? Have global logistics companies set up local operations?

Indicators	Examples of questions to ask in order to measure administrative distance
• Distribution dynamism	Do large retail chains exist in the country? If so, do they cover the entire country or only the major cities? Do they reach all consumers or only wealthy ones?
• Regulation enforcement	What kind of product-related environment and safety regulations are in place? How do the authorities enforce regulations?
Labor markets	
• Education infrastructure	How strong is the country's education infrastructure, especially for technical and management training? Does it have a good elementary and secondary education system as well? Are data available to help sort out the quality of the country's educational institutions?
• International languages	Do people study and do business in English or in another international language, or do they mainly speak a local language?
• Workforce protection	How are the rights of workers protected? How strong are the country's trade unions? Do they defend workers' interests or only advance a political agenda?
Capital markets	
• Decision making transparency	Are financial institutions managed well? Is their decision making transparent? Do noneconomic considerations such as family ties, influence their investment decisions?
• Access to financing	Can companies raise large amounts of equity capital in the stock market? Is there a market for corporate debt? *Does a venture capital industry exist? If so, does it allow individuals with good ideas to raise funds?*
• Information availability	Do independent financial analysts, rating agencies, and the media offer unbiased information on companies?

Source: Selected questions from Khanna and Palepu (2005, Table B)

6.2.3 Legal System

Why is it important to know about the legal environment of each foreign market? International marketers must pay particular attention to the laws of each country within which they operate, mainly because no single, uniform international commercial law exists that governs foreign business transactions. There is high diversity in legal systems across the world, as they vary for historical, cultural, religious, and political (e.g., colonial ties) reasons (Griffin & Pustay, 2015). Laws affect which markets firms can serve and a vast array of marketing elements, such as the prices they can charge (because of the cost of necessary inputs such as labor, raw materials and technology), product, distribution, and promotion policies.

196   *Administrative Distance*

What are the main legal systems in the world? Griffin and Pustay (2015) propose to regroup legal systems according to four types of law: common law, civil law, religious law, and what they call *bureaucratic* law. Each type is briefly presented here:

Common law—The basis of the *common law* system is past practices and precedents. As new decisions are rendered, the reasons offered by judges to rule in trials become part of the body of law and set precedents for future rulings. Examples of countries that are under this system include the UK and many of its former colonies, such as the US, Canada, Australia, India, and New Zealand.

Code law—By comparison, *civil or code law* is an all-inclusive system that has codified all the rules into a written body of texts. This system has its origins in biblical times with the Romans and was later strengthened by the French Napoleonic Code. As common law countries place more emphasis on practice and past decisions, civil law countries refer to a number of rules that are already codified. Among the many dissimilarities between common and code systems, one striking difference can be found in the laws governing the compliance of contracts. Under common law, companies must comply with a contract unless it is impossible because of circumstances deemed "acts of God" (e.g., floods, lightning, and earthquakes). Under code law, acts of God are extended to include "unavoidable interference with performance, whether resulting from forces of nature or unforeseeable human acts." The latter include such things as labor strikes and riots. These are some of the intricacies that MNCs operating global value chains across different legal systems must master (and the source of much disarray in Anglo-Saxon firms when they do business in Latin countries!). Many Internet sources, such as Legal Language Services (LLS), can help us gain a basic understanding of differences between these two major legal systems. The role of lawyers, for instance, is another one of these differences, since in common law systems it is the responsibility of lawyers to ask questions of witnesses and demand production of evidence, while in civil law systems, these are judges' responsibility (LLS, 2013). This explains why the number of lawyers in countries like the UK and the US is so much higher than in Japan and France (see Table 6.2).

Table 6.2 Comparing the number of judges, lawyers, and suits filed across selected countries

Number of	Australia	Canada	France	Japan	UK	US
(Per 100,000 people; numbers are rounded)						
• Judges	4	3	12	3	2	11
• Lawyers	360	25	70	25	250	390
• Suits filed	1,540	1,450	2,420	1,770	3,680	5,810

Source: Adapted from Ramseyer and Rasmusen (2010)

Religious law—As for religious law, one of the most important examples is Islamic law. Typically, *religious law* encompasses duties and obligations stemming from a holy book. For instance, the Sharia is a comprehensive code governing Muslim conduct in all areas of life, including business. It is based on the Koran and the Hadith (itself based on the life, sayings, and practices of the Prophet Muhammad). Examples of countries that are governed by Islamic law include Afghanistan and Saudi Arabia, while many other Muslim countries in North Africa and the Middle East have mixed systems relying on both Islamic and civil law. Among the unique aspects of Islamic law is the prohibition of the payment of interest. This feature affects banking and business practices, but Islamic finance has developed to allow business transactions and still adhere to Islamic law.

Bureaucratic law—Finally, *bureaucratic law* is a term designating the legal system that is in place in dictatorships and countries where the law basically depends on the people in power. Then, the ability of international business managers to conduct business in an efficient way is often compromised by bureaucrats. For instance, contracts can be made or broken at the whim of those in power.

Other classifications, such as the one proposed by JuriGlobe (a website developed by the World Legal Systems Research Group at the University of Ottawa in Canada) distinguish between civil, common, Muslim, and customary law systems, as well as mixed systems. *Customary law* is founded on custom (either rooted in wisdom born of concrete daily experience or in spiritual and philosophical traditions) and plays a role in many countries in Africa, as well as China and India (JuriGlobe, 2017b). *Mixed systems* then refer to hybrid or composite law systems in countries where two or more systems apply either in combination or in juxtaposition.

Figure 6.6 situates these various legal systems in the world and shows homogeneity in some regions (e.g., South America, most of Europe, and the former Soviet Union countries) and fragmentation in others (e.g., Asia and Africa). It also highlights the existence of mixed systems in many countries and, more rarely, in regions within countries such as the Canadian province of Quebec (mixing civil and common law).

What is the rule of law? One core concept to assess in the legal environment of countries is the extent to which the rule of law applies. In simple terms, the *rule of law* means the extent to which law is governing in a country, as opposed to arbitrary decisions of people in power. The World Justice Project (WJP, 2017a), a nonprofit US-based organization since 2009, defines it as a system in which the following four universal principles are upheld:

- The government and its officials and agents as well as individuals and private entities are accountable under the law;
- The laws are clear, publicized, stable, and just; are applied evenly; and protect fundamental rights, including the security of persons and property and certain core human rights;
- The process by which the laws are enacted, administered, and enforced is accessible, fair, and efficient; and

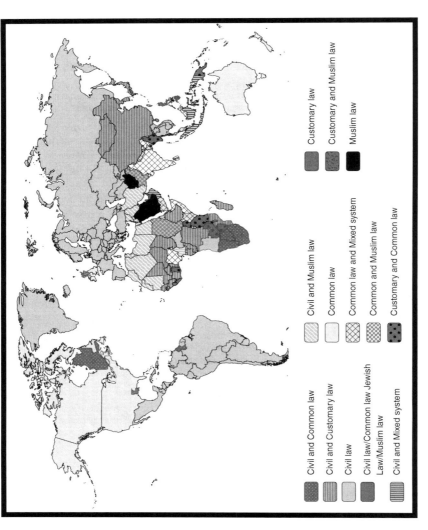

Figure 6.6 Mapping legal systems in the world

Source: Based on JuriGlobe (2017a)

For the color version, see the eResource at www.routledge.com/9781138202344

Administrative Distance 199

- Justice is delivered timely by competent, ethical, and independent representatives who are of sufficient number, have adequate resources, and reflect the makeup of the communities they serve.

Which information sources can we use to assess differences in terms of rule of law across countries? One of the available information sources is the WJP's *Rule of Law Index*. The 2016 edition covered one hundred and thirteen countries and jurisdictions in the world. To measure and compare how the rule of law is experienced in everyday situations by the general public worldwide, the index relied on more than one hundred thousand household and expert surveys. It is based on the following eight factors:

- Constraints on government powers (e.g., "government powers are effectively limited by: the legislature/ the judiciary/ independent auditing and review," "government officials are sanctioned for misconduct," "transition of power is subject to the law");
- Absence of corruption ("government officials in the executive/ judicial/ legislative/ police and military branch do not use public office for private gain");
- Open government (e.g., "publicized laws and government data," "right to information," "complaint mechanisms");
- Fundamental rights (e.g., "equal treatment and absence of discrimination," "freedom of opinion and expression/ belief and religion/ arbitrary interference with privacy/ assembly and association is effectively guaranteed," "fundamental labor rights are effectively guaranteed");
- Order and security (e.g., "crime is effectively controlled," "civil conflict is effectively limited," and "people do not resort to violence to redress personal grievances");
- Regulatory enforcement (e.g., "government regulations are: effectively enforced/ applied and enforced without improper influence," "administrative proceedings are conducted without unreasonable delay," "the government does not expropriate without lawful process and adequate compensation");
- Civil justice (e.g., "people can access and afford civil justice," "civil justice is free of: discrimination/ corruption/ improper government influence,","civil justice is not subject to unreasonable delay," "alternative dispute resolution is accessible, impartial, and effective"); and
- Criminal justice (e.g., "criminal investigation system is effective," "correctional system is effective in reducing criminal behavior," "criminal system is impartial," "due process of law and rights of the accused").

In 2016, the countries with the worst rule of law index scores were: Venezuela, Cambodia, Afghanistan, and Egypt (at par with Cameroon and Zimbabwe), while the five countries with the best scores were the Netherlands, Sweden, Finland, Norway, and Denmark (WJP, 2017b).

200 *Administrative Distance*

6.2.4 *Regional Integration*

What are the main regional integration forms between countries? As seen in Chapter 1, *regional integration* has been defined as the process in which nations enter an agreement in order to improve regional cooperation through institutions and norms (Rosamond, 2000). Signing trade agreements leads to collective governance and interdependence between nations to different degrees. Five main forms of regional integration between countries exist. They are listed hereafter from the least to the most integrated form: free trade areas, custom unions, common market, economic union, and finally, political union. Figure 6.7 illustrates central differences among them and their possible evolution over time.

The WTO distinguishes *regional trade agreements* (RTAs) (i.e., reciprocal trade agreements between two or more partners) from *preferential trade arrangements* (PTAs) (such as unilateral trade preferences under which developed countries grant preferential tariffs to imports from developing countries). In terms of RTAs, the WTO distinguishes only two types: *free trade areas* (FTAs) and *customs unions* (CUs). According to its glossary, an FTA is characterized by duty free trade within the group but members set their own tariffs on imports from non-members (e.g., AFTA in Asia, and CISFTA in former Soviet Union). In turn, a CU is an agreement where members not only remove internal barriers to trade within the group, but also apply a common external tariff to trade with non-members (e.g., CACM in Central America, and CEMAC in Central Africa). The WTO lists all more extensively integrated groups (e.g., the EU) under the label Economic Integration Agreement (EIA). Any FTA or CU with more advanced integration mechanisms is deemed an EIA.

Which are the important regional trade agreements around the planet? Figure 6.8 situates several (but far from all) regional trade agreements in the world with different degrees of integration. The map represents existing signatories in 2016 and presents the respective date of entry into force of these RTAs. For simplicity purposes, many countries appear as part of only one agreement, when in fact they belong to muliple blocks (e.g., India is simultaneously part of the SAFTA since 2006 and linked with the ASEAN since 2015). The main objective here is to point out that when we think of trade agreements, we tend to think of only a few ones, perhaps five or ten, when there are literally hundreds of them. The WTO (2016b) lists no less than three hundred and eight RTAs (including bilateral agreements, FTAs, CUs, and EIAs). What is important to remember here is that regional integration is a worldwide phenomenon. Every single region on the planet is the host to multiple integration agreements.

Americas—In the Americas, we usually think of the NAFTA (i.e., the North American Free Trade Agreement, including Canada, USA, and Mexico) and the Mercosur (i.e., the Southern Common Market, including Argentina, Brazil, Paraguay, and Uruguay). There are several other RTAs, such as the CAN (i.e., the Andean Community regrouping Bolivia, Colombia, Ecuador, Peru, and Venezuela), the CACM (i.e., the Central American Common Market with Costa Rica, El Salvador, Guatemala, Honduras, and Nicaragua), the

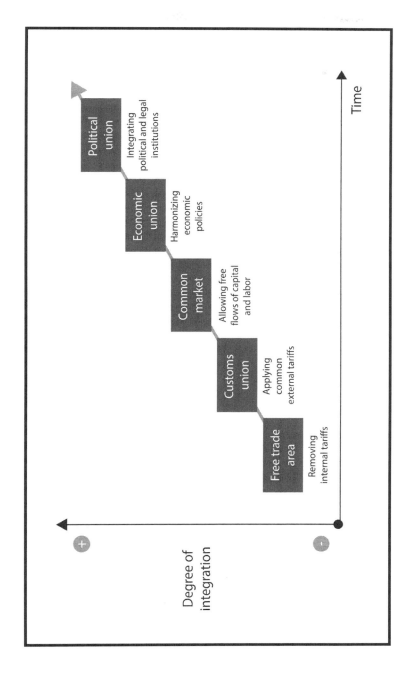

Figure 6.7 Illustrating varying degrees of integration in regional trade agreements

Source: Adapted from Griffin and Pustay (2015)

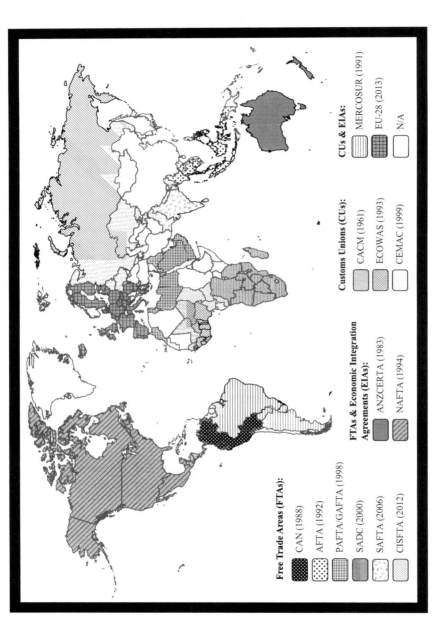

Figure 6.8 Mapping the geographic diversity of regional integration with selected agreements

Source: Based on WTO (2016b)

For the color version, see the eResource at www.routledge.com/9781138202344

CARICOM (i.e., the Caribbean Community and Common Market regrouping Antigua and Barbuda, Bahamas, Barbados, Belize, Dominica, Grenada, Guyana, Haiti, Jamaica, Montserrat, Saint Kitts and Nevis, Saint Lucia, Saint Vincent, and the Grenadines, Suriname, and Trinidad and Tobago) and the Pacific Alliance (Chile, Colombia, Mexico and Peru). Other integration initiatives that are not (yet) listed by the WTO are also present in the political agendas of countries. An example is the UNASUR (i.e., the Union of South American Nations which regroups the twelve countries in South America since 2008 with headquarters in Ecuador, a parliament in Bolivia, and a central bank in Venezuela), which is aspiring to eventually replicate the European Union model. Like most ambitious regional integration proposals, the UNASUR has encountered many delays and setbacks.

Europe and parts of Eurasia—In Europe, the European Union (EU) comes to mind as one of the most advanced examples of integrated block. First formed in the 1950s with six members (Belgium, France, Italy, West Germany, Luxembourg, and The Netherlands), the union was then extended to nine members during the 1970s (with the addition of Denmark, Ireland, and the UK) and then to twelve members in the 1980s (with the inclusion of Greece, Portugal, and Spain) (Griffin & Pustay, 2015). Three additional members joined in the 1990s: Austria, Sweden, and Finland. In the 2000s, the EU grew from fifteen to twenty-eight members with the addition of ten countries in 2004 (Cyprus, Czech Republic, Estonia, Hungary, Latvia, Lithuania, Malta, Poland, Slovenia, and Slovakia), two more in 2007 (Bulgaria and Romania), and one more in 2013 (Croatia). In 2016, the UK started a transition to exit the EU, the so-called "Brexit." It is still represented on the map as a part of the EU, due to a lengthy transition process. In terms of integration, this is one major setback but it is only one of the many challenges that has paved the history of the EU for more than sixty years. Regional integration is an extremely difficult and long process, and the EU is probably the most advanced and comprehensive example, with its ups and downs. The EU was awarded the Nobel Peace Prize in 2012 because it has contributed "to the advancement of peace and reconciliation, democracy and human rights in Europe" (Nobel Prize, 2012). In addition, the EU has signed more than forty RTAs with individual nations (e.g., Norway, Syria, and Georgia). Aside from this major block, other RTAs exist in Europe such as the EFTA (i.e., the European Free Trade Area among Iceland, Liechtenstein, Norway, and Switzerland) and the CEFTA (i.e., the Central European Free Trade Agreement regrouping Albania, Bosnia and Herzegovina, Kosovo, Moldova, Montenegro, Serbia, and Macedonia).

Extending to the East from Europe, we find many RTAs, such as the CIS-FTA (i.e., Treaty on a Free Trade Area between members of the Commonwealth of Independent States, which includes Armenia, Belarus, Kazakhstan, the Kyrgyz Republic, Moldova, the Russian Federation, Tajikistan, and Ukraine), the CEZ (i.e., Common Economic Zone with Belarus, Kazakhstan, the Russian Federation, and Ukraine), and the EAEU (i.e., Eurasian Economic Union including Armenia, Belarus, Kazakhstan, the Kyrgyz Republic, and the Russian Federation).

204 *Administrative Distance*

Middle East and Africa—In the Middle East and Arab countries, we also find various RTAs. Examples include the GCC (i.e., Gulf Cooperation Council with Bahrain, Kuwait, Oman, Qatar, Saudi Arabia, and the United Arab Emirates) and the PAFTA (i.e., Pan-Arab Free Trade Area regrouping Bahrain, Egypt, Iraq, Jordan, Kuwait, Lebanese Republic, Libya, Morocco, Oman, Qatar, Saudi Arabia, Sudan, Syria, Tunisia, the United Arab Emirates, and Yemen).

The African continent is host to the CEMAC (i.e., Monetary and Economic Community of Central Africa including Cameroon, the Central African Republic, Chad, Congo, Equatorial Guinea and Gabon), the SADC (i.e., Southern African Development Community with Angola, Botswana, Lesotho, Madagascar, Malawi, Mauritius, Mozambique, Namibia, Seychelles, South Africa, Swaziland, Tanzania, Zambia and Zimbabwe) and, among other trade agreements, the ECOWAS (i.e., Economic Community of West African States, regrouping Benin, Burkina Faso, Cabo Verde, Côte d'Ivoire, Gambia, Ghana, Guinea, Guinea-Bissau, Liberia, Mali, Niger, Nigeria, Senegal, Sierra Leone, and Togo). Several individual African countries have also developed bilateral deals with the EU (e.g., Cameroon, Côte d'Ivoire, and South Africa).

Asia and Australasia—Finally, the Asia-Pacific region undergoes similar integration processes with, for instance, the AFTA, which is the FTA of the ASEAN (i.e., the Association of Southeast Asian Nations including Brunei Darussalam, Cambodia, Indonesia, Lao People's Democratic Republic, Malaysia, Myanmar, Philippines, Singapore, Thailand, and Vietnam) and the ANZCERTA (i.e., the Australia New Zealand Closer Economic Relations Trade Agreement). Countries like China and Japan have signed a great number of bilateral FTAs. For instance, China has deals with countries as diversified as Iceland, Chile, Costa Rica, Pakistan, Peru, South Korea, and Switzerland (and many more). In turn, Japan also has deals with Chile, Peru, and Switzerland, as well as with Mexico, Mongolia, and India (and a great number of other countries in Asia-Pacific).

Will regional integration keep increasing? Overall, regional integration is entirely dependent upon the evolution of politics. It is deepened by liberalism and slowed down—or reverted—by national protectionism. Interestingly, those two antagonist trends—spanning decades—tend to follow the same pendulum pattern as discussed in Chapter 5 about cultural convergence and divergence. The turn of 2016–2017 has been marked by a beginning of "disintegration," with the exit of the UK from the EU and of the US from the TPP (i.e., Trans-Pacific Partnership between remaining Australia, Brunei, Canada, Chile, Japan, Malaysia, Mexico, New Zealand, Peru, Singapore, and Vietnam). The drastic change of political direction that has occurred in the US with Donald Trump as president (leading to reconsider even well-established agreements like the NAFTA and impose new barriers) may—or may not—initiate a major slowdown in regional integration. This needs to be assessed over the following decades and benchmarked against the thirty-nine agreements that were recently signed or are under negotiation all over the world (WTO, 2017b). Whether regional integration keeps increasing or not, the next question remains relevant (see "Food for Thought").

Administrative Distance   205

Food for Thought 6.2

- In your opinion, why is regional integration a driver of administrative distance?

6.3 Central Role of Governments and Global Organizations

In this section, we discuss the central role of governments and global institutions in facilitating (or inhibiting) international trade and thereby in impacting administrative distance between countries. In a nutshell, this role is twofold: administrating international trade and solving disputes. To this purpose, we address the following questions:

- Which are the global organizations with an active role in administrating trade?
- What can international organizations and national governments do to set the rules of international trade?
- How can national governments intervene in international trade? To what extent are governments' decisions affecting companies with international activities?
- How can international disputes be resolved?
- Who are the actors involved in helping firms solve disputes with international counterparts?

6.3.1 Administrating International Trade

Administrating trade can mean two things: first, defining the rules of the game (e.g., establishing international classifications and standards), and second, intervening in trade (e.g., by promoting or controlling trade). Before tackling these two aspects, we take a quick look at some of the main global organizations involved in international trade.

Which are the global organizations with an active role in administrating international trade? Before reading further, do you happen to recognize the logos of some of the main global organizations presented in Figure 6.9?

WTO—The World Trade Organization (WTO) was established in 1995 and is located in Switzerland. As of July 2016, it regrouped one hundred and sixty-four countries, and its main functions include: administering trade agreements and being a forum for trade negotiations, monitoring national trade policies, providing technical assistance and training for developing countries, and handling international trade disputes (WTO, 2017c). Overall, it promotes trade flows by encouraging nations to adopt non-discriminatory and predictable trade policies. Its website is a gold mine to understand anything related to international trade, from trade of goods and services (e.g., anti-dumping measures, import licensing, quantitative restrictions, tariff and non-tariff measures, rules of origin, sanitary measures) to trade-related

206 *Administrative Distance*

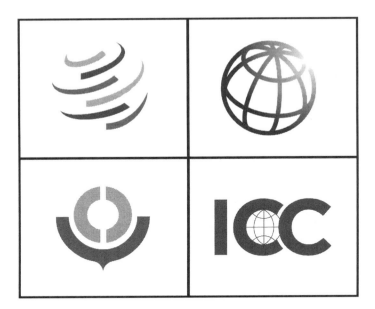

Figure 6.9 Presenting the logos of important international organizations
Source: Courtesy of the World Trade Organization, the World Bank, the World Customs Organization, and the International Chamber of Commerce

investment measures, regional trade agreements, preferential trade arrangements, and dispute settlement.

WIPO—Also headquartered in Switzerland, the World Intellectual Property Organization (WIPO) has existed since 1967 and counts with one hundred and eighty-nine state members (WIPO, 2017). Its role is to inform about topics related to intellectual property (IP), define and promote international rules for IP protection, offer legal and technical assistance, and, finally, establish procedures to solve disputes about IP. It works closely with national agencies such as the US Patent and Trademark Office (USPTO), the Canadian Intellectual Property Office (CIPO), and the French Institut National de la Propriété Industrielle (INPI).

WCO—The World Customs Organization (WCO) is located in Belgium and has been an independent intergovernmental body since 1952. Its mission is to enhance the effectiveness and efficiency of one hundred and eighty customs administrations across the globe (collectively processing approximately 98 percent of world trade). Founded on the principles that "Borders divide, Customs connects," the WCO provides support to customs administrations to facilitate legitimate trade, realize revenues, and protect society (WCO, 2017). Among many other services, it has developed the "Harmonized Commodity Description and Coding System," generally referred to as Harmonized System (HS). This international product nomenclature's purpose is further described in the next subsection.

Administrative Distance   207

World Bank—The World Bank was founded in 1944 and is headquartered in the US. It consists of the following five organizations: the International Bank for Reconstruction and Development (lends money to governments of middle- and low-income countries), the International Development Association (provides interest-free loans and grants to governments of the poorest countries), the International Finance Corporation (helps developing countries achieve sustainable growth by financing investment, mobilizing capital in international financial markets, and providing advisory services to businesses and governments), the Multilateral Investment Guarantee Agency (promotes FDI into developing countries by offering political risk insurance to investors and lenders), and the International Centre for Settlement of Investment Disputes (provides international facilities for conciliation and arbitration of investment disputes) (World Bank, 2017b). As such, its mission is heavily geared toward reducing poverty and supporting economic and social development. In addition to providing financial and technical assistance, the World Bank is also a major source of information (studies, raw data, etc.). It does not administrate international trade per se, but because it closely monitors it, its existence is of major interest for international marketers.

IMF—The International Monetary Fund (IMF) is another US-based organization founded in 1944. Regrouping one hundred and eighty-nine countries, its goals are to: foster global monetary cooperation, secure financial stability, facilitate international trade, promote high employment and sustainable economic growth, and reduce poverty around the world (IMF, 2017). As a source of information for marketers, the IMF's *World Economic Outlook Reports*, *Regional Economic Reports*, and *Principal Global Indicators* (e.g., exchange rates, interest rates, and consumer and producer price indices) are particularly useful.

ICC—Located in France, the International Chamber of Commerce (ICC) dates as far back as 1919. It has members in one hundred and thirty-five countries, and national committees in ninety countries. In addition, the ICC connects twelve thousand chambers of commerce worldwide through the World Chambers Federation (WCF). Although it resembles any other major intergovernmental organization, the delegates that are governing the ICC are business executives and not government officials. The ICC provides a variety of services to companies, including—but not limited to—delivering certificates of origin and Temporary Admission (ATA) carnets or "merchandise passports" (for duty-free temporary imports of goods such as commercial samples or goods for use at trade fairs), defining Incoterms® rules (see Chapter 4), offering dispute resolution mechanisms, e-learning courses, and online certifications for business professionals (ICC, 2017).

What can international organizations and national governments do to set the rules of international trade? One way for governmental and non-governmental organizations to be defining the rules of the game is through *classifications*. Classification systems help monitor flows across borders by providing a specific code for each industrial good. Customs agents use this code to know how to tax the merchandise. For goods, the main classification system is the HS (i.e., Harmonized System). It allows identifying goods and

208 *Administrative Distance*

shipments that pose a risk to the health, safety, and security, determining appropriate duty rates, negotiating trade agreements, and compiling trade statistics (CBSA, 2017). For the latter, one of the best information sources is COMTRADE, the United Nations' online database. Other systems exist, such as the SITC (i.e., Standard International Trade Classification, maintained by the UN), or more regional ones, such as the NAICS (i.e., the North American Industrial Classification System, with 5-digit codes standardized for Canada, Mexico, and the US, and a 6-digit allowing for national specificities). An example of how detailed the information can get is provided in Table 6.3 with crop production in the agriculture, forestry, fishing and hunting sector being broken down to the 6-digit level. What is important to note here is that all classification systems have a similar hierarchical structure with several digits, used to identify specific products.

Table 6.3 Illustrating the NAICS hierarchical structure with a focus on the Agriculture, Forestry, Fishing and Hunting sectors

Code					Sector
2-digit					
11	**3-digit**				Agriculture, forestry, fishing and hunting
⮕	111	**4-digit**			Crop production
	⮕	1111	**6-digit**		Oilseed and grain farming
		⮕	1111110		Soybean farming
			1111120		Oilseed (except soybean) farming
			1111130		Dry pea and bean farming
			1111140		Wheat farming
			1111150		Corn farming
			1111160		Rice farming
			1111190		Other grain farming
	⮕	1112			Vegetable and melon farming
	⮕	1113			Fruit and tree nut farming
	⮕	1114			Greenhouse, nursery and floriculture production
	⮕	1119			Other crop farming
⮕	112				Animal production and aquaculture
⮕	113				Forestry and logging
⮕	114				Fishing, hunting and trapping
⮕	115				Support activities for agriculture and forestry

Code	Sector	Code	Sector
2-digit		53	Real estate and rental and leasing
21	Mining, quarrying, and oil and gas extraction	54	Professional, scientific and technical services
22	Utilities	55	Management of companies and enterprises
23	Construction	56	Administrative and support, waste management and remediation services
31–33	Manufacturing	61	Educational services
41	Wholesale trade	62	Health care and social assistance
44–45	Retail trade	71	Arts, entertainment and recreation
48–49	Transportation and warehousing	72	Accommodation and food services
51	Information and cultural industries	81	Other services (except public administration)
52	Finance and insurance	91	Public administration

Source: Statistics Canada (2017)

Since more than one industrial classification system exists, it can be quite confusing when we look for duty rates information across markets. To find this information, the WCO recommends searching its website or the following websites: the Market Access Map, (created by the International Trade Center, which is the joint agency of the WTO and the UN dedicated to supporting the internationalization of SMEs since 1964), the European Union's Market Access Database, and the websites of the UNCTAD (i.e., the United Nations Conference on Trade And Development) and of the BITD (i.e., the International Customs Tariff Bureau).

Now, what more can international organizations do to set the rules of international trade? Another way for governmental and nongovernmental organizations to define the rules of the game is through *standards*. Setting industrial standards facilitates trade because it helps firms to benchmark products and services internationally. A well-known example is the International Organization for Standardization (ISO), which is the world's largest developer of voluntary international standards. ISO standards are developed through the consensus of globally established experts. They "provide a strong basis that can be applied in the development of national and international regulation. Not only do they help save time, they are essential tools for reducing barriers to international trade" (ISO, 2017). Popular standards include: ISO 9000 (quality management), ISO 14000 (environmental management), ISO 22000 (food safety management), ISO 26000 (social responsibility), ISO 31000 (risk management), and ISO 50001 (energy management).

210   *Administrative Distance*

How can national governments intervene in international trade? The new economic models of international trade developed in the 1980s—known as global strategic trade theory (see Chapter 4)—justify the need for government trade intervention. Everywhere, governments (at the levels of countries, states/provinces, and regions) routinely promote, restrict, and control international trade (Griffin & Pustay, 2015).

First, they can enhance trade flows by giving incentives to companies (e.g., subsidies in the form of tax rebates or attractive loans and other financing mechanisms to help them export) and by facilitating their operations with free trade zones (FTZ), geographic areas in which imported or about-to-be-exported goods receive preferential tariff treatment (Griffin & Pustay, 2015). Along with industrial associations, they also organize trade missions abroad, combining diplomatic and business interests. For instance, a Quebec premier traveled to Cuba for the first time in September 2016. He was accompanied by forty company representatives, in the context of a trade mission organized by Export Quebec (Montreal Gazette, 2016). Export Quebec is the provincial agency in charge of helping companies expand into foreign markets. Most governments have implemented such agencies. Another example is Export.gov, operated by the US Department of Commerce's International Trade Administration and nineteen other US government agencies. Among many other activities, Export.gov organizes trade missions for companies wishing to explore and pursue export opportunities (Export.gov, 2017).

Then, governments have the power to restrict inbound and outbound flows of goods using two main instruments: tariffs and non-tariff measures. Tariffs are customs duties on merchandise imports or exports. In addition to raising revenues for governments, tariffs can give a price advantage to locally-produced goods over imported goods (WTO, 2017e). Non-tariff measures include quotas, product and testing standards, restricted access to distribution networks, local purchase requirements, currency controls, and other measures (Griffin & Pustay, 2015). The WTO website is probably one of the best sources of information to understand the meaning and functioning of these instruments, in particular the "trade topics" section. Overall, governments decide on the intensity with which products enter and leave countries (see Chapter 4 for a few of the main international trade theories).

Finally, governments play a controller role, verifying that regulations are enforced and that trade agreements are respected. In particular, they keep an attentive eye on unfair trade practices (e.g., unfair pricing strategies such as dumping and subsidies by foreign governments that would distort trade). In the WTO agreement, the tool they mainly use in this role are "countervailing measures." Indeed, a country can use the dispute-settlement procedure to seek the withdrawal of the subsidy or the removal of its adverse effects, and ultimately charge countervailing duty (i.e., extra duty) on imports that are found to be hurting domestic producers (WTO, 2017f). We further discuss the resolution of disputes in the next subsection.

To what extent are governments' decisions affecting companies with international activities? It is safe to say that decisions by governments have a tremendous impact on companies. Governmental policies emerge as international managers' predominant concern. This is well illustrated in annual

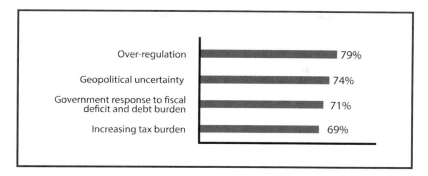

Figure 6.10 Presenting selected threats in the business world as perceived by global CEOs

Source: Adapted from PwC (2016)

surveys of CEOs in MNCs by PricewaterhouseCoopers (PwC) in which perceived threats related directly or indirectly to governmental decisions are always ranking high. For instance, a large proportion of surveyed CEOs consider over-regulation, geopolitical uncertainty, government response to fiscal deficit and debt burden, and increasing tax burden as key threats to their respective organization's growth prospects in a globalizing world, as illustrated in Figure 6.10. Over the years, other important perceived threats have included: exchange rate volatility, availability of key skills, social instability, and shifting consumer spending and behaviors. To a large extent, these threats also depend on governmental policies (labor protection, investment in research and development, regulations on product consumption, etc.).

6.3.2 Solving International Disputes

How can international disputes be resolved? The three main forms of dispute resolution include mediation (also called conciliation), arbitration, and litigation (Figure 6.11). First, companies can ask a third party to *mediate* their differences and agree on whatever solution is found by this third party. However, it is a nonbinding agreement. *Arbitration* also involves finding a disinterested and informed third party to act as a referee but the disputants agree to honor the judgment made. Contrary to mediation, arbitration results in a binding agreement. Finally, *litigation* is the last resort when everything else has failed. The WIPO website offers several examples of mediation and arbitration cases about patents, copyrights, and other disputes related to intellectual property.

Who are the actors involved in helping firms solve disputes with international counterparts? Legal disputes can arise between companies, between a company and a government or, finally, between governments. When companies are involved, disputes are solved at local courts or through mediation or arbitration. The most clear-cut decision can be made when international contracts include a jurisdictional clause, for example: "The parties hereby

Figure 6.11 Illustrating international commercial disputes
Source: Own image

agree that the agreement is made in Madrid, Spain, and that any question regarding this agreement shall be governed by the laws of Spain." At the level of governments, disputes are generally solved at the level of the WTO and the International Court of Justice (ICJ). The latter is the principal judicial organ of the UN and has been operating since 1946 from The Netherlands. An example of pending cases, as of March 2017, is the dispute between Bolivia and Chile for Bolivia to obtain access to the Pacific Ocean (obviously, such access would drastically increase the country's opportunity to participate in international trade). Other actors include the PCA (i.e., Permanent Court of Arbitration, established as early as 1899) and the ICCA (i.e., International Council for Commercial Arbitration, an NGO also located in The Netherlands).

In terms of resources, the WTO website offers an interactive tool to learn more about all kinds of disputes (e.g., measures affecting exports, patent protection, antidumping measures, safeguard measures, etc.). The "Dispute Map" is particularly useful and offers a quick overview on the number of cases that each country has pending (as complainant or respondent) with the WTO settlement body, as illustrated in Figure 6.12. The US and EU have

Figure 6.12 Mapping disputes between WTO members

Source: © World Trade Organization. Accessed April 2017 from WTO (2017a)

For the color version, see the eResource at www.routledge.com/9781138202344

214 *Administrative Distance*

the highest number of disputes pending. For cases that have been settled, the website offers the possibility of accessing settlements with detailed panel reports.

6.4 Issues at Stake

In this section, we take a look at some important issues, including the evolution over time of administrative distance (is it decreasing?), its impact on marketing, and possible remedies. To this purpose, we address the following questions:

- Are trade agreements and international standards always positive? Are they "building blocks" or "stumbling blocks" in the path toward global rules? Is administrative distance increasing or decreasing?
- To what extent does administrative distance impact marketers' decisions? What about laws with an impact on entry modes, product/brand decisions, pricing, distribution, and promotion?
- Is administrative distance always negative? What is one of the main challenges in overcoming administrative distance? How can companies overcome it? In particular, how can they reduce their vulnerability to risk in foreign countries?

6.4.1 Administrative Convergence

Are trade agreements and international standards always positive?[1] There is a debate in the current literature on whether free trade agreements (both bilateral and multilateral), regional agreements (e.g. EU or NAFTA), and international standards (e.g., ISO or International Labor Organization (ILO) norms) are beneficial for the participating parties, or if they create extra levels of complexity, sometimes with no evident gains. As far as the global economy is concerned, the phenomenon of integration appears to facilitate international trade and investment flows by ensuring common rules of the game and unified standards (e.g., Melitz, 2003). At the same time, many scholars of economic development, as well as of economic geography, argue that there are important nuances, as some agreements are more beneficial than others, and that certain types of countries and actors gain disproportionate benefits at the expense of other economic players (e.g., Rodrik, 2011).

For instance, Couillard and Turkina (2015) evaluate the effects of trade liberalization by analyzing the effects of free trade agreements on the dairy sector's competitiveness across seventy-six countries over a twenty-year period (1990–2009). With a longitudinal econometric model, the results demonstrated that when a country had an established comparative advantage, free trade agreements positively influenced several indicators of competitiveness (e.g., production, market share, and trade balance). The results also indicated that multilateral free trade agreements were more beneficial than bilateral agreements. Finally, they showed that the agreements were more beneficial to developed countries than to developing countries.

Administrative Distance 215

At the firm level, some authors argue that small or medium enterprises (SMEs) often lose from these agreements vis-à-vis powerful MNCs (Stiglitz, 2002). Additionally, several studies demonstrate that even though weaker actors tend to derive smaller benefits from the international arrangements, actors that happen to be outside these agreements (e.g., least developed countries) are losing even more from not being part of these initiatives (Hornok & Koren, 2016).

Another issue about agreements and standards concerns their role in the path toward global rules (see "Food for Thought").

Food for Thought 6.3

- Are trade agreements and international standards "building blocks" or "stumbling blocks" toward global rules for a truly global business?

Overall, is administrative distance increasing or decreasing? To this day, there is no agreement in the literature on whether we are converging toward similar political, legal, and institutional environments.

On the one hand, some scholars argue that strong evidence suggests a considerable degree of convergence at the regional level (e.g., Haas, 1971). Additionally, due to the network-based structure of the modern society (people-to-people networks, interfirm, and other interorganizational networks), many norms and standards penetrate via these network linkages, thereby resulting in changes in regulations. Therefore, changes are not only occurring in a top-down manner (when imposed by governments). For instance, Turkina and Postnikov (2012, 2014) investigate cross-border interfirm networks and found that the diffusion of organizational practices and norms is occurring within these networks. Using a social network analysis approach, they have also found instances when these norm and practice transfers resulted in convergence in legislation as a bottom-up process (e.g., firms actively lobbied for a change in regulations in their domestic market when the legislation did not favor the newly acquired knowledge and practices from foreign partners).

At the same time, other researchers note that even within well-established trading blocs (e.g., NAFTA, EU) there is a great deal of divergence (e.g., Lee, 2003). For instance, there are significant differences in legal standards, procedures and implementations between Mexico and the US policies, and environmental norms among EU countries are marked by heterogeneity, especially between the old members and countries in Eastern and Southern Europe. Moreover, some scholars argue that globalization, leading to increasing competition, does not favor all the actors involved in an equal manner (e.g., Schiff & Winters, 2003). This is why we witnessed a surge against integration, with members leaving the blocks (e.g., Brexit in 2016). According to these researchers, these tendencies may considerably increase administrative distance.

216   Administrative Distance

6.4.2 Impact on Marketing Decisions

To what extent does administrative distance impact marketers' decisions? This type of distance has a strong impact on marketing, both at the strategic and tactical levels. Among all the possible drivers of administrative distance, looking at examples related to regulations helps us to realize that marketing is particularly impacted in terms of: entry modes (e.g., anti-trust and competition regulations which can prevent companies from acquiring local firms, as well as laws against corruption), targeting (e.g., laws protecting vulnerable consumers such as children), product policies (e.g., laws on environmental practices, consumer safety, labeling and packaging, and intellectual property protection), pricing (e.g., laws against collusion among competitors to fix prices, use of monopolistic position to increase prices, price discrimination, and surge pricing), distribution (e.g., regulations about potentially dangerous products or about retailing business hours), and promotion (e.g., regulation of sales promotion, competitive advertising, and cyber law). The following paragraphs provide examples of companies who were found guilty of disrespecting local regulations. They illustrate that punishment can result in large or small fines, even for large MNCs.

What about laws with a possible impact on entry modes? Laws protecting competition (e.g., against trusts and cartels, price fixing, and corruption) often prevent companies from acquiring or partnering with foreign companies in a way they would normally. For instance, anticompetitive agreements are agreements between companies that restrict competition, such as cartels—where companies agree to avoid competing with each other or agree on the prices at which their products will be sold. Antitrust refers to the action of preventing or controlling trusts or other monopolies (European Commission, 2014). Examples of regulations and infringement are presented here:

- Carrefour (French retailer) was fined more than 14 million USD in 2010 for imposing resale price restrictions among members of its franchise network in Greece (European Commission, 2010).
- Intel (US chipmaker) was fined a record 1.06 billion euros (~1.2 billion USD) by the EU's antitrust regulation body in 2009. Among other faulty practices, the company was accused of obstructing its only competitor (Advanced Micro Devices) by giving rebates to computer makers (e.g., Acer, Dell, Hewlett Packard, and Lenovo) from 2002 until 2005, on the condition that they buy at least 95 percent of chips for personal computers from Intel (Bloomberg, 2016).
- Qualcomm Inc. (US mobile technologies company) was fined 975 million USD by China's National Development and Reform Commission in 2015 because it violated China's anti-monopoly law (The Globe and Mail, 2015).
- Rio Tinto (Anglo-Australian mining group) bid to buy Canadian Alcan in 2007 for 38.1 billion USD. As the deal would result in the world's largest maker of aluminum and bauxite, the bid had to also be approved by US antitrust authorities (BBC News, 2007).

Administrative Distance 217

- Servier (French pharmaceutical company) and five generic drug manufacturers were fined by the European Commission in 2014 for an amount of 430 million Euros (~490 million USD) because they had agreed to delay the entry into the European market of generic drugs in order to protect Servier's flagship drug Perindopril (European Union, 2016).

In the same vein, companies cannot agree to fix prices, divide up markets among themselves, or abuse a dominant position in a particular market to squeeze out smaller competitors (European Union, 2016). The examples below illustrate various punishments received by companies for price fixing:

- Apple (US technology company) was accused in 2015 by the US Justice Department of colluding with five publishers (Hachette, HarperCollins, Penguin, Simon & Schuster, and Macmillan) to eliminate retail price competition and raise e-book prices. The practice occurred in 2010 and prices increased to 12.99–14.99 USD (from 9.99 USD previously charged by Amazon.com) with the objective of breaking up Amazon.com's low-cost dominance in the digital book market. The company was forced to pay 450 million USD as part of a settlement (The Guardian, 2016a).
- Bridgestone (Japanese tire and rubber producer) was charged with conspiring to allocate sales, rig bids and fix prices of parts sold to Toyota, Nissan, Suzuki, Isuzu, and Fuji Heavy Industries in the US (2001–2008). The company had to pay a 425 million USD criminal fine (a particularly high amount because of its previous conviction for conspiring to fix prices in the marine hose industry). Overall, a three-year investigation by the US Justice Department's Antitrust Division has yielded more than 2 billion USD in criminal fines as more than two dozen Japanese automotive suppliers pleaded guilty to conspiring to fix the prices of parts sold to automakers in the US and abroad (New York Times, 2014).
- Mercedes-Benz (German car manufacturer) was fined almost 60 million USD in China in 2015 because the carmaker pressured local dealers into setting a minimum sales price on some of its car models (BBC News, 2015).
- Samsung (South Korea), Philips (The Netherlands) and Infineon (Germany) were fined a total of 138 million Euros (~150 million USD) in 2014 following a European antitrust investigation regarding a price-fixing scheme for chips used in mobile SIM cards between 2003 and 2005 (The Wall Street Journal, 2014).

Finally, corruption rigs competition. It is the object of much debate because of differences in values and beliefs across cultures. Consequently, behaviors (such as favoring long-term business partners over other players) can be judged as totally unacceptable in some countries, while being frowned upon but tolerated or perceived as entirely normal in others. In international business, corruption has long been regulated but is under increasing scrutiny with, for instance, the OECD's Convention on Combating Bribery of Foreign Public Officials in International Business Transactions (1997) and the Anti-Bribery Recommendation (2009) (OECD, 2017).

218   *Administrative Distance*

At the country level, the Sarbanes-Oxley Act (US) and the Corruption of Foreign Public Officials Act (Canada) are examples of regulations constraining national firms' potential misbehavior. The latter, for instance, states that a person (e.g., a manager or employee in a company) commits an offence when he or she offers a loan, reward, advantage, or benefit of any kind to a foreign public official (or to any person for the benefit of a foreign public official), in order to obtain a direct or indirect advantage in the course of business. This offence is punishable with up to fourteen years in prison (Government of Canada, 1998). Examples of corruption allegations and punishments are presented below:

- Dumex (an infants' and children's nutrition company, part of French Groupe Danone) has been accused of bribing hospital staff in China with payments of up to 10,000 Yuan (~1,500 USD) in the form of "sponsorship fees" to promote its baby formula (BBC News, 2013).
- Griffiths Energy International (Canadian oil and gas company) was fined 10 million CAD (~7.5 million USD) in 2013, for a bogus consulting contract with the wife of Chad's ambassador to Canada, a contract that was deemed equivalent to a bribe (The Globe and Mail, 2013).
- SNC-Lavallin (engineering company from Canada) was accused of paying 160 million CAD (~115 million USD) to the son of dictator Muammar Gaddafi in Libya in order to obtain major contracts in the country (National Post, 2013).

What about laws with an impact on product/brand decisions? Laws ensuring company and consumer protection (e.g., IP protection and packaging restrictions) can have important effects on decisions related to international product policies. For instance, examples of infringement abound when it comes to regulations aimed at protecting firms' intellectual property (one of their core assets). Sometimes, the protection mechanisms in place can seem disproportionate to the risks involved, such as in a few of the examples presented here:

- Louis Vuitton (French luxury company) filed a suit in 2015 against a restaurant in Seoul (South Korea) because it was named "Louis Vuiton Dak." Specializing in fried chicken, the restaurant name was a play on the word *tongdak* which means "whole chicken" in Korean. Its owner first responded to the legal threat by tinkering with the restaurant name ("chaLouisvui tondak") but Louis Vuitton complained again and the court judged the name was not different enough. It ordered the restaurant's owner to pay the fashion house 14.5 million won (~12,500 USD) for the twenty-nine days that the amended name was displayed (South China Morning Post, 2016).
- Nivea (a brand of cosmetics belonging to German group Beiersdorf) pursued Vinea (a German fitness and wellness park) for trademark infringement in 2014 due to the similarity in brand names. Ultimately, Vinea changed its name to Vivana (Rheingau Echo, 2014).

Administrative Distance 219

- Starbucks (US coffee chain) complained against trademark infringement by Star Box Coffee (UK), a small coffee outdoor kiosk located close to a London underground station. The owner and sole employee of the kiosk removed the word Star from his main sign, menus, posters, and stickers to avoid "weakening Starbucks' global brand" (Daily Mail, 2017).

Regulations aiming to protect and inform consumers (e.g., against health issues or misinformation and false claims from companies) also give way to a number of violations, illustrated below:

- Apple was fined 2,500 CAD (~1,800 USD) in 2012 because an employee in a Quebec city store offered AppleCare to a customer instead of following the required information procedure (e.g., mentioning that the product was already protected with a warranty according to local regulations) (Le Soleil, 2014).
- Chevron (US oil giant) was fined in Ecuador for an amount of 8.6 billion USD in 2011 for polluting a large part of the country's Amazon region between 1972 and 1992 (BBC News, 2011).
- Taiwan banned Japanese food imports from areas near Fukushima in 2011 after the earthquake and tsunami that triggered a nuclear meltdown at a power plant in order to protect consumers from health problems (Reuters, 2015).
- The "plain tobacco packaging" regulation forces tobacco companies to remove logos and colors that would allow consumers to recognize brands (brand names are authorized but have to be written in a uniform plain style) (CNTC, 2017)(Figure 6.13). It has been implemented in Australia (2011), as well as in France and the UK (2016) (Framework Convention Alliance, 2016). In 2012, this regulation was challenged by several tobacco exporting countries (e.g., Honduras, the Dominican Republic, Cuba, and Indonesia) with a formal complaint at the WTO; by the end of 2017, and due to complex legal and factual issues, the panel in charge of examining the case had still not issued its final report, thus exceeding by far the usual 6-month period allocated for making a recommendation to the dispute settlement body (WTO, 2017d).
- The COOL (Country of Origin Labeling) regulation became mandatory in the US in 2008 for certain meats, vegetables, fruits, and nuts sold to private consumers. It has been taken to the WTO by Canada (joined by Mexico) since the cost associated with adding a country of origin label has proven to significantly impact the retail price. It also affected business practices, since American meat transformation plants used to mix Canadian and American cattle. Impeding this practice resulted in lowering considerably Canadian meat procurement. Overall, this regulation was accused of creating an unfair trade environment (Mullins, 2010).
- The US, Canada, and Argentina complained in 2003 against the EU for measures affecting the approval and marketing of biotech products and genetically modified organisms (WTO, 2010).

220 *Administrative Distance*

Figure 6.13 Example of plain packaging for cigarettes
Source: Courtesy of the CNTC (Comité National Contre le Tabagisme) in France

What about laws with an impact on pricing? Pricing is a marketing activity that is under intense scrutiny by regulators because it can lead to unfair situations for consumers or competitors. Whether because of unclear pricing or price discrimination, many companies have been punished for minor or major infringements. Examples are provided here:

- Amazon (US online retailer) was fined 1 million CAD (~750,000 USD) by Canada's competition bureau in 2017 relative to pricing practices on its local website between 2014 and 2016. Indeed, the company used to compare its own prices to a regular "list price," without verifying that the list prices provided by its suppliers were accurate. In doing so, it suggested a savings incentive for consumers and created the impression that its prices were lower than prevailing market prices (Financial Post, 2017).
- Ryanair (Irish low cost airline) was fined 330,000 GBP (~372,000 USD) in 2013 by the Netherlands Consumer Authority for unclear prices at the start of online booking procedures. After getting into legal troubles in the UK for the same reason, the company's UK website started

presenting passengers with a total price including their fare and other "hidden charges" (e.g., a web check-in fee, an administration fee, an Emissions Trading Scheme levy, and a credit card payment charge) (The Telegraph, 2013).

- Sephora (French company of cosmetics) received an 18,000 CAD fine (~13,500 USD) in 2010 because one of its stores in Montreal violated Quebec's accurate pricing law (2001). According to this law, retailers must display prices on shelves, have a scanner at the cash register, and a bar code on each product. Prior to this case, Costco and Walmart were fined for the same reason (17,500 CAD and 32,510 CAD, respectively) (Toronto Sun, 2015).

Dumping is considered international price discrimination. It occurs when the price of a product in the importing country is less than the price in the exporting country, or when the importing country can prove that the price is unfair to local manufacturers. As such, retaliation is allowed and anti-dumping measures often take the form of compensatory import duty rates to level off the price difference (WTO, 2016a). Interestingly, many countries are accused of wrongly imposing anti-dumping measures to protect their own manufacturers, as illustrated in some of the examples provided below:

- Chinese solar panels exported to the US were found to be sold below production costs; for this reason, the US imposed a compensatory measure (31–250 percent duty rate) in 2012 to level the playing field (ProSun, 2012).
- EU steel producers have complained about a flood of products from China sold for less than they cost to make, due to Chinese overcapacity. Consequently, the EU imposed import duties on different types of Chinese made steel (for instance, 65–74 percent for heavy-plate steel) (Euronews, 2016).
- Recent complaints at the WTO include: China against Taiwan for dumping practices on USB flash drives (2015); the Russian Federation against Ukraine for anti-dumping measures on ammonium nitrate (2015); Canada against China for its anti-dumping duties on imports of cellulose pulp (2014); and Argentina against the EU regarding anti-dumping measures imposed on biodiesel (2013).

What about laws with an impact on distribution? Regulations aiming at protecting consumers' safety, local manufacturers, the environment, or a specific set of beliefs in society (e.g., religious rest, food surplus) often impact distribution and retail activities (e.g., controlled products, opening hours, local sourcing, waste management), as illustrated below:

- The recreational use of marijuana is prohibited in many countries. A change in legislation in Canada could legalize it in 2018. It would give the right to provinces to decide how the drug is distributed and sold (including pricing and minimum age requirements). As for Canadians

222   *Administrative Distance*

growing their own marijuana, they would be limited to four plants per household (CBC News, 2017).

- While alcohol importations are private in many European countries, it is restricted under provincial authorities in Canada. In Quebec, for instance, any importations must be made through Société des Alcools du Québec (SAQ, 2017). The provincial-owned corporation gives a large but controlled selection of brands and types of alcohol to restaurants and bars, drugstores, and grocery stores.
- In Sweden, Systembolaget is the only retail store that sells alcoholic beverages, but unlike the SAQ in Quebec, Systembolaget does not have the right to directly import products, but must do it through authorized importers (Resnick & De Roany, 2014).
- Many countries maintain restrictive retail opening hours. For instance, Germany rejected pleas in 2004 from retailers to be allowed to open on Sundays and public holidays (BBC News, 2004). In Jerusalem (Israel), several grocery stores were forced to close on Shabbat following a city decision in 2016 to apply religious law more strictly (The Jerusalem Post, 2016). Meanwhile, shops and restaurants in some touristic places like downtown Montreal (Canada) are permitted to operate 24/7 (Montreal Gazette, 2015b)—which does not mean that they all do.
- To ensure customer satisfaction, supermarkets often throw away good-quality food approaching its "best-before" date. To avoid food poisonings from items removed from the bins, reportedly, some do not hesitate to purposefully spoil the food (e.g., by dosing it with bleach). In 2016, France became the first country in the world to make this type of food waste illegal. Supermarkets with a footprint of 400 square meters (4,305 square feet) or more are required to sign donation contracts with charities or else face fines of 3,750 euros (~4,000 USD) (The Guardian, 2016b).
- In India, foreign retailers are obliged by law to sell a minimum of 30 percent of locally-sourced goods if they want to open wholly owned stores. In 2015, a change in legislation exempted retailers of high-tech goods. Yet, Apple did not qualify right away for this exemption, one of the reasons why the company struggled with its expansion in the country (Reuters, 2016).

What about laws with an impact on communication and promotion? Laws aiming at protecting consumers (e.g., privacy) and, in a larger perspective, the interests of society as a whole (e.g., cultural specificity, religion) or of specific groups of citizens (e.g., women rights) often differ internationally and restrict companies in the way they can communicate and promote their offerings. Examples of issues in this regard include the following companies:

- Benetton (Italian fashion company) had to withdraw an advertising image included in their "Unhate" campaign showing the pope kissing a senior Egyptian imam after the Vatican protested and called the campaign totally unacceptable (Daily Mail, 2011).

- Dolce & Gabbana (Italian luxury company) saw one of its campaigns banned in Spain after complaints from womens' rights defense organizations. The controversial image featured a woman in a submissive position surrounded by several men, possibly suggestive of collective rape. Consequently, the company made the decision to stop advertising in Spain in order to protect their own creative freedom (Le Nouvel Observateur, 2007).
- Laws against Internet spamming forces companies to ask and obtain consent from consumers before sending newsletters and other communications. For instance, Canada's new anti-spam law (passed in 2010, entered into force in 2014 and reinforced in 2015) prohibits the sending of commercial electronic messages without the recipient's permission, including messages to email addresses and social networking accounts, and text messages sent to a cell phone (Government of Canada, 2017).
- MNCs such as Nestlé (Switzerland), and Heinz and Abbott (US) were accused by the Breastfeeding Promotion Network of India (BPNI) and the International Baby Food Action Network (IBFAN) of breaking baby milk laws by promoting milk formula and infant cereals over breastfeeding, which is considered a more accessible way of ensuring babies' health (Reuters, 2013).
- To safeguard the French idiom, the Charter of the French language in Quebec (Canada) imposes that public signs, posters, and commercial advertising be either in French or in both French and another language, provided that French is markedly predominant. In this way, Kentucky Fried Chicken translated its brand name (*Poulet Frit Kentucky*) and McDonald's translated product names like Happy Meal into *Joyeux Festin* (Business Insider India, 2016). In turn, Second Cup changed its name to Second Cup Café & Cie (Montreal Gazette, 2015a). Interestingly, France does not impose similar protection mechanisms for safeguarding its language.

6.4.3 Challenges and Opportunities in Overcoming Administrative Distance

Is administrative distance always negative? It is possible to argue that administrative distance is not always negative. It has a "direction," i.e., it can be negative or positive depending on the firms' starting point, in other words, their country of origin. Firms from countries with less-efficient political, legal, and institutional environments (such as developing and emerging countries) could find it easier to commercialize their offerings in developed economies, characterized by better administrative conditions. This assumption needs more research to be ascertained as these firms' capability to navigate uncertainties and find creative ways around hurdles may not be exploitable anymore. Tighter regulatory frameworks might prevent them from doing business the way they are used to. However, it is reasonable to assume that more stability and transparency, and easier access to information, and the presence of key institutional actors (e.g., analyzers and credibility enhancers)

224 *Administrative Distance*

facilitate the decision-making process of these firms. The other way around, administrative distance could represent a systematic barrier for firms from developed economies venturing into less-developed economies, with poorer administrative conditions. Yet, here again, we can take the devil's advocate position and argue that many MNCs have not hesitated to exploit interesting "institutional voids," in particular less-constraining regulations (e.g., on consumer and environmental protection). This calls to observe one of the main challenges to take into account about administrative distance.

What is one of the main challenges in overcoming administrative distance? One of the main challenges is to first come with a fine-tuned understanding of its importance and implications, according to the business in question, before even trying to overcome it. The difficulty stems from the sheer number of factors to take into account to assess differences between countries, as well as from finding accessible, reliable, and industry-specific information sources. We have seen that differences in institutional landscapes and legal systems are important drivers. We have also seen the role played by lower or higher degrees of risks and regional integration in decreasing or increasing barriers to international business. For each one of these drivers, we have highlighted multiple indicators and sources.

In research, the way administrative distance is captured is quite simplistic, compared to the task at hand. It also often involves creative ways of finding relevant proxies. For instance, Brewer (2007) operationalizes the measure of administrative distance—while capturing psychic distance (see Table 4.1, in Chapter 4)—by relying on three indicators for political ties (i.e., number of bilateral or regional free trade agreements, value of aid programs, and number of trade representations offices), and two indicators for historic ties (i.e., colonial relationships—measured as either direct colonial relationship, membership of the same empire or no colonial relationship, and shared wars for both World War I and II—as either allies, neutral or enemies).

In turn, Xu et al. (2004) measures differences in terms of "regulative institutions" using single items tapping the following seven dimensions: institutional stability ("the chance that the legal and political institutions in your country will change drastically in the next five years is low"), anti-trust laws ("anti-trust or anti-monopoly policy in your country effectively promotes competition"), settlement of disputes ("citizens of your country are willing to accept legal means to adjudicate disputes rather than depending on physical force or illegal means"), legal system ("the legal system in your country is effective in enforcing commercial contracts"), product liability ("legal claims for product liability are not an important cost of business in your country"), impartiality of arbitration ("private business can readily file suits at independent and impartial courts if there is a breach of trust on the part of government"), and finally, effectiveness of police force ("your country's police are effective in safeguarding personal security so that this is an important consideration in business activity").

Finally, Yang et al. (2012) measures "institutional distance" with six items pertaining to: enforceability of business laws, impartiality of arbitration, dispute settlement, intellectual property protection, institutional stability, and number of regulatory bodies of enforcement.

Administrative Distance   225

These examples of scientific investigation show that one of the advantages of such a simplified approach is to get a sense of administrative distance. The disadvantage is that it provides only a limited picture, one on which companies cannot fully rely. As Ghemawat (2001) puts it, administrative distance is among the most ignored dimensions of distance. More than sixteen years later, this seems to still be the case. Yet, it may not be because firms underestimate its importance, but because they lack the tools to assess it in an extensive and time-efficient manner. Complexity is a real issue in assessing administrative distance. Another important issue, one dealing with relevance, is raised in "Food for Thought."

Food for Thought 6.4

- In reference to Ghemawat (2001), to what extent is administrative distance industry-specific?

How can companies overcome administrative distance then? To sum it up, firms can do "extensive homework" about the target-country, carefully choose the entry mode, expand their investment base, and finally, contract insurance.

First, companies must spend time and the necessary resources to do extensive research about as many drivers of administrative distance as possible. Collecting secondary data is one thing, but administrative distance—like cultural distance—is often best captured with primary data that "country scouts" (i.e., employees taking trips and spending time in selected foreign countries, talking to knowledgeable people and observing practices) can bring back home.

Then, choosing an adapted entry mode is one of the best coping mechanisms for a firm willing to enter "administratively challenged" and risky countries. Licensing to local firms and creating joint-ventures with local firms are two entry modes commonly used. In the first case, granting a foreign partner with the responsibility of manufacturing their goods, for instance, prevents foreign companies from being directly affected by any of the factors that increase risk. Second, doing business with a committed local partner helps to acquire information quickly in case of political changes and often minimize hostile decisions from local governments.

Next, the rationale behind expanding the investment base is similar. When companies open their foreign ventures' equity to local governments (whether at the national, regional, or municipal levels) and local investors, these actors become financially interested in the venture's success. This minimizes the risk that the same government will take adversarial decisions against the foreign firm. Disney is a good example of this practice with its amusement park business. For instance, the company did not hesitate to heavily involve the local governments when entering Hong Kong and Shanghai (HKU 885, 2010; UV 7197, 2016).

226 *Administrative Distance*

Finally, a common way to counter vulnerability whenever there is risk, is to contract insurance. It works for our cars or our houses and it also works for businesses when they export or undertake FDI. Many private banks as well as governmental agencies offer specialized insurance services for all sorts of risks abroad (e.g., political and currency risks). Examples include the MIGA (i.e., Multilateral Investment Guarantee Agency, a branch of the World Bank Group), or at the level of countries the OPIC (i.e., Overseas Private Investment Corporation, the US government's development finance institution), EDC (i.e., Export Development Canada, Canada's export credit agency) and COFACE (i.e., Compagnie Française d'Assurance pour le Commerce Extérieur, a French private organization).

One particular type of risk concerns IP protection. To a certain extent, patenting allows reacting against copy of products and manufacturing processes. In most cases, patenting supposes to ask for protection in each country at specific national offices (e.g., the USPTO, CIPO, and INPI). In some instances, there is a facilitated approach to patenting across regional blocks. For instance, companies had to protect their trademarks in each one of the EU countries. Since 2006 and with the Council on the Community Trade Mark, companies only need to apply once for IP protection for the reasonable amount of 1,000 Euros (~1,060 USD, as of March 2017) (EUR-Lex, 2006). The protection lasts ten years and can be renewed. The OHIM (i.e., Office for Harmonization in the Internal Market) is an example of agencies trying to reduce administrative complexity as regards IP protection. We can note here that entering countries that are part of one regional block—i.e., sharing extensive trade agreements—is another way to reduce administrative distance.

Conclusion: Administrative Distance Matters Because It Generates Uncertainty and Complexity. It Could Be Decreasing, Yet. . .

What would a nomological network for administrative distance look like? A *nomological network* has been defined as the representation of the constructs of interest in a study, their observable manifestations and the interrelationships among and between them (Cronbach & Meehl, 1955). Figure 6.14 presents an overview of the proposed nomological network for administrative distance in relation to marketing. In its center, it situates administrative distance as the phenomenon under scrutiny. It reminds us that administrative distance is about contrasting firms' home country and target foreign countries in terms of their political, legal, and institutional environments. On the left-hand side of the figure, we find several important drivers of administrative distance (e.g., differences in political climate, regional integration, legal system, presence of adjudicators, and institutional landscape). In this overview of "causes," we focus on governments (at various levels: national, municipal, etc.), and global organizations, as key actors determining the degree of administrative distance for firms. In turn, the right-hand side of the figure captures the fact that outcomes of administrative distance are found at all levels of marketing. Thus, administrative distance heavily impacts

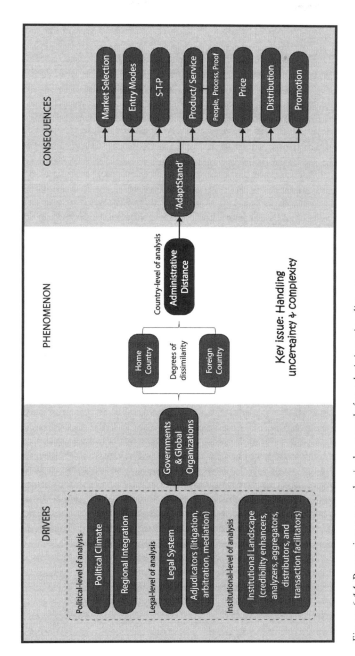

Figure 6.14 Proposing a nomological network for administrative distance

Source: Own elaboration

228 *Administrative Distance*

AdaptStand decisions for marketing (see Chapter 3). Companies have the opportunity to standardize when administrative distance is low, and an obligation to adapt when administrative distance is high. Contrary to other types of distance, firms not only incur the risk of failing if they do not adapt to foreign countries' administrative environments when required, but they can also be entirely denied the opportunity to do business there.

So, why does administrative distance matter for marketing in a globalizing world? Back to our initial question, we have seen that a lack of knowledge and understanding about foreign administrative environments—or else unpredictable changes in these environments—result in major difficulties for firms. Contrary to cultural distance, which requires a fine understanding of subtle and tacit differences among countries, administrative distance is of a technical nature. The differences are explicit and public records are available. However, the complexity (notably due to technical jargon and varying degrees of governmental intervention) renders country comparison equally challenging. Thus, administrative distance matters because it forces companies to deal with elevated degrees of uncertainty and complexity in doing business. Simply put, the key issue for marketers when looking at foreign markets from the angle of administrative distance is then: "**handling uncertainty and complexity**" (see Figure 6.14).

Finally, is administrative distance decreasing worldwide? In Chapter 1, we discussed the phenomenon of globalization as following a pendulum-like movement, with alternative phases of acceleration and deceleration. Integration (at the regional and international levels) is an inherent mechanism of globalization. After reading this chapter, the role of integration as one determinant of administrative distance should be clear. Thus, to a large extent, the reduction of administrative distance between countries signals a trend toward integration, and by extension, globalization. It should come as no surprise that part of the answer to the question of whether administrative distance is increasing or decreasing relies on examining the same pendulum-like movements as we did for globalization.

In this chapter, we have seen that the literature is conflicted on the topic and that evidence of decreasing administrative distance (e.g., trade agreements are consistently signed at the WTO) coexists with evidence of increasing administrative distance (e.g., creation of complex rules and standards unfavorable to some actors, such as developing countries and their firms). Overall, there has been a trend toward decreasing administrative distance since the end of World War II. However, recent events (e.g., the rise of protectionism and far right movements in Europe and the US) may signal a future push toward an increase in administrative distance. This mixed evidence could well be symptomatic of a transition period between two phases. Spanning decades, these pendulum-like phases express at the societal level the very human tension between wanting and fearing what is foreign, between embracing others' ways and protecting one's own territory and habits. Sociologists, equipped to analyze these trends over long periods of time, are surely better positioned to answer this question than marketers. Yet, what we need to remember to make marketing-related decisions is that a definitive "Yes, administrative distance is decreasing" or "No, it's not" are misleading answers. They omit a large part of the complexity of our social reality. Changes in politics guide the evolution of administrative distance and these changes are not cohesive at the global scale. Carefully considering administrative distance between countries when conducting marketing activities abroad remains crucial.

In the next chapter, we look into two interrelated dimensions of distance between countries: economic and technological distances.

Note

1 In Subsection 6.4.1, the paragraphs entitled "Are trade agreements and international standards always positive?" and "Overall, is administrative distance increasing or decreasing?" have been written in collaboration with Ekaterina Turkina, Associate Professor in International Business (HEC Montréal, Canada), whose research interests include state-business relations, socio-cultural, and institutional impact on interfirm networks, as well as on industrial clusters.

References

BBC News (2004, June 9th). Germany Rejects Sunday Shopping. Retrieved from http://news.bbc.co.uk/2/hi/business/3792015.stm

BBC News (2007, August 27th). Rio Tinto's Alcan Deal Approved. Retrieved from http://news.bbc.co.uk/2/hi/business/6965189.stm

BBC News (2011, February 15th). Chevron Fined for Amazon Pollution by Ecuador Court. Retrieved from www.bbc.com/news/world-latin-america-12460333

BBC News (2013, October 15th). Danone in Management Shuffle Amid China Bribery Claims. Retrieved from www.bbc.com/news/business-24530034

BBC News (2015, April 23rd). China Fines Daimler's Mercedes-Benz for Price-Fixing. Retrieved from www.bbc.com/news/business-32426042

Bloomberg (2016, June 21st). Intel Fights Record $1.2 Billion Antitrust Fine at Top EU Court, *By Stephanie Bodoni*. Retrieved from www.bloomberg.com/news/articles/2016-06-21/intel-fights-record-1-2-billion-antitrust-fine-at-top-eu-court

Brewer, Paul (2007). Operationalizing Psychic Distance: A Revised Approach. *Journal of International Marketing, 15*(1), 44–66.

Business Insider India (2016). 15 of Your Favorite Brands That Are Called Entirely Different Things Abroad. Retrieved March 2017, from www.businessinsider.in/15-of-your-favorite-brands-that-are-called-entirely-different-things-abroad/KFC-PFK-in-Quebec-Canada/slideshow/53196743.cms

CBC News (2017, March 26th). Liberals to Announce Marijuana Will Be Legal by July 1, 2018, *By David Cochrane*. Retrieved from www.cbc.ca/news/politics/liberal-legal-marijuana-pot-1.4041902

CBSA (2017). Harmonized Commodity Description and Coding System. Canada Border Service Agency. Retrieved March 2017, from www.cbsa-asfc.gc.ca/trade-commerce/tariff-tarif/hcdcs-hsdcm/menu-eng.html

Cherchye, Laurens & Moesen, Wim (2003). *Institutional Infrastructure and Economic Performance: Levels Versus Catching Up and Frontier Shifts* Discussions Paper Series, No. 03.14. Center for Economic Studies—Leuven Catholic University Retrieved from https://feb.kuleuven.be/eng/ew/discussionpapers/Dps03/Dps0314.pdf

230 *Administrative Distance*

CNTC (2017). Instauration de paquets neutres pour les produits du tabac. Comité National Contre le Tabagisme. Retrieved April 2017, from www. cnct.fr/nos-actions-de-plaidoyers-90/instauration-de-paquets-neutres-pour-les-produits-du-tabac-1–59.html

Coface (2017). Country Risk Assessment Map (1st Quarter). Retrieved April 2017, from www.coface.ca/News-Publications/News/Coface-Country-Risk-Outlook-2017

Couillard, Catherine & Turkina, Ekaterina (2015). Trade Liberalisation: The Effects of Free Trade Agreements on the Competitiveness of the Dairy Sector. *The World Economy, 38*(6), 1015–1033.

Cronbach, Lee Joseph & Meehl, Paul (1955). Construct Validity in Psychological Tests. *Psychological Bulletin, 52*(4), 281–302.

Czinkota, Michael, Ronkainen, Ilkka & Moffett, Michael (2011). *International Business* (8th ed.). Hoboken, NJ: John Wiley and Sons (p. 731).

Daily Mail (2011, November 17th). Benetton Withdraws Ad Campaign Image of Pope Kissing Egyptian Imam After Vatican Complains It Is Disrespectful. Retrieved from www.dailymail.co.uk/news/article-2062423/Benetton-Unhate-advert-Pope-kissing-imam-withdrawn-Vatican-calls-disrespectful.html

Daily Mail (2017, March 16th). Starbucks Forces Tiny Coffee Kiosk to Change Its Name from Star Box Coffee Because It Could 'Weaken' Its Global Brand— but Marxist Owner Refuses £300 'Goodwill Payment', *By Katie French*. Retrieved from www.dailymail.co.uk/news/article-4319260/Starbucks-forces-Star-Box-Coffee-change-name.html#ixzz4dsCd2uUK

EUR-Lex (2006). Community Trade Mark. European Union. Retrieved April 2017, from http://eur-lex.europa.eu/legal-content/EN/TXT/HTML/?uri= URISERV:l26022a&from=FR

Euronews (2016, October 7th). Brussels Sets Import Duties on Some Chinese Steel over Dumping Claims. Retrieved from www.euronews.com/2016/10/07/brussels-sets-import-duties-on-some-chinese-steel-over-dumping-claims

European Commission (2010). Greece: Carrefour Fined for Restrictive Practices in Greek Franchise Network Retrieved March 2017, from http://ec.europa.eu/competition/ecn/brief/04_2010/el_carrefour.pdf

European Commission (2014). The EU Explained: Competition. Luxembourg: Publications Office of the European Union. https://bookshop.europa.eu/en/com petition-pbNA0216161/?CatalogCategoryID=sciep2OwkgkAAAE.xjhtLxJz

European Union (2016). Competition. Retrieved April 2017, from http://europa. eu/pol/comp/index_en.htm

Export.gov (2017). Department of Commerce Organized Trade Missions. Retrieved April 2017, from http://2016.export.gov/trademissions/index.asp

Financial Post (2017, January 11th). Amazon Canada Fined $1 Million plus $100,000 Costs for Misleading Price Claims on Website, *By Hollie Shaw*. Retrieved from http://business.financialpost.com/news/retail-marketing/ama zon-canada-fined-1-million-plus-costs-for-misleading-price-claims-on-website

Framework Convention Alliance (2016). France and UK Join Australia as Plain Packaging Leaders. Retrieved April 2017, from www.fctc.org/fca-news/opinion-pieces/1413-france-and-uk-join-australia-as-plain-packing-leaders#sthash. O5olTwPL.dpuf

Freedom House (2017). Freedom in the World. Retrieved February 2017, from https://freedomhouse.org/report/fiw-2017-table-country-scores

Administrative Distance   231

Ghemawat, Pankaj (2001). Distance Still Matters: The Hard Reality of Global Expansion. *Harvard Business Review*, 79(8), 137–147.

The Globe and Mail (2013, January 25th). Judge Approves $10.35-Million Fine for Griffiths Energy in Bribery Case, *By Kelly Kryderman*. Retrieved from www.theglobeandmail.com/report-on-business/industry-news/the-law-page/judge-approves-1035-million-fine-for-griffiths-energy-in-bribery-case/article7858675/

The Globe and Mail (2015, February 9th). Qualcomm Fined $975-Million in China Antitrust Case, *By Ian King*. Retrieved from www.theglobeandmail.com/report-on-business/international-business/qualcomm-fined-975-million-in-china/article22883526/

Government of Canada (1998). Corruption of Foreign Public Officials Act. Justice Laws Website. Retrieved April 2017, from http://laws-lois.justice.gc.ca/eng/acts/C-45.2/page-1.html

Government of Canada (2017). Canada's Anti-Spam Legislation. Retrieved March 2017, from http://fightspam.gc.ca/eic/site/030.nsf/eng/h_00039.html

Griffin, Ricky & Pustay, Michael (2015). *International Business* (8th ed.). New Jersey: Pearson (p. 624).

The Guardian. (2016a, March 7th). Apple to Pay $450m Settlement over US Ebook Price Fixing. Retrieved from www.theguardian.com/technology/2016/mar/07/apple-450-million-settlement-e-book-price-fixing-supreme-court

The Guardian. (2016b, February 04th). French Law Forbids Food Waste by Supermarkets, *By Angelique Chrisafis*. Retrieved from www.theguardian.com/world/2016/feb/04/french-law-forbids-food-waste-by-supermarkets

Haas, Ernst (1971). The Study of Regional Integration: Reflections on the Joy and Anguish of Pretheorizing. In *Regional Integration: Theory and Research*, Leon Lindberg and Stuart Scheingold (Editors). Cambridge: Harvard University Press (p. 3–44).

Heritage Foundation (2017). Index of Economic Freedom. Retrieved February 2017, from www.heritage.org/index/download

HKU 885 (2010). Disney: Losing Magic in the Middle Kingdom. Case written by: Ali Farhoomand. Hong Kong: Asia Case Research Centre (p. 31).

Hornok, Cecilia & Koren, Miklos (2016). Winners and Losers of Globalisation: Sixteen Challenges for Measurement and Theory. In *Economics without Borders, Economic Research for European Policy Challenges*, Richard Blundell, Laszlo Matyas, Marc Ivaldi, Estelle Cantillon, Barbara Chizzolini, Wolfgang Leininger, Ramon Marimon, and Frode Steen (Editors). Cambridge: Cambridge University Press (p. 238–273).

ICC (2017). About us. International Chamber of Commerce. Retrieved March 2017, from https://iccwbo.org/about-us/

IMF (2017). About IMF. International Monetary Fund. Retrieved March 2017, from www.imf.org/external/about.htm/

ISO (2017). ISO Standards and Better Regulation. International Organization for Standardization. Retrieved March 2017, from www.iso.org/iso-and-policy-makers.html

The Jerusalem Post (2016, January 21st). Grocery Stores to Close on Shabbat in Jerusalem Following City Decision, *By Jeremy Sharon*. Retrieved from www.jpost.com/Israel-News/Politics-And-Diplomacy/Grocery-stores-to-close-on-Shabbat-in-Jerusalem-following-city-decision-442358

232 *Administrative Distance*

JuriGlobe (2017a). Classification of Legal Systems and Corresponding Political Entities. University of Ottawa. Retrieved February 2017, from www.juriglobe. ca/eng/sys-juri/index-syst.php

JuriGlobe (2017b). Customary Law Systems and Mixed Systems with a Customary Law Tradition. University of Ottawa. Retrieved February 2017, from www.juriglobe.ca/eng/sys-juri/index-syst.php

Khanna, Tarun & Palepu, Krishna (2005). Spotting Institutional Voids in Emerging Markets. *Harvard Business Review Background Note 106–014, (August 2005)*, 1–11.

Kostova, Tatiana (1999). Transnational Transfer of Strategic Organizational Practices: A Contextual Perspective. *The Academy of Management Review*, 24(2), 308–324.

Krayenbuehl, Thomas (1985). *Country Risk: Assessment and Monitoring*. Cambridge: Woodhead-Faulkner (p. 180).

La Nación (2015, May 28th). Por el cepo y la nacionalización de YPF, cayó fuerte la inversión extranjera, *By Martín Kanenguiser*. Retrieved from www.lanacion. com.ar/1796474-por-el-cepo-y-la-nacionalizacion-de-ypf-cayo-fuerte-la-inver sion-extranjera

La Nación (2017, February 21st). España espera que el Presidente despeje las dudas que aún existen sobre el país, *By Martín Yebra*. Retrieved from www. lanacion.com.ar/1986402-espana-espera-que-el-presidente-despeje-las-dudas-que-aun-existen-sobre-el-pais

Le Nouvel Observateur (2007, March 14th). Dolce & Gabbana cesse toute publicité en Espagne. Retrieved from http://tempsreel.nouvelobs.com/monde/20070313. OBS6782/dolce-gabbana-cesse-toute-publicite-en-espagne.html

Le Soleil (2014, September 8th). Garantie supplémentaire: amende de 2514 $ pour la boutique Apple de Québec, *By Gilbert Leduc*. Retrieved from www. lapresse.ca/le-soleil/affaires/consommation/201409/08/01-4798286-garantie-supplementaire-amende-de-2514-pour-la-boutique-apple-de-quebec.php

Lee, Margaret (2003). *The Political Economy of Regionalism in Southern Africa*. Boulder: Lynne Rienner Publishers (p. 314).

LLS (2013). Common Law and Civil Law: A Brief Comparison. Legal Language Services. Retrieved February 2017, from www.legallanguage.com/legal-articles/common-law-and-civil-law-a-brief-comparison/

Melitz, Marc (2003). The Impact of Trade on Intra-Industry Reallocations and Aggregate Industry Productivity. *Econometrica*, 71(6), 1695–1725.

Montreal Gazette. (2015a, June 17th). Quebec Will Table New Sign Regulations This Fall, *By Philip Authier*. Retrieved from http://montrealgazette.com/news/local-news/quebec-tables-new-regulations-for-trademark-signs

Montreal Gazette. (2015b, May 22nd). New Tourism Zone Allows Stores to Stay Open Around the Clock, *By Linda Gyulai*. Retrieved from http://montrealga-zette.com/business/local-business/retail/montreal-shops-in-new-tourism-zone-will-be-able-to-set-their-own-hours

Montreal Gazette (2016, September 11th). Quebec Premier Philippe Couillard to Lead Trade Mission to Cuba, *By Julien Arsenault, Presse Canadienne*. Retrieved from http://montrealgazette.com/business/local-business/quebec-premier-philippe-couillard-to-lead-trade-mission-to-cuba

Mullins, Matt (2010). Not COOL: The Consequences of Mandatory Country of Origin Labeling. *Journal of Food Law & Policy*, 6(1), 89–102.

National Post (2013, January 25th). Millions in SNC-Lavalin Bribes Bought Gaddafi's Playboy Son Luxury Yachts, Unsealed RCMP Documents Allege, *By Stewart Bell.* Retrieved from http://news.nationalpost.com/news/millions-in-snc-lavalin-bribes-bought-gaddafi-son-luxury-yachts-unsealed-rcmp-documents-allege

New York Times (2014, February 13th). Bridgestone Admits Guilt in U.S. Price-Fixing Case, *By Jaclyn Trop.* Retrieved from www.nytimes.com/2014/02/14/business/bridgestone-admits-guilt-in-us-price-fixing-case.html?_r=1

Nobel Prize (2012). The Nobel Peace Prize 2012—Press Release. NobelPrize.org. Retrieved February 2017, from www.nobelprize.org/nobel_prizes/peace/laureates/2012/

OECD (2017). OECD Convention on Combating Bribery of Foreign Public Officials in International Business Transactions. Organization for Economic Co-operation and Development. Retrieved April 2017, from www.oecd.org/corruption/oecdantibriberyconvention.htm

ProSun (2012). Dumping. ProSun. Retrieved April 2017, from www.prosun.org/en/fair-competition/trade-distortions/dumping.html

PwC (2016). 19th Annual CEO Survey—Redefining Business Success in a Changing World. PricewaterhouseCoopers. www.pwc.com/gx/en/ceo-survey/2016/landing-page/pwc-19th-annual-global-ceo-survey.pdf

Ramseyer, Mark & Rasmusen, Eric (2010). Comparative Litigation Rates. *Harvard John M. Olin Discussion Paper Series, No. 681.* Harvard Law School. Retrieved from https://dash.harvard.edu/handle/1/30064400

Resnick, Évelyne & De Roany, James (2014). *Guide pratique de l'export du vin* (2nd ed.). Paris, France: Dunod (p. 224).

Reuters (2013, August 1st). India to Probe Claims Multinationals Break Baby Milk Law, *By Nita Bhalla.* Retrieved from http://in.reuters.com/article/india-baby-mil-mncs-law-idINDEE9700E420130801

Reuters (2015, May 15th). Taiwan Enforces Stricter Controls on Japanese Food Imports, *By J.R. Wu and Ami Miyazaki.* Retrieved from www.reuters.com/article/us-taiwan-japan-food-idUSKBN0O00F320150515

Reuters (2016, May 25th). India Says Apple Must Sell Locally-Sourced Goods to Set Up Stores. Retrieved from www.reuters.com/article/us-apple-india-idUSKCN0YG2LW

Rheingau Echo (2014). Aus Vinea wird Vivana. *Rheingau Echo.* Retrieved January 2014, from www.rheingau-echo.de/nachrichten/region/oestrich-winkel/vinea-vivana-id8647.html

Rodrik, Dani (2011). *The Globalization Paradox: Democracy and the Future of the World Economy.* New York: W. W. Norton & Company (p. 368).

Rosamond, Ben (2000). *Theories of European Integration.* Basingstoke: Palgrave Macmillan (p. 240).

SAQ (2017). Import Authorisation Form. Retrieved April 2017, from https://importation.saq.com/ImportationParDesTiers/pageGenerique/login.jsf

Schiff, Maurice & Winters, Alan (2003). *Regional Integration and Development.* Washington, DC: World Bank Publications (p. 321).

Scott, Richard (2014). *Institutions and Organizations: Ideas, Interests and Identities* (4th ed.). Thousand Oaks: Sage Publications (p. 344).

South China Morning Post (2016, April 19th). 'Louis Vuitton Fried Chicken' Owner Fined in South Korea. Retrieved from www.scmp.com/news/asia/east-asia/article/1937087/louis-vuitton-fried-chicken-owner-fined-south-korea

234   *Administrative Distance*

Statistics Canada (2017). North American Industry Classification System (NAICS) Canada 2012. Retrieved March 2017, from http://www23.statcan.gc.ca/imdb/p3VD.pl?Function=getVD&TVD=118464; http://www23.statcan.gc.ca/imdb/p3VD.pl?Function=getVD&TVD=307532&CVD=307533&CPV=11&CST=01012017&CLV=1&MLV=5

Stiglitz, Joseph (2002). *Globalization and Its Discontents*. New York: W. W. Norton & Company (p. 304).The Telegraph (2013, April 24th). Ryanair Fined Over 'Unclear' Fares, *By Oliver Smith*. Retrieved from www.telegraph.co.uk/travel/news/ryanair/Ryanair-fined-over-unclear-fares/

Toronto Sun (2015, March 30th). Sephora Store Hit with $18,000 Fine for Unclear Pricing, *By QMI Agency*. Retrieved from www.torontosun.com/2015/03/30/sephora-store-hit-with-18000-fine-for-unclear-pricing

Transparency International (2017). Corruption Perceptions Index 2016. Transparency International. Retrieved February 2017, from www.transparency.org/news/feature/corruption_perceptions_index_2016

Turkina, Ekaterina & Postnikov, Evgeny (2012). Cross-border Inter-firm Networks in the European Union's Eastern Neighbourhood: Integration via Organizational Learning. *Journal of Common Market Studies*, 50(4), 632–652.

Turkina, Ekaterina & Postnikov, Evgeny (2014). From Business to Politics: Cross-Border Inter-Firm Networks and Policy Spillovers in the EU's Eastern Neighbourhood *Journal of Common Market Studies*, 52(5), 1120–1141.

UV 7197 (2016). *The Walt Disney Company: Mickey Mouse Visits Shanghai*. Case written by: Stephen Maiden, Gerry Yemen, and Elliott Weiss. Charlottesville: Darden School of Business (p. 11).

Wagner, Daniel (2012). *Managing Country Risk—A Practitioner's Guide to Effective Cross-Border Risk Analysis*. Boca Raton: CRC Press, Taylor and Francis Group (p. 308).

The Wall Street Journal (2014, September 3rd). European Union Fines Smart Card Chip Producers Over Price Fixing, *By Tom Fairless*. Retrieved from www.wsj.com/articles/european-union-fines-smart-card-chip-producers-over-price-fixing-1409740220

WCO (2017). About Us. World Customs Organization. Retrieved March 2017, from www.wcoomd.org/en/about-us/what-is-the-wco.aspx

WIPO (2017). Inside WIPO. World Intellectual Property Organization. Retrieved March 2017, from www.wipo.int/about-wipo/en/

WJP (2017a). What Is the Rule of Law? World Justice Project. Retrieved February 2017, from http://worldjusticeproject.org/what-rule-law

WJP (2017b). The Rule of Law Index. World Justice Project. Retrieved February 2017, from http://data.worldjusticeproject.org/

World Bank (2017a). Doing Business. Retrieved February 2017, from www.doingbusiness.org/rankings

World Bank (2017b). About the World Bank. Retrieved March 2017, from www.worldbank.org/en/about

WTO (2010). European Communities—Measures Affecting the Approval and Marketing of Biotech Products. © World Trade Organization. Retrieved March 2017, from www.wto.org/english/tratop_e/dispu_e/cases_e/ds291_e.htm

WTO (2016a). Technical Information on Anti-Dumping. World Trade Organization. from www.wto.org/english/tratop_e/adp_e/adp_info_e.htm

WTO (2016b). Regional Trade Agreements Information System (RTA-IS)—List of All RTAs in Force. © World Trade Organization. Retrieved July 2016, from http://rtais.wto.org/UI/PublicAllRTAList.aspx

WTO (2017a). Map of Disputes Between WTO Members—Selection: European Union. © World Trade Organization. Retrieved April 2017, from www.wto.org/english/tratop_e/dispu_e/dispu_maps_e.htm

WTO (2017b). List of Early Announcements. © World Trade Organization. Retrieved March 9 2017, from http://rtais.wto.org/ui/PublicEARTAList.aspx

WTO (2017c). What We Stand For. © World Trade Organization. Retrieved March 2017, from www.wto.org/english/thewto_e/whatis_e/what_stand_for_e.htm

WTO (2017d). DS435: Australia—Certain Measures Concerning Trademarks, Geographical Indications and Other Plain Packaging Requirements Applicable to Tobacco Products and Packaging. © World Trade Organization—Dispute Settlement. Retrieved April 2017, from www.wto.org/english/tratop_e/dispu_e/cases_e/ds435_e.htm

WTO (2017e). Tariffs. © World Trade Organization. Retrieved April 2017, from www.wto.org/english/tratop_e/tariffs_e/tariffs_e.htm

WTO (2017f). Subsidies and Countervailing Measures. © World Trade Organization. Retrieved April 2017, from www.wto.org/english/tratop_e/scm_e/scm_e.htm

Xu, Dean, Pan, Yigang & Beamish, Paul (2004). The Effect of Regulative and Normative Distances on MNE Ownership and Expatriate Strategies. *Management International Review*, 44(3), 285–307.

Yang, Zhilin, Su, Chenting & Fam, Kim-Shyan (2012). Dealing With Institutional Distances in International Marketing Channels: Governance Strategies That Engender Legitimacy and Efficiency. *Journal of Marketing*, 76(3), 41–55.

7 Economic and Technological Distances

Table of Contents

7 Economic and Technological Distances

Introduction: Why Do They Matter? Are They Decreasing?...........237
7.1   *Definitions*..238
7.2   *Drivers* 243
      7.2.1   *Development Levels*..249
      7.2.2   *Resources*..252
      7.2.3   *Infrastructure*...253
      7.2.4   *Intellectual Property* 253
7.3   *Central Role of Market Attractiveness*...........................258
      7.3.1   *Economic Potential as a Moderator to the Effect of Distance*...258
      7.3.2   *Emerging Markets (BRIC and Other Groupings)*...260
7.4   *Issues at Stake* 266
      7.4.1   *The Persistent Heterogeneity of Economies* 266
      7.4.2   *Economic and Technological Convergence* 270
      7.4.3   *Impact on Marketing Decisions with Corporate Examples: Disney and Volkswagen*..273

Conclusion: "Eco-techno" distance matters because it jeopardizes revenues and profits. To some extent, it is decreasing (but not everywhere).
References

Recommended Readings

- D'Andrea, Guillermo & Marcotte, David (2010). Let Emerging Market Customers Be Your Teachers. *Harvard Business Review*, *88*(12), 115–120.

- Ghemawat, Pankaj (2001). Distance Still Matters: The Hard Reality of Global Expansion. *Harvard Business Review*, 79(8), 137–147. [Also recommended in Chapter 4]
- Malhotra, Shavin; Sivakumar, K. & Zhu, PengCheng (2009). Distance factors and target market selection: The moderating effect of market potential. *International Marketing Review*, 26(6), 651–673.
- Sheth, Jagdish N (2011). Impact of Emerging Markets on Marketing: Rethinking Existing Perspectives and Practices. *Journal of Marketing*, 75(July), 166–182.

Introduction: Why Do They Matter? Are They Decreasing?

Asking the question: **"Why do economic and technological distances matter in marketing activities?"** is about completing the 360° overview of differences existing across countries undertaken in the three previous chapters. Although the focus here is on the differences across countries to better understand what challenges companies face when venturing abroad to market their offerings, the contrast between "rich" and "poor" is also visible within countries. Something that companies cannot ignore when considering entering new markets: there are rich people in poor countries and poor people in rich countries. Images from large cities in emerging economies, such as those from Rio de Janeiro to cite one example among many, illustrate this disparity well. For instance, luxury apartment buildings (featuring individual Jacuzzis on

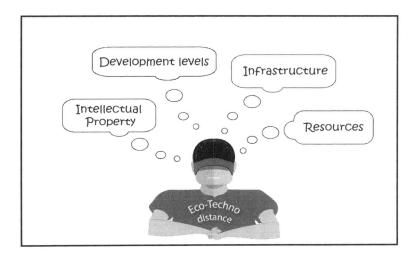

Figure 7.1 Illustrating Chapter 7

Source: Own elaboration

238 *Economic and technological distances*

each balcony, an Olympic-size outdoor swimming pool, and several tennis courts surrounded by well-tended gardens) can be separated by a simple wall from the next door *favela* (i.e., shanty town) where people live under iron sheet roofs, often with limited water distribution, electricity, sewage systems, and garbage collection.

Such images not only capture well the divide in economic and technological conditions, but they also reveal their intricate relationship. We can study economic and technological differences separately, but ultimately, they manifest jointly. Good economic conditions strongly correlate with good technological conditions (and vice versa). This is the reason why, in this chapter, we often refer to the *eco-techno distance*, a term that is proposed here to encapsulate both types of distance and simplify our analysis.

Figure 7.2 situates this chapter in the overall book structure. It indicates that we are now completing the first step in building an international marketing plan: looking at the concepts and tools we need to better understand the general context and the PEST environments in which companies do business in foreign markets.

To answer the question initially raised and ultimately reflect on whether the eco-techno distance between markets increases or decreases in a globalizing world, we first define concepts and review models that help us understand the linkages between economic and technological conditions. Next, we look at some of the important driving factors of this type of distance (development levels for the economic dimension; existing resources and infrastructure, as well as the role of intellectual property for the technological dimension). We then focus on the central role of market attractiveness (i.e., size and growth potential) in explaining why the eco-techno distance might be—or not—an impediment to marketing, in other words: "Why—and when—it matters." Finally, we address some of the issues at stake, such as the debated economic convergence, and whether we are tending toward more inclusion (i.e., a reduction in the gap between the rich and poor), as well as the impact of economic and technological differences on marketing decisions.

7.1 Definitions

In this section, we address the following questions:

- What is economic distance? And technological distance? So, how can we define the eco-techno distance between countries?
- What is Porter's (1990) "national diamond of competitive advantage" model about? How can it help in further defining the eco-techno distance?

Before we start, we can refer to some of the recommended readings and consider how eco-techno distance is approached in the literature (see "Food for Thought").

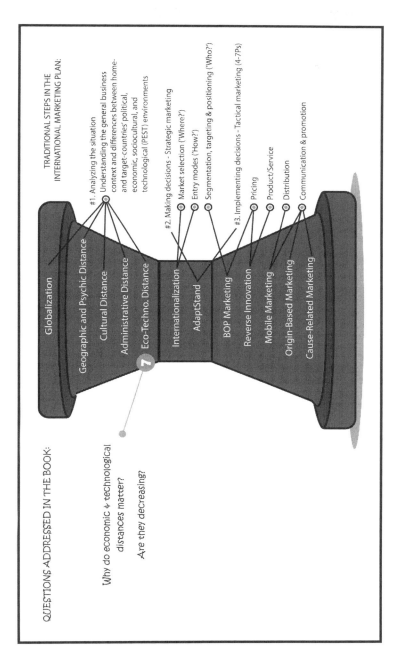

Figure 7.2 Positioning Chapter 7 in the overall book structure

Source: Own elaboration

240   *Economic and technological distances*

Food for Thought 7.1

- In reference to Malhotra, Sivakumar, and Zhu (2009) and Ghemawat (2001), what is economic distance? And technological distance?

What is economic distance? And technological distance? First, *economic distance* is quite simple to understand with only a few factors used to characterize it. Ghemawat (2001)—who has sometimes been credited for pinpointing the exact term—mentions that economic distance stems from differences in consumer incomes, costs, and quality of resources, and information/knowledge. In turn, Tsang and Yip (2007, p. 1156) define economic distance as: "the level of economic development of the host country relative to that of the home country. [. . .]. The economic distance between two countries often reflects differences in factor costs (such as wages) and in technological capability."

As such, *technological distance* appears to be implicitly embedded within most definitions of economic distance. The common PEST framework used for analyzing the general business environment of countries suggests capturing the technological dimension by studying natural and human resources (e.g., available water and land, energy sources and workers' qualifications), R&D activity, and the rate of technological change (all factors related to knowledge).

Although these differences in income, resources, and knowledge have been considered in thousands of studies for their impact on international business, it is surprising that only a handful of articles have taken a narrow focus on economic or technological distance and made them the central variables under study. For instance, a search on scientific database Proquest/ABI Inform found less than fourty articles with "economic distance" or "technological distance" in the title, as of March 2018. Malhotra et al. (2009) have also noted how surprising it is that economic distance received so little consideration. One possible explanation for this lack of specific attention is that, until recently, business was mainly conducted between developed countries (e.g., "the Triad" constituted of Japan, the US, and Western European countries, which dominated the world economy until the late 1990s). Having similar economic and technological backgrounds, there was little need to put eco-techno distance at the center of investigation. However, the irruption on the global scene of emerging economies (e.g., China) since then makes this need much more pressing.

So, how can we define the eco-techno distance between countries? Building on the definition of psychic distance proposed by Katsikeas, Skarmeas, and Bello (2009, p. 154) as "the degree of dissimilarity in the parties' operating environments" (see Chapter 4), we can define the *eco-techno distance* as "the degree of dissimilarity between the home- and foreign-country economic and

Economic and technological distances   241

technological environments." This allows for the inclusion of many more indicators than the few proposed above. Besides the PEST framework previously mentioned, there is another well-known model that can help us better understand what eco-techno distance is and why it matters: the "National Diamond of Competitive Advantage" model.

What is Porter's (1990) "National Diamond of Competitive Advantage" model about? How can it help in further defining eco-techno distance? This model (see Figure 7.3) explains that success in international trade comes from the interaction of four elements: favorable factor conditions (e.g., the presence of educated workers), favorable demand conditions (e.g., the presence of consumers with dispensable purchasing power), healthy competitive rivalry among firms (mainly because it triggers innovation), and the existence of supporting industries (e.g., logistics services).

In addition, the active involvement of the government in enhancing these four elements is key to success. Regarding factor conditions, governments can invest in education and infrastructure for transportation and communication, etc. In terms of demand conditions, a wide array of governmental decisions affects the number of potential consumers, how much money they can spend and when (through subsidies, regulations, etc.). With reference to competitive rivalry, the influence of government is noticeable through, for instance, how much protection is offered against copy infringement or against monopolistic situations. Finally, governments can considerably help the development of supporting and related industries to a specific activity by granting subsidies and favorable taxation conditions.

Although this model is generally used to understand why a country can be more or less competitive internationally, it also helps in structuring our thoughts about eco-techno distance. From Figure 7.3, we can enrich our vision by focusing on two of its core components: factor and demand conditions. To simplify our analysis, we propose looking at "production factors" on the one hand (equivalent to "factor conditions"), and "demand factors" (equivalent to "demand conditions") on the other hand. Economic distance is grounded in differences in demand factors, while technological distance is based in differences in production factors across countries. For instance, differences in demand conditions (i.e., how "sophisticated" consumers can be) stem from differences in consumers' income, saving capacity, access to credit, and product familiarity. In turn, differences in production factors are determined by differences in the availability of high-quality inputs (including financial, human, and natural resources), as well as in the presence of physical, administrative, information, scientific, and technological infrastructures. With this in mind, we refine our definitions: economic distance can be seen as the degree of dissimilarity between the home- and foreign-countries in terms of demand factors, and technological distance as the degree of dissimilarity between the home- and foreign countries in terms of production factors (see Figure 7.15).

Now that we have defined what economic and technological distances are (i.e., eco-techno distance), we can look at some of their important drivers.

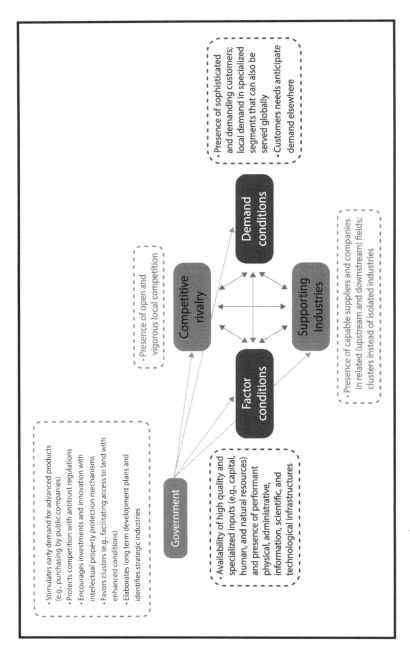

Figure 7.3 Illustrating the interdependence between demand and production factors with the "National Diamond of Competitive Advantage" model

Source: Adapted from Porter (1998)

7.2 Drivers

Which are the important components of the economic and technological environments that may differ across countries (i.e., create distance)? In other words, what are the drivers of eco-techno distance? Among the many indicators used to describe the economic and technological environments of countries, we focus on development levels (for the economic environment) and on infrastructure, resources, and intellectual property (for the technological environment). These indicators have a great influence on the volume and the value of demand and production (i.e., how many customers and competitors, how sophisticated their expectations and outputs are, etc.). Next, we analyze each of these four elements in turn. Questions raised are as follows:

- In which stage of development is the foreign country situated? Are there any other important development indicators beyond average income?
- Where can we find information about countries' economic development?
- How can we compare levels of dotation in production factors (e.g., resources)? And what about infrastructure? Why is it important? What is the global digital divide?
- Why is Intellectual Property (IP) reflective of technological development? How important is IP for firms from developed economies? Where can we find information about countries' technological development in general and about IP in particular?

7.2.1 Development Levels

When considering a foreign country's development level, it is useful to first acknowledge the class or stage of economic development in which this country is situated. Overall, there are "developed" economies and those which are not. Every year, the World Bank updates the cutoff point that separates "developed" economies from the rest. In this way, an economy is seen as emerging if its level of wealth creation, measured as gross national income (GNI) per capita, is below that of developed economies. In 2017, the cutoff point was $12,236 per capita (World Bank, 2017b). Depending on the source, definitions of "developing" and "emerging" economies vary and there is no consensus in the literature on what distinguishes them from one another. We can simplify this discussion by remembering that "emerging" is situated closest to "developed" (the highest stage), before "developing" and "least developed" (the lowest stage) in the economic development scale.

In which stage of development is the foreign country situated? The World Bank proposes a classification of countries according to four income categories (high, upper-middle, lower-middle, and low income) which is presented in Figure 7.4 (numbers are rounded to facilitate memorization). For the 2018 fiscal year and using the World Bank Atlas method (in current USD), a GNI per capita of: 1,005 USD or less defined low-income economies; between 1,006–3,955 USD defined lower-middle-income economies; between 3,956–12,235 USD defined upper-middle-income economies; and 12,236 USD or more defined high-income economies (World Bank, 2017b). The figure also

244 *Economic and technological distances*

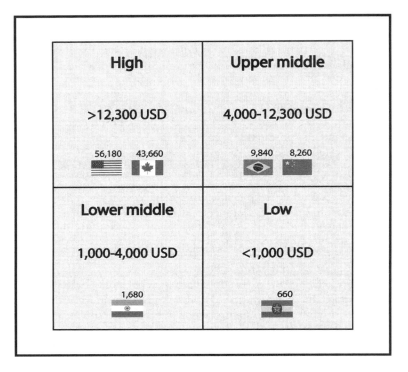

Figure 7.4 Classifying countries by income levels (2016)
Source: Own elaboration based on World Bank (2017a, 2017b)

shows examples of countries in the high income category (Canada and the US), the upper-middle-income category (Brazil and China), the lower-middle-income category (India), and the low-income category (Ethiopia) for the year 2016 (World Bank, 2017a).

Next, Figure 7.5 shows that the least developed economies are concentrated in large parts of Africa and Asia, while developed economies are concentrated in the Northern hemisphere (in particular in Western Europe, North America, Japan, and South Korea), as well as several Middle Eastern countries (e.g., Saudi Arabia), and finally, Australia and New Zealand. Overall, this figure represents the world's fragmentation in terms of economic development levels.

Are there any other important indicators beyond average income? Although it is quite convenient to use one simple criterion to define economic development (income per capita), this choice is often criticized. To enrich our understanding of a country's development level, we can rely on: income distribution, income inequality, and other indicators presented here:

- Income distribution (i.e., the proportion of people falling into different income categories) is interesting to contemplate. Taking the example of

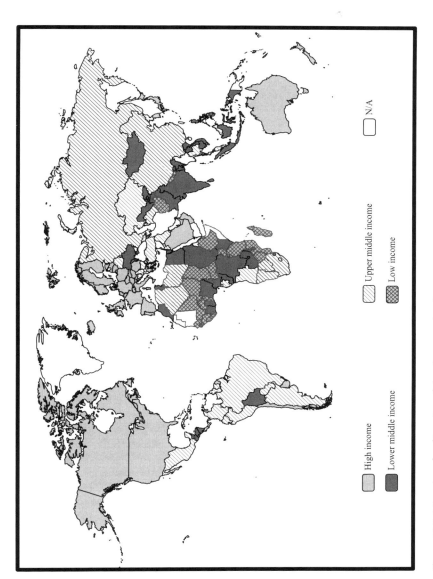

Figure 7.5 Mapping the diversity of development levels

Source: Own elaboration based on World Bank (2017a)

For the color version, see the eResource at www.routledge.com/9781138202344

Canada, Figure 7.6 shows that the proportion of people with revenues above 100,000 CAD (~75,000 USD) in 2010 was approximately 14 percent of the Canadian population (i.e., nearly five million people). This indicator is thus useful to estimate market size, for instance, according to targeted customers' revenue levels. Overall, the need for segmentation and differential targeting depends a lot on income distribution.

Worldwide, revenue distribution is also revealing. Figure 7.7 represents the global income distribution in 2010, based on deciles (i.e., when we divide income into ten equal parts, so that each part represents one tenth of the population). This data illustrates how unequal income distribution is worldwide, with the tenth richest capturing more than half of global income. In Chapter 8, we further address the topic of global inequality when we study the notion of "bottom of the pyramid marketing."

- Inequality is also an important indicator to monitor at the country level. A well-known measure of inequality is the Gini coefficient developed by Corrado Gini, an Italian statistician who died in 1965 (BBC News, 2015). It is a measure of dispersion applied to the distribution of income that shows economic inequality within a country. The Gini index proposed by the World Bank measures the extent to which the distribution of income among individuals or households within an economy deviates from a perfectly equal distribution (World Bank, 2017c). Thus, a Gini index of 0 represents perfect equality, while an index of 100 implies perfect inequality.

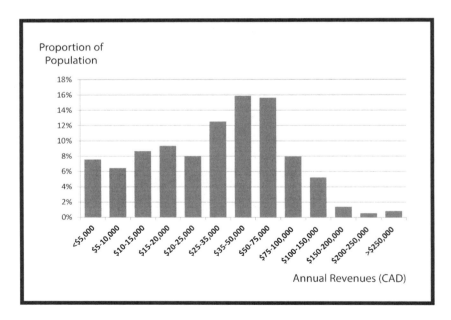

Figure 7.6 Representing the income distribution within one country: the example of Canada

Source: Statistics Canada (2014)

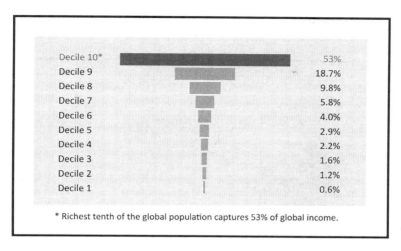

Figure 7.7 Representing the global income distribution in 2010

Source: Adapted from Dikhanov (2005) and updated with 2010 data, courtesy of Yuri Dikhanov, Senior Economist in the Development Data Group of the World Bank

To give a sense of the range, Gini scores were the following for the year 2010: Norway (~26), Canada (~33), and the US (~40); and for the year 2011: Chile (~51) and South Africa (~63) (World Bank, 2017d). Thus, countries can be marked by striking differences in terms of inequality, even at similar levels of economic development. For instance, Canada and its southern neighbor, the US, are both highly developed economies but there is less economic inequality in Canada. In Africa, wild discrepancies are observed across the continent, with some countries presenting high rates of inequality (e.g., South Africa and Botswana), while others present more equal income distribution (e.g., Tanzania and Ethiopia). Considering the low level of incomes, it does not mean that people are better off but that income distribution is more homogenous across the population.

- Finally, the United Nations proposes the Human Development Index to capture an enlarged notion of development by taking into consideration people's life expectancy and years of schooling, in addition to GNI per capita (PPP). Figure 7.8 shows that in several countries deemed to have lower incomes (e.g., Argentina, Chile, and many others located in Latin America, as well as countries in North Africa, the Middle East, Eastern Europe, and the former Soviet Union), the level of human development is higher than what income levels would suggest. This means that—despite limited incomes—people have access to important services (e.g., health and education) that improve their living standards.

Where can we find information about countries' economic development? The most comprehensive and free data is available on the World Bank's website. In addition, the data is provided in several languages, including English, Spanish, French, Arabic, and Japanese. Table 7.1 lists various indicators that

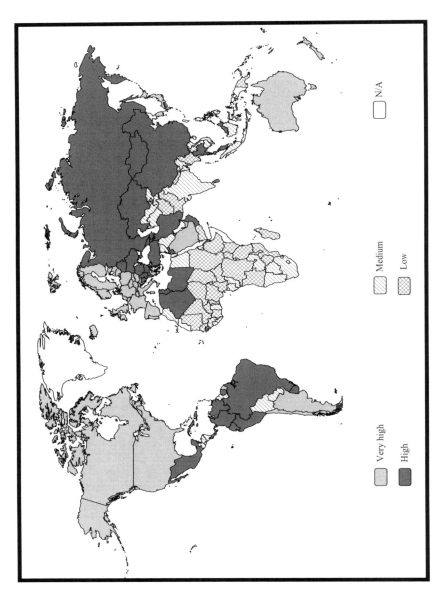

Figure 7.8 Mapping Human Development Index scores (2014)

Source: Adapted from UNDP (2015)

For the color version, see the eResource at www.routledge.com/9781138202344

Economic and technological distances   249

Table 7.1 Measuring differences in development levels with selected indicators from the World Bank's "Economy and Growth" category

---

Economy & Growth

- Agriculture, value added (% of GDP)
- Cash surplus/deficit (% of GDP)
- Central government debt, total (% of GDP)
- Current account balance (BoP, current USD)
- Exports of goods and services (% of GDP)
- External debt stocks (% of GNI)
- Foreign direct investment, net inflows (BoP, current USD)
- GDP at market prices (current USD)
- GDP growth (annual %)
- GDP per capita (current USD)
- GDP per capita growth (annual %)
- GDP per capita, PPP (current international dollar)
- GNI, Atlas method (current USD)
- GNI per capita, Atlas method (current USD)

- GNI per capita, PPP (current international dollar)
- Gross capital formation (% of GDP)
- Gross savings (% of GDP)
- Imports of goods and services (% of GDP)
- Industry, value added (% of GDP)
- Inflation, consumer prices (annual %)
- Inflation, GDP deflator (annual %)
- Net official development assistance received (% of GNI)
- Net official development assistance received per capita (current USD)
- Net official development assistance received (current USD)
- Services, etc., value added (% of GDP)
- Short-term debt (% of total reserves)
- Total debt service (% of exports of goods, services and primary income)
- Total reserves (includes gold, current USD)

Source: World Bank (2016b)

belong to the "Economy and Growth" category. The website allows the ability to build graphs (e.g., bar charts, line charts, and maps) to compare the structure and wealth of foreign economies with indicators as important as the GNI at purchasing power parity (PPP), inflation, the percentage of GDP represented by various economic sectors such as industry and services, and so on. The graph function is particularly useful as it allows us to visually compare the evolution of any indicator overtime while proposing a world average that we can then benchmark against other countries. Figure 7.9 offers an example of such a comparison by contrasting the GNI per capita of Armenia, Ethiopia, the Russian Federation, Spain, and Sweden, with the world average.

7.2.2 Resources

How can we compare levels of dotation in production factors? The capacity of countries to produce any type of goods largely depends on their access to resources. According to Keegan and Green (2008), resources include: natural and physical resources (e.g., access to land, water, and raw materials, such as

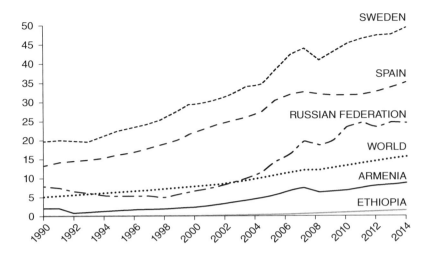

Figure 7.9 Comparing the GNI per capita at PPP (in current international dollar): the examples of Armenia, Ethiopia, the Russian Federation, Spain, and Sweden

Source: World Bank (2016c)

wood and coal), human resources (not only the volume of available workforce but also its value in terms of education, qualification, experience, training, etc.), technological resources (e.g., available technologies and patented intellectual property), financial resources (access to capital through banks, public and private investors, stock markets, etc.), and finally organizational resources (e.g., the number of companies and the structure of the business landscape with either large, medium, or small firms).

For a foreign company, it is also important to determine the level of competitive rivalry (volume and value of competitors) as well as the available suppliers, distributors, and other needed collaborators. If the presence of local firms with valuable brands and established reputations can be a hurdle because it represents more-intense local competition, it can also facilitate entry by ensuring the presence of reliable business partners.

Table 7.2 presents a selection of the long list of available indicators from the World Bank's website. Information about natural resources can be found in the "Agriculture and Rural Development" category (e.g., proportion of arable land area or forest area), and in the "Energy and Mining Category" (e.g., fossil fuel energy consumption and presence of alternative and nuclear energy).

A company interested in human resources can investigate how educated the workforce is in a foreign country, with indicators presented in the "education" category (e.g., government expenditure on education either as a percentage of total government expenditure or as a percentage of GDP).

Table 7.2 Measuring differences in resources with selected indicators from the World Bank's "Agriculture and Rural Development," "Energy and Mining," and "Financial Sector" categories

Agriculture & Rural Development

- Agricultural irrigated land (% of total agricultural land)
- Agricultural land (% of land area)
- Agricultural machinery, tractors per 100 sq. km of arable land
- Agriculture, value added (% of GDP)
- Arable land (hectares per person)
- Arable land (% of land area)
- Cereal yield (kg per hectare)
- Crop production index (2004–2006 = 100)
- Employment in agriculture, female (% of female employment)
- Employment in agriculture, male (% of male employment)
- Fertilizer consumption (kilograms per hectare of arable land)
- Food production index (2004–2006 = 100)

- Forest area (sq. km)
- Improved sanitation facilities, rural (% of rural population with access)
- Improved water source, rural (% of rural population with access)
- Land area (sq. km)
- Land under cereal production (hectares)
- Livestock production index (2004–2006 = 100)
- Permanent cropland (% of land area)
- Rural population
- Rural population (% of total population)
- Rural poverty gap at national poverty lines (%)
- Surface area (sq. km)

Energy & Mining

- Access to electricity (% of population)
- Access to non-solid fuel (% of population)
- Alternative and nuclear energy (% of total energy use)
- Electric power consumption (kWh per capita)
- Energy imports, net (% of energy use)
- Energy use (kg of oil equivalent per capita)
- Fossil fuel energy consumption (% of total)

- Fuel exports (% of merchandise exports)
- Investment in energy with private participation (current US$)
- Ores and metals exports (% of merchandise exports)
- Renewable electricity output (% of total electricity output)
- Renewable energy consumption (% of total final energy consumption)
- Time required to get electricity (days)
- Total natural resources rents (% of GDP)

Financial Sector

- Account at a financial institution, female (% age 15+)
- Account at a financial institution, male (% age 15+)
- Automated teller machines (ATMs) (per 100,000 adults)
- Bank capital to assets ratio (%)

- Interest rate spread (lending rate minus deposit rate, %)
- International migrant stock, total
- Lending interest rate (%)
- Listed domestic companies, total

(Continued)

252 *Economic and technological distances*

Table 7.2 (Continued)

Agriculture & Rural Development

- Bank nonperforming loans to total gross loans (%)
- Commercial bank branches (per 100,000 adults)
- Deposit interest rate (%)

- Domestic credit provided by financial sector (% of GDP)
- Domestic credit to private sector (% of GDP)
- Foreign direct investment, net inflows (BoP, current USD)
- Inflation, consumer prices (annual %)

- Market capitalization of listed domestic companies (current USD)
- Market capitalization of listed domestic companies (% of GDP)
- Official exchange rate (LCU per US$, period average)
- Real interest rate (%)

- Risk premium on lending (lending rate minus treasury bill rate, %)
- Stocks traded, total value (% of GDP)

- Stocks traded, turnover ratio of domestic shares (%)

Source: World Bank (2016b)

Finally, indicators used to estimate the financial landscape of the country can be found in the "Financial Sector" category on the World Bank's website (e.g., lending interest rate, market capitalization of listed domestic companies as a percentage of GDP, real interest rate, and stocks traded as a percentage of GDP).

7.2.3 Infrastructure

What about infrastructure? Why is it important? A country's infrastructure includes all necessary elements to support production and marketing (e.g., paved roads, railroads, seaports, communications networks, and energy supplies). The quality of an infrastructure directly affects economic growth potential and the ability of a company to engage effectively in business (Cateora, Gilly, & Graham, 2011). Table 7.3 presents a few of the available indicators on the World Bank's website in the "Infrastructure" category (e.g., air transport freight, investment in energy with private participation, mobile cellular subscriptions, and rail lines). In turn, Table 7.4 compares a few technological indicators for several countries giving a sense of the technological distance existing between them.

What is the global digital divide? Access to the digital world has grown drastically in the past decade with ~44 percent of the world population using the Internet in 2015, up from only ~16 percent in 2005 (World Bank, 2016a). Nevertheless, the *global digital divide* captures existing inequality in terms of access around the world. It can be measured by the number of computers per one hundred people, the Internet users per one hundred people, or by the proportion of households with (or without) access to the Internet. Figure 7.10 illustrates this digital divide or gap by revealing significantly lower proportions of households with Internet access in developing and least-developed countries (LDCs). These households are particularly located

Economic and technological distances 253

Table 7.3 Measuring differences in technological development with selected indicators from the World Bank's "Infrastructure" category

Infrastructure

- Air transport, registered carrier departures worldwide
- Annual freshwater withdrawals, total (% of internal resources)
- Container port traffic (TEU: 20 foot equivalent units)
- Electric power consumption (kWh per capita)

- Fixed broadband subscriptions (per 100 people)
- Fixed telephone subscriptions (per 100 people)
- Improved water source, rural (% of rural population with access)
- Improved water source, urban (% of urban population with access)
- Internet users (per 100 people)

- Investment in energy with private participation (current USD)
- Investment in telecoms with private participation (current USD)
- Investment in transport with private participation (current USD)
- Investment in water and sanitation with private participation (current USD)
- Mobile cellular subscriptions (per 100 people)
- Rail lines (total route-km)

- Renewable internal freshwater resources per capita (cubic meters)
- Renewable internal freshwater resources, total (billion cubic meters)
- Secure Internet servers (per 1 million people)

Source: World Bank (2016b)

Table 7.4 Assessing technological distance between selected countries (China, Japan, South Korea, and Vietnam)

Country	Investment in energy with private participation—current Bn USD (2012)	Air transport freight—million ton-km (2015)	Mobile cellular subscriptions—per 100 people (2015)	Rail lines—total route-km (2013)
India	9.4	1,833	78	64,460
China	3.2	19,805	93	66,298
Vietnam	0.317	384	130	2,347
South Korea	N/A	11,296	118	3,650
Japan	N/A	8,868	125	20,140

Source: World Bank (2012, 2013, 2015a, 2015b)

in Africa, Asia-Pacific, and the Middle East. Obviously, one must take into account the abundant and rural populations in some of these regions. Nevertheless, it reveals fewer opportunities to access online information and electronic marketplaces, a significant disadvantage for the population.

7.2.4 Intellectual Property

Why is IP reflective of a country's technological development? In Chapter 6, levels of intellectual property (IP) protection were scrutinized in the

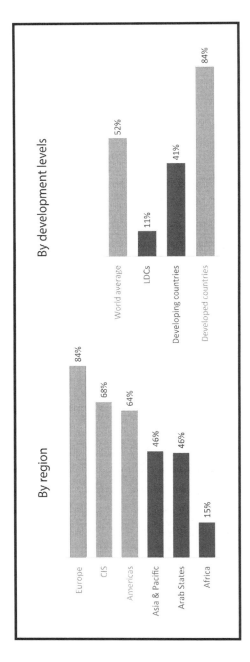

Figure 7.10 Illustrating the global digital divide by looking at the proportion of households with Internet access in various regions

Source: Adapted from ITU (2016)

Economic and technological distances 255

context of administrative distance (i.e., laws and regulations aimed at protecting companies' IP). Here, we look into IP once more, but this time as an important pillar of the technological environment of countries. IP refers to "creations of the mind" (e.g., inventions, literary and artistic works, designs, symbols, names and images used in commerce) that are materialized into patents, copyrights, trademarks, industrial designs, and geographical indications (WIPO, 2017). IP usually forms the basis of firms' competitive advantage.

It is important to understand that firms are motivated to innovate (e.g., by developing new products and technologies) and develop their business (e.g., by building valuable brands) insofar as they can benefit from it. Protection of their IP is, thus, crucial. Yet, differences between countries in terms of the intensity, degree of sophistication, and encouragement of innovation (e.g., by governments incentives) are also important and drive eco-techno distance. In particular, assessing the state of IP development in foreign countries helps companies to evaluate the presence of local competitors as well as of potential collaborators (e.g., valuable suppliers, universities, and laboratories for R&D).

How important is IP for firms from developed economies? Taking the anecdotal example of toothbrushes, we can infer a lot about the importance of intellectual property protection for companies from developed economies. Indeed, we may not always realize how technological toothbrushes can be. The packaging of an Oral-B toothbrush shows us the amount of effort put into developing the technology and protecting the related IP. Oral-B is commercialized by Gillette, which merged with Procter & Gamble in 2005. First, Figure 7.11 illustrates the registered trademarks Oral-B® and 3DWhite™ and the patents developed to protect the appearance of the bristles (US4802255), their design (USD434563), and the handle (USD347736) (Google Patents, 2017). Second, Figure 7.12 presents excerpts of these patents (held by Gillette Canada), which hint at the level of detail required in these technical and legal documents (each three to six pages long). Former packaging of this product also presented a copyrighted text describing the properties of the toothbrush (the sign ©—which stands for copyright and protects literary, musical, and artistic works—was then visible next to the text).

This Oral-B toothbrush packaging reveals the time, money, and resources (e.g., engineers and lawyers) invested. Surely, this IP helps in differentiating the product and gaining a competitive advantage. But if IP for toothbrushes is this sophisticated, what then of airplane parts and surgical robots? This anecdotal example suggests that for many firms from developed economies, the level of IP development and protection is highly important and central to the "rule of the business game." Companies protect what they own, and this protection is what motivates them to keep developing their intellectual and technological assets. This may not be the case for firms from emerging or developing economies. Favored at home where the legal context is less restrictive, these companies find high entry barriers when trying to enter developed markets. IP protection may not even be the future of the business game either with the phenomenon of "open innovation." In all cases, understanding the situation in regard to differences in IP development and

256 *Economic and technological distances*

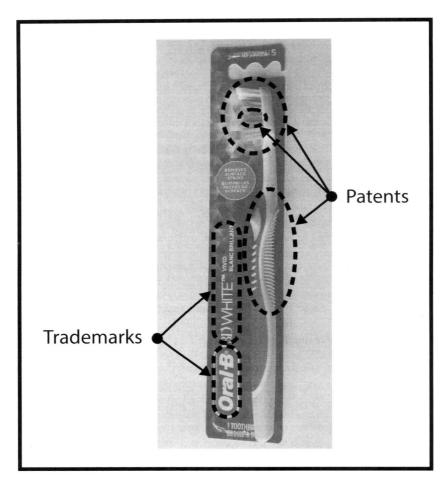

Figure 7.11 Illustrating the importance of intellectual property protection with trademarks and patents for an Oral-B toothbrush

Source: Own elaboration with the courteous permission of P&G

protection between home- and target-markets is required for a good assessment of eco-techno distance.

Where can we find information about IP? The World Intellectual Property Organization (WIPO) (see Chapter 6 for a presentation) provides core information about IP, such as protection mechanisms in the world (e.g., international agreements), dispute resolution, policy making, and more. When it comes to contrasting different countries in terms of IP development, the World Bank website offers a "Science and Technology" category that presents data on patent and trademark applications, R&D expenditures, numbers of researchers and technicians involved in R&D, and numbers of scientific and

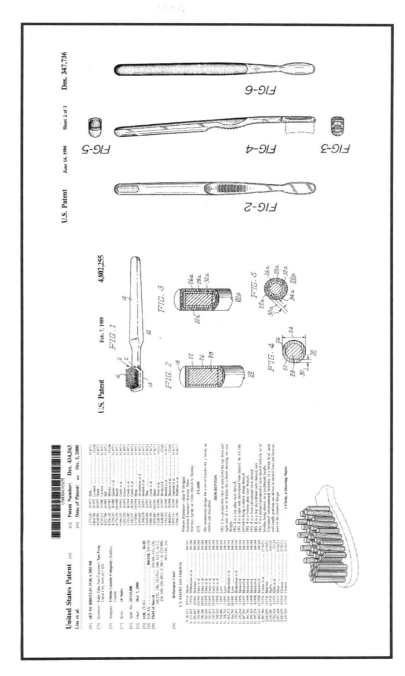

Figure 7.12 Presenting selected excerpts of US4802255, D434563, and D347736 patents, held by Gillette (in charge of commercializing Oral-B toothbrushes and a company belonging to P&G)

Source: Google Patents (2017)

258 *Economic and technological distances*

Table 7.5 Measuring differences in intellectual property development with selected indicators from the World Bank's "Science and Technology" category

Science & Technology

- Charges for the use of intellectual property, payments (BoP, current USD)
- Charges for the use of intellectual property, receipts (BoP, current USD)
- High-technology exports (current USD)
- High-technology exports (% of manufactured exports)
- Patent applications, nonresidents
- Patent applications, residents

- Research and development expenditure (% of GDP)
- Researchers in R&D (per million people)
- Scientific and technical journal articles
- Technicians in R&D (per million people)
- Trademark applications, direct nonresident
- Trademark applications, direct resident

Source: World Bank (2016b)

technical articles, to name a few, to get a sense of a country's productivity in this domain. Table 7.5 presents a selection of the available indicators.

7.3 Central Role of Market Attractiveness

Now that we have a better idea of what eco-techno distance is and its determinants, we move on to questioning the reasons why it matters by addressing the following questions:

- When trying to understand the impact of distance in general (and of eco-techno distance in particular) on marketing decisions, why would market attractiveness (e.g., size and potential) matter?
- Why resort to market grouping? Which are the groupings of emerging markets that are particularly monitored nowadays?
- How different are emerging markets from developed markets in general? And are these emerging markets really attractive to firms from developed economies?

7.3.1 Economic Potential as a Moderator to the Effect of Distance

When trying to understand the impact of distance in general (and of eco-techno distance in particular) on marketing decisions, why would market attractiveness (e.g., size and growth potential) matter? This question brings us back to concepts reviewed in Chapter 4 about the persistent effect of geographic distance in international trade. Specifically, we think of the gravity model of international trade, which stipulates that the intensity of trade flow between two countries varies according to the physical distance that separates them and according to their economic size (measured by their GDP,

Economic and technological distances 259

for instance) (Isard, 1954; Tinbergen, 1963; Alexander, Rhodes, & Myers, 2011).

From this theory, we understand that if foreign markets are far away but particularly attractive due to their size (i.e., potential gains with high volumes of sales), then the negative effect of distance tends to fade. This is typically the case with the US market for Chinese companies and the Chinese market for US companies. Both countries are quite distant, but the volume and value of trade flows are huge (see Figures 4.12 and 7.14). In other words, market size can "moderate" the effect of physical distance: when the foreign market is highly attractive, the negative effect of distance is reduced; when the foreign market is not attractive, a full-fledged negative effect of distance on trade flows is then observed.

Largely studied from an economic perspective with objective data, this moderation mechanism is also quite interesting to study from a sociological perspective, with subjective data, including dimensions of distance other than just geographic distance. In this vein, Durand, Turkina, and Robson (2016) argue that theories of motivation, such as the _expectancy-value theory_ (Atkinson, 1957; Vroom, 1964), could explain why the effect of psychic distance in international business is sometimes found to have: a negative effect on international business (the mainstream assumption following the Uppsala theory of internationalization, see Chapter 3), a positive effect, or no effect at all. When managers are highly motivated to do business somewhere— because of foreseen economic gains—their efforts and persistence in overcoming distance (in all its forms) eventually pay off, even if the target-country is extremely distant and different. Thus, a tentative answer to the question raised (i.e., "Why would market attractiveness matter in explaining the impact of eco-techno distance on marketing decisions?") is that market size and potential determine degrees of motivation and the consequent efforts that managers are willing to undertake to overcome distance. Eco-techno distance could be a real barrier only when market attractiveness is low.

Since this assumption has received little empirical attention so far, we can only rely on the few existing studies conducted on the effect of distance (at large, not just geographic distance) and the role of market attractiveness in marketing decisions. Malhotra et al. (2009) examine the effect of the CAGE distance on one entry mode in foreign markets: cross-border acquisitions. Their findings about the role of market size and the role of different types of distance are quite revealing. Can we infer anything about the importance of "directionality" in studying eco-techno distance and other types of distance (see "Food for Thought")?

Food for Thought 7.2

- In reference to Malhotra et al. (2009), what is the combined impact of market potential and distance on foreign entry modes (acquisitions)? Can we infer anything about the importance of "directionality" in studying eco-techno distance and other types of distance?

260 Economic and technological distances

Why resort to market grouping? Even though market attractiveness has received little scientific attention in relation to the effect of an enlarged notion of distance (the CAGE distance), one common practice in country analysis exposes its importance: market grouping. *Market grouping* simply refers to the habit of economists and marketers to group markets that present similar characteristics together in order to simplify analyses and decisions. For us marketers, examples of questions involved in the market selection process include: "For our next expansion move abroad, should we target this country or this other country?" and, "If we target this country, why not this other one which presents a rather similar profile?"

The principles of market grouping indeed lie in "proximity" (i.e., the opposite of distance), since the absence of differences is assumed to make our task easier and cheaper: less time and fewer resources and effort are dedicated to adapting to specificities and a more standardized approach can be implemented (see Chapter 3 for the AdaptStand debate). In this way, market groupings are often formed on either cultural proximity (similar cultures favor understanding of needs and expectations), administrative and political proximity (comparable political aspirations and preferential—or common—tariff treatment facilitate trade within the group of countries), geographic proximity (transportation networks are likely to be interrelated and greatly enhance trade within the group), or economic proximity (purchasing power similarity is likely to induce similar demand characteristics) or any combination of these types of proximity. Proximity within a group of countries means a higher attractiveness for foreign firms.

Recent market groupings rely mainly on economic proximity, especially when it comes to making decisions about entering emerging markets. For instance, Brazil and China are hardly close when it comes to geography, culture, and regulations, but their level of market attractiveness explain why they can be grouped together and studied jointly. In the next section, we look into several of these recent groupings of emerging markets (e.g., the BRIC, CIVETS, and MIST). What is interesting to remember here is that it is because of the central role of market attractiveness that emerging countries are grouped together and often presented as the "next go-to destination."

7.3.2 Emerging Markets (BRIC and Other Groupings)

Which are the groupings of emerging markets that are particularly monitored nowadays? For more than fifteen years, the BRIC countries have often made headlines in business news and corporate reports. Other groupings such as the Next 11, MIST, MINT, CIVETS, and E7 countries have also received some degree of interest. The reason for this attention is the same as previously mentioned: market analysts foresee the economic weight of the grouped countries becoming particularly important in the future. Despite the existence of various types of distance between the group members—and between them and developed economies—these countries are under scrutiny for both the opportunities they represent (as market and resource pools) and for the threats they represent (as sources of fierce competition in both developed

Economic and technological distances   261

economies and in other developing economies). These market groupings are briefly presented here:

- In 2001, Jim O'Neil, a British economist, proposed that the BRIC acronym regroup Brazil, Russia, India and China. At the time, he was head of the Asset Management team at Goldman Sachs (he later became a politician in the UK). Goldman Sachs (US) is a leading global investment banking, securities, and investment management firm. Among several other common characteristics, the BRIC countries were grouped together because they featured gigantic resources (e.g., just the four of them represented more than 40 percent of the world population and more than 25 percent of the land area) and held the promise of spectacular growth (e.g., they could eclipse the combined economies of the richest countries in terms of GDP by 2050) (Goldman Sachs, 2001). As stated in a subsequent report, "the BRICs story is not simply about developing country growth successes. What makes the BRICs special is that they have the scale and the trajectory to challenge the major economies in terms of influence on the world economy." (Goldman Sachs, 2005, p. 7). The potential for the growth of South Africa was also recognized early on (e.g., Goldman Sachs, 2003). In 2011, South Africa started to attend the BRIC Summit, an annual event initiated in 2009, where heads of states meet to discuss trade and other issues. Consequently, it has often been added to this particular grouping to form the BRICS (adding South Africa), although this is mainly motivated by political reasons. In regards to its size, South Africa is hardly "in the same league" as the other four heavyweights. Nevertheless, it is a leading country in the African continent—host to more than one billion people—which, in turn, deserves to be regarded as the next possible "economic giant" (Brand South Africa, 2011).
- In 2005, Jim O'Neil and his team introduced the "Next 11" market grouping (also known by the numeronym N-11). The N-11 shows broad representation by region and includes: Bangladesh, Egypt, Indonesia, Iran, Korea, Mexico, Nigeria, Pakistan, Philippines, Turkey, and Vietnam (Goldman Sachs, 2005). These countries were identified by running projections of GDP, real GDP growth, income per capita, incremental demand, and exchange rate paths for each of these economies but also by focusing on demographic profiles. According to Goldman Sachs (2005), a successful growth story is unlikely to have a global impact without a substantial population. The work by O'Neil and colleagues was indeed clearly meant to identify trends that could considerably modify the balance of global economic powers, established in the post-World War II era.
- In 2011, O'Neil's team highlighted the importance of the four largest N-11 countries (i.e., Mexico, Indonesia, South Korea, and Turkey) and adopted the term *growth markets*, arguing that the traditional labels of "developed" and "emerging" countries no longer reflected the fundamental nature of the global economy (Goldman Sachs, 2011). *Growth*

262   *Economic and technological distances*

markets included any country outside the developed world that was responsible for at least 1 percent of global GDP. Along with favorable demographics, these were the economies that were most likely to experience rising productivity and a faster growth rate than the world average. The MIST acronym (sometimes labeled the MIKT) was born. Nigeria was spotted as potentially making this list in the short term and the MINT acronym (Mexico, Indonesia, Nigeria, and Turkey) was used later on, substituting South Korea with Nigeria. Let us remember that South Korea has long been cited in another grouping of emerging markets in the 1990s: the four Asian "dragons" or "tigers" (along with Hong Kong, Singapore, and Taiwan), and has been falling into the "developed economy" category for a long time. On the other hand, Nigeria is increasingly regarded as a new growth engine in Africa.

- The CIVETS acronym regroups Colombia, Indonesia, Vietnam, Egypt, Turkey and South Africa. It was proposed in 2008 by the editorial editor at *The Economist* Intelligence Unit (Financial Times, 2012). *The Economist* is a leading British magazine-format newspaper and has been published since 1843. The rationale for grouping these countries together is similar: they were seen as the next generation of emerging markets. Incidentally, good acronyms help us memorize a list and actually mean something (e.g., BRIC, MIST). Civets are small, catlike mammals found in Asia and Africa (The Economist, 2009).

- Finally, the E7 countries—a numeronym standing for 'Emerging' market economies—include the BRIC countries, along with Indonesia, Mexico, and Turkey. This grouping was proposed in 2006 by analysts at PricewaterhouseCoopers (PwC, 2008). Headquartered in the UK, PwC is one of the largest "professional services" company in the world (e.g., services related to insurance, strategy and management consulting, data and analytics, financial, legal and actuarial advisory, and auditing). The rationale for this market grouping is, once more, the economic growth potential of the member countries. Recent estimates for the E7 forecast the average annual growth rate of GDP (in USD terms, including any projected real exchange rate changes versus USD) at 7.1 percent for the 2014–2020 period and 5.1 percent for the 2020–2030 period (PwC, 2015b, Table 2.b). This average growth rate is, thus, projected to be far superior to those of the G7 countries (i.e., Canada, France, Germany, Italy, Japan, the UK, and the US), estimated at 2.1 percent (2014–2020) and 1.9 percent (2020–2030).

Whether introduced by analysts in investment banks, newspapers or consulting firms, these market groupings aim to tell us a similar story: in the 2000s, the irruption of large and fast growing economies from the developing world started to challenge the economic dominance of the richest nations. Table 7.6 contrasts several of the above-mentioned groupings with the G7 (i.e., Canada, France, Germany, Italy, Japan, UK, and US)—another well-known numeronym standing for "the group of 7"—on indicators related to growth and population.

Economic and technological distances   263

Table 7.6 Comparing several market groupings on selected indicators: the G7, BRIC, MIST, and CIVETS

	G7	*BRIC*	*MIST*	*CIVETS*
	Canada, France, Germany, Italy, Japan, UK, US	*Brazil, Russia, India, China*	*Mexico, Indonesia, South Korea, Turkey*	*Colombia, Indonesia, Vietnam, Egypt, Turkey, South Africa*
Aggregated GDP at PPP (Tn USD)	36.9	36.7	8.9	7.8
Average GDP real growth rate (%)	1.24	2.50	3.25	3.43
Average GDP per capita at PPP (USD)	~44,500	~15,500	~22,500	~13,000
Average inflation rate (%)	0.56	5.28	3.85	6.50
Average median age (years)	43	34	32	28
Aggregated population (Mn people)	760	2,989	513	630
Average population growth rate (%)	0.34	0.58	0.87	1.21

Source: Own elaboration inspired by Canadian Business (2012) and based on CIA World Factbook (2016a)

Before moving on to important limitations of these emerging market groupings, we spend a little more time reflecting on their characteristics (see "Food for Thought") and their attractiveness to firms from developed economies.

Food for Thought 7.3

- In reference to D'Andrea and Marcotte (2010) and Sheth (2011), how different are emerging markets from developed markets?

Are these emerging markets really attractive to firms from developed economies? A pessimistic answer would emphasize the fragile political structures in emerging economies, as well as unreliable judicial systems (as states are often deficient in law enforcement, for instance), macroeconomic instability (e.g., fiscal imbalances, defaults, and devaluations), and social unrest (Griffin & Pustay, 2015; Cateora, Gilly, Graham, & Money, 2016). In the same vein, Khanna and Palepu (2010, p. 5) describe "persistent headaches of doing business in emerging markets": intellectual property rights

264 Economic and technological distances

are insecure, navigating government bureaucracies can be thorny, product quality is unreliable, local talent is insufficient to staff operations, reliably assessing customer credit is difficult, overcoming impediments to distribution can be frustrating, sorting through investment opportunities or performing due diligence on potential partners is often a guessing game, and finally, corruption may be so endemic that the risks can simply outweigh the potential rewards. In addition, the majority of consumers in emerging markets are characterized by lower revenues, with entirely different needs and consumption patterns. To adapt to such radically different consumers and hope to "get it right," firms from developed economies need to invest significant resources, time, and effort in doing things differently (see Chapter 8 on "Bottom of the Pyramid Marketing"). This adaptation comes to a cost that some deem too high, notwithstanding the fact that it can also divert companies' attention from where it is most needed (i.e., from competitive and "money-making markets"). Finally, recent years have shown that the path to economic success forecasted for emerging economies in the early 2000s is not a straightforward one. Taking the example of the BRIC countries, several setbacks have motivated the publications of articles with evocative titles, such as "India: A Bric Hits the Wall" (The Economist, 2012), "Russia: A Wounded Economy" (The Economist, 2014), "The Mirage Behind Brazil's Economic Miracle" (Bloomberg, 2014), "Brazil's Fall: Disaster Looms for Latin America's Biggest Economy" (The Economist, 2015), and "Has the BRICS Bubble Burst?" (The Guardian, 2016).

On the contrary, an optimistic answer would emphasize the following facts: emerging economies are opening their large markets and having more vigorous growth rates than developed economies; they have deregulated their economy and have been undergoing the privatization of public services for some years; and finally, their participation in regional integration (i.e., trading blocs) is growing, which reinforces their attractiveness by also opening up to trade the other countries that are part of the signed agreements (Griffin & Pustay, 2015; Cateora et al., 2016). In addition, they are characterized by a growing middle-class, an ideal target for consumption goods (see Chapter 8). Another attractive characteristic of emerging economies is their increasing contribution to global wealth, with the so-called "shift in global economic power" (PwC, 2016). This is one of five megatrends or long-term global trends identified by PwC—along with demographic and social change, rapid urbanization, technological breakthroughs, and resource scarcity and climate change. This shift is based on projections until 2050 that show the decline of the relative contribution of the G7 countries compared to the E7 countries (PwC, 2015a). Figure 7.13 relies on GDP projections in real market exchange rate (MER) terms (in constant 2014 USD). It illustrates the steady decrease of the G7 contribution to global GDP (from 43 percent in 2014 to a projected 27 percent in 2050), and, conversely, the steady increase of the E7 contribution to global GDP (from 24 percent in 2014 to a projected 42 percent in 2050) (PwC, 2015b). The shift is projected to occur during the 2030 decade.

So, the answer to whether emerging markets are really attractive to companies from developed economies heavily depends on managers' degree of risk aversion. Risk aversion is not necessarily a bad thing. It may prevent

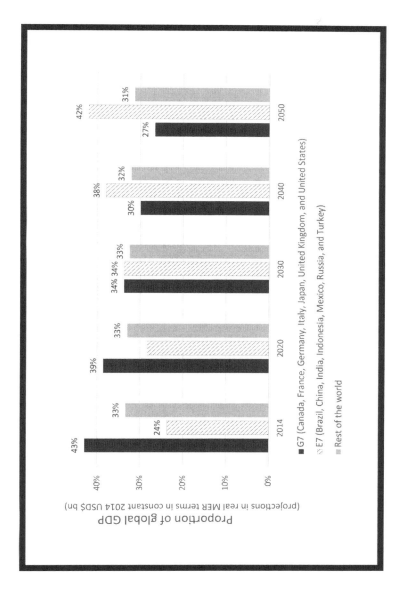

Figure 7.13 Illustrating the anticipated shift in global economic power from developed to emerging economies

Source: Adapted from PwC (2015b, Table 2.a)

266 *Economic and technological distances*

some companies from entering emerging markets unprepared, run head-on into significant hurdles, and exit only after a few years, having incurred losses and damaged reputation. The type of industry and the organizational structure (determining to some extent the freedom to adapt to local contingencies, see Chapter 3) are also important factors that will weigh in the answer. Finally, it all boils down to examining the question as if it were any foreign expansion move (see Chapter 2). The factors driving decisions of where firms internationalize (emerging markets or else) include:

- Managers' vision and attitude toward risk
- The available resources (e.g., financial and human resources)
- How much control is desired
- How much knowledge of target markets is possessed

7.4 Issues at Stake

Studying eco-techno distance is necessary to complete our situation analysis (first step in an international marketing plan, see Figure 7.2) and gain a well-rounded understanding of the challenges associated with firms' expansion into foreign environments. This dimension of distance also gains particular momentum because of the current rise of emerging markets and their potential to disrupt the established global economic order.

After defining the phenomenon and highlighting some of its main drivers, we have emphasized the role of market attractiveness in determining whether eco-techno distance is really a barrier for foreign expansion. In this section, we discuss some connected issues by raising the following questions:

- Are market groupings really homogeneous? Instead of using a national perspective to estimate market attractiveness, should we rather rely on a regional or even an urban perspective?
- Is economic distance between countries increasing or decreasing? In other words, are we heading toward global economic convergence?
- Are there any other differences between economies to take into account by firms with a global presence?
- What is the impact of eco-techno distance on marketing activities in an international context? How can companies adjust?

7.4.1 The Persistent Heterogeneity of Economies

As previously explained, one of the main rationales for resorting to market grouping is to simplify analyses and decisions. This practice is only relevant if the degree of commonality between markets is high. We have to question if this is always the case.

Are market groupings really homogeneous? First, the reliability of market groupings based on geographical proximity alone has long been questioned (e.g., Griffin & Pustay, 2015). Nevertheless, the organizational structure of

Economic and technological distances   267

Table 7.7 Illustrating "intra-regional heterogeneity" with selected countries in the Americas

REGION	*POPULATION*	*GDP PER CAPITA*
(Selected countries)	*(Million, 2016)*	*(Thousand current USD, PPP, 2016)*
NORTH AMERICA		
Canada	35.36	46.2
Greenland	0.57	(2008) 37.9
Mexico	123.16	18.9
US	323.99	57.3
CENTRAL AMERICA		
Costa Rica	4.87	16.1
Honduras	8.89	5.3
Nicaragua	5.96	5.3
Panama	3.70	22.8
SOUTH AMERICA		
Argentina	43.88	20.2
Bolivia	10.96	7.2
Brazil	205.82	15.2
Chile	17.65	24.0
Paraguay	6.86	9.4

Source: Own elaboration based on CIA World Factbook (2017)

many companies reflect the fact that it still is seen as a convenient lens. Other companies have reconsidered their organizational design and restructured to also account for economic proximity in the markets they serve (e.g., developed markets versus emerging markets). The point here is a note of caution regarding the practice of market grouping (even based on economic proximity) as the degree of homogeneity within country groups is not always as high as we can believe *a priori*. Table 7.7 and Figure 7.14 illustrate this point by looking at the heterogeneity of economies based on geographic and economic proximity, respectively.

First, Table 7.7 presents two economic indicators (size of population and GDP per capita) for selected countries in the Americas. If "North American" markets are often grouped together, we can see that there is little commonality between the population sizes of Canada and the US, for instance, and little commonality between the income of people in Mexico and people in the US. Markets in Central America are also often targeted as one whole. If their small population size is indeed similar, the income of consumers in Panama or Costa Rica is by far superior to that of Nicaragua or Honduras, the former being "high income" economies, while the latter are barely out of the "lower-middle income" category, as defined by the World Bank (see Figure 7.4).

In turn, Figure 7.14 takes the example of the BRIC countries to illustrate the presence of heterogeneity between their economies, although they have been grouped together on the basis of many economic indicators, showing similar patterns. For instance, their respective level of activity in exports reveals disparate situations. Choosing a few commercial partners located in

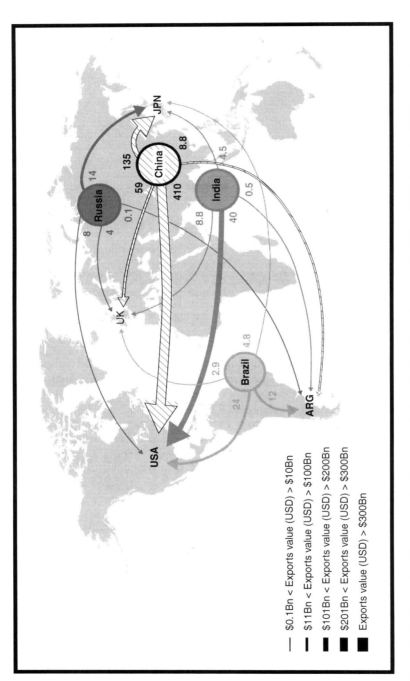

Figure 7.14 Illustrating "intra-grouping heterogeneity" with the value of exports (in Billion USD) from the BRIC countries toward selected trade partners

Source: Own elaboration based on UN Comtrade (2015)

For the color version, see the eResource at www.routledge.com/9781138202344

Economic and technological distances 269

various regions of the world (namely, Argentina, Japan, the UK, and the US), we see why China is often referred to as a "giant among giants" or "dwarfing the other BRICs": the value of its exports is tenfold compared to the other three member countries (reaching the hundreds of billion dollars when the others are, at best, reaching 30–40Bn threshold). Of course, the choice of trade partners is imperfect here. For instance, the top export destinations of Russia are not the US, UK, or Argentina, but rather The Netherlands, China, and Germany (OEC, 2017). Still, the value of Russian exports to these countries remains well under the 40Bn USD mark, far from the value made by China in exports. The figure just hints at the significant differences existing within the grouping.

However tempting, grouping of emerging markets can be misleading. Criticism comes from the fact that, growth potential aside, the grouped countries are notably diverse (e.g., in terms of culture and political systems). An article in the Financial Times (2012) even describes the proliferation of acronyms such as BRIC and CIVETS as a "marketing ploy" used by analysts to convince investors to put their money in countries they know relatively little about. Indeed, most investment banks have started offering products related to these groupings (e.g., Standard & Poor has launched a CIVETS 60 index, HSBC offers a CIVETS-based fund, and Goldman Sachs offers a Next-11 fund) (Financial Times, 2012). Overall, we just need to remember to use caution when resorting to market grouping, and be careful with the conclusions we derive from this exercise in assessing the attractiveness of markets.

Instead of using a national perspective to estimate market attractiveness, should we rather rely on a regional or even an urban perspective? In 2007, McKinsey—a leading management consulting firm from the US—argued that it was time to look at the world's economy at a finer level of granularity than nations and started to monitor the attractiveness of cities with the 'Cityscope' database. According to the McKinsey Global Institute (2012, p. 16): "Choosing the right urban markets requires combining granular market intelligence with company-specific information on the potential of different urban geographies and the cost of reaching them. A strategy based on clusters of cities is an attractive option for many companies, particularly in large countries like China and India that have significant regional differences in their market characteristics."

The Cityscope database covers more than 2,600 cities across the world, and maps the evolution of global urban consumption with projections until 2030. GDP growth between 2010 and 2025 is forecasted to be driven largely by cities in emerging markets—either those that are called "megacities" (e.g. Mexico, Sao Paulo, Shanghai, Jakarta, Istanbul, and Lagos), or "middleweight cities" (whose populations are comprised between 200,000 and 1 million inhabitants). A group of 443 cities located in emerging economies (including twenty megacities) is expected to contribute 47 percent of global growth by 2025 (McKinsey Global Institute, 2012).

Other market research firms have also picked up on the phenomenon and emphasized the rising importance of looking at cities in emerging economies (and in developed economies as well, for that matter) to better assess economies' attractiveness. For instance, Euromonitor International—a leading

270 Economic and technological distances

market intelligence provider based in the UK—ranked thirty megacities in the world in terms of growth of consumer expenditure in 2015–2016. In this ranking, only seven out of thirty megacities were from developed economies (i.e., New York, Los Angeles, and London in the three first positions; Tokyo and Seoul in sixth and seventh position, respectively; Paris in fifteenth position; and Osaka in twenty-seventh position). The remaining twenty-three megacities were all from emerging economies (e.g., Shanghai and Beijing in fourth and fifth position, respectively; Buenos Aires in tenth position; and Jakarta in twelfth position, to name a few) (Euromonitor International, 2016). This approach also reveals some of the important limitations of market grouping and opens up new ways of looking at the world's economy and the eco-techno distance between countries (or cities!). Choosing the appropriate level of analysis for our evaluation of distance between markets might be key in producing relevant information for companies' international marketing plans.

7.4.2 Economic and Technological Convergence

Beside development levels, are there any other differences between economies to take into account by firms with a global presence?[1] An interesting source of diversity across countries, due to a combination of different economies, cultures, and institutions, is found in the notion of corporate governance. Corporate governance concerns "the structure of rights and responsibilities among the parties with a stake in the firm" (Aoki, 2000, p. 11). In this definition, the term *parties* refers to managers, shareholders, the board of directors, and other stakeholders (e.g., employees, suppliers, and consumers).

On the one hand, a certain degree of convergence is observed in terms of corporate governance norms (e.g., the appointment of independent board members to monitor managers and institutional investors' activism), generally tending toward the Anglo-Saxon model (Aguilera & Cuervo-Cazurra, 2004; Davis, 2012). For instance, Germany was seen as the prototypical coordinated market economy in the 1990s, but public firms then began to advertise their commitment to "shareholder value" to attract foreign investors (Fiss & Zajac, 2004). At the same time in Japan, foreign institutional investors increasingly replaced domestic shareholders. Japanese firms became more focused on financial return, and less attached to forming long-term relationships with their stakeholders. They started to reconsider permanent employment—one of the cornerstones of the postwar Japanese economy—and began to downsize (Ahmadjian & Robbins, 2005).

On the other hand, the literature shows that corporate governance practices are still far from being unified across the world. For instance, country characteristics explain most of the variance in firms' governance ratings (Doidge, Karolyi, & Stulz, 2007). Since corporate governance shapes firms' fund raising abilities (Leuz, Lins, & Warnock, 2009), but also top managers' remuneration (Chhaochharia & Grinstein, 2009) and investment horizons (Lee & O'Neill, 2003), it influences firms' strategies and their ability to internationalize, innovate, and deploy tactics against their competitors.

As a result, managers in MNCs should carefully consider local corporate governance norms and practices when they decide to enter new markets, design joint-venture agreements with domestic firms, and consider the acquisition of local targets.

Is technological distance between countries increasing or decreasing?[2] In Chapter 1, we have introduced globalization and its consequences for marketing. To build on this chapter and several of the subsequent chapters (Chapters 4 and 6, in particular), we can see the modern stage of globalization as the result of some "forces" or important changes of the twenty-first century: 1) the reduction in transportation and communication costs, 2) the multiplication of multilateral free-trade policies, and 3) the improved political and institutional stability in emerging countries, leveraged in particular by one special case: the opening of China and its entry into the WTO (2001). As a result, MNCs can move firm-specific assets across national boundaries (Dunning, 1998).

If we were to only consider the above-mentioned forces, we could conclude that eco-techno distance is reduced and that the world is getting smaller. Indeed, there are signs of macro-economic convergence across countries, notably due to an improved global infrastructure (Hadengue & Warin, 2014). Still, the twenty-first century brings a unique phenomenon: the Fourth Industrial Revolution, with its incredible set of new technologies and their multiple applications in manufacturing. The question of whether technological distance will increase or decrease is, thus, central to answering the question of eco-techno distance convergence. In a macroeconomic perspective, technological distance stems from two factors: distance created by different development levels of technological infrastructures across countries, and distance created by different levels of technological applications (or implementation).

While there is a scenario in which technological distance increases due to the location of R&D centers in capital intensive places, there is also a scenario where technological distance decreases due to the low costs of replicating these new technologies. Instead of finding capital-rich locations with highly developed infrastructures, the key variable is then to have access to trained human capital to replicate and use these innovations at an industrial scale. As further discussed in Chapter 9, innovations are increasingly seen as coming from emerging countries (e.g., Hadengue, De Marcellis-Warin, & Warin, 2015). In short, the *technological infrastructure* distance may increase but it can be balanced by the decrease in the *technological application* distance. In an open world—where more people have access to knowledge, collaborations, and technology transfers—eco-techno distance might be reduced. However, this type of distance may also be recreated by the emergence of local-specific innovations or inventions, before they spread again to other parts of the world and level the playing field.

What about economic distance between countries, is it increasing or decreasing? In other words, are we heading toward global economic convergence?[3] The fast pace of economic growth in the developing world—and, by contrast, sluggish growth in the developed world—suggests that the fall of economic distance between poor and rich countries is only a matter of time.

272   *Economic and technological distances*

For instance, the average GDP real growth rate in the richest countries was around 1 percent in 2016 (e.g., 1.24 percent in the G7), while it was well above 3 percent in many emerging countries (e.g., 3.25 percent in the MIST and 3.43 percent in the CIVETS), as detailed in Table 7.6. Countries such as China and India even presented spectacular growth rates of 9 percent and 5.6 percent, respectively, in terms of their GDP per capita (average over the 2000–2015 period) (UNCTAD, 2017). In addition, the average income in developed economies narrowed from twelve to nearly fifteen times higher than in developing economies in the past decade—a significant but closing gap. Indeed, the average GDP per capita for developing and developed economies in 2008 was 2,504 USD and 36,558 USD, respectively (at constant prices of 2005), while it was 3,174 USD and 37,915 USD in 2015 (own calculations based on *UNCTADStat*).

In growth research, the notion of *conditional convergence* refers to the trend that sees lower-income countries catching up with the richest countries if "the right conditions are in place" (Goldman Sachs, 2005, p. 10). The assumption that these favorable conditions (e.g., political stability) will continue has underlined all the projections made about the BRIC and other groupings in bridging the gap with developed economies. Countries with more favorable conditions for growth (e.g., China, Mexico, Russia, South Korea, and Vietnam) were expected to exhibit the highest speed of convergence, while the speed of convergence for other countries (e.g., Brazil and India) was deemed slower, but was expected to increase in the future ((Goldman Sachs, 2005), p. 13). More broadly, Asia has shown consistent progress toward convergence since the 1970s, whereas Africa and Latin America have experienced a rising convergence gap between 1970 and the early 2000s (Rodrik, 2011). As of 2016, the size of the Chinese economy has, in fact, already surpassed the US economy (21 and 20 trillion USD in GDP at PPP, respectively) (CIA World Factbook, 2016b). In turn, the size of the Indian economy far exceeds the Japanese economy (9 and 5 trillion USD in GDP at PPP, respectively). By 2060, the OECD projects that the sum of the GDPs of China and India will exceed that of its thirty-five member countries, and the total GDP of developing countries will prevail over the total GDP of developed economies (OECD, 2012a).

Signs of economic convergence are also visible in other areas aside from income. For instance, Dowrick and DeLong (2003) studied economic convergence looking at the following indicators: common technology, similar capital-labor ratios, real wage levels, productivity levels, and standards of living (see Chapter 1). Sound markets and entrepreneurial spirit are among other factors that lead to higher growth, and, thus, faster convergence (Financial Times, 2011). Interestingly, the "green economy" also drives convergence. In addition to its contribution to a more sustainable environment, green growth is said to result in more efficient use of natural resources, higher diversification of the economy (less risk), more innovation (e.g., green technologies), and less inequality, which ultimately yields faster convergence for countries pursuing sustainable development policies (OECD, 2012b).

However, the idea that economic convergence between poor and rich countries is only a matter of time, and is thus inevitable, is far from being

Economic and technological distances 273

consensual. Since the Great Recession (2008–2009), the growth outlook has rather improved for advanced economies and deteriorated for the developing world (IMF, 2016). Even as far as 2060, the OECD estimates that the GDP per capita in emerging countries will rise no higher than 20–60 percent of the level of income in advanced economies (OECD, 2012a).

First, the "right conditions" supporting the notion of conditional convergence for emerging economies have hardly proven to be sustainable, as the evolution of Latin American economies have illustrated since the 1970s (Rodrik, 2011). Many key challenges are seen as simply blocking the path to economic convergence. The reliance on natural resources, endemic corruption, political instability, and, more broadly, the weakness of institutions are persistent barriers to a more prosperous future in poor countries (e.g., Khanna & Palepu, 2010). In turn, developed nations also face their own set of challenges, including the integration of new labour force (Boudarbat & Ebrahimi, 2016) and the rise of income inequality (Piketty, 2014).

Second, mechanisms of wealth redistribution, across and within nations, hardly converge. Taxation systems are still widely disparate (Zucman, 2015). The existence of tax havens (e.g., Bermuda and Liechtenstein), the tax incentives provided to foreign companies and individuals by governments highly willing to attract FDI, capital, and talents (e.g., Ireland and Chile), and the practice of transfer pricing within MNCs (i.e., when subsidiaries purchase goods/services from other subsidiaries at prices that are either far below or above market prices; a practice designed to help MNCs reduce tax contributions by increasing profits in locations with lower tax rates and decreasing profits in locations with higher tax rates) have been the object of much debate. Doubts about the power of trade liberalization in actually reducing inequalities (among and within countries) have also widely been expressed (e.g., (Stiglitz, 2012).

Finally, criticism about the economic system itself cannot be ignored. Indeed, the way neo-liberal capitalism has evolved during the past decades suggests that to be sustained over time, the system actually needs sources of cheaper labor and resources (hence, "poorer" locations). Movements of delocalization and outsourcing are acute manifestations of this ingrained characteristic. The textile industry is a case in point: US brands that once outsourced their manufacturing to China in search of cheaper labor costs now invest in production in other countries (e.g., Vietnam and Indonesia), where wages are even lower (New York Times, 2016). From this perspective, it is almost as if the economic system is designed to prevent convergence, always requiring economic differentials to maintain themselves.

7.4.3 Impact on Marketing Decisions with Corporate Examples: Disney and Volkswagen

To what extent does eco-techno distance with a foreign country impact marketers' decisions? Like other dimensions of distance (e.g., cultural and administrative distances) that affect most aspects of marketing in international settings, the impact of eco-techno distance is quite widespread.

274   *Economic and technological distances*

At the strategic level, it heavily affects market selection and the STP process. If differences in the economic and technological environments of a foreign country are particularly marked, it is unlikely that companies will be willing to absorb the high costs of adaptation—or renounce the revenues and profit margins they need—and consequently avoid selecting and entering this particular market altogether. In regard to the STP process, a foreign country whose population presents largely different socio-economic characteristics (e.g., poorer, more rural, less educated or aspirational) requires reconsidering segmentation. Then, targeting different customer segments (e.g., with more purchasing power) might result in having to reposition the offerings (e.g., upscale positioning instead of a mainstream one for affordable products). The impact of eco-techno distance on entry modes is less obvious but is still observable when we reflect on the level of control and internalization that companies need to be competitive (see Chapter 2). In a market characterized by low purchasing power, for instance, it is unlikely that a foreign offering will be competitive through exports (due to price escalation, as discussed in Chapter 2). Instead, FDI might be recommended. In turn, the choice of local partners (e.g., in a joint-venture setting) versus a greenfield investment (which ensures full control) in countries characterized by intensive technological development or by poorly enforced IP protection can be a matter of long-term survival. Another important impact on entry mode is that of technological distance alone. Depending on the local infrastructure, available resources, IP development levels, and presence of valuable collaborators, a foreign company might be enticed to locate production facilities in a foreign country (either through acquisitions or greenfield projects). Here, the "directionality" of distance (see Question 7.2) plays an important role (i.e., from developed to developing environments— what we could call a "negatively charged distance"—or from developing to developed environments—a "positively charged distance"). For instance, a company from a developed economy can be interested in undertaking FDI in a less-developed environment to access "cheaper" production factors (e.g., human and natural resources) and "easier" demand factors (e.g., less sophisticated customer tastes). A company from an emerging economy can be interested in undertaking FDI in a more developed environment to access "better" production and demand factors (e.g., financing of R&D and higher disposable income).

At the tactical level, differences in the economic environment between home- and target-countries can force companies to modify their product and pricing policies (e.g., tweaking existing products—or developing new ones—to make them more affordable to consumers with lower incomes, and introduce better installment payments for consumers with limited access to savings and credit). In turn, product, distribution, and promotion policies can be heavily affected by differences in the technological environment (e.g., limited or unreliable access to electricity severely constrains the distribution of products requiring a cold chain or the promotion of offerings using TV advertising, for instance). We look at the tactical impact of eco-techno distance in more detail in the next two chapters (Chapter 8 "Bottom of the Pyramid Marketing" and Chapter 9 "Reverse Innovation").

Coming back to the impact of differences in economic and technological environments at the strategic level of marketing, we now consider a few examples that illustrate how companies from developed economies have adjusted their STP process when entering emerging markets (i.e., when facing a "negatively charged distance").

Disney[4]—Previously, we presented the internationalization process of the Walt Disney Company's amusement parks (Chapter 2), the degrees of Adapt/Stand for its parks in Tokyo, Paris, and Hong Kong (Chapter 3), and the impact of cultural distance on marketing decisions for its park in Shanghai (Chapter 5). Here, we focus on the example of Hong Kong Disneyland (launched in 2005) to illustrate initial difficulties due to a poorly evaluated eco-techno distance (among other problems).

First, we review important criteria for market selection. For a foreign country to be attractive to build a Disneyland, the economic environment must present the following characteristics: a growing economy and a growing middle-class (in particular the presence of a significant middle- to upper-middle-income segment with growing disposable income), large size and high density of population (including surrounding countries; ideally with a large tourism industry), a social organization including large numbers of families with young children, and finally, easy access to financing and availability of local partners (e.g., suppliers for machinery and food, and, most importantly, local labor with the appropriate skills, in particular a mastery of several languages, including English). The technological environment also needed to present favorable conditions, including: a developed transport infrastructure (for easy and cheap access to the country via airports/harbors and for easy access to the site via highways/trains). The level of local competition had to be reasonable. Other dimensions of distance were also taken into account for market selection, such as geographic aspects (e.g., the availability of land to build the park and sufficient distance from other Disney parks to avoid cannibalization, a temperate and reasonably warm climate all year long for outdoor activities), cultural aspects (e.g., familiarity with Disney characters and openness to US culture) and administrative aspects (e.g., a friendly government to facilitate access to land and financing).

Second, we examine one possible explanation for the poor performance of Hong Kong Disneyland in its first years of operation: the underestimated eco-techno distance and its disastrous impact on STP and pricing decisions. At first, most attractions were targeting families with young children. Yet, market research was showing that the segment of the Hong Kong population aged under fourteen years old was less than 14 percent in 2006, and was even expected to decrease overtime. A core difference in consumer behavior between teens and adults versus families is that the former tend to visit amusement parks only once, limiting "repurchase frequency." In addition, the company had targeted local people for 40 percent, Chinese mainland tourists for 33 percent, and overseas tourists for 27 percnt of total customers. Yet, at the time of opening (2005), mainland China had received little prior exposure to Disney culture. As a result, the company had clearly overestimated potential sales from local and mainland visitors. Another miscalculation was the pressure incurred from local competition that resulted in

276 Economic and technological distances

a misguided pricing strategy. Indeed, "Ocean Park" had been located close to Hong Kong since 1977, and featured many attractions (aquariums with dolphins and sharks, a bird garden, giant pandas, and rollercoaster rides). Its strong conservation and education mission resonated well with cultural values. In 2006, Disneyland entry fees during peak days were 68 percent more expensive for consumers over twelve years old and 143 percent more expensive for consumers under twelve years old! Considering that nearly half of the households in Hong Kong earned at the time less than 2,000 USD per month, it is not surprising that many were reluctant to spend 200 USD for a single-day visit to Disneyland (estimated expenses for a four-member family including food and drink), a sum which roughly amounted to 10 percent of their monthly income. Finally, Disney had clearly overestimated its bargaining power with travel agents in charge of promoting the park and distributing tickets. As a result, these important collaborators preferred supporting Ocean Park, which offered higher commissions and less-stringent business terms.

In conclusion, Honk Kong Disneyland provides a good example of a company's expansion that is heavily affected by eco-techno distance. It also shows the marketing issues arising from a suboptimal evaluation of this important dimension of distance.

Volkswagen[5]—The case of Volkswagen served to illustrate the internationalization process (Chapter 2) and efforts in local adaptation (Chapter 3) of companies entering foreign markets. What was not mentioned yet, is that the group resorts to a portfolio of twelve brands that attend to different needs related to transportation (i.e., from motorcycles to passenger and commercial vehicles) and appeal to a vast range of consumer segments. Each of these brands have "an individual identity and a common goal: mobility. For everyone, all over the world." Volkswagen (1937) is the flagship brand of the Volkswagen Group which, over the years, also integrated: Audi from Germany (1964), Seat from Spain (1986), Skoda from the Czech Republic (1991), Bentley from the UK (1998), Bugatti from France (1998), Lamborghini from Italy (1998), and Porsche from Germany (2012).

Now, to illustrate how economic distance affected the company's STP process, we take the example of its entry into India with the Skoda brand (2001), then followed by Audi (2004) and Volkswagen (2007). As in other markets, the company meant to position Volkswagen as more premium than Skoda, while Audi aimed to be positioned on par with BMW and Mercedes. Nevertheless, the marketing team encountered an unexpected situation with the Volkswagen brand which, upon entry, was perceived by consumers as less up-market than Skoda. This was explained by the fact that Skoda had been launched with premium models (Octavia first, and then Laura and Superb), which quickly became CEOs' cars. Consumer perceptions about Skoda were then formed on this basis and it took a while to change them (in particular by lowering prices for Skoda models introduced later).

In terms of competition, the company realized that car manufacturers' brands (e.g., Hindustan Motors, Suzuki, and Tata Motors) positioned for the budget market were grabbing the lion's share of the car market, with 64 percent of overall sales. Next, brands like Hyundai, Ford, Fiat, Nissan, and

Economic and technological distances 277

Chevrolet were positioned for the lower premium market (with 27 percent market share). Then came the brands positioned for the premium market (Volkswagen, Skoda, Toyota, and Honda), with only 8 percent market share, while the brands positioned for the luxury market (e.g., Audi, BMW, Jaguar, Mercedes, Porsche, Rolls-Royce, etc.) were selling limited volumes (1 percent market share).

Thus, the STP process was reconsidered to not only adjust to local competition (and stay out of the budget market), but also to take into account Indian consumers specificities. To segment the Indian market, the company used a combination of demographic and psychographic segmentation techniques, relying in particular on revenues and social strata on the one hand, and on lifestyle and values on the other hand. In this way, it built a two-by-two matrix in order to identify relevant target segments. On the Y-axis, it situated consumers ranging from middle, upper-middle, and high levels of revenues. On the X-axis, it distinguished between "traditional" consumers (with marked attachment to religion, caste system, respect for elders, and property, for instance), "traditional/modern" consumers (motivated by wealth and achievement, and characterized by conspicuous consumption), and "modern" consumers (characterized by individualism and cosmopolitanism, open to inter-caste marriage, and sensitive to environmental protection). In this way, the company defined nine segments that were interesting to target and estimated their relative size within the population under scrutiny. At the level of middle income/class and spanning the "traditional" and "traditional/modern" categories, they situated: "traditional young aspirers (15 percent)" and "new middle-class" (18 percent) consumers. In turn, "traditional merchants" (25 percent) were clearly positioned as "traditional" consumers but spanned the middle and upper-middle income categories. In the upper-middle income category, the company identified a "self-made milieu" segment (9.5 percent) with "traditional/modern" values, and a "young progressives" segment (10 percent) spanning over the "traditional/modern" and "modern" values categories. Finally, in the high income/class category, and ranging from very "traditional" to very "modern," they identified the following segments: "supreme corporate India" (5 percent), "new business leaders" (5 percent), "modern urban elite" (6 percent) and "metropolitan smart" (6 percent).

We see here the obvious efforts made by Volkswagen AG to rebuild their segmentation matrix according to local specificities. The large economic distance with India explains why a brand like Skoda (perceived in developed economies as for limited budgets) would be perceived as premium there, forcing the company to adjust and work hard at repositioning its brands until it reached the desired coherence in its brand portfolio.

How can companies adjust to eco-techno distance? First, we need to remember that many companies choose not to adapt to eco-techno distance. They do that by taking the strategic decision to avoid selecting and entering a market that is too different from what they need in terms of demand and production conditions. Then, if they decide to actually do business in such distant environments, they have to choose an entry mode that ensures maintaining control over costs and prices (so that profits are not impaired), on the one hand, and maintaining control over important proprietary assets such as

278   *Economic and technological distances*

IP, on the other (so that their competitiveness is sustained). Finally, they have the option to adapt their existing marketing activities by carefully segmenting the market, and elaborating a targeting and positioning strategy that fits with their sales objectives. Adjusting the 4/7Ps policies is then a must, in particular pricing, which has direct consequences on the product that can be commercialized and budgets that can be allocated to distribution and promotion. However, they also have the option to consider an entirely different business model (not just alter the existing one). This is the object of the next chapter, entitled "Bottom of the Pyramid (BOP) Marketing."

Conclusion: "Eco-techno" Distance Matters Because It Jeopardizes Revenues and Profits. To Some Extent, It Is Decreasing (but Not Everywhere)

What would a nomological network for these types of distances look like? A *nomological network* has been defined as the representation of the constructs of interest in a study, their observable manifestations and the interrelationships among and between them (Cronbach & Meehl, 1955). Figure 7.15 encapsulates the concepts reviewed in this chapter by proposing a nomological network for both types of distance in relation to marketing. Because of the strong interrelation of the economic and technological environments, we could have represented "eco-techno" distance as one and only one phenomenon at the center of the figure. Instead, we have kept separate the presentation of both phenomenon to highlight that some driving factors are more associated with economic distance (i.e., demand factors as determined by economic development levels, with a direct link to the volume and value of clients and competitors), whereas others are more associated with technological distance (i.e., production factors determined by levels of infrastructure, resources, and IP development, with a direct link to the volume and value of collaborators, such as suppliers and financing partners). In terms of outcomes, the impact of eco-techno distance can be found at all levels of marketing. Yet, the figure highlights the particular importance of its effect on market selection, the segmentation-targeting-positioning (STP) process, and pricing. Indeed, depending on their assessment of the eco-techno distance, companies will either choose or refuse to enter specific markets, will rethink entirely the way they position their offerings and for whom, and finally adapt pricing strategies and tactics. Ultimately, these decisions have major consequences on corporate revenues and profits.

So, **why do economic and technological distances matter for marketing decisions in a globalizing context?** Throughout this chapter, we have reviewed a variety of factors belonging to the eco-techno environment with an impact on marketing decisions at both the strategic and tactical levels of marketing. Overall, we can conclude that eco-techno distance matters because it jeopardizes revenues and profits in foreign markets, particularly in the case of a "negatively charged" eco-techno distance (for firms from developed economies expanding in less-developed economies). Simply put, the key issue for marketers when looking at foreign markets from the angle of eco-techno distance is then: correctly "**assessing market attractiveness**" in terms of size and growth potential, for both revenues and profits (see Figure 7.15).

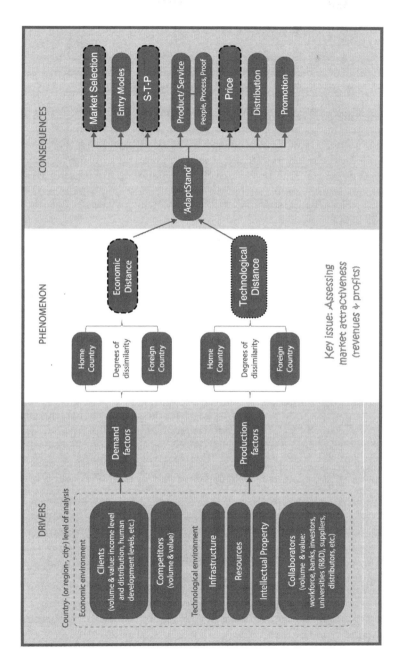

Figure 7.15 Proposing a nomological network for economic and technological distances
Source: Own elaboration

280 *Economic and technological distances*

Finally, are economic and technological distances decreasing? This question is equivalent to wondering about convergence, as discussed in Section 7.4.2. Overall, we can find arguments and data to support either standpoint: "Yes, it seems that we are heading toward eco-techno convergence" or "No, there is no way this is going to happen." Such mixed evidence and ambivalence is unsettling because it makes the decision process that much harder. However, it is also typical of transition periods in society like the one we seem to be experiencing: we are not in the "modern" era anymore, but in a "postmodern" era (see Chapter 1). This means that we find ourselves in a period of time (decades and even centuries) that is not "what it was" but that is still not clearly defined and cannot be named yet after a specific set of characteristics. Consequently, the evolution of eco-techno distance is hard to predict, quite similarly to cultural and administrative distances (Chapters 5 and 6). Once more, the take away for us marketers and marketing analysts is to avoid rooting our analyses in both unchecked certainty and a short timeframe, while ignoring the existence of solid counter-arguments to our positions.

Notes

1 In Section 7.4.2, the subsection entitled "Are there any other differences between economies to take into account by firms with a global presence?" has been written in collaboration with Aude Le Cottier, Assistant Professor in International Business (HEC Montréal, Canada), whose research focuses on international corporate governance and the impact of ownership structure on firms' strategies and performance.
2 In Section 7.4.2, the subsection entitled "Overall, is eco-techno distance between countries increasing or decreasing?" has been written in collaboration with Thierry Warrin, Associate Professor in International Business (HEC Montréal, Canada), whose research focuses on industrial organization as well as international finance and economics.
3 In Section 7.4.2, the subsection entitled "Is economic distance between countries increasing or decreasing? In other words, are we heading toward global economic convergence?" has been written in collaboration with Pouya Ebrahimi, PhD candidate in International Business at HEC Montréal (Canada), whose research focuses on international taxation and global supply chain management.
4 The example of Disney relies on: HKU 885 (2010).
5 The example of Volkswagen is based on: IMB 443 (2013); Volkswagen (2017).

References

Aguilera, Ruth & Cuervo-Cazurra, Alvaro (2004). Codes of Good Governance Worldwide: What Is the Trigger? *Organization Studies*, 25(3), 415–443.

Ahmadjian, Christina & Robbins, Gregory (2005). A Clash of Capitalisms: Foreign Shareholders and Corporate Restructuring in 1990s Japan. *American Sociological Review*, 70(3), 451–471.

Alexander, Nicholas, Rhodes, Mark & Myers, Hayley (2011). A Gravitational Model of International Retail Market Selection. *International Marketing Review*, 28(2), 183–200.

Aoki, Masahiko (2000). *Information, Corporate Governance, and Institutional Diversity: Competitiveness in Japan, the USA, and the Transnational Economies*. New York: Oxford University Press (p. 186).

Economic and technological distances 281

Atkinson, John (1957). Motivational Determinants of Risk-Taking Behavior. *Psychological Review*, 64(6), 359–372.

BBC News (2015, March 12th). Who, What, Why: What Is the Gini Coefficient? Retrieved from www.bbc.com/news/blogs-magazine-monitor-31847943

Bloomberg (2014, January 23rd). The Mirage Behind Brazil's Economic Miracle, *By Meghan McArdle*. Retrieved from www.bloomberg.com/view/articles/2014-01-23/the-mirage-behind-brazil-s-economic-miracle

Boudarbat, Brahim & Ebrahimi, Pouya (2016). L'intégration économique des jeunes issus de l'immigration au Québec et au Canada. *Cahiers québécois de démographie*, 45(2), 121–144.

Brand South Africa (2011). New Era as South Africa Joins BRICS. Retrieved June 2017, from www.brandsouthafrica.com/investments-immigration/business/trends/global/brics-080411

Canadian Business (2012). How BRIC and Other Economic Groups Compare. Retrieved July 2017, from www.canadianbusiness.com/investing/infographic-how-bric-and-other-economic-groups-compare/

Cateora, Philip, Gilly, Mary & Graham, John (2011). *International Marketing* (2nd ed.). New York: McGraw-Hill/Irwin (p. 742).

Cateora, Philip, Gilly, Mary, Graham, John & Money, Bruce (2016). *International Marketing* (17th ed.). New York: McGrawn-Hill/Irwin (p. 704).

Chhaochharia, Vidhi & Grinstein, Yaniv (2009). CEO Compensation and Board Structure. *The Journal of Finance*, 64(1), 231–261.

CIA World Factbook (2016a). Country Comparison: GDP, GDP Growth Rate, GDP per Capita, Unemployment Rate, Inflation Rate, Median Age, Population Growth Rate. Retrieved June 2017, from www.cia.gov/library/publications/the-world-factbook/rankorder/rankorderguide.html

CIA World Factbook (2016b). Country Comparison: GDP (Purchasing Power Parity). Retrieved June 2017, from www.cia.gov/library/publications/the-world-factbook/rankorder/2001rank.html

CIA World Factbook (2017). Field Listing: Country Profile—People and Society/Economy. Retrieved May 2017, from www.cia.gov/library/publications/the-world-factbook/geos/bl.html

Cronbach, Lee Joseph & Meehl, Paul (1955). Construct Validity in Psychological Tests. *Psychological Bulletin*, 52(4), 281–302.

D'Andrea, Guillermo & Marcotte, David (2010). Let Emerging Market Customers Be Your Teachers. *Harvard Business Review*, 88(12), 115–120.

Davis, Gerald (2012). Politics and Financial Markets. In *The Oxford Handbook of the Sociology of Finance*, Karin Knorr Cetina and Alex Preda (Editors). Oxford: Oxford University Press (p. 33–51).

Dikhanov, Yuri (2005). Trends in Global Income Distribution, 1970–2000, and Scenarios for 2015. United Nations Development Program. www.rrojasdatabank.info/globalincometrends1970-2000.pdf

Doidge, Craig, Karolyi, Andrew & Stulz, René (2007). Why Do Countries Matter so Much for Corporate Governance? *Journal of Financial Economics*, 86(1), 1–39.

Dowrick, Steve & DeLong, Bradford (2003). Globalization and Convergence. In *Globalization in Historical Perspective*, Michael Bordo, Alan Taylor, and Jeffrey Williamson (Editors). Chicago: University of Chicago Press (p. 191–226).

Dunning, John (1998). Location and the Multinational Enterprise: A Neglected Factor? *Journal of International Business Studies*, 29(1), 45–66.

282 *Economic and technological distances*

Durand, Aurélia, Turkina, Ekaterina & Robson, Matthew (2016). Psychic Distance and Country Image in Exporter-Importer Relationships. *Journal of International Marketing*, 24(3), 31–57.

The Economist (2009). BRICS and BICIS. Retrieved June 2017, from www.economist.com/blogs/theworldin2010/2009/11/acronyms_4

The Economist (2012). A Brick Hits the Wall. Retrieved March 2018, from www.economist.com/blogs/newsbook/2012/05/indias-economy

The Economist (2014). Russia: A Wounded Economy. Retrieved March 2018, from www.economist.com/news/leaders/21633813-it-closer-crisis-west-or-vladimir-putin-realise-wounded-economy

The Economist (2015). Brazil's Fall: Disaster Looms for Latin America's Biggest Economy. Retrieved March 2018, from www.economist.com/news/leaders/21684779-disaster-looms-latin-americas-biggest-economy-brazils-fall

Euromonitor International (2016). Cities for Success. *By Ugne Saltenyte*. http://blog.euromonitor.com/2016/02/top-megacities-for-growth-in-2016.html

Financial Times (2011, January 4, 2011). In the Grip of a Great Convergence. *By Martin Wolf*. Retrieved from www.ft.com/content/072c87e6-1841-11e0-88c9-00144feab49a?mhq5j=e1

Financial Times (2012, June 8th). Civets, Brics and the Next 11. *By Elaine Moore*. Retrieved from www.ft.com/content/c14730ae-aff3-11e1-ad0b-00144feabdc0?mhq5j=e1

Fiss, Peer & Zajac, Edward (2004). The Diffusion of Ideas Over Contested Terrain: The (Non) Adoption of a Shareholder Value Orientation Among German Firms. *Administrative Science Quarterly*, 49(4), 501–534.

Ghemawat, Pankaj (2001). Distance Still Matters: The Hard Reality of Global Expansion. *Harvard Business Review*, 79(8), 137–147.

Goldman Sachs (2001). Building Better Global Economic BRICs. By Jim O'Neill—Global Economics Paper No: 66. www.goldmansachs.com/our-thinking/archive/archive-pdfs/build-better-brics.pdf

Goldman Sachs (2003). Dreaming With BRICs: The Path to 2050. By Dominic Wilson and Roopa Purushothaman—Global Economics Paper No: 99. www.goldmansachs.com/our-thinking/archive/archive-pdfs/brics-dream.pdf

Goldman Sachs (2005). How Solid Are the BRICs? By Jim O'Neill, Dominic Wilson, Roopa Purushothaman and Anna Stupnytska—Global Economics Paper No: 134. www.goldmansachs.com/our-thinking/archive/archive-pdfs/how-solid.pdf

Goldman Sachs (2011). Introducing "Growth Markets". Retrieved June 2017, from www.goldmansachs.com/our-thinking/archive/intro-growth-markets/index.html

Google Patents (2017). Patents for Toothbrush Bristles and Handle: US4802255, D434563 and D347736. Retrieved June 2017, from https://patents.google.com/patent/US4802255A/en; https://patents.google.com/patent/USD434563S/en; https://patents.google.com/patent/USD347736S/en

The Guardian (2016, March 27th). Has the BRICS Bubble Burst?, *By Simon Tisdall*. Retrieved from www.theguardian.com/business/2016/mar/27/brics-bubble-burst-brazil-russia-india-china-south-africa

Griffin, Ricky & Pustay, Michael (2015). *International Business* (8th ed.). New Jersey: Pearson (p. 624).

Hadengue, Marine, De Marcellis-Warin, Nathalie & Warin, Thierry (2015). Reverse Innovation and Reverse Technology Transfer: From Made in China to Discovered in China in the Pharmaceutical Sector. *Management International*, 19(4), 49–69.

Hadengue, Marine & Warin, Thierry (2014). Patterns of Specialization and (Un)conditional Convergence: The Cases of Brazil, China and India. *Management International*, *18*, 123–141.

HKU 885 (2010). *Disney: Losing Magic in the Middle Kingdom*. Case written by: Ali Farhoomand. Hong Kong: Asia Case Research Centre (p. 31).

IMB 443 (2013). *Volkswagen in India*. Case written by: Seema Gupta. Bangalore: Indian Institute of Management (p. 33).

IMF (2016). World Economic Outlook—October 2016. International Monetary Fund. www.imf.org/external/pubs/ft/weo/2016/02/

Isard, Walter (1954). Location Theory and Trade Theory: Short-Run Analysis. *Quarterly Journal of Economics*, *68*(2), 305–320.

ITU (2016). ICT Facts and Figures—Percentage of Households with Internet Access. ICT Data and Statistics Division, Telecommunication Development Bureau. www.itu.int/en/ITU-D/Statistics/Documents/facts/ICTFactsFigures2016.pdf

Katsikeas, Constantine, Skarmeas, Dionysis & Bello, Daniel (2009). Developing Successful Trust-Based International Exchange Relationships. *Journal of International Business Studies*, *40*(1), 132–155.

Keegan, Warren & Green, Mark (2008). *Global Marketing* (5th ed.). New Jersey: Pearson Prentice Hall (p. 643).

Khanna, Tarun & Palepu, Krishna (2010). *Winning in Emerging Markets: A Road Map for Strategy and Execution*. Boston: Harvard Business Review Press (p. 272).

Lee, Peggy & O'Neill, Hugh (2003). Ownership Structures and R&D Investments of U.S. and Japanese Firms: Agency and Stewardship Perspectives. *Academy of Management Journal*, *46*(2), 212–225.

Leuz, Christian, Lins, Karl & Warnock, Francis (2009). Do Foreigners Invest Less in Poorly Governed Firms? *The Review of Financial Studies*, *22*(8), 3245–3285.

Malhotra, Shavin, Sivakumar, K. & Zhu, PengCheng (2009). Distance Factors and Target Market Selection: The Moderating Effect of Market Potential. *International Marketing Review*, *26*(6), 651–673.

McKinsey Global Institute (2012). Urban World: Cities and the Rise of the Consuming Class. McKinsey & Company 77. www.mckinsey.com/global-themes/urbanization/urban-world-cities-and-the-rise-of-the-consuming-class

New York Times (2016). Is China Stealing Jobs? It May Be Losing Them, Instead, *By Michael Schuman*. Retrieved from www.nytimes.com/2016/07/23/business/international/china-jobs-donald-trump.html

OEC (2017). Country profile—Russia. Observatory of Economic Complexity, Massachussets Institute of Technology (US). Retrieved July 2017, from http://atlas.media.mit.edu/en/profile/country/rus/

OECD (2012a). Looking to 2060: Long-Term Global Growth Prospects. Economic Policy Paper Series No.3, Organisation for Economic Co-operation and Development. www.oecd.org/eco/outlook/2060%20policy%20paper%20FINAL.pdf

OECD (2012b). Green Growth and Developing Countries: A Summary for Policy Makers. Organisation for Economic Co-operation and Development. www.oecd.org/dac/50526354.pdf

Piketty, Thomas (2014). *Capital in the Twenty-First Century*. Cambridge: Harvard University Press (p. 696).

284   *Economic and technological distances*

Porter, Michael (1990). The Competitive Advantage of Nations. *Harvard Business Review*, 68(2), 73–93.

Porter, Michael (1998). The Competitive Advantage of Nations. Free Press. Retrieved July 2017, from www.caneval.com/vision/innovation/innovation2.html

PwC (2008). The World in 2050—Beyond the BRICs: A Broader Look at Emerging Market Growth Prospects. By John Hawksworth and Gordon Cookson. PricewaterhouseCoopers. www.pwc.com/la/en/publications/assets/world_2050_brics.pdf

PwC (2015a). The World in 2050: Will the Shift in Global Economic Power Continue? By: John Hawksworth and Danny Chan of PwC's Economics and Policy (E&P), PricewaterhouseCoopers. www.pwc.com/gx/en/issues/the-economy/assets/world-in-2050-february-2015.pdf

PwC (2015b). Download Key Projections. PricewaterhouseCoopers. Retrieved November 2016, from www.pwc.com/gx/en/issues/economy/the-world-in-2050.html

PwC (2016). Mega Trends—Shift in Global Economic Power. PricewaterhouseCoopers. Retrieved February 2017, from www.pwc.co.uk/issues/megatrends/shift-in-global-economic-power.html

Rodrik, Dani (2011). The Future of Economic Convergence. NBER Working Paper, No.17400. National Bureau of Economic Research. Retrieved from www.nber.org/papers/w17400.pdf

Sheth, Jagdish (2011). Impact of Emerging Markets on Marketing: Rethinking Existing Perspectives and Practices. *Journal of Marketing*, 75(4), 166–182.

Statistics Canada (2014). Individuals by Total Income Level, by Province and Territory CANSIM, Table 111–0008. Retrieved December 2016, from www.statcan.gc.ca/tables-tableaux/sum-som/l01/cst01/famil105a-eng.htm

Stiglitz, Joseph (2012). *The Price of Inequality: How Today's Divided Society Endangers Our Future*. New York: W. W. Norton & Company (p. 560).Tinbergen, Jan (1963). Shaping the World Economy. *The International Executive*, 5(1), 27–30.

Tsang, Eric & Yip, Paul (2007). Economic Distance and the Survival of Foreign Direct Investments. *Academy of Management Journal*, 50(5), 1156–1168.

UN Comtrade (2015). Exports from Reporters (Brazil, Russia, India, China) to Partners (Argentina, Japan, UK, USA) in Current USD. Retrieved May 2017, from https://comtrade.un.org/data/

UNCTAD (2017). Gross Domestic Product per Capita, Constant (2005) Prices, 2000–2015. *United Nations Conference on Trade and Development*. Retrieved July 2017, from http://unctadstat.unctad.org/wds/TableViewer/tableView.aspx?ReportId=96

UNDP (2015). Human Development Data (1980–2015). United Nations Development Programme. Retrieved December 2016, from http://hdr.undp.org/en/data#

Volkswagen (2017). Brands and Models. Retrieved July 2017, from www.volkswagenag.com/en/brands-and-models.html

Vroom, Victor (1964). *Work and Motivation*. New York: John Wiley and Sons (p. 331).

WIPO (2017). What Is Intellectual Property? World Intellectual Property Organization. Retrieved July 2017, from www.wipo.int/about-ip/en/

Economic and technological distances   285

World Bank (2012). Investment in Energy With Private Participation (Current US$). Retrieved December 2016, from http://data.worldbank.org/indicator/IE.PPI.ENGY.CD?view=chart

World Bank (2013). Rail Lines (Total Route-km). Retrieved December 2016, from http://data.worldbank.org/indicator/IS.RRS.TOTL.KM

World Bank (2015a). Air Transport, Freight (million ton-km). Retrieved December 2016, from http://data.worldbank.org/indicator/IS.AIR.GOOD.MT.K1

World Bank (2015b). Mobile Cellular Subscriptions (per 100 people). Retrieved December 2016, from http://data.worldbank.org/indicator/IT.CEL.SETS.P2

World Bank (2016a). Individuals Using the Internet (% of Population). Retrieved May 2017, from http://data.worldbank.org/indicator/IT.NET.USER.ZS

World Bank (2016b). Indicators. Retrieved July 2017, from http://data.worldbank.org/indicator

World Bank (2016c). GNI Per Capita, PPP (Current International $). Retrieved May 2017, from http://data.worldbank.org/indicator/NY.GNP.PCAP.PP.CD?locations=AM-ET-RU-ES-SE-1W

World Bank (2017a). GNI Per Capita in 2016, Atlas Method (Current US$). Retrieved June 2017, from http://data.worldbank.org/indicator/NY.GNP.PCAP.CD

World Bank (2017b). Country Classification—World Bank Country and Lending Groups. Retrieved June 2017, from https://datahelpdesk.worldbank.org/knowledgebase/articles/906519-world-bank-country-and-lending-groups

World Bank (2017c). GINI Index (World Bank Estimate)—Details. Retrieved June 2017, from http://data.worldbank.org/indicator/SI.POV.GINI

World Bank (2017d). GINI Index for Selected Countries: Norway, Canada, US, Chile and South Africa. Retrieved June 2017, from http://data.worldbank.org/indicator/SI.POV.GINI?locations=US-CA-ZA-NO-CL

Zucman, Gabriel (2015). *The Hidden Wealth of Nations: The Scourge of Tax Havens*. Chicago: University of Chicago Press (p. 129).

8 Bottom of the Pyramid Marketing

Table of Contents

8 Bottom of the Pyramid Marketing

Introduction: Should Companies Target Consumers with
Low Revenues? 287
    8.1   *Background Information* 289
        8.1.1   Segmenting and Targeting 289
        8.1.2   Positioning 294
    8.2   *Definitions* 296
        8.2.1   Changing Consumption Patterns in
               Emerging Economies 296
        8.2.2   The TOP, MOP and BOP Segments and
               BOP Marketing 302
    8.3   *Corporate Examples* 306
        8.3.1   Cemex 306
        8.3.2   Danone 307
        8.3.3   Nokia 310
        8.3.4   Philips 311
        8.3.5   Schneider Electric 312
        8.3.6   Telenor 315
        8.3.7   Unilever 318
        8.3.8   Vodafone 319
    8.4   *Issues at Stake* 320
        8.4.1   Size and Attractiveness of the BOP Segment 322
        8.4.2   Responsibility 324
        8.4.3   Impact on Marketing Decisions and
               Feasibility 324
        8.4.4   Outcomes 325

Conclusion: Targeting low revenue consumers with BOP marketing
can be a solution to overcome the eco-techno distance but it requires
careful consideration and long-term investments.
References

Recommended Readings

- Prahalad, Coimbatore Krishnao & Hammond, Allen (2002). Serving the World's Poor, Profitably. *Harvard Business Review*, *80*(9), 48–59.
- Karnani, Aneel (2007). The Mirage of Marketing to the Bottom of the Pyramid: How the Private Sector Can Help Alleviate Poverty. *California Management Review*, *49*(4), 90–111.
- Human, Gert; Ascott-Evans, Byron; Souter, William & Xabanisa, Steven (2011). Advertising, Brand Knowledge and Attitudinal Loyalty in Low-Income Markets: Can Advertising Make a Difference at the "Bottom-Of-the-Pyramid"? *Management Dynamics*, *20*(2), 33–45.
- Van Den Waeyenberg, Sofie & Hens, Luc (2012). Overcoming Institutional Distance: Expansion to Base-Of-the-Pyramid Markets. *Journal of Business Research*, *65*(12), 1692–1699.

Introduction: Should Companies Target Consumers with Low Revenues?

In the 2000s, the irruption of emerging markets on the global business scene has become undeniable. Whether large or small countries (e.g., China and Vietnam), these newcomers have represented both a source of threats (due to competition) and opportunities (resources, markets, efficiency, and strategic-assets) for companies from developed economies. In terms of market-seeking opportunities, companies are now confronted with a sizeable difference compared to what they know at home: a much higher proportion of the population in emerging economies is considered poor. Traditionally, companies have developed offerings for a range of budgets. Yet, when it comes to selling in emerging and developing markets, many companies have faced seemingly unbreakable barriers: affordability of products and services for poor consumers, and other challenges related to eco-techno distance (see Chapter 7). **Bottom of the Pyramid (BOP) marketing has emerged as a possible solution to overcome eco-techno distance** (see Chapter 7), although it is not without hurdles. We then ask the question: "**Should companies target consumers with low revenues?**"

The objectives of this chapter are to define, illustrate, and discuss the topic of BOP marketing. First, we cover the basics of segmenting, targeting, and positioning, before defining BOP marketing. Indeed, implementing BOP marketing starts with a targeting decision: Who should companies be targeting: consumers with low, middle, or high income? At the strategic level, this is one of the three core questions (along with the "where" and "how") that we, as marketers, must answer: Who are our customers? Next, we look into definitions and drivers of BOP marketing, in particular the attractiveness of emerging economies and changes in consumption patterns. Then, we present

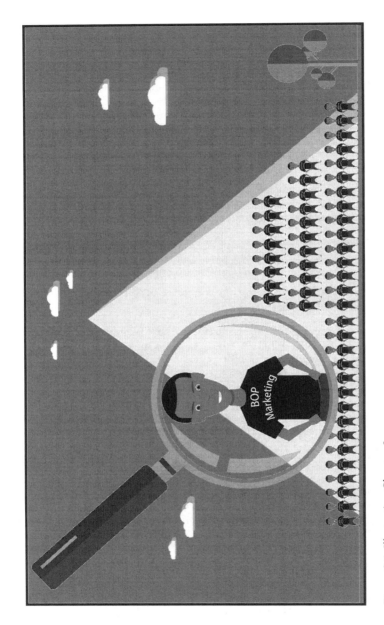

Figure 8.1 Illustrating Chapter 8

Source: Own elaboration

Bottom of the pyramid marketing   289

examples of MNCs from both developed and emerging economies adopting this approach, and highlight its impact on marketing decisions. Finally, we discuss the issues at stake with BOP marketing: its relevance, key success factors and outcomes (both positive and negative).

Figure 8.2 situates the present chapter in the overall book structure. It indicates that BOP marketing is an approach at the crossroads between strategic marketing and tactical marketing. At the strategic level, it relates directly to the question of segmenting, targeting, and positioning. At the tactical level, we will see that it touches all aspects of the 4/7Ps of the marketing-mix, but the figure emphasizes the importance of pricing, to solve the affordability issue, as mentioned above.

8.1 Background Information

In order to understand the issues at stake with BOP marketing, it is useful to have a basic notion of how to answer the following questions:

* What is segmentation? And how can we segment international markets?
* What are the attributes of a "good" market segment?
* How can a value offering be positioned in foreign markets?

8.1.1 Segmenting and Targeting

What is segmentation? *Segmentation* is the process that companies use to divide large heterogeneous markets into smaller markets (as illustrated in Figure 8.3) that can be reached more efficiently and effectively with products and services that match their unique needs (Kotler & Armstrong, 2005—Chapter 7).

How can we segment international markets? Segmentation for international markets relies on techniques similar to the ones used in domestic markets. Factors influencing segmentation include: geographic location, political and legal factors, and economic and technological factors, as well as socio-cultural factors. *Intermarket segmentation* refers to dividing consumers into groups with similar needs and buying behaviors when they are located in different countries. Thus, the main segmentation techniques are based on consumers' geographic, demographic, psychographic, and behavioral characteristics.

Starting with *geographic segmentation*, the idea is to divide consumers according to different geographical units (e.g., nations, regions, states, counties, or cities) or according to other features belonging to the broader domain of geography (e.g., climate, population density, topography, etc.). Figure 8.4 matches spending habits and ZIP codes.

In turn, *demographic segmentation* divides consumers into groups based on variables such as age, gender, family size, family life cycle, income, occupation, education, religion, race, generation, and nationality. It is often the most popular segmentation method, because data (e.g., age, income, and so on) is relatively easy to collect.

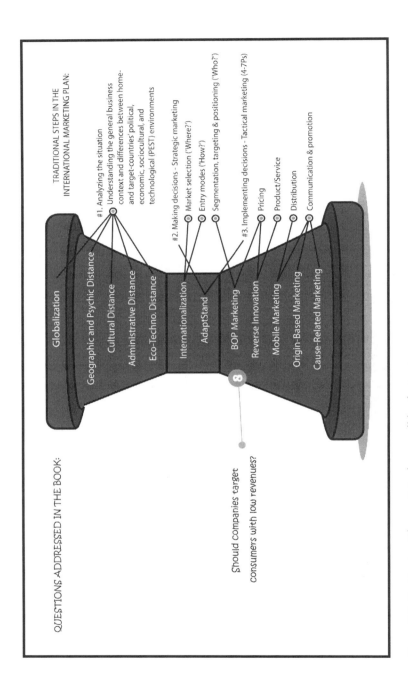

Figure 8.2 Positioning Chapter 8 in the overall book structure

Source: Own elaboration

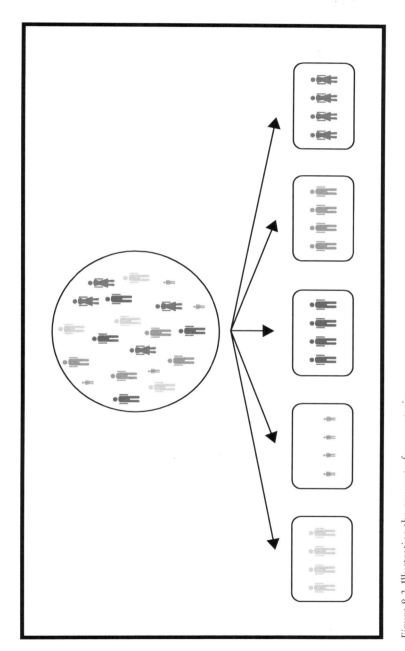

Figure 8.3 Illustrating the concept of segmentation
Source: Own elaboration

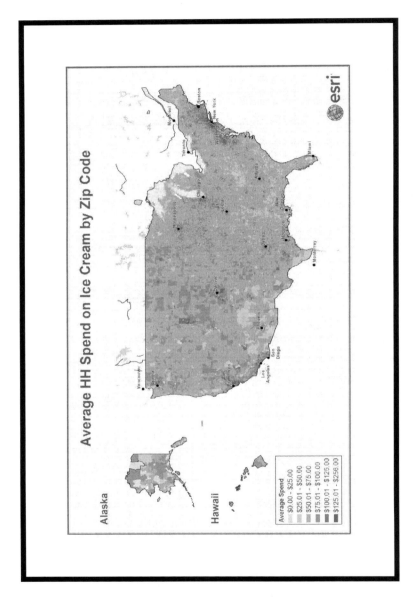

Figure 8.4 An example of geographic segmentation with ice cream spending in the US
Source: Esri (2012). Used by permission. Copyright © 2016 Esri, Pam Allison. All rights reserved.
For the color version, see the eResource at www.routledge.com/9781138202344

Bottom of the pyramid marketing 293

In regards to *psychographic segmentation*, this technique divides buyers into different groups based on social class, lifestyle, or personality traits. An example of such segmentation is a tool called the Values and Lifestyles System (VALS™), developed by Strategic Business Insights, a US market research and consulting firm. This tool groups consumers into eight categories, according to their primary motivations and resources. For the US market, segments have been labeled: innovators, thinkers, believers, achievers, strivers, experiencers, makers, and survivors. This segmentation is replicated with adaptation in countries like China, Japan, Nigeria, the UK, Venezuela, and the Dominican Republic. Visuals illustrating the relative importance of each segment in the overall population of each country (a useful insight to estimate market potential) are available on the company website.

Finally, *behavioral segmentation* divides buyers into groups based on their knowledge, attitudes, uses, or responses to a product (Kotler & Armstrong, 2005). It is common to differentiate these behaviors according to the occasion (i.e., specific moments in which products are particularly consumed, such as flowers on Valentine's Day or for weddings, dates during Ramadan, etc.), benefits sought (e.g., cleaner breath, taste, and teeth, as illustrated in a Colgate commercial—available on YouTube with search keywords: "1950s Colgate Toothpaste Commercial Vintage"), user status (e.g., first-time female voters, as illustrated by a promotional video made for the Barack Obama presidential campaign—available on YouTube with search keywords: "Lena Dunham: Your First Time"), and usage rate (e.g., weekly cigarette consumption distinguishes light from heavy smokers).

Multiple segmentation (i.e., combining several of the above-mentioned segmentation techniques) is used to identify smaller, better-defined target groups. Nielsen's market segmentation tool (PRIZM™) is a good example of such an approach. Sixty-six segments for American households exhibit unique characteristics and buying behaviors based on a host of geographic and demographic factors. The company website offers the possibility to browse segment profiles. For instance, clicking on one segment in particular, such as "01—Upper Crust" shows that it is composed of people over age fifty, without kids, living in the suburbs, owning their home, with higher levels of education, shopping at Saks Fifth Avenue, going on vacation in Europe, watching the Golf Channel, and driving a Lexus LS. Such detailed profiling gives good insights for marketers to customize products, pricing, distribution, and promotion according to targeted segments.

What are the attributes of a "good" segment? According to Kotler and Armstrong (2005), a good market segment is: measurable (i.e., it is possible to learn about the size, purchasing power, and profiles of the people concerned), accessible (i.e., the segment can be effectively reached and served), substantial (i.e., markets are large and profitable enough to serve), differentiable (i.e., groups of people are conceptually distinguishable and actually respond differently to various marketing-mix decisions), and actionable (i.e., effective programs can be designed for attracting and serving the segment). This will be an important question when we discuss the relevance of BOP marketing.

294 *Bottom of the pyramid marketing*

8.1.2 Positioning

What does positioning refer to? *Positioning* is the way the value offering (i.e., products and services) is perceived by consumers on important attributes in comparison with competing offerings (Kotler & Armstrong, 2005). Figure 8.5 illustrates the idea of "standing out." Perceptions are based on individual subjectivity and have little to do with objective reality.

Positioning value offerings in foreign markets relies on the same techniques as in domestic markets. A useful tool is the positioning map, which situates consumer perceptions of offerings (or brands and organizations) versus competing offerings. Figures 8.6 and 8.7 present positioning maps for various brands in the automotive and cosmetics industries. They are not the result of formal studies but are a simple illustration of how one could, arguably, situate these brands with respect to one another. The interesting aspect of these maps is the choice for the X- and Y-axes. Typically, we think of positioning maps in terms of price and quality. There are, however, no limitations or rules about which product attributes or segmentation criteria we should choose in order to compare brand perceptions. Here, we contrast cars on levels of environmental friendliness and security versus fun. Alternatively, automotive brands could be compared on whether they are conservative or sporty, practical, or classy. For cosmetics, we chose two demographic segmentation variables: age, and whether the brands were positioned for the mass or premium segments (related to price). Other axes

Figure 8.5 Illustrating the concept of positioning
Source: Own elaboration

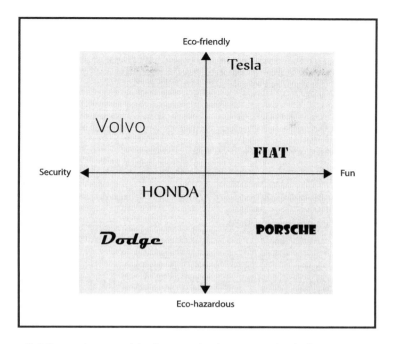

Figure 8.6 Proposing a positioning map in the automotive industry
Source: Own elaboration

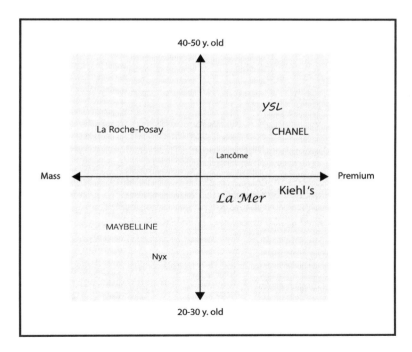

Figure 8.7 Proposing a positioning map in the cosmetics industry
Source: Own elaboration

296 Bottom of the pyramid marketing

could help position the brands on whether they are nature or science based, or whether they are animal tested or not, for instance. Again, the positioning map, as a tool, reveals its usefulness when the comparison axes are strategically chosen.

8.2 Definitions

In this section, we address the following questions:

- What makes emerging economies particularly attractive? In particular, what is one of the main trends characterizing emerging economies in terms of growth potential?
- Why is the middle class in emerging markets an engine for growth? How does the middle class compare against other income segments of the population?
- In such economies, should companies target the Top of the Pyramid (TOP), Middle of the Pyramid (MOP), or Bottom of the Pyramid (BOP) segments?
- What is Bottom of the Pyramid (BOP) marketing?

8.2.1 Changing Consumption Patterns in Emerging Economies

What is one of the main trend characterizing emerging economies in terms of growth potential? In Chapter 7, we have shown that with growth rates maintained over 5 percent annually, various groupings of emerging economies (e.g., the BRIC, MIST, CIVETS, and the E7) are regarded as more attractive than are developed economies in terms of growth potential. Besides economic growth, another trend draws a lot of attention: the development of a large middle class.

Definitions of the middle class at the global level are not consensual (for a literature review, see OECD, 2010). For instance, *middle class* includes people with incomes comprised between 10 and 20 USD daily (Pew Research Center, 2015), between 10 and 100 USD daily (OECD, 2010), and between 6,000 and 30,000 USD annually (Goldman Sachs, 2010). According to the OECD (2010, p. 10): "globally comparable data is not very accurate. We can probably be more confident of changes over time than in levels of income when comparing across countries. It is therefore less interesting to place too much emphasis on a precise definition of the middle class range. The focus should be on changes over time of the number of individuals falling into a specific category, even if that has an element of arbitrariness about its boundaries."

The global middle class is expected to grow from 1.8 billion people in 2009 to 3.2 billion by 2020, and to 4.9 billion by 2030, with 85 percent of this growth coming from Asia (OECD, 2010). Based on the Pew Research Center (2015), Figure 8.8 reveals significant increases with the number of middle-income people growing from 124 to 396 million in Asia and the South Pacific (this number grew from 32 to 235 million in China alone—a 634 percent increase over ten years!). Figure 8.9 reveals the particular weight

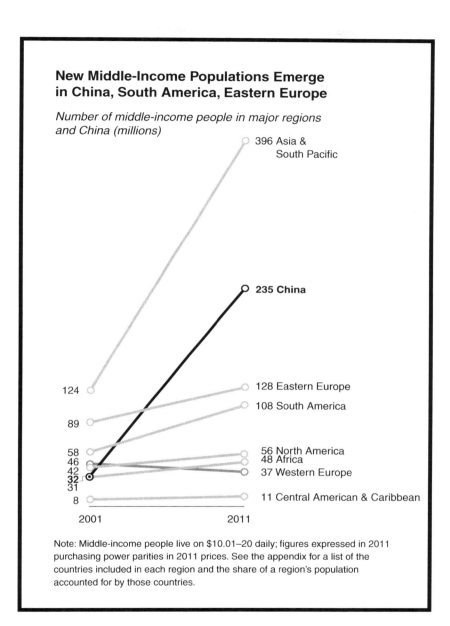

Figure 8.8 Illustrating the drastic growth of middle-income populations in Asia, South America, and Eastern Europe

Source: Pew Research Center (2015)

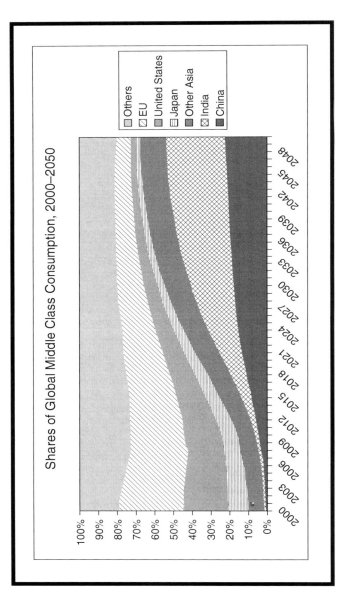

Figure 8.9 Contrasting the shares of several developed and emerging economies in global middle-class consumption (2000–2050)

Source: OECD (2010)

Bottom of the pyramid marketing 299

of China and India in global middle-class consumption and the projected decrease in the EU and US respective shares.

Why is the middle class in emerging markets an engine for growth? According to Goldman Sachs (2009), savings and investments are extremely limited in countries with a GDP per capita below 1,000 USD, and consumption represents a very high share within total GDP. In these countries, consumption is directed toward basic necessities, such as food and non-alcoholic beverages. When countries pass through industrialization and reach a GDP per capita of around 1,000–3,000 USD, savings and investments typically rise and the share of consumption within total GDP falls. In countries with GDP per capita above the 3,000 USD threshold, domestic demand becomes a more important engine of growth, and the share of consumption in total GDP starts to rise again. In addition, people turn toward more-discretionary product categories, such as health, restaurants and hotels, recreation, and culture. Figure 8.10 illustrates different spending patterns among income levels.

In all, the middle class has always provided opportunities for companies to expand sales as people strive to increase their quality of life and own more-comfortable homes, filled with higher-value-added goods (e.g., cars and telecom equipment). Since two billion people could join the global middle class by 2030 (Goldman Sachs, 2008), this trend represents a major driver for growth.

Aren't reports from consulting firms overly optimistic? Consider this generic note from Goldman Sachs (2009, p. 1): "The Goldman Sachs Group, Inc. does and seeks to do business with companies covered in its research reports. As a result, investors should be aware that the firm may have a conflict of interest that could affect the objectivity of this report. Investors should consider this report as only a single factor in making their investment decision." It is, thus, crucial to rely on several sources of information when making decisions about market attractiveness. We ought to seek out data provided by public institutions (such as the World Bank and OCDE), independent and nongovernmental research organizations (such as the World Resource Institute and the Pew Research Center), as well as university researchers, especially when they are bluntly criticizing market potential estimates, such as Karnani (2007). Reviewing both optimistic and pessimistic analyses is a sure way to balance out global consulting firms general enthusiasm and make informed decisions.

How does the middle class compare against other income segments of the population? Over the 2001–2011 decade, the middle-income population has increased from 7 percent to 13 percent of the global population (Pew Research Center, 2015). In turn, the proportion of poor people (living on 2 USD or less daily) has decreased significantly (from 29 percent to 15 percent of the global population). However, low-income people (2.01–10 USD daily) constitute the largest segment by far, with 56 percent of the overall population in 2011 (Pew Research Center, 2015). In other words, more than two-thirds of the world population earns less than 10 USD daily in 2011, as represented in Figure 8.11.

In this context, whom should companies target: people with high, middle, or low incomes? Asking this question (see "Food for Thought") requires visiting the concepts of the Top, the Middle, and the Bottom of the Pyramid (TOP, MOP, and BOP) segments.

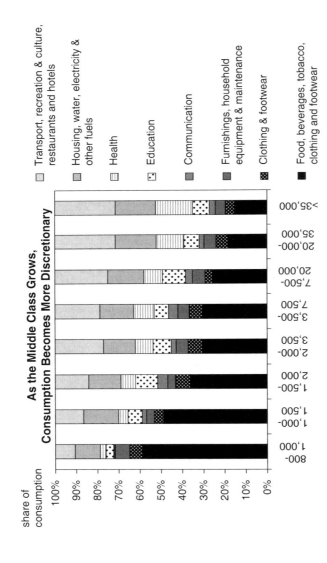

Figure 8.10 Contrasting spending patterns among various income levels

Source: Goldman Sachs (2010, p. 3). Reproduced with permission. Copyright 2010 Goldman, Sachs & Co. All rights reserved.

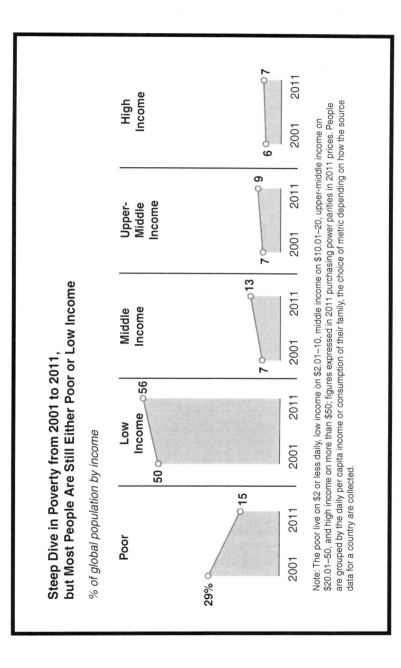

Figure 8.11 Comparing the proportion of various income segments in the global population

Source: Pew Research Center (2015)

> **Food for Thought 8.1**
>
> - In the context of emerging and developing economies, whom should companies target: people with high, middle, or low incomes?

8.2.2 The TOP, MOP, and BOP Segments, and BOP Marketing

What is Bottom of the Pyramid (BOP) marketing? This concept was put forward by Coimbatore Krishnao Prahalad (1941–2010) with other colleagues in a book entitled *The Fortune at the Bottom of the Pyramid* (2004), as well as in a prior *Harvard Business Review* article (2002).

The idea is to represent annual individual incomes by the world population, in the shape of a pyramid. Prahalad and Hammond (2002) consider that people earning more than 20,000 USD annually (i.e., the rich) constituted the top of the pyramid (TOP), people earning between 2,000 and 20,000 USD represented the middle of the pyramid (MOP), and people earning less than 2,000 annually (i.e., the poor) were at the bottom of the pyramid (BOP). This initial cut reportedly included 0.1 billion people at the TOP, 2 billion people at the MOP, and 4 billion people at the BOP.

Figure 8.12 Portrait of Coimbatore Krishnao Prahalad (1941–2010)

Source: Screen capture from a YouTube video available with search words: "C.K. Prahalad: How do you think about sustainability?" posted by: FastCompany, retrievable at www.YouTube.com/watch?v=sQgWNWJ7UTM

Bottom of the pyramid marketing   303

However, the thresholds used to segment the income pyramid vary greatly, and consequently, the size of the BOP market has received diverging evaluations. While Prahalad and Hammond (2002) estimate the market size to be 4 billion people with revenues under 2,000 USD per year (i.e., 6 USD per day), the World Bank evaluates it at 2.7 billion (in 2001) and The Economist (2004) at only 0.6 billion, as reported in Karnani (2007) and Pitta, Guesalaga, and Marshall (2008). The Pew Research Center uses the following thresholds of daily earnings: 50 USD or more for high incomes; 20–50 USD for upper-middle incomes; 10–20 USD for middle incomes; 2–10 USD for low incomes; and under 2 USD for poor people (Pew Research Center, 2015). Annually, the thresholds (for a household of four people) are up to ~3,000 USD to be considered poor; up to ~15,000 USD for low incomes; up to ~30,000 USD for middle incomes; and up to ~73,000 USD to move from upper-middle to high incomes. As illustrated in Figure 8.13, this categorization suggests that, in 2011, the TOP comprised nearly 500 million people (only 7 percent of the overall population, then estimated at 7.007 billion people), while the MOP (upper-middle and middle incomes) comprised ~1.5 billion people, and the BOP (low incomes and poor people) comprised ~4.9 billion people (representing as much as 71 percent of the global population). A stricter evaluation of the BOP would limit the segment size to people in deep poverty (i.e., earning less than 2 USD daily). The estimated size of the BOP in 2011 would then be around 1 billion people (15 percent of 7.007 billion).

Regardless of the chosen threshold, data shows that the vast majority of people live with annual incomes that are far below those in "rich" economies.

Another way of considering the numbers at the BOP is to take a regional level of analysis. World Resources Institute (2007) reports that 65 percent of Eastern Europeans (i.e., 254 million), 70 percent of South Americans (i.e., 360 million), 85 percent of Asians (i.e., 2.8 billion), and 95 percent of Africans (i.e., 486 million) were living at the BOP.

Finally, Credit Suisse (2015) provides data considering adults only, which allows for a finer analysis but unfortunately relies on different thresholds. This study finds that 3.4 billion people (71 percent of the global population) earn less than 10,000 USD annually, and about one billion adults (21 percent) earn between 10,000 and 100,000 USD. Combined, it is about 4.4 billion people who concentrate only ~15 percent of global wealth (~40 trillion USD in annual earnings). In turn, the segment of rich people—composed of 34 million adults (0.7 percent of the overall adult population) who earn more than one million USD annually and 349 million adults (7.4 percent) who earn between 100,000 and $1 million USD—accounts for nearly 85 percent of global wealth (with ~210 trillion USD in annual earnings). Incidentally, just sixty-two billionaires had the same wealth as 3.6 billion people in 2015 (Oxfam, 2016).

Overall, it is still rather difficult to find public data with up-to-date estimates to compare the size and evolution of the TOP, MOP, and BOP segments. Figure 8.14 illustrates the significant disproportion of income distribution in the world between the rich and the poor.

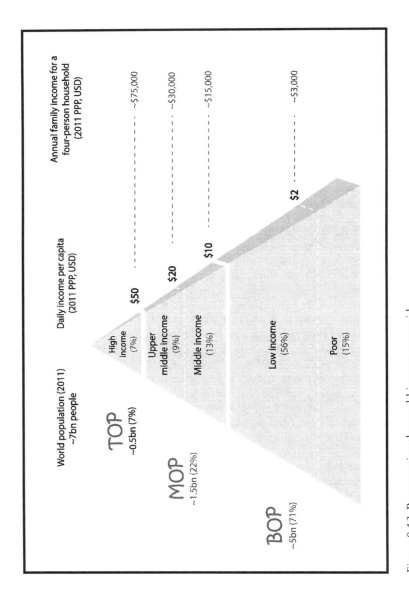

Figure 8.13 Representing the world income pyramid
Source: Adapted from Prahalad and Hammond (2002) and Pew Research Center (2015)

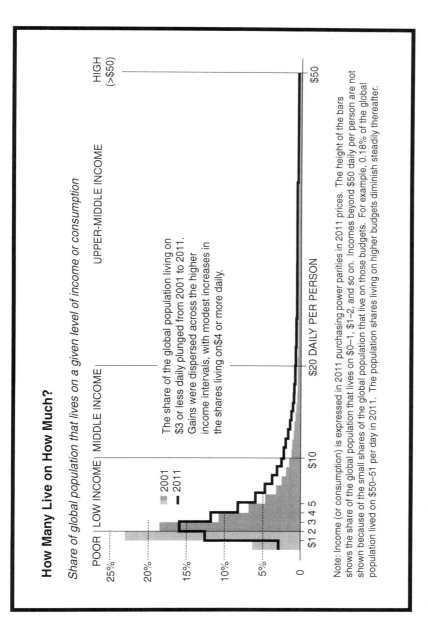

Figure 8.14 Illustrating the distribution of income in the world

Source: Pew Research Center (2015)

306 Bottom of the pyramid marketing

8.3 Corporate Examples

This section addresses the following questions:

- What are known corporate examples of BOP marketing?
- Who are the actors involved and where are these examples from?

Below, the examples are presented in alphabetical order but the companies have very different profiles and origins. Can you tell (see "Food for Thought")?

Food for Thought 8.2

- Among the examples listed below (and others that you may have heard of), what type of companies adopt BOP marketing? Where are these companies from and where do they implement BOP marketing?

8.3.1 Cemex

Patrimonio Hoy[1]—A Mexican company, Cemex was founded in 1906 as a cement manufacturer and has since become a large MNC (see Table 8.1). Among other social initiatives, it has launched a program called *Patrimonio Hoy* in its home country (1998) which helps people at the BOP build their own home (Figure 8.15). A video presenting the program is available on YouTube with search words: "Patrimonio Hoy, CEMEX Mexico sustainability program."

With this initiative, the company answers to both tangible and intangible problems encountered by consumers at the BOP. Tangible problems include lack of savings, limited knowledge of building technology, the inability to store materials, and limited access to both financing and quality building materials. Intangible problems include the local cultural values that do not encourage long-term planning. To address these problems, the company has

Table 8.1 Profiling Cemex (Mexico)

Who:	Cemex
Since:	1906
What:	Cement and construction materials
From:	Mexico
Sales (Bn USD):	13.4
Employing (people):	41,000
Manufacturing in (countries):	~30
Selling in (countries):	50

Source: Cemex (2016a)

Bottom of the pyramid marketing 307

Figure 8.15 A Cemex BOP initiative: Patrimonio Hoy
Source: Cemex (2016b)

developed solutions with access to micro-financing and makes no demands for financial collateral or letters of recommendation for credit purposes. It also makes available staff architects, offers a masonry training program, and unlimited and free storage of materials. The company negotiates with distributors and aggregates volume so that distributors remain motivated to service poor customers, insuring regular deliveries of material.

In the past twenty years, the initiative has been successfully replicated in Colombia, Panama, Costa Rica, Nicaragua, and the Dominican Republic. For instance, between 2005 and 2017, about 7,900 families in Nicaragua have benefited from the program. In the Dominican Republic, between 2009 and 2016, more than three thousand families have used *Patrimonio Hoy* to build their homes. These families could ask Cemex for a line of credit with weekly payments of either 700 Dominican pesos (DOP) (~15 USD), 1,000 DOP (~21 USD), or 1,500 DOP (~31 USD). Obtaining loans through this channel is often the only chance for these low revenue customers since many work informal jobs that traditional banks would not consider as employment. Although it experienced a 20 percent rate of losses on loaned money in the Dominican Republic, the company still considered the experience a positive one.

8.3.2 Danone

Grameen Danone Foods[2]—Danone (France) is a large MNC with 2016 global sales close to 25 billion USD (see Table 8.2). In 2006, Danone has created a joint-venture with Grameen Bank, the Grameen Danone Foods (launched in Bangladesh) (Figure 8.16).

The business model of Grameen Danone Foods for targeting children with malnutrition with the local production of nutritive yogurt (named "Shokti Doi") is described in multiple videos on YouTube (e.g., search words: "Grameen Danone Foods Limited Part 2"). TV commercials also show the product benefits and its positioning (e.g., "Shokti Plus Doi TVC"). Obtaining

308 *Bottom of the pyramid marketing*

Table 8.2 Profiling Danone (France)

Who:	Danone
Since:	1919
What:	Dairy products, waters and beverages, baby and medical nutrition
From:	France
Sales (Bn USD):	24.5
Employing (people):	99,000
Manufacturing in (countries):	N/A
Selling in (countries):	130

Source: Danone (2016a)

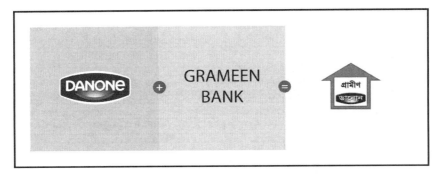

Figure 8.16 Presenting Grameen Danone Foods, a joint-venture between Danone and Grameen Bank

Source: Own elaboration based on images courtesy of Danone and Danone Grameen Foods Limited

a sufficient supply of milk has been a challenge and the joint-venture has worked hard at organizing deliveries to the transformation facility and establishing a supply chain with local micro-producers. This helped to create local jobs and reinforced the social acceptability of the project. Another salient point in this successful initiative at the BOP is the way the product is distributed: a radical departure from what Danone is used to in developed economies: sales are made in small shops or by local women (proudly called "Grameen Ladies") carrying a small number of items in coolers and going on foot selling door-to-door.

Grameen Bank was founded by Muhammad Yunus (Figure 8.17), who is considered to be the "father" of micro-credit and was awarded the Nobel Peace Prize in 2006 for his work in fostering development "from below." Enlightening speeches by Yunus are available on YouTube (e.g., with search words: "Muhammad Yunus—Grameen Bank").

In their 2012 sustainable development report, the company stated the following: "Danone has inventoried the key learnings to be drawn from the BOP project in India, namely: the importance of thoroughly understanding local food culture and eating habits to better integrate these into the

Bottom of the pyramid marketing 309

Figure 8.17 Portrait of Muhammad Yunus with Aurélia Durand (book author) at the first Social Business Forum held at HEC Montréal on May 24, 2017

Source: Photography by Katrina Albert, Social Business Creation—IDEOS

development process; the correct target population size (cities, rural areas) in an emerging country; controlling distribution circuits and costs and the various intermediaries to reach the target economically; and the importance of the management and education model for enhancing the product's image and use. These lessons have been shared and are already used in other projects, in particular the micro-distribution projects conducted as part of the Danone Ecosystem Fund" (Danone, 2012, p. 24).

Other BOP initiatives by Danone include "1001 Fontaines" (Cambodia), "NutriGo" (China), "La Laiterie du Berger" (Senegal), and "El Alberto" (Mexico). For instance, "1001 Fontaines" (established in the early 2000s) provides a drinking water system to isolated villages in partnership with the UV + Solaire company. As of December 31, 2016, this project had been implemented in more than one hundred and fifty Cambodian villages, and was replicated in fourteen villages in Madagascar and five villages in India, giving more than 420,000 people access to drinking water. In turn, La Laiterie du Berger (2005) works with local Fula herders by manufacturing yogurt

310 *Bottom of the pyramid marketing*

and cream from fresh milk, which are then sold at competitive prices on the Senegalese market. Herders are also provided with feed for their cattle and training to improve productivity. NutriGo (2011) relies on a partnership with the NGO Shanghai NPI Social Innovation Development Center to market a powdered food supplement, called YingYangBao. This product provides children with key nutrients (such as proteins, vitamins, iron, and calcium) in the economically disadvantaged rural areas of China. Finally, El Alberto (2011) is a project that brings clean and affordable water to the indigenous communities of the El Alberto region of Mexico. It results from a partnership between the Porvenir Foundation, HOD Mexico, and the Mexican government. At the end of 2016, the project supplied drinking water to nearly thirty thousand people.

8.3.3 *Nokia*

Nokia Life Tools[3]—Nokia, today a global leader in creating the technologies at the heart of our connected world (see Table 8.3), previously marketed affordable phones for the BOP market and extremely valuable services to attend to these customers. For instance, Nokia Life Tools, an SMS-based, subscription information service, was launched in India in 2009 (Figure 8.18). Among other services related to agriculture, it allowed farmers in rural India to connect with their mobile phone and get market prices instantly. Having real-time information represented a great opportunity to ensure getting fair prices and being less dependent on traders. This line of services also included education and entertainment services, with a system to learn how to speak English, for instance. In the following years, it was deployed in Indonesia, China, Nigeria, and Kenya, and has been experienced by more than 95 million people. The service was discontinued after Microsoft bought Nokia's handset division for 7.2 billion USD in April 2014. Today, the Finnish company HMD Global Oy is Nokia's exclusive brand licensee for mobile phones, smartphones, and tablets.

Table 8.3 Profiling Nokia (Finland)

Who:	*Nokia*
Since:	1865
What:	Technologies (information and communication), fixed and mobile broadband, IP and optical networks, software, services, digital health and media, intellectual property and technology licensing
From:	Finland
Sales (Bn USD):	26.8
Employing (people):	101,000
Manufacturing in (countries):	N/A
Selling in (countries):	130 countries

Source: Nokia (2016)

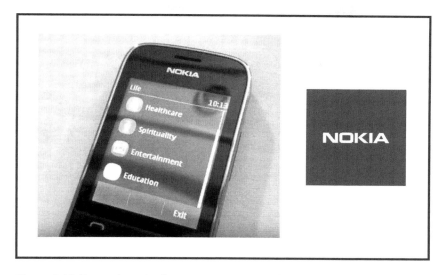

Figure 8.18 Presenting a Nokia BOP initiative: Nokia Life Tools
Source: Screen capture from a YouTube video available with search words: "Nokia Life Tools Demo," posted by Martin Gicheru, retrievable at www.YouTube.com/watch?v=afftxqjb85k

8.3.4 Philips

LifeLight[4]—Philips, also known as Royal Philips, was established in The Netherlands (1891) and has become one of the major global players in areas of electronics, healthcare, and lighting (see Table 8.4).

Philips Lighting (listed as an independent company since 2016) has developed a solar home lighting system called LifeLight in Kenya (2014). For this, the company has participated in an initiative of the World Bank Group, called Lighting Global, to increase energy access to people disconnected from electricity. As of 2015, an estimated 1.3 billion people worldwide and 560 million in Africa alone did not have access to electricity. When the sun goes down, people with no electricity can only pursue their activities by candlelight or by using kerosene lamps. In both cases, the low light output makes it difficult to read or be productive in any way. In addition, kerosene lanterns represent safety and health risks, as well as high costs (around $50 per year).

Philips's LifeLight is one of fourteen products having obtained the Lighting Global Quality Standards (i.e., technical norms aiming to guarantee quality, durability, truthfulness of advertising, consumer and IP protection). Figure 8.19 illustrates the LifeLight range of products. These products were developed by the Nairobi-based Philips Africa Innovation Hub, which is a center for developing innovations "in Africa–for Africa" in the areas of healthcare, lighting, and healthy living. For instance, the LifeLight Home is a solar-powered LED lighting system with two pendant luminaires and a USB port for phone charging that is connected to a solar panel.

312   *Bottom of the pyramid marketing*

Table 8.4 Profiling Royal Philips (Netherlands)

Who:	Royal Philips
Since:	1891
What:	Lighting, Consumer lifestyle, Healthcare
From:	Netherlands
Sales (Bn USD):	27.3
Employing (people):	105,000
Manufacturing in (countries):	22
Selling in (countries):	100

Source: Philips (2016)

After the initial launch in Kenya (with a dedicated roadshow "Maisha ni Mwelekeo," shown in a YouTube video available with search words: "Phillips launch of Home lighting systems-Nakuru county"), Philips Life-Light range was rolled out in other African markets during 2015 (e.g., in the Democratic Republic of Congo, as shown in a YouTube video available with search words: "Philips Gift of Light Project—Solar LED Lighting"). Prices vary from country to country but in Kenya, the LifeLight Home, the LifeLight Plus, and the LifeLight were priced at approximately 100, 45, and 25 USD in 2014, respectively.

8.3.5 Schneider Electric

Access to Energy program[5]—Schneider Electric, a French-based MNC (1836), is today a global leader in energy management and automation (see Table 8.5).

In 2009, President and CEO Jean-Pascal Tricoire supported the launch of the BipBop program by the Sustainable Development division, in order to improve the company's societal commitment and to reaffirm its innovation capacity. BipBop stands for "Business, Innovation, and People at the Base of the Pyramid." The program aims to enhance universal access to modern energy for low-income populations living mostly in rural areas of Sub-Saharan Africa, India, and South-East Asia. Since its inception, the program was built on a combined approach of philanthropy and business. The program relies on the following pillars: developing the local economy via impact investments (Business); deploying a commercial access to energy products and solutions that is as wide as possible (Innovation); and promoting long-term competencies by sponsoring the creation of technical and vocational training in energy-related trades with non-profit partners (People). Figure 8.20 presents a visual of these three pillars.

In 2009, the first initiatives were mostly philanthropic, aligned with the objectives of Schneider Electric's Foundation, whose mission is: "Building sustainable communities through energy knowledge and leadership." Following a series of pilot projects in India and Madagascar, the access to energy program took a stronger commercial path. Considered as an internal "start-up," the business pillar of the program saw a constant revenue growth, linked with yearly increased commercial and societal objectives. In 2014, the

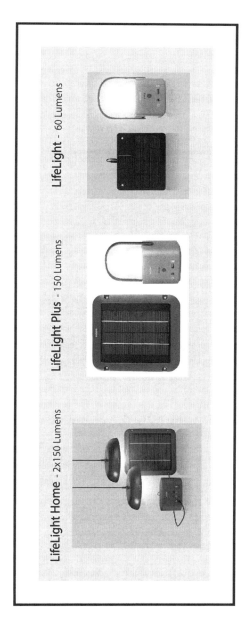

Figure 8.19 Presenting a Philips's BOP initiative: the LifeLight range of products

Source: Courtesy of Philips Lighting

Table 8.5 Profiling Schneider Electric (France)

Who:	Schneider Electric
Since:	1836
What:	Energy management and automation solutions
From:	France
Sales (Bn USD):	27.6
Employing (people):	144,000
Manufacturing in (countries):	45
Selling in (countries):	100

Source: Schneider Electric (2016)

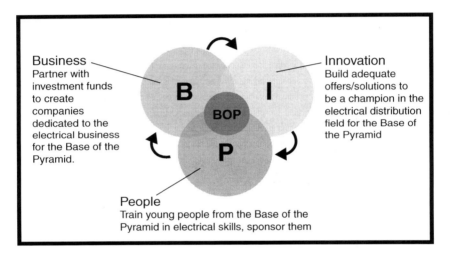

Figure 8.20 Illustrating the three pillars of Schneider Electric's Access to Energy program (formerly called the BipBop program)

Source: Courtesy of Schneider Electric

top management decided that it was time for the BOP segment to actually become a business opportunity and be managed as such (André & Ponssard, 2015). Governance of the program then extended from the Sustainable Development division to include the different business units and local operations centers in foreign countries. This is when the BipBop program transitioned to the Access to Energy program.

Reasons for the success of this program lie in the organizational structure and management. First, the Sustainable Development central division was already interlinked with the global corporate strategy on existing environmental value propositions. This guaranteed that the program could initially evolve in a preserved environment and adopt discretionary rules to innovate and question the status quo. This stage was intended to build experience and provide evidence of the profitability of BOP activities. It also permitted progressive interaction with other functional and business entities within

Schneider Electric, including R&D teams (to design new offers), purchasing teams and manufacturing plants (to develop affordable and quality products), the internal supply chain (to make these products globally available), and local sales operations (to commercialize them).

The Access to Energy program is now acting as a small business unit, developing a wide portfolio of products and solutions—ranging from solar lanterns to community electrification microgrids through solar home systems, water pumping systems, and street lighting—with the goal of answering all energy needs at the BOP. It supports business development activities in more than twenty countries across Africa, Asia, and South America, where the company has a presence. Jointly with the local sales force, the program builds innovative access channels to overcome some of the key barriers in BOP markets, listed next.

First, the company links with distributors active in rural areas such as gas stations, solar distributors or agricultural cooperatives in order to overcome geographic distance and make the products physically available in these remote areas,. Second, the company partners with microfinance institutions or savings groups in order to overcome economic distance and make the products financially affordable for low-income customers (often characterized by non-recurrent revenues). Third, the company developed additional services for locally adapting and manufacturing the technologies into packaged solutions, as well as for training technical staff in operation and maintenance facilities (e.g., for large community electrification projects), with the purpose of overcoming technological distance. Finally, the BipBop program had to rethink its marketing materials in order to better raise awareness about the benefits of turning away from polluting and expensive sources of energy and create aspirational demand for solar products. For instance, communication materials, such as posters, leaflets, and point-of-sale displays, were translated into local languages or dialects and included in-situ comic strips explaining the use of products. In a way, this helped breach cultural distance with end-consumers who had little prior exposure to the benefits of technological innovation for the environment and for their own health. YouTube videos are available to further describe the achievements of the program (e.g., search words: "Access to Energy: Our Ambition for Tomorrow").

Initial low levels of profitability with this BOP initiative were later balanced with the generation of extra-financial and indirect business returns (e.g., increased intimacy with existing customers, improved brand image, screened and incubated innovations, and motivated employees and talent attraction). Nevertheless, profitability level remains a key question if the program is to expand. This is particularly the case in countries where the Access to Energy turnover represents a significant part of the company's revenue, thus potentially downgrading its local profit and loss statement.

8.3.6 Telenor

Grameenphone and the Village Phone program[6]—Established in 1855, Telenor (Norway) became Telenor Group in 2012, with a clear strategy of targeting developing markets (see Table 8.6).

316 *Bottom of the pyramid marketing*

Table 8.6 Profiling Telenor (Norway)

Who:	*Telenor Group*
Since:	1855
What:	Mobile services
From:	Norway
Sales (Bn USD):	15.4
Employing (people):	37,000
Manufacturing in (countries):	N/A
Selling in (countries):	13

Source: Telenor Group (2016)

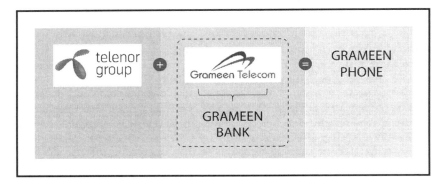

Figure 8.21 Presenting Grameenphone a joint-venture between Telenor and Grameen Telecom

Source: Own elaboration based on images courtesy of Telenor and Grameen Telecom

As early as 1996, Telenor built a joint venture with Grameen Telecom from Bangladesh (created in 1995) to create Grameenphone, registered in Dhaka (see Figure 8.21). Through a successful bidding, Grameenphone was awarded a license for operating GSM mobile phones in Bangladesh, which at the time was a luxury in urban areas and something of a fairy tale for rural areas.

The business model for Grameenphone followed the inspiration of Mohammad Yunus and Grameen Bank's microcredit model by lending a small amount of money to women in rural villages (selected among the members of Grameen Bank and who became known as the "Village Phone Ladies") so that they could buy a mobile phone, a small solar recharger unit, and receive training in using and servicing the equipment. Then, they could sell phone usage on a per-call basis at an affordable price to others in their villages. Beside Yunus, other actors involved also include Iqbal Quadir— a Bangladeshi who experienced poverty in childhood and later became a banker in New York—who held financial responsibilities in the first years of operations before selling his shares in 2014.

In a nutshell, the Village Phone program was launched in 1997 with a symbolic call to the then-Prime Minister of Bangladesh by the first Village Phone Lady, Laily Begum (from Patira, Dakhinkhan). Her story is quite striking.

Bottom of the pyramid marketing   317

Living in poverty, Laily Begum first took a 4,500 BDT (~55USD) loan from Grameen Bank to buy a cow. Selling milk was a start, but the money was not sufficient for meeting her family's subsistence needs. After repaying the initial loan, she obtained an 8,000 BDT (~100 USD) loan for growing crops, and later another 15,000 BDT (~ 185 USD) loan to build a solid roof for her house. Being a good borrower of the bank with an excellent loan repayment track record, Begum then obtained a loan for a phone and became the first phone operator in the Village Phone program. Yet, she faced difficulties in the beginning, with young fellows of the area refusing to pay their phone bills, other women teasing her, and many forcing her to come to their homes so that they could make phone calls. To solve these problems, her husband stopped his work as a day laborer and started to get involved as well (for instance, he built a separate room for the mobile phone business and purchased an antenna to receive better signal coverage). This is when Begum's income started to grow significantly, as she had no competitors yet (in this early phase, her monthly income could be as high as 26,000 BDT per month, roughly 325 USD). Later on, when people started using other mobile phones in the area, her income from the phone booth stabilized around 7,000–8,000 BDT per month (~85–100 USD), of which she could save up to 40 percent. Investing the monthly savings, Begum and her husband then acquired two grocery stores, one laundry shop on rent, one shop used as a pharmacy, and also owned and operated a restaurant. From these businesses, their monthly income was about 13,000 BDT (~160 USD), which allowed the couple to live in much more comfortable conditions and to ensure the education of their children.

For women like Laily Begum, being a Village Phone Lady meant becoming respected entrepreneurs, contributing financially to the well-being of their families, and gaining importance both in their own home and in their communities. For the villages in question, the program has really helped in bridging the digital gap. For Grameen Telecom, the business model also proved to be highly profitable, since rural phones generated about 100 USD per month compared to 30 USD for urban phones. The involvement of Grameen Telecom in the program helped provide training, SIM distribution, and technical services, while Grameenphone provided network coverage support and regulatory compliance.

Building upon this success, the Village Phone program was first replicated in Uganda by the Grameen Foundation (2003) and later diffused to Cambodia, Haiti, Indonesia, Nigeria, Rwanda, and the Philippines. Grameenphone is now the largest mobile operator in Bangladesh, with a vision to "provide the power of digital communication, enabling everyone to improve their lives, build societies and secure a better future for all" (Grameenphone, 2014, p. 3).

In 2016, Telenor Mobile Communications owned about 55 percent of this joint-venture, Grameen Telecom held ~35 percent, and the remaining 10 percent was publicly held. First incorporated as a private limited company, Grameenphone converted to a public limited company in 2007 and was listed on the Dhaka and Chittagong Stock Exchanges in 2009. As of 2016, the company counted 58 million customers, nearly 25 million mobile data users, and more than 357,000 points of sale that generated about 1.4 billion USD in revenues.

8.3.7 Unilever

Pureit[7]—Unilever (UK/Netherlands) is one of the global leaders in the consumer goods industry, including food, beverages, cleaning agents, and personal care products (see Table 8.7 and Figure 8.22).

Hindustan Unilever, the Indian subdivision of Unilever, has developed Pureit, a water cleaning system (launched in 2008 in India and perfected until 2010). The company targets several consumer segments with a range of products in the Pureit line (see Figure 8.23). The Pureit Compact is aimed at the BOP with a price at 22 USD. In terms of competition, Pureit Compact's biocide-cum-filter technology is much more affordable than ultraviolet technology-based products (125–230 USD) or reverse osmosis

Table 8.7 Profiling Unilever (US)

Who:	Unilever
Since:	1929
What:	Food, refreshments, personal and home care
From:	UK/Netherlands
Sales (Bn USD):	58.7
Employing (people):	169,000
Manufacturing in (countries):	69
Selling in (countries):	190

Source: Unilever (2016)

Figure 8.22 Presenting Unilever's logotype
Source: Reproduced with kind permission of Unilever PLC and group companies

Bottom of the pyramid marketing 319

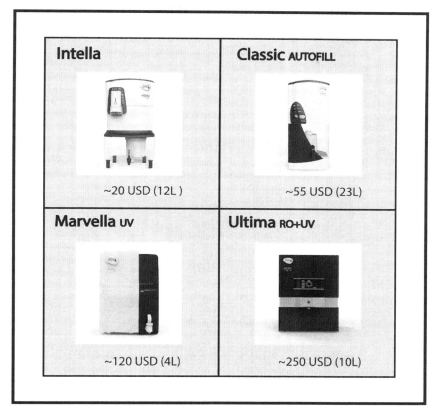

Figure 8.23 Presenting a range of products: Unilever's "Pureit" water purifiers

Source: Own elaboration inspired by HBS 9–511–067 (2011) and based on data retrieved from Hindustan Unilever (2017), all images reproduced with kind permission of Unilever PLC and group companies.

technology-based products (170–710 USD). In comparison to possibly cheaper alternatives (such as other biocides, resin, and filter technology-based products), Pureit Compact offers higher safety from germs.

8.3.8 Vodafone

M-Pesa[8]—With British origins, Vodafone is another mobile services company that is behind a large BOP initiative: "M-Pesa." Table 8.8 provides an overview of Vodafone (Figure 8.24).

Launched in Kenya in 2007 and in Tanzania in 2008, M-Pesa is a phone-based payment system that allows people to transfer money and pay for services by phone (see Figure 8.25). Starting in 2014, Vodafone has replicated these very successful services to the bottom of the pyramid in eleven countries, including

Table 8.8 Profiling Vodafone (UK)

Who:	Vodafone
Since:	1991
What:	Mobile services
From:	UK
Sales (Bn USD):	52.2
Employing (people):	107,000
Manufacturing in (countries):	N/A
Selling in (countries):	26

Source: Vodafone (2016)

Figure 8.24 Presenting Vodafone's logotype
Source: Courtesy of Vodafone, the Vodafone logo is a registered trademark of Vodafone Group

Afghanistan, India, and several Eastern European countries. The company website presents a map detailing their international presence, revealing that the company specifically targets developing countries. It is interesting to mention that the product was discontinued in South Africa as of June 30, 2016, mainly because of a demographic reason. Indeed, there are fewer young and old people (the specific targets for this service) in South Africa compared to Kenya.

8.4 Issues at Stake

In order to look into several of the main issues at stake with BOP marketing, we address the following questions:

- Is the BOP segment really attractive?
- What are the key success factors of BOP marketing? What is the impact of BOP marketing on traditional marketing activities?
- Who should be held responsible for addressing poverty at the BOP: governments, companies, or NGOs?
- In terms of outcomes, is BOP marketing positive, or can it be negative?

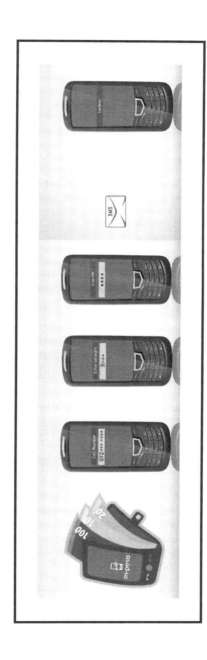

Figure 8.25 Illustrating the M-Pesa mobile phone-based money transfer

Source: Screen capture from a YouTube video available with search words: "Vodacom m-pesa: Sending money," posted by Vodacom SA, retrievable at www.YouTube.com/watch?v=s0BNYxK3dns

322 *Bottom of the pyramid marketing*

Before we start, we should look at the points of contention in the literature about BOP marketing (see "Food for Thought").

Food for Thought 8.3

- In reference to Prahalad and Hammond (2002) and Karnani (2007), what are the points of contention (i.e., main issues and debates) about BOP marketing?

8.4.1 *Size and Attractiveness of the BOP Segment*

Is the BOP segment attractive? The question about whether the BOP is a measurable segment remains open to this day. The World Resources Institute (2007) estimate the BOP market value at 5 USD trillion, which is a gigantic number. To have a comparison point, this sum represents more than the combined value of exports of the top three exporters in 2016: China (2.1 USD trillion), the US (~1.5 USD trillion), and Germany (1.3 USD trillion) (CIA World Factbook, 2016). These figures suggest an attractive market size.

Beyond overall estimates based on aggregate purchasing power (and putting aside the costs to reach this segment), it is important to subsegment the BOP to gain a better evaluation of its market potential. Low-income communities are, in fact, highly heterogeneous. They are located in different countries and regions with different socio-economic contexts and cannot be restricted to a homogenous global segment (Dawar & Chattopadhyay, 2002). Priorities in consumption are quite different with incomes below 2 USD/day or up to to 6 USD/day (Pitta et al., 2008).

The World Resources Institute (2007) propose a subsegmentation of the BOP market with people with income of 3,000 USD/year (i.e., the "BOP3000"), 2,500 USD/year, 2,000 USD/year, 1,500 USD/year, 1,000 USD/year, and 500 USD/year (i.e., the "BOP500"). As illustrated in Figure 8.10, the proportion of income that is spent on basic necessities, such as food, beverages, clothing and footwear, decreases from around 70 percent of earnings of the BOP1000 to under 40 percent of the BOP3500's earnings while spending on transport, recreation, culture, restaurants, and hotels doubles from about 10 percent to 20 percent of incomes (Goldman Sachs, 2010).

Furthermore, the structure of the BOP varies greatly from country to country, as illustrated in Figure 8.26, which contrasts four selected countries. The larger subsegments are the BOP3000 and 2500 in Russia; the BOP2000, 1500, and 1000 in India; the BOP1000 in Indonesia; and the BOP 1000 and 500 in Burkina Faso. Not only should companies pay attention to these differences in composition, but also in magnitude. For instance, the estimated annual expenditure of the largest BOP subsegment is ~2 USD billions in Burkina Faso (BOP500), ~40 USD billions in Russia (BOP3000), ~87 USD billions in Indonesia (BOP1000), and ~395 USD billions in India (BOP1500). Overall, the BOP in each country represents quite different market sizes,

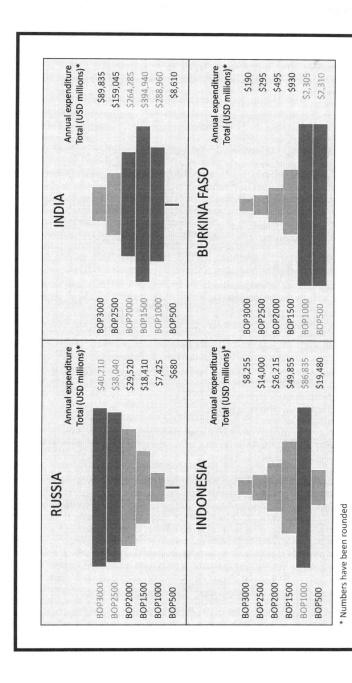

Figure 8.26 Illustrating the heterogeneity of the BOP segment
Source: Adapted from World Resources Institute (2007)

324 Bottom of the pyramid marketing

varying from ~5.5 USD billions in Burkina Faso, ~134 USD billions in Russia, ~205 USD billions in Indonesia, and a staggering 1,205 USD billions in India (World Resources Institute, 2007).

Finally, one of the realities at the BOP is that "The poor are scattered," requiring that distribution systems be entirely redesigned (Prahalad & Hammond, 2002). The question of attractiveness of this segment is, therefore, to be put in perspective with its profitability, since costs increase when customers are hard to reach.

8.4.2 Responsibility

Who should be held responsible for addressing poverty at the BOP, governments, companies, or NGOs? This question raises the role that MNCs have to play in eradicating poverty. Prahalad and Hammond (2002, p. 11) make it clear that "big corporations should solve big problems." On the contrary, Karnani (2007) argues that governments should assume their role in improving infrastructures, guaranteeing efficiency of markets, and also protecting the development of local businesses against foreign MNCs. The role of individuals at the BOP also must be questioned. Prahalad and Hammond (2002) position the individuals downstream of value chains as consumers only. Karnani (2007) makes a clear argument that individuals should be considered upstream of value chains as workers if their living conditions are to be improved. Later work by Seelos and Mair (2007) shows the interest of combining these perspectives and seeing individuals as both consumers and producers for alleviating poverty. What do you think (see "Food for Thought")?

Food for Thought 8.4

- Do you believe that MNCs should take on a significant role in trying to alleviate poverty?

8.4.3 Impact on Marketing Decisions and Feasibility

What is the impact of BOP marketing on traditional marketing activities? The literature shows that massive adaptation is required from companies willing to undertake this approach. In fact, most authors—and the examples seen previously—talk in favor of redesigning entire business models instead of just adapting practices used in developed economies. When a company decides to follow this path, it affects most decisions at the strategic and tactical levels of marketing.

First, BOP marketing requires a careful country selection and targeting process in order to focus on a population that is sufficiently attractive in terms of economic mass but also reachable in a profitable manner. Entry modes have to be carefully considered since local knowledge has been found

Bottom of the pyramid marketing   325

to be crucial. Joint-ventures with local partners (including governmental and nongovernmental actors) are regularly privileged. The marketing-mix often requires a complete redesign. Innovation extends from products to processes and business models in order to allow drastically reduced prices. People need to get specific training and be nurtured in adopting new ways of doing business. Distribution is often the biggest challenge, since low-revenue consumers tend to be hard to reach (scattered in remote areas, or else concentrated in suburbs but drastically lacking of infrastructure, etc.). Finally, promotion should not assume product familiarity and media selection needs to be tailored to local culture and conditions.

What are the key success factors of BOP marketing? For all the above-mentioned reasons, inclusion is a first key success factor. This notion emphasizes the importance of partnerships between firms and local governments, NGOs, and individuals (as both consumers and producers) for successfully implementing BOP marketing. Innovation (in products and business models) is another obvious key success factor. Affordability and accessibility come next. Finally, education plays an important role, not only for poor consumers in target-countries (in terms of sustainable consumption and savings, for instance), but for MNCs as well (in order to fight against preconceived ideas about the BOP segment and put forward the importance of ethical issues and environmental protection while trying to make a profit). These factors are visually represented in the nomological network proposed in the conclusion of this chapter.

8.4.4 Outcomes

In terms of outcomes, is BOP marketing only positive?[9] As always, such a complex question should require a follow-up question: "For whom?" From a critical perspective, the emergence of the BOP approach might be seen as a discourse developed by researchers and practitioners dealing with multinational enterprises (MNEs) (Dawar & Chattopadhyay, 2002). Indeed, the BOP approach was progressively integrated within the already strong and fashionable trend of corporate social responsibility (CSR). Such a perspective suggests that CSR can create value when long-term financial and social goals are integrated into the strategy of MNEs (Porter & Kramer, 2006). BOP marketing tries to convey that MNEs undertaking strategic CSR initiatives in developing countries might generate competitive advantages, such as integrating poor communities in production processes or by obtaining a license to operate, namely the broad consent of a community, and thereby legitimizing their role and presence in those countries.

Yet, the BOP approach is not an unquestionable avenue for MNEs to contribute to alleviating poverty. In addition, the vast majority of low-income economic activities in developing regions take place in the informal economy, and is thus not accounted for by traditional economic indicators, such as purchasing power or gross domestic product (De Soto, 2000). In sum, doing business "well" while dealing with low-income populations requires a different and deeper mindset, something that BOP marketing should learn how to do from a truly social-oriented perspective.

326 *Bottom of the pyramid marketing*

Conclusion: Targeting Low-Revenue Consumers with BOP Marketing Can Be a Solution to Overcome the Eco-Techno Distance, But It Requires Careful Consideration and Long-Term Investments

What would a nomological network for BOP marketing look like? A *nomological network* has been defined as the representation of the constructs of interest in a study, their observable manifestations and the interrelationships among and between them (Cronbach & Meehl, 1955). Figure 8.27 aims to encapsulate important variables in relation to the adoption of BOP marketing by companies.

First, it underlines the four main issues raised about: 1) the size and attractiveness of the BOP segment (with conflicting views on potential revenues and profitability for MNCs); 2) the responsibility of various types of actors (with debates about the respective role of firms of all sizes, including entrepreneurs, SMEs, and MNCs, as well as governmental and nongovernmental organizations) in helping low-revenue consumers accessing a better quality of life; 3) the feasibility of BOP marketing (in order to be successful, companies undertaking BOP marketing must focus on the following key factors: inclusion, innovation, affordability, accessibility, and education); and 4) the actual outcomes of BOP marketing (with divided opinions in regards to the potential improvement or degradation of various success indicators).

Then, the figure shows that BOP marketing is mainly a market-seeking activity (one of the four main motivations for firms to go abroad, discussed in Chapter 2). It can be argued that a strong driver is also the willingness to innovate and learn about new business models (strategic asset-seeking) in order to serve entirely different markets. We will develop this point in more detail in the next chapter, dealing with reverse innovation, an approach that is close in essence to BOP marketing. Among other causes explaining why companies undertake BOP marketing is the notion of distance. Distance plays a dual role. On one hand, the existence of a large economic and technological distance between developed and developing/emerging economies is what motivates companies to take a different marketing approach. On the other hand, the very existence of this type of distance, as well as other types—such as administrative, cultural, and psychic distance—represents barriers to the successful implementation of BOP marketing.

Finally, the figure illustrates that the consequences of BOP marketing can be ambivalent. At the level of analysis of the firm, a successful implementation contributes to performance by bringing in a significant source of new revenues. The ability to tap into large and underserved markets is also likely to increase competitiveness (by learning new ways of doing business). Contributing to improving the quality of life of poor people can benefit the corporate reputation worldwide. However, BOP marketing is paved with challenges and examples of companies failing in their attempts to profitably serve low revenue consumers are documented. Therefore, an unsuccessful implementation can have the contrary effect on performance, competitiveness and reputation. Interestingly, companies undertaking BOP marketing tend to stay quiet on financial results. We can think of two explanations for

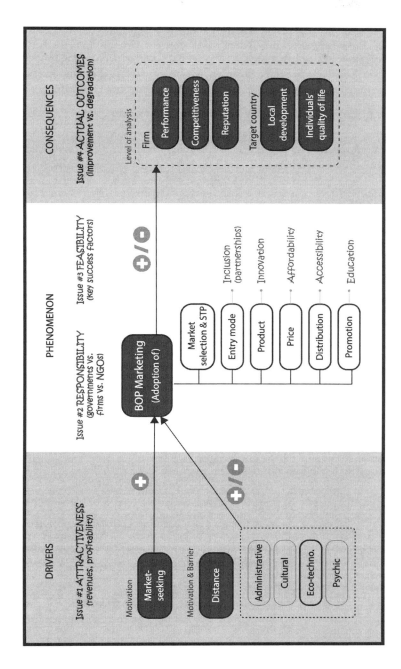

Figure 8.27 Proposing a nomological network for BOP marketing

Source: Own elaboration

328 Bottom of the pyramid marketing

this silence: results are either poor (draining resources and possibly jeopardizing the overall competitiveness) or results are good (companies are then at risk of being accused of exploiting poverty). In both cases, the performance, competitiveness, and reputation of companies may be at stake. At the level of analysis of the target-country where BOP marketing is implemented, the literature displays arguments in favor of and against its capacity to help local industries develop and actually improve poor people's quality of life. For instance, knowledge transfer from MNCs to local entrepreneurs can boost local economies. On the contrary, the mere presence of MNCs can deter initiatives from local companies. In turn, individuals in poverty can greatly benefit from accessing products or services that were out of reach before, thanks to BOP marketing. However, they can also be led to make purchases that are not in their best interest in the long term, due to a lack of education.

So, should companies target low revenue consumers with BOP marketing? In all, targeting low-revenue consumers with BOP marketing is a market-seeking opportunity that requires significant investments in terms of time and resources. **It provides a solution to overcome a "negatively charged" eco-techno distance** (see Chapter 7). In all cases, it suggests proceeding carefully. If successful, this approach can bring tremendous benefits for future growth. Yet, companies should balance the gains against the potential harm caused to their own business as well as to local economies and targeted consumers. BOP marketing should stay closely connected to the overall CSR strategy.

Notes

1 The example of Patrimonio Hoy, an initiative of Cemex, is based on: Cemex (2016b); El Dinero (2016); El Nuevo Diario (2017); WDI W92C02 (2012).
2 The example of Danone and Danone Grameen Foods is based on: Danone (2012, 2016b); Nobelprize.org (2006).
3 The example of Nokia Life Tools, an initiative of Nokia relies on: information provided by Nokia
Trademarks, Domain Names & Designs department (2017); HBS 9–710–429 (2011); New York Times (2016); Nokia (2009, 2013); (Nokia, 2014, 2016).
4 The example of LifeLight, an initiative of Philips, is based on: information provided by Philips's Press Office and Philips (2015).
5 In Section 8.3.5, the example of Schneider Electric's Access to Energy program has been written in collaboration with Thomas Andre, Access to Energy Strategy Director at Schneider Electric.
6 In Section 8.3.6, the example of Telenor and Grameenphone has been written in collaboration with Ashraful Hassan, Managing Director at Grameen Telecom, Grameen Distribution and Grameen Shamogree; it also relies on: information provided by Telenor's Brand Design & Digital Experience department (2017); Grameenphone (2014, 2016, 2017); Hart and Christensen (2002); Telenor (2016).
7 The example of Pureit, a product of Unilever, is based on: HBS 9–511–067 (2011).
8 The example of M-Pesa, an initiative of Vodafone, is based on: Standard Digital News (2016).
9 In Section 8.4.4, the paragraph entitled "In terms of outcomes, is BOP marketing only positive?" has been written in collaboration with Marlei Pozzebon, Professor in International Business Management (HEC Montréal, Canada),

Bottom of the pyramid marketing   329

whose research interests include the social economy, sustainable development, and the political and cultural aspects of technology transfer.

References

André, Thomas & Ponssard, Jean-Pierre (2015). *Managing Base of the Pyramid as a Business Opportunity: A Longitudinal Field Study*. HAL. Retrieved from https://hal.archives-ouvertes.fr/hal-01221651/document

Cemex (2016a). Annual Report—Integrated Strategy for a Better Future. Retrieved from http://archive.cemex.com/InvestorCenter/files/2016/IntegratedReport2016.pdf

Cemex (2016b). Patrimonio Hoy. Retrieved June 2017, from www.cemexmexico.com/DesarrolloSustentable/PatrimonioHoy.aspx

CIA World Factbook (2016). Country Comparison: Exports. Retrieved June 2017, from www.cia.gov/library/publications/the-world-factbook/rankorder/2078rank.html

Credit Suisse (2015). Global Wealth Databook. Credit Suisse Research Institute. Retrieved from https://publications.credit-suisse.com/tasks/render/file/?fileID=F2425415-DCA7-80B8-EAD989AF9341D47E

Cronbach, Lee Joseph & Meehl, Paul (1955). Construct Validity in Psychological Tests. *Psychological Bulletin*, 52(4), 281–302.

Danone (2012). Rapport de développement durable 2012. Retrieved from www.danone.com/fileadmin/user_upload/Rapport_de_developpement_durable_Danone_2012.pdf

Danone (2016a). Annual Financial Report—Welcome to the Alimentation Revolution. Retrieved from http://danone-danonecom-prod.s3.amazonaws.com/user_upload/info_reglementees_NIV/Danone_-_DDR_2016_-_VENG.pdf

Danone (2016b). Company Report—Registration Document. Retrieved from http://danone-danonecom-prod.s3.amazonaws.com/user_upload/Investisseurs/DDR_2017/ANG/Danone_-_DDR_2016_-_VENG.pdf

Dawar, Niraj & Chattopadhyay, Amitava (2002). Rethinking Marketing Programs for Emerging Markets. *Long Range Planning*, 35(5), 457–474.

De Soto, Hernando (2000). *The Mystery of Capital: Why Capitalism Triumphs in the West and Fails Everywhere Else*. New York: Basic Books (p. 278).

The Economist (2004, March 11th). More or Less Equal. *The Economist*. Retrieved from www.economist.com/node/2498851

El Dinero (2016, July 14th). Patrimonio Hoy, el plan responsable de Cemex para construcción de viviendas, *By Rossbell de la Rosa*. Retrieved from www.eldinero.com.do/25451/patrimonio-hoy-el-plan-responsable-de-cemex-para-construccion-de-viviendas/

El Nuevo Diario (2017, January 26th). Facilitan construcción de viviendas. Retrieved from www.elnuevodiario.com.ni/economia/empresas/416797-facilitan-construccion-viviendas/

Esri (2012). Average HH Spend on Ice Cream by Zip Code. Environmental Systems Research Institute, Pam Allison. Retrieved June 2017, from www.pamallison.com/2012/06/12/ice-cream-who-buys-it/

Goldman Sachs (2008). The Expanding Middle: The Exploding World Middle Class and Falling Global Inequality. (Global Economics Paper No. 170), By Dominic Wilson and Raluca Dragusanu, Employees of Goldman, Sachs & Co. www.ryanallis.com/wp-content/uploads/2008/07/expandingmiddle.pdf

330   *Bottom of the pyramid marketing*

Goldman Sachs (2009). The BRICs Nifty 50: The EM & DM Winners. Goldman Sachs Global Economics, Commodities and Strategy Research. Retrieved from www.goldmansachs.com/our-thinking/archive/archive-pdfs/nifty-fifty.pdf

Goldman Sachs (2010). Is This the "BRICs Decade"? By Dominic Wilson and Raluca Dragusanu, Employees of Goldman, Sachs & Co.—BRICs Monthly No. 10/03. Retrieved from www.goldmansachs.com/our-thinking/archive/archive-pdfs/brics-decade-pdf.pdf

Grameenphone (2014). Annual Report 2014. Retrieved from www.grameen phone.com/sites/default/files/investor_relations/annual_report/Full-Report-2014.pdf

Grameenphone (2016). Annual Report—Welcome to an Unbound World. Retrieved from https://cdn01.grameenphone.com/sites/default/files/investor_relations/annual_report/GP_Annual_Report_2016_Optimized.pdf

Grameenphone (2017). Corporate Information. Retrieved June 2017, from www.grameenphone.com/about/investor-relations/corporate-factsheet/corporate-information

Hart, Stuart & Christensen, Clayton (2002). The Great Leap: Driving Innovation From the Base of the Pyramid. *MIT Sloan Management Review*, 44(1), 51–56.

HBS 9–511–067 (2011). *Hindustan Unilever's 'Pureit' Water Purifier*. Case written by: Kasturi Rangan and Mona Sinha.Boston: Harvard Business School (p. 26).

HBS 9–710–429 (2011). *Emerging Nokia?* Case written by: Juan Alcacer, Tarun Khanna, Mary Furey, and Rakeen Mabud. Boston: Harvard Business School (p. 23).

Hindustan Unilever (2017). A Purity Promise That Will Last You a Lifetime. Retrieved July 2017, from www.pureitwater.com/IN/pureit-water-purifiers

Human, Gert, Ascott-Evans, Byron, Souter, William & Xabanisa, Steven (2011). Advertising, Brand Knowledge and Attitudinal Loyalty in Low-Income Markets: Can Advertising Make a Difference at the "Bottom-Of-the-Pyramid"? *Management Dynamics*, 20(2), 33–45.

Karnani, Aneel (2007). The Mirage of Marketing to the Bottom of the Pyramid: How the Private Sector Can Help Alleviate Poverty. *California Management Review*, 49(4), 90–111.

Kotler, Philip & Armstrong, Gary (2005). *Principles of Marketing*. New Jersey: Prentice Hall (p. 768).

New York Times (2016). Nokia Phones May Find Life After Microsoft. Retrieved June 2017, from www.nytimes.com/2016/05/19/business/international/nokia-microsoft-foxconn-android.html?_r=0

Nobelprize.org (2006). Muhammad Yunus—Facts. Retrieved June 2017, from www.nobelprize.org/nobel_prizes/peace/laureates/2006/yunus-facts.html

Nokia (2009). Nokia Life Tools Launched Across India. Press release. Retrieved June 2017, from http://company.nokia.com/en/news/press-releases/2009/06/12/nokia-life-tools-launched-across-india

Nokia (2013). Nokia Life Services to Expand to Kenya. Press release. Retrieved June 2017, from www.nokia.com/en_int/news/releases/2013/02/26/nokia-life-services-to-expand-to-kenya

Nokia (2014). Annual Report 2014. Retrieved from http://company.nokia.com/sites/default/files/download/investors/nokia_uk_ar14_full.pdf

Nokia (2016). Annual Report 2016—Rebalancing for Growth. Retrieved from www.nokia.com/sites/default/files/files/nokia_20f16_full_report_2_1.pdf

Bottom of the pyramid marketing 331

OECD (2010). The Emerging Middle Class in Developing Countries. (Working Paper No. 285). By Homi Kharas. Retrieved from www.oecd.org/dev/44457738.pdf

Oxfam (2016). An Economy for the 1%—How Privilege and Power in the Economy Drive Extreme Inequality and How This Can Be Stopped. (210 Oxfam Briefing Paper), By Deborah Hardoon, Sophia Ayele, and Ricardo Fuentes-Nieva, Oxfam International (UK). Retrieved from http://policy-practice.oxfam.org.uk/publications/an-economy-for-the-1-how-privilege-and-power-in-the-economy-drive-extreme-inequ-592643

Pew Research Center (2015). A Global Middle Class Is More Promise than Reality. Washington, DC. Retrieved July 2015, from www.pewglobal.org/files/2015/08/Global-Middle-Class-Report_8-12-15-final.pdf

Philips (2015). Solar-Powered LED Luminaires from Philips Can Brighten the Homes of Millions. Retrieved June 2017, from www.philips.com/a-w/about/news/archive/standard/news/press/2015/20150319-Solar-powered-LED-luminaires-from-Philips-can-brighten-the-homes-of-millions.html

Philips (2016). Annual Report—A Focused Leader in Health Technology. Retrieved from www.philips.com/static/annualresults/2016/PhilipsFullAnnual-Report2016_English.pdf

Pitta, Dennis, Guesalaga, Rodrigo & Marshall, Pablo (2008). The Quest for the Fortune at the Bottom of the Pyramid: Potential and Challenges. *Journal of Consumer Marketing*, 25(7), 393–401.

Porter, Michael & Kramer, Mark (2006). Strategy and Society: The Link Between Competitive Advantage and Corporate Social Responsibility. *Harvard Business Review*, 84(12), 78–92.

Prahalad, Coimbatore Krishnao & Hammond, Allen (2002). Serving the World's Poor, Profitably. *Harvard Business Review*, 80(9), 48–59.

Schneider Electric (2016). Financial and Sustainable Development Annual Report 2016. Retrieved from www.schneider-electric.com/ww/en/documents/finance/2017/03/2016-annual-report-tcm50-288816.pdf

Seelos, Christian & Mair, Johanna (2007). Profitable Business Models and Market Creation in the Context of Deep Poverty: A Strategic View. *The Academy of Management Perspectives* 21(4), 49–63.

Standard Digital News (2016, May 15th). Five Reasons M-Pesa Failed in South Africa, *By XN Iraki*. Retrieved from www.standardmedia.co.ke/business/article/2000201831/five-reasons-m-pesa-failed-in-south-africa

Telenor (2016). Global Presence. Retrieved June 2017, from www.telenor.com/about-us/global-presence

Telenor Group (2016). Annual Report 2016. Retrieved from www.telenor.com/wp-content/uploads/2017/03/Annual-Report-2016-Q-960dfcfa007ceee404c193b48ad20cff.pdf

Unilever (2016). Annual Report and Accounts 2016—Making Sustainable Living Commonplace. Retrieved from www.unilever.com/Images/unilever-annual-report-and-accounts-2016_tcm244-498744_en.pdf

Van Den Waeyenberg, Sofie & Hens, Luc (2012). Overcoming Institutional Distance: Expansion to Base-Of-the-Pyramid Markets. *Journal of Business Research*, 65(12), 1692–1699.

Vodafone (2016). Annual Report 2016—Confidence in the Future. Vodafone Group Plc. Retrieved from www.vodafone.com/content/annualreport/annual_report16/index.html

332 *Bottom of the pyramid marketing*

WDI W92C02 (2012). *Constructing a Base-of-the-Pyramid Business in a Multinational Company: CEMEX's Patrimonio Hoy Looks to Grow.* Case written by: Ted London. Ann Arbor: Michigan Ross School of Business (p. 22).

World Resources Institute (2007). The Next 4 Billion People: Market Size and Business Strategy at the Base of the Pyramid. By Allen Hammond, William Kramer, Julia Tran, Rob Katz, and Courtland Walker. Retrieved from www.wri.org/publication/next-4-billion

9 Reverse Innovation

Table of Contents

9 Reverse Innovation

Introduction: Should Companies Develop New Offerings
from Developing Economies to Sell Worldwide?........................334
- 9.1 Background Information..335
  - 9.1.1 Extended Marketing-Mix (from 4Ps to 7Ps) 335
  - 9.1.2 Attributes and Cues 341
  - 9.1.3 International Product Policies..........................344
- 9.2 Definitions..345
  - 9.2.1 Diffusion of Innovation and the International
    Product Life Cycle (Rogers, Vernon)................346
  - 9.2.2 Reverse Innovation (Govindarajan) 351
- 9.3 Corporate Examples...352
  - 9.3.1 Fiat 355
  - 9.3.2 General Electric 357
  - 9.3.3 Narayana Health 357
  - 9.3.4 Harman 360
  - 9.3.5 Tata Group 361
  - 9.3.6 Vestergaard 363
- 9.4 Issues at Stake 366
  - 9.4.1 Origin of Innovation and International
    Diffusion..366
  - 9.4.2 Impact on Marketing Decisions and
    Feasibility..368
  - 9.4.3 Outcomes 368

Conclusion: Companies should develop new offerings from developing economies to then sell worldwide (i.e., undertake reverse innovation) to overcome a negative eco-techno distance and enhance competitiveness, but they should be aware that it can also bring disruption in developed markets.

References

334 *Reverse Innovation*

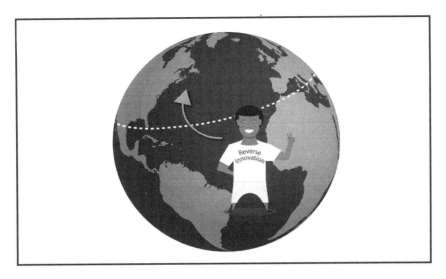

Figure 9.1 Illustrating Chapter 9
Source: Own elaboration

Recommended Readings

- Govindarajan, Vijay (2012). A Reverse-Innovation Playbook. *Harvard Business Review*, 90(4), 120–124.
- Govindarajan, Vijay & Ramamurti, Ravi (2011). Reverse Innovation, Emerging Markets, and Global Strategy. *Global Strategy Journal*, 1(3–4), 191–205.
- Immelt, Jeffrey; Govindarajan, Vijay & Trimble, Chris (2009). How GE Is Disrupting Itself. *Harvard Business Review*, 87(10), 56–65.
- Vernon, Raymond (1966). International Investment and International Trade in the Product Cycle. *The Quarterly Journal of Economics*, 80(2), 190–207.
- Wells, Louis (1968). A Product Life Cycle for International Trade? *Journal of Marketing*, 32(3), 1–6.

Introduction: Should Companies Develop New Offerings from Developing Economies to Sell Worldwide?

Traditionally, innovation has been seen as diffusing from developed economies into developing economies. The concept of reverse innovation captures the phenomenon that these flows are changing and moving backward, from the developing to the developed world. As this reversal occurs, it not only

Reverse Innovation 335

challenges preconceptions about "less developed" countries but can also bring major disruption into the home markets of firms from developed economies. **Reverse innovation can arguably be seen as a strategy that companies use to overcome eco-techno distance issues** (see Chapter 7). By addressing the question: **"Should companies develop new offerings (products and services) from developing economies to sell worldwide?"** this chapter aims to discuss the opportunities and challenges companies face in adopting reverse innovation.

Figure 9.2 situates the topic of reverse innovation in the book structure and shows that, in relation to the different steps in an international marketing plan, this topic can be particularly discussed when considering product and price policies.

Overall, the objectives of this chapter are to define, illustrate, and discuss the topic of reverse innovation. First, we look into background information about the notion of international product management by reviewing the extension of the marketing-mix from 4Ps to 7Ps (called the *extended marketing-mix*), and pay particular attention to product attributes and cues. The AdaptStand issue (i.e., adaptation and standardization) of international product policies is broached next. Second, we define several important concepts and present Vernon's and Roger's theories, which help understand the fundamentals of how innovation diffuses internationally. We then discuss the concept of reverse innovation (proposed by Govindarajan and colleagues) in further detail, before moving on to present examples of firms that have adopted this approach. Finally, we conclude with an overview of the issues debated when it comes to reverse innovation, including discussions about diffusion patterns and globalization, key success factors and the overall impact on marketing decisions, and whether its outcomes are only favorable for firms from developed economies.

9.1 Background Information

When thinking about products and services in an international environment, it is useful to keep in mind important concepts. We begin by addressing the following questions:

- What is the extended marketing-mix?
- What is a "product"? What are important product attributes and cues?
- What is special about services?
- What are international product policies about? Should product policies be standardized or adapted? What about new product development (NPD)?

9.1.1 Extended Marketing-Mix (from 4Ps to 7Ps)

What is the extended marketing-mix? The addition of three "Ps" to the marketing-mix comes from the necessity to consider more aspects when delivering a service, as opposed to a product. Indeed, defining policies about the *product*, the *price*, the *promotion*, and the *place* (i.e., the traditional 4Ps)

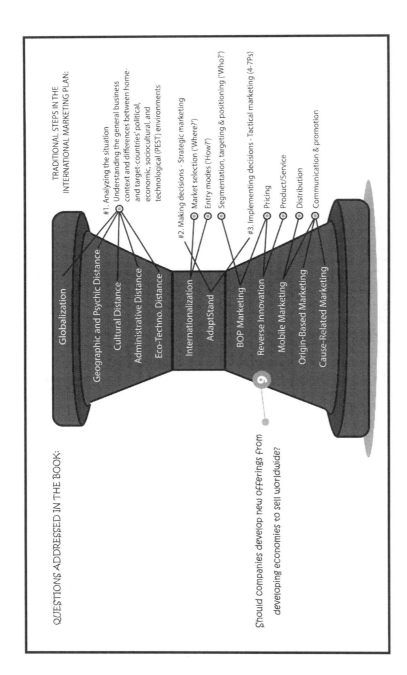

Figure 9.2 Positioning Chapter 9 in the overall book structure
Source: Own elaboration

is still very useful but when delivering services, firms are also interested in understanding how the *process, people*, and *physical evidence* will affect the value of these services, as perceived by customers.

In the P that corresponds to *process*, firms should understand well the steps through which their service is delivered to customers. Different steps, and different numbers of steps, may or may not differentiate the service from competition and add value for customers. The notion of process includes waiting times, information given to customers (i.e., customer direction), procedures, mechanization, the overall flow of activities, policies, and customer involvement (Rafiq & Pervaiz, 1995). Figure 9.3 illustrates different types of food services (clockwise, it shows scenes in a fast-food restaurant, a European-style restaurant, a pizza delivery, and finally, a Korean restaurant serving hot pot). It helps us to realize that the steps through which customers receive the service and end up eating are entirely different. In fast-food restaurants, customers are educated so that they know to wait in line to order from a board, pay, receive their food on a tray, and either take it out or sit at the next table available. In European-style restaurants, customers are educated to be seated at a table—with some variations across countries, since in North America, for instance, one is supposed to wait to be assigned a table, whereas in Europe or Latin America customers often choose their table on their own—then order their food from a menu that is handed to them and wait for the food to be served, already prepared. Korean restaurants are an example of restaurants where the food can be brought unprepared to the table and cooked by customers themselves in a hot pot. Finally, pizza can be ordered by phone or online, delivered at home, and paid for by cash or card. In all these examples, waiting times, information, and attention provided to customers can make for a valuable or disastrous experience. These examples illustrate the importance of the *process* in adding value to services.

In turn, the P that corresponds to *people* (also called *participants*) refers to the direct or indirect interaction that may occur between customers and the staff operating the service, since the behavior of employees performing a service might be a source of value creation. This includes training, discretion, commitment, incentives, appearance, and general attitudes (Rafiq & Pervaiz, 1995). To illustrate the importance of employees as brand ambassadors, the case of Southwest Airlines is interesting (see the YouTube video where a staff member of the airline raps the safety briefing, available with search words: "Flight Attendant Rapping the Safety Briefing! Southwest Airlines!"). Employees' behavior should be congruent with the brand image and the desired positioning of the service performed.

Finally, *physical evidence*, also called *proof*, includes anything in the environment surrounding the service, such as furnishings, color schemes, layout, noise level, or any other tangible clues (Rafiq & Pervaiz, 1995). It can be the type of music, as well as smells and other sensorial elements, that add value for customers and/or help them differentiate the service in question from that of competitors. Figure 9.4 illustrates a traditional setting and an

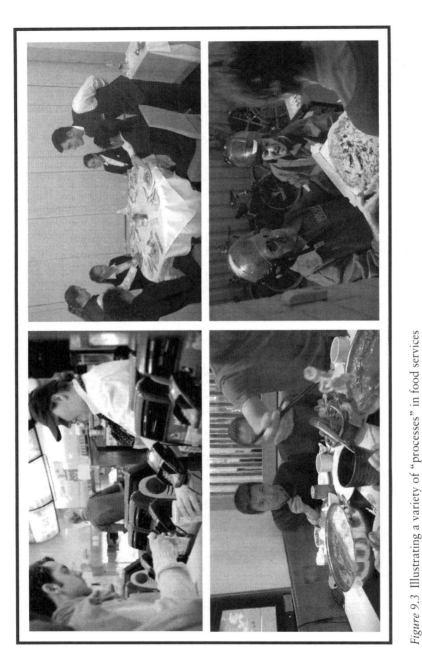

Figure 9.3 Illustrating a variety of "processes" in food services

Source: Own elaboration based on screen captures from YouTube videos available with search words: "Milestone Restaurants t/a McDonald's—customer service," posted by BrightStarPR, retrievable at www.YouTube.com/watch?v=Dl912AI3JQc; "Table Setup and Sequence of Service," posted by FB Cesar Ritz, retrievable at www.YouTube.com/watch?v=5pK1owmRemQ; "How to Properly Eat Hotpot," posted by Off the Great Wall, retrievable at www.YouTube.com/watch?v=EzOxAeqoCso; and "Quand on est livreur de pizza—Palmashow," posted by Palmashow, retrievable at www.YouTube.com/watch?v=dUXbW2u1nA

Figure 9.4 Representing regular and augmented "proof" for transportation services

Source: Own elaboration based on screen captures from YouTube videos available with search words: "21st Century Bus Shelter," posted by STM MouvementCollectif, retrievable at www.YouTube.com/watch?v=Nk7CJZROTq8 and "Cool and Creative Bus Stop Advertisements," posted by MovieCarScene, retrievable at www.YouTube.com/watch?v=9vG01R7f5pE

340   *Reverse Innovation*

enhanced setting at a bus stop—an environment where the customer waits prior to receiving a service (urban transportation). It shows how transportation companies can be creative in offering shelter while their customers wait for their bus. This is an additional way to differentiate from direct and indirect competition. Hospital rooms and pediatric clinics are other examples where the physical evidence (e.g., lights, shades, and color of fabric, as well as integration of games and entertainment within the design of the room) can be significantly enhanced to increase the value of the service offered (for sick children and concerned parents).

An overview of the elements that are comprised in the extended marketing-mix is presented in Table 9.1.

What is a product? An encompassing definition of a *product* presents goods, services, persons (e.g., celebrities), events (e.g., concerts), or places (e.g., tourist destinations) as bundles of satisfactions or utilities that buyers receive. It might not be intuitive as to why celebrities can be described as products. Yet, when you think about buying a music album or attending a performance by a famous artist, you receive more satisfaction than just listening to or watching the delivered performance. You also purchase an experience about which to tell your friends, and associate with values and attributes of the celebrity with which you identify, etc.

9.1.2 Attributes and Cues

What are important product attributes? To answer this question, we refer to a central marketing theory which was developed by Olson (1972) and called the *cue utilization theory*. Richardson, Dick, and Jain (1994, p. 29) summarize it in the following extract:

> Products consist of an array of cues that serve as surrogate indicators of quality to shoppers [. . .] Cues can be classified as extrinsic or intrinsic to the products [. . .] Intrinsic cues are product-related attributes (e.g., ingredients) that cannot be manipulated without also answering physical properties of the product [. . .] Extrinsic cues are product-related attributes (e.g., price, brand name and packaging) which are not part of the physical product.

In this way, we can say that the physical form, taste, color, odor, and texture of a product, how it functions, its conditioning, packaging, and labeling, as well as its warranty, the manufacturer's and retailer's servicing, the manufacturer's reputation, and country of origin are all important product attributes. They are often "signaled" by price and brand, which act as summarizing cues. The variety and level of precision that an analysis of intrinsic and extrinsic cues holds are illustrated in Figure 9.5, with an example specific to food products.

Intrinsic cues correspond to the first layer in the "product component model" by Cateora, Gilly, Graham, and Money (2016, p. 395), i.e., the core components of products (e.g., the product platform, design features, and functional features).

Table 9.1 Overview of the extended marketing-mix (7Ps)

Marketing-mix element	Mainly relevant for goods	Relevant for both (products and services)	Mainly relevant for services
Product	Product line; Features and options; Style; Packaging; Service level	Quality; Brand name; Warranty	Service line; Capabilities; Facilitating goods; Tangible clues; Physical environment; Personnel; Process of service delivery
Price		Level; Discounts and allowances; Payment terms; Customer's own perceived value; Quality/price interaction; Differentiation	
Place	Inventory levels and locations; Outlet locations; Sales territories; Transport carriers	Distribution channels and coverage	Accessibility; Location
Promotion		Advertising; Personal selling; Publicity; Sales promotion	Facilitating goods; Tangible clues; Physical environment; Personnel; Process of service delivery
People/Participants			Personnel: training, discretion, commitment, incentives, appearance, interpersonal behaviour; Attitudes; Customer contact
Physical evidence/Proof			Environment: furnishings, colour, layout, noise level, facilitating goods; Tangible clues
Process			Mechanization; Policies; Procedures; Customer involvement; Customer direction; Flow of activities

Source: Adapted from Rafiq and Pervaiz (1995, p. 6)

342   *Reverse Innovation*

Extrinsic cues correspond to the second layer, labeled the "augmented product" or the packaging component (including price, quality, package, styling, trademark, and brand name), as well as the third layer, the "support services component," composed of attributes related to services around the physical product (e.g., deliveries, warranty, instructions, spare parts, installation, and repair and maintenance).

It is interesting to note that competitive rivalry was taking place on core components extensively in the 1950s–1970s. In the 1980s–1990s, firms started to compete aggressively on attributes belonging to the augmented component, such as brand and price. In subsequent decades, support services became prominent in defining successful companies. Nowadays, for many industrial products, the revenues from support services largely exceed the revenues from the products themselves. For instance, telecommunication companies practically give away cellular phones in order to gain the phone services contracts (Cateora et al., 2016).

What is special about services? Services have four unique characteristics that distinguish them from products: they are *intangible, inseparable* (i.e., service creation cannot be separated from its consumption), *heterogeneous* (i.e., service is individually produced and is thus unique and difficult to reproduce), and *perishable* (i.e., once created, a service cannot be stored). These characteristics suggest that services, when performed at the international scale, must be handled in a different way as opposed to products that can be stored, for instance (Cateora, Gilly, & Graham, 2011, Chap. 11). Besides, it is often not intuitive to imagine services crossing borders, but a great number of service industries (see Figure 9.6 for a few well-known brands) are now widely international, such as:

- Transportation services (e.g., Air Canada, Casual Cruise Asia, Greyhound Lines in North America, Eurolines in Europe, and Uber)
- Information, communications, and audiovisual services (e.g., Associated Press, AVI-SPL, Facebook, Google, LinkedIn, News Corporation, Reuters, and Twitter).
- Entertainment services (e.g., eOne, Le Cirque du Soleil, Netflix, and Vivendi).
- Tourism and leisure services (e.g., Accor, Airbnb, Club Med, Disney Parks and Resorts, Expedia, Madhvani Group, and MGM Resorts International).
- Education services (e.g., EF Education First, HEC Paris Qatar, Project Management Institute and University of Cambridge International Examinations).
- Health care services (e.g., Abbott, GE Healthcare, McKesson and Mercury Healthcare International).
- Financial services (e.g., Banco Santander, BNP Paribas, HSBC, ING, Société Générale and Sumitomo Mitsui Banking Corporation).
- Insurance services (e.g., AXA, Allianz, Aegon, Generali Group, Prudential, Munich Re and Zurich Insurance Group).

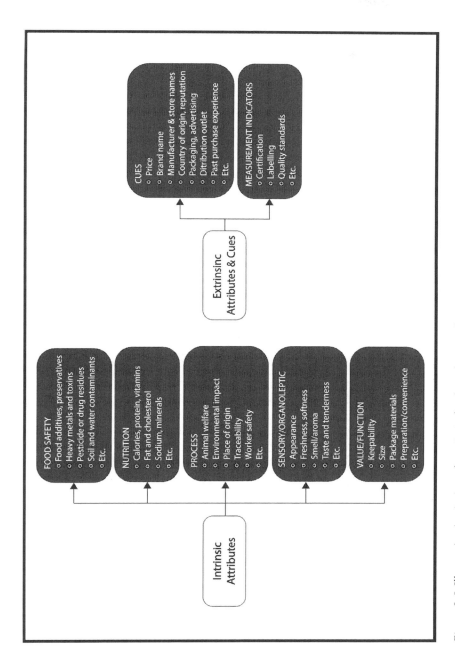

Figure 9.5 Illustrating intrinsic and extrinsic food product attributes

Source: Adapted from Caswell, Noelke, and Mojiduszka (2002, p. 227)

344 *Reverse Innovation*

Figure 9.6 Examples of firms offering international services

Source: Courtesy of Air Canada, KPMG International (KPMG is a registered trademark of KPMG International. KPMG International's Trademarks are the sole property of KPMG International and their use here does not imply auditing by or endorsement of KPMG International or any of its member firms), Netflix, and Société Générale

- Management consulting (e.g., Accenture, Deloitte, Ernst & Young, KPMG and PWC).
- Computer and information services (e.g., Apple, Cisco, IBM, Microsoft, Oracle, TATA Consulting Services and Unisys).

9.1.3 *International Product Policies*

What are international product policies about? International product policies consist of a set of decisions around the desired degree of standardization and adaptation of all product attributes (e.g., quality, design, labeling, conditioning, packaging, brand name, and range). The term *product range* refers to the portfolio of products that companies develop, such as the Elvive line by L'Oréal, which includes shampoo, hair conditioner, styling mousse, mask pot, and oil with UV filters for all hair types. In international markets, we can decide to commercialize the full range or else limit the range to only a few products. Like for any other marketing policies, decisions are thus made at the tactical level and concern AdaptStand degrees.

Should product policies be standardized or adapted? To the question whether product policies should be standardized or adapted to international markets, the answer is: "It depends." The factors on which this decision depends rely heavily on existing resources of the firm and target markets (see Chapter 3) as well as on the concept of distance. Taking the example of conditioning and labeling, types of distance that can force companies to adapt to local conditions include: *geographic distance* (e.g., physical and climatic constraints such as humidity, heat and transport conditions), *administrative distance* (e.g., regulations constraints such as rules of origin and waste management), and *cultural distance* (e.g., local usage of distributors and consumers in terms of size, shape and color codes).

The concept of *environmental sensitivity* (Keegan & Green, 2016, pp. 127–128) offers an intuitive way of understanding that products need to be adapted to specific national contexts according to varying degrees. Food, for example, is the most culturally sensitive category of consumer goods. For this reason, dehydrated Knorr Soups did not gain popularity in North America because of a marked preference for canned soups. Food requires more product adaptation than do computers or integrated circuits, in terms of cultural environments. However, environmental sensitivity varies according to the relative importance of CAGE differences (Chapter 4). Integrated circuits may require minimal cultural adaptation, but significant technical or administrative adaptation (in terms of voltage and quality certification, for instance).

What about new product development (NPD)? Traditionally, textbooks about international product policies and product management have put a lot of emphasis on new product development and innovation. However, little emphasis was placed—until recently—on where the innovation was taking place. Indeed, it was assumed that innovation occurred in firms' home markets (usually developed economies), and later diffused to foreign countries with a certain degree of AdaptStand (i.e., the principles of *glocalization* —see Chapter 3). This has been changing over the past few years with the rise of "reverse innovation."

9.2 Definitions

To understand *reverse innovation*, we first look into the ways innovation diffuses in general and, more specifically, on international markets with the concept of the "international product life cycle." The questions addressed are the following:

- How does innovation diffuse?
- New product development (NPD): what is the international product life cycle?
- Where was innovation diffusing from? And now: what is reverse innovation?
- Where can we see evidence of changing patterns in the diffusion of innovation?

9.2.1 Diffusion of Innovation and the International Product Life Cycle (Rogers, Vernon)

How does innovation diffuse? The "diffusion of innovations theory" was proposed by Everett Rogers in 1962 in his seminal book entitled *Diffusion* *of Innovations*, which has had several editions since then. Core elements of this theory are presented hereafter: "The main elements in the diffusion of new ideas are: i) an innovation, ii) which is communicated through certain channels, iii) over time, iv) among the members of a social system." (Rogers, 1983, p. 35). The notion of time is thus central here (see Chapter 4, when we discussed the nature of knowledge as being tacit and requiring time to reach others). A video presentation of the theory is available on YouTube with the word search: "Roger's Diffusion of Innovation." A visual example consists in the diffusion of Twitter in the US (available on YouTube using the word search: "US Twitter Adoption"). It shows—as the theory predicts—the curve slowly increasing at first, then speeding up when the early and late majorities adopt the innovation, then slowing down. Figure 9.7 illustrates the five categories of people according to their behavior in regards to innovation adoption and their respective proportion in the overall population (i.e., innovators, 2.5 percent; early adopters, ~15 percent; early majority, ~35 percent; late majority, ~35 percent, and finally laggards, ~15 percent). It also shows the curve representing the innovation diffusion in terms of market share—a curve in the shape of an S (called the S-Curve) because of the rapid increase in market share with adoption by the early and late majorities.

What is the international product life cycle? Figure 9.8 illustrates the life cycle of a product moving on from the initial phase of product development to

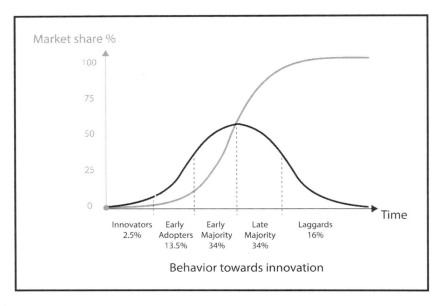

Figure 9.7 Illustrating Roger's theory of innovation diffusion

Source: Adapted from Rogers (2003)

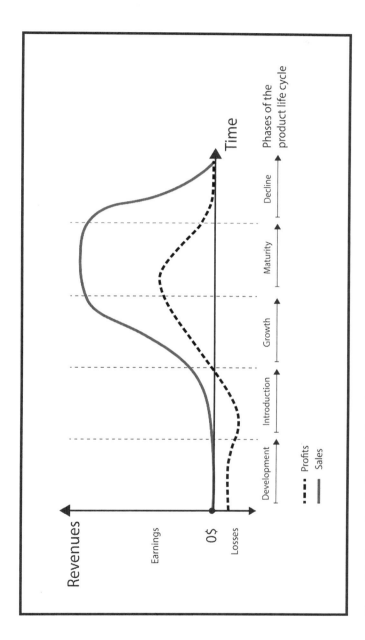

Figure 9.8 Illustrating the Product Life Cycle (PLC)
Source: Adapted from Kotler and Keller (2016, p. 153)

348   *Reverse Innovation*

the phase of market introduction, then growth, maturity, and finally decline. The figure also illustrates that sales and profits do not coincide. Indeed, product development and introduction phases usually cost firms money before they can make any profit—which explains the high rate of product launches failures in start-ups.

Figure 9.8, however, does not speak much to the *international product life cycle* (IPLC) theory, proposed by Raymond Vernon in 1966 to explain patterns of imports and exports (see Chapter 4). This theory assumes that innovation flows from more-advanced to less-advanced countries in terms of economic development levels. In the introduction and growth phases of the novel product, consumption levels are usually higher than local production levels—thus inviting other advanced countries to import—with a reversion of the pattern in the standardized phase. Finally, the theory predicts that less-developed countries import products, all the while increasing local production until they reach maturity and then start exporting (see Figure 9.9).

An important assumption in this theory is that developing economies—when their turn comes—export innovative products to even-less-developed countries (not back to advanced countries). This is well illustrated by the following extract:

> Despite the fact that so many MNCs have created producing networks all over the globe, the subsidiaries of such firms located in the developing countries have yet to acquire all of the products that their parents and affiliates produced in richer and larger markets. Most of the developing countries, therefore, are still in process of absorbing the innovations of other countries introduced earlier, according to patterns that remain reasonably consistent with product cycle expectations. [. . .] Firms operating in the more rapidly industrializing group—in countries such as Mexico, Brazil, India and Korea—are demonstrating a considerable capability for producing innovations that respond to the special conditions of their own economies. Once having responded to those special conditions with a new product or process [. . .], firms of that sort are in a position to initiate their own cycle of exportation and eventual direct investments; their target according to the hypothesis would be the markets of the other developing countries that were lagging a bit behind them in the industrialized pecking order.
>
> (Vernon, 1979, p. 266)

So to the question "Where was innovation diffusing from?" the answer is unequivocally: from developed economies. Figure 9.10 illustrates another important aspect of this theory, which is that foreign competition for innovative countries starts at the beginning of the mature phase of the product.

The prior quotation clearly states that developing countries could only aspire to innovate and diffuse their newer product toward lesser developed economies. The assumption was that to innovate, countries must have performant infrastructures, consumers with high purchasing power, and sophisticated expectations. Recent observations have started to seriously question this assumption (see "Food for Thought").

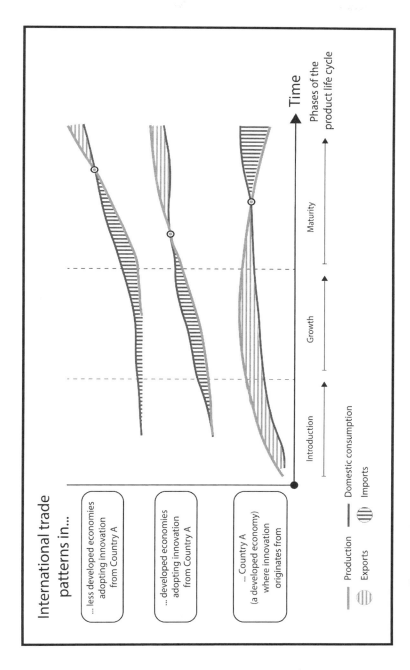

Figure 9.9 Illustrating the International Product Life Cycle (IPLC)
Source: Adapted from Vernon (1966, p. 199)

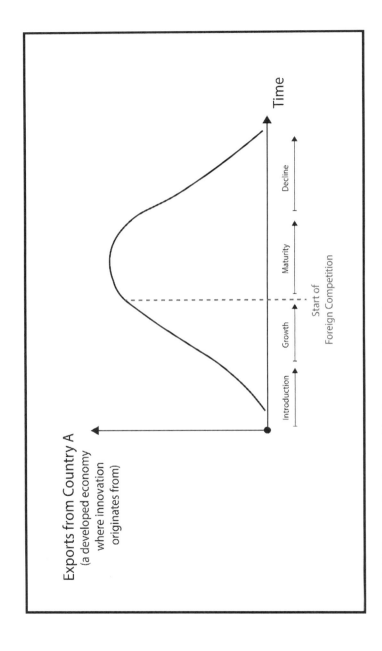

Figure 9.10 Representing the rise of foreign competition in the export cycle

Source: Adapted from Wells (1968, p. 3)

Food for Thought 9.1

*   In reference to Wells (1968) and Vernon (1979) on the one hand, and to Govindarajan and Ramamurti (2011) and Govindarajan and Trimble (2012) on the other hand, why is reverse innovation such a disruption?

9.2.2 Reverse Innovation (Govindarajan)

What is reverse innovation? *Reverse innovation* was proposed by Govindarajan and colleagues in the beginning of the 2010s as a way to capture a new phenomenon: innovations coming from emerging economies (e.g., China, India, and Brazil). Immelt, Govindarajan, and Trimble (2009) define reverse innovation or *trickle-up innovation* as an innovation seen first, or likely to be used first, in the developing world before spreading to the industrialized world. A general presentation of the article is available on YouTube with the search words: "Vijay Govindarajan: How GE Is Disrupting Itself." Figure 9.11 illustrates the idea of reverse innovation stemming from poor and developing economies and expanding into rich and developed economies, while the traditional view was presenting the reverse flow of innovation diffusion.

The topic of reverse innovation being still emergent in the marketing literature, the definition of the concept has not yet reached a consensus. Von Zedtwitz, Corsi, Soberg, and Frega (2015) focus on the location—in either developed or developing economies—of the concept ideation, product development, and first and secondary markets. Their typology include no fewer than sixteen different routes for global innovation flows, distinguishing *spillback innovation* from *cost/capacity innovation* or *reverse spillover*, *reverse product life cycle*, and more. Most importantly, they differentiate between "weak" and "strong" reverse innovation, depending on where the ideation of the product happens. In their view, having advanced economies as the secondary market is a marker of a strong reverse innovation.

Where can we see evidence of changing patterns in the diffusion of innovation? Figures 9.12 and 9.13 illustrate the evolution over time of two indicators proposed by the World Bank that can help us measure the extent to which innovation is possibly stemming from either developed or developing economies. First, we turn our attention to the degree of high-technology integrated in exported products, i.e., the ratio of high-technology exports over total manufactured exports. Looking at Japan and the US as representative examples of developed economies, we observe a high and rather stable ratio between 1992 and 2000 at around 25 percent and 35 percent, respectively, and a steady decline over time, down to about 17 percent and 19 percent in 2015. On the contrary, China provides an eloquent example for emerging economies with an increase from 6 percent in 1992 to 31 percent in 2005 (when it was at its peak), and a slight decrease in subsequent years

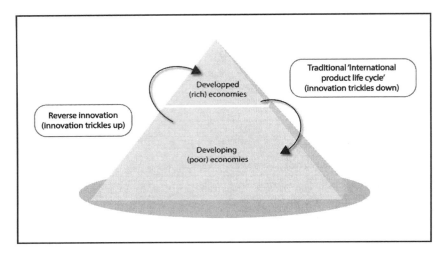

Figure 9.11 Illustrating the concept of reverse innovation
Source: Adapted from Govindarajan and Ramamurti (2011)

down to 26 percent in 2015 (World Bank, 2017a). This data, and much more of this nature, is easily retrievable using the World Bank "indicators," available on their website. Looking next at the number of patents applications by residents during the 1985–2014 period (last data available as of March 2017), the rise of China is tremendous compared to other countries, even traditionally innovative ones such as Japan and the US. Over this time frame, the number of patent applications in China rose from about 4,000 to 800,000. Both of these indicators are imperfect and might reflect the massive delocalization of production and outsourcing trend toward emerging economies (e.g., exported goods from China contain a lot of innovations designed elsewhere). Although the ownership of these high-tech goods remains in the hand of firms from developed economies, capabilities and facilities to produce them seem to have moved to developing countries. Thus, these indicators depict an interesting picture of profound changes which have occurred in the 2000–2010 decade, with new patterns of flows between developed and emerging economies that traditional theories did not forecast.

9.3 Corporate Examples and Counterexamples

The number of corporate examples of reverse innovation has been increasing in recent years but is far from being as high as in other practices studied in this book (e.g., mobile marketing and cause-related marketing). In addition, there is often a debate about whether the examples provided are actual cases of reverse innovation, an issue that Von Zedtwitz et al. (2015) framed as

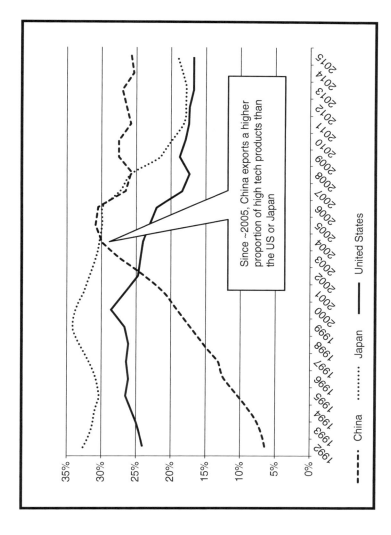

Figure 9.12 Comparing high-technology exports of China, Japan, and the US (1991–2015)
Source: World Bank (2017a)

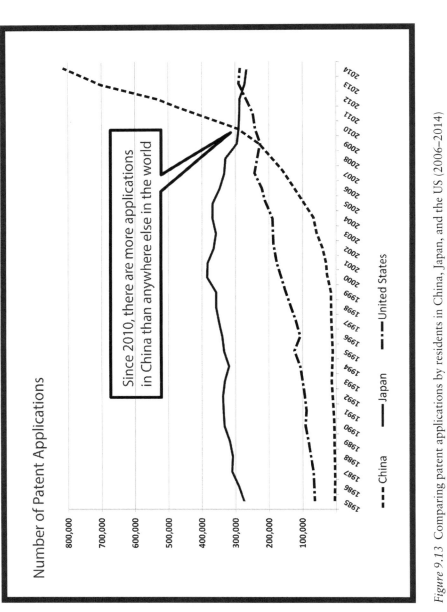

Figure 9.13 Comparing patent applications by residents in China, Japan, and the US (2006–2014)

Source: World Bank (2017b)

Reverse Innovation   355

"weak" or "strong" reverse innovation. Their topology of global innovation flows, with selected corporate examples, is presented in Table 9.2.

What are known examples of reverse innovation? Contrary to BOP marketing (Chapter 8), discussions about reverse innovation include different sizes of companies and different origins (from both developed and developing economies). This section examines several examples with a critical eye (see "Food for Thought").

Food for Thought 9.2

- Among the examples listed below (and others that you may have heard of), which are examples of "true" or "strong" reverse innovation? Are there any examples of failed attempts at reverse innovation?

9.3.1 Fiat

MultiAir technology[1]—Founded in 1899, FIAT (Fabbrica Italiana Automobili Torino) is one of Italy's most successful automobile manufacturers. It has merged with Chrysler (US) in 2014 to become Fiat Chrysler Automobiles (FCA). Among its many accomplishments, FIAT is recognized for its "Multi-Air System," a fuel technology for engines that maximizes power and torque and reduces gasoline consumption levels and CO_2 emissions.

This technology was developed in 2009 by its Brazilian subsidiary MM Cofap. Fiat had acquired Cofap in 1997 (one of the largest auto-parts producer in Latin America) for its products' excellent performance and unique engineering customer support. Incorporated in Magneti Marelli (MM), one of Fiat Group's companies specialized in high-tech systems and components for cars, MM Cofap soon became Fiat's favored supplier. Its Brazilian engineering team retained authority over the coordination of its R&D activities, a decision that reinforced the subsidiary's role as a center of excellence. The subsidiary designed a completely original system, drawing inspiration from Brazil's focus on fuel efficiency innovation. With this technology, Fiat went beyond adaptation as it engaged in the design of regional products based on global platforms, provided inputs related to local requirement and designed derivatives to suit local preferences. Among other examples, the subsidiary also developed a shock absorber technology in Brazil to suit the specific needs of consumers of developing countries with poor road quality, which was later implemented as part of its standard 500X package worldwide.

After being successfully tested and adopted in FIAT models sold in Brazil, the MultiAir technology was first integrated in the Alfa Romeo Mito (2009) for the EU market and in the Fiat 500 (2011) for the US market. As of 2017, the technology is present at the global scale in multiple models of various FCA brands (e.g., Alfa Romeo, Lancia, Dodge, and Jeep). The example of Fiat and its Brazilian subsidiary MM Cofap illustrates the importance of

Table 9.2 Differentiating among types of reverse innovation and corporate examples

Company	Innovative Product	Concept Ideation	Product Development	First Entry Market(s)	Subsequent Market(s)
Strong reverse innovation					
☐ Bosch	Impact screwdriver	Malaysia	Malaysia	Japan	Germany
☐ Fiat	Flexible-fuel vehicle	Brazil	Italy	Brazil	Europe
☐ General Electric	Electrocardiogram	India	India	India	US
☐ Nokia	Mass-market phones	Finland	China	China	Europe
☐ P&G	Vicks Honey Cough	Venezuela	Venezuela	Mexico	US/Europe
☐ Vestergaard	LifeStraw	Denmark	Vietnam	Africa/Asia	Europe/US
Weak reverse innovation					
☐ Eli Lilly	Oncovin	Madagascar	US	US	Africa
☐ Parmalat	Milk in a pouch	Italy	Italy	Colombia	Canada
☐ SAP	Hana In-Memory apps	Germany	China/India	US/Europe	China/India
Not reverse innovation					
☐ Grundfos	Lifelink	Denmark	Denmark	Kenya	Africa
☐ Imvubu Projects	Hippo Roller	South Africa	South Africa	South Africa	Africa
☐ JAC	Tojoy	China	Italy	China	Egypt/Syria
☐ PSA	Metropolis (DS9)	France	China	China	China
☐ Volkswagen	Santana	Germany	Germany	Germany	China
☐ Xechem	Nicosan	Nigeria	US	Nigeria	Africa

Source: Adapted from Von Zedtwitz et al. (2015, p. 20)

Reverse Innovation   357

the parent–subsidiary relationship, with good communication flow between them, as a key success factor in facilitating technology transfer and diffusing innovation from developing to worldwide markets.

9.3.2 General Electric

Mac 400 ECG machine[2]—Founded in 1892 in the US, General Electric (GE) is one of the largest companies in the world (see Table 9.3). It developed the Mac 400 EKG machine in India (2008) which was presented in a seminal article about reverse innovation by Immelt et al. (2009). ECG and EKG are two common abbreviations for "electrocardiograms," which are tests used to measure electrical activity and collect data on heart health. As ECGs are the most widely performed cardiac tests in the developed world, GE aimed to create a product that would also be suitable for the economic and infra-structural realities of India. Resulting from this effort, the Mac 400 ECG was designed as a lightweight, compact electro-cardiograph for 60 percent of its wholesale cost (~800 USD in India, as opposed to 2000–10,000 USD in US hospitals). It was first intended to be used for India's predominantly rural population. After its initial launch, the GE team kept innovating by downsizing the printer size and battery threshold to 500 ECG readings, making the cost of each test comparable to that of a bottle of water. Since its launch, the Mac 400 ECG has continued to be used across India and the rest of the world.

Figure 9.14 illustrates that, when "reversed," this product has been employed in different settings than when initially deployed in India. For instance, it equipped emergency medical teams in North America with quick diagnostic capability when encountering traffic accidents. The portability of this ECG machine has thus come as a breakthrough innovation in the developed world, stemming directly from needs found in rural India.

9.3.3 Narayana Health

Health City Cayman Islands[3]—The hospital chain Narayana Health (NH) was founded in India (2001) by Dr. Devi Shetty. Due to India's economic

Table 9.3 Profiling General Electric (US)

Who:	General Electric
Since:	1892
What:	Power, renewable energy, oil & gas, energy management, aviation, healthcare, transportation, appliances and lighting
From:	US
Revenues (Bn USD):	~124
Employing (people):	295,000
Manufacturing in (countries):	40
Selling in (countries):	180

Source: General Electric (2016)

358   *Reverse Innovation*

Figure 9.14 Illustrating the use of an ECG machine in developing vs. developed economic contexts

Source: Screen capture from YouTube videos available with search words: "MAC Series ECG Brings Cardiac Monitoring to Rural India and the World," posted by GE Healthcare, retrievable at www.YouTube.com/watch?v=TBjvCU9tdfQ; "Really Bad RV Accident with Car, Helicopter called," posted by Robert Brown, retrievable at www.YouTube.com/watch?v=oKe-WmesQJI

situation and large rural population (i.e., dispersed and difficult to reach), millions of people have no access to healthcare. Patients with access often have to pay more than 50 percent of their health care expenses themselves, or decline treatment entirely. In this challenging context, NH is dedicated to delivering high-quality healthcare services at the lowest cost. It does so with an innovative business model that has been extensively documented (e.g., a six-minute overview from a German television program, available on YouTube with search words: "Global 3000 Social Entrepreneurs").

Reverse Innovation   359

In summary, the hospital chain employs a hub-and-spoke configuration of assets, i.e., hospitals are established in urban hubs where they locate their best talent and equipment, while the spoke facilities are located in rural towns and villages. The business model relies on scale economies with a high volume of operations, as well as many practices leading to cost reductions, learning, and expertise. For instance, hospitals are characterized by construction practices and layouts that save a lot on energy consumption and a variety of costs (e.g., waiting areas located outside of buildings require less floor space; low rise buildings with prefabricated materials and metal sheet roofing reduce fire safety and elevator costs; the design of buildings is kept minimalist, with large windows to allow for natural ventilation and light, thereby reducing air conditioning and electricity costs; multiple Intensive Care Unit or ICU beds in an open-bay environment—as opposed to individual rooms—makes observation easier by fewer nurses; and finally, the use of ICT and mobile technology allows for tele-diagnosis and remote monitoring of patients (in particular at night). Management practices are also quite innovative. For instance, cross-subsidization allows for patients with higher incomes to finance procedures for lower-income patients (even performed for free, when necessary). Work practices include task-shifting (i.e., routine tasks are performed by less-experienced staff), multitasking (e.g., nurses perform duties of respiratory therapists), and the reuse of medical devices (e.g., steel clamps are sterilized before reuse).

NH expanded internationally with a first move to the Caribbean region, inaugurating Health City Cayman Islands in 2014. The target segments were both individuals from lower-income countries (Caribbean Islands and Central America) and individuals and companies (employers and insurance companies) in the broad region's high-income countries (Canada and the US). Indeed, the hospital in Cayman Islands offered shorter waiting times and far more affordable surgeries compared to standards in North America. Because it was positioned to attract customers from developed economies, it can be argued that the NH case represents a case of reverse innovation. As of March 2017, the World Bank's GNI per capita (Atlas Method) was not available but a GDP per capita of nearly 59,000 USD (United Nations, 2014) suggests that the population income is well above the 12,000 USD threshold of developed economies (see Chapter 7). In addition, the fact that customers from developed economies travel to benefit from the innovation reinforces the idea that the services provided by Health City Cayman Islands are diffusing in a reverse logic (from "South to North")—from a poor country like India to a richer country like Cayman Islands first, and perhaps to even richer countries later. Besides, the business model has started to be an inspiration in other countries, starting with the US. For instance, CareMore (a Southern California Medicare group) adopted the task-shifting approach; Iora Health clinics (in Las Vegas and Brooklyn) reformed their health care system by hiring athletic trainers and school teachers to aid patients in behavioural rehabilitation, allowing physicians to focus on diagnostic and medical treatment procedures; and Boston-based Steward Health Care has implemented a tele-ICU system in ten hospitals.

In terms of marketing decisions, pricing required particular attention when diffusing the innovative business model from "South to North." For

360 *Reverse Innovation*

instance, one of the routine cardiac surgeries performed, the Coronary Artery Bypass Graft (CABG), was priced 3,000 USD at NH Bangalore, whereas it was performed for 80,000–120,000 USD in US hospitals (the same procedure, with the same excellent standards of care and outcomes). How the CABG should be priced in Cayman Islands—considering the need to take into account differences in demand and competition, and to adapt the business model to geographic, administrative, cultural, economic, and technological conditions—had thus been a crucial decision. Too high (e.g., 70,000 USD), and NH could lose sight of its corporate philosophy and a competitive positioning compared to other medical tourism destinations in the region (e.g., Costa Rica and Colombia). Too low (e.g., 10,000 USD), and it would risk sending the wrong signal in terms of quality for the wealthy target segment, among other risk factors. The first year of operation for Health City Cayman Islands confirmed that setting the right price for a reverse innovation was difficult, as the hospital struggled with pricing adjustments.

9.3.4 Harman

The Saras and Nalanda platforms[4]—Harman (US) develops navigation telematics, infotainment, and multimedia equipment for the car industry (see Table 9.4). In 2009, the company's R&D center located in India developed two cost-effective platforms, called Saras and Nalanda. The company explained that a 30–40 percent price reduction was achieved for Saras through smarter ways of developing the software and hardware, greater integration and scaling down some features (e.g., from 3D to 2D). What also allowed Harman to circumvent traditional processes and innovate was having local teams generate radical change from below and the CEO implement companywide changes from above, at the same time.

Harman's products are now integrated into the most sophisticated cars, including the "connected car," such as the Rinspeed Σtos concept (demonstration available on YouTube with search words: "The Rinspeed Etos—The

Table 9.4 Profiling Harman (US)

Who:	Harman International Industries
Since:	1980
What:	Augmented navigation, telematics, infotainment, multimedia, safety and security systems for the car industry; infotainment, audio, lighting, video switching and control systems for the entertainment and enterprise markets
From:	US
Revenues (Bn USD):	6.2
Employing (people):	25,000
Manufacturing in (countries):	10
Selling in (countries):	N/A

Source: Harman (2015)

First Car with Its Own Drone?"), presented at the 2016 Consumer Electronics Show in Las Vegas (US). Other YouTube videos are available in which similar applications are highlighted in what appears to be one of the most significant and latest innovations for cars (e.g., "HARMAN Infotainment: A Seamless Experience," and "HARMAN next-generation scalable Infotainment Platform").

The example of Harman's Saras and Nalanda platforms illustrates a B2B setting where innovation is "reversed" in developed economies, perhaps more easily than if it were in a B2C setting. Indeed, final customers (here, car buyers) are not always aware of the provenance of the many technological components found in the product they purchase. Beyond awareness, they might simply not care about the origin of components because they trust the car manufacturer's brand. Nevertheless, products—and especially high technology ones—originated from the developing world are likely to suffer from a negative "country-of-origin effect" (see Chapter 11). Even though industrial purchasers are also exposed to this effect and may be suspicious at first of innovations coming from countries they see as "less developed" than their own, they are more knowledgeable and educated technically. With time, the superior ability to compare on facts rather than solely on perceptions could lead to a higher acceptance of reverse innovation by industrial buyers than by final customers. Furthermore, the integration of innovative products coming from emerging economies into the offerings of well-established brands from the developed world could act overtime as a "seal of approval," and thus contribute to slowly changing perceptions of final customers and greatly facilitating the reversal of innovation flows.

9.3.5 Tata Group

The Nano car[5]—A controversial example of reverse innovation is the Nano, developed in India (2008) by Tata Motors, a member of the Tata Group, which is one of the world's largest conglomerates (see Table 9.5). Tata Motors has been manufacturing passenger vehicles since the 1990s and reached a net revenue of nearly 43 billion USD in 2016 while employing more than 76,500 people.

Table 9.5 Profiling Tata Group (India)

Who:	*Tata Group*
Since:	1868
What:	Steel, motors, consultancy services, power, chemicals, global beverages, teleservices, branded watches, jewelry and eyewear, communications and hotels
From:	India
Revenues (Bn USD):	103
Employing (people):	661,000
Operations in (countries):	100
Selling in (countries):	150

Source: Tata Group (2016)

362 *Reverse Innovation*

Ratan Tata, chairman of the group from 1991 to 2012 (and then for an interim term in 2016), considered improving safety conditions on Indian roads an important project. Indeed, the sight of a family of four riding on a motorbike is very common, with babies often seen bouncing on the knees of sari-clad women sitting side-saddle behind the driver. Added to the danger, the discomfort of such a transportation mode (because of rain, dust, exhaust fumes from other vehicles, and so on) made a strong case for people to switch and adopt a family car. Due to economic conditions, this would only become possible with a car significantly cheaper than the alternative options. This was the promise held by the Nano, initially positioned as "the world's cheapest car." Indeed, the basic model could sell for a little less than a three-wheel auto-rickshaw, and not much more than many motorbikes sold in India. Informative videos available on YouTube include a documentary by the National Geographic (search keywords: "Megafactories Tata Nano") and the presentation of the car version released in 2015, the TATA Nano GenX AMT (search keywords "2015 TATA Nano GenX AMT—First Drive Review").

From the start in 2008, the low price strategy was made possible by an intense effort in frugal innovation. Among the three models initially launched, the basic model included a tiny 624cc engine capable of a top speed of just over 95 kilometers (~60 miles) per hour. This engine was positioned in the back of the car, making it trunkless. It had no air-conditioning, power-steering, or automatic windows, and featured only one windscreen wiper and side mirror. Tires were also smaller, and less steel than average was used in the car's construction. Costs were also reduced because some parts were designed to have two functions instead of just one (e.g., the seat rails acted as side impact protection bars). Finally, low-cost Indian labor played a central role in keeping the Nano price as minimal as possible. In 2009, assembly line workers at the Nano plant earned about 215 USD on average per month, a salary that was fair by Indian standards.

Foreign expansion into Europe was planned for 2011 with the Europa Nano, a model upgraded to meet higher expectations of customers in terms of comfort (e.g., climate control and infotainment system) and tougher safety and environmental standards. The publicized price point was 2,000 euros (~2,200 USD), making it by far the cheapest car on the market. The launch was first delayed to 2015 and then cut short when the car failed to pass crash tests in Germany or the essential UN safety requirements.

As of 2017, the Nano cannot be considered an example of reverse innovation, since it did not penetrate markets in developed economies. It is even considered by many as a definitive failure in its home market. Beyond the initial technical hurdles (e.g., the car was catching fire), the positioning of the Nano as "the cheapest car" did not attract customers. It appears that even low-income customers have aspirational motives when considering purchasing a car. Furthermore, the low price could only be reached with massive economies of scale, and for this, the company targeted a minimum production of 250,000 units per year. Between October 2015 and September 2016, sales were only about 14,000 cars, largely missing the target. The profitability and, hence, the viability of the Nano car are definitely questioned.

So, why talk about the Nano in the context of reverse innovation? Because this example shows us that it could have happened. An Indian-made car attempted to penetrate the European market, an enterprise that was hard to imagine ten years back. Furthermore, it may still happen if the vision of leaders such as Ratan Tata prevail and if administrative distance gives leeway to the interest of poorer customers. With the Nano case, it is actually quite interesting to ponder the extent to which these administrative barriers set in developed economies (e.g., safety and environmental regulations) protect customers or protect car manufacturers from competition coming from the "less developed" world.

9.3.6 Hippo Roller

The Hippo Roller—The Hippo Roller was developed in the mid-1990s by a medium-sized company from South Africa to facilitate water transportation (see a video presentation on YouTube with search words: "GOOD:Hippo Rollers" published by *GOOD* Magazine). Indeed, people in Africa—and particularly women—spend significant time every day fetching the water their families need to drink, cook, and clean. Carrying large buckets on their heads over long distances is not only a time-consuming and difficult task, it is also a daily activity that regularly results in long-term health consequences (e.g., neck and spine injuries). The Hippo Roller offers a safe and practical solution, with a simple mechanism to roll a barrel (carrying five times more water than a simple bucket) along the ground while walking. Several You-Tube videos (search words: "hippo roller") show the product in use. This innovation has been distributed to more than twenty countries. Nevertheless, Von Zedtwitz et al. (2015) did not classify it as reverse innovation since it is found solely in developing economies, particularly in African countries. Because water access is usually not an issue in developed economies, the need for this product does not exist. Yet, the question remains whether the product could be used by different market segments or if it could be sold for an entirely different use. Indeed, the commercialization of Verstergaard's Lifestraw in developed economies—presented next—shows that rethinking targeting and positioning can be key to successfully "inverting" the innovation flow from poor to rich countries.

9.3.7 Vestergaard

LifeStraw[6]—A company that few have heard about is Vestergaard (Switzerland), a SME with many activities surrounding humanitarian help (see Table 9.6). It commercializes its products in Africa, Europe, and North and Central America, as well as in many countries in South America and Asia, and has offices in India, Kenya, Switzerland, the US, and Vietnam.

Among its activities, Vestergaard has developed a technology for purifying drinking water in Kenya (from 1996 to 2005) and incorporated it into a line of products (see Figure 9.15). Drinkable water is a central issue across the world, as an estimated 0.8 to 1 billion people do not have access to clean water sources and 1.5 million children die every year because of the resulting

364 *Reverse Innovation*

Table 9.6 Profiling Vestergaard (Switzerland) in 2015

Who:	*Vestergaard*
Since:	1957
What:	Initially a manufacturer of uniforms for workmen. As of 2007, the company has focused solely on humanitarian products: PermaNet® (insecticide-treated bed net); LifeStraw® (water cleaning technology); ZeroFly® (defence against insect pests for livestock and crop protection; and CarePack® (health interventions targeting AIDS programs, prevention campaigns, and maternal health, among other initiatives)
From:	Initially from Denmark and now incorporated in Switzerland
Sales (Bn USD):	0.25
Employing (people):	170
Manufacturing in (countries):	5
Selling in (countries):	150

Sources: Devex Impact (2016); Vestergaard (2017a)

diarrhea. The technology has been incorporated into a basic straw (the LifeStraw) and into equivalent products of different sizes, including family and community sizes. It is also embedded in a carry-on bottle (the LifeStraw Go). It removes 99.9999 percent of water-borne bacteria, as well as many other parasites (e.g., E-coli and salmonella).

This is an interesting example of reverse innovation due to the adaptation of the targeting and positioning strategy when repatriating the technology developed in Kenya into developed economies. While the company targets consumers with survival objectives in developing economies, it targets hikers and campers for leisure and recreational purposes in rich countries, with the same technology. YouTube videos illustrate the very different positioning of the product according to customers' location, whether in developing economies (e.g., with search words: "LifeStraw" published by Global Issues Summit Africa) or developed economies (e.g., with search words: "The LifeStraw—Can you REALLY trust it?" published by Backpacking Bananas). Accordingly, distribution and pricing of the product are also vastly adapted. In developing economies, it is often sold to NGOs and governments that in turn grant free access to their final consumers, who are usually in poverty. In developed economies, the product can be found in typical outlets for outdoor sports (e.g., Decathlon in France and Mountain Equipment Coop in Canada), or online retailers like Amazon, for about 35 USD.

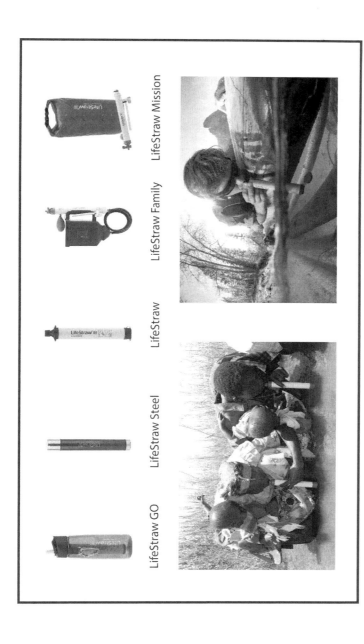

Figure 9.15 Presenting the LifeStraw line of products and different uses in developing and developed contexts

Sources: Vestergaard (2016); Screen captures from YouTube videos available with search words: "LifeStraw," posted by Global Issues Summit Africa, retrievable at www.YouTube.com/watch?v=HoH2STgvEbc; " The LifeStraw® Personal Water Filter," posted by EartheasyTV, retrievable at www.YouTube.com/watch?v=i82YD7uvi2s.

366   *Reverse Innovation*

9.4 Issues at Stake

We conclude this chapter by presenting three main issues related to the origin of innovation and its international diffusion, the feasibility of reverse innovation (key success factors) and its actual outcomes. Questions covered are:

- Is reverse innovation such a disruption in the way we conceptualize innovation diffusion? Is there a common point between the two visions of innovation diffusion internationally?
- What are the key success factors for reverse innovation and what are its implications for marketing decisions?
- What are the actual outcomes of reverse innovation: positive or negative?
- When it comes to new products and business models, are there any other major trends aside from reverse innovation that represent a challenge for marketers?

For starters, can you form an opinion about the relevance of reverse innovation for companies (see "Food for Thought")?

Food for Thought 9.3 & 9.4

- Should companies develop new products/services from developing economies to sell worldwide?
- In your opinion, does reverse innovation allow firms to better face globalization and its consequences?

9.4.1 Origin of Innovation and International Diffusion

Is reverse innovation such a disruption in the way we conceptualize innovation diffusion? Is there a common point between the two visions of innovation diffusion internationally? The literature has yet to further establish commonalities between the two visions of how innovation diffuses internationally, and how reverse innovation relates to globalization. For instance, Govindarajan and Trimble (2012) present reverse innovation as a subsequent step to globalization, as illustrated in Figure 9.16.

As discussed in Chapter 1, the idea that corporations sell "the same things in the same way everywhere" (Levitt, 1983, p. 92) captures what globalization entails. In turn, the "think global, act local" lemma supports the notion of glocalization. Both steps mean implicitly that innovation stems from developed economies and that the way to expand abroad is to take these same products and decide to either standardize them or adapt them to some degree. Govindarajan and Trimble (2012) explain that reverse innovation is different in that products are designed locally for emerging economies and are really built starting from the unique needs in these countries. Then, innovation diffuses back to developed economies. However, the opposition is not so clear between the concepts of globalization/glocalization and reverse

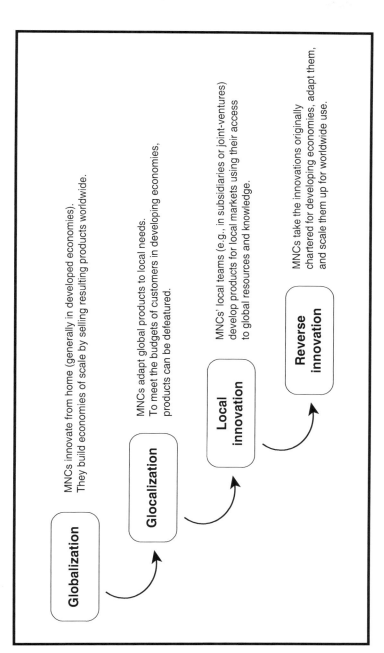

Figure 9.16 Highlighting linkages between globalization and reverse innovation

Source: Adapted from Govindarajan and Trimble (2012)

368   Reverse Innovation

innovation. Although the direction of innovation diffusion is clearly contrary, there is one important commonality. Either traditional or reversed, innovation diffusion first happens in similar markets before going to more "distant" markets, either downward or upward (in terms of economic development of countries). In a way, the concept of distance (or proximity) is central to explaining international innovation diffusion.

9.4.2 Impact on Marketing Decisions and Feasibility

What is the impact of reverse innovation on marketing activities? Reverse innovation has direct links to international product policies, yet such an approach obviously forces companies to equally revise their marketing strategies; for example, market selection and entry modes, targeting and positioning. Von Zedtwitz et al. (2015) show the importance of the location of the four steps of innovation (i.e., ideation, product development, product launch, and diffusion) in defining the nature of innovation (i.e., whether or not it is a traditional or reverse innovation). Therefore, different markets will be selected in sequence, starting with developing markets and then moving to developed markets. Entry modes will also be affected, since foreign investment is recommended in order to innovate far away from developed home markets. Acquisitions have been used as a preferred entry mode to quickly acquire local knowledge. Finally, targeting and positioning is a central question at the moment of repatriating the innovation from developing to developed economies. In terms of the tactical marketing, the product and brand management are obviously affected, as well as price, communication, and promotion when it comes to taking the product back to more developed economies, especially because of a possible negative effect of origin. It is not clear, however, if distribution management is affected by reverse innovation, more research is needed in this regard.

What are the key success factors of reverse innovation? For firms adopting reverse innovation, a key success factor revolves around their organizational structure. Indeed, relations between headquarters and subsidiaries need to allow sufficient autonomy to subsidiaries in developing innovative ideas and products. The support of headquarters to later diffuse the resulting products worldwide is then needed. The entry mode is also important since the quality of partnerships with local actors will determine success. Finally, a central question about products is that it has to be an actual innovation (with the following characteristics: performance, durability, perceived usefulness, and ease of use). The effect of origin is important to consider in the sense that the innovation should benefit from a coherent product-country image that will not constitute a barrier at the moment of exporting or repatriating the innovation in developed economies.

9.4.3 Outcomes

In terms of outcomes, is reverse innovation only positive?[7] For MNCs headquartered in developed countries, reverse innovation generally brings positive outcomes, associated with the opening of new markets in developing countries. However, positive effects are not guaranteed, since it can represent disruptive innovation that cannibalizes existing products already sold in developed countries. Thus, MNCs have to pay great attention to the business model associated with reverse innovation and reconsider targeting and positioning. A successful example is the Logan car produced by French company Renault. First produced in Romania (under the Dacia brand) in 2004 for local consumers, it was later commercialized abroad in many other emerging countries and then reached the most developed countries of Europe by disrupting the used-car market. Wealthy consumers preferred buying a cheap and robust new Logan as a second car, instead of buying a used car. In this way, the success of the Logan did not cannibalize the other new Renault models (Jullien, Lung, & Midler, 2013).

When "repatriating" an innovation from a developing economy into developed economies, targeting and positioning should be carefully reconsidered but not necessarily adapted. Often, reverse innovation offers affordable products to the lower-income classes and poorest regions in developed economies. With increasing income inequalities, the lowest categories of income in rich countries can indeed be under the level of the highest income categories in developing countries. Paying attention to income distribution reminds us of the existence of a BOP market (see Chapter 8) in the richest countries.

For MNEs headquartered in developing countries (e.g., Tata Group), reverse innovation is generally positive and contributes to building domestic capabilities as a more likely vehicle toward prosperity and poverty reduction. For the local population in emerging markets, reverse innovation may help in solving social problems. However, despite some identified benefits, there is no clear evidence that reverse innovation results in large-scale prosperity and poverty reduction (Radojevic, 2015). Reverse innovation is by no means synonymous with corporate social responsibility.

When it comes to new products and business models, are there any other major trends, aside from reverse innovation, that represent a challenge for marketers? Reverse innovation is a disruptive trend that has been observed during the past few years but it is only one facet of a tremendous change in the way new product development is occurring nowadays. Many more innovations in terms of products and business models are to come. Open innovation and peer-to-peer (P2P) business models are appearing, often with little insight on how to market the resulting products. Indeed, they are produced in an open-source setting by people who are distributed all around the world, and more importantly who are not bound legally by the structure of a formal organization. The P2P Foundation offers interesting resources that give a better idea of what P2P business models are all about. Some of the resulting products are extremely performant (e.g., the Wikispeed car that consumes only 2L/100 km of petroleum fuel), even though the issue of large-scale production has not yet been solved for most of them. Another hint at the disruption to come is the Bitcoin, which seriously questions traditional pricing and payment methods. A large number of questions remain unanswered when it comes to marketing the products resulting from such initiatives. For instance, how do we fix a price tag and reward people internally for the value created? How do we organize for distribution and promotion? Finally, the takeaway

370   *Reverse Innovation*

here is that with reverse innovation and open innovation, new product development is under considerable change. Production managers are already well aware of this change. As marketers, we are only starting to see the challenges ahead, at both the strategic and tactical levels of marketing.

Conclusion: Companies Should Develop New Offerings from Developing Economies to Then Sell Worldwide (i.e., Undertake Reverse Innovation) to Overcome a Negative Eco-Techno Distance and Enhance Competitiveness, But They Should Be Aware That It Can Also Bring Disruption in Developed Markets

What would a nomological network for reverse innovation look like? A *nomological network* has been defined as the representation of the constructs of interest in a study, their observable manifestations and the interrelationships among and between them (Cronbach & Meehl, 1955). Figure 9.17 aims to encapsulate important variables in relation to the adoption of reverse innovation by companies.

First, it underlines the three main issues raised in the chapter about: 1) the actual origin of innovation and whether it has really been "reversed"; 2) the feasibility of reverse innovation (in order to be successful, companies need to pay specific attention to the following key factors: a relationship between their headquarters and local subsidiaries which offer support and autonomy, an adequate entry mode through FDI that allows for strong partnerships with local actors; and a truly performant innovation that is not stigmatized by an unfavorable product-country image); and finally, 3) the actual outcomes of reverse innovation (with questions raised in regards to the potential for increased competitiveness or for disruption due to competition from low-cost economies in developed markets and the cannibalization of existing offerings).

Next, the figure shows that reverse innovation is not only a market-seeking activity (one of the four main motivations for firms to go abroad, discussed in Chapter 2) but is also a strong strategic-asset seeking opportunity for firms from developed countries (with the acquisition of new technologies and products/services). For firms from developing countries, it represents mainly a market-seeking activity. Among other causes explaining whether companies undertake reverse innovation or not is the notion of distance. Unlike for BOP marketing, distance plays a less ambivalent role and is mainly a barrier to the successful adoption of reverse innovation. The existence of economic and technological distance between developing and developed economies makes it difficult for firms to develop truly innovative products that respond to unsatisfied needs in developed markets. Furthermore, we have seen corporate examples (e.g., the failure of the Tata Nano to penetrate European markets) where regulations and local standards (i.e., administrative distance) prevented the reversal of innovations for which the demand was potentially strong. Psychic distance should also be accounted for since preconceptions often impede managers' ability, in developed economies, to believe in the potential of developing economies as sources of innovation for the world.

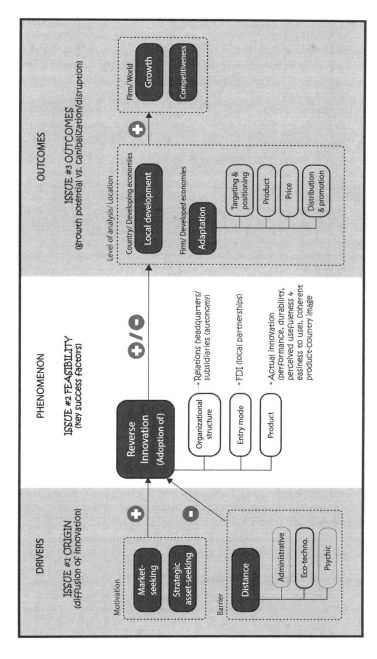

Figure 9.17 Proposing a nomological network for reverse innovation

Source: Own elaboration

372   *Reverse Innovation*

Finally, the figure illustrates that the consequences of reverse innovation, although mainly positive, can also be ambivalent. At the level of analysis of the country from where the innovation originates, there are reasons to believe that this practice is favorable to local development (e.g., through FDI, foreign firms develop capacities with the employment and training of local people who get exposed to new knowledge, ideas, and skills). Yet, questions remain about the extent to which the presence of large foreign MNCs impedes the growth of local entrepreneurs. At the level of the firm and in the context of developed economies, adopting reverse innovation requires rethinking most aspects of marketing, from redefining the target segments of the population and the desired positioning (e.g., the extent to which the country of origin of the innovation is put forward), to adapting the offering (product or service), its price, distribution and promotion. The costs and challenges associated with readapting the innovation are seen as problematic. In many cases, firms need to pay specific attention to avoid cannibalizing their existing offerings with a "better and cheaper" product. For this, a different branding is often recommended. In summary, a successful implementation of reverse innovation—for firms from either developed or developing economies—contributes to significant growth and global competitiveness but bears the risk of creating disruption once repatriated in developed markets.

So, should companies develop new offerings from developing countries in order to sell them worldwide? In other words, should companies undertake reverse innovation? The answer to this question is a tentative "Why not, if . . .," and the conditions are key: reverse innovation can be highly beneficial if companies can develop a true innovation with a marked competitive advantage and carefully revisit their marketing strategies and tactics before bringing back the innovation in developed markets. It is a market- and strategic asset-seeking opportunity from which companies from developed economies should not shy away. In their own quest for internationalization, firms from emerging and developing economies will certainly not. As economic distance within countries also increases (see Chapter 7), the common belief that consumers from "rich countries" would never adopt products developed "for the poor" is slowly starting to erode. Psychic distance, and perhaps more importantly administrative distance, might keep firms from the developing world at bay for a few years longer, but the mechanisms of globalization (i.e., integration and convergence) are likely to continue paving the way for the worldwide adoption of new offerings from developing countries. Like BOP marketing, reverse innovation thus **provides a solution to overcome a "negatively charged" eco-techno distance** (see Chapter 7).

Notes

1   The example of Fiat's MultiAir technology relies on: Athreye, Tuncay-Celikel, and Ujjual (2014); Costa, Bruno, Vasconcellos, and Da Silveira (2015); FCA (2014); Schmidt (2011); WardsAuto (2011)
2   General Electric's Mac 400 ECG machine example is based on: Forbes (2017); General Electric (2011); Immelt et al. (2009)
3   The Narayana Health initiative with Health City Cayman Islands is based on: Govindarajan and Ramamurti (2013); HBS 9–505–078 (2011); HBS 9–712–402 (2012); HBS 9–714–510 (2016)

4 The example of Harman's Saras and Nalanda platforms relies on: Govindarajan (2012); Harman (2012)
5 The example of Tata's Nano car is based on: Autocar India (2016); Green Car Reports (2012); Reuters (2016); Tata Group (2016); Tata Motors (2016); The Guardian (2014a, 2014b); The Telegraph (2009)
6 The example of Vestergaard's LifeStraw relies on: Daily Mail (2016); Devex Impact (2016); New York Times (2011); Vestergaard (2016, 2017a, 2017b)
7 In Section 9.4.3, the paragraph entitled "In terms of outcomes, is reverse innovation only positive?" has been written in collaboration with Patrick Cohendet, Professor in International Business Management (HEC Montréal, Canada), whose research interests include the economics of knowledge, knowledge and innovation management, as well as the management of technological transfers.

References

Athreye, Suma, Tuncay-Celikel, Asli & Ujjual, Vandana (2014). Internationalisation of R&D into Emerging Markets: Fiat's R&D in Brazil, Turkey and India. *Long Range Planning, 47*(1–2), 100–114.

Autocar India (2016, October 27th). Does the Tata Nano Have a Future? *By Hormazd Sorabjee* Retrieved from www.autocarindia.com/auto-news/does-the-tata-nano-have-a-future-403375.aspx

Caswell, Julie, Noelke, Corinna & Mojduszka, Eliza (2002). Unifying Two Frameworks for Analyzing Quality and Quality Assurance for Food Products. In *Global Food Trade and Consumer Demand for Quality*, Barry Krissoff, Mary Bohman, and Julie Caswell (Editors). Boston: Springer (p. 43–61).

Cateora, Philip, Gilly, Mary & Graham, John (2011). *International Marketing* (2nd ed.). New York: McGraw-Hill/Irwin (p. 742).

Cateora, Philip, Gilly, Mary, Graham, John & Money, Bruce (2016). *International Marketing* (17th ed.). New York: McGrawn-Hill/Irwin (p. 704).

Costa, Renato Machado, Bruno, Marcos, Vasconcellos, Eduardo & Da Silveira, Luiz (2015). MNC's Subsidiaries in Emerging Countries Driving Internationalization and Innovation: A Case Study in Brazil. *International Journal of Automotive Technology and Management, 15*(4), 381–400.

Cronbach, Lee Joseph & Meehl, Paul (1955). Construct Validity in Psychological Tests. *Psychological Bulletin, 52*(4), 281–302.

Daily Mail (2016, May 9th). Would YOU Drink from a Puddle? $20 LifeStraw Lets You Sip Safely from Dirty Water—and It's Saving Millions of Lives, *By Sarah Griffiths for MailOnline*. Retrieved from www.dailymail.co.uk/sciencetech/article-3580985/Gasping-drink-20-LifeStraw-lets-drink-safely-murkiest-pools-hiking-saving-millions-lives.html#ixzz4klCcB9KL

Devex Impact (2016). How a Textile Company Became a Development Powerhouse. Retrieved June 2016, from www.devex.com/news/how-a-textile-company-became-a-development-powerhouse-87556

FCA (2014). The Group History. Fiat Chrysler Automobiles. Retrieved June 2017, from www.fcagroup.com/en-US/group/history/Pages/default.aspx

Forbes (2017). The World's Biggest Companies. Retrieved June 2017, from www.forbes.com/companies/general-electric

General Electric (2011). Market-Relevant Design: Making ECGs Available Across India. Retrieved June 2017, from http://newsroom.gehealthcare.com/ecgs-india-reverse-innovation/

374 *Reverse Innovation*

General Electric (2016). Annual Report—Leading a Digital Industrial Era. 264. www.ge.com/ar2016/downloads

Govindarajan, Vijay (2012). A Reverse-Innovation Playbook. *Harvard Business Review*, 90(4), 120–124.

Govindarajan, Vijay & Ramamurti, Ravi (2011). Reverse Innovation, Emerging Markets, and Global Strategy. *Global Strategy Journal*, 1(3–4), 191–205.

Govindarajan, Vijay & Ramamurti, Ravi (2013). Delivering World-Class Health Care, Affordably. *Harvard Business Review*, 91(11), 117–122.

Govindarajan, Vijay & Trimble, Chris (2012). *Reverse Innovation: Create Far From Home, Win Everywhere*. Boston: Harvard Business Review Press (p. 229).

Green Car Reports (2012, October 16th). Tata Nano Hits U.S. & Europe by 2015: How Will It Look? *By Richard Read*. Retrieved from www.greencarreports.com/news/1079856_tata-nano-hits-u-s-europe-by-2015-how-will-it-look

The Guardian (2014a, January 31st). Tata Nano Safety Under Scrutiny After Dire Crash Test Results, *By Philip Oltermann*. Retrieved from www.theguardian.com/global-development/2014/jan/31/tata-nano-safety-crash-test-results

The Guardian (2014b, February 3rd). Tata Nano: The Car That Was Just Too Cheap, *By Vanessa Able*. Retrieved from www.theguardian.com/commentisfree/2014/feb/03/tata-nano-car-cheap-poor-safety-rating

Harman (2012). Indian R&R Centre Has Come to Develop Two Cost-Effective Platforms—Saras and Nalanda. Retrieved June 2017, from www.harman.in/about-us/innovation/innovation-stories-2/cost-effective-platform/

Harman (2015). Harman International Industries Incorporated. Retrieved from http://investor.harman.com/secfiling.cfm?filingid=1193125-13-329239&cik=

HBS 9–505–078 (2011). *Narayana Hrudayalaya Heart Hospital: Cardiac Care for the Poor (A)*. Case written by: Tarun Khann, Kasturi Rangan and Merlina Manocaran. Boston: Harvard Business School (p. 24).

HBS 9–712–402 (2012). *Narayana Hrudayalaya Heart Hospital: Cardiac Care for the Poor (B)*. Case written by: Tarun Khann and Tanya Bijlani. Boston: Harvard Business School (p. 6).

HBS 9–714–510 (2016). *Health City Cayman Islands*. Case written by: Tarun Khanna and Budhaditya Gupta. Boston: Harvard Business School (p. 19).

Immelt, Jeffrey, Govindarajan, Vijay & Trimble, Chris (2009). How GE Is Disrupting Itself. *Harvard Business Review*, 87(10), 56–65.

Jullien, Bernard, Lung, Yannick & Midler, Christophe (2013). *The Logan Epic: New Trajectories for Innovation*. Paris, France: Dunod (p. 288).

Keegan, Warren & Green, Mark (2016). *Global Marketing* (9th ed.). New Jersey: Pearson (p. 624).

Kotler, Philip & Keller, Kevin (2016). *A Framework for Marketing Management* (6th ed.). London: Pearson (p. 352).

Levitt, Theodore (1983). The Globalization of Markets. *Harvard Business Review*, 61(3), 92–102.

New York Times (2011, September 26th). LifeStraw Saves Those Without Access to Clean Drinking Water, *By Jascha Hoffman*. Retrieved from www.nytimes.com/2011/09/27/health/27straw.html

Olson, Jerry (1972). *Cue Utilization in the Quality Perception Process: A Cognitive Model and an Empirical Test*. (Doctoral dissertation), Purdue University (US).

Radojevic, Nebojsa (2015). *Essays on Reverse Innovation*. (Doctoral dissertation), International Business Management—HEC Montréal, Montréal (Canada).

Rafiq, Mohammed & Pervaiz, Ahmed (1995). Using the 7Ps as a Generic Marketing-mix: An Exploratory Survey of UK and European Marketing Academics. *Marketing Intelligence & Planning*, 13(9), 4–15.

Reuters (2016, November 5th). India's Tata Motors Defends Strategy for $1500 Nano Car, *By Sankalp Phartiyal and Aditi Shah*. Retrieved from www.reuters.com/article/us-tata-sons-management-nano-idUSKBN13006Q

Richardson, Paul, Dick, Alan & Jain, Arun (1994). Extrinsic and Intrinsic Cue Effects on Perceptions of Store Brand Quality. *Journal of Marketing*, 58(4), 28–36.

Rogers, Everett (1983). *Diffusion of Innovations* (3rd ed.). New York: Free Press (p. 453).

Rogers, Everett (2003). *The Diffusion of Innovations* (5th ed.). New York: Free Press (p. 576).

Schmidt, David (2011). Chrysler Brings MultiAir to North America. Chrysler Group LCC 28. Retrieved from www.ukintpress-conferences.com/uploads/SPEXNA11/Day1_7_David_Schmidt.pdf

Tata Group (2016). Tata Leadership with Trust—Group Overview. Retrieved from www.tata.com/pdf/Tata_Group_presentation.pdf

Tata Motors (2016). Annual Report—Toward Tomorrow. Retrieved from www.tatamotors.com/investors/financials/71-ar-flipbook/files/assets/basic-html/page-1.html

The Telegraph (2009, March 23rd). Tata Nano, World's Cheapest Car, Launched in India, *By Dean Nelson*. Retrieved from www.telegraph.co.uk/news/worldnews/asia/india/5039397/Tata-Nano-worlds-cheapest-car-launched-in-India.html

United Nations (2014). Country Profile: Cayman Islands. Retrieved March 2017, from http://data.un.org/CountryProfile.aspx?crName=Cayman%20Islands

Vernon, Raymond (1966). International Investment and International Trade in the Product Cycle. *The Quarterly Journal of Economics*, 80(2), 190–207.

Vernon, Raymond (1979). The Product Cycle Hypothesis in a New International Environment. *Oxford Bulleting of Economics and Statistics*, 41(4), 255–267.

Vestergaard (2016). LifeStraw. Retrieved May 2017, from www.vestergaard.com/our-products/lifestraw

Vestergaard (2017a). About Us. Retrieved June 2017, from www.vestergaard.com/about-us

Vestergaard (2017b). Where We Work. Retrieved June 2017, from www.vestergaard.com/where-we-work

Von Zedtwitz, Max, Corsi, Simone, Soberg, Peder & Frega, Romeo (2015). A Typology of Reverse Innovation. *The Journal of Product Innovation Management*, 32(1), 12–28.

WardsAuto (2011). Schaeffler Expects Other Takers for MultiAir Technology. By David Zoia. Retrieved April 2017, from http://wardsauto.com/news-analysis/schaeffler-expects-other-takers-multiair-technology

Wells, Louis (1968). A Product Life Cycle for International Trade? *Journal of Marketing*, 32(3), 1–6.

World Bank (2017a). High-Technology Exports (% of Manufactured Exports). Retrieved March 2017, from http://databank.worldbank.org/data/reports.aspx?source=2&type=metadata&series=TX.VAL.TECH.MF.ZS#

World Bank (2017b). Number of Patent Applications by Residents (1985–2014). Retrieved March 2017, from http://data.worldbank.org/indicator/IP.PAT.RESD/countries/US-IN-CN-BR-RU-JP?display=graph

10 Mobile Marketing

Table of Contents

10 Mobile Marketing

Introduction: Should Companies Reach Consumers
Wherever and Whenever? 378
    10.1   *Background Information*..378
          10.1.1   International Distribution Policies................380
          10.1.2   Online Distribution and Promotion..............384
    10.2   *Definitions and Drivers* 389
          10.2.1   Mobile Marketing...391
          10.2.1   Technology Acceptance As a Behavior..........394
    10.3   *Corporate Examples*..398
          10.3.1   Costco, Danone, and FIAT...........................398
          10.3.2   Frank And Oak 403
          10.3.3   IKEA 406
          10.3.4   Nivea and FCB 407
          10.3.5   Uber 410
    10.4   *Issues at Stake* 413
          10.4.1   The Newly Empowered Consumer 414
          10.4.2   Impact on Marketing Decisions
                    and Feasibility...415
          10.4.3   Outcomes 419

Conclusion: Reaching consumers wherever and whenever with mobile
marketing is a good idea to help bridge geographic, technological,
and temporal distances. Nevertheless, companies should also mitigate risks in implementing this approach.
References

Recommended Readings

- Berthon, Pierre; Pittb, Leyland; Planggerb, Kirk & Shapiro, Daniel (2012). Marketing meets Web 2.0, social media, and creative consumers: Implications for international marketing strategy. *Business Horizons*, 55(3), 261–271.
- Davis, Fred; Bagozzi, Richard & Warshaw, Paul (1989). User acceptance of computer technology: A comparison of two theoretical models. *Management Science*, 35(8), 982–1003.
- Gao, Tao; Rohm, Andrew; Sultan, Fareena & Pagani, Margherita (2013). Consumers Un-tethered: A Three-Market Empirical Study of Consumers' Mobile Marketing Acceptance. *Journal of Business Research*, 66(12), 2536–2544.
- Kaplan, Andreas (2012). If You Love Something, Let It Go Mobile: Mobile Marketing and Mobile Social Media 4x4. *Business Horizons*, 55(2), 129–139.
- Shankar, Venkatesh; Venkatesh, Alladi; Hofacker, Charles & Naik, Prasad (2010). Mobile Marketing in the Retailing Environment: Current Insights and Future Research Avenues. *Journal of Interactive Marketing*, 24(2), 111–120.

Figure 10.1 Illustrating Chapter 10
Source: Own elaboration

378 *Mobile Marketing*

Introduction: Should Companies Reach Consumers Wherever and Whenever?

Contrary to BOP marketing and reverse innovation (Chapters 8 and 9), unfamiliar notions for many of us, it is likely that mobile marketing already plays a daily part in our lives as consumers, workers, and citizens. If we own a smartphone or any other mobile device (e.g., a tablet or wearable technology, like a smartwatch), we are indeed constantly exposed to mobile marketing activities from different organizations (from firms providing us with goods and services, to our employers, to governmental agencies with whom we interact for taxes, social benefits, etc.). **Mobile marketing can be seen as a solution to overcome issues related to geographic and technological distances** (see Chapters 4 and 7). By addressing the question: **"Should companies reach consumers wherever and whenever?"** this chapter plants the idea that this fast-rising practice is, however, not without risks.

Figure 10.2 situates the topic of mobile marketing in the overall book structure. It highlights that, in relation to the different steps in an international marketing plan, mobile marketing can be particularly discussed when considering distribution and promotion policies.

Overall, the objectives of this chapter are to define, illustrate, and discuss the topic of mobile marketing, set in the larger context of online marketing. First, we go over some concepts about international distribution and then zoom in on online distribution and promotion through electronic commerce and digital marketing. Next, we review definitions of mobile marketing and look into drivers for its adoption. In particular, we study the notion of "technology acceptance" and look back at the reasoned action theory (Chapter 5) to position the acceptance of mobile marketing as a behavior. We then present several examples of companies using mobile marketing and illustrate their creativity in doing so. Finally, we discuss issues at stake for corporations in regards to mobile marketing, including the risk of consumer retaliation, the impact of this approach on regular marketing decisions, and the extent to which this practice is truly beneficial.

10.1 Background Information

In order to better understand the issues at stake with mobile marketing, it is useful to have a basic notion about international distribution and promotion. First, we discuss the following questions:

- What is the purpose of distribution? What are international distribution decisions about?
- Which are some of the common intermediaries for international distribution through exports? What are some of the important differences across countries in terms of channel structure? And in terms of competitive rivalry?
- How has the Internet impacted international distribution and promotion? And what should an e-vendor be concerned about when expanding abroad?

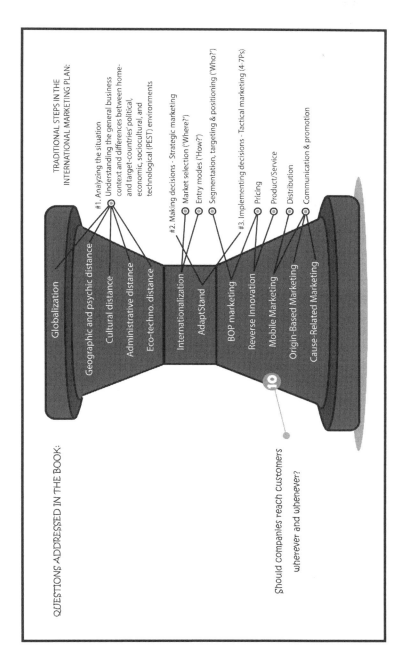

Figure 10.2 Positioning Chapter 10 in the overall book structure

Source: Own elaboration

380   *Mobile Marketing*

10.1.1 International Distribution Policies

What is the purpose of distribution? And what are international distribution policies about? *Distribution* is all about providing customers with access to companies' offerings (products or services). In an international context, distribution thus requires that companies give foreign customers access to products and services across national borders. When we talk about a distribution channel, we refer to all the intermediaries involved in bringing the product or service from the producer to the consumer. Overall, international distribution policies consist of a set of decisions about the desired degree of standardization vs. adaptation (see Chapter 3) in terms of three main areas: channel structure, channel management, and logistics. Figure 10.3 illustrates important decisions that the firm has to make in terms of international distribution. Each of these decisions is influenced by external factors such as existing regulations, levels of competition, the nature of the product and demand (e.g., customer characteristics) (Hollensen, 2016). We recognize easily that these factors can be classified as various elements of the CAGE distance (in particular, administrative, cultural, and eco-techno distances).

Among other differences, we now pay particular attention to varying conditions across countries in terms of channel structure and competitive rivalry.

Which are some of the common intermediaries for international distribution through exports? A wide range of intermediaries is available to handle companies' exports according to their size, experience, and industry, including: agents, merchants, brokers, freight forwarders, trading houses, and export management companies. Figure 10.4 illustrates different lengths of channels from "direct" (manufacturer to final customer) to "one-step" or "two-step" intermediate channels (from manufacturer to wholesaler to retailer, for instance). It also illustrates intermediaries such as group purchasing organizations, often used for online and catalogue sales.

What are some of the important differences across countries in terms of channel structure? In terms of structure, *international distribution channels* can be surprisingly complex, with a high number of possible paths for products to reach customers across borders. For instance, Lefaix-Durand (2008) count no less than eleven different routes for Canadian wood products to make their way into US homes, from the land owner to the homebuilder and with the involvement of various intermediaries (e.g., sawmillers, brokers, framers, subcontractors, component manufacturers, and pro-dealers). Thus, an important difference lies in the "level of intermediation" between countries (i.e., how lengthy and complex channel structures are). In the automotive industry, Cateora, Gilly, and Graham (2011, Exhibits 12.1–2) note that, in North America, parts for cars can have up to six primary channels and two secondary channels to reach end-users from the carmaker (through intermediaries such as warehouse distributors, jobber buying groups and jobbers, installers, mass merchandiser and repair specialists), while they can follow more than thirty different paths in Japan (through a multitude of actors such as independent parts makers, repair parts makers, wholesalers, second-level wholesalers, special agents, dealers, subdealers, cooperative sales companies, large users, gasoline stations, and automobile repair shops). This example

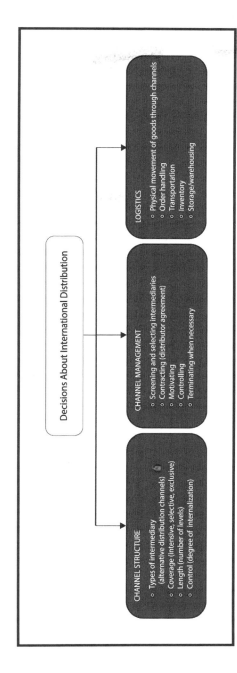

Figure 10.3 Listing important decisions involved in international distribution policies

Source: Adapted from Hollensen (2010, p. 551)

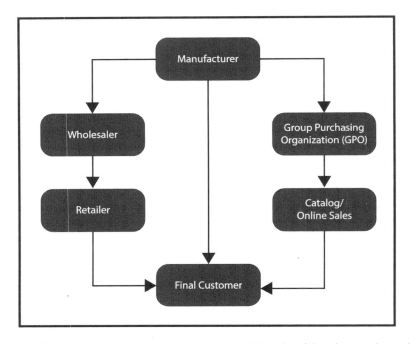

Figure 10.4 Presenting various intermediaries and lengths of distribution channels
Source: Adapted from Pasco-Berho (2008)

illustrates well why entering the Japanese market is reputed for being highly challenging (efforts in understanding and penetrating the very different structure of distribution channels have kept foreign competitors at bay for a long time).

When it comes to competitive rivalry, what are some of the important differences across countries? In terms of competitive rivalry in the distribution business, it is also common that companies face wildly diverse situations abroad. Taking the example of the retailing industry, we start by portraying a few of the well-known retailers such as Costco, Target and Walmart (US), Tesco (UK), Aldi (Germany), and Carrefour (France). Table 10.1 shows information provided in one of the latest available rankings and reveals the massive size of these players in terms of revenues.

Although these leading companies are called "global" retailers, the number of countries in which they have a commercial presence is surprisingly low, compared to other companies in the fast-moving consumer goods (FMCG), fast-food or beverage industries like Coca-Cola, McDonald's, and Procter & Gamble (see Chapter 2). The one with the highest number—i.e., the "most internationalized" retailer in this global Top 10—is Carrefour, with a presence in "only" thirty-three countries in 2013 (Deloitte, 2015). Other companies in the same ranking, and not operating in the hypermarket/

Mobile Marketing   383

Table 10.1 Ranking global retailers

	Company	Net Retail Revenue (Mn USD, 2013)	Country of Origin	Country of Operations (#)
1	Walmart	476,294	US	28
2	Costco	105,156	US	9
3	Carrefour	98,688	France	33
4	Schwarz	98,662	Germany	26
5	Tesco	98,631	UK	13
6	Kroger	98,375	US	1
7	Metro	86,393	Germany	32
8	Aldi	81,090	Germany	17
9	Home Depot	78,812	US	4
10	Target	72,596	US	2

Source: Adapted from Deloitte (2015, p. 11)

superstore format, have stores in more countries (e.g., H&M and IKEA from Sweden with a presence in fifty-four and forty-three countries, respectively, or Marks and Spencer from the UK with forty-eight countries). This is far from the count of 130, 150, or even 200+ countries often publicized by companies in other industrial sectors—just as a reminder, the UN counts ~195 member states and the WTO has ~165 members, so anything above 195 might be slightly incorrect. The fact that the degree of internationalization is not as extensive in the retailing business as in other industries takes us back to the difficulty of distinguishing "global" from "international" companies (Chapter 2). It is a good illustration that the number of countries in which companies operate is not sufficient to make this distinction. Finally, we can explain this observation by looking at the difficulty of standardizing distribution across borders and reaching large economies of scale due to distances (in particular administrative, cultural, and eco-techno distances). Furthermore, the degree of competitive rivalry plays a major role in limiting the extent to which retailers can internationalize. Retailers using the supermarket/superstore format tend to develop regionally and are extremely powerful in their home markets (e.g., with a long tradition and history, as well as many established outlets). Their control of distribution channels makes it very difficult for foreign competitors to come and "steal" market shares.

When it comes to studying the intensity of competition, and its effect on international distribution decisions, we must also be careful and rely on objective data and the right indicators to assess the situation. For instance, the total number of retailers in a given country can be misleading. Indeed, the intensity of competition in 2010 was higher in countries like Argentina or Poland (with a count of ~420,000 and ~330,000 retailers) than in China or the US (~4,500,000 and ~945,000 retailers, respectively). When calculated not in absolute but in relative numbers considering the population size, the number of people served per retailer was: 322 for the US, 294 for China, 115 for Poland, and only 91 for Argentina (Cateora et al., 2011, Exhibit 12.3). This means that the retailing scene was much more competitive in the latter markets, a rather counter-intuitive observation that highlights the need, for

384   *Mobile Marketing*

us marketers, to do our homework in terms of data analysis when studying international markets.

Next, we look into another important source of differences across countries in terms of distribution and promotion: the role of the Internet.

10.1.2 Online Distribution and Promotion

How has the Internet impacted international distribution and promotion? Since the mid-1990s, the Internet has had three important consequences:

- It drastically increased efficiency in managing imports and exports due to integrated software application systems. For instance, Enterprise Resource Planning (ERP) and Vendor Managed Inventories (VMI) are computerized systems based on the Internet that allow companies to communicate with other companies and facilitate "just-in-time" manufacturing and inventory management.
- It has suppressed many intermediaries needed for products to reach consumers, a phenomenon known as *disintermediation* or *shortening* of supply chains. For instance, publishing houses and clothing companies do not need retailers anymore (e.g., bookstores and shops) if they have a transactional website where customers can order directly, pay for the items, and receive their order a few days later by post. However, the phenomenon of *reintermediation* also now occurs, with the emergence of new types of intermediaries, such as Amazon.
- Finally, the Internet has allowed the development of electronic commerce. Figure 10.5 reveals the impressive increase of global Internet retailing sales and growth since the early 2000s. For instance, online retail sales grew from an estimated 100 billion USD in 2003 to more than 500 billion USD in 2012 (Euromonitor International, 2013). Asia-Pacific is by far the most active region in the world when it comes to online sales, followed by North America, Western Europe, Latin America, Eastern Europe, Australasia, and finally the Middle East and Africa. Although the annual growth rate of online sales dropped from an astounding 50 percent to about 20 percent over that decade, it remained far superior to offline sales for grocery and non-grocery retailers (roughly around 5 percent) (Euromonitor International, 2013).

What should an e-vendor be concerned about when expanding abroad? With the possible exception of services, some type of local contact abroad may be required for different activities related to online selling (e.g., payments where credit cards and other modern instruments are not widely available, delivery of the purchased product, addressing consumer queries and complaints, and merchandise returns). All of these activities are impacted in various ways by the CAGE distance.

For instance, an e-vendor should be aware that technological distance between countries is likely to impinge on its expansion. Obvious differences lie in the variety of bandwidth, technology generations (2G/3G/4G), and

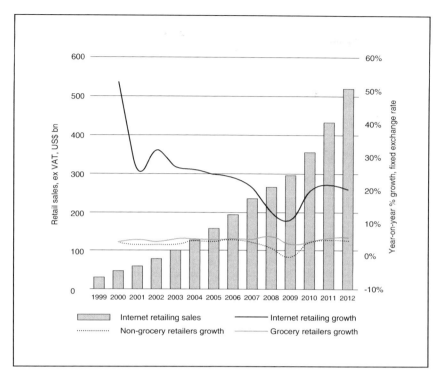

Figure 10.5 Illustrating the growth of global Internet retailing (1999–2012)
Source: Euromonitor International (2013, p. 56), reproduced with permission

Internet penetration rates (i.e., the rate of users considering the total population). The latter differ greatly across the planet, with some regions presenting high rates of penetration (e.g., North America and Europe with rates close to 90 percent and 80 percent, respectively), and others low rates (e.g., Asia and Africa with rates below 30 percent and 50 percent, respectively) (Internet World Stats, 2017). Figure 10.6 provides data that allows us to compare regions and realize that the underpinning conditions for online distribution and promotion are far from being equivalent everywhere. Using various indicators is once more useful in order to gain a broader perspective. If the penetration rate in Africa was only ~28 percent in the first quarter of 2017, the number of users was already above 345 million people, more than in North America (~320 million). In addition, with a cumulated growth rate of more than 7,500 percent over a seventeen-year period, Africa could well become much more interesting for online selling in the future than the penetration rate let us suppose at first. Finally, the evolution over time of these statistics should be frequently reviewed for a better assessment, as conditions change fast in this field.

WORLD INTERNET USAGE AND POPULATION STATISTICS

MARCH 25, 2017—Update

World Regions	Population (2017 Est.)	Population % of World	Internet Users 31 Mar 2017	Penetration Rate (% Pop.)	Growth 2000–2017	Users % Table
Africa	1,246.504,865	16.6 %	345,676,501	27.7 %	7,557.2%	9.3 %
Asia	4,148,177,672	55.2 %	1,873,856,654	45.2 %	1,539.4%	50.2 %
Europe	822710,362	10.9 %	636,971,824	77.4 %	506.1%	17.1 %
Latin America/Caribbean	647,604,645	8.6 %	385,919,382	59.6 %	2,035.8%	10.3 %
Middle East	250,327,574	3.3 %	141,931,765	56.7 %	4,220.9%	3.8 %
North America	363.224,006	4.8 %	320,068,243	88.1 %	196.1%	8.6 %
Oceania/Australia	40,479,846	0.5 %	27,549,054	68.1 %	261.5%	0.7 %
WORLD TOTAL	7,519,028,970	100.0 %	3,731,973,423	49.6 %	933.8%	100.0 %

(1) Internet Usage and World Population Statistics updated as of March 30, 2017. (2) CLICK on each world region name for detailed regional usage information. (3) Demographic (Population) numbers are based on data from the *United Nations—Population* Division. (4) Internet usage information comes from data published by *Nielsen Online*, by ITU, the *International Telecommunications Union*, by *GfK*, by local ICT Regulators, and other reliable sources. (5) For definitions, navigation help and disclaimers, please refer to the *Site Surfing Guide*. (6) Information in this site may be cited, giving the due credit and placing a link back to www.Internetworldstats.com. Copyright © 2017. Miniwatts Marketing Group. All rights reserved worldwide.

Figure 10.6 Contrasting Internet statistics in different regions

Source: Internet World Stats (2017), reproduced with permission

An e-vendor should also be aware that administrative distance represents a barrier because Internet laws (e.g., for privacy protection and cookies) differ widely, as each nation or integrated regional block defines its own rules. Examples of governmental bodies in charge of regulating online activities are: France's Commission Nationale de l'Informatique et des Libertés (CNIL), the Canadian Radio-Television and Telecommunications Commission (CRTC), Quebec's Commission d'Accès à l'Information, and the European Union's Privacy and Electronic Communications Directive. While cyber-laws are converging, to some extent, there is often a time lag and remaining discrepancies across countries. For instance, anti-spam regulations have been applied at different points in time and under different conditions. Since 2002, the European Parliament has adopted the "Directive 2002/58/EC" which includes Article 13 concerning unsolicited communications and makes mandatory the "opt-in" option (EUR-Lex, 2002). Implemented in 2003, Australia's Spam Bill does not require the "opt-in" option, but a clear "unsubscribe link" is mandatory (Commonwealth of Australia Bills, 2003). In Canada, the law only came into effect in 2014 and recipients who agree to accept communications from a company must also be able to unsubscribe easily. Violators may face fines of 1,000,000 CAD (~770,000 USD) if the victim is an individual and 10,000,000 CAD (~7 700 000 USD) if the victim is a business (Government of Canada, 2016). In Japan, violators of the law could even face up to one year of imprisonment (The Government of Japan, 2002).

Cultural distance has also proven to matter as people from different cultures display various usage habits (e.g., different navigation schemes when browsing the Internet and visiting websites). The fact that Arabic speakers tend to browse from right to left, for instance, invites e-vendors to position website menus and other navigation tools on the right-hand side. Websites must be promoted through search engine registration, press releases, local newsgroups and forums, mutual links, banner advertising, and the use of social networks. In this regard, it would be a mistake to think that the social media landscape is similar in all countries. The diffusion of networks among the population could well be impacted by cultural factors. Looking at the example of the professional social network LinkedIn, its adoption varied greatly across countries, with 128 million users in the US in 2016 (i.e., more than 30 percent of the country population), 2 million users in Sweden (~21 percent), 25 million in Brazil (~12 percent), 5 million in Russia (~0.03 percent), and 20 million in China (~0.01 percent) (Statista, 2016). Although Facebook is one of the truly global social networks, many others are favorites in their home countries. In this way, Vkontakt (VK) in Russia, Qzone and Renren in China, or Mixi in Japan have all gained significant national popularity. Figure 10.7 presents the logotypes of six among the main social media networks and instant messengers, some of these we recognize instantly, others not, depending on where we are from. In turn, Table 10.2 provides statistics about the penetration rate (i.e., the ratio of social media users to Internet users) according to own claimed/reported activity based on a survey of Internet users aged sixteen to sixty-four by GlobalWebIndex and reported by We Are Social (2016). As mentioned previously, Facebook is the most popular network in countries like Argentina, France, and the US, but

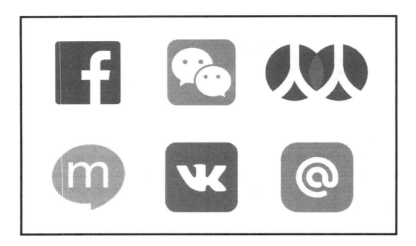

Figure 10.7 Illustrating global diversity in terms of popular social media networks and instant messengers

Source: Own elaboration with permission of Facebook (US), WeChat (China), Renren (China), Mixi (Japan), Vkontakte (Russia), and Line (South Korea)

Table 10.2 Comparing social media penetration rates in selected countries

	Argentina	China	France	Germany	India	Japan	Russia	US
Social Networks								
• Facebook	42%	5%	43%	38%	13%	17%	24%	41%
• LinkedIn	10%	–	6%	3%	7%	–	–	11%
• Mixi	–	–	–	–	–	5%	–	–
• Qzone	–	21%	–	–	–	–	–	–
• Renren	–	6%	–	–	–	–	–	–
• Twitter	18%	–	11%	7%	8%	15%	11%	17%
• VK	–	–	–	–	–	–	39%	–
Messenger/Chat App/VOIP								
• Facebook Messenger	29%	4%	22%	15%	11%	3%	6%	26%
• Line	–	–	–	–	–	25%	–	–
• Skype	13%	–	8%	10%	10%	–	19%	9%
• Viber	–	–	–	–	–	–	15%	–
• WeChat	–	24%	–	–	6%	–	–	–
• WhatsApp	37%	–	7%	39%	12%	–	15%	–

Source: Adapted from We Are Social (2016)

not in countries like Russia or China. Adoption rates for Twitter, however successful, remain modest across the board (under 20 percent). This allows the Twitter *aficionados* to observe that this particular social network is not as widely diffused as they might have initially thought. It thus provides a communication channel to specific targets, but not to the overall population.

Mobile Marketing 389

"Line" is a very successful messenger in Japan, while WhatsApp is used by almost half the population in Argentina. While Viber is a tool of choice in countries such as Russia, it is unheard of in many other countries.

In conclusion, "social media is a function of a country's technology, culture, and government" (Berthon et al., 2012, p. 265). This too is valid for mobile marketing.

10.2 Definitions and Drivers

In order to study mobile marketing, we first look at the broader field of digital and online marketing, with several definitions to differentiate concurrent approaches. We then cover some of the main drivers of mobile marketing acceptance. The following questions are addressed:

- What is digital marketing? And how is it different from online marketing?
- How different is digital media compared to traditional media?
- Which are two important trends that characterize the evolution of digital marketing?
- What is mobile marketing? Then, what difference is there between digital, online, mobile, social and viral marketing?
- What drives the adoption of mobile marketing? How extensive and fast is the adoption of mobile devices? How heterogeneous is mobile adoption across countries?

What is digital marketing? And how is it different from online marketing? Here, *digital marketing* is understood as marketing activities that rely on digital media, i.e., any medium that uses computers and their 'binary' language (one/zero binary digits or 'bits'). Digital media can be 'offline', i.e., not connected to the Internet (e.g., SMS and video) or 'online', when relying on an Internet connection (e.g., websites and QR codes). Table 10.3 presents

Table 10.3 Listing traditional and digital media

Traditional Media		Digital Media
Classified ads (in newspapers)	≈	Classified ads (e.g., www.craigslist.org)
Directories (e.g., Pages Jaunes)	≈	Directories (e.g., www.pj.ca)
Movie theaters (e.g., AMC Entertainment, UGC)	≈	Movie streaming (e.g., www.netflix.com)
Newspapers (e.g., New York Times)	≈	Newspapers (e.g., www.nytimes.com)
Magazines (e.g., The Economist)	≈	Magazines (e.g., www.economist.com)
Mail and catalogs	≠	Emails and SMS
Outdoor (e.g., billboards on highway)	≈	Outdoor (e.g., screens at bus stops)
Radio (e.g., CBS, RTL, Virgin, etc.)	≈	Radio streaming (e.g., www.iheart.com)
Phone	≈	Phone function on a smart phone

(Continued)

390 Mobile Marketing

Table 10.3 (Continued)

Traditional Media		Digital Media
Television (e.g., CNN)	≈	Television streaming (e.g., http://go.cnn.com)
	≠	Blogs
	≠	Social networks and instant messengers
	≠	Video and games

Source: Own elaboration

an overview of the main traditional and digital media. The center column indicates which digital media have a traditional equivalent and which do not.

How different is digital media compared to traditional media? One of the main characteristics of digital media is that it is interactive (by getting consumer feedback almost instantaneously with ratings and comments, for instance) and far more targeted and customized than is traditional media. Targeted advertising, for instance, refers to advertising displayed in the form of banners on websites and apps. These banners show us advertisements from companies which websites we have visited in the prior hours or days (e.g., for the coveted pair of boots or trip abroad that surprisingly appear on our preferred newspaper website). Behind them lies a sophisticated bidding contest, where companies literally fight to reach us, whenever we fall into their target customers. This approach makes advertising efforts so much more efficient because it is highly relevant to targeted segments. For a detailed comparison between traditional and social media, see Armelini and Villanueva (2011).

Now that we have started differentiating among terms that are often used interchangeably, we can push the exercise further and question the conceptual difference between digital, mobile, social, and viral marketing (see "Food for Thought").

Food for Thought 10.1

- What difference do you see between digital, online, social, mobile, and viral marketing?

Which are two important trends that characterize the evolution of digital marketing? In the past decade or so, digital marketing has become more "social" and more "mobile." For instance, the terms *S-commerce* and *M-commerce* have been created to refer to Internet retailing sales generated through mobile devices (such as smartphones and tablets) on the one hand, and through social networks (both offline and online) on the other hand (Euromonitor International, 2013). Using social networks (e.g., Facebook and Renren) for marketing activities is called *social media marketing*, and sometimes *social marketing*. The latter term must be used with caution, as it can be confused with the marketing approach that relies on corporate social responsibility (Chapter 12). In this chapter, *social media marketing* refers to the use of social networks to market offerings. Berthon et al. (2012, p. 263) define social media as "the product of Internet-based applications that build on the technological foundations of Web 2.0" and the Web 2.0 as a platform that allows consumers to create and consume information (instead of merely retrieving it as in the earlier state of the World Wide Web), thereby emphasizing the importance of user-generated content (UGC) in social media. Because of the strong interrelation between digital marketing and the two trends of social and mobile, Lamberton and Stephen (2016) group them together in studying "DSMM marketing" (an acronym standing for Digital, Social Media, and Mobile marketing). Their article provides an impressive literature review of the phenomenon. Retracing the evolution of research over more than fifteen years on DSMM, it distinguishes between three eras: 2000–2004 (when digital marketing started facilitating buyers' behavior), 2005–2010 (when consumers started shaping DSMM with the rising importance of social networks and Word Of Mouth or WOM), and 2011–2014 (when social media took the stage). YouTube videos offer attractive presentations of social media evolution (e.g., with search words: "Social Media 2013 New Music"). Next, we focus on mobile marketing.

10.2.1 Mobile Marketing

What is mobile marketing? In their systematic literature review of the topic, Varnali and Toker (2010) conclude that a common conceptualization of mobile marketing is still missing. As this observation still seems valid several years later, we review various definitions to get a better sense of the phenomenon. *Mobile marketing* has been defined as:

- "the use of a wireless medium to provide consumers with time- and location-sensitive, personalized information that promotes goods, services, and ideas" (Scharl, Dickinger, & Murphy, 2005, p. 165);
- "the use of wireless media (primarily cellular phones and PDAs) as an integrated content delivery and direct response vehicle within a cross-media marketing communications program" (Jayawardhena, Kuckertz, Karjaluoto, & Kautonen, 2009, p. 475; Zhang & Mao, 2008)
- "the two- or multi-way communication and promotion of an offer between a firm and its customers using a mobile medium, device, or technology" (Shankar & Balasubramanian, 2009, p. 118);
- "Any marketing activity conducted through a ubiquitous network to which consumers are constantly connected using a personal mobile device" (Kaplan, 2012, p. 130);
- "Organizations', companies', and brands' efforts to promote, inform, sell, or otherwise drive consumers to take some type of action using a mobile platform" (Rohm, Gao, Sultan, & Pagani, 2012, p. 486).
- "A set of programs and practices that firms employ to communicate and engage, in an interactive manner, with consumers and enable them to access information, download content, or purchase products on mobile

392   *Mobile Marketing*

devices" (Gao et al., 2013, p. 2536, based on a definition from the Mobile Marketing Association).

The absence of consensus does not seem to be a major barrier to a sufficient understanding of the phenomenon. Indeed, several common aspects are salient in these definitions: the use of wireless media to allow communication wherever and whenever (i.e., time- and location-sensitive information, constant connection), the fact that the transmitted information is personal, and that communication and promotion is bi- or multidirectional ("many to many").

Then, what difference is there between digital, online, mobile, social, and viral marketing? As seen previously, *digital marketing* can be social and/or mobile but it can also be viral or not. As defined by Ho and Dempsey (2010, p. 1000), *viral marketing* "typically starts with the marketer creating some form of electronic content such as a video or a mini-site, the aim of which is usually brand-building. The URL (web address) for the electronic content is made available to Internet users, who after viewing the content will decide whether they want to pass the URL along to their friends." The example of Dave Caroll—an unhappy musician and customer of United Airlines—and his "United Breaks Guitars" song is a good illustration of a video gone viral (see Berthon et al., 2012 for further details). Posted on YouTube in 2009, the video has been shared widely on social networks and has received more than 17.9 million views (as of March 2018). The fundamental characteristic for a message to become viral is the transmission by consumers themselves. The emitter can be consumers themselves or companies (e.g., communicating through their corporate Facebook accounts or YouTube channels) but it is when the content spreads like a virus from person to person (i.e., literally imitating a contagion), that messages, advertisements, and campaigns go viral. Then, a snowball effect is observed: their diffusion in the targeted population is likely to be much greater than through traditional media.

Figure 10.8 offers a visual representation of a basic distinction we can make between the concepts of traditional, digital, online, social, mobile, and viral marketing. Five questions help delimit these concepts, each at different levels of analysis: signal, connection, device, media, and emitter. First, is the communication digitized? In other words, does it rely on the binary language of computers and a "finite" signal conveyed by bits? The answer to this question is positive for *digital marketing* and negative for *traditional marketing*. Second, is the Internet used to transmit the communication? When the answer is positive, we can talk about *online marketing*. It is important to note that digital marketing is not necessarily online. Like traditional marketing, it can be offline (e.g., SMS are transmitted via phone operators' networks, not an Internet connection). This is why it is better to avoid using the terms *digital marketing* and *online marketing* interchangeably. Next, we can ask the question: which type of devices do consumers use to get access to the communication? We can only talk about *mobile marketing* when the device is mobile (e.g., mobile phone or tablet). Mobile marketing is necessarily digital (but not online). Now, to understand how to situate *social media*

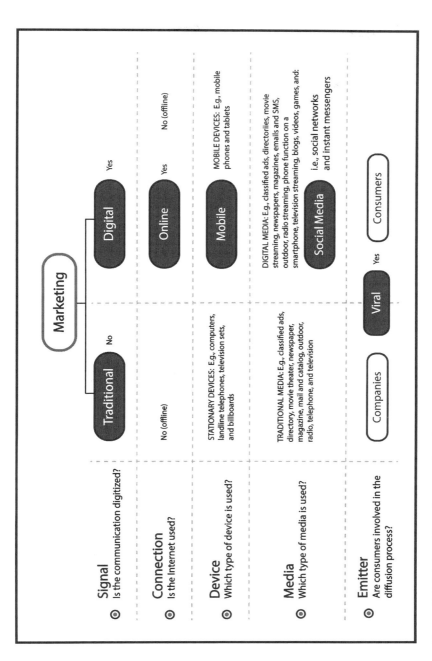

Figure 10.8 Distinguishing between digital, online, mobile, social, and viral marketing

Source: Own elaboration

394 *Mobile Marketing*

marketing, we need to ask: "Which type of media is used?" See Table 10.3 for a non-exhaustive list of traditional and digital media. Social media is only a part of the digital media list. We can then talk about *social media marketing* when marketing activities are conducted on this specific type of media (i.e., through social networks like Facebook). In this case, we understand that social media marketing is necessarily digital and online but it can be mobile or not, viral or not. Finally, the question of whether consumers are involved in the diffusion process is key to situate *viral marketing*. The emitter for messages gone viral can either be companies or consumers. When we talk about activities related to marketing products or services, emitters are usually companies but the involvement of consumers (notably in promotion) is essential for them to be described as viral marketing. *Viral marketing* is then digital, online or not, mobile or not, but necessarily a part of social media marketing.

After defining important concepts to better situate mobile marketing, we go back to the theoretical background that explains why it is adopted by companies and consumers.

10.2.1 *Technology Acceptance As a Behavior*

What drives the adoption of mobile marketing? To answer this question, we need to remember that adopting mobile marketing requires first adopting mobile devices (and, thereby, mobile technology). From there, it is easy to refer to the countless studies in the field of Information Systems that have investigated technology adoption. One specific model, called the Technology Acceptance Model (TAM) has been particularly used to explain the adoption of, among other technologies, mobile technology, and devices. It was introduced by Fred Davis in his doctoral dissertation (1986) and later developed in Davis, Bagozzi, and Warshaw (1989). According to a search in Google Scholar, this widely popular article has been cited nearly 20,300 times as of March 2018. Illustrated in Figure 10.9, the model situates *perceived usefulness* and *perceived ease-of-use* as the two central variables that shape the attitude toward technology, which in turn, influences its adoption and use. A concrete example of this mechanism can be found in the adoption of the electric car, which was delayed, to some extent, due to issues with perceived ease-of-use (other factors include political reasons and the role of oil and gas industry lobbyists). A lot of effort has been dedicated to improving consumer perceptions (e.g., YouTube video available with search words: "U.C. Berkeley Study Says Battery Switching Model Would Accelerate EV Acceptance"). The TAM also takes into account the existence of external variables (e.g., consumer characteristics such as age, knowledge, culture, etc.).

The link established here between perceptions, attitudes, and behaviors is a clear reminder of another model that we have seen in Chapter 5 (Figure 5.13), depicting the planned behavior or reasoned action theory (Fishbein & Ajzen, 1975; 2010). Adopting a new tool, technology, or device can indeed be considered as a behavior. The TAM is thus an adaptation of this theory and is "specifically tailored for modeling user acceptance of information systems. The goal of TAM is to provide an explanation of the determinants of computer acceptance that is general, capable of explaining user behavior across a

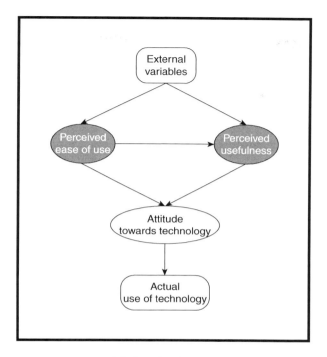

Figure 10.9 Presenting a simplified Technology Acceptance Model (TAM)
Source: Adapted from Davis et al. (1989)

broad range of end-user computing technologies and user-populations, while at the same time being both parsimonious and theoretically justified" (Davis et al., 1989, p. 985). In terms of parsimony, the only two variables introduced here were indeed proven to have a very strong explanatory power and were used in many subsequent studies, separately and together (Bauer, Reichardt, Barnes, & Neumann, 2005; Rohm et al., 2012).

In addition to perceived usefulness and perceived ease-of-use, we can reflect on other important mobile marketing drivers based on recommended readings for this chapter (see "Food for Thought").

Food for Thought 10.2

- In reference to Shankar, Venkatesh, Hofacker, and Naik (2010) and Gao et al. (2013), what are other key drivers for mobile marketing adoption?

396　Mobile Marketing

How extensive and fast is the adoption of mobile devices? In terms of adoption, we can look at several indicators to get a sense of how large mobile marketing is and how fast it is growing (e.g., the number of mobile phone users and of devices, as well as revenues from mobile advertising).

First, the number of mobile phone users worldwide is estimated to rise from 4.15 to 4.78 billion between 2015 and 2020, an increase in proportion from about 57% to 62% of the global population (eMarketer, 2016). Globally, the number of mobile users increased from 200 to ~1,900 million between 2007 and 2015, at a much faster growth pace than the number of desktop users (which grew from 1,100 to 1,700 million in the same time frame) with a 32% compared to 6% Compound Annual Growth Rate (CAGR) (Smart Insights, 2017). For instance, it is at the turn of 2015 that the number of mobile-only Internet users exceeded desktop-only Internet users in the US (ComScore, 2015).

Second, sales of smartphones (i.e., mobile phones that integrate personal data, touch panel functions, and advanced Internet capabilities) have grown drastically since the introduction of the first model by Apple in 2007, as they accounted for more than half of global shipments of all mobile phones in 2013 (Shen, 2015). In 2016, around 1.5 billion smartphones were sold worldwide, a major increase since 2007 when only about 120 million units were sold—thus representing a CAGR above 32 percent annually! (Statista, 2017a). Global unit shipments of tablets are less impressive or steady, but still increased from 125 to 233 million between 2012 and 2014 (i.e., 23 percent CAGR) (Statista, 2017b).

Finally, eMarketer (2017a) projects that the mobile ad spending worldwide will increase from about 140 to 278 billion USD between 2017 and 2021 (i.e., ~19 percent CAGR). In the US only, revenue from digital advertising on non-mobile devices was forecasted to stagnate at around 40 billion USD between 2013 and 2018, while revenue from advertising on mobile devices was estimated to increase from ~45 to more than 80 billion USD (i.e., ~12 percent CAGR) (Business Insider, 2015).

How heterogeneous is mobile adoption across countries? To answer this question, we can look into similar indicators (e.g., number of mobile subscriptions, and growth and penetration rates of mobile phone users, as well as smartphones sales), but this time according to different geographies.

Starting with mobile-broadband subscriptions, we observe wide discrepancies between regions in the world and between economic development levels. In Europe and the Americas, the number of subscriptions per one hundred inhabitants exceeds 75 percent, while it is averaging 45–50 percent in the Commonwealth of Independent States (CIS), Arab States, and Asia-Pacific region, and only reach about ~30 percent in Africa (ITU, 2016). According to the same source, this penetration rate contrasts sharply when comparing developed countries and LDCs (90 percent and 20 percent subscription rates per one hundred inhabitants, respectively), while the world's average is close to 50 percent. In this way, a correlation between income and mobile phone subscriptions is documented. In 2015, the average number of subscriptions per one hundred inhabitants was one hundred and twenty-four in high-income countries, one hundred and five in upper-middle-income countries,

Mobile Marketing 397

ninety in lower-middl- income countries, and sixty in low-income countries (World Bank, 2017).

At the national level, the number of subscriptions per one hundred inhabitants also varies tremendously (e.g., Eritrea: 7/100, Afghanistan: 66/100, Canada: 84/100, India: 87/100, Honduras: 91/100, China: 97/100, France: 103/100, South Africa: 142/100, Indonesia: 149/100, United Arab Emirates: 204/100, Hong Kong: 234/100) (ITU, 2017). Some numbers can surprise us if we expect emerging and developing countries to always be lagging behind. The examples of South Africa, Indonesia, and even Honduras should remind us to systematically search for factual data before assuming anything, as repeated many times throughout this book. Other types of differences among countries can explain the variation observed in the above-mentioned numbers. For instance, why is France only slightly above the saturation threshold of 100 percent, while places like the Emirates and Hong Kong are far into "hyper-saturation," with penetration rates of more than 200 percent? One likely explanation lies in administrative differences: in some countries, customers are locked into multiple-year plans with specific mobile carriers. They have no financial incentives in obtaining more than one mobile subscription. In other countries, people can easily get mobile subscriptions from two, three, or more carriers and benefit from specific deals offered when communicating with friends using the same networks.

Logically, the growth rate of mobile users (i.e., users of smartphones and regular mobile phones) varies inversely to penetration rates. Where penetration rates are already high (i.e., where a large percentage of the population already uses mobile devices), lower growth rates are to be expected. According to eMarketer (2017c), developed countries tended to display slow growth rates for mobile users in 2017 (e.g., France: 1.0 percent, Germany: 0.8 percent, Japan: 0.4 percent, UK: 1.4 percent, US: 1.4 percent), while some emerging countries had limited or moderate growth (China: 2.3 percent, Russia: 0.5 percent), and others experienced significant growth spurts (e.g., India: ~7 percent). As expected, these numbers reflect high penetration rates (e.g., France: ~79 percent, Germany: ~82 percent, Japan: 84.5 percent, UK and US: ~81 percent), moderate penetration rates (e.g., China: ~71 percent, Russia: ~73 percent), and limited penetration rates (e.g., India: 57 percent).

Some countries are particularly hungry for smartphones. This was the case in China and in a group of countries from the emerging Asia-Pacific region (including Cambodia, India, Indonesia, Malaysia, Philippines, Thailand, and Vietnam) in 2016. With 450 and 210 millions of units sold that year in these countries—over a total of 1.4 billion units worldwide—sales represented no less than ~32 percent and ~15 percent, respectively, or put together, nearly half of the number of smartphones sold everywhere (eMarketer, 2017b)! Interestingly, Latin American and Central and Eastern European countries led sales revenue growth from smartphones in 2015–2016 with 18 percent growth rates each (followed closely by China with 15 percent), while growth was nonexistent or barely noticeable in North America (0 percent) and Western Europe (1 percent) (eMarketer, 2017b).

These numbers illustrate, once more, the diversity that characterizes the world. Even for a relatively new and trendy practice like mobile marketing,

398 *Mobile Marketing*

marketers should avoid taking for granted its widespread and uniform diffusion.

10.3 *Corporate Examples*

In this section, we address the following questions:

- How can companies deploy mobile marketing?
- Among available examples of mobile marketing, which are more successful, and why?

How can companies deploy mobile marketing? The two main ways for companies to implement mobile marketing are through mobile applications and the use of mobile technology in store and in promotional material. A *mobile application* or "app" stands for a software application that is basically a computer program that can be downloaded on a mobile (or stationary) device. Among the variety of apps, mobile apps constitute one of the fastest-growing segments in downloads (Lee & Raghu, 2014).

By 2013, mobile application platforms such as Apple's App Store (henceforth AppStore) and Google Play had grown exponentially. For instance, the AppStore was launched in 2008 with only 500 apps and a dozen developers. Five years later, the numbers speak for themselves: 500 million users in 155 countries, nearly 846,000 apps available, around 40 billion app downloads, and more than 7 billion USD paid to more than 200,000 app developers (Shen, 2015).

We can now look into the many examples of firms, from all kinds of industries, that have developed mobile apps or used creative ways to employ mobile technology in stores and promotional material (e.g., paper catalog and magazines).

Among the examples of mobile marketing you known about, which are more successful and why? Next, we look at a few examples of mobile marketing practices. Can you tell why some are more likely than others to be successful (see "Food for Thought")?

Food for Thought 10.3

- Among the examples of companies undertaking mobile marketing listed below (and others that you may have heard of), which ones are bound to be more successful than others and why?

10.3.1 *Costco, Danone, and Fiat*

We briefly review the proposition of three companies that have developed mobile apps around their core business with the main purpose of enhancing customer experience.

First, we look at one of the largest global retailers, Costco Wholesale Corporation (see Table 10.4 for an overview of the company). Since we have provided background information on distribution and retailers earlier in this chapter, it is noteworthy to acknowledge that most large retailers offer mobile apps that allow consumers to shop faster (e.g., using shopping lists), get digital coupons, and personalized deals instantly. For instance, Costco's mobile app in Canada is presented as "the easiest way to save time and money on the go" (Costco Wholesale Corporation, 2017). Members get access to the latest Warehouse Offers right on their mobile device and can easily clip their favorite offers. They can also access a unique and expanded selection of items that are not necessarily available at local warehouses, and benefit from home delivery. In addition, the app offers a navigation system to the nearest Costco warehouse. For customers of the Costco Photo Center, it provides a simpler way to upload photos straight from a mobile phone, and then format and order prints for pickup. Figure 10.10 presents a visual of the app to download from either iTunes or Google Play.

Next, Danone illustrates the case of companies for which the use of mobile technology is not a straightforward endeavor. Because of the multiple business units (i.e., dairy products, baby and medical nutrition, as well as waters and beverages), the many subsidiaries and brands carried by the company (e.g., Actimel, Volvic, Évian, Badoit, Blédina, Danette, and Taillefine), and the nontechnological nature of products, there were many opportunities for the group to use mobile technology, and at the same time not one obvious way to do so. To enhance the customer experience, Danone chose to develop "Dan-On," an app that facilitates the organization of meals (from cooking to planning for healthy nutrition), adjusted to each customer's lifestyle and family size, with smart recipes. Promotion deals for Danone's products via a monthly coupon system are also available to the app users. A video presentation of the app is available on YouTube with search words: "DANONE—DanOn—Customized, balanced and easy meals." This example (see Figure 10.11) shows how an app can be developed around the unifying mission of such a large and diversified group like Danone ("bring health through food to the greatest number of people") (Danone, 2017).

Finally, the Ciao Fiat mobile app developed by FIAT (Italy) reveals the case of an industry where mobile technology is perhaps easier to use in adding

Table 10.4 Profiling Costco (US)

Who:	*Costco*
Since:	1983
What:	Membership warehouse club
From:	US
Sales (Bn USD):	116
Employing (people):	218,000
Manufacturing in (countries):	N/A
Selling in (countries):	9

Source: Costco Wholesale Corporation (2016)

400 *Mobile Marketing*

Figure 10.10 Presenting Costco's mobile application

Source: Courtesy of Costco Wholesale (this image remains the property of Costco Wholesale and may be used only with express permission)

value to customers' experience (most carmakers have developed similar apps). Here is a list of selected functionalities that the app provides to car owners (Ciao Fiat Mobile, 2017):

- personalize the application with their particulars and those of their vehicle and handle important due dates for renewal or maintenance (e.g., driving licence, insurance, warranty, and inspection)
- find their car after parking it (the app shows where the vehicle was left on a map and how to get there)
- find Fiat dealers and book test drives for the current models on sale
- obtain faster help in the event of a breakdown or an accident (the car's position is located automatically through the app and its confirmation is followed by the immediate transmission of a call for help, an SMS for confirmation, and immediate recontact for assistance)
- benefit from augmented reality (AR) technology to better understand extracts of their car model's Handbook explaining how to perform certain tasks (e.g., open and close the hood and change a wheel)

Figure 10.12 shows one functionality available through the app for the electric Fiat 500 model: localizing charging stations, a valuable complementary service.

Figure 10.11 Presenting a visual of Dan-On

Source: Courtesy of DANONE

Figure 10.12 Illustrating one functionality of the FIAT 500e mobile app: location of charging stations

Source: Courtesy of Fiat Chrysler Automobile US LLC

Table 10.5 Profiling Fiat Chrysler Automobile (Italy)

Who:	Fiat Chrysler Automobiles
Since:	1899
What:	Automobile manufacturer
From:	Italy
Sales (Bn USD):	124
Employing (people):	231,000
Manufacturing in (countries):	N/A
Selling in (countries):	140

Source: FCA (2016)

10.3.2 Frank And Oak

Frank And Oak's integration of online, mobile, and brick-and-mortar marketing[1]—Founded in 2012 by two childhood friends, Ethan Song and Hicham Ratnani, Frank And Oak is a Montreal-based (Canada) clothing designer and online retailer with an innovative approach to customer service. The company's main customer targets are millennial men (born between 1980 and 2000, roughly), and, since 2016, women. It largely relies on online sales and a mobile app that offers styling advice and maintains a constant link with customers, notably sending push notifications about promotions and monthly notices with highly personalized offerings. However, stores are also a place for customers to live through a unique community experience with direct access to the most recent collection of clothes and accessories, a styling consultation service, a coffee bar, and a barber salon. A short video presentation of the business model by City Television can be watched on YouTube with search words: "Episode 22—Frank And Oak."

Three years after inception, the start-up already employed about one hundred people and commercialized in all of North America (with 30 percent sales in its domestic market and 70 percent in the US). It opened a temporary office in New York to facilitate initial steps in their US expansion (now closed) and operated wholly owned stores in some of the main metropolises (e.g., Boston, Calgary, Chicago, Edmonton, Halifax, Montreal, Ottawa, Toronto, Vancouver, and Washington, DC). Several of them were in the format of "pop-up stores" (e.g., stores intended to stay open only a few weeks or months). In 2017, pop-ups in Boston, Chicago, Halifax, and Washington, DC, were still active.

Figure 10.13 Presenting Frank And Oak's logotype
Source: Courtesy of Frank And Oak

404 *Mobile Marketing*

Data on sales is not available, but in 2015 more than thirty-five thousand orders were dealt with each month, among which 30 percent were through mobile phones. A spectacular four-year revenue growth rate of 18,480 percent earned the first position in Deloitte's 2015 "Technology Fast 50" ranking of Canadian tech companies. This award not only recognizes companies for rapid growth but also for innovative technology, entrepreneurship, and leadership.

Frank And Oak indeed differentiates from the competition by creating a unique shopping experience and by bridging digital and physical spaces. A few examples of the initiatives implemented to achieve these objectives, starting with community building and consumer involvement, are presented here:

- When it first entered the US market, the company asked customers to vote via the mobile app and help them decide where the six stores planned should open (in either Manhattan, Brooklyn, Chicago, Washington, DC, Philadelphia, Atlanta, San Francisco, Seattle, Austin, or Portland).
- The company also introduced community managers at each location. In order to create a deeper sense of meaning and community, these people were charged with organizing in-store events (e.g., workshops, whisky tastings, and live shows).

Moving on to the use of mobile technology to enhance personalization and the purchasing and after-sale experience, here are a few examples of what Frank And Oak does:

- Through the online and mobile platform, the company collects data on consumers' usage and response to products. When customers come in contact (either online or in-store), personal stylists—equipped with tablets when in stores (see Figure 10.14)—have immediate access to their purchasing history (frequency and length of visits, preferences, amounts spent, etc.) and can thus personalize recommendations accordingly.
- In addition, Apple's iBeacon (a geo-localization tool) was used from April 2015 to May 2016—alongside the release of Frank And Oak's new app and branding—to send push notifications to customers' mobile phones whenever they were physically close to a store (i.e., within a perimeter of 150 meters or ~500 feet). These notifications invited them to pay a visit to the store and offered specific promotions.
- With a positioning that combines uniqueness and affordability, a great deal of care is put into personalizing not only the purchasing experience but the after-sale experience, as well. For instance, all shipped orders are wrapped up in silk paper and marked with a sticker signed by the employee in charge. When buying online, consumers can have the purchased items delivered directly to the store where they can try them on, or they can buy in store and have the items delivered to their home.
- To enhance services, Frank And Oak developed several partnerships with other companies. For instance, telecommunication companies, such as Virgin Mobile, promoted the company's mobile app to their clients in

Mobile Marketing 405

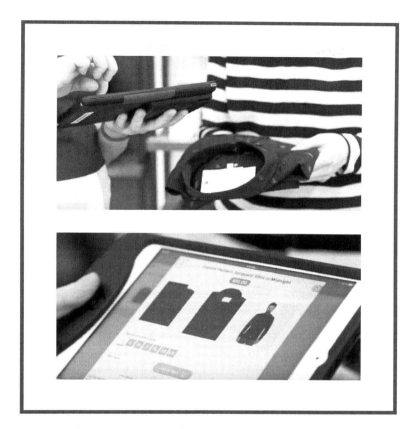

Figure 10.14 Illustrating the use of mobile technology by Frank And Oak

Source: Screen capture from a YouTube video available with search words: "Tulip Retail featuring Frank & Oak," posted by Tulip Retail, retrievable at www.YouTube.com/watch?v=vutljrk9VNg

January 2015 and offered exclusive deals. Affiliation of resident barbers and various partnerships with local vendors (e.g., Monthly Barber and Café Névé in Montreal, Jimmy's Coffee House in Toronto, and Barber Ha in Edmonton) support the services offered in selected stores.
- For targeted postal codes in Montreal, Toronto, and Vancouver, Frank And Oak partnered with Canada Post to allow for same-day delivery of orders.
- In 2015, the company launched a pre-roll advertising campaign on YouTube. Played just before the videos users wanted to see, the 15–30 second ads were interactive and allowed direct purchase (Mobile Commerce Daily—Mobile Commerce Daily, 2015).
- Frank And Oak also offered the "Hunt Club," a program in which registered consumers received a selection of up to five items (corresponding to individual responses given to a questionnaire inquiring about needs,

406 *Mobile Marketing*

preferences, musical tastes, etc.) at home by postal delivery every month. This service came with a ninety-day free trial period and a yearly fee of 20 USD. Customers could then try on the items in the comfort of their own environment and have up to five days to decide which ones to buy and keep, and which ones to return thanks to a prepaid parcel box. Several customer reviews are available on YouTube (e.g., with search words: "Frank And Oak: The Hunt Club | Unboxing | HDStyles," and "Big Unboxing From FRANK AND OAK! My "Hunt Club" Box! Promo Code!"). The Hunt Club was replaced in 2017 by a similar program called the "Style Plan," addressing both male and female millennials. In Canada, membership was priced at 19 CAD (~15 USD) per month and while the system worked a little differently, the spirit remained the same: every month, members would get a Style Plan token redeemable for products at members-only pricing (up to 25 percent off). They would then select the items of their choice from personalized recommendations with free shipping, and keep only what they want with free returns. Any unused tokens would roll over to the next month. Membership could be cancelled at anytime.

In all, the example of Frank And Oak illustrates well how online and mobile marketing can be combined with a grassroots approach (emphasizing gatherings and community building), and unleash companies' creativity in providing a high-quality customer experience. After Canadian male millennials, targeting US male millennials most likely facilitated the first international expansion step of the company (since they share many similar characteristics). From there, market expansion was twofold: targeting a new segment (women of the same generation and style) and pursuing new geographic destinations. In 2017, Frank And Oak already offered shipping to forty countries around the world, but did not have any stores outside of North America yet. The future will tell whether the company can replicate its successful combination of online, mobile, and brick-and-mortar marketing and the types of CAGE distances with which it will be confronted.

10.3.3 IKEA

IKEA's augmented reality app[2]—For promotion, the Swedish furniture company has relied heavily on the distribution of a printed catalog since 1951. In 2016, this catalog has become a three hundred-plus-page book printed in seventeen languages and distributed in twenty-eight countries (Nigam & Jain, 2017). Nevertheless, IKEA took advantage of the advent of mobile technology to innovate in the way it reached its customers. In 2010, they introduced a mobile application consisting of an interactive catalogue available for free on the Apple Store. The application allowed customers to consult the catalogue directly on their smartphone or tablet. Like many other apps seen previously, it offered the basic functionalities of managing shopping lists, making purchases at a distance as well as scanning products while at the store. All of this definitely contributed to enhancing the customer experience.

Mobile Marketing   407

In 2013, the company found an even more creative way to fully benefit from the new opportunities offered by mobile technology. It developed an augmented reality (AR) application that gives clients the opportunity to assess the fit between coveted items (e.g., armchairs, tables, and carpets) and their own homes. Placing the printed catalog in specific positions in a room and using the camera on their tablets or smartphones, customers could scan the printed catalog through the app (using QR codes technology), access collection and product information, and then compare products on the screen while visualizing them in 3-D, positioned as desired in the room. A presentation of this app is available on YouTube with search words: "The New IKEA Catalog App: Create Your Space." Offering access to the virtual catalog and all of the online payment options, the app definitely helps in reducing uncertainty in the online buying process. In 2015, 54 million people used the app to access IKEA's catalog (an increase of 17 percent compared to the previous year). The app, presented in Figure 10.15, is cited as one of the most popular applications and won an Effective Mobile Marketing Award (organized by the *Mobile Marketing Magazine*).

In 2016, IKEA decided to introduce virtual reality (VR) and take the experience to a whole new level. They launched a pilot VR app called "IKEA VR Kitchen Experience" which allows customers—equipped with a VR headset and two wands—to immerse themselves in a virtual life-size IKEA kitchen and walk around freely while testing different materials (e.g., counter tops, flooring, cabinets, and so on). As of 2017, the app has only been released on Valve's game platform Steam, but the company expects that within five to ten years, VR will become an integrated part of people's lives, allowing for the extensive diffusion of the app.

With these initiatives, IKEA managed to build brand awareness and enrich customers' shopping experience and creativity. To a larger extent than ever before, they addressed the well-known pitfall of any online environment: the inability to see, touch, smell, and feel physical products before buying. Importantly, IKEA also made sure to combine and integrate its traditional and online/mobile promotion tools.

10.3.4 Nivea and FCB

The Nivea Protects mobile app[3]—If most brands propose mobile apps nowadays, some are being so creative that they earn advertising industry recognition. This is the case of the German brand Nivea when they hired the Foote Cone & Belding agency (US) based in São Paulo (Brazil) to develop the "Protection Ad" campaign during the summer of 2013. For this, a mobile app called "Nivea Protects" was developed as an extension of the advertising campaign. This campaign earned a Lion award in 2014, from the Cannes Lions International Festival of Creativity (France), which is one of the largest gatherings of worldwide advertising professionals, designers, digital innovators, and marketers. Working around the main product attribute of Nivea cream (i.e., skin protection), and in particular the sunscreen cream, the advertising agency wanted to address the challenge of further protecting

Figure 10.15 Presenting IKEA's store app
Source: Used with the permission of Inter IKEA Systems B.V.

Mobile Marketing 409

children. They had the idea of looking into the problem of children getting lost on crowded beaches.

To address this problem (and fulfill the corresponding need), they developed a campaign combining a printed ad in magazines, a detachable bracelet, and a mobile app. The targeted customer segment, parents, could purchase the magazine and read it on the beach. On the ad page, they would find a detachable paper bracelet with Bluetooth 4.0 technology that they could then attach to their child's wrist and stop worrying about them wandering out of sight. Indeed, the bracelet could be synchronized with the mobile app once downloaded on the parents' mobile phone. After having set the warning distance, parents would receive an alarm on their phone if their child was outside the radius they considered safe.

This campaign was not directly related to purchasing sunscreen, yet it generated a lot of positive word of mouth (WOM). As a result, NIVEA Sun Kids enjoyed a 62 percent increase in sales in Rio de Janeiro. A presentation of the app is available on YouTube with search words: "NIVEA Sun Kids FCB Brasil." The interest of this example also lies in who is behind the advertising campaign: Foote Cone & Belding (FCB). This is one of the most prominent global advertising agency networks (see Table 10.6).

The agency believes that a "Never Finished Idea" is one that can be expressed in a multitude of ways over long periods of time, creating richer equity and lasting returns for brands. In the years that followed, FCB evolved the "Protection Ad" campaign to continue telling the Nivea Sun Kids brand story and was the team behind the creation of "Doll" and "Sun Slide." Beyond Nivea, FCB has worked with brands such as Kotex, Palmolive, and Sunkist to create new consumer behaviors, embodying the principles behind the theory of planned behavior (or reasoned action), discussed previously (see Section 10.2.1 as well as Chapter 5). As marketers, we can only hope to influence behaviors by modifying attitudes, through changing beliefs. For many years, the company's website clearly highlighted this core objective with a central page stating in large font: "What behavior do you want to change?" and, written underneath in smaller font: "At FCB we believe that

Table 10.6 Profiling Foote Cone & Belding (US)

Who:	*Foote, Cone & Belding*
Since:	1873
What:	Advertising, experiential event, sponsorship, promotion, retail and shopper marketing, digital, social media, mobile, direct marketing and CRM
From:	US
Sales (Bn USD):	N/A (FCB is part of the Interpublic Group of Companies)
Employing (people):	8,000
Offices in (countries):	80
Selling in (countries):	200

Source: Foote Cone & Belding (2016a)

410 *Mobile Marketing*

changing attitudes can be helpful, but changing behavior is what we're paid to do and has to be the end goal. We believe asking what appears to be a simple question makes a remarkable difference. So, what behavior do you want to change?"

At the turn of 2017, FCB transformed the message from "change behaviors" to "create behaviors," also displayed prominently on their website. We can reasonably assume that the psychological mechanisms behind this message remain the same as professed by the planned behavior theory (schematically, consumers' beliefs influence their attitudes, which determine their behaviors). Following the new tagline, website visitors could read: "Yes, get people's attention. Yes, make them think, feel, emote. And then move them to do something. To act, to change, to go from there to there." However, the novelty lies in introducing the fact that behaviors can be created (i.e., that new beliefs can be suggested for consumers to embrace). This bring us back to a discussion held in Chapter 2 about whether the essence of marketing was "answering" (the traditional view) or "creating" customer needs (a more recent and disruptive view of marketing). The example of FCB illustrates well this evolution in marketing thinking, especially at a time where new technologies, such as mobile technology, unleash unlimited creative possibilities.

10.3.5 *Uber*

Uber's mobile application[4]—Launched in 2010 in San Francisco (US), Uber's mobile app was originally developed by one of the two founders, Garrett Camp, to allow users to connect directly with luxury vehicle drivers in virtually all locations any time of day, avoiding directly entering the traditional taxi space where passengers must either call into a centralized dispatch or hail a cab on the street. The app evolved into a free mobile application for individuals to fulfil various transportation needs in real-time. The demand for Uber is increasing exponentially, with an estimated gross booking (roughly equivalent to the total value of ride fares) of under one billion USD in 2013, ~3 billion in 2014, ~9 billion in 2015, and ~20 billion USD in 2016. For that same year, net revenue was 6.5 billion USD and Uber's valuation a staggering $69 billion USD (ten to eleven times its net revenue). Table 10.7 presents an overview of the company.

Uber's primary service connects users with private drivers using location-based technology through smartphone devices. As the company operates in major urban areas, usually with higher population concentration, its services aim to provide an alternative for personal transportation. In this way, the company mainly targets business people, travelers, and university students. Uber's clients are capable smartphone users. They can order a service of their choice, based on their specific needs (e.g., UberX, UberGo, UberBlack, UberLimo, and UberPop). Once a vehicle is selected, they will receive an instant quote of the trip fare on their mobile phone, view feedback and ratings of the drivers available, track the vehicle as it arrives, pay for the trip through the app, receive the receipt directly to email, and revisit trip history information (for example, to track items they may have lost in a driver's car). At each stage of the interaction, Uber customers have a high level of power

Mobile Marketing   411

Table 10.7 Profiling Uber (US)

Who:	Uber
Since:	2009
What:	Personal transportation and delivery services
From:	US
Sales (Bn USD):	6.5
Employing (people):	N/A
Operating in (countries/cities):	75/500+

Source: Adapted from Bloomberg (2017) and Uber (2017)

and autonomy compared to traditional taxi customers. From the on-demand model, to the type of service provided, and feedback and rating systems, customers have a greater voice than ever before. However, customers in this industry are also characterized by low loyalty and can easily switch to other leading ride-hailing app (e.g., Easy Taxi in Brazil, Didi Chunxing in China, Ola Cabs in India, Gett in Israel, Mytaxi in Germany and Spain, Yandex Taxi in Russia, Careem in United Arab Emirates, and many others).

In terms of offerings, Uber has a different product-mix across countries, based on local regulations and the availability of partners. In more competitive locations, the company opted for a wider range of vehicles in order to capture greater market share and increase brand awareness through referral marketing. By 2014, Uber began expanding its offerings with logistical operations. For instance, certain cities in the US saw a messenger service called UberRush; "Corner Store," an on-demand delivery service for everyday essentials; UberFresh, a food delivery service with a rotating menu; and UberPool, a carpooling option that facilitated super-cheap pickups for people traveling similar routes. Depending on its geographical region, Uber also does seasonal or occasion-specific deliveries of on-demand ice cream, Christmas trees, roses, and kittens. One example is UberHEALTH: a one-day program in which the company partnered with medical professionals to bring house calls to thirty-five cities across the US, providing wellness packs for $10 per request, as well as up to ten influenza vaccinations by a registered nurse, free of charge. Founder Travis Kalanick described the company as the forerunner of a comprehensive "on-demand economy," in which the push of a smartphone button triggers the almost instantaneous arrival of any physical thing. "If we can get you a car in five minutes," he has said, "we can get you anything in five minutes."

Since Uber does not operate like a traditional transportation service, it has relatively low capital investment in assets. The company's business model revolves around technology and algorithms (e.g., fare estimator, arrival ETA, and wallet-less payment), which is one of the main factors explaining its phenomenal expansion. This model creates a unique set of strengths (e.g., decentralization of operations allows for the company to grow at an exponential rate; positive WOM results in minimal expenditures in traditional promotion) and weaknesses (e.g., issues in enforcing company policies). If we now look into the *People* aspect of the 7Ps, Uber has a limited number of

412   *Mobile Marketing*

employees compared to traditional taxi services. This is due to drivers being defined as "partners" and not as employees, since they operate as independent agents. Actual Uber employees are mostly at the executive and management levels of the organizational structure. For drivers, Uber provides the platform and technology, and in exchange takes a percentage of ride fares (e.g., ~15 percent in Montreal in 2013). Like for customers, the mobile app provides drivers with more freedom and autonomy than they would have in a traditional taxi company. The model also considerably reduces costs for them as they do not have to purchase a taxi license or pay dispatch fees. Taxi licenses are not only extremely expensive (e.g., the price of a license to offer taxi services in Montreal increased from ~52,000 USD to ~144,000 USD between 2000 and 2015, but they are scarce too, drastically limiting the offer. Uber has often been described as "democratizing" the personal transportation industry.

In terms of pricing, Uber offers standard local rates in many locations and also uses dynamic pricing, what the company calls "surge-pricing" (i.e., prices follow spikes or drops in demand). Many other online sellers use the same tactic (e.g., Amazon). This is one opportunity offered by the online environment that brick-and-mortar settings can hardly replicate. Indeed, changing prices for products on shelves on a moment-by-moment basis would be far too impractical and costly (although possible, if regulations were to permit companies the ability not to display prices in store). In the online environment, algorithms can change prices in the blink of an eye.

As for promotion, the company mainly relies on WOM from current users, and has found many creative ways to incentivize referrals. For instance, in 2015, existing customers could offer new users the ability to register using their own user code and as a result both the new and existing customer got a 20 USD credit. This discount deal was then publicized by several celebrities like Neil Patrick Harris and Lindsay Lohan in the US (the latter tweeted the deal to her 7.7 million followers). In other instances, opinion leaders and celebrities have spontaneously endorsed Uber (e.g., Ashton Kutcher), using their Twitter accounts, but this time without any financial incentives. Launching their services in new cities, Uber also resorted to promotional campaigns, such as providing new users with three free rides, for instance. Uber regularly sends promotion codes to users based on historical usage and preferences, while also partnering with companies and organizing events to build brand awareness. Recently, Uber has taken to partnering with other companies to allow the driver request service to be included within their native platforms (e.g., Foursquare, Breathometer, Bluesmart, and Microsoft), in a form of cross-promotion.

In Chapter 2, we described Uber's fast pace of internationalization as largely due to the ease with which a business model based on mobile technology can be replicated across borders. High degrees of technological standardization helped overcome issues related to geographic and economic distance. If technological distance remains a challenge for Uber in developing countries (the app requires certain standards to function well), it is yet another dimension of the CAGE distance that has represented, by far, the most significant hurdle in Uber's internationalization: administrative distance. The taxi

Mobile Marketing   413

industry is a phenomenally difficult arena for new entrants (strict regulations and deep-rooted incumbents made it virtually impossible for new companies to succeed). Furthermore, it is structured and regulated differently across markets, with policies usually determined at the municipal or regional level, increasing the level of complexity. Prior to the emergence of Uber, few innovations or changes had been seen in the traditional taxi industry for decades. Since the disruption of peer-to-peer ridesharing, taxi companies have tried to remain relevant and competitive by introducing their own ride-hailing apps. Entrenched players in many countries (e.g., Canada, France, Romania, and the UK) have also fiercely lobbied and protested against the American company, seen as an unfair competitor.

To counter administrative differences (see Chapter 6), Uber has often embraced an "expand-now, negotiate-later" approach. Arguing that Uber is not a taxi company but a technological platform, it falls within a legislative "gray area." The company usually enters markets without prior notification to the host country, attracts new clientele, garners their support . . . and then works to find a middle ground with local regulators. It was often met with severe reactions and in many cases confronted with cease-and-desist injunctions from governments, with fines imposed on drivers. Using the vast amounts of capital raised, Uber picked up the penalties, also covering legal repercussions that a driver might receive from the authorities. In addition, Uber pushed for new legislations at the state level that would legalize its operations, often successfully.

In conclusion, the example of Uber illustrates well that, with mobile technology, geographic distance is no longer an issue, but "distance still matters" (see Chapter 4) with other types of distance (in this particular case, administrative distance) imposing a significant amount of added costs (time, energy, and money). It also reveals several new opportunities offered to companies embracing mobile marketing, in particular implementing innovative practices in terms of pricing (dynamic pricing) and promotion (WOM) policies.

10.4 Issues at Stake

In this section, we address the following questions:

- Did the online environment establish a new power balance between firms and consumers? What happens when customers feel angry or betrayed?
- What are some of the challenges and key success factors for selling online? How should companies communicate with customers in public online environments?
- What is the impact of adopting mobile marketing on regular marketing activities?
- In terms of outcomes, is mobile marketing only positive? Then, what are the key success factors for mobile marketing?

Before answering these questions, can you form an opinion about the following (see "Food for Thought")?

414   *Mobile Marketing*

Food for Thought 10.4

- In reference to Berthon, Pitt, Plangger, and Shapiro (2012) and Gao, Rohm, Sultan, and Pagani (2013), what are the key issues at stake when considering mobile marketing in an international context?

10.4.1 *The Newly Empowered Consumer*

Did the online environment establish a new power balance between firms and consumers? What happens when customers feel angry or betrayed?[5] While firms use mobile marketing to reach their target audience, customers increasingly turn to their mobile phones to express their anger or frustration when they perceive they have been unfairly treated (Nepomuceno et al., 2017).

Indeed, customers experiencing a situation of *double deviation* (i.e., failed service followed by failed recovery) are likely formulating negative judgments against the firm. Believing that a company displays negative motives is also key in driving negative emotions such as betrayal or anger (Joireman et al., 2013). These negative beliefs and emotions then lead customers to hold grudges against the faulty company and demonstrate a desire for avoidance and/or revenge (Grégoire et al., 2009). Here, the notion of *desire for avoidance* refers to customers' motivation to keep their distance and withdraw from any relationship with the firm (Grégoire et al., 2009). In turn, *desire for revenge* refers to the customers' motivation of bringing the firm down and punishing them to get justice after a service failure (Bechwati & Morrin, 2003). As a result, aggrieved customers can engage in different forms of vengeful behaviors from *direct revenge behaviors,* such as vindictive complaining (e.g., insulting staff) and marketplace aggressions (e.g., slamming the door or damaging companies' property), to *indirect revenge behaviors,* such as negative WOM and online public complaining that happens "behind companies' backs" (Grégoire et al., 2010).

Online customer complaints, which is among the most salient form of customer vengeful behaviors, must be carefully managed by firms. Otherwise, they can tarnish corporate credibility, reputation, and brand equity (Grégoire et al., 2015). For instance, in the recent case where United Airlines violently removed one of its passengers from a flight against his will, the airline suffered serious public relations humiliation and brand damages. The video of the incident captured by another passenger went viral and it was re-tweeted sixteen thousand times just in the first day. The customers' online action resulted in a legal settlement and the placement of four staff on leave (Stevens, 2017). Tripp and Grégoire (2011) outline useful strategies to handle such situations. First, firms should respond within an immediate timeframe and genuinely express their understanding of the difficulties that the customer has experienced. Second, they should tailor a fair response to the complainer. Indeed, occasional customers respond better to financial incentives and restitution values but loyal and relationship-focused customers are more concerned about a firm's genuine recovery efforts and sincere apologies. Finally, customers rarely forgive wrongdoings occasioned by greed. Firms should own up to their honest mistakes, avoid ambiguity, and provide clear and sufficient information about the reasons behind the failure.

In conclusion, customers do complain when feeling angry or betrayed. Doing so in online forums give them enough power to actually "hurt" companies. This opportunity rebalances the power relationship between firms and their customers in favor of the latter. Before that, consumers had limited options: file a formal complaint with the company (which may or may not be taken into consideration), try and attract traditional media attention, or undergo an expensive and risky litigation procedure. Thanks to mobile devices and other ICT tools, revenge is now possible.

10.4.2 Impact on Marketing Decisions and Feasibility

What are some of the challenges and key success factors for selling online?[6] Among the challenges faced by marketers in e-commerce, one of the greatest is undoubtedly its uniquely intangible setting. Indeed, items sold through websites cannot be touched, felt, or smelled (Lee & Tan, 2003; Lin, Jones, & Westwood, 2009). This is also the case for items sold through mobile apps and social media networks. Consequently, many consumers resist shopping online because they find it difficult to evaluate physical cues regarding the goods they are purchasing (Featherman & Pavlou, 2003). Not only is there a physical dimension to intangibility but a mental one as well. *Mental intangibility* refers to the degree to which a product or service can be easily defined, formulated, or grasped mentally (Laroche, Bergeron, & Goutaland, 2001). Thus, a physical tangible product can be mentally intangible. This is particularly true for products with which consumers are not familiar. For example, someone not familiar with a smartphone may be able to touch it, but he might have a hard time defining what it can be used for.

This intrinsically intangible setting leads to an increased perception of risk (Mitchell & Greatorex, 1993; Laroche et al., 2001; Brasil, Sampaio, & Perin, 2008). In addition to intangibility and perceived risk, past research has also identified privacy and security concerns as inhibitors of online shopping (Bart, Shankar, Sultan, & Urban, 2005; Taylor, Davis, & Jillapalli, 2009; Mothersbaugh, Foxx, Beatty, & Wang, 2012; Nepomuceno, Laroche, Richard, & Eggert, 2012). In short, consumers are concerned that private information might not be well protected in e-commerce and that malicious individuals can breach one's sensitive data via the Internet.

In order to reduce perceptions of intangibility and risk, as well as to overcome privacy and security concerns, Nepomuceno et al. (2014) find that marketers should engage in the following best practices: obtain and show recognized third-party seals, improve order checking systems (allowing customers to track the expected date and time of delivery), and improve customer service experiences. In addition, they find that product knowledge is more important than brand familiarity when shopping online, and that dealing with mental intangibility is more important than with physical intangibility.

416   *Mobile Marketing*

Given these findings, Nepomuceno et al. (2014) stress that marketers should give as much information as possible about products sold online (e.g., providing a direct link to the manufacturer's user manual or a detailed description of the parts that compose a given good), as this will increase product information and reduce mental intangibility.

Examples of companies succeeding in implementing these best practices include Amazon and Zappos. Amazon goes to great lengths to ensure customers that their goods are underway. At any time, a customer can identify whether their package has been sent, where it was processed last by the shipping service, and when it will arrive at the destination. Amazon has even integrated their order checking systems with customers' personal calendars to more easily inform them of deliveries. A subsidiary of Amazon, Zappos is an online retailer of shoes also widely recognized as an example of great customer service. A remarkable illustration occurred in 2011 when a customer who was going to be the best man in a wedding did not receive his shoes in time. Zappos was swift to deal with the situation, not only by offering to overnight a new pair of shoes at no cost, but also by upgrading the customer to a VIP account and giving him a complete refund on the purchase (Consumerist, 2011). This example illustrates well how the company avoided a "double deviation" situation (as discussed previously): a swift and generous reaction ensured the customer "recovery" and most likely limited any enduring anger and negative WOM.

In conclusion, overcoming the challenges of selling online is feasible but requires significant time and resource commitment from companies, perhaps offsetting some of the costs reduction associated with the online environment.

Therefore, how should companies communicate with customers in public online environments?[7] Because the rise of social media creates a public conversational environment, companies must carefully choose how to interact with consumers. The type of communication that brands use when exchanging with clients and prospects can indeed become a factor critical to success. Along with message content, the style of the message plays an important role in forming consumers' perceptions about brands.

From the perspective of message content, one of the biggest advantages of the online world is *personalization*. Examples of companies that successfully do so are Amazon (e.g., contents of webpages are individually adapted according to the browsing and purchase history of each client) and Netflix (e.g., users can create multiple profiles in order to enjoy a customized online experience). The benefits of using personalization are numerous. For instance, research has shown that personalization fosters loyalty and positive WOM behaviors (Dantas & Carrillat, 2013). Research also suggests that customized products foster willingness to pay and purchase intention (Franke, Keinz, & Steger, 2009).

In terms of style, two choices are generally available to companies: apply an informal (or "human") tone of voice or a more-formal (also called "corporate") tone of voice. A company's tone of voice can be defined as the communication style it adopts when interacting with customers. For example, conversational human tone of voice is defined as "an engaging and natural style of organizational communication as perceived by an organization's public based on interaction between individuals in the organization and individuals in publics" (Kelleher, 2009). A certain numbers of factors bound the choice between human or corporate tone of voice (or any combination between them). For example, using a human tone of voice on social media is recommended under the following conditions: the brand's products and services are of the hedonic type (i.e., those products or services which provide emotional benefits, as opposed to utilitarian benefits), the context is characterized by low risk and situational involvement (e.g., the relative importance of the purchase is low), and the posts about the brand are mostly positive. In turn, the use of a more-corporate tone of voice is advisable when the brand's products and services are associated with contexts of risk and high situational involvement (Barcelos, Dantas, & Sénécal, Work in Progress). Some companies in the same industry have adopted different tones of voice, such as Mastercard and Visa. Mastercard's Facebook page adopts a more human tone of voice (e.g., using a more casual and informal style, and calling customers by their first name) than Visa's, which is more formal.

In all, choosing the right communication style is important for congruency purposes (e.g., aligning communication with the desired positioning), especially in an online context where words spread very quickly and consumers now have a lot of power.

What is the impact of mobile marketing on regular marketing activities? Looking at marketing activities, we can distinguish between the strategic and tactical level of analysis.

At the strategic level, mobile marketing does not disrupt fundamentally the decisions that companies need to make. However, it adds new criteria to make decisions for either *market selection* (e.g., choosing markets where the technology is well accepted and reliable) or *targeting and positioning* (e.g., user characteristics such as age, innovativeness, knowledge, and connectedness becoming of central importance). The impact of mobile activities on entry modes has not attracted much attention in the literature. This suggests that mobile marketing does not affect and is not affected much by the chosen type of entry mode (e.g., exports or FDI). If anything, mobile marketing also adds to the important criteria that need consideration when choosing the right *entry mode*. What matters is establishing a reliable and performant distribution system for the products/services, regardless of whether these are distributed and promoted via stationary or mobile devices.

At the tactical level, the question of how mobile marketing affects the 4/7Ps is somewhat complex to answer because of the multiplicity of approaches adopted by companies. Many companies will maintain the exact same *product policies* but use mobile technology to enhance customer service and experience (e.g., Costco and IKEA). In this case, a performant app can become a competitive advantage for firms and clearly helps them differentiate from competition. Others will do the same but because of the type of industry they are in and the products they commercialize, customer experience can only be moderately enhanced. The mobile app, for instance, becomes a "nice to have" addition but does not make for a real differentiation point (e.g., Danone, Fiat, and Starbucks). For other companies, mobile technology is embedded in the business model to various degrees, moderately in the case

418 *Mobile Marketing*

of Frank And Oak, for instance, or extensively in the case of Uber. In this configuration, mobile technology becomes a core asset and represents a clear competitive advantage. Finally, other companies develop apps for a fee and these apps become products among others, not a support to pre-existing value offerings. The case of Nivea also illustrated the temporary use of mobile technology to develop a product and its app (i.e., bracelets for tracking kids with a mobile phone while vacationing at the beach) that were only indirectly related to the main product (sunscreen). This is only one example of boundless creativity in developing products with a mobile marketing perspective, and it would be pointless to try and describe them all here. What is important for us to remember is that when companies adopt mobile marketing, the rest of the marketing-mix can be impacted in many different ways. General observations are presented hereafter for some important elements of the marketing-mix.

Pricing is likely to be unaffected for companies using mobile technology to enhance service and customer experience (i.e., the price of furniture at IKEA purchased via a mobile phone or in-store is likely to be similar— notwithstanding any promotion deals). On the contrary, companies with mobile technology at the core of their business models are often adopting different pricing strategies, notably based on localization- and/or time-based factors (e.g., Frank And Oak's push notifications with special deals for customers passing within the vicinity of a store or Uber's surge pricing).

Distribution and processes, in turn, are more strongly impacted when orders are made through online and mobile channels. In particular, there is often the need to offer additional options for collecting purchased items: home-delivery either by owned or contracted logistics fleets or else by private or public carriers (e.g., UPS, Purolator, or the National Post) and pick-up by customers themselves in own stores or in partners' stores (e.g., Sears in Canada partners with stationary shops and other retailers to offer more pick-up points to customers).

Finally, companies need to carefully rethink *promotion* on mobile devices. Adaptation of the design and format of communications is often necessary to improve the ease of reading on smaller screens. Companies also need to choose the digital media used for promotion (see Table 10.2) that are either specific to mobile devices (e.g., SMS and QR codes) or accessible through both mobile and stationary devices (e.g., videos and messages on social media, movie streaming, magazines, newspapers, etc.). Most importantly, companies need to figure out how communications through mobile devices fit within their overall communication strategy, following the principles of "integrated marketing communications." Pinkton and Broderick (2005, p. 22) describe these principles as follows: "the greatest communications impact will be achieved if all the elements involved are integrated into a unified whole. By integrating the range of promotional mix elements so that they work in harmony or synergy with each other, opportunities are created to improve the effectiveness of the total marketing communication effort." Communication through mobile devices abides by the same logic.

10.4.3 Outcomes

In terms of outcomes, is mobile marketing only positive? Although mobile marketing definitely appears as a great opportunity for growth (notably in terms of increased sales and enhanced reputation), it also comes with issues in regards to efficiency of campaigns. For instance, return on investment and conversion in sales are not always as evident as companies would think (perhaps more so for social media marketing than mobile marketing but both being often combined, companies end up investing money in initiatives with little to no ability to forecast results). Besides, there are significant risks in saturating consumers with offers and invading their privacy. In addition, social media marketing has generated an unprecedented shift of power from the firm to the consumer. The risk of angering consumers and eventually provoking their decision to retaliate (the new "consumer revenge" phenomenon) is real regardless of whether consumers use stationary or mobile devices.

The upside of consumers having outlets in voicing their opinions is that it forces companies to act more responsibly. The downside, however, is that consumers can have a limited understanding of how businesses are run. This can result in ambivalent situations for companies in the long term. For instance, Loblaws (a Canadian supermarket chain) had decided to disrupt the commercialization of the Canadian ketchup brand "French's." This was motivated by sales that were below the company's standards. Faced with an uproar of criticism from consumers keen on defending French's and local producers of tomatoes, Loblaws backtracked on its decision to stop selling the ketchup brand, hoping that the enthusiasm for defending the brand displayed online would translate into actual future sales (CBC News, 2016). It is unclear if it has. This is one of many examples where companies now have to handle ambivalent situations between decisions motivated by their bottom line on the one hand, and by reputation on the other hand. Videos presenting the pros and cons of mobile marketing are available on YouTube (e.g., with search words: "The Pros and Cons of Mobile Marketing | Fiverr").

Then, what are the key success factors for mobile marketing? The *key success factors* (KSF) for mobile marketing pertain to the elements mostly impacted in the marketing-mix: product, distribution, and promotion policies (see Figure 10.20). First, successful adoption of mobile marketing requires the offering to be highly relevant to customers. They may want to use their mobile devices to purchase yes, but not only: getting real-time information and sharing ideas and opinions are also high on their list of priorities. Throughout the articles and examples seen in this chapter, customization and interactivity have also appeared essential. In terms of distribution, all examples of successful mobile marketing (whether with the development of apps or the integration of mobile technology in stores) have pointed to actually improving customer experience and lowering perceived risk (of purchasing and sharing private information). As for promotion, the integration of mobile marketing activities with other initiatives (in the spirit of true "integrated marketing communication" strategies) have proven to be highly important, leveraging the combined power of advertising and social media, in particular.

420   *Mobile Marketing*

Other key success factors include: using permission-based communications and a tone of voice that is appropriate according to the desired positioning, as well as obtaining as much positive WOM as possible.

Using different terms and focusing on mobile social media, Kaplan (2012) offers a summary aligned with the above-mentioned KSF with what he has labelled "the 4Is" (i.e., Integrate, Individualize, Involve, and Initiate). In his own words: "First—and to the greatest extent possible—companies should try to integrate their mobile social media activities into the lives of users, to avoid being a nuisance. Second, such integration can be achieved by individualizing activities to take account of each user's preferences and interests, and provide the opportunity to, third, involve the user through engaging in conversation. If firms are really lucky, they might, fourth, even initiate the creation of user-generated content and word-of-mouth, which allows for tighter integration of activities into users' lives" (Kaplan, 2012, p. 134).

Conclusion: Reaching Consumers Wherever and Whenever with Mobile Marketing Is a Good Idea to Help Bridge Geographic, Technological, and Temporal Distances. Nevertheless, Companies Should Also Mitigate Risks in Implementing This Approach

What would a nomological network for mobile marketing look like? A *nomological network* has been defined as the representation of the constructs of interest in a study, their observable manifestations and the interrelationships among and between them (Cronbach & Meehl, 1955). Figure 10.16 aims to encapsulate important variables in relation to the adoption of mobile marketing by companies.

In the case of mobile marketing, we can start summarizing the main issues related to outcomes and feasibility, as they have been detailed previously. The outcomes of mobile marketing are largely positive, with a strong potential for growth through increased sales and enhanced reputation. Nevertheless, there is always a risk for companies investing in mobile activities with low efficiency issues (e.g., lower return on investment than expected and difficulty converting consumer activity into actual sales). Furthermore, the risk for companies to expose themselves to consumer revenge is real. This risk needs to be handled with care (e.g., with dedicated processes and people to avoid situations of double deviation where recovering a disappointed customer fails after experiencing poor service).

In order to be successful, companies must focus on the following key factors: proposing mobile initiatives that are highly relevant and in accordance with consumers' expectations, actually enhancing customer experience, customizing to the largest extent possible, allowing customers to voice their opinions and easily interact with companies and their offerings, asking for permission while communicating with them and using an accurate tone of voice, lowering perceived risk, and integrating mobile with other marketing activities.

When it comes to the drivers of mobile marketing, one of the issues is the variety of factors affecting its acceptance. Based on the articles and examples discussed in this chapter, we can remember that different user's characteristics

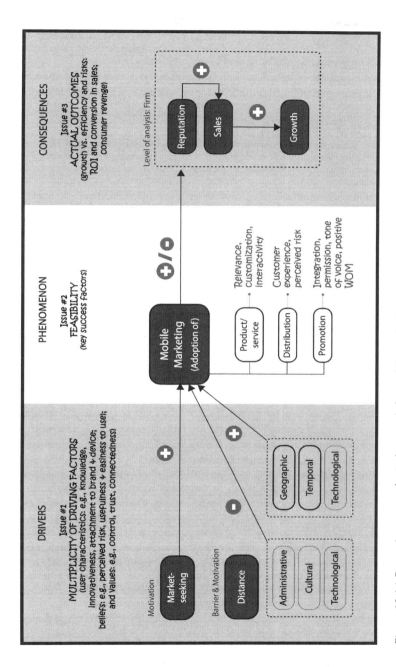

Figure 10.16 Proposing a nomological network for mobile marketing

Source: Own elaboration

422 Mobile Marketing

(e.g., knowledge, innovativeness, attachment to brand and device), beliefs (e.g., perceived risk, usefulness and perceived value, easiness to use), and values (control, trust, connectedness) are all considered important drivers of mobile marketing acceptance, with fluctuations across countries. This variety—and the impact of cultural distance—makes it a complex task for marketers interested in implementing mobile marketing activities.

In terms of general motivation, mobile marketing is first and foremost a market-seeking activity. Among other causes explaining why companies may undertake mobile marketing, we find the notion of distance. As is often the case, distance plays a dual role in both inhibiting and motivating companies. On one hand, the existence of a large technological, cultural, and administrative distance between countries can hinder the replication of mobile marketing activities in foreign markets (i.e., because of insufficient mobile phone penetration, consumers' aversion to risk for sharing location and payment information, or regulations against new entrants and the free flow of information). On the other hand, overcoming technological, geographic, and temporal distance is precisely what motivates companies to undertake mobile marketing activities. Indeed, the use of mobile devices—and in particular mobile phones—has proven to rapidly diffuse (including in emerging countries), allowing companies to reach otherwise-isolated populations (e.g., in rural villages where landlines have not been deployed or where television, newspaper and Internet cable penetration rates are low). Often, online and mobile marketing have proven useful to commercialize products and services in places where both technological infrastructures and geographic conditions (e.g., harsh climates, difficult topography, and remoteness) made it too costly for companies to set up shop. Finally, *temporal distance* is a dimension of psychological distance that we have not broached specifically yet but it has its importance. Cited nearly eight hundred times according to Google Scholar (as of July 2017), an article by Trope, Liberman, and Wakslak (2007) explains why time affects consumers evaluations and behaviors: it plays a central role in shaping perceptions and mental representations of events (hence beliefs, attitudes, and behaviors).

Temporal distance is defined as the distance arising from time and is traditionally measured by comparing near-future versus distant-future events (Kim, Park, & Wyer, 2009). Research on mobile marketing has recently introduced the concept of temporal distance (e.g., Goh, Chu, & Wu, 2015; Luo, Andrews, Fang, & Phang, 2014; Tan & Chang, 2015). While recognizing that this application to the domain of mobile marketing is still in its infancy, it is reasonable to think that mobile marketing helps overcome temporal distance with consumers. As frequently observed, one important characteristic of mobile technology is that it offers real-time information and that mobile devices, being highly personal, are constantly at consumers' reach, often day and night (Sultan, Rohm, & Gao, 2009; Rohm et al., 2012; Gao et al., 2013). This means that mobile marketing reduces considerably the time lag between exposure to a promotional message, for instance, and purchasing decisions (e.g., push notifications using geo-localization features on mobile phones as in the example of Frank And Oak). Traditional advertising campaigns and other promotional events used to reach consumers a certain amount of time before

Mobile Marketing 423

they would find themselves in a buying situation (from several hours to a few days or weeks), thus leaving room for interferences (e.g., competing offers) and distractions. To some extent, temporal distance also relates to administrative distance, when we think of labor regulations which subject companies to open and close at certain hours, observe certain holidays, and so on. With mobile marketing, companies are now "open for business" 24/7 (e.g., through the continuous possibility to order online or live chat with sales or technical representatives), thus reducing the time needed for attending to consumers' needs. All of these expected benefits represent strong motivators for companies to adopt mobile marketing and prompt us to raise the next question.

So, should companies reach consumers whenever and wherever with mobile marketing? The short answer to this question could be: "Absolutely, but . . ." Mobile marketing is a market-seeking opportunity that has proven to be tremendously promising in less than a decade, but is not without dangers. Companies must pay attention to actually enhancing customer experience and to a plethora of key success factors highlighted in this chapter. **Among other benefits, mobile marketing is a practice that can help in bridging geographic, technological, and temporal distances between companies and customers in local as well as foreign markets.**

Notes

1 In Section 10.3.2., the example of Frank And Oak relies on: information provided by the company's Public Relations department; Ici Radio Canada (2015); Les Affaires (2015a, 2015b, 2015c); Mobile Commerce Daily (2015); Mobile Marketer (2015); The Globe and Mail (2015, 2016a, 2016b); Virgin Mobile (2017)
2 In Section 10.3.3, IKEA's example is based on: Burt, Johansson, and Thelander (2011); Business Insider (2014); IKEA (2016a, 2016b); Nigam and Jain (2017).
3 In Section 10.3.4, the example of Nivea and FCB relies on: B2C (2015); Foote Cone & Belding (2016a, 2016b, 2017)
4 In Section 10.3.5, the example of Uber relies on: Bloomberg (2017); CBSNews (2017); CTV News (2015); Digiday (2015); (Montreal Gazette, 2016); New York Post (2014); Ramaswami and Lyons (2013); Slate (2014a, 2014b); The Guardian (2016a, 2016b); The Michael Report (2015); Toronto Star (2017); Uber (2015, 2017); Wall Street Survivor (2017).
5 In section 10.4.1, the subsection entitled: "What happens when customers feel angry or betrayed?" has been written in collaboration with Mina Rohani, Assistant Professor of Marketing at the Edwards School of Business (University of Saskatchewan, Canada). Her research interests revolve around service marketing, online public complaining, and consumer revenge and forgiveness.
6 In Section 10.4.2, the subsection entitled "What are some of the challenges and key success factors for selling online?" has been written in collaboration with Marcelo Vinhal Nepomuceno, Associate Professor in Marketing (HEC Montréal, Canada), whose research interests in consumer behavior include social media, anti-consumption lifestyles, consumer resistance, hormones, and materialism.
7 In Section 10.4.2, the subsection entitled "Therefore, how should companies communicate with customers in public online environments?" has been written in collaboration with Danilo Dantas, Associate Professor in Marketing (HEC Montréal, Canada), whose research interests include database marketing, music marketing, and electronic commerce.

424 *Mobile Marketing*

References

Armelini, Guillermo & Villanueva, Julián (2011). Adding Social Media to the Marketing-mix. *IESE Insight, Second Quarter 2011*(9), 29–36.

B2C (2015). Simply the Best: 6 Great Mobile Marketing Campaigns. *Business 2 Community, By Chloe Basterfield*. By Yngve Andresen, Raymond Hass and Jason Ding. Retrieved July 2017, from www.business2community. com/mobile-apps/simply-best-6-great-mobile-marketing-campaigns-01303500#i7SqAs4AoHVy3Dhs.97

Barcelos, Renato, Dantas, Danilo & Sénécal, Sylvain (Work in Progress). Watch Your Tone: How a Brand's Human Tone of Voice on Social Media Influences Consumer Responses.

Bart, Yakov, Shankar, Venkatesh, Sultan, Fareena & Urban, Glen (2005). Are the Drivers and Role of Online Trust the Same for All Web Sites and Consumers? A Large-Scale Exploratory Empirical Study. *Journal of Marketing, 69*(4), 133–152.

Bauer, Hans, Reichardt, Tina, Barnes, Stuart & Neumann, Marcus (2005). Driving Consumer Acceptanceof Mobile Marketing: A Theoretical Framework and Empirical Study. *Journal of Electronic Commerce Research, 6*(3), 181–192.

Berthon, Pierre, Pitt, Leyland, Plangger, Kirk & Shapiro, Daniel (2012). Marketing Meets Web 2.0, Social Media, and Creative Consumers: Implications for International Marketing Strategy. *Business Horizons, 55*(3), 261–271.

Bechwati, Nada Nasr & Morrin, Maureen (2003). Outraged Consumers: Getting Even at the Expense of Getting a Good Deal. *Journal of Consumer Psychology, 13*(4), 440–453.

Bloomberg (2017, April 14th). Uber, Lifting Financial Veil, Says Sales Growth Outpaces Losses, *By Eric Newcomer*. Retrieved from www.bloomberg. com/news/articles/2017-04-14/embattled-uber-reports-strong-sales-growth-as-losses-continue

Brasil, Vinícius, Sampaio, Cláudio & Perin, Marcelo (2008). A relação entre intangibilidade, o risco percebido e o conhecimento. *Revista de Ciências de Administração, 10*(21), 31–53.

Burt, Steve, Johansson, Ulf & Thelander, Åsa (2011). Standardized Marketing Strategies in Retailing? IKEA's Marketing Strategies in Sweden, the UK and China. *Journal of Retailing and Consumer Services, 18*(3), 183–193.

Business Insider (2014). How Audi, Ikea, And Nike Are Turning Ads Into Services. *By James Connelly*. Retrieved July 2017, from www.businessinsider. com/audi-ikea-nike-turn-ads-into-services-2014-2

Business Insider (2015). Mobile Advertising Is Exploding and Will Grow Much Faster than All Other Digital Ad Categories. Retrieved July 2017, from www. businessinsider.com/mobile-is-growing-faster-than-all-other-ad-formats-2014-10

Cateora, Philip, Gilly, Mary & Graham, John (2011). *International Marketing* (2nd ed.). New York: McGraw-Hill/Irwin (p. 742).

CBC News (2016, May 12th). Loblaws' French's Ketchup Snub Sparks Patriotic Backlash, *By Sheena Goodyear*. Retrieved from www.cbc.ca/news/business/frenchs-ketchup-canadiana-1.3491952

CBS News (2017, July 24th). How Amazon Uses "Surge Pricing," Just Like Uber. *By Kathy Kristof*. Retrieved from www.cbsnews.com/news/amazon-surge-pricing-are-you-getting-ripped-off-small-business/

Ciao Fiat Mobile (2017). How Does It Works? Retrieved July 2017, from www. ciaofiatmobile.it/en/come_funziona.html

Mobile Marketing 425

Commonwealth of Australia Bills (2003). Spam Bill. Retrieved May 2016, from http://www5.austlii.edu.au/au/legis/cth/bill/sb200376/

ComScore (2015). Number of Mobile-Only Internet Users Now Exceeds Desktop-Only in the U.S. Retrieved July 2017, from www.comscore.com/Insights/Blog/Number-of-Mobile-Only-Internet-Users-Now-Exceeds-Desktop-Only-in-the-U.S

Consumerist (2011). Zappos Saves Best Man From Going Barefoot At Wedding. By Ben Popken. Retrieved July 2017, from https://consumerist.com/2011/05/19/zappos-saves-best-man-from-going-barefoot-at-wedding/

Costco Wholesale Corporation (2016). Annual Report. http://phx.corporate-ir.net/phoenix.zhtml?c=83830&p=irol-reportsannual

Costco Wholesale Corporation (2017). Download the Costco Canada App to Your Smartphone! Retrieved July 2017, from www.costco.ca/costco-app.html

Cronbach, Lee Joseph & Meehl, Paul (1955). Construct Validity in Psychological Tests. *Psychological Bulletin, 52*(4), 281–302.

CTV News (2015). Toronto Cab Drivers to Hold Anti-Uber Protest, Delays Expected. Retrieved July 2017, from http://toronto.ctvnews.ca/toronto-cab-drivers-to-hold-anti-uber-protest-delays-expected-1.2692645

Danone (2017). Our Mission in Action. Retrieved July 2017, from www.danone.com/en/

Dantas, Danilo & Carrillat, François (2013). The Relational Benefits of Personalized Communications in an Online Environment. *Canadian Journal of Administrative Sciences, 30*(3), 189–202.

Davis, Fred, Bagozzi, Richard & Warshaw, Paul (1989). User Acceptance of Computer Technology: A Comparison of Two Theoretical Models. *Management Science, 35*(8), 982–1003.

Deloitte (2015). Global Powers of Retailing 2015—Embracing Innovation. Retrieved from https://www2.deloitte.com/content/dam/Deloitte/global/Documents/Consumer-Business/gx-cb-global-powers-of-retailing.pdf

Digiday (2015). Kate Upton, Neil Patrick Harris and Ashton Kutcher Are Tweeting Support for Uber. *By Jordan Valinsky*. Retrieved July 2017, from https://digiday.com/marketing/uber-swears-arent-paying-celebrities-tweet-positively/

eMarketer (2016). Global Mobile Landscape 2016: A Country-by-Country Look at Mobile Phone and Smartphone Usage. Retrieved from www.emarketer.com/Report/Global-Mobile-Landscape-2016-Country-by-Country-Look-Mobile-Phone-Smartphone-Usage/2001859

eMarketer (2017a). Worldwide Ad Spending: The eMarketer Forecast for 2017. Retrieved from www.emarketer.com/Report/Worldwide-Ad-Spending-eMarketer-Forecast-2017/2002019

eMarketer (2017b). Smartphone Sales Worldwide, by Country/Region, 2015 & 2016 Retrieved July 2017, from www.emarketer.com/Chart/Smartphone-Sales-Worldwide-by-CountryRegion-2015-2016/205096

eMarketer (2017c). Mobile Phone User Penetration Worldwide, by Country. Retrieved July 2017, from www.emarketer.com/Article/Mobile-Phone-Smartphone-Usage-Varies-Globally/1014738

EUR-Lex (2002). Directive 2002/58/CE du Parlement européen et du Conseil du 12 juillet 2002 concernant le traitement des données à caractère personnel et la protection de la vie privée dans le secteur des communications électroniques (directive vie privée et communications électroniques) Retrieved May 2016, from http://eur-lex.europa.eu/legal-content/FR/TXT/HTML/?uri=CELEX:32002L0058&from=fr

426 *Mobile Marketing*

Euromonitor International (2013). Emergence of S-Commerce and Impact on Consumer Goods Industries. www.euromonitor.com/emergence-of-s-commerce-and-impact-on-consumer-goods-industries/report

FCA (2016). Annual Report 2016. Fiat Chrysler Automobiles. www.fcagroup.com/en-US/investors/financial_regulatory/financial_reports/files/FCA_2016_Annual_Report.pdf

Featherman, Mauricio & Pavlou, Paul (2003). Predicting E-Services Adoption: A Perceived Risk Facets Perspective. *International Journal of Human-Computer Studies*, 59(4), 451–474.

Fishbein, Martin & Ajzen, Icek (1975). *Belief, Attitude, Intention, and Behavior: An Introduction to Theory and Research*. Reading: Addison-Wesley (p. 578).

Fishbein, Martin & Ajzen, Icek (2010). *Predicting and Changing Behavior—The Reasoned Action Approach*. New York: Taylor and Francis (p. 538).

Foote Cone & Belding (2016a). Our Work. Retrieved May 12, 2016, from www.fcb.com/our-work

Foote Cone & Belding (2016b). Change Behavior. Retrieved July 2017, from www.fcb.com/who-we-are/introduction

Foote Cone & Belding (2017). Where We Are. Retrieved June 2017, from www.fcb.com/where-we-are/locations

Franke, N., Keinz, P. & Steger, C. J. (2009). Testing the Value of Customization: When Do Customers Really Prefer Products Tailored to Their Preferences? *Journal of Marketing*, 73(5), 103–121.

Gao, Tao, Rohm, Andrew, Sultan, Fareena & Pagani, Margherita (2013). Consumers Un-Tethered: A Three-Market Empirical Study of Consumers' Mobile Marketing Acceptance. *Journal of Business Research*, 66(12), 2536–2544.

The Globe and Mail (2015, November 12th). Montreal Men's Fashion Retailer Tops This Year's Technology Fast 50 List *By Sarah Efron*. Retrieved from www.theglobeandmail.com/report-on-business/small-business/sb-growth/montreal-mens-fashion-retailer-tops-this-years-technology-fast-50-list/article27206146/

The Globe and Mail (2016a, June 24th). Frank and Oak's Ethan Song on Reinventing Retail for the Digital Era *By Ethan Song*. Retrieved from www.theglobeandmail.com/report-on-business/small-business/sb-managing/frank-oaks-ethan-song-on-reinventing-retail-for-the-digital-era/article30350175/

The Globe and Mail (2016b, November 28th). Frank and Oak's Millennial Look Now Also for Women, *By Guy Dixon*. Retrieved from www.theglobeandmail.com/report-on-business/frank-and-oaks-millennial-look-now-also-for-women/article33061406/

Goh, Khim-Yong, Chu, Junhong & Wu, Jing (2015). Mobile Advertising: An Empirical Study of Temporal and Spatial Differences in Search Behavior and Advertising Response. *Journal of Interactive Marketing*, 30, 34–45.

Government of Canada (2016). Frequently Asked Questions About Canada's Anti-Spam Legislation. Retrieved May 12, 2016, from www.crtc.gc.ca/eng/com500/faq500.htm

The Government of Japan (2002). Act on Regulation of the Transmission of Specified Electronic Mail. Retrieved May 2016, from http://measures.antispam.go.jp/pdf/Japanese%20anti-spam%20law.pdf

The Guardian (2016a, January 26th). France Hit by Day of Protest as Security Forces Fire Teargas at Taxi Strike, *By Angelique Chrisafis*. Retrieved from www.theguardian.com/world/2016/jan/26/french-taxi-drivers-block-paris-roads-in-uber-protest

Mobile Marketing 427

The Guardian (2016b, February 10th). Black-Cab Drivers' Uber Protest Brings London Traffic to a Standstill, *By Gwyn Topham*. Retrieved from www.theguardian.com/technology/2016/feb/10/black-cab-drivers-uber-protest-london-traffic-standstill

Ho, Jason & Dempsey, Melanie (2010). Viral Marketing: Motivations to Forward Online Content. *Journal of Business Research*, 63(9), 1000–1006.

Hollensen, Svend (2010). *Global Marketing: A Decision Making rocess* (5th ed.). London: Prentice Hall.

Hollensen, Svend (2016). *Global Marketing* (7th ed.). London: Pearson (p. 872).

Ici Radio Canada (2015, January 24th). Vers une révolution dans le commerce de détail? *By Bruno Coulombe*. Retrieved from http://ici.radio-canada.ca/nouvelles/economie/2015/01/23/004-revolution-commerce-detail-desautels.shtml

IKEA (2016a). Ikea Mobile. Retrieved May 12, 2016, from www.ikea.com/ms/en_CA/mobile/mobile_splash.html

IKEA (2016b). IKEA Group Yearly Summary. 51. www.ikea.com/ms/en_CA/pdf/yearly_summary/IKEA_Group_Yearly_Summary_2016.pdf

Internet World Stats (2017). World Internet Users and 2017 Population Stats. Retrieved June 2017, from www.Internetworldstats.com/stats.htm

ITU (2016). The ICT Facts and Figures 2016. ICT Data and Statistics Division, Telecommunication Development Bureau. www.itu.int/en/ITU-D/Statistics/Documents/facts/ICTFactsFigures2016.pdf

ITU (2017). Country ICT Data (Until 2016)—Mobile-Cellular Subscriptions Retrieved July 2017, from www.itu.int/en/ITU-D/Statistics/Pages/stat/default.aspx

Jayawardhena, Chanaka, Kuckertz, Andreas, Karjaluoto, Heikki & Kautonen, Teemu (2009). Antecedents to Permission Based Mobile Marketing: An Initial Examination. *European Journal of Marketing*, 43(3/4), 473–499.

Joireman, Jeff, Grégoire, Yany, Devezer, Berna & Tripp, Thomas (2013). When Do Customers Offer Firms a "Second Chance" Following a Double Deviation? The Impact of Inferred Firm Motives on Customer Revenge and Reconciliation. *Journal of Retailing*, 89(3), 315–337.

Kaplan, Andreas (2012). If You Love Something, Let It Go Mobile: Mobile Marketing and Mobile Social Media 4x4. *Business Horizons*, 55(2), 129–139.

Kelleher, Tom (2009). Conversational Voice, Communicated Commitment, and Public Relations Outcomes in Interactive Online Communication. *Journal of Communication*, 59(1), 172–188.

Kim, Yeung-Jo, Park, Jongwon & Wyer, Robert (2009). Effects of Temporal Distance and Memory on Consumer Judgments. *Journal of Consumer Research*, 36(4), 634–645.

Lamberton, Cait & Stephen, Andrew (2016). A Thematic Exploration of Digital, Social Media, and Mobile Marketing: Research Evolution From 2000 to 2015 and an Agenda for Future Inquiry. *Journal of Marketing*, 80(6), 146–172.

Laroche, Michel, Bergeron, Jasmin & Goutaland, Christine (2001). A Three-Dimensional Scale of Intangibility. *Journal of Service Research*, 4(1), 26–38.

Lee, Gunwoong & Raghu, Santanam (2014). Determinants of Mobile Apps' Success: Evidence From the App Store Market. *Journal of Management Information Systems*, 31(2), 133–170.

Lee, Khai & Tan, Soo (2003). E-Retailing Versus Physical Retailing: A Theoretical Model and Empirical Test of Consumer Choice. *Journal of Business Research*, 56(11), 877–885.

Lefaix-Durand, Aurélia (2008). *Customer-Supplier Relationships as a Means of Value Creation*. (Ph.D), Management—Université Laval, Québec (Canada).

428 *Mobile Marketing*

Les Affaires. (2015a, October 14th). Commerce électronique: livraison le soir même maintenant possible, *By Martin Jolicoeur*. Retrieved from www.lesaffaires.com/blogues/martin-jolicoeur/commerce-electronique-livraison-le-soir-meme-maintenant-realite-a-montreal/582396

Les Affaires (2015b, March 16th). Frank & Oak prépare une nouvelle expansion, *By Martin Jolicoeur*. Retrieved from www.lesaffaires.com/secteurs-d-activite/commerce-de-detail/frank-et-oak-prepare-une-nouvelle-expansion/577086

Les Affaires (2015c, March 26th). Frank & Oak se lance aux États-Unis, *By Martin Jolicoeur*. Retrieved from www.lesaffaires.com/secteurs-d-activite/commerce-de-detail/frank-et-oak-se-lance-aux-etats-unis/577390

Lin, Pei-Jung, Jones, Eleri & Westwood, Sheena (2009). Perceived Risk and Risk-Relievers in Online Travel Purchase Intentions. *Journal of Hospitality Marketing & Management*, 18(8), 782–810.

Luo, Xueming, Andrews, Michelle, Fang, Zheng & Phang, Chee Wei (2014). Mobile Targeting. *Management Science*, 60(7), 1738–1756.

The Michael Report (2015). Finally Revealed: This Is Ethically Questionable Strategy Uber Uses To Win Its Wars. Retrieved December 2015, from http://themichaelreport.com/2015/02/25/the-uber-playbook/

Mitchell, Vincent-Wayne & Greatorex, Mike (1993). Risk Perception and Reduction in the Purchase of Consumer Services. *Service Industries Journal*, 13(4), 179–200.

Mobile Commerce Daily (2015, March 31st). Frank & Oak Grabs Viewers With mCommerce-enabled Interactive Video Ads, *By Brielle Jaekel*. Retrieved from www.mobilecommercedaily.com/frank-oak-grabs-viewers-with-interactive-video-ads

Mobile Marketer (2015, January 16th). Frank & Oak Exec: Leverage iBeacon for Complete User Profile, *By Lauren Johnson*. Retrieved from www.mobilemarketer.com/cms/news/software-technology/16990.html

Montreal Gazette (2016, February 9th). Montreal-Area Taxi Permits Got More Expensive, Not Less, After UberX Started: Data, *By Jason Magder*. Retrieved from http://montrealgazette.com/news/local-news/taxi-licences-dont-seem-affected-by-ubers-arrival

Mothersbaugh, David, Foxx, William, Beatty, Sharon & Wang, Sijun (2012). Disclosure Antecedents in an Online Service Context: The Role of Sensitivity of Information. *Journal of Service Research*, 15(1), 76–98.

Nepomuceno, Marcelo, Rohani, Mina & Grégoire, Yany (2017). Consumer Resistance: From Anti-Consumption to Revenge. In *Consumer Perception of Product Risks and Benefits*, Emilien G., Weitkunat R., and Lüdicke F. (Editors). Berlin: Springer (pp. 345–364)

Nepomuceno, Marcelo, Laroche, Michel & Richard, Marie-Odile (2014). How to Reduce Perceived Risk When Buying Online: The Interactions Between Intangibility, Product Knowledge, Brand Familiarity, Privacy and Security Concerns. *Journal of Retailing and Consumer Services*, 21(4), 619–629.

Nepomuceno, Marcelo, Laroche, Michel, Richard, Marie-Odile & Eggert, Axel (2012). Relationship Between Intangibility and Perceived Risk: Moderating Effect of Privacy, System Security and General Security Concerns. *Journal of Consumer Marketing*, 29(3), 176–189.

New York Post (2014, January 14th). Celebs Using Twitter Fans for Uber Discounts, *By Carl Campanile*. Retrieved from http://nypost.com/2014/01/14/celebs-using-twitter-fans-for-uber-discounts/

Nigam, Shreya & Jain, Aadit (2017). Digital Marketing Campaigns By Furniture Retailers to Generate Online and Offline Sales: With Specific Reference to Ikea, Pepperfry and Urbanladder. *International Educational Scientific Research Journal*, 3(1), 40–43.

Pasco-Berho, Corinne (2008). *Marketing international*. Paris: Dunod (p. 368).

Pinkton, David & Broderick, Amanda (2005). *Integrated Marketing Communications*. Harlow: Pearson Education Limited (p. 801).

Ramaswami, Vivek & Lyons, Connor (2013). Disrupting the Dispatch: How Uber Can Succeed in the Race for Mobile Taxi Supremacy. Retrieved July 2017, from http://iveybusinessreview.ca/cms/1773/disrupting-the-dispatch/

Rohm, Andrew, Gao, Tao, Sultan, Fareena & Pagani, Margherita (2012). Brand in the Hand: A Cross-Market Investigation of Consumer Acceptance of Mobile Marketing. *Business Horizons*, 55(5), 485–493.

Scharl, Arno, Dickinger, Astrid & Murphy, Jamie (2005). Diffusion and Success Factors of Mobile Marketing. *Electronic Commerce Research and Applications*, 4(2), 159–173.

Shankar, Venkatesh & Balasubramanian, Sridhar (2009). Mobile Marketing: A Synthesis and Prognosis. *Journal of Interactive Marketing*, 23(2), 118–129.

Shankar, Venkatesh, Venkatesh, Alladi, Hofacker, Charles & Naik, Prasad (2010). Mobile Marketing in the Retailing Environment: Current Insights and Future Research Avenues. *Journal of Interactive Marketing*, 24(2), 111–120.

Shen, George Chung-Chi (2015). Users' Adoption of Mobile Applications: Product Type and Message Framing's Moderating Effect. *Journal of Business Research*, 68(11), 2317.

Slate (2014a, December 30th). The Year in Uber: The World's Brashest Startup Spent 2014 Expanding Aggressively and Infuriating Just About Everyone, *By Alison Griswold*. Retrieved from www.slate.com/articles/business/moneybox/2014/12/uber_spent_2014_expanding_aggressively_and_pissing_off_just_about_everyone.html

Slate (2014b, November 23rd). What's Really Wrong With Uber? Maybe the Company's Not Evil, Just Inept, *By Alison Griswold*. Retrieved from www.slate.com/articles/business/moneybox/2014/11/uber_s_problem_rapid_growth_decentralization_and_a_pr_team_ill_equipped.html

Smart Insights (2017). Mobile Marketing Statistics Compilation. Retrieved July 2017, from www.smartinsights.com/mobile-marketing/mobile-marketing-analytics/mobile-marketing-statistics/

Statista (2016). Registered Members of LinkedIn Worldwide as of 1st Quarter 2016, by Country (In Millions). Retrieved June 2016, from www.statista.com/statistics/272783/linkedins-membership-worldwide-by-country/

Statista (2017a). Number of Smartphones Sold to End Users Worldwide from 2007 to 2016 (In Million Units). Retrieved July 2017, from www.statista.com/statistics/263437/global-smartphone-sales-to-end-users-since-2007/

Statista (2017b). Global Unit Shipments of Tablets from 2012 to 2017 (In Millions). Retrieved July 2017, from www.statista.com/statistics/203703/global-unit-shipments-of-netbooks/

Stevens, Matt. (2017, July 12th). Chicago Airport Security Officers to Shed unit-shipments-of-netboited Airlines Dragging Episode. *The New York Times*. Retrieved from www.nytimes.com/2017/07/12/us/united-chicago-airport-security.html

430 Mobile Marketing

Sultan, Fareena, Rohm, Andrew & Gao, Tao (2009). Factors Influencing Consumer Acceptance of Mobile Marketing: A Two-Country Study of Youth Markets. *Journal of Interactive Marketing*, 23(4), 308–320.

Tan, Wee-Kheng & Chang, Yun-Ghang (2015). Electronic-Word-of-Mouth Performance in Different Psychological Distances and Familiarity. *Online Information Review*, 39(4), 449–465.

Taylor, David, Davis, Donna & Jillapalli, Ravi (2009). Privacy Concern and Online Personalization: The Moderating Effects of Information Control and Compensation. *Electronic Commerce Research*, 9(3), 203–223.

Toronto Star (2017, April 26th). Hundreds of Taxi, Bus Drivers Loudly Protest Uber in Romania, *By The Associated Press*. Retrieved from www.thestar.com/business/2017/04/26/romanian-government-plans-to-better-regulate-taxi-industry-after-drivers-protest-uber.html

Tripp, Thomas & Grégoire, Yany. (2011). When Unhappy Customers Strike Back on the Internet. *MIT Sloan Management Review*, 52(3), 37–44

Trope, Yaacov, Liberman, Nira & Wakslak, Cheryl (2007). Construal Levels and Psychological Distance: Effects on Representation, Prediction, Evaluation, and Behavior. *Journal of Consumer Psychology*, 17(2), 83–95.

Uber (2015). Outsmart the Flu With UberHEALTH. Retrieved December 2015, from http://newsroom.uber.com/2015/11/uberhealth/

Uber (2017). Find a City. Retrieved July 2017, from www.uber.com/en-CA/cities/

Varnali, Kaan & Toker, Ayşegül (2010). Mobile Marketing Research: The-State-of-the-Art. *International Journal of Information Management*, 30(2), 144–151.

Virgin Mobile (2017). Members Lounge—Step-Up Your Staples With 20% Off at Frank and Oak. Retrieved July 2017, from www.virginmobile.ca/en/members-lounge/benefit1.html?benefit=frankandoak-20percentoff

Wall Street Survivor (2017). Uber: The Road to a $69 Billion Valuation. Retrieved July 2017, from http://blog.wallstreetsurvivor.com/2017/07/17/uber-road-69-billion-valuation/

We Are Social (2016). Digital, social & mobile worldwide in 2015. By Simon Kemp. January 27, 2016. http://wearesocial.com/special-reports/digital-in-2016

World Bank (2017). Mobile Cellular Subscriptions (Per 100 People). International Telecommunication Union, World Telecommunication/ICT Development Report and Database. Retrieved July 2017, from http://data.worldbank.org/indicator/IT.CEL.SETS.P2

Zhang, Jing & Mao, En (2008). Understanding the Acceptance of Mobile SMS Advertising Among Young Chinese Consumers. *Psychology and Marketing*, 25(8), 787–805.

11 Origin-Based Marketing

Table of Contents

11. Origin-Based Marketing

Introduction: Should Companies Rely on a Geographic Origin to Differentiate from Competition and Attract Customers?..433

11.1 *Background Information*..*435*

    11.1.1 *Cue Utilization and the Use of the "Origin" Cue*...*435*

    11.1.2 *Branding (Aaker)*...*437*

11.2 *Definitions and Drivers*..*438*

    11.2.1 *Origin-Based Marketing and the Country-of-Origin Effect*...........................*439*

    11.2.2 *Place branding*...*444*

11.3 *Examples*...*450*

    11.3.1 *Corporate Examples of Origin-Based Marketing: Canada Goose, IKEA, Victorinox, and Volkswagen*.........................*450*

    11.3.2 *National Examples of Place Branding: Argentina, Australia, Chile, and Slovenia*......*462*

11.4 *Issues at Stake*..*472*

    11.4.1 *Evolution of Country Image Over Time and Provenance Paradox*....................*473*

    11.4.2 *Relevance of the Effect (Dilution and Recognition)*...*479*

    11.4.3 *Outcomes*..*483*

    11.4.4 *Impact on Marketing Decisions and Feasibility*...*484*

Conclusion: With attention paid to key success factors, companies should still consider adopting origin-based marketing, as it can bridge geographic and psychic distances and increase their competitiveness abroad and at home.

References

432 *Origin-Based Marketing*

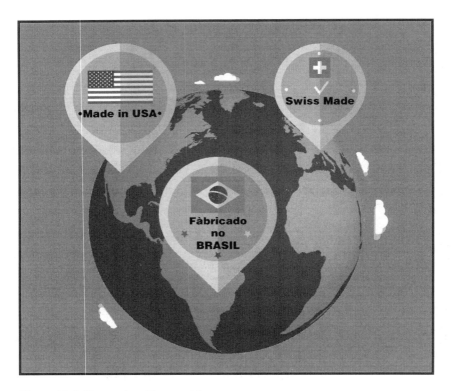

Figure 11.1 Illustrating Chapter 11
Source: Own elaboration

Recommended Readings

- Deshpandé, Rohit (2010). Why You Aren't Buying Venezuelan Chocolate. *Harvard Business Review*, 88(12), 25–27.
- Durand, Aurélia; Turkina, Ekaterina & Robson, Matthew (2016). Psychic Distance and Country Image in Exporter-Importer Relationships. *Journal of International Marketing*, 24(3), 31–57.
- Koschate-Fischer, Nicole; Diamantopoulos, Adamantios & Oldenkotte, Katharina (2012). Are Consumers Really Willing to Pay More for a Favorable Country Image? A Study of Country-of-Origin Effects on Willingness to Pay. *Journal of International Marketing*, 20(1), 19–41
- Papadopoulos, Nicolas (2004). Place Branding: Evolution, Meaning and Implications. *Place Branding*, 1(1), 36–49.

Introduction: Should Companies Rely on a Geographic Origin to Differentiate From Competition and Attract Customers?

Using a geographic origin to promote products and services is nothing new. Producers have put forward the famous "Made-In" and used other geographic cues to distinguish their products for centuries (if not millenniums). Obvious examples are found in food products, for instance, with mentions like "wine from Italy," "olive oil from Greece," and "cotton from Egypt," immediately informing consumers about the alleged superiority of these products compared to competing goods. The *country-of-origin effect* generated by the origin cue has been extensively studied in consumer behavior research. In parallel, a phenomenon known as *place branding* has emerged in the past decades and targets the systematic promotion of places (such as countries and cities). To encompass research on both the effect of origin and place branding, we propose the term *origin-based marketing*. *Origin-based marketing* refers to the consistent use of geographic cues in communication and promotion activities.

Origin-based marketing can be seen as a solution to overcome geographic, cultural, and psychic distance (see Chapters 4, 5 and 7). It is, however, necessary to wonder if this marketing approach continues to be relevant in an accelerated phase of globalization characterized by such ambivalence (see Chapter 1). On the one hand, products can now be designed, manufactured, assembled, and sold in multiple countries, which inevitably dilutes the effect of origin, thereby lowering the interest of relying on specific origin cues. On the other hand, the appeal of exotic products and experiences (e.g., travelling abroad) is now much easier to fulfill. This increases the relevance of using geographic cues to attract customers from all around the world. Furthermore, the impact of nationalist and protectionist movements as well as "buy local" movements on origin-based marketing are rather obscure. Addressing the question: **"Should companies rely on a geographic origin to differentiate from competition and attract customers?"** this chapter re-examines this long-standing practice in light of current developments.

Figure 11.2 situates the topic of origin-based marketing in the book structure and shows that, in relation to the different steps in an international marketing plan, this topic can be discussed particularly when considering communication and promotion policies.

Overall, the objectives of this chapter are to define, illustrate, and discuss the topic of origin-based marketing. As background information, we first examine basic concepts about branding and brand value, as well as the use of cues to market offerings (products/services). This helps in understanding the origin cue before moving on to presenting how places can be used for promotion or be promoted themselves with place branding. Next, we look into examples of companies using origin-based marketing and examples of countries having invested in place branding. Finally, we examine the main issues at stake with origin-based marketing.

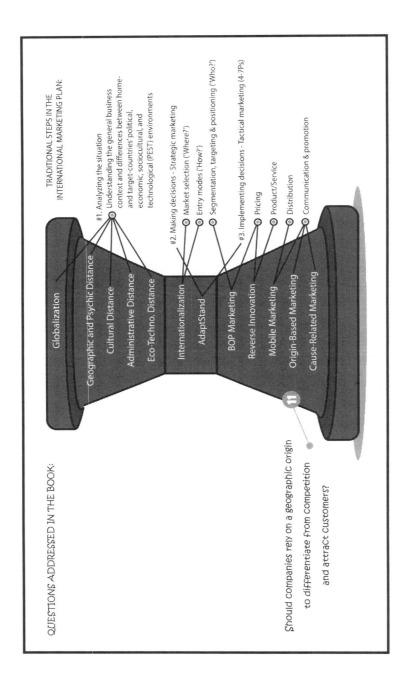

Figure 11.2 Positioning Chapter 11 in the overall book structure

Source: Own elaboration

11.1 Background Information

In order to better understand origin-based marketing in the context of international promotion and communication policies, we address the following questions:

- Which are the main cues used by consumers to make a purchasing decision? Are all of these cues used simultaneously?
- Why would the origin cue affect consumer decision-making?
- What is a brand? And a global brand?
- How are brands valued?

11.1.1 Cue Utilization and the Use of the "Origin" Cue

Which are the main cues used by consumers to make a purchasing decision? In Chapter 9, we introduced the cue utilization theory developed by Olson (1972) and presented the *origin cue* as one of the most common extrinsic cues (i.e., a cue that is not part of the physical product, but that plays a role in influencing customer perceptions). As a reminder, "products consist of an array of cues that serve as surrogate indicators of quality to shoppers" (Richardson, Dick, & Jain, 1994, p. 29). To illustrate this point, Figure 11.3 features a car with no descriptive text to guide us. Even without written information, we are able to evaluate this car, forming an approximate idea of its quality and its price (most likely very high in both cases), by simply

Figure 11.3 Illustrating the use of cues (product category: cars)
Source: Courtesy of Audi AG

436 *Origin-Based Marketing*

looking at its design and recognizing its brand and origin. In this way, design, price, origin, brand and other cues are useful for customers to learn about products, inform purchasing decisions and on which to base other behaviors (e.g., recommendations to others). In Chapter 12, we focus on one of these other cues, the *process cue*, which has taken prominence in recent years with the rise of corporate social responsibility, sustainable development, and responsible consumption.

Are all of these cues used simultaneously? Yes, consumers do infer information from all of these cues simultaneously. From a marketer's point of view, though, the emphasis on specific cues has evolved overtime. Differentiation over quality and price was central in the 1960–80s. In the 1990s and early-2000s, major corporate efforts were put into branding as a means to outrun competition. Since then, the focus has shifted toward responsible processes. This evolution seems to follow a cumulative logic since companies need to keep setting the right price for the chosen positioning, maintaining high-quality offerings, and developing valuable brands in order to remain competitive. In turn, the long-standing origin cue gained new momentum in the 1990s with globalization accelerating (see Chapter 1). Indeed, competition among local and foreign companies increased tenfold, with national borders further opening up and allowing for offerings and investments to flow in from all around the world. Not only did the need to differentiate from competitors become even more crucial, but regulations and safety standards in relation to global supply chains (e.g., in the food and automotive industries or in any other sector where consumers' well-being could be endangered) made the tracking of products' country of origin all the more important. Consequently, firms need to handle a variety of cues in their promotion activities while emphasizing one in particular or several of them in line with their competitive strategies. Before providing background information about the other cue of interest in this chapter—the brand, which helps to better understand place branding—we complete this overview of the origin cue with the mechanisms that explain why the origin cue has the power to influence consumer decisions.

Why would the origin cue affect decision-making? Fishbein and Ajzen's (1975; 2010) *theory of planned behavior* (detailed in Chapter 5) is used to explain the effect of origin and why the origin cue affects decision-making, and ultimately behaviors. Indeed, the image that countries have internationally—the term *image* refers to a mental representation or picture (Jaffe & Nebenzahl, 2001)—is first and foremost a belief that is highly subjective (Nagashima, 1970; Martin & Eroglu, 1993). One country can be seen as having an excellent reputation or the worst one depending on whom is asked. The *theory of planned behavior* explains that beliefs, values, and norms translate into attitudes that then guide behaviors. As such, believing that a country is either good or bad (e.g., at producing a particular product or in specific sectors, such as education) affects attitudes toward products and people coming from this country, and, in turn, generates different behaviors (e.g., purchase or avoidance). Thus, when customers become aware of from where offerings originate, it affects their perceptions, particularly in regard to quality. Although more complex, the brand cue—detailed next—relies on the same mechanisms.

11.1.2 Branding (Aaker)

What is a brand? And a global brand? According to Cateora, Gilly, and Graham (2015, p. Chap. 11), a *brand* essentially encapsulates everything that an offering is and stands for, reflecting everything from its design and its price to its symbolic elements and reputation. In turn, a *global brand* refers to the worldwide use of a name, term, sign, symbol (visual and/or auditory) design, or combination thereof intended to identify goods or services of one seller and to differentiate them from those of competitors. One example of a global brand is easily illustrated by mentally picturing a black circle crowned by two smaller black circles. Many—if not most—of us instantaneously associate this simplistic drawing featuring the back of Mickey Mouse's head with the Disney brand, regardless of our country of origin. Over the years, the consistency with which the Walt Disney Company has used the same graphics (including the famous font and pastel color schemes) across the world and across business units (e.g., entertainment parks, resorts, movies, animated cartoons, and TV channels) contributed to creating a homogeneous image and enhanced recognition. A high degree of awareness is one of the criteria that defines a valuable brand, as detailed next.

How are brands valued? The concept of brand equity has been developed to capture the value of brands. *Brand equity* is defined by Aaker (1991, p. 15) as "the value consumers associate with a brand, as reflected in the dimensions of brand awareness, brand associations, perceived quality, and brand loyalty." Figure 11.4 illustrates the various dimensions of brand equity.

Rankings that compare brand equity of well-known companies rely on similar dimensions to capture the value that cannot be explained by the

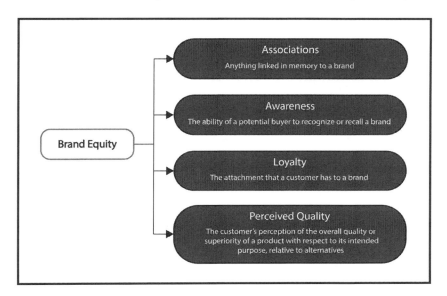

Figure 11.4 Presenting the four dimensions of brand equity
Source: Adapted from Aaker (1992)

438   *Origin-Based Marketing*

physical and financial assets of firms only. An example of such ranking is Interbrand's "Best Global Brands," which relies on a methodology that complies with the requirements of ISO 10668 for monetary brand valuation. This methodology relies on three main measures: the brand's competitive strength (i.e., the ability of the brand to create loyalty), the role the brand plays in purchasing decisions, and the financial performance of the branded offerings (Interbrand, 2017a). First, the brands' strength is measured based on ten factors (i.e., authenticity, clarity, commitment, consistency, differentiation, engagement, governance, presence, relevance, and responsiveness). Second, the portion of the purchase decision attributable to the brand—as opposed to other attributes, such as price and product features—is captured by the *Role of Brand Index*, based on either primary research, a review of historical roles of brands for companies in that industry, or expert panel assessment. Finally, the valuation relies on estimates of the brand's economic profit (i.e., the after-tax operating profit of the brand, minus a charge for the capital used to generate the brand's revenue and margins) (Interbrand, 2017a). In 2017, Apple, Google, Microsoft, Coca Cola, and Amazon were featured as the top five most-valuable global brands, respectively estimated to be worth 185, 140, 80, 70, and 65 million USD (numbers are rounded) (Interbrand, 2017b). Going back to Aacker's model, these global brands not only benefit from a high degree of global awareness, but they are also generally qualified with adjectives such as: excellent design, performant, innovative, creative, sophisticated, etc. These are examples of positive associations with various attributes related to perceived quality. These brands also benefit from high degrees of loyalty, reaching in some cases (like Apple for instance) a "cult" status. Aficionados would never be caught purchasing a competing brand.

Having set the stage with background information about two important cues, origin and brand, we now move on to defining origin-based marketing and examining its drivers.

11.2 *Definitions and Drivers*

In order to situate origin-based marketing, we look at the country-of-origin effect and place branding by addressing the following questions:

- What is the country-of-origin effect (COE)? What are the main drivers and outcomes of the COE?
- What is place branding? What are the different types of places that can be branded?
- What are the motives behind developing a country brand? And who are the stakeholders involved in country branding?
- Overall, what is the difference between origin-based marketing and place branding?

Before examining possible answers, we can start by reflecting on the general differences existing between the effect of origin and place branding (see "Food for Thought").

Origin-Based Marketing 439

> **Food for Thought 11.1**
>
> - In reference to Durand, Turkina, and Robson (2016), Koschate-Fischer, Diamantopoulos, and Oldenkotte (2012), and Papadopoulos (2004), what is the effect of origin? And how is marketing based on a geographic origin different from place branding?

11.2.1 Origin-Based Marketing and the Country-of-Origin Effect

What is the country-of-origin effect (COE)? Like Figure 11.1, presented at the beginning of this chapter, Figure 11.5 is meant to illustrate the notion of COE. Here, it features markings referring to China and Switzerland as the countries of manufacture of two products. At the sight of these mentions, and depending on where we are from (as well as other factors reviewed below), we are likely to have an immediate response, an *a priori* evaluation of these products. Being from the Americas or from Europe, the attitude formed toward the watch from Switzerland is likely to be positive, while the one formed toward the featured product from China (textile) is likely to be somewhat negative. As its name indicates, the COE is an *effect*. It stems from a specific attitude toward a country and affects a wide range of behaviors (Durand, 2016; Durand et al., 2016). It has been defined as any influence that the country of manufacture, assembly, design, or other association of a product may have on a consumer's positive or negative perception of it (Cateora et al., 2015, p. Chap. 11).

Not only does Figure 11.5 illustrate the COE, but it also highlights one particular facet of country image: the product-related country image (also

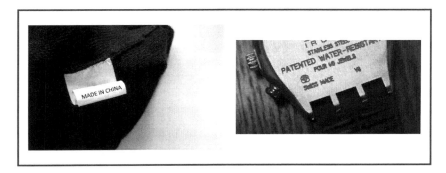

Figure 11.5 Illustrating the effect of origin: China vs. Swiss-made (product categories: watches and textiles)

Source: Own image

called the product-country image or PCI). The pairing between product categories and countries is indeed powerful. If one of the products pictured in Figure 11.5 had been tea, for instance, the markings "from China" and "from Switzerland" would most likely have triggered radically different evaluations (e.g., "tea from Switzerland, really?"). Defined as an individual's beliefs about a country in connection to a specific product category, the PCI is captured by measuring the extent to which a country is capable of conceiving, designing, engineering, producing, or assembling a given product category or by the extent to which products from a specific country are characterized by, for instance: quality, reliability, innovativeness, design, prestige, and workmanship (Durand et al., 2016). Figure 11.6 presents two other formative facets of the much studied country image construct: the people- and environment-related country images.

What are the main drivers of the COE? Some of the main drivers of the COE are: country image, cognitive and affective factors, and promotion and communication activities (corporate and governmental). For starters, *country image* is a core driver of the COE. Among the hundreds of scientific articles published on the topic (see Durand, 2016), there is no consensus on how exactly country images form, but studies have emphasized the role of cognitive processes (e.g., beliefs formed on the basis of information), affective processes (e.g., emotions), normative processes (e.g., pressure from important others), and, finally, conative processes (i.e., a motivational and volitional component reflecting consumers' desired level of interaction with a country) (Roth & Diamantopoulos, 2009). In terms of *cognitive factors*, the knowledge gathered about countries (through TV documentaries, readings, stories from relatives and friends, etc.) and direct international experience

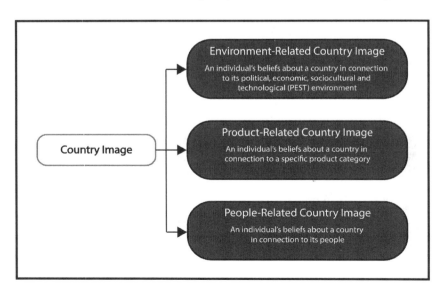

Figure 11.6 Distinguishing the three facets of country image
Source: Adapted from Durand et al. (2016)

play an important role. *Affective factors* such as admiration toward or, on the contrary, animosity against other cultures and countries (e.g., due to historical alliances or wars) affect country images and the attitude (positive or negative) toward countries. Finally, *promotion and communication activities* play an important role in allowing customers to associate offerings with a country of origin. Promotion activities include all of the efforts deployed by governments and industrial associations in putting forward the strengths and capabilities of their country of origin, in particular through place branding (reviewed in more detail in the next section). *Communication activities*—undertaken by the same actors—mainly consist of the visual display of information on offerings. Labels, denominations of origin (e.g., "Scottish Salmon" or "Cafe de Colombia"), and markings (including the famous "made-in") offer a wide range of options to inform customers about the provenance of products. Figure 11.7 presents an example of markings (in this case, an origin cue that is mandatory by law).

Indeed, rules of origin are regulations that governments use, not only to inform customers (increasing traceability, reassuring and giving them a choice based on the origin) but also to establish duties according to the provenance. In Chapter 6, we discussed regional integration and its consequence on product taxation. Consequently, identification is extremely important. It is required to distinguish products from countries with specific trade agreements. In turn, the use of "controlled designation of origin" (e.g., "Champagne") is a practice that is common in certain regions of the world (in particular Europe) and rather scarce in others (e.g., North America). One of the few examples in Canada is the Vintners Quality Alliance, an *appellation* system that guarantees the high quality and authenticity of origin for Canadian wines made in the provinces of British Columbia and Ontario. It is similar to controlled designations of origin from France ("Appellation d'Origine Controlée" or AOC), Italy ("Denominazione di Origine Controllata" or DOC), and Germany ("Qualitätswein mit Prädikat" or QmP), among others. In European

Figure 11.7 Illustrating markings (product category: cameras)
Source: Own image

442 *Origin-Based Marketing*

countries, controlled designations of origin are found by the dozen—not only for wine but for many other food products, such as poultry (e.g., "Poulet de Bresse"), honey (e.g., "Miel de Corse") and of course, cheese. An introduction found on the homepage of the "Cheese from Spain" website illustrates well the spirit of and rationale for this practice: "You sense it immediately . . . The heady aroma. The palate pleasing textures and flavors of centuries-old artisan cheese-making tradition are there for the taking. Spain's fine cheeses express the unmistakable characteristics of their origin . . . milk, grazing lands, climate, production . . . even the microbiology of the region. Their unique qualities are protected by each D.O.—the Denomination of Origin symbol that certifies the authenticity of each variety . . . tangy Manchego, sharp rich Zamorano, smokey Idiazábal, savory Majorero, Mahón—with its paprika-scented rind, mild Tetilla and robust Cabrales—a world-renowned blue cheese. Ask for any Cheese from Spain by name—wherever you buy fine cheese." One possible explanation for why the practice of controlled denominations of origin is so widespread in Europe and not so much in other parts of the world lies in both geography and in the competitive forces stemming from history and demography. First, the geographic diversity of *terroirs* (combinations of meteorological and topographical related factors, as well as know-how and experience) is particularly high in these small territories— small relative to other countries (for instance, Spain is smaller than the state of Texas in the US and is nearly eighteen and nineteen times smaller than the territories covered by Brazil and Canada, respectively)—most of them being characterized by the simultaneous presence of sea coasts, plains, valleys, and mountains with strong variations in temperatures. This diversity actually allows for products to be authentically different. Second, these terroirs have a long history of human settlements and migratory movements, combined with a high population density. For instance, Spain counted in recent years nearly 93 inhabitants per square kilometer while the population density of Texas, Brazil and Canada, was respectively about 34, 25 and 4 people per square kilometer of land area (World Bank, 2016b, c; World Population Review, 2017). In these conditions, the level of competitive rivalry is thus much higher, explaining the need, in many European countries, to resort to all kinds of techniques to differentiate products and services from competing offerings. To conclude, facing competition is the core motive of promotion and communication activities of companies and governments based on the origin cue, with the intent of driving a positive COE.

And what about the outcomes of the COE? As stated previously, Fishbein and Ajzen's (1975; 2010) theory of planned behavior help us understand how beliefs, values, and norms (i.e., cognitive, affective, and normative factors)—related to, for instance, patriotism, ethnocentrism, and attractiveness of a foreign culture—can influence the extent to which the COE, as the result of an attitude, is favorable or unfavorable. In turn, the attitude (e.g., like/ dislike) toward a specific country determines behaviors (e.g., seek/avoid) in relation to its people or products (Jaffe & Nebenzahl, 2001; Roth & Diamantopoulos, 2009). Although some degree of debate still exists about the relevance and strength of the COE (further discussed in Section 11.4), extensive research has shown that a favorable country image can lead to positive attitudes from end-consumers (and business people) toward products from a specific country, which, in turn, promote favorable intentions and behaviors (e.g., Jaffe & Nebenzahl, 2001; Pharr, 2005).

Overall, the COE affects consumer evaluations, purchase intention, and willingness-to-pay. In an integrative literature review, Durand (2016) distinguishes—among a non-exhaustive list of 355 articles on the topic of COE—no fewer than 112 articles dealing specifically with its impact on consumer behavior, and an additional 50 articles on organizational behavior. More specifically, some 89 articles dealt with linkages between COE and the evaluation of products (59), services (8), brands (18), and advertising (4) by consumers. In contrast, the interest raised by purchasing intention (16) and willingness to pay (7) as dependent variables has been limited. Nevertheless, the latter is of particular interest, as it gives companies interested in using a positive origin a tangible reason to do so: they can drive premium prices (Koschate-Fischer et al., 2012). In regard to organizational behavior, investigation of industrial buyers' purchasing behavior mirrors research on consumer behavior, with several studies showing the impact of the country of origin on procurement policies. Furthermore, other outcomes of the COE are accounted for with the reported existence of an impact on financing and banking activities (e.g., links between the country of origin of companies with the performance of initial public offerings or with borrowing opportunities), human resources management (e.g., employment practices in MNCs, organizational attractiveness for job seekers, and employees' work commitment), strategic management (e.g., competitiveness and the development of a first-mover advantage depending on firms' country of origin, and links between the country of origin and the choice of entry modes, as well as the centralization versus delegation dilemma in the management of MNCs), and finally marketing and sales (e.g., effect of the country of origin on the role of salespersons, on firms' policies in terms of standardization versus adaptation of the marketing-mix, and, most of all, on pricing decisions—considering that specific origins can command price premiums) (Durand, 2016). Thus, the impact of the COE is much wider in scope than is generally acknowledged. And this is just for its direct impact. An indirect impact has also been reported, as detailed next.

Can the COE take a moderating role?[1] Yes, it can moderate or mitigate the relationship between other variables (i.e., reinforce or weaken an effect, whether positive or negative). For instance, Wang and Yang (2008) investigate the relationship between brand personality and purchase intentions for cars in China and in Japan. They find that a favorable country image could enhance brand personality's positive impact on purchase intention, whereas a negative country image could significantly decrease the positive brand personality effect on purchase intention. In turn, Purmehdi (2015) studies the mitigating effect of country of origin in the case of product recalls. Overall, consumer product incidents cost more than 1 trillion USD every year in the US alone. It is important for companies to try and keep them to a minimum. Purmehdi (2015) observes that a positive country image in terms of manufacturing quality had the power to limit the negative effect of product recalls on the value of firms. The results from this study, based on 243 product recalls from the US market between 1973 and 2013, revealed that when a

444   *Origin-Based Marketing*

publicly traded firm manufactured its products in Germany (a country associated with higher manufacturing quality), it faced a loss in value in the two days following the product recall that was 7.8 percent lower than a company manufacturing in China (usually associated with lower manufacturing quality). This might seem like a small difference, but it represents millions of dollars in equity. In addition to revealing a moderating role, this study clearly shows that the COE has an impact not only on products or product lines, but also on entire companies.

11.2.2 Place Branding

What is place branding? *Place branding* is a relatively new research field. In the 1990s, researchers started to theorize about the long-lasting practice of promoting places under the name "place marketing." In particular, Kotler, Haider, and Rein (1993b, p. 18) define place marketing as "all the activities promoting the values and images associated with a place in order for potential users to know about its distinctive advantages." Simon Anholt (1961–), a British Honorary Professor at the University of East Anglia and—among other achievements—founder and Editor Emeritus of the *Journal of Place Brand and Public Diplomacy* (University of East Anglia, 2016) largely influenced the burgeoning field of place branding. In an editorial for this journal titled "Definitions of Place Branding—Working Toward a Resolution," Anholt (2010, p. 2) quotes the definition provided by the American Marketing Association's Dictionary for *place marketing*: "Marketing designed to influence target audiences to behave in some positive manner with respect to the products or services associated with a specific place." In his view, place marketing differs from *place branding*. The former is seen as a tool for selling the products, services, and attractions of a given place more effectively, and the latter is meant to tackle the overall image or reputation of a place, in a more direct way.

Anholt has often acknowledged the intricacies in distinguishing various types of activities related to promoting places and enhancing their image abroad. In this particular editorial, he argued that the term *branding* was often confused with the mere development of a catchy tagline and a logo to ornate official communications. In his own words: "Branding [. . .] is a process that goes on largely in the mind of the consumer—the accumulation of respect and liking for the brand—and cannot be seen as a single technique or set of techniques that directly builds respect or liking" (Anholt, 2010, p. 10). For this reason, he justified the use of the term *nation brand* but debated the use of the term *branding* in relation to places (going as far as calling the notion of place branding a chimera). One of his main arguments was that it was nearly impossible for governments to deliberately use branding techniques and significantly enhance the international image of their countries. In his view, it is mainly through the equivalent of "product development" that nations can enhance their international image, that is with good products and services, good people (e.g., highly qualified workers, world-class athletes, and talents in general), and attractive destinations. This is likely why Anholt undertook a turn in his research in 2014 with the *Good Country*

Origin-Based Marketing   445

Index, moving on from work on improving countries' reputation for their own sake to evaluating countries on the basis of their contribution to humanity and to the planet. We examine this evaluation scheme as well as other indexes and rankings in more detail later in this chapter. Here, following Anholt in dismissing the use of *branding* as a term applicable to places seems excessive. Although he raised some valid points, governments actually do implement various branding techniques to enhance the international image of the place they govern (by developing visual identities, using social media to share positive stories, and writing "brand books" with details on the place "personality," for instance), among other promotional techniques (e.g., organizing trade missions and hosting major international events in sports, politics and culture). This view aligns with Papadopoulos (2004, p. 36) who defines *country branding* as the "broad set of efforts by country, regional and city governments, and by industry groups, aimed at marketing the places and sectors they represent." Whether this strategy is chimeric is yet another question that we raise in Section 11.4 ("Issues at Stake") when discussing our ability to evaluate the outcomes of such branding efforts.

Building upon definitions of brands seen earlier in this chapter and inspired by the work of Aaker (1991, 1996), we define *place branding* as the use of branding techniques to promote places. It involves the development of a brand (including a visual identity) triggering positive associations with the place, and the consistent use of this brand across communications in order to enhance recognition, awareness, and perceptions of quality, as well as to encourage loyalty. In spite of the above-mentioned difficulties in finding a consensual definition of place branding—a very common problem for a "young" research field—Anholt and other researchers did agree on the importance of enhancing the international reputation of places, prompting the following questions.

What are the different types of places that can be branded? As mentioned in several of the definitions presented previously, different places can be "branded." Even though country or nation branding receives more attention, other territories, such as states, provinces, regions, counties, cities, and neighborhoods, can all be the object of place branding. Figure 11.8 illustrates different levels of place branding with three examples of visual identities, including protected logos and taglines:

- "Keep exploring/*Explorez sans fin*," a brand for Canada featured in both English and French since the country is officially bilingual; this brand is managed by Destination Canada, a wholly owned corporation by the Government of Canada to promote international demand and tourism export revenue for Canada.
- The iconic "I Love NY" brand, which is owned by the New York State Department of Economic Development and is used to promote all regions of New York State in the US (not just New York City).
- "*Osez la difference*" (meaning "Dare to be different") for the Limousin, a region in France that is traditionally agricultural but interested in attracting workers and industrial companies.

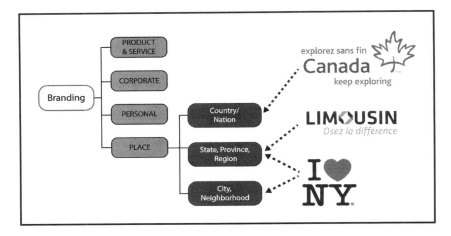

Figure 11.8 Contrasting different levels of place branding

Source: Own elaboration based on brand logo "Keep exploring/*explorez sans fin*" courtesy of Destination Canada; "I Love NY" logo, a registered trademark/service mark of the New York State Department of Economic Development, used with permission; and La Marque Limousin, courtesy of Region Limousin (France)

What are the motives pursued with place branding in general and country branding in particular? In an article entitled "There's No Place Like Our Place! The Marketing of Cities, Regions, and Nations," Kotler and his colleagues have clarified the motivation underlying *place marketing*: "All places must think more like businesses if they hope to win the 'place wars'—the worldwide competition for businesses, tourists, sports teams, and conventions." (Kotler, Haider, & Rein, 1993a, p. 14). Place branding shares a similar purpose. For instance, Papadopoulos (2004, p. 36) explains that country branding pursues one or more of the following objectives: "enhance the place's exports, protect its domestic businesses from 'foreign' competition [. . .], attract or retain factors of development, and position the place for advantage domestically and internationally in economic, political and social terms." Overall, the motivation for place branding is to differentiate places that are competing for the same resources and capabilities. These can be financial, technological, or human—e.g., generating revenues from both exports and local sales (including, but not limited to, tourism), attracting FDI (representing capital injections as well as the possible arrival of new knowledge and technologies), and attracting and retaining talent (e.g., through the temporary or permanent immigration of foreign students, skilled workers, athletes, and artists, all the while avoiding the emigration of local talent and brain drain movements).

Who are the stakeholders involved in country branding? In his book entitled *Nation Branding: Concepts, Issues and Practice*, Dinnie (2008) presents important actors in building a nation brand: the public sector (in particular governmental agencies in charge of tourism, foreign investments, and

Origin-Based Marketing   447

economic development), the private sector (including trade associations, chambers of commerce, as well as product, service, and corporate brands), and, finally, citizens at large (including nongovernmental organizations and the diaspora). He situates a nation brand as an *umbrella brand* that encompasses what he calls *endorsed brands* (e.g., tourism, exports, inward investment, talent attraction, and sports) and *standalone brands* found in places within countries (such as regions, cities, and landmarks), products and services, universities, and national sport teams, as well as cultural and political figures.

This diversity among stakeholders prompted Anholt to point out another limitation of nation branding (Figure 11.9). In his own words, some of the main difficulties in developing a place branding strategy for countries lie in "reconciling the needs and desires of a wide range of different national actors into a more or less single direction, and finding a strategic goal that is both inspiring and feasible, since these two requirements are frequently contradictory" (Anholt, 2008, p. 3).

Overall, what is the difference between origin-based marketing and place branding? *Origin-based marketing* refers to the use of the origin cue in all marketing activities (i.e., product, price, communication, and promotion policies, including branding) in order to benefit from a positive effect of origin. The actors are companies. *Place branding* is about promoting a place of origin. In this case, the actors are mainly governments and industrial associations (although companies also take part in promoting their place of origin through joint activities or their mere reputation). Thus, differences lie in "who" is behind the action and in the purpose of the action. Origin-based marketing is undertaken by companies with the purpose of promoting themselves. Place branding is undertaken by governments and industrial associations with the purpose of promoting the place. In this chapter, we mainly take the perspective of companies who rely on the reputation of their country of origin. In fact, both practices mutually benefit one another. Indeed, a few studies have also shown that countries benefit from the reputation of their local firms (e.g.,Lopez, Gotsi, & Andriopoulos, 2011).

To conclude, Figure 11.10 presents a visual summary of the antecedents and outcomes of the COE for companies. It situates place branding as a promotion activity undertaken by governments to enhance country image, one of the main determinants of the COE.

Furthermore, it is important to notice that the linkages presented in Figure 11.10 do not stop at consumer and organizational behaviors and the resulting success indicators (either measured at the level of individuals with satisfaction and loyalty or at the level of firms with revenues and competitiveness, for instance). An arrow going back from the "success" variable to the "country of origin" variable points to the existence of feedback loops in which the COE outcomes have the power to change the situation in any given country and, therefore, modify its image and international reputation overtime. With consumers buying products, foreign companies investing, and tourists visiting, for instance, a country's economy can thrive. In turn, a positive economic situation is bound to improve infrastructures and healthcare, reduce criminality, fund the arts, etc. Success, or lack thereof, thus affects

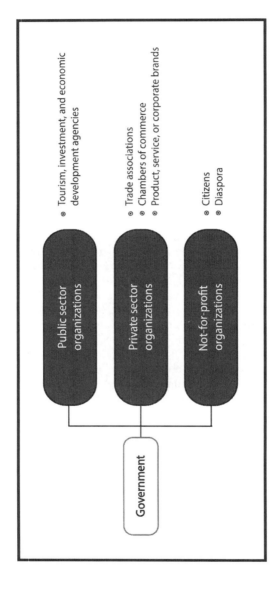

Figure 11.9 Illustrating the diversity of stakeholders in managing a country brand

Source: Adapted from Dinnie (2008, Figure 8.4)

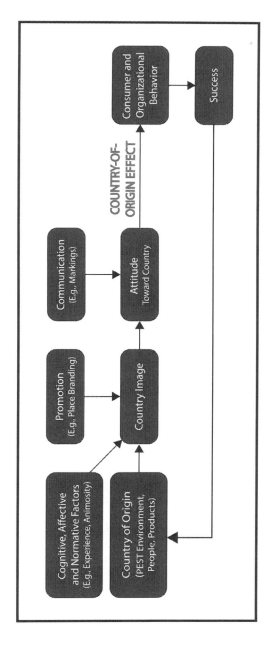

Figure 11.10 Situating place branding as one of the antecedents of the country-of-origin effect (COE)

Source: Own elaboration

450 *Origin-Based Marketing*

positively or negatively the state of the PEST environment and a country's capacity to manufacture products, in turn enhancing or weakening its international image. The evolution overtime of country image and the resulting COE is one of the main issues at stake discussed later on in this chapter.

Next, we provide examples of both origin-based marketing and place branding.

11.3 Examples

11.3.1 Corporate Examples of Origin-Based Marketing: Canada Goose, IKEA, Victorinox, and Volkswagen

While examining the following cases (picked among dozens of available examples), we can ponder which of the depicted strategic and tactical marketing decisions (e.g., from market selection, choice of entry modes, and STP to the 4/7Ps) are most affected by the use of the origin cue (see "Food for Thought").

Food for Thought 11.2

- Among the examples listed below (and others that you may have heard of), which strategic and/or tactical marketing decisions seem most affected by the use of the *origin cue?*

Canada Goose Inc.[2]—Founded in 1957 in Toronto (Canada) by Sam Tick, Canada Goose is best known for its warm winter garments. The company's mission is "To free people from the cold, no matter where they live, and empower them to experience." In 2016, it had sales in nearly forty countries and more than one thousand employees worldwide (see Table 11.1).

Table 11.1 Profiling Canada Goose (Canada)

Who:	*Canada Goose*
Since:	1957
What:	Apparel and textile products
From:	Canada
Sales (Bn USD):	0.2
Employing (people):	1,192
Manufacturing in (countries):	1
Selling in (countries):	37

Source: Canada Goose (2016); The Globe and Mail (2013a)

Origin-Based Marketing 451

First named Metro Sportswear Ltd., the company primarily focused on customer-ordered down-filled coats for people working in frigid conditions (e.g., adventurers embarked on polar expeditions, oil riggers, and police officers). It also manufactured woolen vests, raincoats, snowmobile suits, and other functional outerwear. In the 1970s, David Reiss, the founder's son-in-law, invented a revolutionary volume-based down filling machine that enabled the company to create superior garments. In 1985, high-end down-filled parkas were officially registered under the brand name of Snow Goose. Shortly afterward, Metro Sportswear started selling Snow Goose parkas in Europe under the name of Canada Goose.

In 2001, David Reiss's son, Dani, took over the company as CEO and made the decision to only produce under the name Canada Goose and to keep manufacturing in Canada—even though, at the time, retailers massively relocated production facilities abroad.

Interviewed about his branding decision, Dani Reiss said: "People hate being cold. And who should know more about keeping out the cold than a Canadian?" He further justified the decision by stating: "We picked Canada Goose [instead of Snow Goose] because of the affinity that people have for Canada, not just in Canada, but around the world. We're lucky that we live in a country that people love and romanticize." Cold weather is presented as part of the Canadian identity. The country is indeed often seen as a mythic place and its culture built around *nordicity*—a term coined in 1979 by a Canadian geographer, Louis-Édmond Hamelin—which refers to the perceived, real or imagined, condition of high-latitude regions. A video available on YouTube with search words: "In our elements" illustrates the way the company communicates the Nordic imagery while presenting the company's commitment toward polar bear preservation in the context of its partnership with Polar Bears International.

In relation to keeping manufacturing at home, Dani Reiss was quoted saying: "People who own a Canada Goose jacket around the world feel like they even in fact own a piece of Canada. It's so dynamically tied to the point of manufacturing that we decided that it was very important to stay here." He also felt it was necessary for the company to keep control over the design, manufacturing, and distribution of products. Interestingly, success in Canada came after the brand had been successful in Europe. Due to its history, Canadian customers thought about the brand as a utilitarian one, whereas retailers in Europe saw it almost as a luxury one. Customers there associated the "Made-in-Canada" origin with quality outerwear, and since the company had an authentic story to tell, sales increased quickly.

In 2004, Canada Goose products were featured in two American large-budget movies: *The Day After Tomorrow* and *National Treasure*. From then on, an increasing number of celebrities were photographed in the down-filled coats (e.g., actors Daniel Craig, Emma Stone, and Hugh Jackman). This new interest from celebrities and fashionistas across the world made Dani Reiss realize that there was a market for highly functional but fashionable outerwear.

452 *Origin-Based Marketing*

In terms of promotion, Canada Goose rarely makes use of traditional methods and privileges word-of-mouth publicity, social networking, movie placement, and sponsorship (e.g., with Lance Mackey, a dog musher and dog sled racer from Alaska, who, among other achievements, is a four-time winner of the 1,000-mile Yukon Quest). The company also worked at establishing a brand community, stressing the importance of people. For instance, they published a collectors' book entitled *Goose People* that contains stories that demonstrate Canada Goose's commitment to "Free People from the Cold." Values like entrepreneurship, accountability, passion, respect, and innovation were put forward. In addition to their partnership with Polar Bears International, the company developed alliances with other preservation groups, such as The Conservation Alliance.

Beyond the brand name (which cannot be a more-explicit reference to the country of origin), products are named after Canadian places, such as the coat Montebello (a Quebec municipality), the Victoria (British Colombia's provincial capital), and the Dawson (a city in Yukon), to name a few. In line with the Nordic culture, the brand logo features the Artic continent (see Figure 11.11). A former version of the logo included a goose in the shape of Canada, which was abandoned to avoid creating confusion and possible doubt about the authenticity of the "Made-in-Canada" claim, since the Canada Goose (*Branta Canadensis*) is also found in Alaska, Greenland, the northern US, and occasionally Northern Europe.

Figure 11.11 Presenting Canada Goose's logotype
Source: Courtesy of Canada Goose Inc.

Origin-Based Marketing 453

To maintain its image, the company follows a strict distribution policy. In North America, selected retailers pass through an extensive approval process before being authorized to sell Canada Goose products. In Europe, the company owns the distribution outlets. Pricing policy is also set accordingly. Products are always sold at regular price (promotions and discounts are not available anywhere), with only minor adaptation to different geographic markets. Retail prices for jackets range from ~500 to 1,500 USD.

IKEA[3]—Throughout this book, the example of IKEA served to illustrate central concepts, including: a classic internationalization process (Chapter 2), an AdaptStand marketing strategy with high degrees of standardization (Chapter 3), and cultural adaptation as well (Chapter 5), an innovative mobile application (Chapter 10), and initiatives supporting children and other social causes (Chapter 12). Here, we look at the company as one of the most obvious cases of origin-based marketing.

Starting with the product-country image (PCI) for Sweden and the furniture industry, we need to remember that Swedish design has exercised an international influence on modern architecture and interior furnishings since the early-twentieth century. Indeed, the "functionalism" movement was established during the Stockholm Exhibition (1930). It describes the essence of Swedish designs and architecture, for they aim at function over decoration. More generally, Scandinavian designs are known for their emphasis on ergonomics and practicality, while combining hand craftsmanship, unpretentious form, and utilitarianism. Organic shapes, natural elements, and user-friendly furniture are their products' other characteristics.

Founded in 1943 in Småland (southern Sweden), IKEA's story relies on a powerful narrative originating from this small region where people are known for their grit and determination. At the time, life in that area was not easy and inhabitants had to make a lot out of a little in order to make ends meet. Inspired by its Swedish heritage, IKEA offers affordable and trendy home furnishing products, all combining function, quality, design, and value. IKEA's values (i.e., good design at an affordable price for as many people as possible, produced in a sustainable manner) align perfectly with those of Swedish people (e.g., equality and respect). The name of the company itself reveals a profound attachment to geographic roots. Indeed, it is an acronym composed of the initials of its founder (Ingvar Kamprad), his parents' farm (Elmtaryd), and his hometown in Småland (Agunnaryd). The first store opened in the neighboring town of Älmhult, where product design is still located today. In this context, IKEA has relied on the positive PCI of Sweden in the furniture industry since its inception. It uses the origin cue in many instances, including the overarching color scheme, product names, food offerings, and symbols in advertising. The blue-and-yellow color scheme is obviously chosen after the Swedish flag and is not only used only in the logotype (characterized by blue lettering against a yellow-and-blue backdrop), but also on the outer walls of stores, indoor signalization, printed and digital communications, reusable bags, employee uniforms, etc. Figure 11.12 presents the well-known logotype.

The use of the Swedish language to name all products, with no translation whatsoever in nearly thirty countries is another powerful reference to the

Figure 11.12 Presenting IKEA logotype
Source: Used with the permission of Inter IKEA Systems B.V.

country of origin. Occasional adjustments are made, however, when unfortunate connotations occur in other languages (e.g., the "Jerker" computer desk or the "Fartfull" workbench in English). The story behind this decision is a personal one, since Ingvar Kamprad struggled with dyslexia. Instead of using a numerical system to identify products, he decided to use actual Swedish names and adjectives to help him memorize the vast list of products sold. For example, bathroom articles are named after Scandinavian lakes, rivers, or bays (e.g., Dalskär, Kalkgrund, and Hamnviken), children's items are called after animals and adjectives (e.g., Påhittig, Svärta, and Silkig), and chairs and desks are named after men's names (e.g., Malkolm, Volmar, and Hemnes).

Each IKEA store features a restaurant serving traditional Swedish food, including the famous Swedish meatballs, served with boiled potatoes, cream sauce, and lingonberry jam. In certain countries, the menu is adapted to satisfy customers' preferences or dietary restrictions (e.g., the meatballs are made of salmon in China and Iceland, and made with halal meat in Muslim countries). Regardless of this effort in adaptation, going to a store represents a unique opportunity for customers around the world to discover Swedish food (and is an attraction in and of itself). Following a customary practice in Sweden, all refills of coffee, tea, soft drinks, and water are free of charge, a gesture that positively surprises clients in countries where this is not business as usual. Additionally, stores have a Swedish food market where it is possible to buy Swedish food products (mainly produced in Sweden), under the company's label and based on national recipes and traditions.

Finally, IKEA commercials often include some references to the origin, such as actors speaking with a Swedish accent or spots featuring mid-summer traditions. An example is available on YouTube with search words: "Catch the Swedish Light —IKEA."

Beyond IKEA's use of the origin cue in product and promotion policies, it is interesting to look at the mutual influence that the company and the country have had on one another's reputation. While IKEA has definitely benefited from Sweden's worldwide positive image, the reverse is also true. In

Origin-Based Marketing 455

a 2010 article entitled "The Symbiosis of Sweden & IKEA" and published in online Public Diplomacy Magazine, Olle Wästberg (then Director-General of the Swedish Institute and former Sweden Member of Parliament, State Secretary of Finance, and Consul-General in New York) stated: "IKEA is doing more for the image of Sweden than all governmental efforts combined." In other words, IKEA may have significantly contributed to Sweden's brand as countless consumers across the world came into contact with Swedish culture for the first time by visiting their local IKEA store. These linkages between corporate and nation branding are further examined in Section 11.4 "Issues at Stake." Table 11.2 provides key data about the company.

Victorinox[4]—In 1884, twenty-four-year-old Karl Elsener established a knife cutler workshop in Ibach (Switzerland). In 1921, the thriving company gained a new name from the combination of his mother's name (Victoria), who had always actively supported him, and the newly invented stainless steel, also known as "inox." Interestingly, most people do not realize they know about Victorinox' products until they hear "Swiss Army Knife." The multipurpose knife is indeed famous worldwide with sales in approximately one hundred countries for an estimated 500,000 million USD in 2015 (precise information is kept private by the family-owned company).

Victorinox could not be a more obvious example of reliance on the origin cue: a nationality included in the name of two of its distinctive products (the Swiss Army Knife and the Swiss Card, a credit card-shaped ten-function instrument) and a logotype featuring the iconic cross-and-shield emblem, often presented in white on red, a direct reminder of Switzerland's flag (see Figure 11.14). The PCI is highly favorable between a functional piece of cutlery like the pocket knife that requires reliability, sometimes even in life-or-death situations, and Switzerland, which is often associated with attributes like excellence, innovation, stability, reliability, and functionality.

The story goes that Elsener invented the all-in-one knife in 1891, called it the Swiss Officer's and Sports Knife or, for short, the Officer's Knife ("Offiziersmesser" in German) and patented it in 1897. After supplying the Swiss Army for decades, the company also supplied the US Army, Navy, and Air Force during World War II. A possible explanation as to why the knife became known as the Swiss Army Knife is that American soldiers found its German name too difficult to pronounce. The simplification held and, to this

Table 11.2 Profiling IKEA (Sweden)

Who:	*Ikea*
Since:	1943
What:	Home furnishing products
From:	Sweden
Sales (Bn USD):	39
Employing (people):	163,000
Manufacturing in (countries):	~11
Selling in (countries):	28

Source: IKEA (2016)

Figure 11.13 Presenting Victorinox logotype
Source: Courtesy of Victorinox

Figure 11.14 Presenting the logotype used for the Volkswagen car brand from 2007 to 2015
Source: Courtesy of Volkswagen Aktiengesellschaft

day, the knife is known as the Swiss Knife in many countries (e.g., *Couteau Suisse* in France and *Schweizer Messer* in Germany and Austria). It is still the official pocket knife for fifteen armies around the world, including the US military. A video available on YouTube with search words: "Victorinox 2017 brand movie" gives a good overview of the company's history, products, and distribution outlets. As in many advertising materials, one of the final images is presented with an Alpine landscape in the background, typical of Switzerland. Table 11.3 presents an overview of the company.

Over one hundred and thirty years, the flagship product has evolved greatly and, as of 2017, there were more than four hundred models of the pocket knife, which now can include a USB drive, computer maintenance tools, and a laser pointer. Though it still made up about 40 percent of the company sales in 2013, Victorinox has diversified its business into household and professional knives, watches, travel gear, and fragrances. The positive associations between the country and cutlery can be transmitted to most of these other product categories. The cutlery brand targets cooks and professionals and is, therefore, similarly praised by individuals desiring quality, ergonomics, and maneuverability. The travel gear product line is designed for frequent travelers who value the brand for its sophisticated technicality that offers greater functionality and longevity. The timepiece collection targets customers seeking mechanical performance, craftsmanship, and functionality. Interviewed in 2013 about the challenges of expanding the timepiece line of a brand that is usually associated with pocket knives (just as Mont Blanc is with pens), Victorinox's international sales director Michael Meier said: "Primarily, Swiss Army Knife is an icon of Switzerland. It is widely recognizable all over the world. Second, it is characterized by the highest quality, which lets us ensure the lifetime warranty. If we take into consideration the above features, we feel obliged to produce timepieces of the utmost quality. We treat our advertising slogan—'Companion for Life'—very seriously. Whatever we produce in Victorinox, it is supposed to serve its role for years instead of being just a fad." Questions have been raised, however, regarding whether or not the inferences made from the country image could benefit the fragrance

Table 11.3 Profiling Victorinox (Switzerland)

Who:	Victorinox
Since:	1884
What:	Army, professional and pocket knives, sport tools, multi-tools cutlery, timepieces, travel gear, fashion, and fragrances
From:	Switzerland
Sales (Bn USD):	~0.56
Employing (people):	1,800
Manufacturing in (countries):	N/A
Selling in (countries):	100

Source: Victorinox (2017)

458 *Origin-Based Marketing*

business. This illustrates one of the limitations of origin-based marketing: it does not always go well with diversification, since PCIs vary greatly from one product category to another.

Geographic market selection is wide, since Victorinox is present around the world while exporting more than 90 percent of its production. In 2013, North America generated about 40 percent of total sales at the time, followed by Switzerland, Germany, and the UK. The company had subsidiaries in twelve countries (Brazil, Canada, Chile, China, Germany, Hong Kong, Japan, India, Mexico, Peru, Poland, and the US). In terms of distribution, the company uses multiple channels: in 2013, it owned seventy-five stores (and planned to open one hundred and twenty additional ones through 2016), it used more than forty-six hundred points of sale (e.g., airports and outdoor gear shops), and also increasingly commercialized its offerings through the Internet. Promotional activities included the temporary establishment of "pop-up stores" in mountainous locations (e.g., Rio de Janeiro's Sugarloaf Mountain in Brazil and Whistler in Canada). Advertising (billboards, magazines, etc.) regularly featured the products on a mountainous background, adapted to the target market (e.g., Kobe's Mount Rokko in Japan). Mountains are an obvious link to Switzerland's landscape.

Major issues for the company related to their use of the origin cue related to the protection of its trademark and claim to be "Made-in-Switzerland." Regarding the trademark, regulations vary from country to country. In Switzerland, a product must be made in the Helvetian country for the product to be allowed to include "Swiss" in the product name. This is not the case in the US, for instance, where products can be legally manufactured in any country while bearing this term. In addition, low-price and low-quality pocket knives with shapes and logos that somewhat resemble the Victorinox's logo are legally sold across the world. This exacerbates a situation in which low-quality counterfeit products bearing the exact same trademark are illegally sold everywhere. Since maintaining its reputation of quality is core to Victorinox's brand image, the company fights imitators with vigor (e.g., monitoring websites commercializing its products to verify that they are operated by authorized resellers). It also spends considerable resources avoiding confusion. In 2005, Victorinox chose to acquire its main competitor, Wenger (located in the francophone part of Switzerland), which had also been selling multipurpose knives since 1893, including their flagship "Genuine Swiss Knife." Finally, the implementation of global regulations by the WTO also created concerns. In 2007, for instance, the Swiss Army wanted sixty-five thousand of the pocket knives with new specifications (for an estimated value of 1.7 million Swiss Francs, i.e., ~1.75 million USD). Due to the high value of the contract and under WTO regulations, it had to open an international tendering process with manufacturers from China, Taiwan, and Bulgaria thought to be in good positions to win the bid, which generated consternation in Switzerland and became a hot political matter. If the knives purchased by the Swiss Army were made somewhere else, would Victorinox lose some of its brand equity? In conclusion, these examples illustrate some unexpected hurdles that companies adopting origin-based marketing, like Victorinox, can face.

Volkswagen[5]—The Volkswagen Group (see Table 11.4 for an overview of key data) has served as an example to illustrate various concepts in this

Origin-Based Marketing 459

Table 11.4 Profiling the Volkswagen Group (Germany)

Who:	Volkswagen
Since:	1937
What:	Car manufacturer
From:	Germany
Sales (Bn USD):	217
Employing (people):	~625,000
Manufacturing in (countries):	~30
Selling in (countries):	~150

Source: Volkswagen AG (2016)

book, including the sequence of internationalization and choice of entry modes (Chapter 2), the standardization and adaptation issue (Chapter 3), and the impact of economic and technological distances between markets (Chapter 7). Here, we use the example of this group in general and of the Volkswagen brand in particular to illustrate the notion of product-country image (PCI), the evolving use of the origin cue over time, and the dilemma of using this cue in the context of growth by international acquisitions.

First, we can establish the obvious: the strong product-country image of Germany when it comes to car manufacturing. Indeed, many sources have emphasized that German cars benefit from the strongest COE in the industry, particularly due to the following positive associations: Germany has the know-how and capacity to produce heavy machinery, German engineers receive first-class education, and values in the country include performance, attention to detail, inventiveness, and reliability. Thus, the stereotypical image is that Germany is good at producing well-engineered and well-assembled performing cars. Understandably, the company heavily relied on the origin cue to rip off the benefits of such positive COE.

A first example is found in the "Das Auto." tagline (i.e., "The car." in German—with a dot at the end, conveying the assertiveness in this statement) which was used in combination with the Volkswagen brand logo from 2007 to 2015 in multiple countries, without being translated (see Figure 11.15). Using a recognizable native language is a simple and smart way of informing foreign consumers about the country of origin.

Other examples of the use of the origin cue are found in TV commercials diffused in the US for the Passat model, for instance, which featured the taglines: "That's the Power of German Engineering" (2012) and, "Isn't it time for German engineering?" (2015). These commercials can be screened on YouTube with search words: "Safety First: All-New 2012 Passat" and "2015 Volkswagen Passat | German-engineered Midsize Sedan" (in both cases, the taglines appear at the very end of the spots). We can hardly imagine a more-direct way to refer to the positive PCI. Quite logically, these taglines were never used in Germany, because for them to be well-received over there, the degree of ethnocentrism and nationalism of consumers would need to be extremely (and quite worrisomely) high. Additionally, there is no need to educate potential buyers about the origin of the cars in Germany. Using the

460 Origin-Based Marketing

origin cue when relevant and according to the receptiveness of target audiences is important.

Second, it is quite interesting to wonder why the company decided to stop using the "Das Auto." slogan in the US in 2016. As early as 2009, business magazines forecasted that promotion of Volkswagen cars in the US would put less emphasis on the German origin of the brand. Consumers seemed to be more favorable to an All-American approach and a new assembly plant that opened in 2011 in Chattanooga (Tennessee, US) was an opportunity for the company to take a first step in this direction. For instance, one of the Volkswagen's displays at the North American International Auto Show held in Detroit that same year—one of the largest annual show in the country— was adorned by the words "Born in the U.S.A." A tacit reference to Bruce Springsteen's cult song but also a somewhat stronger statement than the famous "made-in." Interestingly, the emphasis was still put on the origin, but the geographic cue had shifted from the country of manufacture to the country of assembly. Nevertheless, the company struggled in this market, quite atypically. While the Volkswagen brand sold more than 2.9 million cars around the world in the first half of 2016, only 149,000 of them were sold in the US, a small number considering the size of the market. US consumers' tendency toward national preference and the presence of fierce competition from both local and foreign players (e.g., Ford and Toyota) are part of the reasons why the company is experiencing these commercial difficulties.

Yet, other events contributed to the need for a change in communications. In September 2015, a huge scandal shook the international reputation of Volkswagen when the company admitted to equipping more than 11 million diesel-powered cars with software designed to cheat emissions tests worldwide. This scandal hurt the brand and reduced consumers' goodwill in quite a dramatic fashion. In addition, when consumer reports and professional publications like JD Power's 2016 "Vehicle Dependability Survey" ranked Volkswagen cars below the industry average, it was all the more damaging. Reliability is indeed one of the strongest association with the brand's German origin. Finally, the company experienced issues with the positioning of its Volkswagen models. In the US, like in other international markets, consumer perceptions were different than first expected. For instance, the Volkswagen brand was perceived by Indian consumers as less up-market than Skoda at first (see Chapter 7). In the US, while Volkswagen intended to position itself as a rival to Toyota and Ford, US consumers saw the brand as a near-luxury product, for its European origins and because of a close association to its corporate siblings, such as Audi and Bentley. Therefore, they approached the buying process differently and expected more options from a Passat sedan, for instance, than from a Honda Accord or Toyota Camry. In spite of the brand's efforts to be more attractive to value shoppers, its price point was near the top in many of the segments in which it competed and a typical Volkswagen costed more than its competitors. The capacity to demand a premium price due to a positive COE is usually an advantage. When competitive rivalry is high, however, and other market segments are covered by multiple brands from the same group, it can become a liability.

Origin-Based Marketing   461

In this context, it is understandable that the brand would decide to move away from origin-based marketing in the US and drop the use of the origin cue (e.g., the "Das Auto." slogan) in its communications. Interestingly, the overall group communications also seem to have shed any obvious reference to its origin (see, for instance, the contents of the "strategic plan for 2025," available on the group's website). Nevertheless, this does not mean that the Volkswagen brand cannot still rely on its origin in markets where conditions are more favorable to origin-based marketing. Audi, for instance, also maintains strong roots with its origin in communications, keeping its longstanding and worldwide signature "*Vorsprung durch Technik*" (or "advancement through technology") in native German. The positive COE is then more consistent with the positioning of the brand, since Audi targets high-end segments of the market and thus can appeal to consumers' willingness to pay for high-quality products.

The Volkswagen case is interesting because it illustrates the difficulty to maintain an origin-based marketing approach not only in multiple geographies but over time as well. While the reference to German origins really helped the company in many locations for its positive COE, it came across difficulties in markets where "buy local" policies and nationalist preferences were strong. In addition, the occurrence of scandals (or poor customer reviews) linked to the brand attributes (e.g., trustworthiness and reliability) most associated with the geographic origin can have devastating effects on brand equity.

To conclude, we can also reflect on the complexities for a group like Volkswagen to grow through acquisitions while maintaining a close association to its origin. As of 2017, the group managed a portfolio of twelve brands, only three of which were German: Volkswagen, Audi, and Porsche. The other brands were from a number of countries in Europe (e.g., British Bentley, French Bugatti, Italian Lamborghini, Spanish Seat, Czech Skoda, and Swedish Scania). In these conditions, the relevance of origin-based marketing for the group as a whole, or for some of its brands only, becomes increasingly questionable. This could hide an interesting branding problem since the group and the flagship brand bear the same name and are often confused for one another. Perhaps the name of the group could evolve toward something less reminiscent of its geographic origin. Beyond the difficulty of the task, such a decision would bring forward the dilemma that many global companies face: staying close to their origin as a sign of authenticity (and rip off the benefits of a positive COE, wherever possible) or evolving toward a truly cross-border organization in which the concept of origin loses its meaning.

11.3.2 *National Examples of Place Branding: Argentina, Australia, Chile, and Slovenia*

Brand Argentina: From "More Than One Reason" to "Indescribable Fascination"[6]—Tango. Polo. Lionel Messi. Savory steaks. Argentina had the luxury, even prior to starting country branding efforts, to be associated with

462 Origin-Based Marketing

strong images among the international general public. Nestor Kirchner, president of Argentina (2003–2007), could foresee the potential of his country's brand when he mandated a special taskforce to work on the topic in 2004.

Inprotur (*Instituto Nacional de Promocion Turistica or National Institute for Tourism Promotion*), acting as a dedicated country branding team, was created that same year as a special body within the Ministry of Tourism. A second team also joined the taskforce: *Fundación ExportAr* (ExportAr), the export promotion agency, which had the knowledge and experience to help Inprotur include a business perspective to their touristic one.

By 2005, the Argentine country branding team had recruited new participants to add different points of view to the ideation and brainstorming phases. They invited not only governmental actors (e.g., representatives of the Ministry of Foreign Affairs) but also external contributors from the media and communications fields. The first step in creating a country brand was to lead a national and international survey among the general public as well as with leaders and opinion influencers. Surprisingly, the international survey revealed limited awareness of the country, with opinions scattered on a spectrum. While a majority of respondents had a relatively positive (50 percent) and very positive (26 percent) opinion of Argentina, another group (23 percent) held a relatively negative image. Within the country, leaders and influencers had a worse opinion of the country than the general public (47 percent versus 33 percent, respectively, saw the country as having a rather negative image). Country branding efforts were thus necessary not only to assert Argentina's position internationally but also to revive its internal image. Inprotur, ExportAr, and their collaborators wanted to create a brand that would be comprehensive, not only focusing on specific products or tourism. Adding to the survey efforts, benchmarks were conducted, especially against Brand Australia and Brand New Zealand for their novel communication strategies. The result of the ideation process was to create five strategic touristic and business segments around which Brand Argentina could revolve. These segments were represented by the following adjectives, conducting positive associations: Active, Authentic, Natural, Gourmet, Meetings, and High-End.

In 2008, Inprotur developed a marketing campaign around the theme "Diversity that adds value" to better reflect the great diversity of resources and people Argentina has to offer. It focused on three main axes: nature, culture, and knowledge. Various segments were proposed to reflect such diversity: active, authentic, natural, gourmet, meetings, and high-end. In collaboration with the *Asociación Argentina de Agencias de Publicidad* (Argentine Association of Advertising Agencies), the tagline "*Mas de una razón*" ("More than one reason") was created to encapsulate the diverse reasons why one should visit, invest in, or buy from Argentina. The logo was then developed as a result of a contest among forty-five teams of marketing and design students across the country. The winning logo was used between 2008 and 2012 and exhibited three ribbons expanding from a common origin. The common origin represented the unity of people having roots in migratory movements as a starting point and the ribbons—also looking like dynamic

Origin-Based Marketing 463

waves—symbolized links between people and the idea of a nation in motion. Two of the ribbons were blue (one the same shade as the national flag, the other one darker). The third one was silver and was meant to represent the industrial power of Argentina ("Industria Argentina," another promoted brand), also evocative of the following attributes: quality, innovation, and sophistication.

By 2012, Inprotur and ExportAr had budgets of 28 and 32 Million USD, respectively, which allowed them to return to the brainstorming phase and better define the country brand's orientation. Indeed, managers at Inprotur found out that the country brand tagline and logo did not connect well with the Argentines. For instance, many citizens were surprised by the absence of a sun or at least of some yellow in the logotype, an important reference to the national flag and identity. It was time to put the Argentines at the heart of this brand. The two organizations came up with four new fundamental characteristics defining the Argentine essence: 1) Argentina is a land full of imagination, 2) it is characterized by its excesses, 3) it is a country of chemistry (between people, between people and nature), and 4) the country has the capacity to surpass itself. A new tagline arose, "*Indescribable fascinación*" ("Indescribable fascination"). Indescribable, because you have to come to Argentina to understand what the country is all about. And fascination, because Argentines are very emotional people. By 2013, a new logo was developed: it exhibited more space for the word Argentina, it had a more appealing ribbon design and offered a new unique typography. A yellow ribbon replaced the grey one, to better reflect the sun on the national flag and the warmth of the people. A YouTube video presenting the redesign process is available in Spanish with search words: *Rediseño de Marca País Argentina*. Another video explaining the need for a country brand is also available, along with many other visual clips supporting the brand, on the Ministry of Tourism webpage.

In addition, online resources—in particular a comprehensive guide entitled *Manual Marca Pais*, were made available, with other country brand material, for companies willing to use the logotype in their own communications. The idea of putting tags with the country brand logo on non-agrifood products emerged during the benchmark phase after looking at best practices from Brand Australia. Specializing in polo-inspired apparel and successful in international markets, La Martina was one of the participating companies, for instance. Nontraditional marketing initiatives were also launched and included: organizing the "Week of Argentine Products" in foreign supermarkets and stores (e.g., Auchan in France, and Harrods in England); decorating the metro station "Argentine" in Paris to promote tourism; and inviting Argentine chefs to cook in established hotel chains abroad (e.g., Sheraton and Hyatt) so that Argentine food producers could invite potential buyers to taste their products in five-star settings.

In 2015, the new Government of Mauricio Macri proceeded to restructure several agencies, including *Fundación ExportAr*, which became responsible for attracting FDI the following year, in addition to promoting international trade. It is now known as *Agencia Argentina de Inversiones y Comercio*

464   *Origin-Based Marketing*

Internacional, or Argentine Agency for Investment and International Trade. Inprotur has remained in place but its online portal has changed for the brand name "Argentina. World Friendly" and now puts the following words and adjectives at the forefront: nature, food, snow, passion, night, urban. With these changes, efforts in promoting Argentina within and outside of its national borders are as important as ever.

Australia Unlimited[7]—While some of the examples in this chapter feature small or developing economies, the case of Australia is different. For one, the country has a fairly large economy—the fourteenth largest GDP in 2016, according to the World Bank—and has been taking part in international exchanges for many decades. Therefore, it does not need to develop its visibility in order to participate in global business as emerging economies do. Furthermore, it does not suffer from a negative country of origin effect. On the contrary, Australia is generally well known and its name generates positive associations, in particular with landscapes and wildlife (e.g., the Outback, beaches, Great Barrier Reef, kangaroos, and koalas). Still, the Australian government felt it was important to invest in building a stronger nation brand, thereby pursing the same objective as other countries—i.e., to support Australian exporters seeking international buyers, as well as investors and universities in attracting capital and students—but for different reasons. First, the country was widely known for its natural assets, but such a reputation has its limitations when it comes to supporting long-term economic and social development. Second, Australia's remote physical location requires significant efforts in engaging with the rest of the world (e.g., absorbing extra transportation costs and adjusting to considerable time differences when dealing with foreign partners). An excellent reputation can make these efforts worthwhile and motivate business people, workers, and students to engage with the country, and, in turn, help the country in engaging with the world.

Thus, enhancing the country's international positioning with a focus on innovation, creativity, technology, and science became a priority, and in 2009, the Australian Government allocated 20 million AUD (~16 million USD) over four years to the "Building Brand Australia Program." Administrated by "Austrade" (the Australian Trade and Investment Commission, which is responsible for promoting trade, investment, tourism, and education), this program relies on a new brand identity, called "Australia Unlimited" (see Figure 11.15).

The advertising agency network M&C Saatchi (UK) was hired to help develop the brand. Extensive industry consultation, a public tender, and both international and domestic research were used to make sure the brand effectively conveyed strong associations, with values like collaboration, capability, confidence, creativity, enterprising spirit, resilience, and optimism. Overall, the brand was tested among fourteen thousand people in twelve markets. It was then placed at the center of a promotion campaign and deployed using a website (Australia Unlimited) that centralizes articles, research results, photography, and videos (e.g., the "2015 Australia Unlimited Video"), as well as social media channels (e.g., Facebook, Twitter, and YouTube). Instead of putting forward the country's natural assets, this campaign highlighted the work of its world-class scientists, designers, entrepreneurs, artists, and

Origin-Based Marketing 465

Figure 11.15 Presenting Australia's country brand
Source: "Australia Unlimited" is Australia's nation brandmark and is reproduced with permission from the Australian Trade and Investment Commission (Austrade)

humanitarians located both at home and abroad (e.g., exporters, business leaders, expats, and alumni) by showcasing more than four hundred and fifty personal stories.

This strategy is an interesting example of place branding that focuses on the "people-related" facet of country image, as opposed to the more commonly emphasis on the "environment-related" country image (see Figure 11.6). According to recent research, a focus on people is indeed an efficient way to change perceptions and successfully improve a country's international image. Indeed, Durand et al. (2016) found that a positive people-related country image reinforces both decision-makers' appreciation of products made in the country and of its general political, socio-economic, technological, and cultural environment. Although this study only examined perceptions of exporters and importers in the global wine industry and its findings cannot be generalized to the general population at this stage, it points to the existence of a powerful mechanism: people are true ambassadors for their country of origin. We can all understand this principle intuitively but it is most often ignored in place branding strategies. One of the reasons for this surprising omission possibly lies in the difficulty of establishing an actual correlation between the way people are perceived outside of their country of origin and the reputation of the country in question (e.g., its capacity to manufacture certain product categories such as those including high technology, host major events such as the Olympics and international political and cultural forums, or attract MNCs and global investments). Current research methodologies face severe limitations in this regard because too many factors would need to be controlled. Facing this challenge, we are left with observing the few place branding initiatives that situates people at the core of

466 *Origin-Based Marketing*

their campaigns, and estimate their effectiveness subjectively. In the case of Australia, this strategy seems to have paid off, in particular in Asian markets.

In China for instance, networks of *daigou* (i.e., individuals outside of the country who shop on behalf of mainland inhabitants who are interested in safer products than those manufactured locally or cheaper imported products, in particular luxury goods, thereby effectively avoiding local taxes) consider Australia as being a trustworthy country of manufacture. According to Bain and Company (2016), cross-border shoppers in China were 1.6 times more likely to associate Australia with health and nutrition than the US, Germany, Japan, and South Korea. Customer-to-customer (C2C) business might seem anecdotal at first, but *daigous* are in the tens of thousands and represent a considerable market (a reported 12 billion USD worth of business in 2013 and booming ever since). A "people-based" approach to promoting a country might just have been the right strategy to help shape beliefs and influence behaviors in C2C relationships.

India also represents an important trade partner for Australia. For instance, two-way investment as well as two-way exports of goods and services ranged in the 20–25 billion USD each in the past few years. In 2016, India was Australia's sixth-biggest export market, while Australia represented an important supplier of energy and food for India. In a 2017 Forbes India article, Brand Connect—a company specializing in distributing high-end drinks in all the Asia-Pacific region—wrote the following: "Australia is one of the world's most efficient food producers and its agricultural technology and expertise is generating strong interest as India looks to increase the productivity of its own food sector. Meanwhile Australian design, planning, transport, water solutions and building technology can help improve living standards for India's increasingly urbanised population. Close to seventy thousand Indians studied in Australia last year, making Australia one of the top international destinations for Indian students. Now Australian universities are seeking to grow Masters and PhD candidate exchanges via stronger university-to-university partnerships, as well as work with India's corporate sector to support R&D collaboration and technology commercialisation. Australia's world-leading health and medical technology companies are also looking to form strategic partnerships, joint research, and accelerated product development with Indian counterparts." This paragraph entirely aligns with the efforts conducted by the Australian government to promote the country under a different light, and is indicative of a successful repositioning.

Promotion efforts of the Australian government also rely on traditional tools, such as trade missions. It is noteworthy to observe that the brand is then consistently used on these occasions. During the 2017 Australia Business Week in India, for instance, Austrade partnered with CNBC-TV18 (India's premier business channel) to develop a show. Entitled "Australia India Unlimited Opportunities," this three-part series showcased academia and business ties between the two countries. Other initiatives include the annual mission to the Middle East and North African (MENA) region, held since 2012 and entitled the "AU MENA Roadshow" (AU standing for Australia Unlimited). Relying on high-profile forums, targeted roundtables, and official meetings, the 2017 event aimed at introducing Australian companies

Origin-Based Marketing 467

and key government officials, industry stakeholders, and projects (in particular in the mining and healthcare sectors) in Egypt, Saudi Arabia, and the United Arab Emirates.

In conclusion, these examples reveal that the use of the Australia's "Unlimited" tag extends far beyond one single promotion campaign and can be activated overtime and in various settings.

Brand Chile: From "All Ways Surprising" to "Chile Is Good for You" to "Diversity, Tradition, Progress, and Trustworthiness"[8]—Contrary to neighboring Argentina, Chile had to put in significant effort over the past decade into building positive associations with its name. Until recently, the evocation of Chile with foreigners outside of Latin America was often met with a blank stare (e.g., many Europeans and North Americans could not even readily position the country on a map). At first, this effort was undertaken by ProChile, the government's export promotion agency that has been active for more than thirty years, helping exporters promote their offerings abroad, particularly in the agricultural, forestry, and mining sectors, but also in services such as architecture, information technology, and cinema.

In 2005, ProChile undertook the task of promoting the country in a more systematic way, with the input of associations of exporters and the Ministries of Tourism and Economy, among other actors. A first campaign titled "Chile, All Ways Surprising" resulted from this effort. Interestingly, the equivalent of this slogan in Spanish, "*Chile Sorprende Siempre*," only conveys the idea that the country can consistently surprise over time, without the play on words about the country being surprising in many ways. This detail speaks to one of the choices that non-English speaking countries have when developing a slogan: should they prioritize the local language or English for the international community? Here, the slogan was most powerful in English, an indication that it was mainly destined for foreigners, outside of the hispanophone world. Videos of the campaign are available on YouTube (e.g., with search words: "Chile ★ All Ways Surprising Vicente Rogers").

In 2009, a dedicated agency for country branding was created and called *Fundación Imagen de Chile* (Chile Brand Foundation). To have a rough idea of the financial resources available, this agency had a budget of about 6 million USD in 2012, while ProChile relied on a budget of a little under 50 million USD for the same year. One of the first initiatives by *Fundación Imagen de Chile* at the time of its creation was to hire a foreign consulting company to help with collecting primary data about perceptions of Chile, through surveys implemented both locally and abroad. Discussions with similar organizations in other Latin American countries (e.g., Argentina, Colombia, Peru, Mexico, Honduras, and Guatemala) were also an opportunity to learn about common challenges (e.g., foreigners tend to ignore differences within Latin America, going as far as to believing that all inhabitants, typically, like to dance, sing, and eat spicy food), and differentiation strategies. In addition, a content analysis targeted the media outlets in about fifty countries to learn about what was reported on Chile. This work revealed that there was limited awareness of Chile and that, overall, its image was rather neither positive nor negative. Finally, benchmarks against country brands from other countries were also conducted, in particular against direct competitors in specific

468   *Origin-Based Marketing*

sectors (e.g., wines, fruits, and wood products) such as Australia, Canada, New Zealand, South Africa, and Sweden.

In 2010, Fundación Imagen de Chile decided to unveil a new branding campaign with the following slogan: "*Chile hace bien*" or "Chile is good for you." Again, this translation illustrates the difficulty of conveying the same meaning in different languages, this time, with a play on words in the Spanish version. "*Chile hace bien*" also means "Chile does well," referring to the wealth and know-how of the country—a meaning that is entirely lost in the chosen English version. At this time, fruitful collaborations between the agency and national companies with an international presence took place. For instance, *Concha y Toro*—a leading Chilean wine producer representing about one-third of all wine exports from the country and a very successful company in international markets with, among others, a brand like *Casillero del Diablo*—has created advertising spots jointly with *Fundación Imagen de Chile*. Informed about the brand and associated with its development process, *Concha y Toro* is one of many Chilean companies that transmits the desired message in its own communications and acts as a *de facto* country brand ambassador. In addition, *Fundación Imagen de Chile* circulated the results of the local and international surveys they conducted on perceptions about the country, which helped local companies adjust their communication strategies accordingly, depending on the importance of the COE in their business. Beside companies, other target groups that help publicize positive messages about Chile were identified in political and cultural leaders as well as in sports representatives. The idea defended by *Fundación Imagen de Chile* was that these famous people could share some of their visibility and good reputation with the country. The foundation also acted with the government to influence policies and decision-making accordingly with issues identified in surveys. For instance, it lobbied the government for the preservation of Mapuche territory in Patagonia, a long-standing issue whose resolution would reflect well on the country. Finally, online communications and social media were important channels of information dissemination, as they reach a wide audience—easily and for a minimal cost—and provide the ability to receive feedback on featured messages and activities. Indeed, brand managers looked at web analytics in order to measure the impact of these activities, as well as other indicators, both abroad (e.g., the Country Brand Index) and locally (e.g., popularity among citizens).

In 2016, a new campaign was launched with the theme: "Diversity, Tradition, Progress, and Trustworthiness" or "*Diversidad, Tradición, Progreso y Confiabilidad*." In this case, the simple reference to several preferred country attributes reduced the translation issue (adjectives find equivalents in other languages more readily than ideas and plays on words).

The renewal of slogans and communication axes every five years or so can be seen as both a source of strength and weakness. On the one hand, renewing the brand image contributes to energizing the work of the foundation and maintaining an active dialogue with stakeholders. On the other hand, this rather frequent change can be a source of concern, since it potentially limits brand recognition, especially abroad. Some countries have used the same message and visuals for more than ten years. To palliate this issue, an element of constancy was introduced in the visual identity. From early on, several stars were featured in the country brand logo (a reminder of the Chilean flag as well as the fact that the country is an international hub for astronomy, with clear skies over the Andes). These stars and the font remained rather identical, while color schemes and slogans changed.

In addition, the other governmental organizations involved in promoting the country, such as InvestChile and ChileTravel (aiming to attract FDI and tourism, respectively) also now use the 2016 logo with only limited variations in the background color. The resulting unity across actors and actions conveys a sense of professionalism and well-coordinated implementation of a successful country branding strategy.

I Feel Slovenia[9]—Located in Central Europe where the Alps meet the Mediterranean and vast Pannonian plains, Slovenia is bordered by Italy to the west, Austria to the north, Hungary to the northeast, Croatia to the south and southeast, and the Adriatic Sea to the southwest. It covers an area of 20,000 square kilometers (~7,700 square miles)—which is roughly the size of New Jersey in the US—and had an estimated population of about 2 million inhabitants in 2016. Yet, the diversity found in a territory of such modest proportions is enticing. First, Slovenia's biological and topographical diversity is remarkable (e.g., high mountains in the Julian Alps, vast forests and karst underground watercourses forming impressive caves, home to the Carniolan honeybees and Lipizzaner horses, etc.). In terms of history, Slovenia has been successively part of the Roman Empire, the Habsburg Monarchy, and various formations of Yugoslavia involving the Croats and Serbs (after also being annexed by Germany, Italy, and Hungary during World War II). After a plebiscite vote in 1991 in which a massive 88 percent of voters opted for independence (with a turnout of 90 percent), it has become one of the youngest countries in the world by seceding from Yugoslavia. Economically, Slovenia became the first formerly communist country to adopt the euro (2007) after joining the European Union (2004). It later became a member of the OECD (2010), and with an estimated GDP of about 33,000 USD per capita in 2016, it ranks well among high-income economies. Culturally, the Slovenian language became the bastion of the country's identity (even though people often speak several other languages). It has some marked specificities, such as the dual verbal form used when two people perform an action (e.g., love one another). Typical beehive paintings, hay racks (*kozolec*), and walnut rolls (*potica*) are a few more examples of the highlights of Slovenia. Artists such as poetry and theater writer Ivan Cankar and internationally recognized people such as the architect Jože Plečnik, and, more recently, hockey player Anže Kopitar and Olympic skier Tina Maze, complete this brief portrayal of Slovenia, a small country with lots to offer.

In spite of this diversity and richness, the Slovenian government noticed the lack of international recognition of the country, beyond neighboring regions. Starting in the early 1990s, several efforts in promotion with various logos, slogans, and campaigns were made but failed to achieve significant changes. Indeed, the country continued to face challenges, including a certain amount of ignorance and stereotypes due to its location in the Balkans, a tendency in foreigners to confuse Slovenia with Slovakia, and the lack of recognition of

470 Origin-Based Marketing

national symbols (e.g., renowned cities, commercial brands, national dishes and drinks). Believing that a strong trademark was the best marketing tool for modern countries faced with increased competition, the Government of Slovenia decided to step out of the box and adopt a more holistic strategy to promoting the country. It launched a public call in 2006 for a slogan and logotype that would best represent Slovenia, and every citizen was given the opportunity to send a proposal. The winning slogan was "I Feel Slovenia" with a visual emphasis on the letters "love." Slovenia appears to be the only country in the world with "love" in its name. A positioning based on such a strong and positive emotion, with a resolute experiential element—one has to experience and not just "learn about" what the country has to offer—resonated well with what Slovenia is about and what its population stands for.

In 2007, a decision was made to develop a nation brand by adopting an innovative bottom-up approach, building the brand identity starting from the slogan. This was done with the help of local communication agency Pristop and professionals from different fields as well as with international expert Leslie de Chernatony, Honorary Professor at Aston University (UK) and brand management specialist. In order to build the brand, they followed a process inspired from the Delphi method. In its purest form, this method—traditionally used in trend forecasting—is based on the answers of a panel of experts to questionnaires in successive rounds. With anonymous summaries of findings provided after each round, participants can then revise their earlier answers in light of the other experts' opinions. Ultimately, answers from the group converge toward one particular answer. In the case of Slovenia's brand building process, a first open-ended questionnaire was sent out to thirty high-ranked representatives (including experts in the fields of economy, tourism, culture, heritage, sports, and so on). A second questionnaire was then implemented among some seven hundred other representatives from the same key areas. Finally, a web questionnaire was deployed in order to collect data directly from the public. Slovenians were questioned about how they perceived themselves and were also asked to provide their input about the new brand. The idea of a new country brand was well received and as many as 6,900 Slovenians participated, giving feedback on how they see themselves and other ideas for the brand. Overall, the brand development process took around six months and involved a team of about ten people. Figure 11.16 presents the brand.

The resulting brand contents are presented in detail in Slovenia's country brand book, available on the website of the government's Communication Office. In addition, Konecnik Ruzzier and de Chernatony (2013) explain how Slovenia's branding identity was developed and implemented, also proposing a model that captures the mission, vision, and values, as well as core associations and elements of the country's personality. An important aspect is that the brand story speaks for Slovenians, who are assiduous and approach everything they love with passion. Characterized by a pronounced individualism, they also enjoy ties to the local environment and show a deep attachment to the country, society, and family. At the same time, they are open to ideas and people from elsewhere. The choice of the specific shade of green ("Slovenian Green") in the visual identity, the bold reference to

Origin-Based Marketing   471

Figure 11.16 Presenting Slovenia's country brand
Source: Courtesy of the Government Communications Office from the Republic of Slovenia

"love" in the logo (that ingeniously merges with the slogan), and the mission statement ("Forward with Nature") all reflect the unique positioning of Slovenia as a country orientated toward organic development and balance in all things. The involvement of all stakeholders in the brand-building process, particularly citizens, was instrumental in the successful implementation of the brand. Not only did the "I Feel Slovenia" brand contribute to increased recognition abroad and achieve other expected outcomes (e.g., increase in tourist attendance and FDI attraction), but it also helped citizens strengthen their sense of national identity.

However, some issues were faced, including a limited budget for developing the brand identity and launching the implementation (200,000 euros) and a few critics raising the issue that the slogan was in English and not in Slovenian, for instance. It was an opportunity to educate the public about the main objective of the brand: promote Slovenia abroad! Another problem arose after the 2008 parliamentary elections, since political support of the country brand was no longer as strong. The economic and financial turndown of 2008 left its toll in Slovenia as well. In just a few years, Slovenia had several political leaders and it took some persistence from the team managing the brand "I Feel Slovenia" to save it. Eventually, they were able to pursue their objectives and started deploying the brand.

In terms of implementation, state authorities, nongovernmental and commercial organizations, various associations and individuals knew to present themselves to foreign investors and partners under the brand "I Feel Slovenia." The brand was introduced in successive waves, first in tourism, second in the area of sports and business, then to other areas, such as culture and science.

472 Origin-Based Marketing

In sports, the brand was well received and the green color was welcomed by athletes and fans alike. Additionally, athletes were found to be excellent promoters, true ambassadors of their country, for their influence on fans and the public in general. At the same time, they could increase their own value and credibility by using the brand. Close cooperation with the Slovenian Olympic Committee and other federations (e.g., hockey, skiing, basketball, handball, soccer and, white-water kayaking) helped diffuse the brand. An example of another initiative is the presence of hospitality houses at important sporting events such as the Olympic Games (in Whistler, London, and Pyeongchang).

In business, some Slovenian products and services benefited from a better image in international markets than did the country itself. Several co-branding arrangements were thus established with Slovenian companies, whether large exporters or start-ups. In this way, there is an "I Feel Slovenia" line of Gorenje fridges and an "I Feel Slovenia" line of Elan skis. Numerous food and wine producers also decided to add an extra label onto their products with the brand. Connecting with the strongest Slovenian brands helped to build the country brand's value in all markets that were strategic for the Slovenian economy.

An example of implementation of the brand in the area of culture lies in partnerships developed for international events, such as the annual Frankfurt Book Fair, the world's largest trade fair for books.

Finally, two surveys took place in 2015 and 2016 in order to measure the success of the "I Feel Slovenia" brand. The first survey served to assess how entrepreneurs and business people perceived the brand, to what extent it was used, and the key motivators for a more active use. Results showed notably that procedures for companies to participate and start using the "I Feel Slovenia" brand were not clear enough. As a result, more effort was employed in communicating with stakeholders. In the 2016 survey results, companies indicated that the brand identity was no longer representing the country well in the area of business, which led to conducting new in-depth interviews and refreshing the brand. For instance, more emphasis was placed on the green economy, sustainable development, the growing importance of design in the final product, and the integration of information and communication technologies into processes. The intended business image for Slovenia was one of strategic orientation toward niche areas and value co-creation in the field of sustainable technologies, top design, and smart solutions.

11.4 Issues at Stake

In the literature about origin-based marketing and place branding, many perspectives and definitions have been discussed for more than twenty-five years. Research often tends to approach these two phenomena in isolation. Here, we link them together while addressing the following questions:

- How can we evaluate the image of countries (simply put, their reputation)? Is this evaluation stable over time? What does that mean for

Origin-Based Marketing   473

companies, in other words, what is the provenance paradox and how can companies overcome it?

- How many origins can a product have? Is there a risk of dilution of the effect of origin in case of multiple origins?
- Is the origin of products, services, and companies always accurately recognized? What does it mean in terms of the strength and relevance of the effect of origin?
- What are the outcomes of origin-based marketing? Can we really measure them?
- What is the impact of origin-based marketing on traditional marketing activities? And what are the key success factors for origin-based marketing?

11.4.1 Evolution of Country Image Over Time and Provenance Paradox

One of the first issue at stake with origin-based marketing is the evolution over time of country image. To learn about this evolution, we first examine the way country image has been assessed in practice, after having seen its conceptualization.

How can we evaluate the image of countries (simply put, their reputation)? In the background information of this chapter, we have seen how to measure brand equity for brands in general. Similar measures have been developed to capture the value of country brands as well.

Country Brand Index—Developed in 2004 by FutureBrand (UK), a creative company that is part of the major advertising organization Interpublic Group of Companies (along with Foote Cone & Belding presented in Chapter 10, McCann Worldgroup, and Lowe and Partners). This index relies on a model that further extends Aaker's (1996) seminal work. Figure 11.17 presents the 2015 edition of the *Country Brand Index,* which measures the associations that people make with a given country (in terms of values, quality of life, business potential, culture, tourism, and products), levels of familiarity with and awareness of the country, as well as affective and conative factors such as preferences, considerations, and decisions relative to a visit.

The method for this index relies on both quantitative and qualitative data collected from more than 2,500 opinion-formers and frequent international business or leisure travellers in seventeen countries spanning Europe (Germany, France, and the UK), the Americas (Argentina, Brazil, Canada, Mexico, and the US), Eurasia, Asia, and the Pacific (Australia, China, India, Japan, Russia, and Thailand) as well as the Middle East and Africa (Turkey, South Africa, and the United Arab Emirates) (FutureBrand, 2015, p. 7). The latest ranking available (2015) featured the following Top Ten countries, in this order: Japan, Switzerland, Germany, Sweden, Canada, Norway, US, Australia, Denmark, and Austria.

Nation Brand Index—Other examples are found in the work of Simon Anholt, introduced earlier in this chapter (see Section 11.2.2). First, he helped develop the *Nation Brands Index* with collaborators at GFK Roper (a

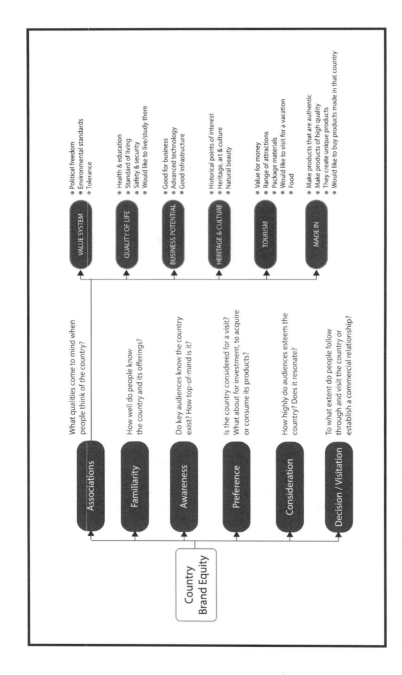

Figure 11.17 Measuring country brand equity
Source: Adapted from FutureBrand (2015)

leading marketing research and consulting firm, headquartered in Germany). The measure relies on what Anholt called the "nation brand hexagon" and captures perceptions about the following six dimensions:

- people (i.e., the population's reputation for competence, openness, friendliness, and other qualities)
- governance (i.e., the reputation of the government's competency, fairness, and commitment to solving global issues)
- exports (i.e., the image of products and services)
- tourism (i.e., the level of interest in visiting the country in question and the draw of natural and man-made attractions)
- investment and immigration (i.e., the power to attract people to live, work or study and the country's quality of life and business environment)
- culture and heritage

The Good Country Index—In 2016, Simon Anholt proposed a new approach aiming to "start a global debate about what countries are really for. Do they exist purely to serve the interests of their own politicians, businesses and citizens, or are they actively working for all of humanity and the whole planet? The debate is a critical one, because if the first answer is the correct one, we're all in deep trouble," as explained in an introductory text on the Good Country website. The finality of this new index (a "bigger picture with purpose") is a departure from traditional measures of nation brand equity. Another point of originality is that it takes the size of the economy (as measured by the GDP) into account. Some of the dimensions covered are rather similar to other measures while others are unique to this index:

- science and technology (measured in terms of the number of foreign students studying in the country; exports of periodicals, scientific journals, and newspapers; number of articles published in international journals; number of Nobel prizes, and number of International Patent Cooperation Treaty applications)
- culture (measured by the exports of creative goods and services, UNESCO dues in arrears as a percentage of contribution, freedom of movement, and freedom of the press)
- international peace and security (e.g., measured by the number of peacekeeping troops sent overseas for UN missions, dues in arrears to financial contributions to UN peacekeeping missions as a percentage of contribution, exports of weapons and ammunition, etc.)
- world order (measured by the percentage of population that gives to charity, number of refugees hosted, number of refugees overseas, population growth rate, and number of UN treaties signed as proxy for diplomatic action and peaceful conflict resolution)
- planet and climate (measured by the National Footprint Accounts Biocapacity reserve, exports of hazardous waste, and organic water pollutant, CO_2, and other gas emissions)

476   *Origin-Based Marketing*

- prosperity and equality, measured by the trading across borders (open trading performance compared to best practice; i.e., IFC distance to frontier score), number of aid workers and volunteers sent overseas according to UNV, fairtrade market size according to Fairtrade International, FDI outflow according to UNCTAD, and development cooperation contributions aid according to Development Initiatives)
- health and well-being (measured by, for instance, exports of pharmaceuticals, voluntary excess contributions to World Health Organization, humanitarian aid contributions, and drug seizures).

The full list of indicators and information sources is available on the website. Finally, another difference between this approach and traditional ways of measuring country brand equity lies in the type of data collection. Rankings aiming to assess the reputation of countries usually rely on primary data, and particularly on surveys to capture individuals' perceptions. Country image is indeed highly subjective. Here, the ranking relies on secondary data (with indicators from UNESCO, the World Bank, etc.), and provides a more objective assessment of the contribution of each country, relative to its size, to the well-being of the planet and its inhabitants. This difference underlines the divergent objective pursued with the notion of a "Good Country." Although it departs from country branding, pioneering work by Anholt is interesting to monitor. Indeed, the idea of assessing countries on how much they are offering to the world instead of just how they are perceived across the world might be a precursor of a radical change in the field. The future will say.

For now, we can just observe and compare: the US, for instance, was ranked twentieth in the *Good Country Index* in 2016, while it was at the top of the list in Anholt-GFK Roper's *Nation Brands Index*. This is a major difference in result. Other countries appear in good position in both rankings. Overall, the *Nation Brands Index* ranking featured the following Top Ten countries for 2016: US, Germany, UK, Canada, France, Italy, Japan, Switzerland, Australia, and Sweden. In turn, the ranking of Top Ten "good countries" for that year were: Ireland, Finland, Switzerland, Netherlands, New Zealand, Sweden, UK, Norway, Denmark, and Belgium. One year later, the countries making the top of the list were: Sweden, Denmark, Netherlands, UK, Switzerland, Germany, Finland, France, Austria, and Canada. In turn, the latest available ranking of FutureBrand (2015) featured: Japan, Switzerland, Germany, Sweden, Canada, Norway, US, Australia, Denmark, Austria. Here again, there are some differences but also many similarities in the countries that make the top of these rankings. Understanding the evolution of these rankings is not always easy and it prompts us to wonder about the next question.

Is this evaluation stable over time? What does that mean for companies? To give another example of the evolution of rankings, Figure 11.18 shows the FutureBrand's ranking at two-year intervals, over a period of four years (2010–2014). It illustrates that the evaluation of a country's reputation or image is not stable over time. In these rankings, countries can gain or lose position rather easily. For instance, Canada was positioned second in 2012 in the world, and

Origin-Based Marketing 477

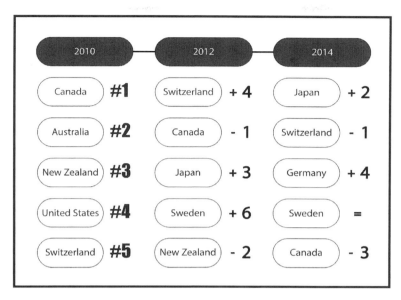

Figure 11.18 Illustrating the evolution of country brands rankings
Source: FutureBrand (2011, 2013, 2015)

was demoted to the fifth place in 2014. We could argue that this downturn is possibly due to the country's involvement in war and some political decisions that were made in favor of the oil and gas industry to the detriment of environmental concerns, among other things. Nevertheless, the reason why such demotion (and promotion) movements occur is not well documented. In addition, we can wonder about the relevance of losing or gaining a few positions; however, the trend over several years seems more important.

Here, we touch some of the limitations of the practical evaluation of country image: first, available rankings are "only" a decade old (which is insufficient if we want to explore the long-term evolution of reputations), and second, as their methodologies evolved, these rankings have relied on different questions over the years, making comparisons—even annual ones— difficult. There is still much research needed to reach a reliable assessment of the evolution of countries' reputation.

This is linked to another problem: the evaluation of country branding efforts. Indeed, logically, one would assume that successful nation branding translates into improved nation brand rankings. So far, no correlation between the time and resources invested in country branding and results (as seen in the evolution of rankings, for instance) has been clearly established. Questioned on this aspect, representatives of the agencies in charge of the country brands given as examples in this book tend to remain vague. As nicely put in a comprehensive article on the topic of nation branding: "The metabolism of a country is longer

478   *Origin-Based Marketing*

and slower than that of a product or a company, so it's still too early to say if any of these top-down reorientations of identity have stuck in a meaningful way" (The Guardian, 2017). In any case, the fact that a country's reputation can change over time means one thing for companies: there is a need for caution and thought before deciding to rely on the origin cue. If the country image is positive, it is not immune to a fallout. If the image is poor, it will take years, if not decades, before it eventually improves.

What can companies do if their country of origin has a negative image in foreign markets? This question can be examined under the lens of the *provenance paradox*, a term coined by Deshpandé (2010) (see "Food for Thought").

Food for Thought 11.3

- In reference to Deshpandé (2010), what is the provenance paradox and what can companies do to overcome a negative COE?

In an article entitled "Why You Aren't Buying Venezuelan Chocolate," Deshpandé (2010) illustrates different strategies adopted by companies suffering from a negative COE. For instance, the case of Toyota and other automotive brands from Japan is illustrative of the evolution of country image, and, by corollary, of the effect of origin, over time. Thirty years ago, Japan was not recognized for its technology and quality manufacturing. It is now considered one of the global leaders in this arena. The reputation of today's China in the Western world reminds us of this evolution. The Chinese image has already started to evolve in this direction and its transformation will possibly go much faster. Only a few years back, and in this part of the world, China was solely associated with negative attributes such as "cheap," "low quality," and "disrespectful of the environment." To some extent, it might still be the case, but more and more, China is also internationally recognized for its entrepreneurial spirit, its massive use of technologies (e.g., mobile phones and solar energy), and other achievements (e.g., investing massively in Africa, acquiring major assets in developed countries, such as Lenovo's purchase of IBM's PC business and Google's Motorola mobile business). Promotion efforts have also been dedicated to counter negative associations and enhance China's image. One example lies in a campaign that did not try to convince audiences that they were wrong in their perceptions about products "made-in China," if they thought they were of poor quality. Instead, the campaign associated the "made-in China" with other countries who had positive PCIs, using the tagline: "Made in China, Made with the World" and showing visuals of different product categories, such as clothing with the label "Made in China with French designers," and shoes with the label "Made in China with American technology" (see YouKu video with search keywords: "视频: made in China"). The message was that Chinese manufacturing and service capabilities were enhanced by the presence of multinationals from all around the world. A way to work at changing beliefs.

From obliterating their geographic origin (e.g., Techint from Argentina), toning it down (e.g., Corona from Mexico), or on the contrary flaunting their provenance (e.g., Juan Valdez from Colombia) and building a brand for the long haul (e.g., Honda from Japan), various strategies are available to companies in their efforts to counter a negative COE—even though they have excellent factors endowment for the product category in question. Beyond these corporate examples, only a handful of scientific studies have directly tackled the problem of a negative country image, with a focus on countries like China, Russia, and Vietnam (e.g., Johansson, Ronkainen, & Czinkota, 1994; Speece & Duc Phung, 2005; Po-Young, Chang, Chia-Yi, & Wang, 2010; Kabadayi & Lerman, 2011).

11.4.2 Relevance of the Effect (Dilution and Recognition)

How many origins can a product have? Is there are risk of dilution of the effect of origin in case of multiple origins? Products (and services) can have multiple origins, depending on where the design, component sourcing, manufacturing, assembly, delivery, and brand (and even ownership) are located. For instance, products that have two origins are said to be *binational* or *hybrid* products. Examples of multiple origins include the iPhone (Apple made a specific effort in displaying information on the back of the product stating, "Designed by Apple in California, Assembled in China") and IKEA clocks (for instance, labels on certain models can specify up to three origins: "Design from Sweden, movement from Japan, and case from China"). In this context, it is reasonable to wonder how multiple origins impact consumer behavior. Are the various origins balancing each other out, resulting in a diluted, or weak, effect of origin? Is one dominating consumers' evaluation (e.g., manufacturing over assembly)? Chao (1993) examines the influence of country-of-design (COD) and country-of-assembly (COA) on consumer evaluations. He concludes that "a careful choice of design and assembly locations is warranted if one wishes to ensure more positive consumer product evaluations. Different strategic combinations involving several countries with different stereotypes appear to exhibit different impacts of COD, COA, and price on consumer product design and product quality perceptions. More specifically, while a good design country location cannot be used to compensate for a poorly perceived country assembly location in terms of product quality, it certainly can be used to boost design quality perception. It can also be used to circumvent the traditional price-quality relationship, in the sense that a lower price does not necessarily connote a lower perceived quality if a good design country location is carefully selected" (Chao, 1993, p. 303). In addition to the traditional efficiency and strategic asset seeking motives (e.g., costs reduction and technology acquisition), results from this study invite companies to consider these partitioned origin effects when choosing locations for alliances with or investments in foreign firms.

Since this early work, researchers continued to investigate the potential dilution of the COE (e.g., Insch & McBride, 2004; Chowdhury, 2010) but attention has mainly shifted from "product origin" (the famous "made-in") to the effect of "brand origin." Indeed, it is impossible for consumers to keep track of design, part, and assembly origins and, instead, they are thought to

480 Origin-Based Marketing

rely on the origin of brands to infer information about products (e.g., Apple and Louis Vuitton are brands associated with the US and France, respectively, although their products have multiple origins) (Magnusson, Westjohn, & Zdravkovic, 2011b). Nevertheless, this invites us to consider whether consumers actually recognize the country of origin of brands.

Is the origin of brands always accurately recognized? This question has only been raised recently and, surprisingly, the answer is negative. Magnusson, Westjohn, and Zdravkovic (2011a) find that consumers are only able to correctly identify brands' country of origin about one-third of the time. Table 11.5 illustrates the case of several international brands, like Haier

Table 11.5 Illustrating the variability in brand origin recognition

BRANDS	COUNTRY OF ORIGIN	RECOGNITION ACCURACY RATE (%) Numbers are rounded
Television Brands		
Haier	China	25
LG	South Korea	16
Philips	The Netherlands	8
Polaroid	USA	80
Samsung	South Korea	25
Sharp	Japan	26
Sony	Japan	68
Toshiba	Japan	80
Automobile Brands		
Audi	Germany	82
Buick	USA	97
Dodge	USA	97
Hyundai	South Korea	50
Kia	South Korea	52
Land Rover	UK	48
Mazda	Japan	65
Mini	UK	66
Nissan	Japan	86
Volvo	Sweden	55
Volkswagen	Germany	95
Fashion Brands		
Burberry	UK	43
Christian Dior	France	47
Calvin Klein	USA	77
Gucci	Italy	71
H&M	Sweden	16
Hugo Boss	Germany	18
Louis Vuitton	France	50
Prada	Italy	60
Ralph Lauren	USA	71
Shiseido	Japan	55
Tag	Switzerland	31

Source: Adapted from Magnusson et al. (2011a)

Origin-Based Marketing   481

(China), LG (South Korea), Philips (The Netherlands), Sharp (Japan), and Hugo Boss (Germany) with recognition rates below 30 percent. The authors noted that regardless of recognition accuracy, the effect of brand origin on consumers' perceptions was significant. They concluded that there is a need to further educate consumers about the correct brand origin.

Some companies would disagree with this conclusion, as they purposefully rely on an origin that is not theirs. Some see this practice as deceitful but no law prevents it, assuming that the actual origin is not hidden. Consumers are then free to get themselves informed about the correct origin. The case of the ice cream brand Häagen-Dazs is well known for misleading consumers into thinking that products have Danish origins, when the company is from the Bronx in New York (US). Many other such examples are available, some more subtle than others in the way they seek to benefit from a positive COE without actually being from the country put forward in communications. For instance, Grissol (a brand of Dare-Food, a Canadian food manufacturing company) sells packages of toasts that feature the name "Baguettes" on a blue-white-red background. Ask anyone who does not know and recognize the company to take a wild guess about its origin and they will tell you "France." This is what Aichner, Forza, and Trentin (2017) call "foreign branding strategy" (i.e., neither the company nor the product originate from the advertised country). While they found that foreign branding had a positive impact on brand performance, they also observed that willingness-to-buy and willingness-to-pay decreased when customers found out that they were misled with regard to the origin of the product. Nevertheless, some companies have managed to successfully maintain their foreign image over time, indicating that—surprisingly—authenticity may not be a key success factor for origin-based marketing.

What does it mean in terms of the relevance of the effect of origin? Indeed, the above-mentioned observations prompt us to ponder: is using the origin cue still relevant for companies in the context of globalization (see "Food for Thought")?

Food for Thought 11.4

* In your opinion, is using the origin cue in a context of globalization still relevant?

This question brings us back to one of the reasons why research on the COE has been so extensive: capturing the COE represents significant methodological challenges. Here is a brief review of the evolution of the literature on the topic of the COE's relevance.

In the 1980s, researchers first focused on showing to managers that the origin cue was important. For instance, Bilkey and Nes (1982) reveal that the political climate and level of economic development of the country of origin affected perceptions of product quality. This was valuable knowledge at the

482 *Origin-Based Marketing*

time, in particular for reflecting on the choice of manufacturing locations, in a context of booming outsourcing and production offshoring.

Starting in the 1990s, much attention was dedicated to isolating the effect of the origin cue from other cues (e.g., price, brand, warranty). This has proven to be difficult and the source of much contradictory findings. Some authors have found that country-of-origin information was more important in affecting product quality assessments than were price and brand information (e.g., Wall, Liefeld, & Heslop, 1991). Others pointed out that overseas buyers may be sensitive to the country of origin, but that their sensitivity could be enhanced or offset by other cues such as price or warranty (e.g., Lee, Kim, & Miller, 1993). When global brands gained prominence, the possible dilution of the COE attracted attention but, again, a variety of methods and mixed empirical evidence resulted in a rather confusing portrayal of the situation. Contrary to the general notion that a well-known global brand would likely override the COE, Tse and Gorn (1993), for instance, find that the country of origin was an equally salient and more enduring factor than brand in consumer product evaluation. This was contradicted by many other authors and, to this day, the confusion remains.

Indeed, the 2000s and 2010s are marked by a renewed debate about the relevance of the origin cue. For instance, Samiee (2011, p. 473) states that: "Revelations regarded limited interest and knowledge of consumers regarding origins of products and brands they purchase questions the appropriateness of using traditional CO [Country of Origin] type research designs [. . .] Additionally, given the global production of an increasing number of brands, contract manufacturing (e.g., IBM) and international sourcing (e.g., Sony), strategic alliances involving parts and components (e.g., Fiat, Volkswagen), as well as the emergence of design only firms that market branded products, but lack any manufacturing facilities (e.g., AMD, Broadcom, Rambus), CO has essentially lost its validity as an important issue with a managerial relevance."

This confusion even translated into "epistolary feuds," with back-and-forth exchanges between authors, mentioned by name—a practice that is not unheard of but that seldom occurs in business research. For instance, Usunier (2006) writes a highly critical piece about studies on country of origin. Josiassen and Harzing (2008) proposes counter arguments to this piece and defended the relevance of the construct which quickly prompts Usunier and Cestre (2008) to backfire with their own arguments. In turn, Samiee (2011) proceeds to overtly criticize the piece by Magnusson et al. (2011a) about country-of-origin recognition. In a rejoinder, Magnusson et al. (2011b) defends their research and the relevance of country-of-origin research. Diamantopoulos, Schlegelmilch, and Palihawadana (2011) also conclude that the criticism against the country-of-origin construct was largely unfounded. They found that country image impacted purchase intentions only indirectly since brand image evaluations already encapsulated consumers' perceptions of the country of origin. Nevertheless, they concluded that the country of origin remained a relevant and powerful influence in today's business world.

In all, there is a marked ambivalence about whether the country-of-origin cue has a positive effect or no significant effect at all. With Deshpandé

Origin-Based Marketing   483

(2010), we also see that there is such a thing as a negative COE and that, consequently, companies coming from countries plagued with an unfavorable image could face negative consequences for relying on their origin. They have to implement specific strategies to overcome this challenge. This ambivalence about the outcomes of the COE (positive, negative, or null) reveals the limit of the methods available to study such a complex phenomenon. Next, we broach this issue by taking a broader perspective and discuss the outcomes of origin-based marketing (and not just the COE per say).

11.4.3 Outcomes

What are the outcomes of origin-based marketing? In terms of outcomes, origin-based marketing combines those of the COE and those commonly associated with successful branding. On the one hand, the outcomes of origin-based marketing follow those of the COE (see Section 11.2.1 and above). Indeed, origin-based marketing aims to influence the behavior of individuals (as either consumers or decision-makers in organizations) by exploiting a positive COE. The expected benefits are thus similar (i.e., a higher willingness-to-pay, more favorable evaluations from consumers, and stronger purchasing intentions). On the other hand, its outcomes are also similar to those of branding because it relies heavily on communication and promotion activities. A favorable country image has been established as a determinant of higher brand equity (e.g., Pappu, Quester, & Cooksey, 2007) and it is, thus, expected that firms that rely on such image also benefit from higher perceived quality, positive associations, increased awareness, and loyalty (see Section 11.1).

In all, origin-based marketing can bring a plethora of benefits. To the list above, we can logically add that it also enhances the reputation of a company, its revenues (by allowing a premium pricing strategy), its performance (including its valuation), and overall competitiveness, since it helps differentiate themselves from other players. The only problem is that research has shown its limitations in actually demonstrating these outcomes. As discussed previously, a methodological problem is at the root of ambivalent results in scientific studies about the COE and about place branding. Isolating the effect of the origin cue (used by companies) or the effect of promotion activities for places (by governments) has proven particularly challenging using the quantitative methods and statistical analyses that we have at our disposal. The two phenomena are too complex.

This means that future research opportunities lie in using qualitative methods instead, and in particular longitudinal case studies of companies. It would be particularly interesting, for instance, to study companies that were not relying on the origin cue to market their offerings and then started (like Canada Goose), as well as companies that were relying on the origin cue in some of their markets and then stopped (like Volkswagen). This does not exclude statistical analyses based on customer opinion surveys or on financial results, but these would have to be embedded in larger research designs, and most importantly, repeated over long periods of time (e.g., five to ten years), while the image of their country of origin would be monitored as

484   *Origin-Based Marketing*

well. Academics who claim that research on the COE has become irrelevant, and those who claim that countries cannot deploy branding techniques and expect the same results as if they were products, have certainly made valid points. Nevertheless, companies keep referring to their respective countries of origin, and national governments keep promoting their countries. Next, we look at what it means for companies adopting origin-based marketing in more practical terms.

11.4.4 *Impact on Marketing Decisions and Feasibility*

What is the impact of origin-based marketing on traditional marketing activities? Many companies rely on their origin, to some extent, without a conscious effort to adjust their marketing activities. Even when they do it purposefully, a gradation exists from a limited to an extensive use of the origin cue, and also from an implicit (e.g., using the color scheme of the national flag like IKEA or emblematic animals like Fjällräven, offering local cuisine or keeping the local language untranslated to communicate) to an explicit use of this cue (e.g., including the country in the product or brand name like Canada Goose and using taglines making a direct reference to the country of origin in promotional material, like Volkswagen's "That's the Power of German Engineering.").

In all, origin-based marketing takes many forms. Contrary to other practices studied in this book (in particular, BOP marketing and reverse innovation), there is no need for companies to redesign their whole business model or to make significant adjustments when implementing it. Nevertheless, companies that rely heavily on their country of origin need to carefully consider strategic and tactical marketing decisions.

In terms of strategic decisions, origin-based marketing forces companies to proceed with a careful market selection since their country of origin might be unknown to consumers or, worse, seen in an unfavorable light due to affective factors, like historical animosity. Consumer targeting can also be a matter of deliberation, in particular in relation to degrees of sensitivity to "buy local" campaigns. Different age groups ("generations"), education levels, location within countries (e.g., in the interior or close to borders; in urban vs. rural areas) are also expected to have diverse reactions to the origin cue. Lastly, the choice of entry mode is probably the most affected strategic decision. Indeed, when a company wants to benefit from a favorable country image for manufacturing and put the "made-in" label forward, it has no choice but to produce at home and export. Nevertheless, it is interesting to note that companies have adopted different answers to the question of "Where should production take place?" when relying on the origin cue. Canada Goose made a conscious decision to keep manufacturing in Canada in a bid to remain authentic in the eyes of foreign buyers. Companies like IKEA and Volkswagen rely heavily on the origin cue and yet have many production facilities abroad through FDI. To face negative press for the suspected discrepancy, these companies took steps to educate consumers and reduce criticism (e.g., the labels of Apple's or IKEA's hybrid products stating the

Origin-Based Marketing 485

country of design, manufacture, assembly, and so on; Volkswagen's reference to German "engineering," specifically).

When it comes to tactical decisions, all of the marketing-mix policies can be affected. Not necessarily are, but they can be. Starting with product policies, labelling is, of course, highly affected by origin-based marketing, since the origin cue must be displayed in the forefront. Product and brand names can also reflect the origin, as illustrated by the examples provided in this chapter. Pricing policies are next and, here again, a variety of choices exist, depending on the desired positioning. While a favorable country image helps in commanding premium prices because of specific associations (e.g., Canada Goose for an authentic experience with Canadian harsh winter conditions, and Victorinox for Swiss reliability), it is not the only strategy. Companies can rely on their origin and still aim for competitive prices (e.g., affordability is important for both IKEA and Volkswagen for reasons embedded in national history and culture). In turn, distribution is probably the least-affected function. Yet, the choice of retail locations and number of sales points, for instance, must be set according to the desired positioning—which goes hand in hand with the pricing policy—and can, thus, align with the adoption of origin-based marketing. By contrast, promotion is likely the function that is most strongly affected when companies decide to rely on their place of origin (for simplicity purposes, we have mainly mentioned countries but, as seen in Section 11.2.2, it can be any other type of place as well, such as a city, like the mention of Paris in L'Oréal's visual identity). Once more, there is no limit in the variety of options at a company's disposal. All activities (advertising, personal selling, public relations, trade shows, etc.) can serve to communicate their association with a place.

Lastly, the extended marketing-mix for services invites us to consider the three additional Ps in the 7Ps (see Chapter 9) of people, processes, and physical evidence. Decisions can also reflect the approach, particularly in relation to people and physical evidence, as illustrated by IKEA's in-store signage and salespersons' uniforms featuring Sweden's national colors. In this case, this detail in itself might not be sufficient for consumers to consciously recognize the origin cue, but it complements the other origin-based marketing initiatives (and conscious recognition is not necessary for the origin cue to be efficient). Another anecdotal example in the service industry is found in restaurants across the world proposing French cuisine. Employing French nationals to wait tables, for instance, is sought after as their usual strong accent in other languages (and particularly in English) sends an additional signal to consumers and permits the restaurant to further benefit from the positive PCI between France and gastronomy.

In conclusion, the impact of origin-based marketing on traditional marketing activities is multifaceted. Companies relying on their origin have lots of room for creativity in implementation but they need to carefully consider what makes the approach successful, as detailed next.

What are the key success factors for origin-based marketing? For starters, companies interested in implementing origin-based marketing should only do so if they benefit from a positive country image and/or from a positive

PCI. This seems like an obvious statement, but we have to remember that country image is highly relative and evolves over time. There might be markets where the image is favorable, and others where it is not. One of the biggest dangers for us marketers is to ignore our natural reliance on the self-reference criterion (i.e., the unconscious reference to our own culture and experience to base our decisions) and wrongly assume that a country we know has a universally favorable image across the world. Due to unforeseen events (wars, terrorism, epidemics, natural disasters, etc.), a positive image can also become stained. Adjusting the use of the origin cue then requires an agility that is not always possible (if the cue is present in the brand name, for instance). Thus, companies interested in origin-based marketing can also adopt a cautious approach and use the origin cue in a way that can be downplayed if circumstances dictate.

As for companies from countries with a negative image, it is possible for them to rely on the origin cue, but only if the PCI is positive. Among the strategies proposed by Deshpandé (2010) that do not involve "downplaying the origin" or "hiding behind a front country" in order to overcome a negative country image—i.e., the opposite of origin-based marketing—only one tackles a negative PCI: the "Build a brand for the long haul" strategy. Companies like Japanese car manufacturers Honda, Toyota, and Nissan are thought to have overcome the provenance paradox by building strong brands over time. Although the idea is appealing, it is difficult to disentangle the reasons why these companies managed to overcome the negative image that Japan had at the time: to what extent did the country improve its image over the same period of time independently of the car industry's success? To what extent is this success due to other factors (such as the power of Keiretsus, these typical networks of companies with interlocked shareholdings, for instance)? These questions are left unanswered, due to methodological limitations, as previously discussed. The remaining strategies point to the existence of a positive PCI, in spite of a negative country image ("Sticking to colonial history" with Turkish rugs or Egyptian cotton, and "Flaunt your country of origin," like Colombian Juan Valdez coffee company). In all, carefully assessing—through market research—the extent to which the country image and PCI are favorable in target markets is key to successfully implementing origin-based marketing.

Furthermore, origin-based marketing can also be implemented at home. In this case, an additional determinant must be assessed with particular caution: the belief held by consumers that buying from local companies is best. This belief can stem from high levels of ethnocentrism, nationalism, patriotism, and the like, but also from high penetration of notions like sustainable development and social responsibility. For one, it is obvious that nationalistic movements favor buying from local companies, even if these are highly internationalized. Incidentally, it should not be taken for granted that local companies will be favored everywhere. The case of Canada Goose illustrates this somewhat counterintuitive observation: success in eastern Canada came only after the company met success in Europe, as local consumers look up to European connoisseurs of fashion and apparel products. Second, consumers who abide by the principles of responsible consumption will be sensitive to the "buy local" argument, in particular to reduce the carbon footprint in goods transportation. In Chapter 12, we take a closer look at these notions as background information for cause-related marketing.

Moving on to the second key success factor, efficient place branding will help improve or maintain the international reputation of a country, region, or city of origin. Thus, companies interested in implementing origin-based marketing should work closely with their governments, at any relevant level (national, regional, and municipal) to jointly promote their place of origin. Participating in international trade fairs and trade missions are particularly well-suited occasions for such joint efforts. Lobbying governments and influencing political decisions with international outcomes is another opportunity for companies to enhance a country's reputation or limit its potential downfall. Simply reacting to political decisions can also go a long way. For instance, the stand taken by companies such as Apple, Facebook, Twitter, Microsoft, and Netflix against the Trump administration's so-called "travel ban" on several Muslim countries in 2017 (e.g., BBC News, 2017) helped provide the foreign public with a more balanced view of what US people believed in at the time. Research has revealed that the impact of countries' reputation on companies is mutual: the reputation of national firms also impact the international image of countries (e.g., Kang & Yang, 2010). Thus, companies and governments working together is key for building up a country's reputation and thus ensuring that origin-based marketing brings the expected benefits to firms.

Conclusion: With Attention Paid to Key Success Factors, Companies Should Still Consider Adopting Origin-Based Marketing, As It Can Bridge Geographic and Psychic Distances and Increase Their Competitiveness Abroad and at Home

What would a nomological network for origin-based marketing look like? A *nomological network* has been defined as the representation of the constructs of interest in a study, their observable manifestations, and the interrelationships among and between them (Cronbach & Meehl, 1955). Figure 11.19 aims to encapsulate important variables in relation to the adoption of origin-based marketing.

Starting with the motivations behind origin-based marketing, Figure 11.19 illustrates that, in addition to being a market-seeking opportunity, the approach is driven by the existence of a positive effect of origin that companies want to exploit (the figure features the country level for simplicity purposes but it is still valid for other types of places). Distance, mainly in its geographic and psychic dimensions, represents a motivation when cognitive, affective, or normative factors push individuals to appreciate and seek offerings that are from "far away" and "different." In the contrary case, it acts as a barrier. These cognitive, affective, and normative factors thus play a central role in deciding whether or not relying on the origin cue in marketing activities is a good idea.

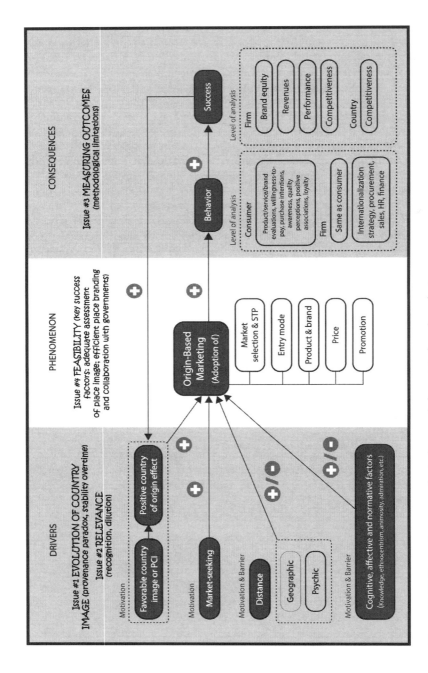

Figure 11.19 Proposing a nomological network for origin-based marketing

Source: Own elaboration

Origin-Based Marketing 489

In terms of implementation and outcomes, Figure 11.19 merely summarizes all the elements seen previously, making clear that most marketing activities at the strategic and tactical levels (to the possible exception of distribution) must be aligned when adopting origin-based marketing. It highlights the many benefits expected from the approach at different levels of analysis: consumer, firm, and country. It also shows the existence of a feedback loop, since success (at both the corporate and national levels) will enhance the international reputation of the place and, thus, reinforce the motivation for relying on this geographic cue.

Finally, the figure offers a reminder of the four main issues at stake with origin-based marketing and discussed in this chapter: 1) the image of the place of origin is not fixed and can improve over time (which is good news for firms suffering from a provenance paradox, i.e., those with good production conditions at home but a lack of recognition and appreciation in international markets due to a poor country image) but can also deteriorate; 2) doubts about the strength of the effect of origin cast a shadow on the relevance for companies to rely on the origin cue, since this cue may not be well recognized or be no longer important in a context of globalization; 3) measuring the outcomes of origin-based marketing is a real challenge due to methodological limitations—which is a problem since it means that lots of financial and human resources can be invested without the security of knowing that it actually pays off; and, finally, 4) companies must correctly assess the image that their place of origin has in target markets across the world (through market research due to high variability and in order to avoid the trap of the self-reference criterion) and participate in place branding activities via an active collaboration with governments.

So, should companies rely on a geographic origin to better differentiate from competition and attract customers? In other words, should companies still adopt origin-based marketing nowadays? The short answer to this question is: "If the origin is liked, it should." The key success factors identified in this chapter and the adjustments needed for implementation are all well within reach. The risks are low if the approach is well planned. More importantly, the effect of origin is likely to persist. The reason is that, more than ever, individual consumers and business decision-makers face complex choices. Because of the battle that local and foreign companies fight to win over clients and the multiplicity of possibilities to satisfy one's needs in an era of global markets and global supply chains, decisions are made arduous. Stereotyping, which lies at the root of the country of origin effect, is a way to reduce this complexity. Relying on a geographic cue is likely to remain a mechanism that decision-makers use, for the foreseeable future, regardless of the issues discussed in this chapter. Depending on what individuals know about and feel about any given country, relying on origin-based marketing can be a tool to **increase competitiveness and bridge geographic and psychic distances between companies and foreign customers (reaching local consumers as well, when sensitive to the "buy local" argument).**

490 *Origin-Based Marketing*

Notes

1 In Section 11.2.1, the paragraph entitled: "Can the COE take a moderating role?" has been written in collaboration with Renaud Legoux, Associate Professor of Marketing at HEC Montréal (Canada). His research interests revolve around consumer behavior, arts marketing, and customer satisfaction.

2 Canada Goose example incorporates the work of M.Sc. students Eve-Gabrielle Bissonnette-Vézina, Astrid Eisterer, Gabriel Garceau, Torben Kessler, Kathrin Seelmann-Eggebert, and Lisa Weber in the context of their 2014 term paper for the "Marketing & Globalization" course, developed and taught by the author of this book at HEC Montreal (Canada). References supporting this example are: Canada Goose (2016, 2017); CBC News (2017); Financial Post (2012); Hulan (2003); New York Post (2015); The Globe and Mail (2010, 2013b); The Star (2013).

3 The IKEA example incorporates the work of M.Sc. students Catherine Blouin-Mainville, Philippine De Giraud d'Agay, Anne-Marie Durand-Tourigny, Gabrielle Fortin-Garant, and Leticia Santos in the context of their 2016 term paper for the "Marketing & Globalization" course developed and taught by the author of this book at HEC Montreal (Canada). References for this example are: Business Insider (2013); Chicago Sun-Times (2004); Edwards (2008); IKEA (2015); (2008); Public Diplomacy Magazine (2010); The Guardian (2008).

4 The example of Victorinox relies on: Bloomberg (2014); CH24.PL (2013); Ivey W14574 (2014); Luxury Activist (2014); Pizzini (n.d.); The Guardian (2007); The Local (2013); Victorinox (2017).

5 Volkswagen example relies on: Business Insider (2016); Car And Driver (2009); Chao (1993); Lawrence, Marr, and Prendergast (1992); Times Free Press (2011); Volkswagen Aktiengesellschaft (2017).

6 In Section 11.3.2, the examples of Argentina and Chile were written in collaboration with Catherine Archambault, PhD Candidate in Strategy at University of Lille (France), whose research focuses on business models, business model innovation, and experimentation. These examples rely mainly on data collected during two study trips in both Argentina and Chile on the topic of country branding, with BAA and M.Sc. students from HEC Montreal in 2012 and 2013. Catherine Archambault was among the M.Sc. students 2012 cohort. She wrote her Master dissertation entitled "How Is a Country Brand Managed? A Comparative Study of Argentina and Chile" (available in French: "*Comment une marque-pays est-elle gérée? Une étude comparative entre l'Argentine et le Chili*") under the supervision of the author of this book. In addition to documentation collected on site, field interviews were conducted with representatives of Fundación ExportAr and Inprotur, as well as of the Asociación de Importadores y Exportadores de la República Argentina, Lumilagro, and Rossi y Caruso (two Argentine companies using the country brand), ProChile, *Fundación Imagen de Chile*, *Comité de Inversiones Extranjeras de Chile*, Gemaex and Bodega Santa Maria (two Chilean companies using the country brand). These study trips were organized and supervised by the author of this book. Information sources for Argentina include: Archambault (2013); Clarin (2016); Minister of Turism Argentina (n.d.).

7 The example of Australia is based on: Australia Unlimited (2017, n.d.); Bain and Company (2016); CNN (2014); Daily News Egypt (2017); Forbes India (2017); Futurebrand (2012, 2015); World Bank (2016a).

8 Same as for Brand Argentina.

9 The example of Slovenia has been written in collaboration with Polona Prešeren, M.Sc., "I Feel Slovenia" Brand Manager and Undersecretary at the Government Communication Office; it also relies on the following sources:

CIA World Factbook (2016); Hlad and Skoberne (2001); Konecnik Ruzzier and de Chernatony (2013); Nicoll and Schoenberg (1998); Slovenian Ministry of Economy (2007).

References

Aaker, David (1991). *Managing Brand Equity*. New York: The Free Press (p. 224).

Aaker, David (1992). The Value of Brand Equity. *Journal of Business Strategy*, 13(4), 27–32.

Aaker, David (1996). Measuring Brand Equity Across Products and Markets. *California Management Review*, 38(3), 102–120.

Aichner, Thomas, Forza, Cipriano & Trentin, Alessio (2017). The Country-of-Origin Lie: Impact of Foreign Branding on Customers' Willingness to Buy and Willingness to Pay When the Product's Actual Origin Is Disclosed. *The International Review of Retail, Distribution and Consumer Research*, 27(1), 43–60.

Anholt, Simon (2008). Place Branding: Is It Marketing, or Isn't It? *Place Branding and Public Diplomacy*, 4(1), 1–6.

Anholt, Simon (2010). Definitions of Place Branding—Working Toward a Resolution. *Place Branding and Public Diplomacy*, 6(1), 1–10.

Archambault, Catherine (2013). *Comment une marque-pays est-elle gérée? Une étude comparative entre l'Argentine et le Chili*. (M.Sc Master dissertation), Management—HEC Montréal, Montréal (Canada).

Australia Unlimited (2017). About Us. Retrieved October 2017, from www.australiaunlimited.com/about-us

Australia Unlimited (n.d.). Building Brand Australia. Retrieved October 2017, from www.australiaunlimited.com/brand-australia/building-brand-australia

Bain and Company (2016). The Hottest Brand in China Is Australia. Brief by Yngve Andresen, Raymond Hass and Jason Ding. Retrieved October 2017, from www.bain.com/publications/articles/the-hottest-brand-in-china-is-australia.aspx

BBC News (2017, January 30th). Trump Travel Ban: Starbucks, Google and Apple Opposed. Retrieved from www.bbc.com/news/av/business-38803789/trump-travel-ban-starbucks-google-and-apple-opposed

Bilkey, Warren J. & Nes, Erik (1982). Country-of-Origin Effects on Product Evaluation. *Journal of International Business Studies*, 13(1), 89–89.

Bloomberg (2014, October 2nd). Swiss Army Knife Maker Victorinox Bets on Own Stores, *By Corinne Gretler and Jan Schwalbe*. Retrieved from www.bloomberg.com/news/articles/2014-10-02/swiss-army-knife-maker-victorinox-bets-on-own-stores

Business Insider (2013, Novermber 13th). There's A Logical System Behind IKEA's Strange Product Name, *By Gus Lubin*. Retrieved from www.businessinsider.com/meaning-of-ikea-product-names-2013-11

Business Insider (2016, August 2nd). 5 Reasons Americans Aren't Buying Volkswagens Anymore, *By Benjamin Zhang*. Retrieved from www.businessinsider.com/why-americans-arent-buying-volkswagen-vw-2016-8

Canada Goose (2016). Annual Report—Form 20-F. Retrieved from http://d18rn0p25nwr6d.cloudfront.net/CIK-0001690511/9109f598-2ac8-4236-8910-6827a1f79021.pdf

Canada Goose (2017). Our History. Retrieved November 2017, from www.canadagoose.com/ca/en/our-history.html

492 Origin-Based Marketing

Car And Driver (2009). Upcoming Volkswagen Models, Lineup to Get Less German. By Jens Meiners. Retrieved November 2017, from www.caranddriver.com/news/upcoming-volkswagen-models-lineup-to-get-less-german-car-news

Cateora, Philip, Gilly, Mary & Graham, John (2015). *International Marketing* (17th ed.). New York: McGraw-Hill/Irwin (p. 704).

CBC News (2017, March 16th). Shares in Coat Maker Canada Goose Soar in Debut on Toronto and New York Markets, *By The Canadian Press*. Retrieved from www.cbc.ca/news/business/canada-goose-ipo-1.4027443

CH24.PL. (2013, July 23rd). Interview of Michael Meier (International Sales Director Victorinox Swiss Army), *By Tomasz Kiełtyka*. Retrieved from https://en.ch24.pl/interview-michael-meier-international-sales-director-victorinox-swiss-army/

Chao, Paul (1993). Partitioning Country of Origin Effects: Consumer Evaluations of a Hybrid Product. *Journal of International Business Studies*, 24(2), 291–306.

Chicago Sun-Times (2004, August 17th). 'Fartfull' Workbench, 'Jerker' Desk: Is Ikea Hiding a Grin? *By Paige Wiser*. Retrieved from https://web.archive.org/web/20060208123705/http://www.findarticles.com/p/articles/mi_qn4155/is_200408/ai_n12556896

Chowdhury, Md Humayun Kabir (2010). The Cognitive Foundations of Partitioned Country-of-Origin: A Causal Path Analysis. *International Journal of Marketing Studies*, 2(2), 258–266.

CIA World Factbook (2016). Country Profile—Slovenia. Retrieved October 2017, from www.cia.gov/library/publications/the-world-factbook/geos/si.html

Clarin (2016, March 28th). La Fundación ExportAr pasa a llamarse de "promoción de inversiones y comercio". Retrieved from www.clarin.com/economia/fundacion-exportar-promocion-inversiones-comercio_0_EywzQXzAx.html

CNN (2014, August 19th). Shoppers or Smugglers? China Cracks Down on "Daigou" Boom, *By Katie Hunt and Serena Dong*. Retrieved from www.cnn.com/2014/08/19/world/asia/china-personal-shoppers/index.html

Cronbach, Lee Joseph & Meehl, Paul (1955). Construct Validity in Psychological Tests. *Psychological Bulletin*, 52(4), 281–302.

Daily News Egypt (2017, March 15th). "Austrade" Hosts 5th Annual "Australia Unlimited MENA" Road Show, *By Reem Hosam El-Din*. Retrieved from https://dailynewsegypt.com/2017/03/15/austrade-hosts-5th-annual-australia-unlimited-mena-road-show/

Deshpandé, Rohit (2010). Why You Aren't Buying Venezuelan Chocolate. *Harvard Business Review*, 88(12), 25–27.

Diamantopoulos, Adamantios, Schlegelmilch, Bodo & Palihawadana, Dayananda (2011). The Relationship Between Country-of-Origin Image and Brand Image as Drivers of Purchase Intentions. *International Marketing Review*, 28(5), 508–524.

Dinnie, Keith (2008). *Nation Branding: Concepts, Issues, Practice*. Burlington: Elsevier (p. 288).

Durand, Aurélia (2016). Building a Better Literature Review: Looking at the Nomological Network of the Country-of-Origin Effect. *Canadian Journal of Administrative Sciences*, 33(1), 50–65.

Durand, Aurélia, Turkina, Ekaterina & Robson, Matthew (2016). Psychic Distance and Country Image in Exporter-Importer Relationships. *Journal of International Marketing*, 24(3), 31–57.

Edwards, Clive (2008). The "Scandinavian Ideal" in Design: Two Distinct Approaches to the Marketing of an Ideal. *Journal of Macromarketing*, *28*(1), 87–96.

Financial Post (2012, May 18th). Canada Goose's Made-In-Canada Marketing Strategy Translates Into Success, *By Hollie Shaw*. Retrieved from http://business.financialpost.com/news/canada-gooses-made-in-canada-marketing-strategy-translates-into-success

Fishbein, Martin & Ajzen, Icek (1975). *Belief, Attitude, Intention, and Behavior: An Introduction to Theory and Research*. Reading: Addison-Wesley (p. 578).

Fishbein, Martin & Ajzen, Icek (2010). *Predicting and Changing Behavior—The Reasoned Action Approach*. New York: Taylor and Francis (p. 538).

Forbes India (2017, September 20th). Celebrating the "Unlimited" in Australia-Indian Ties, *By Brand Connect*. Retrieved from www.forbesindia.com/article/special/celebrating-the-unlimited-in-australiaindian-ties/48205/1

FutureBrand (2011). Country Brand Index 2010–2011. Retrieved from http://sete.gr/_fileuploads/entries/Online%20library/GR/Future%20Brand%20 2010.pdf

FutureBrand (2012). Country Brand Index 2011–2012. 87. Retrieved from www.ontit.it/opencms/export/sites/default/ont/it/documenti/files/ONT_2011-11-29_02777.pdf

Futurebrand (2013). Country Brand Index 2012–2013. Retrieved from https://mouriz.files.wordpress.com/2013/02/cbi-futurebrand-2012-13.pdf

FutureBrand (2015). Country Brand Index 2014–2015. Retrieved from www.mbl.is/media/84/8384.pdf

The Globe and Mail (2010, February 11th). Year of the Goose, *By Grant Robertson*. Retrieved from www.theglobeandmail.com/report-on-business/rob-magazine/year-of-the-goose/article4307839/

The Globe and Mail (2013a, December 13th). Canada Goose Sells a Majority Stake—With a Made-in-Canada Guarantee, *By Iain Marlow, Sean Silcoff, and Susan Krashinsky Robertson*. Retrieved from www.theglobeandmail.com/report-on-business/canada-goose-sells-majority-stake-to-us-private-equity-firm/article15848715/

The Globe and Mail (2013b, April 11th). Canada Goose CEO's 'Aha' Moment: 'I Realized the Brand Was Real', *By Josh O'Kane*. Retrieved from www.theglobeandmail.com/report-on-business/small-business/sb-growth/day-to-day/canada-goose-ceos-aha-moment-i-realized-the-brand-was-real/article10982951/

The Guardian (2007, August 3rd). Made in China: Swiss Army Knife Suffers an Identity Crises, *By Kate Connolly*. Retrieved from www.theguardian.com/business/2007/aug/03/internationalnews

The Guardian (2008, February 4th). Do You Speak Ikea? How the Swedish Giant Names Its Products *By Jon Henley*. Retrieved from www.theguardian.com/lifeandstyle/2008/feb/04/shopping.retail

The Guardian (2017, November 7th). How to Sell a Country: The Booming Business of Nation Branding. Retrieved from www.theguardian.com/news/2017/nov/07/nation-branding-industry-how-to-sell-a-country

Hlad, Branka & Skoberne, Peter (2001). Characteristics of Biological and Landscape Diversity in Slovenia. Environmental Agency of the Republic of Slovenia, Ministry of the Environment and Spatial Planning 13.

494 Origin-Based Marketing

Hulan, Renée (2003). *Northern Experience and the Myths of Canadian Culture.* Montreal & Kingston: Mcgill-Queens University Press (p. 232).

IKEA (2015). IKEA Group Yearly Summary. 39. Retrieved from www.ikea.com/ms/fr_CA/pdf/yearly_summary/IKEA_Group_Yearly_Summary_2015.pdf

IKEA (2016). IKEA Group Yearly Summary. 51. Retrieved from www.ikea.com/ms/en_CA/pdf/yearly_summary/IKEA_Group_Yearly_Summary_2016.pdf

Insch, Gary S. & McBride, J. Brad (2004). The Impact of Country-of-Origin Cues on Customer Perceptions of Product Quality: A Binational Test of the Decomposed Country-of-Origin Construct. *Journal of Business Research*, 57(3), 256–265.

Interbrand (2017a). Methodology. Retrieved October 2017, from http://interbrand.com/best-brands/best-global-brands/methodology/

Interbrand (2017b). Best Global Brands. Retrieved October 2017, from http://interbrand.com/best-brands/best-global-brands/2017/ranking/

Ivey W14574 (2014). *Swiss Army: Diversifying Into the Fragrance Business. Case Written by: Ilan Alon, Marc Fetscherin, and Claudia Carvajal.* London, Ontario: Ivey Publishing 9B14A066 (p. 10).

Jaffe, Eugene & Nebenzahl, Israel (2001). *National Image and Competitive Advantage: The Theory and Practice of Country-of-Origin Effect.* Copenhagen, Denmark: Copenhagen Business School Press (p. 186).

Johansson, Johny K., Ronkainen, Ilkka A. & Czinkota, Michael R. (1994). Negative Country-of-Origin Effects: The Case of the New Russia. *Journal of International Business Studies*, 25(1), 157–157.

Josiassen, Alexander & Harzing, Anne-Wil (2008). Descending From the Ivory Tower: Reflections on the Relevance and Future of Country-of-Origin Research. *European Management Review*, 5(4), 264–270.

Kabadayi, Sertan & Lerman, Dawn (2011). Made in China But Sold at FAO Schwarz: Country-of-Origin Effect and Trusting Beliefs. *International Marketing Review*, 28(1), 102–126.

Kang, Minjeong & Yang, Sung-Un (2010). Comparing Effects of Country Reputation and the Overall Corporate Reputations of a Country on International Consumers' Product Attitudes and Purchase Intentions. *Corporate Reputation Review*, 13(1), 52–62.

Konecnik Ruzzier, Maja & de Chernatony, Leslie (2013). Developing and Applying a Place Brand Identity Model: The Case of Slovenia. *Journal of Business Research*, 66(1), 45–52.

Koschate-Fischer, Nicole, Diamantopoulos, Adamantios & Oldenkotte, Katharina (2012). Are Consumers Really Willing to Pay More for a Favorable Country Image? A Study of Country-of-Origin Effects on Willingness to Pay. *Journal of International Marketing*, 20(1), 19.

Kotler, Philip, Haider, Donald & Rein, Irving (1993a). There's No Place like Our Place! The Marketing of Cities, Regions, and Nations. *The Futurist*, 27(6), 14–21.

Kotler, Philip, Haider, Donald & Rein, Irving (1993b). *Marketing Places: Attracting Investment, Industry, and Tourism to Cities, States, and Nations.* New York: Free Press (p. 388).

Lane, Barbara Miller & Kåberg, Helena (2008). *Modern Swedish Design: Three Founding Texts* New York: The Museum of Modern Art (p. 320).

Lawrence, C., Marr, Norman & Prendergast, Gerald (1992). Country-of-Origin Stereotyping: a Case Study in the New Zealand Motor Vehicle Industry. *European Journal of Marketing*, 26(3), 37–51.

Lee, Hanjoon, Kim, Chankon & Miller, Joseph (1993). The Relative Effects of Price, Warranty and Country of Origin on Consumer Product Evaluations. *Journal of Global Marketing*, 6(1/2), 55–80.

The Local (2013, January 31st). Victorinox Cuts Wenger Swiss Army Knife Brand, *By Malcom Curtis*. Retrieved from www.thelocal.ch/20130131/victorinox-cuts-wenger-swiss-army-knife-brand

Lopez, Carmen, Gotsi, Manto & Andriopoulos, Constantine (2011). Conceptualising the Influence of Corporate Image on Country Image. *European Journal of Marketing*, 45(11/12), 1601–1641.

Luxury Activist (2014, October 24th). Victorinox Opens Pop-Up Store in a Mountain . . . in Rio de Janeiro. Retrieved from http://luxuryactivist.com/luxury/victorinox-opens-pop-up-store-in-a-mountain-in-rio-de-janeiro-switzerland-is-invited-to-the-pao-de-acucar/

Magnusson, Peter, Westjohn, Stanford A. & Zdravkovic, Srdan (2011a). "What? I Thought Samsung Was Japanese": Accurate or Not, Perceived Country of Origin Matters. *International Marketing Review*, 28(5), 454–472.

Magnusson, Peter, Westjohn, Stanford & Zdravkovic, Srdan (2011b). Further Clarification on How Perceived Brand Origin Affects Brand Attitude—A Reply to Samiee and Usunier. *International Marketing Review*, 28(5), 497–507.

Martin, Ingrid & Eroglu, Sevgin (1993). Measuring a Multi-Dimensional Construct: Country Image. *Journal of Business Research*, 28(3), 191–210.

Minister of Turism Argentina (n.d.). Manuel Marca Pais. 96. Retrieved from www.turismo.gov.ar/sites/default/files/Manual_Marca_Pais_Argentina.pdf

Nagashima, Akira (1970). A Comparison of Japanese and U.S. Attitudes Toward Foreign Products. *Journal of Marketing*, 34(1), 68–74.

New York Post (2015, January 26th). The $1,000 Parka That Quietly Took Over Hollywood Fashion, *By Alev Aktar*. Retrieved from https://nypost.com/2015/01/26/the-1000-parka-that-quietly-took-over-hollywood-fashion/

Nicoll, William & Schoenberg, Richard (1998). *Europe Beyond 2000: The Enlargement of the European Union Toward the East*. London: Whurr Publishers (p. 121).

Olson, Jerry (1972). *Cue Utilization in the Quality Perception Process: A Cognitive Model and an Empirical Test*. (Ph.D), Purdue University, West Lafayette.

Papadopoulos, Nicolas (2004). Place Branding: Evolution, Meaning and Implications. *Place Branding*, 1(1), 36–49.

Pappu, Ravi, Quester, Pascale G. & Cooksey, Ray W. (2007). Country Image and Consumer-Based Brand Equity: Relationships and Implications for International Marketing. *Journal of International Business Studies*, 38(5), 726–726.

Pharr, Julie M. (2005). Synthesizing Country-of-Origin Research From the Last Decade: Is the Concept Still Salient in an Era of Global Brands? *Journal of Marketing Theory and Practice*, 13(4), 34–45.

Pizzini (n.d.). Victorinox Swiss Army Knives Info. Retrieved November 2017, from www.pizzini.at/info_sak_engl.htm

Po-Young, Chu, Chang, Chia-Chi, Chia-Yi, Chen & Wang, Tzu-Yun (2010). Countering Negative Country-of-Origin Effects. *European Journal of Marketing*, 44(7/8), 1055–1076.

Public Diplomacy Magazine (2010). The Symbiosis of Sweden & IKEA, *By Olle Wästberg*. Retrieved from www.publicdiplomacymagazine.com/the-symbiosis-of-sweden-ikea/

Purmehdi, Mostafa (2015). *Two Essays on Consumer Protection Initiatives*. (Ph.D Doctoral dissertation), Marketing—HEC Montréal, Montréal (Canada).

496 *Origin-Based Marketing*

Richardson, Paul, Dick, Alan & Jain, Arun (1994). Extrinsic and Intrinsic Cue Effects on Perceptions of Store Brand Quality. *Journal of Marketing*, 58(4), 28–36.

Roth, Katharina & Diamantopoulos, Adamantios (2009). Advancing the Country Image Construct. *Journal of Business Research*, 62(7), 726–740.

Samiee, Saeed (2011). Resolving the Impasse Regarding Research on the Origins of Products and Brands. *International Marketing Review*, 28(5), 473–485.

Slovenian Ministry of Economy (2007). I Feel Slovenia Brand Book. 15. Retrieved from www.ukom.gov.si/fileadmin/ukom.gov.si/pageuploads/dokumenti/arhiv_projektov/IFS/Slovenias_Brand_brand_book.PDF.PDF

Speece, Mark & Duc Phung, Nguyen (2005). Countering Negative Country-of-Origin With Low Prices: A Conjoint Study in Vietnam. *The Journal of Product and Brand Management*, 14(1), 39–48.

The Star (2013, May 29th). Canada Goose Opens First U.S. Office, *By Ashante Ifantry*. Retrieved from www.thestar.com/business/economy/2013/05/29/canada_goose_opens_first_us_office.html

Times Free Press (2011, January 11th). VW's New Passat 'Born in the U.S.A', *By Mike Pare*. Retrieved from www.timesfreepress.com/news/news/story/2011/jan/11/vws-new-passat-born-in-the-usa-chattanooga/39050/

Tse, David K. & Gorn, Gerald J. (1993). An Experiment on the Salience of Country-of-Origin in the Era of Global Brands. *Journal of International Marketing*, 1(1), 57–57.

University of East Anglia (2016). Professor Simon Anholt. Retrieved May 2016, from www.uea.ac.uk/political-social-international-studies/people/profile/s-anholt

Usunier, Jean-Claude (2006). Relevance in Business Research: The Case of Country-of-Origin Research in Marketing. *European Management Review*, 3(1), 60–73.

Usunier, Jean-Claude & Cestre, Ghislaine (2008). Further Considerations on the Relevance of Country-of-Origin Research. *European Management Review*, 5(4), 271–274.

Victorinox (2017). History. Retrieved from www.victorinox.com/ca/en/Explore/Company/History/cms/history

Volkswagen Aktiengesellschaft (2016). Annual Report—We Are Redefining Mobility. Retrieved from http://annualreport2016.volkswagenag.com/service-pages/downloads/files/entire_vw_ar16.pdf

Volkswagen Aktiengesellschaft (2017). Strategy 2025—Together. Retrieved November 2017, from www.volkswagenag.com/en/group/strategy.html

Wall, Marjorie, Liefeld, John & Heslop, Louise (1991). Impact of Country-of-Origin Cues on Consumer Judgments in Multi-Cue Situations: A Covariance Analysis. *Journal of the Academy of Marketing Science*, 19(2), 105–113.

Wang, Xuehua & Yang, Zhilin (2008). Does Country-of-Origin Matter in the Relationship Between Brand Personality and Purchase Intention in Emerging Economies? *International Marketing Review*, 25(4), 458–474.

World Bank (2016a). Ranking of Economies—Gross Domestic Product. Retrieved October 2017, from http://databank.worldbank.org/data/download/GDP.pdf

World Bank (2016b). Population Density (People per Sq. Km of Land Area): Spain, Brazil and Canada. Retrieved October 2017, from https://data.worldbank.org/indicator/EN.POP.DNST?locations=ES-BR-CA

World Bank (2016c). Surface Area (Sq. Km). Retrieved October 2017, from https://data.worldbank.org/indicator/AG.SRF.TOTL.K2?locations=ES-CA-BR

World Population Review (2017). Texas. Retrieved October 2017, from http://worldpopulationreview.com/states/texas-population/

12 Cause-Related Marketing

Table of Contents

12 Cause-Related Marketing

Introduction: Should Companies Rely on Causes to
Differentiate from Competition and Attract Customers? 498
- 12.1 *Background Information*...*499*
  - 12.1.1 *Understanding the "Responsible Process" Cue* *501*
  - 12.1.2 *Business Ethics, Corporate Social Responsibility, and Macromarketing*..............*504*
  - 12.1.3 *Heterogeneity of International Consumption of "Responsible" Products*............................*507*
- 12.2 *Definitions*...*510*
  - 12.2.2 *Cause-Related Marketing*...............................*510*
  - 12.2.2 *Other Initiatives Supporting Causes* *511*
- 12.3 *Corporate Examples*...*514*
  - 12.3.1 *Cause-Related Marketing Initiatives: Coca-Cola, Fjällräven, IKEA, and Subaru* *514*
  - 12.3.1 *Other Initiatives Supporting Causes: Aldo, Fiat, and Procter & Gamble (Dawn, Pampers, and Purifier of Water)*.......*519*
- 12.4 *Issues at Stake* *525*
  - 12.4.1 *Relevance and Trustworthiness*.....................*525*
  - 12.4.2 *Impact on Marketing Activities and Feasibility* *528*
  - 12.4.3 *Outcomes* *534*

Conclusion: Relying on the "responsible process" cue (through cause-related marketing and other CSR-based approaches) can help companies increase their competitiveness, and possibly bridge cultural and psychic distances. Yet, it requires extreme caution.
References

498 *Cause-Related Marketing*

Figure 12.1 Illustrating Chapter 12
Source: Own elaboration

Recommended Readings

- Berglind, Matthew & Nakata, Cheryl (2005). Cause-Related Marketing: More Buck than Bang? *Business Horizons*, 48(5), 443–453.
- La Ferle, Carrie; Kuber, Gayatri & Edwards, Steven (2013). Factors Impacting Responses to Cause-Related Marketing in India and the US: Novelty, Altruistic Motives, and Company Origin. *Journal of Business Research*, 66(3), 364–373.
- Kotler, Philip & Lee, Nancy (2005). Best of Breed: When It Comes to Gaining a Market Edge while Supporting a Social Cause, "Corporate Social Marketing" Leads the Pack. *Social Marketing Quarterly*, 11(3–4), 91–103.
- Varadarajan, Rajan & Menon, Anil (1988). Cause-Related Marketing: A Coalignment of Marketing Strategy and Corporate Philanthropy. *Journal of Marketing*, 52(3), 58–74.

Introduction: Should Companies Rely on Causes to Differentiate from Competition and Attract Customers?

In reference to businessmen speaking about the social responsibilities of business, US economist and Nobel Prize winner Milton Friedman wrote: "The businessmen believe that they are defending free enterprise when they declaim that business is not concerned 'merely' with profit but also with promoting desirable 'social' ends; that business has a 'social conscience' and takes seriously its responsibilities for providing employment, eliminating discrimination, avoiding pollution and whatever else may be the catchwords of the contemporary crop of reformers. In fact they are—or would be if they or anyone else took them seriously—preaching pure and unadulterated social-ism." (New York Times, 1970, p. 17). Socialism, then, was meant as a seri-ous insult by this fierce advocate of market deregulation and advisor of US President Ronald Reagan and UK Prime Minister Margaret Thatcher.

Nearly fifty years later, the idea that corporate social responsibility (CSR) could not be taken seriously in the business world is prone to make us smile. Indeed, an ever-increasing number of companies, large or small, in developed and developing economies, now issue annual CSR or sustainability reports and commit to be better "citizens." In the 2010s, cause-related marketing and other CSR-based approaches have emerged as a central line in corporate com-munications. There is no limit to the number of causes—from social (e.g., dis-crimination and poverty) to environmental (e.g., pollution and biodiversity), health, nutrition, animal welfare, etc.—that companies can support. These causes could be instrumental in helping with cultural and psychic distances. Nevertheless, this strategy still raises some concerns—albeit for different rea-sons than evoked by Friedman. We then ask the question: **"Should compa-nies rely on causes to differentiate from competition and attract customers?"**

Overall, the objectives of this chapter are to define, illustrate, and discuss the topic of cause-related marketing and other CSR-based approaches. All of these activities revolve around the notion of a "responsible process" cue that companies can choose to emphasize in their communications, like they do other cues (e.g., brand and origin). To better understand this "new" cue, we start by reviewing important concepts linked to CSR, ethics, and macro-marketing. We then define cause-related marketing in further detail before moving on to present other initiatives supporting causes. Next, we present examples of companies supporting a variety of causes. Finally, we conclude with an overview of the issues debated when it comes to cause-related mar-keting, including discussions about its relevance for firms and potential pit-falls for both firms and the nonprofit organizations (NPOs) that represent the supported causes. Key success factors and the overall impact on marketing decisions of the approach are also covered.

Figure 12.2 situates the topic of cause-related marketing in the book struc-ture and shows that, in relation to the different steps in an international marketing plan, this topic can be particularly discussed when considering communication and promotion policies.

12.1 Background Information

The questions addressed in this section are:

- What are the main cues used by consumers to make a purchase decision? When traditional cues are not enough to differentiate anymore, then what?
- What are the major trends to which a "responsible process" corre-sponds? What types of products result from a "responsible process"?
- How can we define business ethics and how different is it from corporate social responsibility (CSR)? Then, what is CSR precisely?
- What about macro-marketing, is it entirely aligned with CSR principles?

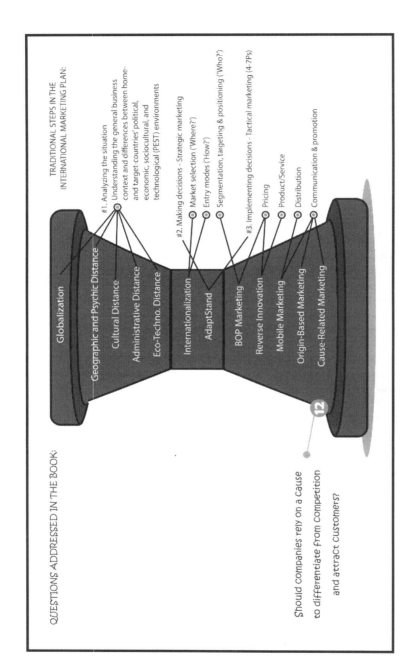

Figure 12.2 Positioning Chapter 12 in the overall book structure

Source: Own elaboration

Cause-Related Marketing 501

12.1.1 Understanding the "Responsible Process" Cue

What are the main cues used by consumers to make a purchase decision? When traditional cues are not sufficient anymore, then what? As discussed in Chapter 11, *cue utilization theory* (Easterbrook, 1959; Olson, 1972) positions cues as surrogate indicators of quality. For many years, companies have focused on differentiating themselves from the competition based on cues like price, design, brand, and origin. When the competition keeps stiffening as a result of globalization and when these traditional cues do not suffice to differentiate anymore, then what? Companies have overwhelmingly turned toward another cue, that we propose to call the *process cue*. Here, we use the term *process* to refer to the way business is conducted, from practices to resulting products. There is one particular type of process that has gained momentum in the past fifteen years or so and which is now being predominantly used by companies in the competitive game: the *responsible process*.

What are the major trends that support the rise of the "responsible process" cue? In recent years, a form of doing business that is "responsible," "sustainable," "ethical," "fair," and so on, has gained intense approval. Sustainable development, business ethics, corporate social responsibility (CSR), and macro-marketing are all concepts that support the rise of the *responsible process cue* to prominence. Sustainable development is a concept that lies at the intersection of what Elkington (1997) called the "triple bottom line" (see Figure 12.3), i.e., environmental action (planet), community involvement (people), and economic growth (profits).

In turn, Figure 12.4 presents the virtuous circle of sustainable consumption and production, proposed by the United Nations Environment Program (UNEP). The circle starts with sustainable resource management within firms as well as products designed for sustainability. These, in turn, lead to cleaner production and improved resource efficiency. Then, sustainable transport, eco-labeling and certification, as well as sustainable procurement and marketing practices enhance sustainable lifestyles. Finally, waste management is an important piece of this virtuous circle as it contributes to enhancing sustainable resource management, thereby closing the loop.

In the next section, we provide more background information on the concepts of business ethics, CSR, and macro-marketing. Before that, we look into the tangible aspect of these notions, considering products resulting from a "responsible process."

What types of products result from a "responsible process"? When companies abide by "responsible" principles and put emphasis on their business processes, it can translate into different types of products:

- Processes aiming at better protecting the environment (e.g., energy efficiency and carbon footprint tracking) may allow companies to commercialize "green" products (e.g., "cleaner" cars and domestic appliances).
- Processes aiming at better protecting collaborators, such as workers in supplier companies (e.g., improving working conditions, paying above-market wages) can translate into "fair" products (e.g., "Fair Trade" labels for textiles, coffee, and chocolate).

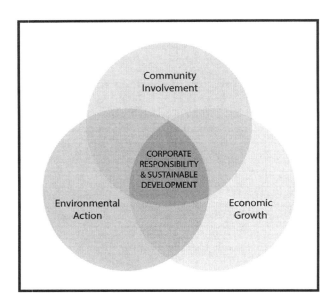

Figure 12.3 Illustrating the three pillars of sustainable development
Source: Adapted from Elkington (1997)

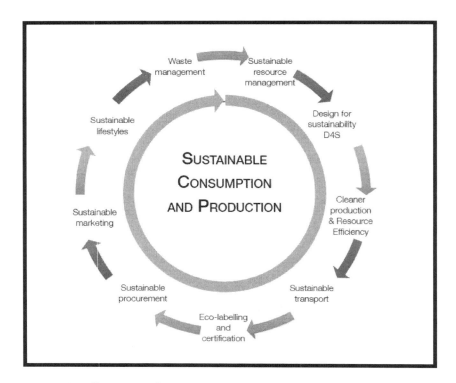

Figure 12.4 Illustrating the virtuous circle of sustainable consumption and production
Source: UNEP (2015, p. 11)

Cause-Related Marketing 503

- Finally, processes aiming at better protecting consumers (e.g., limiting the use of chemicals, allergens, GMOs, and so on) may allow firms to market "organic" products.

Figure 12.5 illustrates one of these products while putting in evidence the prominence of the "responsible process" cue on the packaging itself.

Other examples of products resulting from a so-called responsible process are available on YouTube with advertisements for green products (i.e., "green advertising") by Audi and LG (search words: "2010 Audi Green Car Super Bowl Commercial" and "LG Green Health Commercial"). Some of these examples prompt us to wonder about *green washing*, a term referring to the somewhat abusive use of the environmental cause to help with commercializing products that are not necessarily the most respectful alternatives for protecting the environment (e.g., a car versus other transportation modes like buses and bikes).

Incidentally, a growth spurt in green advertising was observed between 2006 and 2008 when the proportion of green advertisements rose from less

Figure 12.5 Presenting a "responsible" product with emphasis on the "organic" process cue on packaging (product category: juice)

Source: Courtesy of Nestlé

504   Cause-Related Marketing

than 2 percent of the overall number of advertisements and reached almost 6 percent (TerraChoice, 2009). Looking at a longer timeframe, Leonidou, Leonidou, Palihawadana, and Hultman (2011) note that the growth trend is not linear over time but wave-like with peaks in the 1988–94 and 2001–2007 periods. The influence of external events—notably in the realm of politics—can explain such a rise and fall of interest for designing and promoting green products (e.g., the Kyoto Protocol aiming to reduce greenhouse gas emissions was ratified in 1997 and entered into force in 2005). Indeed, environmental policies and regulations will more or less constrain companies to produce (and consumers to buy) responsible products.

For other types of responsible products, a trend toward growth was also observed in the 2000s. For instance, sales of Fair Trade-certified products in the UK alone grew from ~25 to 500 million GBP (~33 to 655 million USD) between 2000 and 2007 (EcoWorld, 2016). In turn, global sales of organic food and drink expanded massively from roughly 18 billion USD in 2000 to nearly 82 billion USD in 2015 (FiBL & IFOAM, 2017).

12.1.2 Business Ethics, Corporate Social Responsibility, and Macromarketing

How can we define business ethics and how different is it from corporate social responsibility (CSR)?[1] Business ethics and CSR are occasionally used interchangeably, or as elements included in one another's definition. For instance, CSR is sometimes included in the definition of ethics (Singer, 1993), while ethics is sometimes included in the definition of CSR (Carroll, 1979, 1983). Through a closer examination, we can see that these notions are conceptually distinct.

On one hand, business ethics is an age-old concept. According to Evans, Haden, Clayton, and Novicevic (2013), the first writing on the topic could be traced back to Johannes Nider, who in 1948 developed certain rules for trade. In particular: "the goods should be lawful and useful, the price of the goods should be fair, and the seller should be honest with the buyer" (Dahlin, 2007, p. 360). In this way, *ethics* deals with the moral issue of what is right and wrong, and also proposes systematic ways of solving moral dilemmas (Crane & Matten, 2016). Business ethics is at the junction of ethics and business: a moral evaluation of an economic system, of the businesses operating within this system, and of the individuals managing and operating within these businesses (Joyner & Payne, 2002). Business ethics deals with a wide array of questions covering the way a company develops its policies with employees, how it solves conflicts, deals with intellectual property rights, communicates its financial information, negotiates with suppliers and clients, develops the values in its mission statement, etc. (e.g., Vallance, 1995).

Corporate social responsibility, on the other hand, is a more recent concept. Its origins can be traced back to an article written by E. Merrick Dodd in 1932 (Post, 2003; Turner, 2006). In this article, the author argues that a firm should have social responsibilities in addition to economic ones because a corporation is "permitted and encouraged by the law primarily because it is of service to the community rather than because it is a source of profit to its owners" (Dodd, 1932, p. 1194). There is no strict consensus on the definition of CSR, and some conclude that it is bound to "evolve in tune with business, political and social developments in the light of ongoing globalization and developments in the field of mass communication" (Taneja, Taneja, & Gupta, 2011, p. 343). However, all agree with Dodd's original focus on the social inclusion of the organization and on its interaction and interdependence with society. As Carroll (1979) suggests, a firm's social responsibility is defined by how a company can identify social issues (e.g. consumerism, environmentalism, discrimination, safety, etc.) and how it can effectively respond to them.

Figure 12.6 presents Carroll's (1991) classic "pyramid of corporate social responsibility." The pyramid illustrates various levels of responsibilities, from the least to the most "responsible" behavior. It starts at the base with economic responsibilities (i.e., be profitable), then legal responsibilities (i.e., obey the law), ethical responsibilities (i.e., do what is right), and finally philanthropic responsibilities (i.e., be a good citizen, by contributing to improving the life quality of employees or consumers, for instance).

Then, what is CSR precisely?[2] CSR is neither new to academic research nor to industry practice. Nevertheless, there is no unanimous understanding of the concept and more than thirty-five definitions have been proposed in the literature over the past sixty years (Dahlsrud, 2008; Matten & Moon,

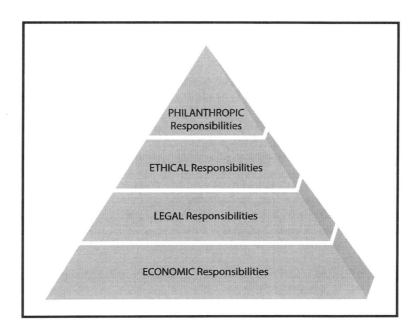

Figure 12.6 Presenting the pyramid of corporate social responsibility
Source: Adapted from Carroll (1991)

2008). Besides business ethics, CSR is also used interchangeably with other concepts, such as "corporate social performance," "corporate sustainability," or "corporate citizenship," to refer to the impact of business on society. In its early days, the nature of CSR was heavily debated but the important role of economic considerations was widely accepted (see the base of Carroll's pyramid, depicted in Figure 12.6). The importance of long-run profit maximization was also emphasized by Levitt (1958) and most famously by Milton Friedman, for whom "there is one and only one social responsibility of business—to use its resources and engage in activities designed to increase its profits as long as it stays within the rules of the game" (2002, p. 133). It is the latter part of the sentence that is important, because the "rules of the game" have dramatically changed in the past decades.

Nowadays, companies must integrate social and environmental concerns into their business operations to be profitable and to maximize shareholder value (Eccles, Ioannou, & Serafeim, 2014). More recent definitions of CSR emphasize this aspect. For instance, CSR has been defined as a voluntary-based set of practices responding to the needs of multiple stakeholders that aligns social and environmental preoccupations with economic objectives (Crane, Matten, & Spencer, 2013). In turn, Griffin and Pustay (2015, Chap. 5) describe CSR as the set of obligations an organization undertakes to protect and enhance the society in which it functions. Öberseder, Schlegelmilch, Murphy, and Gruber (2014, p. 103) summarize it all by stating that "a socially responsible company integrates social and environmental topics in its core business activities and acts responsibly toward its employees, its customers, the environment, its suppliers, the local community, its shareholders and society at large." Thus, a more encompassing definition of CSR provides better guidance for companies gearing up to meet the challenge of being a good corporate citizen.

Consequently, a more holistic understanding of CSR is important for various stakeholders, foremost consumers. This stakeholder group has high expectations of companies and is increasingly willing to reward good corporate behavior by means of advocacy behavior (e.g., positive WOM), willingness to purchase, and willingness to pay (Auger, Burke, Devinney, & Louviere, 2003). CSR should be tied in with a firm's overall strategy and— if performed well—can lead to the creation of greater market value (e.g., Luo & Bhattacharya, 2006; Chernev & Blair, 2015).

In terms of measurement, we find several company rankings assessing MNCs on the basis of CSR. Examples from the US include "Global 100" established by the *Corporate Knights* magazine and "100 Best" by the *Corporate Responsibility* magazine. According to the latter, the top ten most-responsible companies in 2017 included Hasbro, Intel, Microsoft, Campbell Soup, Cisco Systems, and Accenture (CR, 2017). The indicators used to build a CSR index and establish this ranking include ratings on: the environment, climate change, human rights, employee relations, corporate governance, financial performance, and, finally, philanthropy and community support.

Finally, what about macro-marketing, is it entirely aligned with CSR principles? The term *macro-marketing* refers to a conception of marketing that is "larger" than otherwise considered (Bartels & Jenkins, 1977). More than

Cause-Related Marketing   507

thirty years ago, Hunt and Burnett (1982) defined macro-marketing as a multidimensional construct referring to the study of marketing systems, the impact and consequence of marketing systems on society, and the impact and consequence of society on marketing systems. This term opposes the "micro-marketing" concept, defined as all of the activities seeking to accomplish an organization's objectives by anticipating customer needs and directing need satisfying goods toward customers. Micro-marketing corresponds to the generally admitted vision of marketing as the process of planning and executing conception, pricing, promotion, and distribution of ideas, goods, and services to create exchanges that satisfy individual and organizational objectives (American Marketing Association, 2013). With these definitions, we see that the concept of macro-marketing is closely related to that of sustainable marketing. Maignan, Ferrell, and Ferrell (2005) and Rundle-Thiele, Paladino, and Apostol (2008) define *sustainable marketing* as a commitment to conduct marketing activities that minimize the negative and maximize the positive impact on issues important to stakeholders, and, in a more general sense, the adoption of sustainable business practices that create better businesses, better relationships, and a better world. Thus, macro-marketing is entirely aligned with the concept of CSR.

After providing background information about important concepts surrounding the development of "cause-related marketing" (and before focusing on the phenomenon), we briefly present the diversity of situations across countries when it comes to consuming "responsible" products.

12.1.3 Heterogeneity of International Consumption of "Responsible" Products

As with most of the phenomena discussed in this book, diversity across markets is to be expected when it comes to the consumption of "responsible" products. Figure 12.7 ranks countries on the value of per capita consumption of organic and Fair Trade food, as well as the value of sales in these countries (in other words, market size). We can observe the importance that these responsible products have for the Swiss and their propensity to pay, considering that the country ranked first on both counts in 2015 (with an average amount spent of 262 euros for organic food and of 58 euros for Fair Trade products, i.e., ~285 and ~70 USD, respectively). However, the small size of the population explains why the country ranked behind larger markets, such as the US, Germany, France, and China (where consumers are increasingly sensitive to food safety) when it comes to retail sales. In this instance, the US market was by far the largest for organic food, with sales valued at nearly 36 billion euros (~42 billion USD) in 2015, while the UK was significantly bigger than others markets for Fair Trade food with ~2.2 billion euros (i.e., 2.6 billion USD).

In all, we need to remember that companies willing to rely on the responsible process cue should be aware of the widely diverse consumer behaviors and preferences across markets. Neither economic nor geographic distances between the Top Ten countries listed in the figure appear to be straightforward explanations for this diversity. Instead, cultural but also administrative

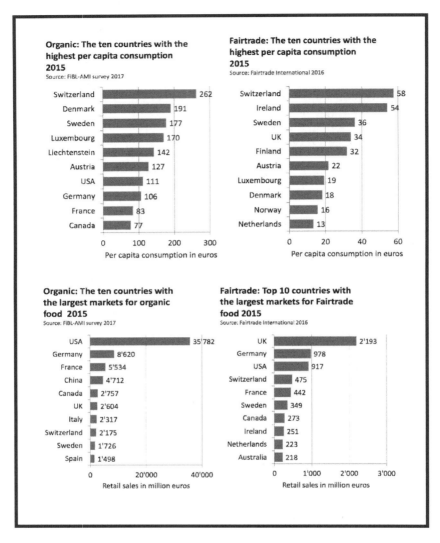

Figure 12.7 Contrasting organic and Fair Trade business (per capita consumption and retails sales) in the top ten consuming countries

Source: FiBL & IFOAM (2017)

distance are more likely reasons as to why consumption differs. An example of a study showing the importance of administrative differences is Thøgersen's (2010) conceptual framework about the determinants of organic food consumption (see Figure 12.8). These determinants can easily be reclassified according to the CAGE distance framework, with cultural factors (e.g., value orientation and food culture), administrative factors (i.e., all political factors

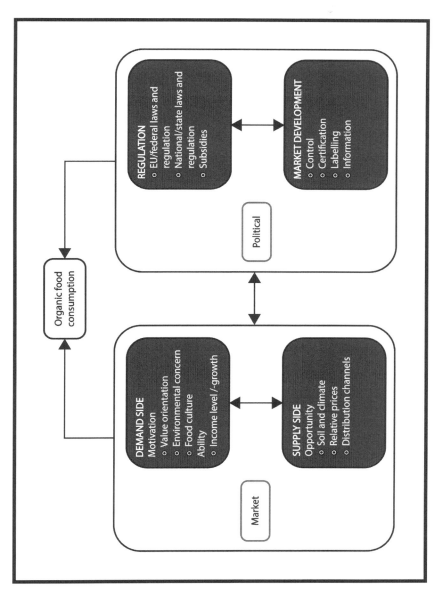

Figure 12.8 Presenting a conceptual framework explaining why organic food consumption differs across countries

Source: Adapted from Thøgersen (2010)

510 Cause-Related Marketing

listed such as regulations, subsidies and certification), geographic factors (soil and climate), and economic factors (e.g., income levels, growth and relative prices) all playing a role in explaining why consumption levels differ across countries.

12.2 Definitions

In order to understand how companies rely on the responsible process cue and, by corollary on "causes," we first reviewed important concepts in regard to corporate social responsibility, macro-marketing and their effect on products. Now, we address the following questions (also see "Food for Thought"):

- What is cause-related marketing?
- How different is cause-related marketing from other initiatives supporting causes?

Food for Thought 12.1

- In reference to Kotler and Lee (2004) and Berglind and Nakata (2005), what is cause-related marketing? How does it differ from other CSR-based approaches?

12.2.2 Cause-Related Marketing

What is cause-related marketing? In a seminal article on the topic, Varadarajan and Menon (1988, p. 60) define *cause-related marketing* as "the process of formulating and implementing marketing activities that are characterized by an offer from the firm to contribute a specified amount to a designated cause when customers engage in revenue providing exchanges that satisfy organizational and individual objectives." In the same vein, Barone, Miyazaki, and Taylor (2000) talk about marketing strategies that link product sales to the support of a charity. Kotler and Lee (2005) add the important notion of a timeframe by defining cause-related marketing as the donation of a percentage of corporate revenues to a cause based on product sales, during an announced period of time. All of these authors agree on a narrow definition of cause-related marketing, adopted in this book as well.

Other authors have defined the approach more broadly. For instance, Marconi (2002) defines it as the practice of marketing a product, service, brand, or company through a mutually beneficial relationship with a nonprofit or social cause organization, a definition endorsed by researchers like Berglind and Nakata (2005). In all, confusion results from the various nuances given to terms used to describe the many ways in which companies support causes. A simple umbrella term to encompass all of them (including cause-related

Cause-Related Marketing 511

marketing) would be *cause marketing* or perhaps *cause-based marketing*. The former term has already been used with specific nuances. For instance, Kotler and Lee (2005) use it interchangeably with *cause promotion* (e.g., sponsorship). The latter term does not appear to have been used yet. However, it is probably best to avoid adding to the confusion by introducing another term. Here, we adopt a narrow definition of *cause-related marketing* and place the transactional aspect between firm and customer in supporting a cause as its core. In this book, we isolate this approach from other approaches, also putting forward the responsible process cue exactly because it involves a greater number of stakeholders: companies, the NPOs that represent causes, and customers. This variety is expected to trigger a richer discussion on issues arising from the ambition of companies to participate in activities that are beyond their traditional economic arena (a possible consequence of globalization, as discussed later on).

12.2.2 Other Initiatives Supporting Causes

How different is cause-related marketing from other initiatives supporting causes? The involvement of customers—i.e., the need for them to purchase something in order to trigger the company's donation—is key in differentiating cause-related marketing from other forms of initiatives supporting causes. A (non-exhaustive) list of these other forms follows, along with examples taken from several companies and in particular from the Coca-Coca Company (which, like many other large MNCs, is active on most of these fronts).

- **Advertising**—when companies use the traditional method of paid advertisements through channels like TV and radio. The Coca-Cola Company, for instance, has developed many large-scale TV commercials featuring cartoons of polar bears drinking soda. In 2013, they launched the "Polar Bowl" spots to coincide with the Super Bowl, the annual championship game of the US National Football League. These spots have created sympathy and awareness, even though they contained no direct mention to the supported cause (polar bears and the environment). A subscription-based chain on YouTube has been created with thirty-four videos (search words: "The Coca-Cola® Polar Bowl—Game Day Moments") to further engage consumers.
- **Facilitated giving**—when companies include a mention or an invitation to encourage donating to a specific charity in their communications. For instance, utility companies (e.g., electricity, gas, water, and phone companies) often include a mention on their monthly paper or electronic bills. Another typical example is initiatives by airlines such as Air Canada's "Every Bit Counts" program. The company collects small change on its flights and in containers in certain airports. The proceeds are then distributed to causes and organizations, such as the Children's Miracle Network and their member pediatric hospitals across the country (Air Canada, 2017).
- **Licensing**—when companies pay a fee to the owners of intellectual property assets (see Chapter 2 for more details on the mechanisms of licensing)

Figure 12.9 Presenting the pink ribbon and logotype of the National Breast Cancer Foundation (US)

Source: Courtesy of the National Breast Cancer Foundation, Inc.

that resonate with the public and display these assets on their own products (often on the packaging). Animal welfare and the fight against breast cancer are examples of causes that receive revenues through the licensing of, for instance, the panda logo and the WWF (World Wildlife Fund) name and the pink ribbon and the NBCF (National Breast Cancer Foundation) logo in the US (see Figure 12.9).

Interestingly, only specific designs of the famous pink ribbon are protected, its generic form being in the public domain. It is, therefore, a logotype that is easy to reproduce without fees, and this may explain its popularity among companies. Incidentally, its sometime abusive use has been dubbed *pink washing* (in reference to *green washing*, a term presented in Section 12.1.1) and has prompted NPOs like Breast Cancer Action (US) to develop resources—under the catchy tagline "Think before you pink"—for consumers to better inform themselves and not unknowingly support flawed campaigns. For instance, the organization acted against Yoplait's pink-lidded yogurt in 2008, since the product was sold to raise money for breast cancer, but was made with dairy stimulated with Recombinant Bovine Growth Hormone (*rBGH*)—a cause factor in breast cancer. The many trademarks owned by the NBCF—e.g., "Pink Ribbon Challenge®," "Help for Today . . . Hope for Tomorrow®," "Helping Women Now™," "Celebrities for the Cause®," "Beyond the Shock®," and "Más allá del Shock®" (NBCF, 2017)—illustrate the importance for NPOs in protecting their IP (an important source of revenues).

- **Philanthropy**—when companies make a direct contribution to a cause. The list of companies donating cash in the form of grants is endless. An example from the 2016 Fortune 500 list (US) is the oil and gas corporation ExxonMobil, which, through its foundation, awarded 1.9 million USD to "Vital Voices" (the international women's group founded by Hillary Clinton), 500,000 USD to the "Medicines for Malaria Venture," and dozens of 80,000 USD grants to science camps at colleges and universities in 2014 (Fortune, 2016). In turn, the Coca-Cola Company awarded grants to no fewer than 262 organizations across the globe in 2016, for a total amount of nearly 73 million USD (The Coca-Cola Company, 2016c).

- **Public relations**—when companies use the tools and techniques of public relations (e.g., blogging, events, newsletters, press releases, and social media accounts) to communicate their support for a cause. For instance, IKEA informs the public about all of its social endeavors with press releases posted on its active online newsroom.
- **Responsible practices**—when companies adopt discretionary business practices that support causes. General examples include the facilitation of recycling (e.g., batteries) in the workplace, or protection of gender equality among employees. In the particular case of the Coca-Cola Company, one example is its Water Stewardship program. Launched in 2004, the program aims to, among other objectives, improve the overall water-use efficiency during production, manage environmental pollution through wastewater and storm-water discharge at production facilities, and replenish the water used in production and distribute it back to communities and the environment (The Coca-Cola Company, 2017).
- **Social marketing**—when companies encourage behavior change through campaigns. Examples given in Kotler and Lee (2005) include workshops organized by Home Depot in Arizona (US) to share water conservation basics, including drought-resistant gardening (supported cause: the environment), and Crest's dental clinics providing affordable oral care for poor children and their families and teaching them how to avoid cavities (supported causes: health and poverty). Another example from The Coca-Cola Company is the initiative undertaken in 2013 to help ease the longstanding political tensions between India and Pakistan. A commercial available on YouTube with search words: "Coca-Cola Small World Machines—Bringing India & Pakistan Together" presents how the company had set up live communication boxes (resembling Coca-Coca vending machines) in commercial areas to encourage people from both sides of the border to interact and "make a friend" (e.g., by touching hands or drawing peace, love, and happiness symbols).
- **Sponsorship**—when companies promote causes through paid sponsorships. Sports traditionally convey values of excellence, sacrifice, and achievement and are often considered noble causes. Major sporting events (e.g., the Olympics and the World Cup in soccer/football) are well-known examples of high-profile sponsorships. An article in Forbes (2016) reveals that a four-year cycle as an Olympic Global Partner costs about 200 million USD. According to the same source, Panasonic (Japan) had recently paid 350 million USD for an eight-year, four-Olympic Game sponsorship. This is indicative of the astounding amount of money that a company like Coca-Cola Company must have given away to no fewer than 204 National Olympic Committees over its ninety-year commitment (since 1928!) as a sponsor of the Olympic Games. In the context of its #ThatsGold global campaign for the 2016 Rio Games, the company's

514 *Cause-Related Marketing*

Vice-President of Global Creative, Rodolfo Echeverria, was quoted as saying: "While the gold medal is an icon of sporting success, Coca-Cola believes that gold moments can happen far beyond the podium. They can happen every day and all around the world. [. . .] For Coca-Cola, gold moments are made of special feelings—joyful, refreshing, sharable— all of those moments that make you feel gold, just like the feeling of drinking an ice-cold Coca-Cola" (The Coca-Cola Company, 2016b).

- **Volunteering**—when companies provide volunteer services in the community performed by employees who are paid to do so. For instance, Microsoft enables its engineers to teach computer science in high schools and matches employee volunteer time in NPOs with 25 USD in cash per hour (Fortune, 2016).

Before moving on to more detailed examples, we can conclude that companies have indeed a vast array of options when it comes to supporting causes and relying on the responsible process cue in their communications.

12.3 Corporate Examples

We now look at examples that illustrate cause-related marketing and other forms of corporate support for causes presented in alphabetical order. Note that some of these companies clearly have a better fit with the causes they support than others. Can you tell (see "Food for Thought")?

Food for Thought 12.2

- Considering the examples listed below (and others that you may have heard of), is there always a good fit between the company and the chosen cause? Why is this important?

12.3.1 Cause-Related Marketing Initiatives: Coca-Cola, Fjällräven, IKEA, and Subaru

Here, we look only into a few of the dozens (if not hundreds) of examples of cause-related marketing available. For many more, see "causerelatedmarketing.blogspot.ca," for instance, a well-documented blog written by Paul Jones from Alden Keene (US), a marketing and communications consultancy serving businesses and nonprofit organizations.

Coca-Cola[3]—The Coca-Cola Company has been used as an example to illustrate firms' internationalization process (Chapter 2) and the challenges of adaptation and standardization across markets (Chapter 3). This massive MNC (see Table 12.1 for key data) also serves as an example in this chapter, since it has countless social initiatives.

Cause-Related Marketing 515

Table 12.1 Profiling The Coca-Cola Company (US)

Who:	*The Coca-Cola Company*
Since:	1886
What:	Beverages
From:	US
Sales (Bn USD):	~42
Employing (people):	100,300
Manufacturing in (countries):	48
Selling in (countries):	200

Source: The Coca-Cola Company (2016a)

One example of an initiative that falls into the cause-related marketing category is Coke's Smile-izer effort. In 2010, the company offered to donate one USD to the National Park Foundation every time someone recorded a laugh for twenty seconds on mycoke.com (up to $50,000). The National Park Foundation is the charitable partner of the National Park Service (US) and aims to gain the support of "private citizens, park lovers, stewards of nature, history enthusiasts, and wilderness adventurers" for national parks and vast protected natural areas. The laugh could be transmitted via all the usual social media outlets and it "floated" around on the mycoke.com website like a Coke bubble.

Another example of cause-related marketing by the company is the "Arctic Home" campaign. Launched in 2011, this initiative conducted in partnership with the WWF targeted the protection of polar bears and their habitat. By derivation, supported causes included the environment and climate change, since polar bears suffer from raising global temperatures and the resulting habitat loss (National Geographic, 2018). Yet, the connection with the arctic mammals largely antecedes these issues, since polar bears made a first appearance in a print ad in 1922 and in a TV commercial in 1993.

Showing their continued support to the cause, the initiative consisted of an initial donation of 2 million USD to WWF and the possibility for consumers to participate (from November 1, 2011, to February 1, 2012) by purchasing limited-edition "Arctic Home" Coke cans and other popular Coca-Cola products (e.g., Coke Zero, Sprite, Fanta, and Minute Maid) identified with white bottle caps. Consumers could then text the package code to a dedicated phone number which triggered donations of 1 USD to the WWF (up to 1 million USD). With this campaign, the Coca-Cola Company contributed 3 million USD overall to the cause.

Fjällräven[4]—In 1950, a fourteen-year-old Swedish boy named Åke Nordin could never find a backpack that was comfortable enough to take during long hikes in the great outdoors and that fulfilled his needs. He decided to take the matter into his own hands. After making a wooden frame, he used his mother's sewing machine to sew a bag out of strong cotton material. A few years later, his time in the military showed him that there was a market for functional and hardwearing outdoor equipment. This is how Fjällräven (roughly pronounced "Fyallraven") was founded in 1960 with the ambition

516 *Cause-Related Marketing*

Figure 12.10 Presenting Fjällräven's logo in the shape of its namesake, the Arctic fox
Source: Courtesy of Fjällräven

to inspire people to enjoy nature. Today, Fjällräven manufactures outdoor equipment (e.g., backpacks, sleeping bags, and tents), hunting equipment, and travel equipment, as well as clothing and accessories (e.g., jackets, tops, trousers, shorts, dresses, skirts, and wallets). Indeed, the brand also appeals to eighteen-to-twenty-seven-year-old customers across the world, who view the company as trendy and young and buy products such as the Kånken backpack to make a fashion statement.

To some extent, Fjällräven is also an example of origin-based marketing (see Chapter 11). The brand name has been kept in the original language—in spite of difficulties for foreigners to pronounce it—and all products feature a small sewn Swedish flag. The company can indeed capitalize on a favorable product-country image (PCI) between Sweden and outdoor equipment. In addition, the company was named after those beautiful white foxes that Åke Nordin spotted during his beloved treks (*Fjällräven* literally translates as Arctic fox). Figure 12.10 presents the company logo in the shape of the Arctic fox.

Here, Fjällräven is presented as an example of commitment to CSR in general, and of cause-related marketing in particular. Its mission statement reads as follows: "develop durable, timeless and functional outdoor equipment, act responsibly toward people, animals and nature, and awaken and maintain an interest in outdoor life." In one particular cause-related marketing activity, it proposes to donate 100 Swedish Krona (~12 USD) for each one of the "Save the Arctic Fox Kånken" special edition backpacks sold (retail price of 99.95 euros, about 120 USD, or should we rather say 119.90 USD, to stay in the logic of "psychological pricing"). The offer is also valid for the mini version of the classic Kånken (retail price of 84.95 euros). These two products then come with a small tag that reads: "When buying this product you support the Swedish Arctic Fox Project with 10 euros. This project aims to preserve the Arctic Fox ('Fjällräven' namesake) today in danger of extinction across mainland Europe."

IKEA[5]—The company—which has also been used to illustrate various concepts discussed in this book (see Chapters 2, 3, 5, 10 and 11)—is an excellent example of cause-related marketing, and more generally, of the use of the responsible process cue. One of its many social initiatives is a series of cause-related marketing campaigns conducted in partnership with UNICEF (i.e., the United Nations International Children's Emergency Fund), an organization dedicated to defending the rights of children worldwide. In 2003, IKEA stores around the globe donated two dollars (or two pounds or two euros) from the sale of each 6.99 USD "IKEA BRUM soft-toy teddy bear" to benefit children living in Angola and Uganda. At first, the campaign was expected to raise 400,000 USD to support UNICEF's "Children's Right to Play" program. The program lasted two years and raised more than 2 million USD.

At the end of 2005, IKEA pursued the same idea with a Christmas campaign (from November 19 through December 24). Under the tagline "One euro is a fortune . . . A child's smile is worth so much," all IKEA stores worldwide donated one euro for each soft toy sold to support UNICEF and "Save the Children" programs in impoverished countries. The company was expected to be able to donate more than 1 million euros (~1.2 million USD) as a result of sales, but ended up raising 2.2 million USD with this campaign. Since then, the company has repeated the experience every year with other types of soft toys, and has been able to donate between 18 and 24 million USD (depending on the sources). The support to UNICEF has also taken other forms, such as direct donations, sales of greeting cards, and in-kind assistance.

Subaru[6]—Subaru is the car manufacturing division of transportation conglomerate Subaru Corporation (Japan), founded in 1953. In 2017, Subaru had net sales of 3,326 trillion yen (~29.3 billion USD) and employed more than 14,700 people. In 2008, the US headquarters (Subaru of America) launched a cause-related marketing initiative called "Share the Love" (see Figure 12.11)

This initiative has the particularity to let consumers decide to which cause the company should give. For each new Subaru purchased or leased, the company committed to giving 250 USD to either one of the following organizations: the American Society for the Prevention of Cruelty to Animals (ASPCA), Make-A-Wish, Meals on Wheels America, or the National Park Foundation. The causes supported by these NPOs are, respectively, animal protection, help to critically ill children, fight against hunger, and preservation of the environment. A YouTube video (search words: "Subaru Share the Love | "Put a Little Love in Your Heart" | :60") presents the spirit of the campaign with characters representative of each cause singing together a song about love. Instead of these four national organizations, consumers could also choose local charities, depending on the participation of retailers (in 2017, more than 660 local organizations benefited from the campaign).

Since its creation in the US less than ten years ago, this campaign has raised an impressive 115 million USD. It has not been implemented in other countries. Instead, the company is involved in sponsoring a varying number of causes, depending on the location. In France, for instance, the company sponsors three national sports federations (the national federations of aviation, aerobatics, and hockey: 'Fédération Française d'Aéronautique,' 'Equipe de France de Voltige Aérienne,' and the 'Fédération Française de Hockey sur Glace'). In Canada, at least six sponsorships are reported on the national

Figure 12.11 Presenting Subaru's "Share the Love" cause-related marketing campaign

Source: Courtesy of Subaru of America, Inc.

Cause-Related Marketing 519

website of the company, including the Subaru Ironman Canadian Series Triathlons and the Subaru Grassroots Triathlon Series, Golf for the Cure, Subaru Centurion Cycling, Canadian Ski Instructors' Alliance, and Ronald McDonald House Charities Toronto. As of the end of the year 2017, the company's websites in Spain, Mexico, and Argentina did not report any social activities, suggesting that marketing did not rely on the responsible process cue there.

This case illustrates that a very successful cause-related marketing campaign by a MNC is not necessarily replicated in multiple locations. The type and number of supported causes may vary according to a number of factors (e.g., cultural and economic, but also historical, reflecting the specific conditions of entry and expansion in foreign markets).

12.3.1 Other Initiatives Supporting Causes: Aldo, Fiat, and Procter & Gamble (Dawn, Pampers, and Purifier of Water)

Aldo[7]—A wholesale distributor and third-party sourcing provider of fashion footwear, handbags, and accessories, Group Aldo was created in 1972 by Aldo Bensadoun in Montreal (Canada). As a private company, financial information is not disclosed but in 2017, the company operated under two signature brands (Aldo and Call It Spring), and a multi-brand retail concept (GLOBO) with three thousand points of sale in more than one hundred countries around the world. From the start, Aldo wanted to create a different kind of company, one built on ethics and compassion, with strong values like love, respect, and integrity. His company has been committed to the fight against AIDS as far back as 1985, when few were willing to take a stand. One of the forefront initiatives is simply called "Aldo Fights AIDS" (see Figure 12.12 for the logos as they appear in the bilingual home country).

In 2014, this movement launched an important fundraising and awareness campaign called #FriendsFight. Three different partners were involved:

Figure 12.12 Featuring the bilingual logos (English/French) of Aldo's campaign against AIDS

Source: Courtesy of Aldo Group Inc.

520   Cause-Related Marketing

Waris Ahluwalia, VFILES, and the beneficiary of the campaign, Partners in Health. Ahluwalia is a New York-based designer, CEO of Waris Loves You and House of Waris. He collaborated on the design of a special collection of friendship bracelets. Each bracelet was sold for 5 USD with the tagline: "Buy it. Wear it. End it." VFILES is a digital fashion community created in 2013 that provides an online and in-person environment for users to socialize, be entertained, and shop. Together with Aldo, to help with diffusion, they created a series of web videos, each one featuring a couple of friends reminiscing about times they fought for each other. These videos are available on YouTube (e.g., with search words: "#BOSSMODE—VFILES + Aldo #FRIENDS-FIGHT"). Finally, Partners In Health is a Boston-based nonprofit health care organization founded in 1987. It received the totality of the bracelet sales to support its HIV/AIDS programs. Information about the amount donated with these bracelet sales is not available, but Partners In Health Canada lists Group Aldo as a contributor for 10,000 CAD or more in its 2015 fiscal year.

Overall, Aldo Group says it raised more than 10 million USD for international AIDS programs. Examples of other initiatives include both large international campaigns and participation in small local events. For instance, the company led an advertising campaign with YouthAIDS involving a number of celebrities, including famous singers, musicians, and actors such as Avril Lavigne, Joel and Benji Madden, Eva Mendes, Charlize Theron, and Michelle Yeoh, to name a few (see a YouTube video with search key words: "Aldo Fights AIDS Campaign Video 1"), and participated in "ÇA MARCHE," a seven-kilometer walk in Montreal organized by Foundation Farha. The company is also involved in an impressive number of activities related to other causes (e.g., breast cancer, children welfare, and supporting the arts).

Fiat—To illustrate the fact that companies also support causes other than health-related ones, we can look at the example of Lancia, a brand owned by FIAT. In 2008, for instance, it sponsored the 9th World Summit of Nobel Peace Laureates. A video (available on the Wall Street Journal website) shows the laureates from around the world arriving at the summit in Lancia luxury models and having their car doors opened for them, one after the other. After showing Lech Walesa (1983 laureate), Mikhaïl Gorbatchev (1990 laureate), and others, one door opens on an empty seat. A text then reads: "Aung San Suu Kyi 1991 laureate," followed by a picture of the Burmese politician (who—before becoming the equivalent of a prime minister—had been placed under house arrest in her home country for a total of fifteen years over a twenty-one-year period) and the two subsequent texts read: "Lancia supports the 9th World Summit of Nobel Peace Laureates," and "Lancia supports Aung San Suu Kyi. Free now."

This is a strong political statement coming from a company. Analyzed from a marketer's point of view, it likely targets a group of educated consumers sensitive to values like freedom of speech and opinion. Sponsoring an event related to Nobel Prizes also contributes to building an association between the brand and attributes of excellence and outstanding performance. Although the political stand taken by the company is bold, it bears limited risk, since opponents to Aung San Suu Kyi are unlikely to weight much in Lancia's or FIAT's markets.

Procter & Gamble[8]—Created in 1837 by William Procter and James Gamble, Procter and Gamble-P&G (US) has become one of the global giants in the FMCG industry. In 2016, it had net sales of 65.3 billion USD and a vast portfolio of about sixty-five brands, organized in five major segments: beauty (18 percent of net sales), grooming (11 percent), health care (11 percent), fabric and home care (32 percent), and baby, feminine, and family care (28 percent). Each of these segments carried several product categories and subcategories, such as, in the beauty segment: hair care with shampoo, conditioner, styling aids, and treatments (e.g., Head & Shoulders and Pantene); and skin and personal care with antiperspirant and deodorant, skin care, and personal cleansing (e.g., Olay, Old Spice and SK-II); in the grooming segment: shave care with female and male blades and razors, pre- and post-shave products, and appliances (e.g., Braun, Gillette, and Venus); in the health care segment: oral care with toothbrushes, toothpaste, and other oral care products (e.g., Oral-B and Crest); personal health care with, for instance, vitamins and minerals, and gastrointestinal, rapid diagnostic, and respiratory products (e.g., Vicks); in the fabric and home care segment: fabric care with enhancers, additives and detergents (e.g., Ariel, and Tide); home care with products for the air, dishes and surface care (e.g., Dawn, Febreze, and Mr. Clean); and in the last segment: baby care with wipes, diapers and pants (e.g., Pampers), pads for feminine care and adult incontinence (e.g., Always and Tampax); and family care with paper towels, tissues, and toilet paper (e.g., Bounty and Charmin). Table 12.2 provides more details about the company.

Like many large MNCs, the company has numerous activities related to CSR (see P&G's sustainability webpage). Its annual *Citizenship Report* details the company's actions for communities and for the environment. Illustrative of the efforts deployed by the company, three cases are described next: the Children's Safe Drinking Program and the P&G Purifier of Water packets (supported causes: health and the environment), the "Pampers 1 Pack = 1 Vaccine" campaign (supported cause: health), and finally, the "Dawn Saves Wildlife" campaign (supported cause: animal welfare and the environment).

First, the dish washing liquid soap Dawn—one of P&G's star products with more than 1 billion USD net sales in 2016—has developed a close association with wildlife protection over the past forty years. The story is an interesting one as, in an unusual turn of events, the cause selected the company (instead of the other way around).

Table 12.2 Profiling Procter & Gamble (US)

Who:	*P&G*
Since:	1837
What:	Consumer packaged goods
From:	US
Sales (Bn USD):	~65
Employing (people):	105,000
Manufacturing in (countries):	39
Selling in (countries):	180

Source: Procter & Gamble (2016)

Back in 1978, the International Bird Rescue Research Center (a US-based NPO dedicated to rehabilitating injured aquatic birds, notably seabirds affected by oil spills) obtained a small grant from oil company Chevron (US) to test all major dish soaps for cleaning birds. Dawn turned out to be the best soap. For the following ten years, the NPO regularly requested to be sponsored by P&G, in vain. Just one year after the company finally accepted (1988), a major spill occurred, the Exxon Valdez, which received massive media coverage. Subsequently, volunteers were shown on TV footage using Dawn soap and saving oil-covered birds from a certain death. The unlikely association between a dishwashing liquid and animals in distress took root.

Between 2002 and 2009, the company highlighted its connection with wildlife protection intermittently until it launched a full-fledged cause-related marketing campaign entitled: "Dawn Saves Wildlife" (see Figure 12.13).

This campaign was supported by a TV spot—realized with the help of Kaplan Thaler Group (US), part of the advertising and PR agency Publicis Group (France)—that showed a baby duck, penguin, and seal being washed with Dawn soap. The company donated 1 USD every time consumers bought a bottle of Dawn Ultra soap and visited a dedicated website to enter a code printed on the back of bottles. In addition to triggering the donation, having to enter a code on the website ensured that educational information was passed along to consumers about the environmental issues at stake. As a

Figure 12.13 Illustrating P&G's "Dawn Saves Wildlife" initiative
Source: Courtesy of Procter & Gamble

Cause-Related Marketing   523

result of this initiative and subsequent campaigns, more than one hundred thousand bottles of soap were facilitated to volunteers dedicated to bird rescue, and more than seventy-five thousand animals were saved from oil spills.

Nowadays, Dawn advertising campaigns still feature marine birds and animals and promote the powerful yet gentle cleaning properties of the product. The brand's YouTube channel "Dawn Dish Soap" features many of the TV commercials used (e.g., with search words: "Dawn Helps Save Wildlife—Home").

Second, P&G launched the "Pampers 1 pack = 1 vaccine" campaign (2006) in partnership with UNICEF (i.e., the United Nations International Children's Emergency Fund, an organization dedicated to defending the rights of children worldwide). Pampers is the worldwide leader in the disposable wipes and training pants industry. The brand alone generated 9 billion USD in 2016, which represented nearly 14 percent of the company's net sales that same year. The cause-related marketing campaign aimed to eliminate tetanus in newborns and mothers. For every marked pack of Pampers diapers and wipes purchased, the company donated about 0.05 USD to UNICEF and helped provide one tetanus vaccine. Examples of commercials are available on YouTube to see how the campaign was presented, mainly targeting mothers, in North America (search words: "1 Pack of Pampers = 1 Vaccine Commercial"), in Europe (search words: "Pampers '1 Pack = 1 Vaccine' Campaign: Happy Birthday Ad," and for comparison, in Pakistan (search words: "Pampers Unicef : 1 pack = 1 vaccine").

In 2012, the campaign had resulted in about 32 million USD in donations and more than 300 million vaccines distributed in seventeen of the world's poorest countries. The partnership between Pampers and UNICEF is credited with helping to eliminate tetanus in seven of the twenty-five countries that have eliminated the disease since 1999. The partnership also benefited UNICEF, as a quote from the organization's partnership profile suggests: "Pampers' marketing expertise has helped UNICEF to simplify a complicated development issue and to bring the issue to the consumer, as well as provide the consumer with opportunities to take action" (UNICEF, 2012, p. 4).

Finally, the case of P&G Purifier of Water packets (Figure 12.14) is interesting because it illustrates cause-related marketing and other forms of support for causes, as well as reverse innovation (Chapter 9). The story behind the product is that scientists working for the Fabric Care category were trying to understand how to reuse dirty laundry water when they discovered a formulation that could make dirty water drinkable. In the context of the Children's Safe Drinking Program launched in 2004, the technology for water purification (e.g., elimination of bacteria, viruses, and parasites, and removal of solid materials) was packaged and first released in African countries where the lack of drinkable water is a life-threatening situation. In only thirty minutes, each four-gram packet can clean 10 liters of water, effectively fulfilling the needs of a family of five for a day. Videos available on YouTube show how the technology works (e.g., with search words: "P&G Purifier of Water Demonstration").

Interestingly, the packets have found their way back into developed economies, thus making a good case of reverse innovation. Indeed, an adaptation

524 *Cause-Related Marketing*

Figure 12.14 Presenting P&G Purifier of Water packets
Source: Courtesy of Procter & Gamble

to the STP strategy led the company to target outdoor and leisure customers (e.g., campers, hikers, fishermen, and hunters) in rich countries. The packets are also sold for emergencies and natural disasters everywhere (e.g., as part of survival kits) and promoted on information websites like "Day One Response."

Among the various techniques employed to help and fund the Children's Safe Drinking Water program, as described on its webpage, we find:

- Cause-related marketing—Consumers from developed economies are invited to order the packets and test the technology as a "fun, family-friendly activity at home." Each purchase of four packets triggers a donation by the company of three months' worth of clean water to a child in a developing country. In 2010, a campaign was also launched stating that P&G would donate a day of safe drinking water to people in need each time consumers redeemed coupons for P&G products.

- Fundraising—Consumers can find a fundraiser toolkit including ideas and information on how to promote and run a fundraiser, as well as how to give a demonstration of the technology with the tagline: "Encourage your friends, family, and community to support the P&G CSDW Program."
- Direct donations—with a direct link to the donation form and the tagline: "It doesn't take a lot to make a big difference. Just 10 cents provides one P&G water purification packet that creates 10 liters of clean water. And: Just $1 gives a child clean water for 50 days. $7.50 gives a child clean water for a year. $30 gives a family clean water for a year."

Since 2004, the program has provided more than 10 billion liters of clean water across seventy-five countries, an equivalent donation of more than 50 million USD. The campaign aims at providing 200 million packets per year by 2020.

12.4 Issues at Stake

In order to consider the issues usually discussed in the literature on cause-related marketing, we now address the following questions:

- Do consumers really care about CSR in general, and supporting causes in particular?
- Which examples of corporate *faux pas* could explain why some customers have become cynical and lost trust in cause-related marketing? In all, is cause-related marketing trustworthy?
- What is the impact of cause-related marketing on regular marketing activities?
- What are the key-success factors of cause-related marketing (and other initiatives based on the responsible process cue)?
- Is cause-related marketing replicable in international markets?
- What are the benefits of cause-related marketing? And what are the downsides of this approach?

12.4.1 Relevance and Trustworthiness

Do consumers really care about CSR in general, and supporting causes in particular?[9] Research shows that consumers increasingly care about CSR and want to know whether companies act responsibly and ethically toward a multitude of stakeholders (e.g., Öberseder et al., 2014). At the same time, CSR is an abstract concept that is often not salient during the moment of purchasing decision-making. When choosing among products, CSR indeed becomes a peripheral criterion and is only influential if other criteria (e.g., price or quality expectations) are satisfied (Öberseder, Schlegelmilch, & Gruber, 2011). Even consumers who generally have a positive predisposition and care about ethical attributes, such as labor practices or environmental

526   *Cause-Related Marketing*

friendliness, might ignore these in the actual purchasing situation. They willfully ignore the ethical information to avoid potential negative emotions and feelings of dissonance in case the preferred product alternative does not correspond to their ethical values (Ehrich & Irwin, 2005). So, while consumers care about CSR, they do not necessarily act upon their values. This fact can reasonably cast some doubt about the relevance for companies in promoting their products based on the responsible process cue in general, and supporting causes more particularly.

On the one hand, cause-related marketing constitutes a potential remedy for consumers taking their values into account when purchasing. The distinctive feature of cause-related marketing is indeed that it is "linked to customers' engaging in revenue-producing transactions with firms (exchange of goods and services for money)" (Varadarajan & Menon, 1988, p. 60). Thus, it truly is a joint effort of both firms and consumers, for whom the purchase of the product might in turn lead to feelings of warm glow because they did something good (Andrews, Xueming, Fang, & Aspara, 2014). Beyond generating positive feelings, tying products to a cause can even affect product evaluations. For instance, Chernev and Blair (2015) found that product perceptions were altered in the case of socially responsible companies: wine of a responsible company tasted better, according to consumer perceptions.

On the other hand, the fact that the practice is dependent on consumers' monetary contribution also triggered some criticism, which denounces CRM as a low-involvement CSR tool that distracts from creating real social value (Porter & Kramer, 2002) and crowds out philanthropy (Krishna, 2011). Finally, it is important to note that a product whose purchase will contribute to a particular cause is not automatically a "responsible product" (Grolleau, Ibanez, & Lavoie, 2016). (Apple) RED, for example, is a cause-related marketing campaign involving (RED) and Apple in which up to 50 percent of the purchasing price of a designated Apple product, such as the iPod touch, goes to the fight against HIV and AIDS ((Red), 2017). At the same time, a recent article of the World Economic Forum points out the horrendous working conditions of miners, often children, in the Democratic Republic of Congo (World Economic Forum, 2017). It is in these mines that the raw material for various technological products, including the iPod touch, are being sourced. Raising this paradox is important because it can further reinforce suspicion about the trustworthiness (among consumers) and the relevance (among companies) of cause-related marketing.

Which examples of corporate faux pas could explain why some customers have become cynical and lost trust in cause-related marketing?[10] Over the recent years, various mistakes, scandals, and critical analyses have led to skepticism about CRM (e.g., Einstein, 2012; King, 2006; Pallotta, 2008). Generally, we can identify five types of wrongdoings that can weaken customers' interest, attitude, and trust in CRM programs and their supporting partners: 1) lack of fit between cause and company, 2) lack of perceived honesty, 3) poor execution, 4) confusing messages and

Cause-Related Marketing   527

positioning, and 5) questionable use of revenues. They are each illustrated with examples:

- As further discussed in the next subsection, a lack of fit between the company and its supported cause has been observed on multiple occasions. For instance, Kentucky Fried Chicken (KFC) and the Susan G. Komen Foundation were heavily criticized in the US after the development of the "Buckets for the Cure" program in 2010, which aimed at donating 0.50 USD per large bucket of chicken to the famous breast cancer foundation (Medscape, 2010). Critics highlighted the poor nutritional value of KFC chicken and the high levels of PhIP, a by-product of the grilling process listed as a potential carcinogen by several health agencies (Think Before You Pink, 2010; US Department of Health and Human Services, 2011). Another wave of criticism came a year after when KFC offered to donate one USD per half-gallon of full-of-sugar soda to the Juvenile Diabetes Research Fund (Food Politics, 2011).
- A lack of perceived honesty in a company's motives in undertaking CRM has also backfired against several companies. For instance, Microsoft and search engine Bing offered to donate 1 USD for every retweet of their #SupportJapan tweet, for a maximum of 100,000 USD, after the 2011 tsunami. Because the tweet contained a link to Bing's website, many people complained that this was just a plain opportunistic move by the company (AdWeek, 2011). Walmart was also criticized for launching an initiative in Ohio (US) to sponsor a food drive during Thanksgiving 2013 to help people in need. The problem was that many of those who actually benefited from this initiative were also Walmart employees, and questions regarding low wages at Walmart were consequently raised by the media (The Plain Dealer, 2013).
- Poor execution is another issue that has limited the success of otherwise-benevolent CRM programs. The example of Starbucks' #RaceTogether campaign after the unfortunate shooting of a black male in Missouri (US) in 2015 illustrates this point well. With this campaign, Starbucks wanted to initiate conversations on racial issues between baristas and customers. However, many customers strongly disliked the company's approach and preferred to order their early morning coffee in silence, instead of engaging in debates about such a sensitive issue (Fast Company, 2015). Additionally, plain bad taste in CRM execution can heat up debate. For instance, the Guns and Gold Pawn Shop (New Mexico, US) organized a Coyote Kill Contest in 2013, for which half of the proceeds were to go to the Children's Outdoor Adventure Association. Around seventy people went out hunting, while protestors called this contest an unsuitable "blood sport" (Non-Profit Quarterly, 2013).
- Confusing messages and positioning in CRM initiatives have received their share of criticism. For instance, doubt was cast upon Unilever's honesty and integrity in 2007 due to the confusion created by its simultaneous support of the Dove Self-Esteem Fund—seeking to help women

528 *Cause-Related Marketing*

accept the beauty of their natural body—and the Axe male deodorant's depiction of ideal women in their commercials as skinny, busty, and particularly stupid (AdvertisingAge, 2007).

- Finally, a questionable use of generated revenues has been at the center of suspicion toward CRM activities. Back in 1999, the state of Georgia in the US forced Yoplait, the yogurt brand jointly owned by General Mills (US) and Sodiaal (France), to make an additional contribution to the Breast Cancer Research Foundation. Yoplait had initially capped its contribution to 100,000 USD after advertising that it would donate fifty cents for every foil lid customers sent to the company. With customers sending in more than 8 million lids, it should have donated more than 4 million ISD (The National Law Review, 2015). In recent years, critics have questioned the scope of McDonald's philanthropic activities. For instance, the company offered a meager 0.8 percent of its annual 5.5 billion USD net income in 2012 to charities, and only donated on average 20 percent of the Ronald McDonald House Charities (RMHC) revenues, despite receiving significant publicity for its name (Huffington Post, 2013). In this way, McDonald's customers contributed 1.5 times more than the company itself to RMHC, by donating 50 million versus 34 million USD by the company (Huffington Post, 2013).

Avoiding these rather common traps is essential and for this, a CRM program must: be sincere, reveal a strong fit between the company and the cause or nonprofit organization supported, be carefully planned and well executed, and must be supported by clear and unambiguous communication.

In all, is cause-related marketing trustworthy? Berglind and Nakata (2005, p. 444) provide a good summary of important questions to raise: "Is the CRM program a diversionary tactic, hiding a product problem through a public relations spin? Is the amount donated to the cause disproportionately small relative to the sales generated for the product? And, most of all, is the CRM campaign a clever manipulation to enrich a corporation's coffers (generating a buck), or is it a sincere way of assisting a charity (creating a bang or social impact)?" Obviously, answering these questions is not straightforward. It will depend greatly on the company under scrutiny. In this context, a possible answer to the question of trustworthiness is: "It depends who implements it." Precedent also has a role to play, as companies undertaking cause-related marketing initiatives or other types of social initiatives for decades raise less suspicion in regard to their possible opportunism.

12.4.2 Impact on Marketing Activities and Feasibility

What is the impact of cause-related marketing on regular marketing activities? While other practices studied in this book have major impacts on most if not all strategic and tactical decisions, cause-related marketing has no obvious influence on market selection, entry modes, or distribution.

Cause-Related Marketing 529

As for the *STP process*, companies are unlikely going to reconsider their overall targeting and positioning strategies when relying on the responsible process cue, but they can certainly adjust their selection of causes to the targeted customer segments, in particular MNCs tapping into a large pool of different segments (e.g., Unilever and Procter & Gamble).

Next, *product and price policies* are affected to some extent, since companies need to decide if they tie their offerings to a cause with their regular products, modified products, or new products, and for which price (markup, proportion of sales that will be directed to the cause, and maximum amount donated). Fjällräven and Subaru, for instance, are examples of companies relying on the responsible process cue with no modifications whatsoever to their regular products. In turn, Coca-Cola's Arctic Home campaign offers an example of "modified" product policy with the development of different conditioning and packaging for the cans (unlike regular cans, they featured the company's logo in red, set against an all-white background and a drawing of three polar bears) (The Telegraph, 2011). Finally, some companies decide to develop an entirely new product for the cause, in line with their regular product lines. For instance, Aldo's friendship bracelets, described previously, fit well with their regular line of fashion accessories. In 2009, Samsung (South Korea) launched its Reclaim phone, an eco-conscious smartphone that is 80 percent recyclable, with a green casing mostly made of corn-based bio-plastics and with fully recyclable packaging (Inhabitat, 2009). Any purchase between August and December in 2009 in the US from service partner Sprint with a two-year plan (for ~50 USD) led Samsung to donate 2 USD to the Nature Conservancy (for a minimum of 250,000 USD and up to 500,000 USD which the campaign achieved) (Cause-Related Marketing Blogspot, 2010a). Others even design virtual products, such as Marriot (US) with the 'Make a Bed' campaign. Consumers could make virtual beds online using Marriot Towne Place's Facebook page, and for each bed made, the hospitality company gave 2 USD to the American Red Cross Disaster Relief (up to 50,000 USD), who then used the money to provide comfort kits to people in need (Cause-Related Marketing Blogspot, 2010c).

Finally, the adoption of cause-related marketing mostly affects *promotion and communication policies*. As shown in Section 12.3, examples reveal a wide range of practices, often conveyed through three types of media channels: traditional press and TV advertising (e.g., Aldo and Coca-Cola Company), public relations tools (e.g., websites and blogs with the publication of newsletters and press releases, like IKEA does), and social media (e.g., Facebook and YouTube corporate accounts, like Marriot and Subaru do). Even digital tools like SMS can be employed. For instance, Snickers, a brand owned by US food manufacturer Mars, launched a campaign to support Feeding America. The selected cause (hunger relief) fit quite well with the famous snack bar (positioned with the motto "Handles your hunger"). Inside Snickers's wrappers, consumers could find a code to text to a dedicated phone number or to enter directly on the brand's website. While the company had already committed to

530   *Cause-Related Marketing*

donate the cost of 2.5 million meals to Feeding America—a gesture that certainly conveys goodwill and lowers risks of criticism—every time someone entered the code, it donated the cost of one additional meal, up to 1 million extra meals, which represented about 500,000 USD (Cause-Related Marketing Blogspot, 2010b). Amid the variety of possibilities to use the responsible process cue, marketers need to pay special attention to the type of message the company sends when supporting a cause, the type of media channels (and combination thereof) used, and how the campaign fits in the overall communication and promotion plan.

What are the key-success factors of cause-related marketing (and other initiatives based on the responsible process cue)? In a nutshell, the KSF for a successful implementation of the approach are: ability to select the right cause, creativity in the design of campaigns, careful execution of campaigns, as well as integration of campaigns in the overall CSR strategy of the company.

Selecting the right type of cause (animal welfare, environmental preservation, fight against diseases, etc.)—one that fits with the company's mission and offerings, as well as with preferences of targeted customer segments—is central. Surveying two thousand Americans representative of the overall adult population and covering seventeen causes (e.g., childhood obesity, domestic violence, gay marriage, and global warming), a study conducted by the Center for Social Impact Communication at Georgetown University (US) and Ogilvy Public Relations Worldwide showed interesting differences in the way gender, ethnicity, and generation affect preferences for certain causes. For instance, findings revealed that women were more supportive of the "feeding the hungry" cause than men (43 percent and 34 percent, respectively). In turn, African Americans and Hispanics were much more supportive of the fight against HIV/AIDS than were Caucasians (24 percent, 21 percent, and 9 percent, respectively), and were significantly more likely to believe that they could contribute to a cause through social media (58 percent and 51 percent, respectively, vs. 34 percent of Caucasians). Finally, Generation Y (people born between 1982 and 1993) were quite a bit less involved in the "feeding the hungry" cause than were Generation X (1966–1981), Baby Boomers (1951–1965), and the Silent Generation (born before 1951), with 30 percent, 37 percent, 42 percent, and 42 percent, respectively, of representatives of each generation very or somewhat involved with the cause. In turn, people from the Silent Generation were more involved in "Supporting our troops" than were those from Generation Y (47 percent vs. 31 percent) (CSIC, 2011). In all, marketers must realize the existence of these differences across segments in order to select the right cause for their target customers. A good fit between company and cause is central to success (e.g., La Ferle et al., 2013).

In addition, companies should also consider the scope (or reach) of the cause (i.e., local, regional, national, or international) to better reflect what they stand for and what their audiences care for. In their early paper entitled "Tactical Considerations for the Effective Use of Cause-Related Marketing," Ross, Stutts, and Patterson (1990) find that consumers were more likely to support local or regional causes as opposed to national or international causes. This result was contradicted by La Ferle et al. (2013), who find—in

Cause-Related Marketing 531

one of the few cross-market data collections available—that the scope of the cause (a local versus worldwide charity) did not impact attitudes toward cause-related campaigns for either US or Indian consumers. However, they also investigated the effect of the company origin (national versus international) and found that Indian consumers were more favorable to campaigns when the company was Indian as opposed to a MNC. In the broader context of CSR communications, Becker-Olsen, Taylor, Hill, and Yalcinkaya (2011) find that they were most effective when MNCs partnered with local NPOs in the context of global initiatives. Although more research is needed to have a clearer picture of the effect of the scope, companies should pay attention to this factor in designing their campaigns.

Furthermore, the apparent solution adopted by Subaru and others (like Amazon Smile, for instance) to give customers a choice of causes and let them decide which one they support is not without hurdles. For instance, Robinson, Irmak, and Jayachandran (2012) find that allowing consumers to select the cause was generally a good idea (since it drove willingness-to-pay and purchase intentions), but that certain conditions in terms of culture and fit affected the approach. Indeed, this strategy was particularly efficient in the context of a high degree of collectivism and a low perceived fit between company and causes. Certain conditions (e.g., when consumers learn that the charities are far from accomplishing their intended goals) even decreased purchase intentions. Therefore, the option to let customers decide which cause they support is not a miracle recipe and needs, like any decision, careful consideration.

Finally, companies must decide whether to engage in only one type of social initiative (e.g., cause-related marketing, sponsorship, or philanthropy) or in multiple types all at once. Size and resources could be influencing factors here, as large MNCs (e.g., Coca-Cola, IKEA, and Procter & Gamble) tend to tackle several social issues using a variety of initiatives, whereas smaller companies (e.g., Fjällräven and Aldo) concentrate their efforts on one cause and a limited number of initiatives (relative to MNCs). Companies have had success with both strategies. One challenge when undertaking simultaneous initiatives though is to avoid confusion and dilution of the impact in the eye of consumers. Engaging the appropriate amount of resources for clear communication is then of the essence.

Moving on to a second type of KSF, creativity in the design of campaigns relying on the responsible process cue in general, and on causes in particular, has become more and more crucial. With the increasing popularity of the approach, customers can easily become unimpressed. To differentiate themselves from the multitude of other companies supporting causes (and often the same cause, through the same NPO), companies must develop imaginative (e.g., Coke's Smile-izer) and powerful (e.g., Aldo's friendship bracelet) campaigns. Companies also need to manage the life cycle (see Chapter 9) of the approach, especially when active in international markets with different levels of maturity in the advertising industry (Cf. (La Ferle et al., 2013)

Clarity is another key-success factor. Companies want to minimize any ambiguity that could arise from supporting a cause and publicizing this support. The contrary inevitably leads to damaging backlash, as illustrated in

532 Cause-Related Marketing

Section 12.4.1. Honesty, transparency, and authenticity are, thus, often cited in the literature as essential in building credible campaigns. For instance, Wicki and van der Kaaij (2007) talk about an "authenticity gap" when companies project an identity that suggests a higher level of corporate citizenship compared to their actual identity. Overtime, communications will only increase consumers' perception of this authenticity gap. This is an important risk to keep in mind, since consumers continue to gain more and more power to manifest their resentment against companies who "betray" them, in particular thanks to social media and mobile technology (see Chapter 10). Finding the right donation frame (e.g., in-kind vs. percentage of sales) is also important to reduce consumers' perceptions that companies have self-centered motives. For instance, Vlachos, Koritos, Krepapa, Tasoulis, and Theodorakis (2016) find that in-kind donations better contained consumers' skepticism. This is best illustrated by the example of Snickers, detailed previously, which guaranteed 2.5 million meals to Feeding America as part of their agreement for a joint campaign (Cause-Related Marketing Blogspot, 2010b).

Overall, a carefully planned execution, and the integration of any initiative into the overall CSR strategy of companies, have been proven necessary for cause-related marketing campaigns to be successful.

Finally, companies must make significant contributions to the causes they support to avoid backlash and to convince the public that these campaigns are more about making a "bang" for causes than a "buck"—in reference to Berglind and Nakata's (2005) article entitled "Cause-Related Marketing: More Buck Than Bang?" This seems obvious, and yet, among the examples provided in this chapter, some companies put a 500,000 USD cap on their donations triggered by customers' purchases, while others had a 50,000 USD threshold. In the latter case, doubt can easily be cast on the motives of companies, especially since they can gross millions of dollars thanks to consumers' goodwill. In addition, companies must avoid confusion in the way they communicate about donation amounts. For instance, Olsen, Pracejus, and Brown (2003) find that consumers could overestimate the amount donated as a result of their purchase, depending on whether this amount was expressed as a percentage of the sale price or as a percentage of profits, the latter of which would result in a much lower donation amount. In this case, the risk of being accused of making a ridiculously small contribution to the cause in comparison to the sales grossed (and thus making a "buck" for themselves) is real, as later detailed in the next section about possible negative outcomes.

Is cause-related marketing replicable in international markets? An interesting question for companies engaged in cause-related marketing is whether they can use the same causes and replicate the same campaigns across markets (since standardization is known to reduce costs, as discussed in Chapter 3). Unfortunately, studies aiming to answer this question are rare, to say the least. As of December 2017, a search on ABI/Inform Collection (ProQuest) resulted in only five peer-reviewed articles with an international lens, and none of these directly addressed the question. We can then try to extrapolate from studies investigating the question in the broader context of CSR to wonder about the internationalization of cause-related marketing (see "Food for Thought").

Cause-Related Marketing   533

Food for Thought 12.3

- Extrapolating from La Ferle et al. (2013), is cause-related marketing easily replicated across international markets? What could enhance or inhibit the internationalization of this approach?

The few studies that look at cause-related marketing from an international perspective indicate that the CAGE distance/proximity (see Chapter 4) could well determine the possibility of adopting the approach and replicating campaigns across markets. In particular, administrative, cultural, and economic factors were found to explain consumers' attitude differentials. For instance, La Ferle et al. (2013) compare reactions to campaigns in the US and India. They found that Indian respondents attributed higher levels of altruistic motives to companies engaging in cause-related marketing and had more positive attitudes toward the approach than did their American counterparts. They explained this observation with the fact that lower levels of economic development and maturity of the advertising industry in India made cause-related marketing seem more novel and original. They then turned toward India's political environment to explain the lack of maturity in marketing and advertising practices. Until the 1990s, this environment indeed favored market protection from foreign competition, the dominance of state-owned corporations in many industries, and high taxes on advertising. In these conditions, the stage of the life cycle in which cause-related marketing is situated—as an innovative practice—is still "development" or "honeymoon," an easier context than in more mature markets. In turn, Robinson et al. (2012) find that certain cultural traits (collectivism versus individualism) affected consumers reactions in cause-related marketing campaigns.

Considering these interesting but limited empirical findings, we can turn toward other types of initiatives to infer the existence of important differences across markets. International variations in sponsorship, for instance, are better documented. For example, the IEG's annual year-end industry review and forecast reveals that company spending for sponsorship varies greatly by region, as illustrated in Table 12.3. North America is by far the region where causes receive more money through sponsorship, followed—to a lesser extent—by Europe and Asia-Pacific. For instance, ~37 percent of the overall amount spent with sponsorship in 2016 was in North America, ~27 percent in Europe, and ~25 percent in Asia-Pacific (IEG, 2017). In comparison, amounts spent in the rest of the world appear almost negligible (~11 percent).

We can also look at studies investigating CSR in an international context. For instance, Becker-Olsen et al. (2011) compare CSR marketing communications in Mexico and the US and their effect on attitudes toward the firm and purchase intentions. They found that MNCs emphasizing global

534   Cause-Related Marketing

Table 12.3 Comparing sponsorship spending in different regions of the world

GLOBAL SPONSORSHIP SPENDING BY REGION

	2015 Spending (Bn USD)	2016 Spending (Bn USD)	Increase from 2015 (%)	2017 Projected Spending (Bn USD)	Projected Increase from 2016 (%)
Asia Pacific	14	14.8	5.7	15.7	5.8
Central/South America	4.3	4.4	3.5	4.5	3.4
Europe	15.3	16	4.6	16.7	4.5
North America	21.4	22.3	4.2	23.2	4.1
All Other Countries	2.5	2.6	3.4	2.7	3.3

Source: Adapted from IEG (2017)

(as opposed to local) CSR efforts benefited from more-positive perceptions, but that local tastes and experiences should shape tactical decisions in the implementation of programs. Similar to La Ferle et al. (2013), they also find that consumers from the country with lower levels of economic development were less suspicious of companies communicating on CSR activities.

Taking the above as a mere indication, and in the absence of sufficient data on international cause-related marketing, we can tentatively answer that replicating the approach across markets seems possible but certainly requires a high degree of adaptation to local CAGE particularities. Future research should tackle the internationalization issue in order to better guide companies interested in adopting the approach across markets.

12.4.3 Outcomes

We can now conclude our analysis of important issues at stake with cause-related marketing by questioning the actual outcomes of the approach, thereby summarizing and complementing several positive and negative consequences seen throughout the chapter.

What are the benefits of cause-related marketing? In general, cause-related marketing represents a strong source of value creation for companies and the causes they support (Austin & Seitanidi, 2012). The perspectives of the three main stakeholders are taken in turn.

For *companies*, benefits are both external (e.g., increased revenues, enhanced brand recognition and corporate reputation, as well as improved customer goodwill and loyalty) and internal (e.g., higher employee morale and better employee retention) (Berglind & Nakata, 2005; Andrews et al., 2014). Westberg and Pope (2014) even show that it was more effective than other approaches, like sales promotion and sponsorship, in building brand equity.

Cause-Related Marketing 535

For *NPOs* and the causes they promote, benefits include increased funding, extended exposure, and enhanced visibility, as well as access to nonfinancial resources (such as expertise in marketing and management from successful MNCs) (Berglind & Nakata, 2005). Allying a cause with a familiar brand also improves the attitude toward the cause, in particular when the cause is unfamiliar (Lafferty & Goldsmith, 2005).

Finally, *consumers* benefit from cause-related marketing because they are given the opportunity to "do good" through their everyday consumption habits. This, in turn, makes them feel good about themselves. Andreoni (1990) proposes the theory of "warm-glow giving" to explain that people get a positive feeling from contributing and doing good (e.g., helping others), which can be considered in economic terms as a "utility." The theory has then been used in a number of articles to explain the drive that consumers have to purchase products tied to a cause (e.g., Andrews et al., 2014).

What are the downsides of this approach? Although cause-related marketing seems to be a win-win-win strategy for companies, NPOs, and consumers, a number of possible negative outcomes also transpired throughout this chapter.

From the perspective of companies, Varadarajan and Menon (1988, p. 69) note that firms walked "a fine line between reaping increased sales, goodwill, and positive publicity and incurring negative publicity and charges of exploitation of causes." This comment is still valid today and the examples of faux pas highlighted in Section 12.4.1 indicate that the lack of perceived honesty, poor execution of campaigns (including confusing messages and positioning), as well as questionable use of revenues, can have serious public backlash against companies.

Beyond the resulting damage made to brand equity, the resources and the time needed to address complaints are not negligible. Since legal action can be taken against companies, finding out and complying with local regulations can be quite time consuming, as the rules governing cause-related campaigns are far from being homogenized within and across nations. In the US, for instance, states have various requirements for alliances between companies and NPOs, in terms of: 1) registration and reporting (some states compel registering with the state which requires filing an annual report with the Attorney General or the department or agency in charge of consumer protection); 2) contract (some states require the establishment of a written contract between the state, the company and the charity); and 3) reporting and accounting (e.g., documenting money transfers at the end of the sales promotion and retaining records for a number of years) (The National Law Review, 2015). In all, cause-related marketing is not without bearing risks nor demanding efforts from companies.

A final downside for companies to take into consideration is the erosion over time of cause-related marketing efficiency. As La Ferle et al. (2013, p. 369) note: "Once consumers become more familiar with the technique, diminishing marginal returns may occur. [. . .] as a greater number of corporations associate with causes, the resulting clutter makes it harder for firms to stand out." Contrary to other marketing practices seen in previous chapters (e.g.,

536 Cause-Related Marketing

origin-based marketing, which gains authenticity as time passes, or mobile marketing, which is unlikely to be a fad due to the general evolution of technology integration into our lives), cause-related marketing could be a short-lived approach. Marketers must take this into account when choosing this type of approach over other types also relying on the responsible process cue.

For NPOs and causes, the downside of cause-related marketing is by far more preoccupying than for the other stakeholders, since perverse effects on donations have been suspected (hence jeopardizing the chances of long-term survival of these organizations). Indeed, having the feeling that they have already made a contribution with the purchase of products associated to causes, people could stop giving directly to charities (Berglind & Nakata, 2005). A risk of discharging consumers from the responsibility of contributing and desensitizing them is then present.

Furthermore, some cause-related marketing campaigns feature "non-responsible" products (see Section 12.4.1), as well as what Grolleau et al. (2016) call "products with negative externalities." These authors give the examples of campaigns encouraging the purchase of plastic water bottles (e.g., the 'Drink 1, Give 10' campaign of Volvic—a brand owned by Danone (France)—in partnership with UNICEF) rather than drinking tap water, the purchase of small plastic containers of yogurt rather than larger ones (e.g., Yoplait's "Save Lids to Save Lives" campaign, presented previously), as well as other campaigns encouraging the purchase of unhealthy products (e.g., fatty food, cigarettes, alcohol, etc.). They conclude that "initiatives by firms to connect socially-responsible projects to their products may have negative side-effects in some circumstances when the product is characterized by a socially irresponsible feature: the positive effect of the donation can be negated through an increase in consumption of the entire product category leading to environmental degradation (for example) and through a reduction in global donations. The crowding-out effect may apply to the overall budget devoted to various causes and an increase in donation to a cause can imply a disproportionate decrease in donations for other causes. In addition, the crowding-out effect may be particularly strong if cause-related products are directed at consumers who were previously offering direct donations" (Grolleau et al., 2016, p. 4329). These are serious negative outcomes that can possibly arise from CRM initiatives.

Finally, negative impacts for consumers have not been widely reported in the literature beyond feelings of confusion in regard to the amount of donations made by companies (Olsen et al., 2003; Grolleau et al., 2016). It is, however, reasonable to assume that these feelings, added to the disappointment and anger directed toward companies suspected of exploiting causes to their own benefit, is a cause of discomfort at a minimum and possibly a cause of psychological distress in worst-case scenarios. These situations can obviously cancel out the warm glow that consumers initially seek, and discourage them from participating in cause-related marketing efforts in the future.

After overseeing the various positive and negative outcomes of cause-related marketing, we can now reflect on the relevance of the approach (and more generally, of CSR-based initiatives) in helping firms face the challenges brought by globalization (see "Food for Thought").

Food for Thought 12.4

- Overall, do you think that relying on the 'responsible process' cue in general and on causes in particular help companies better face globalization?

Conclusion: Relying on The "Responsible Process" Cue (through Cause-Related Marketing and Other CSR-Based Approaches) Can Help Companies Increase Their Competitiveness and Possibly Bridge Cultural and Psychic Distances. Yet, It Requires Extreme Caution

What would a nomological network for cause-related marketing look like? A *nomological network* has been defined as the representation of the constructs of interest in a study, their observable manifestations and the interrelationships among and between them (Cronbach & Meehl, 1955). Figure 12.15 aims to encapsulate important variables in relation to the adoption of cause-related marketing by companies.

In addition to offering a visual summary of the issues at stake tackled in Section 12.4 (i.e., relevance of the approach and key success factors from the perspective of companies, trustworthiness from the perspective of consumers, and outcomes from the perspective of the three main stakeholders), the figure highlights several motivations and barriers to the adoption of cause-related marketing. First, we borrow Dunning's terminology (see Chapter 3) to situate the approach as motivated by market-seeking opportunities and strategic-asset seeking opportunities (in particular, an enhanced reputation). Second, we argue that in an international perspective, distance is likely to act as a barrier (in particular the administrative, cultural and economic dimensions) but also as a motivator. Indeed, countries can be perceived as vastly different (see Chapter 4 on psychic distance) and cultures can be deeply different (see Chapter 5 on cultural distance), relying on causes is a clever way to work around these differences (instead of trying to minimize them or only target similar consumer segments across markets). Many of the causes that companies support are universal (fight against hunger and diseases, safety of water, the protection of children, animal welfare, etc.) and touch people's lives wherever they are and regardless of their cultural identities. Of course, some causes are likely to resonate more than others (and it is important to find the right fit and scope/reach) but, overall, the process of resorting to causes and the responsible process cue—while working on commonalities instead of differences—seems like a winning strategy to bypass psychic and cultural distance issues.

So, should companies rely on a cause (or causes) to better differentiate themselves from competition and attract customers? The short answer to this question could be: "Yes, but with extreme caution and within a certain timeframe."

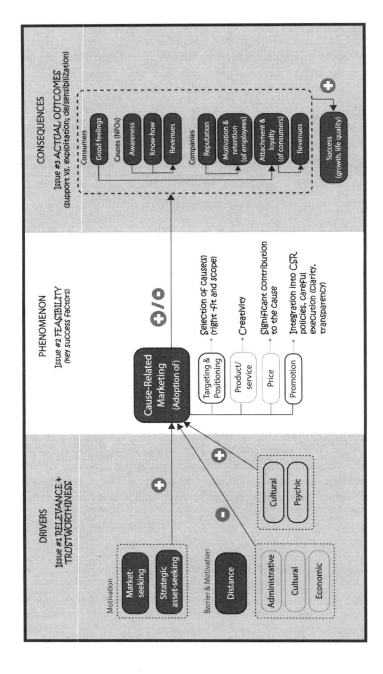

Figure 12.15 Proposing a nomological network for cause-related marketing

Source: Own elaboration

Cause-Related Marketing 539

An increase in competitive rivalry is a direct consequence of globalization (see Chapter 1). Companies with both local and international ambitions face this challenge. The intention to differentiate a firm's products or services from those of competitors is recognized as an underlying driver of CSR leadership (Kotler & Lee, 2004; Lindgreen, Xu, Maon, & Wilcock, 2012). Thus, adopting cause-related marketing can be seen as an adequate response from companies seeking to attract more consumers (and gain market share over competitors). However, its implementation bears a number of risks and pitfalls. To avoid potential backlash, companies must be extra careful when designing and implementing campaigns. Paying attention to selecting the right causes and avoiding all ambiguity in regard to motives are key success factors but they are not sufficient over time. Since the "playing field" has become increasingly crowded with companies engaging in all sorts of CSR-based initiatives, being creative is particularly important, at least in developed economies. On a global scale, there is room to take advantage of the approach's life-cycle, still in an emergent state in less-developed economies (where needs for social initiatives are even greater).

Overall, current research does not allow us to anticipate whether CRM will be an enduring or a short-lived approach among all CSR-based initiatives. The responsible process cue, however, is likely to stay prominent in corporate communications for the foreseeable future. Indeed, the use of cues by companies to keep on differentiating themselves from competition seems to follow a cumulative logic. Schematically, companies seek to compete with an emphasis on multiple cues: price (peak in the 1960s) AND quality (peak in the 1970s-80s) AND brand (peak in the 1990s) AND origin (peak in the 1990s-2000s) AND responsibility (peak in the 2010s). Good corporate citizenship is likely to remain central until it becomes so standard that a new cue is needed in order to stand out. For now, relying on the responsible process cue (through cause-related marketing and other CSR-based approaches) is a tool that companies can use to **increase their competitiveness and possibly bridge cultural and psychic distances in international markets.** Relying on causes (with impeccable ethics) may indeed allow companies to address differences in social background, religion, language or familiarity with foreign offerings in a different manner. People across the world believe in the importance of protecting children, drinking safe water, etc. To varying degrees, they rally around universal causes.

Notes

1 In Section 12.1.2, the paragraph entitled "How can we define business ethics and how different is it from corporate social responsibility (CSR)?" has been written in collaboration with Jonathan Deschênes, Associate Professor in Marketing (HEC Montréal, Canada), whose research interests include nonprofit marketing, donor studies, responsible marketing, and responsible consumer behavior.
2 In Section 12.1.2, the paragraph entitled "What is CSR precisely?" has been written in collaboration with Verena Gruber, Assistant Professor in Marketing (HEC Montréal, Canada), whose research interests include sustainability, sustainable consumption behavior, and corporate social responsibility.

540　Cause-Related Marketing

3 Throughout the chapter, the example of the Coca-Cola Company incorporates the work by M.Sc. students Denise Kolassa, Andriana Hnatykiw, Suvi Ojala, Bailey Wells, and Lana Zamour in the context of their 2014 term paper for the "Marketing & Globalization" course, developed and taught by the author of this book at HEC Montreal (Canada) and relies on: Adweek (2010); CRM Blog (2010); The Coca-Cola Company (2011, 2013, 2016a, 2016b, 2016c, 2017).

4 The example of Fjällräven incorporates the work by M.Sc. students Kenza Ben Driss, Theo Boye, and Paul-Antoine Sagot in the context of their 2017 term paper for the "Marketing & Globalization" course, developed and taught by the author of this book at HEC Montreal (Canada). References supporting this example are: Fjällräven (2017, n.d.).

5 IKEA example in this chapter relies on: IKEA (n.d.); UNICEF (2005, 2017).

6 The example of Subaru is based on: Subaru (2017a, 2017b, 2017c).

7 Aldo example relies on information provided by Aldo's Public Relations and Communication department (2015) and Aldo Group Inc. (2017a) Aldo Group Inc. (2017b); AldoFightsAids (n.d.); News Wire (2014) Partners in Health Canada (2017) CBC News (2015).

8 The example of Procter & Gamble incorporates the work by M.Sc. students Gabriel Bouffard and Saeed Khosravi in the context of their 2017 term paper for the "Marketing & Globalization" course, developed and taught by the author of this book at HEC Montreal (Canada). It relies on the following sources: New York Times (2009); Procter & Gamble—Children's Safe Drinking Water Program (2017); Procter & Gamble (2016, 2017a, 2017b); UNICEF (2012).

9 In Section 12.4.1, the paragraph entitled "Do consumers really care about CSR in general?" has been written in collaboration with Verena Gruber, Assistant Professor in Marketing (HEC Montréal, Canada), whose research interests include sustainability, sustainable consumption behavior, and corporate social responsibility.

10 In Section 12.4.1., the paragraph entitled "Which examples of corporate faux pas could explain why some customers became cynical and lost trust in cause-related marketing?" has been written in collaboration with Jonathan Deschênes, Associate Professor in Marketing (HEC Montréal, Canada).

References

(Red) (2017). Our Partners: Apple. Retrieved October 2017, from https://red.org/our-partners/

AdvertisingAge (2007, November 26th). Dove Viral Draws Heat From Critics, *By Jack Neff*. Retrieved from http://adage.com/article/news/dove-viral-draws-heat-critics/122185/

Adweek (2010, August 3rd). Coke, WNBA Team Up, *By Rebecca Cullers*. Retrieved from www.adweek.com/brand-marketing/coke-wnba-team-102965/

AdWeek (2011, March 14th). Bing Tries to Help Japan on Twitter, Walks Into a PR Nightmare, *By Anne McGraw*. Retrieved from www.adweek.com/digital/bing-tries-to-help-japan-on-twitter-walks-into-a-pr-nightmare/

Air Canada (2017). Air Canada Foundation Programs and Initiatives. Retrieved December 2017, from www.aircanada.com/en/about/community/foundation/programs.html

Aldo Group Inc. (2017a). Leaders. Retrieved June 2017, from www.aldogroup.com/leaders.html

Aldo Group Inc. (2017b). Corporate Statement. Retrieved November 2017, from www.aldogroup.com/corporate-statement.html

AldoFightsAids (n.d.). #friendsfight. Retrieved November 2017, from www.aldofightsaids.com/#friendsfight

American Marketing Association (2013). Definition of Marketing. Retrieved October 2014, from www.ama.org/AboutAMA/Pages/Definition-of-Marketing.aspx

Andreoni, James (1990). Impure Altruism and Donations to Public Goods: A Theory of Warm-Glow Giving. *The Economic Journal*, *100*(401), 464–477.

Andrews, Michelle, Xueming, Luo, Fang, Zheng & Aspara, Jaakko (2014). Cause Marketing Effectiveness and the Moderating Role of Price Discounts. *Journal of Marketing*, *78*(6), 120–142.

Auger, Pat, Burke, Paul, Devinney, Timothy & Louviere, Jordan (2003). What Will Consumers Pay for Social Product Features? *Journal of Business Ethics*, *42*(3), 281–304.

Austin, James & Seitanidi, May (2012). Collaborative Value Creation: A Review of Partnering Between Nonprofits and Businesses: Part I. Value Creation Spectrum and Collaboration Stages. *Nonprofit and Voluntary Sector Quarterly*, *41*(5), 726–758.

Barone, Michael, Miyazaki, Anthony & Taylor, Kimberly (2000). The Influence of Cause-Related Marketing on Consumer Choice: Does One Good Turn Deserve Another? *Journal of the Academy of Marketing Science*, *28*(2), 248–262.

Bartels, Robert & Jenkins, Roger (1977). Macromarketing. *Journal of Marketing*, *41*(4), 17–20.

Becker-Olsen, Karen, Taylor, Charles, Hill, Ronald & Yalcinkaya, Goksel (2011). A Cross-Cultural Examination of Corporate Social Responsibility Marketing Communications in Mexico and the US: Strategies for Global Brands. *Journal of International Marketing*, *19*(2).

Berglind, Matthew & Nakata, Cheryl (2005). Cause-Related Marketing: More Buck Than Bang? *Business Horizons*, *48*(5), 443–453.

Carroll, Archie (1979). A Three-Dimensional Conceptual Model of Corporate Social Performance. *Academy of Management Review*, *4*(4), 497–505.

Carroll, Archie (1983). Corporate Social Responsibility: Will Industry Respond to Cutbacks in Social Program Funding? *Vital Speeches of the Day*, *49*(19), 604–608.

Carroll, Archie (1991). The Pyramid of Corporate Social Responsibility: Toward the Moral Management of Organizational Stakeholders. *Business Horizons*, *34*(4), 39–48.

Cause-Related Marketing Blogspot (2010a, January 28th). Green Up Your Cause Marketing. Retrieved December 2017, from https://causerelatedmarketing.blogspot.ca/2010/01/green-up-your-cause-marketing.html

Cause-Related Marketing Blogspot (2010b, September 24th). A Clever Cause Marketing Campaign from Snickers and Feeding America. Retrieved December 2017, from https://causerelatedmarketing.blogspot.ca/search?q=snickers

Cause-Related Marketing Blogspot (2010c, October 8th). Cause Marketing from Marriott Benefiting the Red Cross. Retrieved December 2017, from https://causerelatedmarketing.blogspot.ca/search?q=red+cross

CBC News (2015, September 27th). Farha Foundation March Raises Money for HIV/AIDS Programs. Retrieved from www.cbc.ca/news/canada/montreal/farha-foundation-ca-marche-2015-1.3245912

Chernev, Alexander & Blair, Sean (2015). Doing Well By Doing Good: The Benevolent Halo of Corporate Social Responsibility. *Journal of Consumer Research*, *41*(6), 1412–1425.

542 Cause-Related Marketing

The Coca-Cola Company (2011). Arctic Home Campaign Fact Sheet. Retrieved December 2017, from www.coca-colacompany.com/stories/arctic-home-campaign-fact-sheet

The Coca-Cola Company (2013). Coke Raises More Than $2 Million to Save Polar Bears. Retrieved December 2017, from www.coca-colacompany.com/our-company/coke-raises-over-2-million-to-save-polar-bears

The Coca-Cola Company (2016a). Annual Report 2016. Retrieved from www.coca-colacompany.com/content/dam/journey/us/en/private/fileassets/pdf/2017/TCCCAR16-final.pdf

The Coca-Cola Company (2016b, July 13th). Press Release: Coca-Cola Goes for Gold in Rio 2016 Olympic Games With Global #ThatsGold Campaign. Retrieved from www.coca-colacompany.com/press-center/press-releases/coca-cola-goes-for-gold-in-rio-2016-olympic-games-with-global-thatsgold-campaign

The Coca-Cola Company (2016c). Grants Paid by the Coca-Cola Foundation. 35. www.coca-colacompany.com/content/dam/journey/us/en/private/fileassets/pdf/our-company/2016-PIDC-Contributions-Report.pdf

The Coca-Cola Company (2017). 2016 Sustainability Report: Water Stewardship. Retrieved December 2017, from www.coca-colacompany.com/stories/2016-water-stewardship

CR (2017). The 2017 100 Best Corporate Citizens. Corporate Responsibility Magazine. Retrieved July 2017, from www.thecro.com/100-best/the-100-best-corporate-citizen/

Crane, Andrew & Matten, Dirk (2016). *Business Ethics: Managing Corporate Citizenship and Sustainability in the Age of Globalization* (4th ed.). New York: Oxford University Press (p. 605).

Crane, Andrew, Matten, Dirk & Spencer, Laura (2013). Corporate Social Responsibility: In a Global Context. In *Corporate Social Responsibility: Readings and Cases in a Global Context*, Andrew Crane, Dirk Matten, and Laura Spence (Editors). London: Routledge (pp. 3–26).

CRM Blog (2010, November 29). Cause Marketing That's Good for a Laugh, *By Paul Jones*. Retrieved from http://causerelatedmarketing.blogspot.com/2010/11/cause-marketing-thats-good-for-laugh.html

Cronbach, Lee Joseph & Meehl, Paul (1955). Construct Validity in Psychological Tests. *Psychological Bulletin*, 52(4), 281–302.

CSIC (2011). Dynamics of Cause Engagement. Ogilvy Public Relations Worldwide and the Center for Social Impact Communication (CSIC) at Georgetown University (US) 40. Retrieved from http://csic.georgetown.edu/research/digital-persuasion/dynamics-of-cause-engagement/

Dahlin, Laurie (2007). Where have all the Ethics Gone? Business Ethics and Corporate Social Responsibility Through the Years. *Proceedings of the Northeast Business & Economics Association*, 360–366.

Dahlsrud, Alexander (2008). How Corporate Social Responsibility Is Defined: An Analysis of 37 Definitions. *Corporate Social Responsibility and Environmental Management*, 15(1), 1–13.

Dodd, Merrick (1932). For Whom Are Corporate Managers Trustees? *Harvard Law Review*, 45(7), 1145–1163.

Easterbrook, James (1959). The Effect of Emotion on Cue Utilization and the Organization of Behavior. *Psychological Review*, 66(3), 183–201.

Eccles, Robert, Ioannou, Ioannis & Serafeim, George (2014). The Impact of Corporate Sustainability on Organizational Processes and Performance. *Management Science*, 60(11), 2835–2857.

EcoWorld (2016). Consumer issues. Retrieved May 16, 2016, from www.ecoworld.org.uk/eco_topics/food/consumer-issues.asp

Ehrich, Kristine & Irwin, Julie (2005). Willful Ignorance in the Request for Product Attribute Information. *Journal of Marketing Research*, 42(3), 266–277.

Einstein, Mara (2012). *Compassion Inc.: How Corporate America Blurs the Line Between What We Buy, Who We Are and Those We Help*. Berkeley: University of California Press (p. 222).

Elkington, John (1997). *Cannibals With Forks—The Triple Bottom Line of 21st Century Business*. Oxford: Capstone Publishing Ltd (p. 424).

Evans, Randy, Haden, Stephanie Pane, Clayton, Russell & Novicevic, Milorad (2013). History-of-Management-Thought About Social Responsibility. *Journal of Management History*, 19(1), 8–32.

Fast Company (2015, June 15th). The Inside Story of Starbucks's Race Together Campaign, No Foam, *By Austin Carr*. Retrieved from www.fastcompany.com/3046890/the-inside-story-of-starbuckss-race-together-campaign-no-foam

FiBL & IFOAM (2017). The World of Organic Agriculture—Statistics and Emerging Trends 2017. Willer, Helga and Julia Lernoud (Eds.) Research Institute of Organic Agriculture (FiBL), Frick and IFOAM. Organics International, Bonn (Germany) 340. https://shop.fibl.org/CHen/mwdownloads/download/link/id/785/?ref=1

Fjällräven (2017). Save the Arctic Fox Kånken. Retrieved November 2017, from www.fjallraven.com/save-the-arctic-fox-kanken

Fjällräven (n.d.). Facts About the Arctic Fox Retrieved November 2017, from www.fjallraven.com/facts-about-the-arctic-fox

Food Politics (2011, June 16th). The Latest in Cause Marketing: KFC, Pepsi, and Diabetes, *By Marion Nestle*. Retrieved from www.foodpolitics.com/2011/06/the-latest-in-cause-marketing-kfc-pepsi-and-diabetes/

Forbes (2016, August 4th). Sponsorship and Advertising Trends in the 2016 Rio Olympic Games: Three Things to Watch for, *By Charles Taylor and John Murphy*. Retrieved from www.forbes.com/sites/onmarketing/2016/08/04/sponsorship-and-advertising-trends-in-the-2016-rio-olympic-games-three-things-to-watch-for/#255d3d4018c7

Fortune (2016, June 22nd). The 20 Most Generous Companies of the Fortune 500, *By Caroline Preston*. Retrieved from http://fortune.com/2016/06/22/fortune-500-most-charitable-companies/

Friedman, Milton (2002). *Capitalism and Freedom*. Chicago: University of Chicago Press; 40th Anniversary Edition (first published in 1962) (p. 230).

Griffin, Ricky & Pustay, Michael (2015). *International Business* (8th ed.). New Jersey: Pearson (p. 624).

Grolleau, Gilles, Ibanez, Lisette & Lavoie, Nathalie (2016). Cause-Related Marketing of Products With a Negative Externality. *Journal of Business Research*, 69(10), 4321–4330.

Huffington Post (2013, October 29th). Clowning Around With Charity: How McDonald's Exploits Philanthropy and Targets Children, *By Michele Simon. In Collaboration With Corporate Accountability International and the Small Planet Fund*. Retrieved from www.huffingtonpost.com/michele-simon/clowning-around-with-charity_b_4174914.html

544 Cause-Related Marketing

Hunt, Shelby & Burnett, John (1982). The Macromarketing/Micromarketing Dichotomy: A Taxonomical Model. *Journal of Marketing*, 46(3), 11–26.

IEG (2017). Sponsorship Spending Forecast: Continued Growth Around the World. IEG Sponsorship Report. Retrieved June 2017, from www.sponsorship.com/IEGSR/2017/01/04/Sponsorship-Spending-Forecast—Continued-Growth-Ar.aspx

IKEA (n.d.). Press Release: Introducing a Bear That Gives. IKEA Helps Support UNICEF's Play Based Programs for Children. Retrieved December 2017, from www.ikea.com/ms/en_US/about_ikea/press_room/press_release/national/brum.html

Inhabitat (2009, August 10th). Samsung Unveils Green Phone Made From Corn, *By Rebecca Paul*. Retrieved from https://inhabitat.com/samsung-unveils-green-phone-made-from-corn/

Joyner, Brenda & Payne, Dinah (2002). Evolution and Implementation: A Study of Values, Business Ethics and Corporate Social Responsibility. *Journal of Business Ethics*, 41(4), 297–311.

King, Samantha (2006). *Pink Ribbons, Inc.: Breast Cancer and the Politics of Philanthropy*. Minneapolis: University of Minnesota Press (p. 157).

Kotler, Philip & Lee, Nancy (2004). *Corporate Social Responsibility: Doing the Most Good for Your Company and Your Cause*. Hoboken, NJ: John Wiley and Sons (p. 320).

Kotler, Philip & Lee, Nancy (2005). Best of Breed: When It Comes to Gaining a Market Edge While Supporting a Social Cause, "Corporate Social Marketing" Leads the Pack. *Social Marketin Quarterly*, 11(3–4), 91–103.

Krishna, Aradhna (2011). Can Supporting a Cause Decrease Donations and Happiness? *Journal of Consumer Psychology*, 21(3), 338–345.

La Ferle, Carrie, Kuber, Gayatri & Edwards, Steven (2013). Factors Impacting Responses to Cause-Related Marketing in India and the US: Novelty, Altruistic Motives, and Company Origin. *Journal of Business Research*, 66(3), 364–373.

Lafferty, Barbara & Goldsmith, Ronald (2005). Cause—Brand Alliances: Does the Cause Help the Brand or Does the Brand Help the Cause? *Journal of Business Research*, 58(4), 423–429.

Leonidou, Leonidas, Leonidou, Constantinos, Palihawadana, Dayananda & Hultman, Magnus (2011). Evaluating the Green Advertising Practices of International Firms: A Trend Analysis. *International Marketing Review*, 28(1), 6–33.

Levitt, Theodore (1958). The Dangers of Social-Responsibility. *Harvard Business Review*, 36(5), 41–50.

Lindgreen, Adam, Xu, Yue, Maon, François & Wilcock, Jeremy (2012). Corporate Social Responsibility Brand Leadership: A Multiple Case Study. *European Journal of Marketing*, 46(7/8), 965–993.

Luo, Xueming & Bhattacharya, Chitra (2006). Corporate Social Responsibility, Customer Satisfaction, and Market Value. *Journal of Marketing*, 70(4), 1–18.

Maignan, Isabelle, Ferrell, O. C. & Ferrell, Linda (2005). A Stakeholder Model for Implementing Social Responsibility in Marketing. *European Journal of Marketing*, 39(9–10), 956–977.

Marconi, Joe (2002). *Cause Marketing: Build Your Image And Bottom Line Through Socially Responsible Partnerships, Programs, and Events*. Chicago: Dearborn: A Kaplan Professional Company (p. 240).

Matten, Dirk & Moon, Jeremy (2008). "Implicit" and "Explicit" CSR: A Conceptual Framework for a Comparative Understanding of Corporate Social Responsibilit. *Academy of Management Review*, 33(2), 404–424.

Cause-Related Marketing 545

Medscape (2010, April 29th). Pink "Buckets for the Cure" Collaboration Between KFC and Komen Draws Sharp Criticism, *By Roxanne Nelson*. Retrieved from www.medscape.com/viewarticle/721024

The National Geographic (2018, February 1st). Polar Bears Really Are Starving Because of Global Warming, Study Shows, By Stephen Leahy. Retrieved from https://news.nationalgeographic.com/2018/02/polar-bears-starve-melting-sea-ice-global-warming-study-beaufort-sea-environment/

The National Law Review (2015, April 14th). Legal Issues in Cause-Related Marketing, *By Jason Kohout*. Retrieved from www.natlawreview.com/article/legal-issues-cause-related-marketing

NBCF (2017). Terms of Service. Retrieved December 2017, from www.nationalbreastcancer.org/terms-of-service

New York Times (2009, September 24th). Tough on Crude Oil, Soft on Ducklings, *By Andrew Adam Newman*. Retrieved from www.nytimes.com/2009/09/25/business/media/25adco.html

News Wire (2014). #FriendsFight: ALDO Launches New Campaign for ALDO FIGHTS AIDS (AFA) Retrieved November 2017, from www.newswire.ca/news-releases/friendsfight-aldo-launches-new-campaign-for-aldo-fights-aids-afa-513567791.html

NonProfit Quarterly (2013, November 18th). Killing Coyotes to Benefit Terminally Ill Kids Sparks Protest, *By Ruth McCambridge*. Retrieved from https://nonprofitquarterly.org/2013/11/18/killing-coyotes-to-benefit-termi nally-ill-kids-sparks-protest/

Öberseder, Magdalena, Schlegelmilch, Bodo & Gruber, Verena (2011). Why Don't Consumers Care About CSR?: A Qualitative Study Exploring the Role of CSR in Consumption Decisions. *Journal of Business Ethics*, *104*(4), 449–460.

Öberseder, Magdalena, Schlegelmilch, Bodo, Murphy, Patrick & Gruber, Verena (2014). Consumers' Perceptions of Corporate Social Responsibility: Scale Development and Validation. *Journal of Business Ethics*, *124*(1), 101–115.

Olsen, G. Douglas, Pracejus, John W. & Brown, Norman R. (2003). When Profit Equals Price: Consumer Confusion About Donation Amounts in Cause-Related Marketing. *Journal of Public Policy & Marketing*, *22*(2), 170–180.

Olson, Jerry (1972). *Cue Utilization in the Quality Perception Process: A Cognitive Model and an Empirical Test*. (Ph.D), Purdue University, West Lafayette.

Pallotta, Dan (2008). *Uncharitable: How Restraints on Nonprofits Undermine Their Potential*. Medford: Tufts University Press (p. 312).

Partners in Health Canada (2017). Our Partners. Retrieved December 2017, from http://pihcanada.org/our-story/our-partners/

The Plain Dealer (2013, November 18th). Is Walmart's Request of Associates to Help Provide Thanksgiving Dinner for Co-Workers Proof of Low Wages? *By Olivera Perkins*. Retrieved from www.cleveland.com/business/index.ssf/2013/11/is_walmarts_request_of_associa.html

Porter, Michael & Kramer, Mark (2002). The Competitive Advantage of Corporate Philanthropy. *Harvard Business Review*, *80*(12), 56–68.

Post, Frederick (2003). A Response to "The Social Responsibility of Corporate Management: A Classical Critique". *American Journal of Business*, *18*(1), 25–36.

Procter & Gamble (2016). Annual Report 2016. Retrieved from www.pginvestor.com/Cache/1500090608.PDF?O=PDF&T=&Y=&D=&FID=1500090608&iid=4004124

Procter & Gamble (2017a). About P&G. Retrieved December 2017, from http://news.pg.com/about/core_strengths

546 Cause-Related Marketing

Procter & Gamble (2017b). Corporate & Brand Programs. Retrieved December 2017, from https://us.pg.com/sustainability/community-impact/brand-corporate-programs

Procter & Gamble—Children's Safe Drinking Water Program (2017). Help Us Share the Power of Clean Water. Retrieved December 2017, from www.csdw.org/csdw/donate.shtml

Robinson, Stefanie Rosen, Irmak, Caglar & Jayachandran, Satish (2012). Choice of Cause in Cause-Related Marketing. *Journal of Marketing*, 76(4), 126–139.

Ross, John K., III, Stutts, Mary Ann & Patterson, Larry (1990). Tactical Considerations for the Effective Use of Cause-Related Marketing. *Journal of Applied Business Research*, 7(2), 58.

Rundle-Thiele, Sharyn, Paladino, Angela & Apostol, Sergio Antonio (2008). Lessons Learned From Renewable Electricity Marketing Attempts: A Case Study. *Business Horizons*, 51(3), 181–190.

Singer, Andrew (1993). Can a Corporation Be Too Ethical? *Across the Board*(April), 17–22.

Subaru (2017a). Annual Report. 102. Retrieved from www.subaru.co.jp/en/ir/library/pdf/ar/ar_2017e.pdf

Subaru (2017b). List of Partners. Retrieved December 2017, from Argentina: www.subaru.com.ar/; Canada: www.subaru.ca/WebPage.aspx?WebSiteID=282&WebPageID=4774&=footlink; France: www.subaru.fr/partenaires-subaru-france.html; Mexico: www.subaru.com.mx/; Spain: www.subaru.es/

Subaru (2017c). The Subaru Love Promise. Retrieved December 2017, from www.subaru.com/love-promise.html

Taneja, Shallini, Taneja, Pawan & Gupta, Rajen (2011). Researches in Corporate Social Responsibility: A Review of Shifting Focus, Paradigms, and Methodologies. *Journal of Business Ethics*, 101(3), 343–364.

The Telegraph (2011, December 3rd). Coca Cola Drops 'Polar Bear' Cans Because Consumers Prefer to See Red *By Jacqui Goddard*. Retrieved from www.telegraph.co.uk/foodanddrink/foodanddrinknews/8933476/Coca-Cola-drops-polar-bear-cans-because-consumers-prefer-to-see-red.html

TerraChoice (2009). The Seven Sins of Greenwashing. Retrieved from www.map-testing.com/assets/files/2009-04-xx-The_Seven_Sins_of_Greenwashing_low_res.pdfThink Before You Pink (2010). What the Cluck?! Retrieved December 2017, from https://thinkbeforeyoupink.org/past-campaigns/buckets-for-the-cure-2/

Thøgersen, John (2010). Country Differences in Sustainable Consumption: The Case of Organic Food. *Journal of Macromarketing*, 30(2), 171–185.

Turner, Richard (2006). Corporate Social Responsibility: Should Disclosure of Social Considerations be Mandatory. Submission to the Parliamentary Joint Committee on Corporations and Financial Services Inquiry. Retrieved from www.aph.gov.au/~/media/wopapub/senate/committee/corporations_ctte/completed_inquiries/2004_07/corporate_responsibility/submissions/sub05_pdf.ashx

UNEP (2015). Sustainable Consumption and Production—a Handbook for Policy Makers. United Nations Environment Programme. Retrieved from www.switch-asia.eu/fileadmin/user_upload/RPSC/Publications/03SCP-Handbook-AP_low-resolution_.pdf

UNICEF (2005). Press Release: IKEA Heralds Promotion to Support UNICEF and Save the Children Activities. Retrieved December 2017, from www.unicef.org/media/media_29933.html

UNICEF (2012). The UNICEF and P&G Pampers Partnership to Support Maternal and Neonatal Tetanus Elimination. 4. Retrieved from www.unicef.org/partners/Partnership_profile_2012_PAMPERS_V2_approved.pdf

UNICEF (2017). UNICEF Corporate and Philanthropic Partnerships. Retrieved December 2017, from www.unicef.org/corporate_partners/index_42735.html?p=printme

US Department of Health and Human Services (2011). Report on Carcinogens. Public Health Service, National Toxicology Program.

Vallance, Elizabeth (1995). *Business Ethics at Work*. Cambridge: Cambridge University Press (p. 191).

Varadarajan, Rajan & Menon, Anil (1988). Cause-Related Marketing: A Coalignment of Marketing Strategy and Corporate Philanthropy. *Journal of Marketing*, 52(3), 58–74.

Vlachos, Pavlos A., Koritos, Christos D., Krepapa, Areti, Tasoulis, Konstantinos & Theodorakis, Ioannis G. (2016). Containing Cause-Related Marketing Skepticism: A Comparison Across Donation Frame Types. *Corporate Reputation Review*, 19(1), 4–21.

Wall Street Journal (2009, January 26th). Fiat Draws Attention to a Cause—Along With Car, *By Aaron O. Patrick*. Retrieved from www.wsj.com/articles/SB123291980298913525

Westberg, Kate & Pope, Nigel (2014). Building Brand Equity With Cause-Related Marketing: A Comparison With Sponsorship and Sales Promotion. *Journal of Marketing Communications*, 20(6), 419.

Wicki, S. & van der Kaaij, J. (2007). Is It True Love Between the Octopus and the Frog? How to Avoid the Authenticity Gap. *Corporate Reputation Review*, 10(4), 312–318.

World Economic Forum (2017). The Dark Secret Powering Your Smartphone. By Mark Viso, CEO of Pactworld. Retrieved October 2017, Published September 19th, 2017, from www.weforum.org/agenda/2017/09/global-battery-alliance-child-labour-congo/?utm_content=bufferac89d&utm_medium=social&utm_source=facebook.com&utm_campaign=buffer%20on%20October%2012th%202017

Overall Book Conclusion

Overall, this book highlights the existence of two main consequences of globalization for companies with direct impacts on marketing. First, competition has increased hundredfold. Second, distances between firms and their markets have evolved in an ambivalent manner: they have decreased (due in large part to the opening of markets, improvements in transportation and communications, and the emergence of a global consumer segment), AND increased at the same time (because companies can reach consumers located further away, they are now left handling more significant differences between markets in terms of culture, regulations, technology, and economy).

International marketers need to embrace this ambivalence and realize that, to overcome competition and distance issues, companies can adopt one, two or more of the five marketing practices presented in this book (such as Danone did with BOP marketing and cause-related marketing, FIAT with reverse innovation, mobile marketing, and cause-related marketing; and IKEA with origin-based marketing, mobile marketing, and cause-related marketing). There are many more marketing solutions available to companies to increase their competitiveness (e.g., experiential marketing, use of Big Data, etc.), but the practices under scrutiny in this book particularly help with distance issues. In summary, companies can adopt BOP marketing and/or reverse innovation to overcome economic and technological distances. Mobile marketing can be key in facing geographic, technological, and temporal distances. Finally, both origin-based marketing and cause-related marketing can help with overcoming psychic distance (the former also helping with geographic distance and the latter with cultural distance).

None of these practices, however, are devoid of adverse repercussions (for companies but also for important stakeholders). It is therefore important to examine their relevance on a case-by-case basis and eventually plan, with care, their implementation.

Acronyms

4Ps	Product, Price, Place, and Promotion
7Ps	Product, Price, Place, Promotion, People, Process, and Physical Evidence
AACSB	Association to Advance Collegiate Schools of Business
AIDS	Acquired Immune Deficiency Syndrome
AFTA	ASEAN Free Trade Area
AMA	American Marketing Association
ANZCERTA	Australia-New Zealand FTA and EIA
AR	Augmented Reality
ASEAN	Association of South East Asian Nations
ASR	Aggregation Services Router
ATA	Admission Temporaire/Temporary Admission
B2B	Business-to-Business
B2C	Business-to-Consumer
BDT	Bangladeshi Taka
Bn	Billion
BOP	Bottom of the Pyramid
BRIC	Brazil, Russia, India and China
BSP model	"Buy-Ship-Pay" model
BITD	International Customs Tariff Bureau
C2C	Consumer-to-consumer
CACM	Central American Common Market
CAGE	Cultural, Administrative, Geographic and Economic
CAGR	Compound Annual Growth Rate
CBSA	Canadian Border Service Agency
CEMAC	Economic and Monetary Community of Central Africa
CDBA	Costs of Doing Business Abroad
CIM	Chartered Institute of Marketing
CIPO	Canadian Intellectual Property Office
CISFTA	Commonwealth of Independent States' FTA
CIVETS	Colombia, Indonesia, Vietnam, Egypt, Turkey and South Africa
CIS	Commonwealth of Independent States
CRM	Cause-Related Marketing
CSR	Corporate Social Responsibility

CU	Customs Union
DSMM marketing	Digital, Social Media, and Mobile marketing
DYI	Do-It-Yourself
ECOWAS	Economic Community of West African States
EIA	Economic Integration Agreement
EIU	Economist Intelligence Unit
EQUIS	European Quality Improvement System
ETA	Estimated Time of Arrival
EU	European Union
FDI	Foreign Direct Investment
FMCG	Fast-Moving Consumer Goods
FTA	Free Trade Area
FTZ	Free Trade Zone
GAFTA	Greater Arab Free Trade Area
GDP	Gross Domestic Product
GMAT	Graduate Management Admission Test
GMOs	Genetically Modified Organisms
GNI	Gross National Income
GSM	Global System for Mobile Communications
HBR	Harvard Business Review
HBS	Harvard Business School
HS	Harmonized System classification
ICC	International Chamber of Commerce
ICCA	International Council for Commercial Arbitration
ICJ	International Court of Justice
ICT	Information and Communication Technologies
Incoterms	International Commercial Terms
INPI	Institut National de Propriété Industrielle
IP	Intellectual Property
IPLC	International Product Life Cycle
ISO	International Organization for Standardization
IT	Information Technology
KIBS	Knowledge-Intensive Business Services
KSF	Key Success Factors
LDCs	Least Developed Countries
LOF	Liability of Foreignness
LOO	Liability of Outsidership
MERCOSUR	Southern Common Market
MENA	Middle East and North Africa
MER	Market Exchange Rate
MIST	Mexico, Indonesia, South Korea, and Turkey
MNC	Multinational Corporation
Mn	Million
N/A	No Answer or Non Available
NAFTA	North American Free Trade Agreement
NGO	Non-Governmental Organization
NPO	Non-Profit Organization

OECD	Organization for Economic Cooperation and Development
OEM	Original equipment manufacturer
P2P	Peer-to-Peer
PAFTA	Pan-Arab Free Trade Agreement
PCA	Permanent Court of Arbitration
PEST	Political, Economic, Sociocultural, and Technological
PLC	Product Life Cycle
PD	Psychic Distance
PCI	Product-Country Image
PDA	Personal Digital Assistant
PDI	Power Distance Index
PPP	Purchasing Power Parity
PwC	PricewaterhouseCoopers
QR codes	Quick Response codes
R&D	Research and Development
ROI	Return on Investment
RTA	Regional Trade Agreement
SADC	Southern African Development Community
SAFTA	South Asian Free Trade Agreement
SMEs	Small and Medium Enterprises
SMS	Short Message Service
STP	Segmenting, Positioning and Targeting
TOEFL	Test of English as a Foreign Language
TPP	Trans-Pacific Partnership
Tn	Trillion
TV	Television
UGC	User-Generated Content
UK	United Kingdom
UN	United Nations
UNCTAD	United Nations Conference on Trade And Development
US	United States (of America)
USD	US Dollars
USPTO	US Patent and Trademark Office
VIP	Very Important Person
VOD	Video on demand
VOIP	Voice Over Internet Protocol
VR	Virtual Reality
WCF	World Chambers Federation
WHO	World Health Organization
WIPO	World Intellectual Property Organization
WOM	Word of Mouth
WTO	World Trade Organization
WWII	World War II

Index

Note: **Bold** page references indicate tables. *Italic* references indicate figures and boxed text.

01-Upper Crust segmentation 293
4Is (Integrate, Individualize, Involve, and Initiate) 420
4Ps (product, price, place, promotion) 56, 278, 335
5Cs (Company, Context, Collaborators, Clients, and Competitors) 56

Aaker, David 437, 445, 473
Abbott 223
Abercrombie & Fitch 59–60, 87–88
ABI/Inform Collection (ProQuest) 240, 532
absolute advantage *109*, 110
Access to Energy program 312, 314–315, *314*
access and internationalization 49
activity costs 55
adaptation *see* AdaptStand decisions; standardization and adaptation
AdaptStand decisions: corporate examples of 87–93, **88**, *90*, **91**; country-level factors and 80–81; firm-level factors and 82–84; geographic distance and 130, 132; glocalization versus 93–94; industry-level factors and 81–82; for McDonald's 91–92, **91**; new product development and 345; organizational design and 86–87; product-level factors and 81–82; psychic distance and 130, 132; *see also* standardization and adaptation
adjudicators 193
administrative costs 116

administrative distance: assessing 182, 215, 228–229; challenges in overcoming 223–225; complexity and 225, 228; convergence and 214–215; corporate examples of 216–223; defining 184–185; disputes and, international 211–212, *212*, *213*, 214; drivers of *182*, 185, 186–204; Food for Thought *185*, *205*, *225*; importance of 182, 226, 228; increasing 215; institutional distance versus 185; institutional infrastructure and 191, 193–194, **194–195**; international organizations and 205–211, *206*, **208–209**; issues at stake and 214–215; legal system and 195–197, **196**, *198*, 199; marketing decisions and, international 216–223, 228; marketing plan and, international *183*; national governments and 210–211; nomological network for 226, *227*; overcoming 225–226; political risk and 186–188, *189*, 190–191; product policies and 344–345; regional integration and 200, *201*, *202*, 203–204; trade and, international 205–211, **208–209**
ad valorem tariff 28
advertising, cause-related 511
affective factors 441
affiliates 62
Africa and regional trade agreements 204
aggregators 193

Index 553

Aichner, Thomas 481
air shipping 119
Ajzen, Icek 164–166, 436, 442
alcohol imports 222
Aldo 519–520, *519*, 529
All-Bran Commercial 171–172
Amazon (tech company) 29, 60, 220, 416
American Marketing Association (AMA) 74
American Red Cross Disaster Relief 529
Americas, regional trade agreements in 200, 203
Anderson, Otto 37
Andreoni, James 535
Anholt, Simon 444–445, 475
Ansoff's Matrix 49, 56, 58
Anti-Bribery Recommendation 217
Apache Open Office's globalization guide 172
Apostol, Sergio Antonio 507
appearance and communication 152
appellation system 441–442
Apple (tech company) 29, 87, **88**, 217, 219, 479
apps 398–400, *400, 401, 402, 408*, 409–413
arbitration 211
Arctic Home campaign 529
Argentina 187, 461–464
Armelini, Guillermo 390
Armstrong, Gary 293
Arrow, Kenneth 122
Asia and regional trade agreements 204
attitudes 159, 394–395, *395*
attributes, product 340, 342, *343*, 344, *344*
audiovisual services 342
auditory cues 150
augmented reality (AR) technology 400, 406–407, *408*
AU MENA Roadshow 466
Aung San Suu Kyi 520
Australasia and regional trade agreements 204
Australia 387, *460*, 464–467
Australia Unlimited *460*, 464–467
automotive industry, positioning in 294, *295*
avoidance, desire for 414

Bagozzi, Richard 394
Bain and Company 466
Barone, Michael 510
Bartlett, Christopher 87
Bathelt, Harald 124
Becker-Olsen, Karen 531, 533
Begum, Laily 317
behavioral beliefs 164
behavioral segmentation 293
behaviors 164–166, *165*
beliefs 159, 161–164, 166
Bello, Daniel 103, 240
Benetton 222
Bensadoun, Aldo 519
Berglind, Matthew 510, *510*, 528, 532
Berreman, Gerald 144
Berthelon, Matias 124
Berthon, Pierre *414*
Best Global Brands 438
Beugelsdijk, Sjoerd 162
Big Data 166
Big Mac Index 91–92
Bilkey, Warren J. 481
binational product 479
Bing (web search engine) 527
biotech products 219
Bird Rescue Research Center 522
blocs, trading 215
Body Shop, The *45*, 46
Boehnke, Klaus 164
Bolivia 187, *188*
border effect 125
borders, concept of 4
Borghini, Stefania 124
born global company 37–39, *39*
Boschma, Ron 100, 102, 121, *121*, 126, *126*
Bottom of the Pyramid (BOP) marketing: attractiveness of segment 322, 324; consequences of 326, 328; corporate examples of 306–320; defining *288, 296*, 299, 302–303; driver of 326; eco-techno distance and 287, 289; emerging markets and 296, *297*, 299; Food for Thought *302, 306, 322*; heterogeneity of segment and 322, *323*, 324; impact of 324–325; issues at stake and 320–325; Key Success Factors of 325; marketing decisions and, international 324–325; middle class and 296, *297, 298, 299, 300*; multinational

554 *Index*

enterprises and 325; nomological network for 326, *327*; outcomes of 325; positioning and 294, *294, 295*, 296; reverse innovation and 326, 369; segmentation and 289, *291, 292, 293*, 299, *301*, 303, *304*; size of segment 213, 322, *323*; targeting 287, 289, *291, 292*, 293, *302*, 328

Bradley, Frank *143*

brand: books 445; endorsed 447; equity 437, *437*; global 437; laws 218–219; nation 444; origin of 480–483, *480*; standalone 447; umbrella 447; *see also* product; *specific name*

Brand Connect 466

branding 437–438, 444; *see also* country branding; place branding

Breast Cancer Action 512

Breastfeeding Promotion Network of India (BPNI) 223

Brewer, Paul 103–104, 224

BRIC (Brazil, Russia, India, and China) countries 12, 260–264, **263**, *265*, 266, 269

Bridgestone 217

Broderick, Amanda 418

brownfield projects 41

Brown, Norman R. 532

Buckets for the Cure program 527

bureaucratic law 196–197

Burgernomics 91–92

Burnett, John 507

business administration and globalization 10–11

Business Environment Risk Intelligence (BERI) 187

business ethics 504–507

Business Risk Reports 187

Buy-Ship-Pay (BSP) model 116–117, *116*

Buzell, Robert 79, *80*, 81–82

CAGE (cultural, administrative, geographic, and economic) framework 58, *102*, 107, 123, 125, 130, 380, 384, 533

CAGR (Compound Annual Growth Rate) 396

Cairncross, Frances 2

Camp, Garrett 63

Canada 246, *246*, 267

Canada Goose Inc. 450–453, **450**, *452*

Canadian Intellectual Property Office (CIPO) 206

Cankar, Ivan 469

CARICOM (Caribbean Community and Common Market) 203

Carrefour 216

Carrière, Céline 124

Carroll, Archie 505

Carroll, Dave 392

castes 144

Cateora, Philip 75–76, 84, 119, 159, 380, 437

cause-related marketing (CRM): assessing 539; benefits of 534–535; business ethics and 504–507; corporate examples of 498–499, 514–525; corporate social responsibility and 499, 504–507, *505*, 525–526, 539; crowding-out effect and 536; customer's care about 525–526; defining 498, 510–511; disadvantages of 535–536; Food for Thought *510*, *514, 533, 537*; green washing and 503; heterogeneity of international consumption of responsible products and 507–508, *508, 509*, 510; international markets and 532–534; issues at stake and 525–537; Key Success Factors of 530–532; longevity of, unknown 539; macro-marketing and 506–507; marketing activities and 528–534; marketing plan and, international 499, *500*; mistakes and 526–528; nomological network for 537, *538*; nonprofit organizations and 499, 535–536; non-responsible product and 536; organic and Fair Trade food consumption and 507, *508, 509*; other initiatives supporting causes and 511–514, 519–525; outcomes of 534–536; relevance of 525–528; reliance on, by companies 498–499, 537, 539; responsible process cue and 501, *502*, 503–504, *503*, 537; responsible product and 503, *503*, 507–508, *508, 509*, 510; sustainable consumption and 501, *502*; sustainable development and 501, *502*; terms for 511; trustworthiness of 525–528; warm-glow giving and 535

Index   555

Cavusgil, Tamer 39, 81
Cemex 306–307, **306**, *307*
champion firms 111, *314*
Chao, Paul 479
Chartered Institute of Marketing (CIM) 74
Charter of the French language in Quebec 223
Chetty, Sylvie 39
Cheung, Fanny 167
Chevron 219
Children's Safe Drinking Program 523–525, *524*
Chile 467–469
China 173, 221, 269, 352, *353*, *354*, 478
chronemics 150
Cityscope database 269
CIVETS (Colombia, Indonesia, Vietnam, Egypt, Turkey, and South Africa) countries 12, 260–264, **263**, *265*, 266, 269
civil law 196
classification systems 207–209, **208–209**
Clayton, Russell 504
Coca-Cola Company 60, 79, 88–89, 513–515, **515**, 529
code law 196
COFACE 187
Cofap 355
cognitive-cultural pillar 184
cognitive factors 440–441
common law 195–196
communication: appearance and 152; costs *114*, 116; eye contact and 152; high context approach to 152–153; laws 222–223; low context approach to 152–153; marketing and, international 154; meaning and 148, 150, *151*; nonverbal 150–152, **150**, *151*, 154; online with customer 416–417; origin-based marketing and 441; posture and 151–152; services 342; stance and 151–152; verbal 147–148, *149*, 150, 154
companies and benefits of cause-related marketing 534, *537*, 539
comparative advantage *109*, 110–112
competition: companies overcoming issues of 548; comparative advantage and *109*, 110–112; competitive advantage and

111–113, *112*, 241; corruption and 217; globalization and 19–20, *20*; product and foreign 348, *350*; rivalry in 382–384
competitive advantage 111–113, *112*, 241
concentrated global marketing 79
conditional convergence 272–273
conservation and values 164
consulting firm reports 299
consumer: avoidance 414; cause-related marketing benefits and 535; laws 219–220; needs 75; newly empowered 414–415; revenge 414, 419
consumption, sustainable 501, *502*
contingency perspective 93
contractual agreements 40
control beliefs 164
Convention on Combating Bribery of Foreign Public Officials in International Business Transactions 217
convergence: administrative distance and 214–215; conditional 272–273; cultural 14, *19*, 167–168, *167*, **168**; defining 167; economic distance and 270–273; Food for Thought 20; globalization and 14, *15*, *16*, *17*, *18*, 19–20, *19*, *20*; technological distance and 270–273; technology and 14, 19–20; of values 167–168, **168**
Convergence Club 14, *15*, *16*, *17*, *18*
COOL (Country of Origin Labeling) 219
Corak, Miles 145
Coronary Artery Bypass Graft (CABG) 360
corporate social responsibility (CSR) 325, 499, 504–507, *505*, 525–526, 539
corruption 190–191, *192*, 217–218
Corruption of Foreign Public Officials Act 218
corruption laws 217–218
Corruption Perceptions Index 190–191
Corsi, Simone 351
cosmetics industry, positioning in 294, *295*
Costa Rica 267
Costco Wholesale Corporation 399, **399**, *400*

556 Index

cost-insurance-and-freight (CIF) term 117
costs: activity 55; administrative 116; communication 114, *114*, 116, *116*; distance perspective of 113, *114*, 116–117, *116*, 119, 121; geographic distance and 113, *114*, 116–117, *116*, 119, 121; transaction 51–53, *53*, 116, *116*; transportation *114*, 116, 119, **119**
costs of doing-business abroad (CDBA) 55
Couillard, Catherine 214
country-based international trade theories 109–110, *109*
Country Brand Index 473, *474*
country branding 445–447, *448*, 477; *see also* origin-based marketing; place branding; *specific country*
country-level factors 80–81, 107
country-of-assembly (COA) 479
country-of-design (COD) 479
country risk 186–187, *189*
county-of-origin effect (COE) 433, 439–444, *439*, *440*, 442–444, 447, 483; *see also* origin-based marketing
Coyote Kill Contest 527
credibility enhancers 193
credit risk 186
Credit Suisse 303
crossvergence 168, **168**
Croucher, Sheila 4
crowding-out effect 536
CSGR Globalization Index 23
cues: auditory 150; extrinsic 342, *343*; intrinsic 340, *343*; origin 435–436, 441, *441*, *450*, *481*; product 150, 340, 342, *343*, 344, 435–436, *435*; responsible process 501, *502*, 503–504, *503*, 537
cue utilization 340, 342, 344, 435–436, *435*, 501
cultural clusters 159, *160*
cultural convergence 14, *19*, 167–168, *167*, **168**
cultural distance: assessing 139–140, 168–169, 174, 176; behaviors and 164–166, *165*; beliefs and 159, 161–164; category of people and 142; convergence of culture and 167–168, **168**; corporate examples of 169–173; cultural clusters and

159, *160*; defining 140, 142; drivers of *139*, 143–164; Food for Thought *143*, *169*; high/low context approach to communication and 152–153; importance of 139, 143, 174; intergenerational elasticity of earnings and 145, *146*; Internet usage and 387; issues at stake and 167–169; language and 147–148, *149*, 150; marketing and, international 169, 174, 176; marketing plan and, international 140, *141*; measuring 161–164; monochronic-time cultures and 153–154; nomological network for 174, *175*; nonverbal communication and 150–152, **150**, *151*; norms and 159, 161–164; orientation and 161; polychronic-time cultures and 153–154; product policies and 344–345; psychic distance versus 142, *143*; religion and 154, 156, *156*, *157*, 158, *158*; social class and 145; social mobility and 145, 147; social organizations and 143–145, 147; social stratification and 144–145, 147; task/relationship model and 154, *155*; values and 159, 161–164, **163**, 166–168, **168**; verbal communication and 147–148, *149*, 150, 154; work-related dimensions and 161–162
cultural proximity 26
Culture's Consequences (Hofstede) 140
Cultures and Organizations (Hofstede) 140
customary law 197
customs unions (CUs) 200
cyber laws 387

D'Andrea, Guillermo *263*
Dan-On app 399, *400*
Danone 307–310, *308*, **308**, 309, 399, *401*
Davis, Fred 394
Dawn soap 522–523, *522*
Death of Distance 2.0, The (Cairncross) 2
Delivered Duty Paid (DDP) 117
delocalization of production 352
DeLong, Bradford 272

Index   557

demand similarity 111, *112*
demographic segmentation 289
De Mooij, Marieke 168
Dempsey, Melanie 392
Deshpandé, Rohit 478, *478*, 482–483, 486
desire for avoidance 414
desire for revenge 414
Detox Challenge 172
development levels 243–244, *244*, *245*, 246–247, *246*, *247*, *248*, 249, **249**
Diamantopoulos, Adamantios 482
Dichtl, Erwin 107
Dick, Alan 340
Dictionary of Gestures, A (Indij) 150
differentiated global marketing 79
Difffusion of Innovations (Rogers) 345
diffusion of innovation 345–347, *346*
digital divide, global 252, *254*
digital marketing 389–391, **389–390**, 392, *393*, 394
Dinnie, Keith 446–447
direct export 41
direct investment 47
directionality 259, *259*
Directive 2002/58/EC 387
direct revenge behaviors 414
Disdier, Anne-Célia 125
disintegration 204
disintermediation 384
Disney *see* Walt Disney Company
displacement and globalization 6
disputes, international organizations resolving 211–212, *212*, *213*, 214
distance: assessing 2, *3*, 31; companies overcoming issues of 548; convergence and 19; evolution of 548; globalization and 2, 31; integration and 19; mobile marketing in overcoming 378; negatively charged 274, 278, 372; origin-based marketing and 433; paradoxes of 126, 128; proximity versus 121–122; reverse innovation and 370; *see also specific type*
distance perspective of costs 113, *114*, 116–117, *116*, 119, 121
"Distance Still Matters" (Ghemawats) 124
distribution: channel structures, cross-country 380, 382, *382*;

income 246–247, *247*, 303, *305*; intermediaries for international 380, *381*; Internet and 384, *385*, **386**; laws 221–222; online 384–385, *385*, **386**, 387–389; policies, international 380, *381*, 382–384, *382*, 418; purpose of 380
distributors 193
divergence 167–168, **168**
Dodd, Merrick 505
Doing Business Index 188, 190
Dolce & Gabbana 223
domestic marketing 74, 76, 77, 78–79, **78**
donations 525
double deviation 414
Dove Self-Esteem Fund 527
Dow, Douglas 103–104, *143*
Dowrick, Steve 272
DSMM (Digital, Social Media, and Mobile) marketing 391
Dumex 218
dumping laws 221
Dunning, John 48, *48*, 113, *121*, 537
Durand, Aurélia 259, *309*, *439*, 443, 465

Echeverria, Rodolfo 514
Eclectic paradigm 50–51
economic distance: adjustment to, by countries 277–278; assessing 238, 271–273, 278, 280; convergence and 270–273; corporate examples of 273–278; defining 240–241; development levels and 243–244, *244*, *245*, 246–247, *246*, *247*, *248*, 249, **249**; directionality and 259, *259*; drivers of *237*, 243–258; economic potential and 258–260; Economy and Growth Category and 247, 249, **249**; emerging markets and 260–264, *263*, **263**, *265*, 266; Food for Thought *240*; growth markets and 261–262; heterogeneity of economies and 266–267, **267**, *268*, 269–270; Human Development Index and 247, *248*; importance of 237, 258, 278; income categories and 243–244, *244*, 247, 249, **249**; income distribution and, global 246–247, *247*; infrastructure and 252–253; issues at stake and

558 Index

266–278; least developed countries and 244, *245*, 252–253; market attractiveness and 258–266, 269, 278, *279*; market groupings and 260, **263**, 266–267, *268*, 269; marketing decisions and, international 273–275; marketing plan and, international 238, *239*; negatively charged 274, 278, 372; nomological network for 278, *279*; resources and 249–250, **251–252**, 252

Economic Freedom Index 190
economic inequality 246
Economist Intelligence Unit (EIU) 23, 25–26, 187, 191
Economist, The 303
eco-techno distance 240–241, *259*, 287, 289; *see also* economic distance; technological distance
Eden, Lorraine 55
education services 342
efficiency seeking and internationalization 49–50
El Alberto project 310
electrocardiograms (ECG or EKG) 357, *358*
Elkington, John 501
Elsener, Karl 455
emerging markets 260–264, *263*, **263**, *265*, 266, 296, 297, 299
endorsed brand 447
Enterprises Resource Planning (ERP) 384
entertainment services 342
entry mode laws 216–217
entry modes of internationalization 39–40, *40*, *42*, 43–47, 53, **120**
environmental sensitivity 345
epistolary feuds 482
EPRG (Ethnocentric, Polycentric, Regiocentric, and Geocentric) orientations 56, 83–84
equity brand 437, *437*
Ericcson 29
Ernst & Young 23, 26
ethics, business 504–507
Eurasia and regional trade agreements 203
Euromoney 187
Euromonitor International 269–270
European Union steel producers 221
Europe and regional trade agreements 203

Evans, Jody 106, 108
Evans, Randy 504
e-vendor 384–385, *385*, 387–389
ExportAr 463
Export.gov 210
Export Quebec 210
exports 40–41, 43, 351, *353*
extended marketing-mix 335, 337, *338*, *339*, 340, **341**
extrinsic cues 342, *343*
Exxon Valdez oil spill 522
eye contact and communication 152

Facebook 13–14, 29, 159, 387, **388**, 417, 487, 529
Facebook AI Research (FAIR) 29–30
facilitated giving 511
Fair Trade-certified product 504, 507, *508*, *509*
fast-moving consumer goods (FMCGs) 9, 382
Feeding America program 529–530
Ferrell, Linda 507
Ferrell, O. C. 507
Fiat 355, 357, 399–400, *402*, **402**, 520
firm-based international trade theories 110–113, *112*
firm-level factors 82–84, 107–108
Fishbein, Martin 164–166, 436, 442
Fjällräven 515–516, *516*, 529
food donations 222
Food for Thought: administrative distance *185*, *205*, *225*; born global *39*; Bottom of the Pyramid marketing and *302*, *320*, *322*; cause-related marketing *510*, *514*, *533*, *537*; consumer needs *75*; convergence *20*; cultural convergence *167*; cultural distance *143*, *169*; cultural versus psychic distance *143*; directionality *259*; economic distance *240*; eco-techno distance and *259*; emerging markets *263*; geographic distance *121*; globalization *10*, *30*; integration *20*; internationalization *48*, *59*; mobile marketing *390*, *395*, *398*, *414*; origin-based marketing *439*, *450*; origin cue *481*; paradox of psychic distance *126*; poverty, alleviating *324*; provenance paradox *478*; psychic distance *54*, *102*; reverse innovation *351*,

355, 366; standardization and adaptation *79, 80, 87*; standardized global marketing *79*; technological distance *240*; trade agreements *215*
Foote Cone & Belding (FCB) 409–410, **409**
foreign direct investment (FDI) 40–41, 47, 274
Fortune at the Bottom of the Pyramid, The (Prahalad et al.) 302
Forza, Ciprino 481
franchise and franchising 45–46, *45*
Frank And Oak 403–406, *403, 405*, 418
Freedom House 190–191
Freedom in the World reports 190
Freeman, Susan 39
free-on-board (FOB) term 117
free trade areas (FTAs) 200
free trade zone (FTZ) 210
Frega, Romeo 351
Freund, Caroline 124
Friedman, Milton 498, 506
Fukushima nuclear meltdown 219
Fundación de Chile 467
fundraising 525
FutureBrand 476

G7 countries 262, **263**
Gamble, James 521
Gao, Tao *395, 414*
General Agreement on Tariffs and Trade (GATT) 113, *115*
General Electric (GE) 357, *357, 358*
General Mills 528
genetically modified organisms 219
geographic distance: AdaptStand decisions and 130, 132; air versus sea shipping and 119; assessing 99–100, 132; Buy-Ship-Pay model and 116–117, *116*; costs and 113, *114*, 116–117, *116*, 119, 121; defining 100, 102; drivers of *99*, 108–124; effects of 124–126; Food for Thought *121*; gravity models and 125–126, *127*; importance of 130, 132; Incoterms® and 117, *118*, 119; issues at stake and 124–130; knowledge and 122–123; marketing decisions and, international 128–130; marketing plan and 100, *101*; measuring 102; nomological network for 130, *131*, 132; paradoxes of 126, 128, **128**;

production and 119, 121; product policies and 344–345; proximity and 121–124, *123*; trade patterns and, international 108–113
geographic origin *see* origin-based marketing
geographic segmentation 289, *292*
Germany 222, 270
Ghemawat, Pankaj 2, 21, *21*, 23, 100, 102, *102*, 107, 123–124, 143, 185, 225, *225*, 240
Gillette 255
Gilly, Mary 75, 119, 159, 380, 437
Gini index 147, 246–247, 249
Global Association of the Exhibition Industry 124
global brand 437
global digital divide 252, *254*
globalization: business administration and 10–11; competition and 19–20, *20*; consequences of 548; convergence and 14, *15, 16, 17, 18*, 19–20, *19, 20*; corporate examples of 26, *27, 28*–30; defining 4, 6, 9; displacement and 6; distance and 2, 31; drivers of 11–14; dynamics of world and 12–14; economic integration and 19–20, *20*, 26, 28; export growth and 6, *7, 8*; Food for Thought *10, 30*; historical perspective of 9–10; issues at stake and 20–26; marketing and, international 2, *2*, 31; marketing plan and, international 4, *5*; measuring 23, 25–26, **25**; outcomes of, ambivalence of 30–31, *30*; politics and 12–13; reverse innovation and 366, *367*; scale and 6, 14, 19–20; scope of 21, 23, *23, 24*; technological integration and 13–14, 28–29
Globalization Index 23, **25**
"Globalization of Markets, The" (Levitt) 10
global marketing 78–79; *see also* marketing, international
global organizations *see* international organizations; *specific name*
global strategic rivalry 111–113, *112*
Global System Mobile (GSM) network 29
GlobalWebIndex 387
GLOBE (Global Leadership and Organizational Behavior Effectiveness) 162
glocalization 93–94
Goldman Sachs 261, 269, 299

560 Index

Golfetto, Francesca 124
Good Country Index 444–445,
  475–476
Goodenough, Ward 140
Google 29
Gorbatchev, Mikhaïl 520
Gorn, Gerald J. 482
Govindarajan, Vijay 351, *351*, 366
Graham, John 75, 119, 159, 380, 437
Grameen Bank 307–310, *308*, **308**
Grameen Danone Foods 307–310,
  308, **308**
Grameenphone program 315–317,
  316
grand corruption 190
gravity models 125–126, *127*
green advertising 503–504
green economy 272
greenfield projects 40–41
Green, Mark 79, 249–250
green product 503
green washing 503
Grégoire, Yany 414
Griffin, Ricky 45, 143, 195–196, 506
Griffiths Energy International 218
Grissol 481
Grolleau, Gilles 536
gross domestic product (GDP) 5,
  8, 12, 21, 91, 125, *127*, 249,
  261–262, 264, **267**, 272, 299, 359,
  464, 469
gross national income (GNI) 243,
  249, *250*, 359
group orientation 161
growth markets 261–262
Gruber, Verena 506
Guesalaga, Rodrigo 303
Guns and Gold Pawn Shop 527
Gustafson, David 167

Häagen-Dazs 481
Haden, Stephanie Pane 504
Haider, Donald 444
Hall, Edward 140, 152–153
Hall, Mildred 152–153
Hamelin, Louis-Édmond 451
Hammond, Allen 303, *322*, 324
haptics 150
Harman 360–361, **360**
Harmonized Commodity Description
  and Coding System (Harmonized
  System or HS) 206–208
Harzing, Anne-Wil 482
Head, Keith 125

headquarters-subsidiaries
  relationships 83, *83*
Health City Cayman Islands 357–360
Heckscher, Eli 110
Heckscher-Ohlin theory 111
Heinz 223
heterogeneity of economies 266–267,
  267, *268*, 269–270
high context approach to
  communication 152–153
Hill, Ronald 531
Hippo Roller 363
Hofacker, Charles *395*
Hoff, Edward 79, 82
Hofstede, Geert 140, 142, *142*,
  161–162, 168
Hofstede Insights 161
Ho, Jason 392
Home Depot 513
Hoorn, André 162
House, Robert J. 162
HSBC 166, 170
Hultman, Magnus 504
Human Development Index 247, *248*
human resources 49
Hunt, Shelby 507
Hutchings, Kate 39
hybrid product 479
Hymer, Stephen 55

ICCA (International Council for
  Commercial Arbitration) 212
Iger, Bob 170
IKEA 61, 89–90, *90*, 171, 406–407,
  408, 453–455, *454*, *455*, 479, 485,
  516–517
Immelt, Jeffrey 351
imports 222
income: categories 243–244, *244*,
  247, 249, **249**; distribution,
  global 246–247, *247*, 303, *305*;
  intergenerational elasticity of 145,
  146; segmentation 299, *301*, 303,
  304
Incoterms® (International
  Commercial Terms) 117, *118*, 119
India 222–223
Indij, Guido 150
indirect export 41, 43
indirect revenge behaviors 414
individual-level factors 107–108
individual role in groups 143–144
industry-level factors 81–82
inequality, economic 246

information analyzers and advisors 193
information and communication technologies (ICT) revolution 113; *see also* communication; technology
information services 342
infrastructure and economic distance 252–253, *253*
innovation: development and diffusion of 176; diffusion of 345–347, *346*; repatriating 369; trickle-up 351; *see also* reverse innovation; technology
innovation-related (I) models of internationalization 37, 41
Inprotur 462–463
Institute for Training in Intercultural Management (ITIM) 161
institutional distance 184
institutional infrastructure 191, 193–194, **194–195**
institutional voids 191
institutions 184; *see also* administrative distance; international organizations
Institutions and Organizations (Scott) 184
Institut National de la Propiété Industrielle (INPI) 206
insurance 226
integration: administrative distance and regional 200, *201, 202,* 203–204; distance and 19; economic 19–20, *20,* 26, 28; Food for Thought *20*; globalization and 13–14, 19–20, *20,* 26, 28; regional 200, *201, 202,* 203–204; technological 13–14, 28–29; of technology 29
Intel 216
intellectual property (IP) 43, 206, 226, 243, 253, 255–256, *256, 257, 258,* **258**
Interbrand 438
intergenerational elasticity of earnings 145, *146*
intermarket segmentation 289
Internalization (I-type) advantage 51–53
International Baby Food Action Network (IBFAN) 223
International Bank for Reconstruction and Development 207
international business management 48

International Centre for Settlement of Investment Disputes 207
International Chamber of Commerce (ICC) 207
International Country Risk Guide (ICRG) 187, 191
International Court of Justice (ICJ) 212
International Development Association 207
international diffusion 366, *367,* 368
International Finance Corporation 207
internationalization: access and 49; corporate examples of 59–64; decision making about 35, *35,* 41, *42,* 58–59, 65; defining 37–39; drivers of 47–55; efficiency seeking and 49–50; entry modes 39–40, *40, 42,* 43–47, *53,* **120**; Food for Thought *48, 59*; gravity models and 125–126, *127*; innovation-related models of 37, 41; issues at stake and 55–59; liability of ownership and 55; marketing plan and, international 35, *36*; market seeking and 49; motives for 48–50, 64–65; OLI framework and 50–53, **54**; process 37–39, *38*; production and 50–53, *53*; psychic distance and 53–54; resource seeking and 49; strategic asset seeking and 50; transaction costs and 51–53, *53*; Uppsala model of 37–38, *38,* 54
"Internationalization Process of the Firm, The" (Johanson and Vahlne) 53–54
International Monetary Fund (IMF) 47, 207
international organizations: classification systems and 207–209, **208–209**; dispute resolution and 211–212, *212, 213,* 214; logos 205, *206*; trade administration and 205–211, **208–209**; *see also specific name*
International Organization for Standardization (ISO) 209
International Product Life Cycle (IPLC) 111, *112,* 345, *347,* 348, *349, 350*
Internet: distribution and 384, *385,* **386**; regulation of 387; spamming 223; URL 392; usage *386,* 387; user-generated content and 391

562　*Index*

intracorporate transfers 43
intrinsic cues 340, *343*
Irmak, Caglar 531
Isard, Walter 125

Jacks, David 125
Jain, Arun 340
Japan 219, 270, 351, *353, 354*
Jayachandran, Satish 531
Johanson, Jan 39, 53–55, *54*, 102, *102*
Josiassen, Alexander 482
JuriGlobe 197

Kalanick, Travis 63
Kamprad, Ingvar 61
Kaplan, Andreas 420
Karnani, Aneel 299, 303, *322*, 324
Karunaratna, Amal 103–104, *143*
Katsikeas, Constantine 84, 103, 240
Keegan, Warren 79, 249–250
Kellogg Company 171–172
Kentucky Fried Chicken (KFC) 527
Kenya 311–312
Key Success Factors (KSFs): of Bottom
of the Pyramid marketing 325; of
cause-related marketing 530–532;
of mobile marketing 414–416,
419–420; of origin-based marketing
485–487; of reverse innovation 368
Khan, Amir 88
Khanna, Tarun *185*, 191, 194
Knight, Gary *39*
knowledge 122–123; *see also*
intellectual property (IP)
Knowledge-Intensive Business Services
(KIBS) 129
knowledge spillovers 122
Koeglmayr, Hans-Georg 107
KOF Index of Globalization 23,
26, **27**
Kopitar, Anže 469
Koritos, Christos D. 532
Kotler, Philip 74, *75*, 293, 444,
510–511, *510*, 513
Krempel, Lothar 126
Krepapa, Areti 532
Krugman, Paul 111

La Ferle, Carrie 530–531, 533–535,
533
Lages, Luis Filipe 106
La Laiterie du Berger 309–310
Lamberton, Cait 391

Lane, Henry 126, *126*
language 147–148, *149*, 150, 154
Latin American economies, evolution
of 273
laws: brand 218–219; bureaucratic
196–197; civil 196; code 196;
common 195–196; communication
222–223; consumer 219–220;
corruption 217–218; customary
197; cyber 387; defining 184;
distribution 221–222; dumping
221; entry mode 216–217;
marijuana 221–222; price fixing
217; pricing 220–221; promotion
222–223; regulatory 216–217;
religious 196–197; *see also* legal
system; *specific name*
least developed countries (LDCs) 244,
245, 252–253, 396
Lee, Julie Anne 144, 166
Lee, Nancy 510–511, *510*, 513
Legal Language Services (LLS) 196
legal system 195–197, **196**, *198*, 199;
see also laws
leisure services 342
Leonidou, Constantinos 504
Leonidou, Leonidas 504
Leontief, Wassily 110–111
Levitt, Theodore 6, 10, *10*, 11, *11*, 12,
72, 74, 79, 506
liability of foreignness (LOF) 55
liability of outsidership (LOO) 55
Liberman, Nira 422
licenses and licensing 43–45, 225,
511–512
LifeLight system 311–312, *313*
LifeStraw 363–364, *365*
Linder, Staffan 111
LinkedIn 387
LintonRalph 140
litigation 211
Loblaws 419
local goods 222
local partners 225
Location (L-type) advantage 51
L'Oréal 50, 344
Louis Vuitton 218
low context approach to
communication 152–153

Mac 400 ECG machine 357, *358*
macro-marketing 506–507
Magnusson, Peter 480, 482
Maignan, Isabelle 507

Mair, Johanna 324
Make a Bed campaign 529
Malhotra, Shavin *240*, *259*, *259*
Malmberg, Anders 124
management contract 46–47
Manual Marca Pais 463
MAR (Marshall-Arrow-Romer) approach 122
Marconi, Joe 510
Marcotte, David *263*
marijuana laws 221–222
market groupings 260, **263**, 266–267, 268, 269
marketing, international: administrative distance and decisions about 216–223, 228; beliefs and 166; Bottom of the Pyramid and decision about 324–325; cause-related marketing's impact on 528–534; communication and 154; concentrated 79; cultural distance and 169, 174, 176; defining 74, 75–76; digital 389–391, **389–390**, *393*, 394; domestic 74, 76, 77, 78–79, **78**; domestic marketing versus 76, 77, 78–79, **78**; economic distance and decisions about 273–275; geographic distance and decisions about 128–130; globalization and 2, 31; global marketing versus 78–79; individual role in groups and 144; Middle of the Pyramid 296, 299, 302–303, *302*; mobile marketing and decisions about 415–418; online 384, *385*, 392, *393*, 394; origin-based marketing and decisions about 484–487; psychic distance and decisions about 129–130; reverse innovation and decisions about 368; social media 390–392, *393*, 394; technological distance and decisions about 273–275; traditional 392; values and 166; viral 392, *393*, 394; word of mouth 391, 412, 414, 416; *see also* Bottom of the Pyramid (BOP) marketing; cause-related marketing; mobile marketing; origin-based marketing
Marketing Management (Kotler) 74
marketing-mix: mobile marketing and 418; reverse innovation and 335, 337, *338*, *339*, 340, **341**

marketing plan, international: administrative distance and *183*; building on 55–56, *57*, *58–59*; cause-related marketing and 499, *500*; cultural distance and 140, *141*; economic distance and 238, *239*; geographic distance and 100, *101*; globalization and 4, *5*; internationalization decision and 35, *36*; mobile marketing and 378, *379*; origin-based marketing and 433, *434*; psychic distance and 100, *101*; reverse innovation and 335, *336*; standardization and adaptation and 72, *73*; technological distance and 238, *239*
market seeking 49, 422, 537
Marriot 529–530
Mars (food manufacturer) 529
Marshall, Alfred 122
Marshall, Pablo 303
Maseland, Robbert 162
Maskell, Peter 124
Mastercard 417
Mavondo, Felix 106
Maze, Tina 469
M-commerce 390
McDonald's 61–62, 90–91, **91**, 173, 528
McKinsey Global Institute 269
meaning and communication 148, 150, *151*
media, traditional 390
Menon, Anil 510, 535
mental intangibility 415
mercantilism *109*, 110
Mercedes-Benz 217
Microsoft 172, 527
middle class 296, *297*, *298*, 299, *300*
Middle East and regional trade agreements 204
Middle of the Pyramid (MOP) marketing 296, 299, 302–303, *302*
MIGA (Multilateral Investment Guarantee Agency) 226
Miller, Stewart 55
MIST (Mexico, Indonesia, South Korea, and Turkey) countries 12, 260–264, **263**, *265*, 266
Mitrany, David 13
mixed legal systems 197
Miyazaki, Anthony 510
mobile applications (apps) 398–400, *400*, *401*, *402*, *408*, 409–413

564   *Index*

mobile marketing: apps and 398–400, *400*, *401*, *402*, *408*, 409–413; benefits of 423; challenges of 415–416; communication with customers and, online 416–417; corporate examples of 398–413; defining *377*, 391–392, *393*, 394; deploying 398; digital marketing versus 389–392, **389–390**, *393*, 394; distance and, overcoming 378; distribution policies and, international 380, *381*, 382–384, *382*, 418; drivers of 394–398; empowered consumers and 414–415; Food for Thought *390*, *395*, *398*, *414*; issues at stake and 413–420; Key Success Factors of 414–416, 419–420; marketing decisions and 415–418; marketing-mix and 418; marketing plan and, international 378, *379*; as market seeking activity 422; mobile devices and, adopting of 396–398; nomological network for 420, *421*; online distribution and 384–385, *385*, 387–389; online marketing versus 384, *385*, 392, *393*, 394; outcomes of 419; regular marketing activities and 417–418; social media and 387–389, *388*, **388**; social media marketing versus 390–392, *393*, 394; Technology Acceptance Model and 394–398, *395*; temporal distance and 422–423; ubiquity of 378; viral marketing versus 392, *393*, 394
monochronic-time (M-time) cultures 153–154
M-Pesa initiative 319–320, *321*
Mueller, Stefan 107
MultiAir technology 355, 357
multinational corporations (MNCs) 9, 41, 43, 50, 113, 196, 271, 273, *324*, 369; *see also specific name*
multinational enterprises (MNEs) 325, 369
multiple segmentation 293
Murphy, Patrick 506

NAFTA (North American Free Trade Agreement) 200, 204
NAICS (North American Industrial Classification System) 208, **208–209**

Naik, Prasad *395*
Nakata, Cheryl 510, *510*, 528, 532
Nalanda platform 360–361
Nano car 361–363
Napoleonic Code 196
Narayana Health (NH) 357–360
National Breast Cancer Foundation (NBCF) 512, *512*, 528
National Diamond of Competitive Advantage model 238, 241, *242*
national governments and international trade 210–211
nationalization 187, *188*
National Park Foundation 515
National Park Service 515
nation brand 444; *see also* place branding
nation brand hexagon 475
Nation Brand Index 473, 475–476
Nation Branding (Dinnie) 446
negatively charged distance 274, 278, 372
Nepomuceno, Marcelo 415–416
Nes, Erik 481
Nestlé 223
Netflix 62, 92
New Balance 28
new product development (NPD) 345
New Trade Theory 50, 111
Next 11 market grouping 261, 269
Nielsen's market segmentation 293
Nike 28
Nivea 218, 407, 409–410, 418
Nobel Prizes 520
Noka 29
Nokia 310–311, **310**, *311*
Nokia Life Tools 310–311, *311*
nomological network: for administrative distance 226, *227*; for Bottom of the Pyramid marketing 326, *327*; for cause-related marketing 537, *538*; for cultural distance 174, *175*; for economic distance 278, *279*; for geographic distance 130, *131*, 132; for mobile marketing 420, *421*; for origin-based marketing 487, *488*, 489; for psychic distance 130, *131*, 132; for reverse innovation 370, *371*; for technological distance 278, *279*

nonprofit organizations and cause-related marketing 499, 535–536; *see also specific name*

non-responsible product 536
nonverbal communication 150–152, **150**, *151*, 154
nordicity 451
normative beliefs 164
normative pillar 184
norms 159, 161–164
Novicevic, Milorad 504
numeronym N-11 261, 269
NutriGo 309–310

Öberseder, Magdalena 506
oculesics 152
O'Grady, Shawna 126, *126*
Ohlin, Bertil 110
OLI framework 50–53, **54**, 113
Olsen, G. Douglas 532
Olson, Jerry 340, 435
Olympic Global Partner 513
O'Neil, Jim 261–262
online communication with customer 416–417
online marketing and distribution 384, *385*, 392, *393*, 394
openness to change and values 164
operational risk 186
opt-in option 387
Oral-B® toothbrush 255, *256*, *257*
organic and Fair Trade food consumption 507, *508*, *509*
Organisation for Economic Development and Co-operation (OECD) 217
organizational design and AdaptStand decisions 86–87
orientation 161
original equipment manufacturers (OEM) 29; *see also specific name*
origin-based marketing: affective factors and 441; appellation system and 441–442; branding and 437–438; cognitive factors and 440–441; communication and 441; corporate examples of 450–472; Country Brand Index and 473, *474*; country branding and 445–447, *448*, 477; country image over time and 473, *474*, 475–479; country-of-assembly and 479; country-of-design and 479; country-of-origin effect and 439–444, *439*, *440*, 442–444, 447, 483; cue utilization and 435–436, *435*; defining 432, 433, 438;

dilution of effect 479–483; distance and 433; drivers of 439–450; Food for Thought *439*, *450*; Good Country Index and 475–476; issues at stake and 472–487, 489; Key Success Factors of 485–487; marketing decisions and 484–487; marketing plan and, international 433, *434*; Nation Brand Index and 473, 475–476; nomological network for 487, *488*, 489; origin of brands and 480–483, *480*; origin cue and 435–436, 441, *441*, *450*, *481*; outcomes of 483–484; place branding and 444–450, *446*, 447, *449*, 450; product-country image and 440, 453; promotion and 441; provenance paradox and 478, *478*, 486, 489; recognition of effect 479–483; reliance on 489; *see also specific place*
origin cue 435–436, 441, *441*, *450*, *481*
Ownership (O-type) advantage 51

P2P Foundation 369
Pagani, Margherita *414*
Paladino, Angela 507
Palepu, Krishna *185*, 191, 194
Palihawadana, Dayananda 482, 504
Pampers 1 pack = 1 vaccine campaign 523
Papadopoulos, Nicolas 445–446
París, José Antonio 23
Parity Purchasing Power theory 91–92, 247, 249, *250*
parties, defining 270
patent applications 352, *354*
patents 255, *257*
Patrimonio Hoy program 306–307, *307*
Patterson, Larry 530
PCA (Permanent Court of Arbitration) 212
peer-to-peer (P2P) business models 369
people or participants 337
perceived ease-of-use variable of technology acceptance 394–395, *395*
perceived usefulness variable of technology acceptance 394–395, *395*

566 Index

Perlmutter, Howard *80*, 83–84
personalization 416
PEST framework 58, 103, 123, 130, 238, 240
petty corruption 190
Pew Research Center 296, 303
philanthropy 512–513, 528
Philips Lighting 311–312, **312**, *313*
physical evidence 337, *339*
physical resources 49
pillars of institutions 184
Pinkton, David 418
pink washing 512
Pinterest 173
Pitta, Dennis 303
Pittb, Leyland *414*
place branding 444–450, *446*, *447*, *449*, *450*; *see also specific place*
place marketing 444, 446
place personality 445
plain tobacco packaging 219, *220*
Planggerb, Kirk *414*
planned behavior, theory of 164–166, 436
Plečnik, Jože 469
Plümper, Thomas 126
political corruption 190–191
political distance 185
political risk 186–188, *189*, 190–191
Political Risk Services (PRS) Group 187, 191
politics and globalization 12–13
polychronic-time (P-time) cultures 153–154
Pope, Nigel 534
Porter, Michael 87, 111, 113, 121–122, *121*, 238, 241
portfolio investment 47
positioning 294, *294*, *295*, 296
Postnikov, Evgeny 215
posture and communication 151–152
poverty, Food for Thought for alleviating *324*
Pracejus, John W. 532
Prahalad, Coimbatore Krishnao 302–303, *302*, *322*, 324
preferential trade arrangements (PTAs) 200
price escalation 119, **120**
price fixing laws 217
pricing 418
pricing laws 220–221
PRIZM™ 293
process 501

process cue 436, 501
processes, food service 337, *338*
Procter & Gamble 255, 521–525, **521**, *522*, *524*
Procter, William 521
product: attributes 340, 342, *343*, 344, *344*; binational 479; biotech 219; competition and, foreign 348, *350*; cues 150, 340, 342, *343*, 344, 435–436, *435*; defining 340; development 444; Fair Trade-certified 504, 507, *508*, *509*; green 503; hybrid 479; laws 218–219; life cycle 82, 111, *112*, 345, *347*, 348, *349*, *350*; local 222; mental intangibility and 415; new development of 345; non-responsible 536; personalization of 416; policies, international 344–345; range 344; responsible 503, *503*, 507–508, *508*, *509*, 510; services versus 342–344; *see also* brand; *specific type*
product-country image (PCI) 440, 453
production 50–53, 119, 121, 352
product-level factors 81–82
promotion 418, 441; *see also* marketing, international
promotion laws 222–223
proof 337, *339*
Proquest/ABI Inform 240, 532
provenance paradox 478, *478*, 486, 489
proxemis 150
proximity: cultural 26; distance versus 121–122; geographic distance and 121–124, *123*; market groupings and 260; non-spatial dimensions of 122–123, *123*; paradoxes of 126, 128, **128**
psychic distance: AdaptStand decisions and 130, 132; assessing 99–100, 132; country-level factors and 107; cultural distance versus 142, *143*; defining 102–104; degree of 103, *103*; drivers of 99, 106–124; firm-level factors and 107–108; Food for Thought *54*, *102*; importance of 130, 132–133; individual level factors and 107–108; internationalization and 53–54; issues at stake and 124–130; marketing decisions and, international 129–130; marketing

plan and, international 100, *101*; measuring of *103*, 104, **104–105**, 106; nomological network for 130, *131*, 132; paradox of *126*
psychographic segmentation 293
public relations 513
Purchasing Power Parity (PPP) 91–92, 247, 249, *250*
Pureit Compact 318–319, *319*
Purmehdi, Mostafa 443
Pustay, Michael 45, 143, 195–196, 506

Qualcomm Inc. 216
Quelch, John *79*, 82

#RaceTogether campaign 527
Ralston, David 167–168, *167*
Ramamurti, Ravi *351*
Ratnani, Hicham 403
Reagan, Ronald 12, 499
reasoned action, theory of 164–166, *165*
Redefining Global Strategy (Ghemawat) 21, *22*
regional integration 200, *201*, *202*, 203–204
regional trade agreements (RTAs) 200, *201*, 203–204
regulation 184, 387; *see also* laws
regulative pillar 184
regulators 193
regulatory law 216–217
Rein, Irving 444
reintermediation 384
Reiss, Dani 451
Reiss, David 451
religion 154, 156, *156*, *157*, 158, *158*
religious law 196–197
Renren 13
resources 49, 249–250, **251–252**, *252*
resource seeking and internationalization 49
responsible practices 513
responsible process cue 501, *502*, 503–504, *503*, *537*
responsible product 503, *503*, 507–508, *508*, *509*, 510
retailers: e-vender 384–385, *385*, 387–389; opening hours for 222; ranking global 382, **383**
revenge behaviors 414, 419
revenge, desire for 414
reverse innovation: attributes and 340, 342, *343*, 344, *344*; Bottom

of the Pyramid marketing and 326, 369; concept of 334–335, *334*, 351–352, *352*; consequences of 372; corporate examples and counterexamples of 352, 355–365, **356**, 370; cues and 340, 342, *343*, 344; decision to undertake 372; defining 345, 351; diffusion of innovation and 345–347, *346*; distance and 370; Food for Thought and *351*, *355*, *366*; 4Ps and 335, 337; globalization and 366, *367*; international diffusion and 366, *367*, 368; international product life cycle and 345, *347*, 348, *349*, *350*; issues at stake and 366–370; Key Success Factors of 368; marketing decisions and, international 368; marketing-mix and, extended 335, 337, *338*, *339*, 340, **341**; marketing plan and, international 335, *336*; nomological network for 370, *371*; origin of innovation and 366, 368; outcomes of 368–370; 7Ps and 335, 337, *338*, *339*, 340, **341**
Ricardo, David 110
Richardson, Paul 340
Rinallo, Diego 124
Rinspeed Etos car 360–361
Rio Tinto 216
rivalry 111–113, *112*, 382–384
Robinson, Stephanie Rosen 531, 533
Robson, Matthew 259, *439*
Rockefeller, John D. III 144
Rogers, Everett 345–346, 3335
Rohm, Andrew *414*
Role of Brand Index 438
Romer, Paul 122
Ronald McDonald House Charities (RMHC) 528
Ronen, Simcha 159, 161
Ross, John K., III 530
Royal Philips 311–312, *312*, *313*
rule of law 197, 199
Rule of Law Index 199
Rundle-Thiele, Sharyn 507
Ryanair 220–221

Samiee, Saeed 482
Samsung 217, 529
Saras platform 360–361
Sarbanes-Oxley Act 218
Save Lids to Save Lives campaign 536

568 *Index*

scale and globalization 4, 6, 14, 19–20
Schiff, Maurice 124
Schlegelmilch, Bodo 482, 506
Schneider Electric 312, 314–315, *314*, **314**
Schultz, Howard 92
Schwartz, Shalom 162, 164
S-commerce 390
Scott, W. Richard 184–185
sea shipping 119
Seelos, Christian 324
segmentation: behavioral 293; Bottom of the Pyramid marketing and 289, *291*, *292*, 293, 299, *301*, 303, *304*; demographic 289; geographic 289, *292*; income 299, *301*, 303, *304*; intermarket 289; multiple 293; psychographic 293; 01-Upper Crust 293
self-enhancement 164
self-transcendence 164
semi-internationalization 21, *23*
Sephora 221
services 342–344, *344*
Servier 217
7Ps (policies of processes, personnel, and physical evidence) 56, 278, 335, 337, *338*, *339*, 340, *341*
Shanghai NPI Social Innovation Development Center 310
Shankar, Venkatesh *395*
Shapiro, Daniel *414*
Sharia 170
Shenkar, Oded 159, 161, 168, *169*
Sheth, Jagdish *263*
Shetty, Devi 357
shortening of supply chains 384
Sivakumar, K. *240*
Skarmeas, Dionysis 103, 240
Slovenia *466*, 469–472
small or medium enterprises (SMEs) 215
Smith, Adam 110
SNC-Lavallin 218
Soberg, Peder 351
social class 145
social economy concept 12
social marketing 513
social media marketing 390–392, *393*, 394
social media and networks 387–389, *388*, **388**; *see also specific name*
social mobility 145, 147

social organization 143–145, 147
social stratification 144–145, 147
Sodiaal 528
solar panels, Chinese 221
Song, Ethan 403
Sousa, Carlos 79, 80, *80*, 83, 106, *143*
Southwest Airlines 337
space perceptions 166
Spam Bill 387
spamming 223
spillovers of knowledge 122
sponsorship 513–514, *533*, **534**
stance and communication 151–152
standalone brand 447
standardization and adaptation: centralized decision making and 86; contingency perspective of 93; corporate examples of 87–93, **88**, *90*, **91**; country-level factors and 80–81; degree of 71–72, 80, 93–94; delegation of decision making and 86; drivers of 80–85, *85*; EPRG framework and 82–84; firm-level factors and 82–84; Food for Thought 79, *80*, 87; industry-level factors and 81–82; issues at stake and 86–87; marketing plan and, international 72, *73*; organizational design and 86–87; product-level factors and 81–82; pros and cons of 71, 79–80
standardized global marketing 79, *79*
Starbucks 62–63, 92, 173, 219, 527
steel producers, European Union 221
Stephen, Andrew 391
STP (segmentation-targeting-position) process 78, 274, 277–278
strategic asset seeking and internationalization 50
Strategic Business Insights 293
stratification 144–145, 147
Stutts, Mary Ann 530
Subaru 517, *518*, 519, 529
subcontracting 46
Subway *45*, 46
Sultan, Fareena *414*
supply chains, shortening of 384
Susan G. Komen Foundation 527
sustainable consumption 501, *502*
sustainable development 501, *502*
Swiss Federal Institute of Technology 23
SWOT (Strengths, Weaknesses, Opportunities, and Threats) 56, 58

synthetic model 166
Systembolaget 222

Taiwan 219, 221
Tan, Qun 79, 80, *80*, 83
task/relationship model 154, *155*
Tasoulis, Konstantinos 532
Tata Motors 28, 361–363, **361**
Tata, Ratan 362
taxation systems 273
Taylor, Charles 531
Taylor, Kimberly 510
technological application 271
technological distance: adjustment to, by companies 277–278; assessing 238, 271, 280; convergence and 270–273; corporate examples of 273–278; defining 240–241; development levels and 243–244, *244*, *245*, 246–247, *246*, *247*, *248*, 249, **249**; digital divide and, global 252, *254*; directionality and 259, *259*; drivers of *237*, 243–258; Food for Thought *240*; heterogeneity of economies and 266–267, **267**, *268*, 269–270; importance of *237*, 258, 278; infrastructure and 252–253, **253**, 271; intellectual property and 253, 255–256, *256*, *257*, 258, **258**; issues at stake and 266–278; market attractiveness and 258–266, 269, 278, *279*; market groupings and 260; marketing decisions and, international 273–275; marketing plan and, international 238, *239*; negatively charged 274, 278, 372; nomological network for 278, *279*
technological integration 13–14, 28–29
technology: acceptance of 394–398, *395*; attitude toward 394–395, *395*; augmented reality 400, 406–407, *408*; convergence and 14, 19–20; digital divide and, global 252, *254*; infrastructure for 252–253, **253**, 271; integration of 29; MultiAir 355, 357; perceived ease-of-use variable of 394–395, *395*; perceived usefulness variable of 394–395, *395*; *see also specific type*
Technology Acceptance Model 394–398, *395*
Telenor Group 315–317, *316*, **316**
Telenor Mobile Communications 317

temporal distance 422–423
Terpstra, Robert 167
Tesla 63
Thanda matlab Coca-Cola 88–89
Thatcher, Margaret 12, 499
Theodorakis, Ioannis G. 532
Theodosiou, Marios 84
Thøgersen, John 508
threats perceived by global CEOS 211, *211*
Tick, Sam 450
time perceptions 166
Tinbergen, Jan 125
Toker, Ayşegül 391
Top of the Pyramid (TOP) marketing 296, 299, 302, *302*
"Tortuous Evolution of the Multinational Corporation, The" (Perlmutter) 83
tourist services 342
trade: administration of international 205–211, **208–209**; administrative distance and, international 205–211, **208–209**; blocs and, trading 215; country-based theories, international 109–110, *109*; fairs, international 123–124; firm-based theories, international 110–113, *112*; free zones of 210; national governments and international 210–211; patterns, international 108–113
trade agreements 214–215, *215*; *see also* regional trade agreements; *specific name*
trading blocs 215
traditional marketing 392
traditional media 390
transaction costs 51–53, *53*, 116, *116*
transaction facilitators 193
Trans-Pacific Partnership (TPP) 28
Transparency International 190–191
transportation costs *114*, 116, 119, **119**
transportation services *339*, 342
Trentin, Alessio 481
trickle-up innovation 351
Tricoire, Jean-Pascal 312
Trimble, Chris 351, *351*, 366
Tripp, Thomas 414
Trope, Yaacov 422
Tsang, Eric 240
Tse, David K. 482
Turkina, Ekaterina 214–215, 259, *439*

570 *Index*

turnkey project 47
Twitter 14, 346, 388, **388**, 412, 487

Uber 3–64, 410–413, **411**
UberFresh 411
Ueda, Keiko 148
umbrella brand 447
UNASUR (Union of South American Nations) 203
UNICEF 523
Unilever 318–319, *318*, **318**, *319*
United Airlines 392
United Nations Conference on Trade and Development (UNC-TAD) 47
United Nations Environment Program (UNEP) 501
United States 28, 351, *353*, *354*
universal values theory 162–164, **163**
University of Warwick 23
Uppsala model (U-model) 37–38, *38*, 54
URL (web address) 392
user-generated content (UGC) 391
US Patent and Trademark Office (USPTO) 206
Usunier, Jean-Claude 144, 166, 482

Vahlne, Jan-Erik 39, 53–55, *54*, 102, *102*
values 159, 161–164, **163**, 166–168, **168**
Values and Lifestyles System (VALS™) 293
van der Kaaij, J. 532
Varadarajan, Rajan 510, 535
Varnali, Kaan 391
Vendor Managed Inventories (VMI) 384
Venkatesh, Alladi 395
verbal communication 147–148, *149*, 150, 154
Vernon, Raymond 335, 348, *351*
Vestergaard 363–364, **364**, *365*
VFILES 520
Vice Media 64
Victorinox 455–458, *456*, **457**
Vietnam 28
Village Phone program 315–317, *316*
Villanueva, Julián 390
Vinters Quality Alliance 441
viral marketing 392, *393*, 394
Visa 417

visual cues 150
Vlachos, Pavlos 532
Vodafone 319–320, *320*, **320**, *321*
Volkswagen 64, 92–93, 276–277, *456*, 458–462, **459**, 485
volunteering 514
Von Zedtwitz, Max 351–353, 363, 368
Vrontis, Demetris 80, *80*, 82, 93–94

Wagner, Daniel 186
Wakslak, Cheryl 422
Walesa, Lech 520
Walmart 527
Walt Disney Company 60–61, 89, 169–170, 225, 275–276
Wang, Xuehua 443
Warhaw, Paul 394
Waris Ahluwalia 520
warm-glow giving 535
Water Stewardship program 513
Wealth of Nations (Smith) 110
wealth redistribution 273
We Are Social 387
Web 2.0 391
Webber, Ross 167
Weber, Max 184
Wells, Louis *351*
Westberg, Kate 534
Westjohn, Stanford A. 480
Wicki, S. 532
Williamson, Oliver 51, *52*
WOM (Word of Mouth) marketing 391, 412, 414, 416
World Bank 207, 243, 246–247, 250, 256, 267, 351–352, 359
World Bank Atlas method 243
World Chambers Federation (WCF) 207
World Customs Organization (WCO) 206, 209
World Intellectual Property Organization (WIPO) 206, 211, 256
World Justice Project (WJP) 197, 199
World Legal Systems Research Group 197
World Resources Institute 303, 322
World Trade Organization (WTO) 113, 200, 205–206, 210, 212, *213*, 221, 271
World Wildlife Fund (WWF) 512, 515

Xu, Dean 224

Yalcinkaya, Goksel 531
Yang, Zhilin 224, 443
YingYangBao product 310
Yip, Paul 240
Yoplait 512, 528, 536

YouTube 29, **91**, 364, 391–392, 405, 511, 523
Yunus, Muhammad 308, *309*

Zappos 416
Zdravkovic, Srdan 480
Zhu, PengCheng *240*